GOLD SEAL
Pinot Chardonnay
NEW YORK STATE
WINE
1964
Produced & Bottled by GOLD SEAL VINEYARDS, INC., Hammondsport, New York

1971
Mirassou
Monterey Santa Clara
White Burgundy

Novitiate
K MUSCAT
 suit Wines
e of Los Gatos
AND BOTTLED BY
GATOS, CALIFORNIA
ALCOHOL 20%
BY VOLUME

BRONTE
SISTER LAKES DISTRICT
PREMIUM MICHIGAN
BACO NOIR
Alcohol 12% By Volume
AT THE BRONTE VINEYARDS, HARTFORD, MICHIGAN

Mother Vineyard
Southern
SCUPPERNONG
WINE
MADE FROM
NORTH CAROLINA SCUPPERNONG GRAPES
MOTHER VINEYARD WINE CO.

MEIER'S
ISLE St GEORGE
OHIO STATE
HAUT
SAUTERNES

MANISCHEWITZ
CONCORD GRAPE
THE TRADITIONAL KOSHER WINE

GUILD VINO DA
TAVOLA
RED
CALIFORNIA TABLE WINE
MADE AND BOTTLED BY GUILD WINE CO., LODI, CALIF. ALC. 12½% BY VOL.

EXTRA QUALITY
PINOT
Canadian Champagne
Brights

Canepa
Select Estate Bottled

Lakes Region
Foch
ROBUST NEW HAMPSHIRE BURGUNDY

F.J.
GALLO
HEARTY BURGUNDY
OF CALIFORNIA

Paul Masson
BLANC de PINOT
California Brut Champagne

Beaulieu
Vineyard
BV
ESTATE BOTTLED
GEORGES DE LATOUR
PRIVATE RESERVE
NAPA VALLEY CABERNET SAUVIGNON
PRODUCED & BOTTLED BY BEAULIEU VINEYARD
AT RUTHERFORD, NAPA COUNTY, CALIFORNIA

PRODUCED AND BOTTLED BY
Boordy Vineyard
Boordyblümchen
A Light White Table Wine Recalling
The Muscatelle Of Austria And Germany
J. & P. Wagner, Props.
Riderwood, Maryland
1965

NATURAL FERMENTED
Produced by
Old Wine
Cellar
Bonded Winery No. 25
AMANA, IOWA
PIESTENGEL
Rhubarb Wine
Alcoholic Content 16-18% by Volume

fetzer
1970
ESTATE BOTTLED MENDOCINO
DRY SAUVIGNON BLANC
fetzer Vineyards

Inglenook

MAISON FONDÉE EN 1880
Hanns Wiederkehr
ARKANSAS
CHAMPAGNE
EXTRA DRY
NATURALLY FERMENTED IN THE BOTTLE

Stone Hill Wine Cellars

Sweet Catawba
GRAPE WINE

NAPA VALLEY
CHARBONO
1968

The Wines of America

THE Wines OF AMERICA

BY LEON D. ADAMS

A San Francisco Book Company/Houghton Mifflin Book

HOUGHTON MIFFLIN COMPANY   BOSTON

ISBN: 0-395-15456-1
ISBN: 0-913374-01-6
Library of Congress Catalog Card Number: 73-75347

Printed in the United States of America.

This SAN FRANCISCO BOOK COMPANY/HOUGHTON MIFFLIN BOOK originated in San Francisco and was produced and published jointly. Distribution is by Houghton Mifflin Company, 2 Park Street, Boston, Massachusetts 02107.

Book design and maps by Anita Walker Scott

FOR TIMOTHY AND SUSAN

Contents

MAPS

Preface

THAT A comprehensive book about American wines is long overdue is obvious from the statistic that nine out of ten bottles of the wines Americans drink are American-grown.

Other writers, who for decades have kept adding to the hundreds of volumes that extol the vintages of Europe, have recently discovered that California wines compare favorably with the Old World kinds and have begun giving them moderate praise. Yet hundreds of other excellent wines produced in California and in the more than a dozen other winegrowing states are still ignored, and the real story of wine in this country has not yet been told.

Meanwhile, a nationwide upsurge in winegrowing is in progress because at long last the civilized custom of dining with wine is spreading across America. An unprecedented boom in grape-planting is opening new vineyard areas and reviving the long-dormant wine industries of states whose wines were famous a century ago, but whose vineyards withered and died before World War I in the path of Prohibition. New champagne cellars are now operating in Michigan, Illinois, and the Ozark grape district of Arkansas, and old wineries have been reopened in Missouri. Vineyards lately planted with unfamiliar grape varieties are yielding wines, as yet unknown outside their localities, in Indiana, Maryland, New Hampshire, Oregon, Pennsylvania, South Carolina, Washington, and other states whose climates long were thought inhospitable to any vines except the native kinds. New fragrances found in grapes are beginning to broaden the taste horizons and expand the wine cellars of a generation thus far acquainted only with traditional wine tastes.

Exploring the wine trails that now crisscross America is a Bacchic voyage of discovery. Wines still unknown to connoisseurs are waiting to be tasted, not only in the showplace wineries of California and New York, which already are visited by hundreds of thousands of tourists each year, but in scores of other hospitable cellars across the continent. Canada and Mexico are important on the borders of the American winescape, and I have included chapters on their wines, which until now have been only sketchily described in English-language publications.

This book is therefore intended for those who would like to know the full range of America's grapes and wines — the new as well as the old, the costly rare vintages and the ones that come in economical jugs — where you can see them produced, the origins of the colorful people who produce them, and the facts behind their romantic stories.

Each of the regions has its own vinous history, rich in human, dramatic quality. In some it is the struggle for survival against local and national dry politics. In others it is a story of victory achieved, after centuries of failure, over vine pests that defeated all past attempts to grow wine grapes. Many fabulous characters, past and present, play leading roles in these dramas. I tell some of their individual stories, because, although the quality of a wine depends first on the grape, it depends no less on the aims and character, than on the talent, of the vintner.

And woven in the strange, stormy history of the wine industry there is another of deeper cultural significance that merits pondering: the evolution of a nation's mores and attitudes toward drinking. In particular, Americans are revising their concept of wine. They once regarded it as merely another intoxicant, one of the trio that connote revelry, "wine, women, and song." Today millions of average families have adopted the light, dry table wines as part of their daily meals, while a younger generation is sampling the new, still lighter kinds that "pop" and compete with beer. Wine use in this country has more than trebled since the Second World War—a change of tremendous social and dietary importance—and yet the trend to wine as an American beverage has just begun.

My forty-plus years of traveling and tasting through America's vineyards have covered most, though not all, of the wineries which both grow grapes and make wines. During the seven years of compiling and writing this book, the meteoric rise in table wine consumption was causing revolutionary changes in the vineyards and wineries. To describe these changes and to include the new vineyards that are springing up across the continent, I have had repeatedly to revise each chapter after it was finished, and only as of press time is the book "complete."

While it might go without saying, I should emphasize that

nearly all of the wines I describe were tasted at the wineries, where they had been stored in dark, cool cellars—not at restaurants or after purchase in stores, where too often the light table and sparkling wines are injured by heat, light, and other improper storage conditions. Such partial spoilage seems to occur most ...en in the Midwest and South, where the perishable nature of ...se types apparently is not yet understood, and especially in ...xico, where, except at the wineries, I found few table wines ...were not at least partially oxidized.

...hat matter, you are unlikely ever to taste the identical wine ...writer describes. For wines, unlike most other alcoholic ..., are constantly changing—not only from vintage to ...the weather in the vineyard changes, but also while they ...r bottles. A taster's description of a wine is merely a ...emoir; the next cask, blend, or even the next bottle ...ifferent product, for this is a characteristic of wine. No ...promise, when a wine has given him a great taste ex-...at another bottle under the same label will deliver ...ste thrill for you.

...ny wine-snob friends denounce me for tolerating the ...cord-grape-juice taste which they find objectionable in ...tive wines, let me point out that we are far outnumbered ...illions of Americans and Canadians who prefer that "real ...ste" in their drinks and even in their grape chewing gum. I have been exposed all my life to European and California wines, which are made of Vinifera grapes, and I therefore prefer them. But I do not find the flavor of the Labrusca grapes objectionable, and I rate the Labrusca wines impartially.

Anyone who presumes to pass judgment on the qualities of wines ought to define his standards and his terminology. Most of our leading connoisseurs, if challenged to do so, would have to confess that they pronounce an American wine "fine," "good," or "ordinary" according to how closely it may or may not resemble a counterpart among the most publicized and costliest of French or German wines. They are therefore unable to appreciate the new taste experiences offered by many American wines. Idolizing the wines of Europe as classic, they seldom recognize any wine of this country as "great." Fame, scarcity, and high prices usually explain their choices of the European wines they cite as models of perfection; and with these they stock their cellars, usually to incite the envy of fellow collectors. This kind of snobbery would be harmless if it were not for the annoying habit most such collectors have of referring to the costly rarities as "the good wines," thereby inevitably classing all other wines under the antonym "bad." Equally unfortunate is their custom of calling good wines "ordinary," a more derogatory term in English than in the French *ordinaire*, which means "regular" or "standard."

Since there has never been a truly international wine jury, consisting of both American and European experts, to taste wines solely on their individual merits (and with the labels hidden), I have had to invent one. My imaginary jury consists of the several hundred connoisseurs of my acquaintance, representing all of the different Old and New World tastes. My ratings of individual wines are what I believe would be the impartial verdicts of this jury if it existed.

And, in my lexicon, a wine that is sound and palatable is "good"; a spoiled, partially spoiled, or otherwise unpalatable wine is "bad"; a wine true to its type and markedly superior in taste, nose, and balance to the "good" ones of that type is "fine"; and a "fine" wine which gives the connoisseur of that wine type such pure delight to his senses as to be unforgettable, deserves to be called "great."

These distinctions are important to the purposes of this book. For among its purposes is to help gain recognition and provide encouragement for the new pioneers of winegrowing in many old and new localities throughout America where I have watched vines being planted lately. For I am one of those who believe that wine finally will become the national mealtime beverage when its production is no longer concentrated in only a few states—when winegrowing becomes truly a nationwide industry.

Sausalito, California   LEON D. ADAMS
January, 1973

The Wines of America

1

America's Surprising Wines

I N THE quantity of wine it produces annually, the United States ranks sixth among the winegrowing nations.* In the average quality of its wines, it ranks first.

The standard wines of America, available everywhere in thrifty jugs, are superior to any that householders in other lands get to drink with their daily meals. The best American wines, produced by the few dozen vineyards which aim for highest quality and premium prices, have equaled many of the Old World's finest. The latter fact, often demonstrated in "blind" comparative tastings with the classic wines of Europe, is all the more surprising when it is remembered that Europe, with its two thousand years of experience, has thousands of vineyards whose vintages are sought after and treasured by connoisseurs, while the United States has had only these few.

This country has two advantages over the Old World in winegrowing. One is in climates more hospitable to grapes—a subject about which a good deal follows, because climate is the key to the fascinating lore of wine. The other advantage is that of having started anew. The American wine industry, reborn when National Prohibition ended in 1933, chose the scientific approach to quality. Rejecting the traditions, cobwebbed cellars, and primitive methods that hinder wine progress in much of Europe, it utilized the new research in viticulture and enology, in which the United States now leads the world—research that has removed the guesswork from winemaking.

Exported now to other countries, where they compete on even

*Commercial wine production in the U.S. averages 275 million gallons yearly, compared to 1.8 billion gallons in Italy, 1.7 billion in France, 639 million in Spain, 579 million in the U.S.S.R., 557 million in Argentina, 275 million in Portugal, 222 million in Algeria, and 185 million in West Germany.

terms with the world-famous wines of France and Germany, American wines are still improving. As yet they have only approached the great quality they can achieve in the future. Already they are a serious challenge to Old World wines sold in this country, to such an extent that European vintners have begun imitating American wine names. (Nor is merely equaling European wines as great an achievement as it might seem because, as is well known in the wine trade, the wines under many famous French and German labels have changed greatly, not necessarily for the better, since the Second World War.) But just as artists in other fields give their best performances for appreciative audiences, this country's winegrowers will continue improving their products to the extent that the wine-buying public will appreciate and pay for them.

There is much to appreciate, not only in the fine wines of California, New York, and Ohio, but also in the vastly improved table wines of Arkansas, Michigan, Oregon, and Washington, which as yet are seldom found outside their borders. Connoisseurs in Maryland, Pennsylvania, Illinois, and Missouri who seek rare and good wines can find them at small vineyards in their own states, and thereby can promote the agricultural economy of their regions. The southern states, the last citadels of the Prohibition movement, can help both their faltering agriculture and the cause of temperance by speeding the revival of their once important winegrowing industry, originally based on the Scuppernong grape. New York and Ohio, whose distinctive wines long have been made of native grapes, merit recognition for their superior new wine types made from exotic grape varieties planted since the 1950s. As for California, that state's premium wineries cannot plant new vineyards fast enough to keep up with the soaring demand for their finest "varietal" table wines. Some of their Chardonnays, Cabernet Sauvignons, and Pinot Noirs are even being rationed, a case or two per month to each of the best stores and restaurants, which reserve single bottles for their favorite patrons.

How little known are some states' wines is evident from the now-famous Department of State wine list, issued in 1966, of American wines which our embassies and consulates were urged to serve "with pride and confidence" to their guests in foreign countries under Former President Lyndon B. Johnson's "drink American" policy. I was one of the six so-called experts whom the Department summoned to Washington to compare our tasting notes and to prepare the list.* From all of our cumulative

*The others were Dr. Maynard Amerine, Creighton Churchill, Harold Grossman, Tom Marvel, and Robert J. Misch.

knowledge, the six of us were able to agree on recommending only eighty-nine wines—seventy from California, sixteen from New York, two from Ohio, and one from Maryland—just four of the twenty-six states in which wine is produced commercially. From my notes on the many excellent wines I have tasted since, it would be easy now to quadruple both the number of wines and the number of states the list represents.

America produces good wines of every type made elsewhere on the globe. It also makes many types that are entirely its own. In fact, this country offers the widest spectrum of wine flavors that can be found anywhere in the world. This results principally from its wide variety of climates. It is climate that principally determines which grape varieties can produce the best wine quality where. The right soil is essential, of course, but good soils for grape growing can be found almost anywhere, while ideal climatic conditions cannot. Each climatic district and each vineyard with its own microclimate will produce, from the same grape variety, a distinctly different wine. The Riesling grown in the warmer parts of the Napa Valley differs appreciably from Riesling grown on the cooler hillsides a few miles to the west, from Riesling grown at Piesport on the Moselle, and from Riesling grown in western Oregon or at Hammondsport, New York. And the Catawba grape makes a different wine when grown on Isle St. George in the middle of Lake Erie from Catawba grown in the Ozark region of Missouri and Arkansas. Differences in the exposure of vines to sunlight even in the same vineyard influence wine flavors, too. (Yes, differences in soil account in part for differences in wines—especially between the wines of single vineyards—but European producers are inconsistent in claiming that soils are the chief reason the wines of their best vineyard districts are unique. Well-drained, warm soils capable of adequately nourishing the vines are essential for quality and yield. It is not true, as they would have us believe, that a special soil component climbs up through the vine, enters into the grape and its juice, and gives the wine a distinctive taste.)

America is one vast Vineland, so named by the Norse explorer Leif Ericson when he landed on Newfoundland *circa* A.D. 1000. Whether the berries he found growing wild there were really grapes as the saga says, or squashberries as some botanists now contend, Ericson was right. For in the expanse of North America between 50° north latitude in Canada and 20° north latitude in Central Mexico are the greatest natural grape-growing areas on earth. More species of the genus Vitis, the grapevine, grow wild here than in all the rest of the world combined. The borders of the United States, which extend from 49° latitude in the State of

Washington to 25° latitude in Texas and Florida, encompass vast regions superior, in terms of growing-season temperatures, to Germany's Rhineland at 50° latitude and to Champagne and Burgundy at 49° and 47° latitude in France. This country has hundreds of such areas, with enough total acreage to accommodate the Rhineland, Moselle, Champagne, Burgundy, and Bordeaux regions several times over.

In California's equable climate, with its long rainless growing seasons and its mild winters, grapes transplanted from Europe thrive as well as, and often better than, in their Old World homelands. This is why California wines resemble those of Europe; they are made from the same grape varieties—the species called *Vitis vinifera*. These Old World grapes also have long made some of the wines of eastern Washington, western Oregon, and southern New Mexico. But in the East and Midwest, the rigorous winters and humid summers make it difficult to grow the delicate Vinifera, and here the hardier native "slip-skin" grapes, which are mostly domesticated varieties of *Vitis Labrusca*, are mainly grown. This is why most eastern wines have, in varying degrees, the fragrant, grapy or foxy flavor you taste in Concord grape juice, jelly, and jam. Only since the 1950s have Vinifera been grown successfully in the East, yielding wines that lately have amazed connoisseurs. In recent decades the climates of many eastern and midwestern states have been found hospitable to still another group of hardy grape varieties, the French-American hybrids. These are crosses of native American grapes with Vinifera, developed by grape breeders in France. Increasingly planted east of the Rockies now, these hybrids are making wines different in taste from both of their parents, but definitely of European, not Labrusca character. The southeastern states, with their humid climates which are inhospitable to most bunch grapes, are the natural home for still another American grape species, the Muscadines, *Vitis rotundifolia*. The Muscadines are more like cherries than like grapes, and the best-known variety is the Scuppernong. Nor are these the complete assortment, as will be seen in the chapters which describe individual wines and the districts where they are grown.

Actually, grapes grow in all fifty states, and any grape can make wine. Next to apples, grapes are the most widely grown fruit in America. This country has almost 700,000 acres of vineyards, about one fortieth of the total in the world. Commercial wine-growing is impractical, however, in areas with growing seasons of less than 120 days between the killing spring and autumn frosts. This rules out only western Montana, Wyoming, Colorado, the northern portions of Maine, of Minnesota, of Michigan, of North

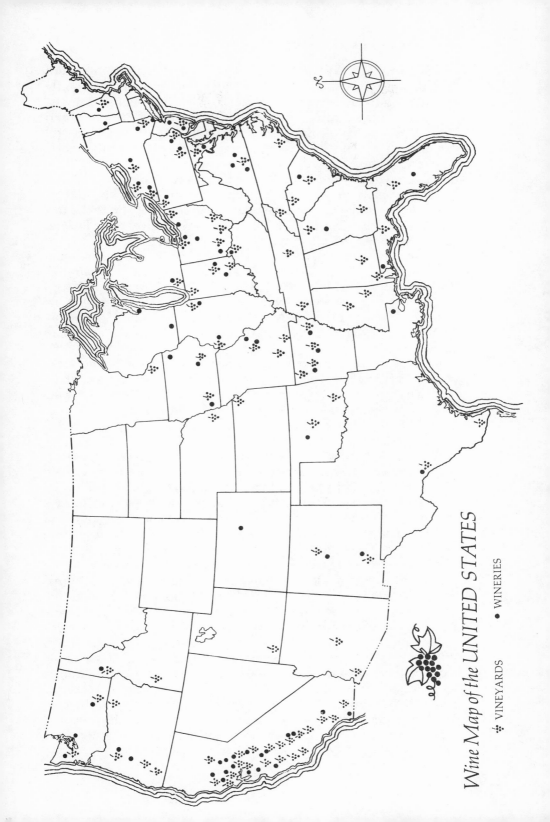

Wine Map of the UNITED STATES

VINEYARDS   • WINERIES

Dakota, and of Wisconsin, and eastern Nevada, southeastern Oregon, and Alaska. Before 1900, wines were grown successfully in such unlikely-seeming states as Idaho, Indiana, Kansas, Kentucky, Mississippi, Nebraska, Oklahoma, Tennessee, and West Virginia. As evidence, the skeletons of old wineries still can be seen in many of the rural areas which once supported their vineyards. These states will produce wines again, when their legislators, departments of agriculture, and their horticultural scientists awake to the exploding new demand for table wine in this country, to the progress being made elsewhere, and to the fact that now, for the first time in three quarters of a century, Federal research money can be obtained to assist them.

California, with half a million acres of vineyards, more than three times the grape acreage of all the other states combined, produces about three million tons of grapes annually and supplies three fourths of the wine consumed in this country. New York, with 36,000 acres, Michigan, with 17,000, Washington, 18,000, Pennsylvania, 9000, Ohio, 4500, and other states with smaller vineyard acreages, produce altogether about a sixth of the wine consumed.* The remainder, about one tenth of the total, consists of foreign wines, imported mainly from France, Italy, Portugal, Spain, and Germany. California also supplies some other states' vintners each year with well over a million gallons of neutral bulk wines, wine spirits, and condensed juice (called grape concentrate) for blending with their own production.

The dominance of California prompts some people in other states to question whether wine can be grown profitably anywhere else, since California can produce the common types more cheaply and until very recent years has had a chronic grape surplus of a quarter-million tons per year. The best answer is the example of other states' thriving wineries, expecially those of New York, a state which has steadily increased its share of the wine market. The eastern states compete by making the kinds of wine California cannot grow. Again it is a matter of climate, for the chief California wine districts do not grow the Labrusca grapes which make the highly flavored eastern wines, such as Catawba, Delaware, Niagara, and Concord. These grapes fail to ripen properly in the mild California weather. In fact, the Concord grape juice which my children drink at breakfast in our California home has to come from grapes grown in eastern Washington. Actually, the California surplus has consisted of leftover raisin and table grapes—not of the fragile, shy-bearing, finest wine-grape varieties of which there is, and probably always will be, a shortage both in California and throughout the world, because they are expensive to grow.

*These acreages include new plantings, which are increasing each year.

The flavor difference between the principal wines of western and eastern America has seldom been better expressed than in these two conversations: A few years ago, as I was leaving home on an eastern tasting trip, a leading California vintner said to me, "You're wasting your time. Eastern wines have no future. Their grapes have that foxy taste that real wine drinkers can't stand." A month later, when I was tasting Labrusca and Scuppernong wines in a Virginia winery, the proprietor, Mack Sands, explained to me why he was expanding his production in three eastern states. "Those California wines have no future," he said, "because their Vinifera grapes lack flavor. Americans want real grape flavor in wine. Our grapes here in the East are the only ones that have got it."

To most Americans, "grape flavor" *means* that foxy taste. It comes chiefly from an ester, methyl anthranilate, which occurs in the Labrusca grapes, and which can also be made synthetically. Completely dry wines made of Labrusca varieties are too harsh for the average palate, but millions of Americans like this flavor in sweet and semisweet wines. Some of the best eastern champagnes and sauternes owe their appeal, I think, to the hint of Labrusca fragrance in their taste, delicately balanced, however, by judicious blending with California wine or with the nonfoxy juice of the French hybrids. These were the kinds of wine the late Captain Paul Garrett had in mind when he tried unsuccessfully in 1934 to convince the California winegrowers that someday blends of Labrusca from the East and Vinifera from the West would help to make this a wine-drinking nation. Thirty-six years later, the biggest California vintners began doing as Garrett advised, bringing Labrusca juices and concentrate from other states to add flavor to their Cold Duck, kosher-type and other wines.

The fact that there are plenty of buyers for both California and other states' wines is obvious from the rate at which the consumption of both has grown. Wine use has more than trebled since the Second World War, and is certain to multiply in the next few decades. As this is written, wineries of both West and East are not only expanding their vineyards, but are urgently searching for new lands with suitable climates in which to plant premium grapes for the vastly greater markets they foresee in the future. Moreover, population growth in California threatens that state's chief fine-wine districts. Real estate subdivisions and rising taxes on farm-land in these favored areas already have crowded many of their oldest vineyards out of existence. As a result, new vineyards are being planted in many localities that have not produced wine for a century, and in others that have never grown wine grapes before.

Yet America still is far from becoming a wine-drinking country.

The chief obstacles that still prevent regular wine use from becoming nationwide are outmoded state laws, relics of Prohibition, that hamper the production and sale of wine. In most states, exorbitant license fees and burdensome red-tape requirements prevent farmers from opening small wineries and selling their grapes to the public in the form of wine. And although wine is now sold in all fifty states, more than half make it difficult to buy. Twenty-five states impose taxes or markups on light table wines at rates ranging from fifty cents to $1.50 per gallon. When added to the seventeen-cent Federal tax, these result in pricing light wines as a luxury or as a sinful indulgence, instead of as an article of food. Twenty states forbid the sale of table wines in groceries, restricting it to liquor outlets. This necessitates an inconvenient extra stop for the housewife when she goes shopping for food, and, furthermore, many liquor stores are not the kind of places where she is willing to be seen. One of the reasons per capita wine use in California is more than double that of the nation as a whole is that virtually all food stores in California sell wine. (When supermarkets in England began stocking wine during the 1960s, table wine consumption in that country jumped 15 percent in a single year.) At this writing, thirty-two states still have many legally dry localities, counties, cities, or towns, and forty-three of the fifty states still have local or state blue laws forbidding the sale of any alcoholic beverage on Sundays. These are some of the reasons why the civilized custom of drinking wine with meals has not yet spread to such states as Alabama, Iowa, Kansas, Kentucky, Mississippi, and West Virginia. Yearly wine consumption in these states still is less than four pints per inhabitant, as compared to one and one half gallons per year average for the nation. Oklahoma and South Carolina still prohibit their restaurants from serving their patrons so much as a glass of table wine with a meal. It is remarkable that in spite of the obstacles to wine-drinking that exist in most of this country, consumption of this beverage has increased as it has. The obstacles will be removed only when enough Americans and enough of their legislators come to realize that wine belongs with food. For table wine is used principally at mealtimes; it is the only true mealtime beverage. This cannot be said of water, coffee, tea, soft drinks, beer, or of milk. Dry table wine, the principal kind of wine used in the world, and cheaper than milk to produce, is the only beverage that has few other uses except to accompany the main course of a meal.

Another impediment to wine use, though a lesser one, is snobbery, which is defined as drinking the label, not the wine. The average American householder still seldom serves any wine and only thinks of doing so for some special occasion, such as the entertainment of important guests. Although more or less content in his daily life with his modest home and moderately-priced automobile, he feels that if he serves a wine he must impress the guests with his affluence. For this purpose a reasonably-priced American wine will not do. Instead, he buys one of the high-priced imports the wine snobs recommend, and the rest of the time lives by bread alone.

No matter how fine an American wine may be, the American snob dares not praise it highly, for fear of being thought naïve, or even chauvinistic, which to him would be worse. Credit this to the fantastically successful propaganda campaign the European vintners have waged throughout the world for more than a century, to the effect that only their climates and soils can produce truly fine wines. They have made it unfashionable in this country to describe any wine as "great" unless it comes from a French château or a German castle.

Most British and American writers of wine books (some of whom are active in the sale of imports) have long helped to spread this attitude as gospel. When they occasionally praise a table wine from Spain, Portugal, or Italy, they are careful first to deny that it possibly can be equal or superior to the classic wines of France or Germany. For many years they sneered at all American wines, comparing them to French *ordinaires*. Lately, however, their tone has abruptly changed. These writers now compete with one another in cautiously worded praise of California wines, with such statements as that "the New World vintages have come of age." British author Hugh Johnson currently leads the competition, declaring that "the best of California's wines today are among the world's best."

The fact is that of the 1.7 billion gallons of wine France produces annually, less than 5 percent is better than ordinary. By artful publicity the French have succeeded in clothing the rest of their output with the glamour of the rare 5 percent. With American wines the reverse has occurred. About 10 percent of this country's wines are of premium quality, but many of the finest vintages are little known and hard to find. Consequently, the nine tenths of American wines that are only of standard quality and are readily available are what most people think of as typifying American wines.

There are two ways to cope with wine snobbery. One is to compare wines with their labels hidden, a method I highly recommend. A California vintner friend of mine secretly switches the contents of bottles and then enjoys hearing his label-drinker friends praise his own wines over imports. The other way is to send American wines to Europe and challenge the imports on their home grounds. Several American vineyards now export their wines to England, Switzerland, Belgium, and to scores of other countries around the world. But not to France, which annually imports millions of gallons from many other countries, but stubbornly refuses to admit any regular commercial shipments from the United States.

Now comes the question most often asked about American wines: how *do* they compare with the wines of Europe? The reply usually given evades the question by pointing out that wines, being farm products, are necessarily individuals, that no two natural wines can ever be identical in taste, and therefore that they should never be compared. This of course is nonsense; part of the fun in wines is in comparing them. What the inquirer wants to know is whether there are any basic differences in flavor or aroma between American wines and imports in general, that he himself can distinguish by taste. The answer is that there is no marked difference between American and European wines of the same types and ages when both are made of the identical grape varieties, grown in similar climates, aged in casks made of the same variety of oak, and when both are given the same treatment and care in the vineyard and winery. The average taster cannot distinguish between a fine American Chardonnay and a fine French White Burgundy, or between the best Napa Gamay Noir and the best French Beaujolais.

But note, please, that I have qualified my answer, and note in particular the reference to the same variety of oak. For if only the grape varieties, the vineyard climates, and the care given the grapes and wines are identical, there still is one difference that even a neophyte taster can distinguish. It is the peculiar, complex bouquet of European wines that are aged in small wooden casks— a bouquet heretofore seldom found in barrel-aged American wines. For more than a century, nobody ever guessed why this difference existed. In recent years, its cause has been learned. It results from the different species of oak trees that grow on the European and American continents, the kinds of oak from which wine barrels are made. The complex bouquet comes from the wood, not from the grapes. How this was discovered accidentally, through the stubbornness of an amateur California winegrower in the late 1950s, will be related in Chapter 13. Now that many American vintners have imported European oak casks and have begun to age some of their wines in them, woody bouquet is no longer an Old World exclusive.

This is not to say that America as yet has any wines closely resembling French sauternes or German moselles, but neither have France and Germany any wines like our Catawba, Sauvignon

Blanc, or Cabernet Sauvignon. Each country, because of differences in climate or in the grape varieties it alone grows, still has some wines that are exclusively its own. Nor does America yet offer any vintages to compete with seventy-five-dollar-a-bottle Romanée Conti 1953 or with a Rheingau Trockenbeerenauslese 1934 at one hundred dollars. One of the drawbacks of American fine wines, besides the fact that they are little known, is that they still generally lack the great bouquet from bottle-aging that connoisseurs exclaim over. Too few years have yet elapsed since Repeal to provide many venerable rarities, and the American system of collecting annual inventory taxes on producers' aging stocks has prevented the wineries from holding back their wines for many years after bottling. The consumer who wants really old American wines must buy them young and age them himself in his cellar. On the other hand, among white wines, which require less age than reds, there are a few California and New York Chardonnays for which true wine lovers are gladly paying higher prices per bottle in preference to well-known imports.

Nomenclature is another reason most American wines compete at a disadvantage with imports in the snob trade. For the bulk of this country's wine is sold as burgundy, sauterne, chablis, rhine wine, champagne, port, and sherry—names which refer to old winegrowing districts in Europe. It is fashionable among Europe-minded connoisseurs to denounce all such wines as "imitations." Behind this charge is the French government, which for many years has been trying to persuade all other wine countries to stop using wine-type names of French origin. Several nations, including Spain and Mexico, have yielded to this pressure officially, though they, too, continue selling most of their wines at home under the French type-names. Spain conducts a campaign abroad similar to that of the French, hoping to acquire a world monopoly on sherry (named by the British, who have trouble pronouncing Latin names, for the Andalusian sherry-producing district around Xérès or Jerez de la Frontera). Germany surrendered to the French on this issue long ago, and calls its sparkling wines *Sekt* (derived from *sec*, the French word for "dry") instead of "champagne," and Italian vintners call their champagnes *spumante*. Russia, however, goes on making vast quantities of its "champanskoe," "portvein," "madera," and "cognac." The United States regulation defines fourteen* wine-type names of European geographic origin as "semigeneric" and requires them to be prominently qualified on labels with the true place of origin, as "American Burgundy," "California Sherry," "Ohio Champagne," "Napa Valley Chablis,"

*The fourteen: burgundy, claret, chablis, champagne, chianti, malaga, madeira, moselle, port, rhine wine, hock, sauterne, sherry, tokay.

etc. If the United States ever could be persuaded to give up the generic names, France, in particular, would reap overnight a monopoly on the vast markets which American vintners have built in this country for champagne, burgundy, sauterne, and chablis by spending countless millions in advertising and promotion during the past century. These wine names have been anchored in the American language for generations, along with French bread, French rolls, French dressing, French fried potatoes, French toast, Danish pastry, English muffins, Russian rye, Swiss cheese, Irish stew, English toffee, hamburger steak, Dutch ovens, Dutch doors, Venetian blinds, India ink, and chinaware. The generic names are the only ones the average wine buyer understands. What else, the American vintners ask, could you possibly call champagne?

A puzzling consequence of such labeling is that American vintners, being individuals, have never agreed on just what the semigeneric European names mean. Sauternes are always white and burgundies are always red (unless labeled white), but these wines can range in taste all the way from bone-dry to semisweet, depending upon which American winery makes them. I wonder how the citizens of the small Burgundian town of Chablis, world-famed solely for its dry white wine, must have felt when they first learned in 1965 that Gallo of California had begun labeling one of its two rosé wines as "pink chablis." And anyone accustomed to drinking California burgundy experiences a shock when he first tastes the foxy New York or Ohio burgundy, while the regular buyers of New York and Ohio burgundies are equally shocked when they taste the California version. (But rather than try to unravel here the mysteries of American wine nomenclature and labeling regulations, I attempt to do so in Chapter 26, where vintage labels, "produced," "made," and "estate-bottled" are also explained.)

As a defense against the criticism of their generic wine-type labels, American vintners are making increased use of grape-variety names for their wines. They find this profitable, because varietal names suggest rarity and quality, intangible elements for which buyers are willing to pay extra. Burgundy brings a higher price when it is labeled Pinot Noir, sauterne when it is sold as Semillon, and chablis when the label calls it Chardonnay. In consequence, as might be expected, the "varietal wine" list has grown considerably in recent years. It once consisted mainly of Riesling, Cabernet, Zinfandel, and muscatel from California, and Catawba and Scuppernong from the East. But now, there are almost one hundred varietal names on American wines, including three different Rieslings, six different Pinots, and even varietally labeled wines of the French hybrid grapes with such names as Baco Noir, Seibel 10878, and Seyval Blanc (formerly Seyve-Villard 5276). The result is delicious confusion—partly because the average grape variety can be called by any of several names—and especially in spelling and pronunciation. The latter is why most restaurants now find it necessary to print a number opposite each tongue-twisting item on their wine lists.

And now the European vintners have begun imitating the American varietal labels, renaming Bordeaux, Burgundy, and Spanish wines for "varietal grapes"—the Old World's ultimate recognition of American success.

Varietally named wines are not necessarily better than those with generic labels. Since under the Federal labeling regulations a wine need only derive 51 percent of its volume from the premium grape variety named on its label, some vintners succumb to the temptation to stretch the quantity with 49 percent of less expensive grapes; and unfortunately, the character of the premium variety is usually lost in such blends. The temptation to do this is great, because in the coast counties of California, for example, the noble Chardonnay grape during the 1971 vintage was scarce at $625 a ton, compared to the plentiful supply of good Burger grapes in the San Joaquin Valley at $80. A premium winery's Chardonnay wine should be superior to its chablis (the principal dry white type it sells), but if the "Chardonnay" is stretched with too much Burger, the same winery's chablis may turn out to be the better wine.* And in the eastern states, the demand for Catawba wine so far exceeded the supply of this grape a few years ago that some vintners asked the Government to rule that Catawba is not really a "varietal" wine, but can be made from any grape. The Government fortunately did not oblige.

Why aren't American wines named for the vineyard districts, as most European wines are? Picture the quandary in which this would place the vintners in such centers as St. Helena, Saratoga, Healdsburg, Hammondsport, and Cincinnati. For each of them makes several, and in some cases thirty or more, different wine types—including some from grapes grown outside their home districts—in order to sell "a complete line" under their brand names. But place-name labeling presents no problem to European vintners, because they sell wines produced by others. European vintners are primarily shippers (*négociants*); they buy their wines

---

*In 1972, the "burgundies" of the California premium producers were among the best buys in red wines on the market, usually better than the same wineries' more expensive Pinot Noirs. Why? Because the burgundies of the premium producers must be of markedly higher quality than popular-priced burgundies, in order to justify the higher prices of the California premium brands.

from producers in many districts. They, too, sell "complete lines" under their names, whereas the American wineries produce most or all of their own.

A third kind of American wine nomenclature, that usually combines some generic, varietal, and district meaning, has emerged in recent years and deserves mention. It is the proprietary name, which identifies both the wine and the brand. Current examples include the Beaumont and Beauclair of Beaulieu Vineyard; the Rubion, Baroque, Emerald Dry, and Rhine Castle of Paul Masson; the Chateau La Salle of The Christian Brothers, and the Lake Country Red, White, and Pink from Taylor of New York. Perhaps such proprietary names, as their numbers grow in years to come, eventually will silence the Europe-minded critics and end the nomenclature wrangle.

In contrast to Europe, with its scores of thousands of small wineries, all of the American wines we are discussing come from fewer than five hundred bonded wineries. These range in size from the few dozen barrels in Melvin Gordon's tiny Conestoga Vineyard cellar at Birchrunville, Pennsylvania, to the mammoth 60-million-gallon Gallo Winery at Modesto, California, which is by far the world's largest. There were more than a thousand bonded wineries in this country as recently as the 1930s. The number has shrunk because large wineries, with the advantages of mechanization, automation, and efficient mass marketing, have grown larger, while many smaller ones who could not afford these things have gone out of business.

But now we have dozens of entirely new winegrowers, who are reversing this trend. Some are opening wineries and acquiring vineyards because they see the wine business expanding and becoming profitable for others. The majority, however, are primarily hobbyists—I call them the oenothusiasts—who are motivated less by hope of profits than by love of fine wines. After the Second World War, home winemaking became widely popular as a hobby in the United States, to such an extent that a new industry was created to supply the hobbyists with materials and equipment. Many of these hobbyists began to grow their own grapes, first planting vines in backyards, and in some cases buying additional land and establishing small vineyards. Then, some of the oenothusiasts, finding their grape crops produced more wine than the two hundred gallons per year the United States Government permits a householder to make and possess, decided to bond their cellars and sell their wines. The result was that while many medium-sized commercial vintners, no longer able to compete with the giants, were closing their wineries during the postwar years, almost as many nonprofessionals were opening new wineries to pursue their avocation. Fascinated by the romance and greatness of wine, many of these new small growers are now striving to produce the world's finest single bottles of wine.

In another industry, such a development might seem unimportant. But as later chapters will show, from Nicholas Longworth, a lawyer, to Philip Wagner, a journalist, avocational vintners have led the way to much of the progress of winegrowing in America. It is the new oenothusiasts who are now pioneering by planting vines and opening little wineries in new districts and in localities that supported wineries a century ago. It is they who may make winegrowing again a nationwide industry.

At hand is an issue of *Fortune* magazine with a lavish spread of pictures of wealthy Americans' great wine cellars—all but one filled entirely with famous-label European wines. As rarities, some of the single bottles named are worth large sums of money. (Philatelists, too, pay fortunes for single postage stamps with which they cannot even mail a letter.) This country now has an increasing number of wines that deserve a place beside Europe's best. If those collectors who stock great cellars will now begin to explore American vineyards and to choose wines for their worth in drinking delight, such collections as those pictured in *Fortune* are certain henceforth to include many American wines.

2

Four Centuries of History

MERICAN wines have entered world competition as youngsters, for most of the present wine industry dates from the repeal of Prohibition in 1933, and most of its best vineyards were not planted until a full generation later. Yet, as Samuel Johnson said, "the present state of things is the consequence of the past," and the wines of today reflect in their flavors many long-forgotten events of the past four centuries.

Single dramatic episodes in American wine history have been portrayed in romantic pageants enacted at local vintage festivals and in several epic novels and motion pictures. But a complete story of winegrowing in this country would require volumes, because it would cover some four hundred years, at least thirty-three states, and a thousand historic vineyards. Its cast of characters would include European despots, American Presidents, senators, and governors, Spanish padres, grape breeders, temperance crusaders, wine-minded journalists, college professors, and a whole procession of eminent vintners, both past and present.

Although winegrowing has influenced the economy and culture of many states, you are unlikely to find wine even mentioned in their histories, because the Prohibitionists erased it. Like the dictators who rewrite nations' histories to blot out other ideologies than their own, the fanatical forces responsible for Prohibition spent years of zealous effort obliterating all of the favorable references to wine they could find in printed texts, failing only to remove them from the Bible.* As a result, few Americans now associate winegrowing with such historic figures as Lord Delaware, William Penn, Thomas Jefferson, the elder Nicholas Longworth, Padre Junípero Serra, General Vallejo, Captain John Sutter, or Leland Stanford. And scarcely anyone now living in Cincinnati,

*They did succeed, however, in getting references to "wine" changed to "cakes of raisins" in *The Short Bible* published by Scribner's in 1924.

18

St. Louis, Pittsburgh, or Los Angeles realizes that these cities were winemaking centers a century ago. Even California, whose oldest industry is winegrowing, has begun only in recent years to designate its most famous old wineries as state historical landmarks because of their growing value as tourist attractions. The official textbook from which school children are taught California's history discusses virtually every product of the state's farms and factories, but never once mentions wine.

Each vineyard region in America has its own romantic story, the highlights of which I include in the later chapters devoted to the wines of the various states. Here I only touch on some of the major developments. Of particular interest are the stormy, tragic happenings during the Prohibition period and the striking changes which since Repeal have revolutionized winegrowing and winedrinking throughout the nation. And because the events influencing wine in this country have occurred at widely separated places and times and might otherwise seem unconnected, I have also prepared a brief Chronology of Wine in North America, which appears as Chapter 27.

· 2 ·

The first American wines were made of wild grapes. Between 1562 and 1564, the first French Huguenots to reach North America made wine of the Scuppernong grapes they found growing near the present site of Jacksonville in Florida. Other early arrivals fermented the native grapes, too: the Jamestown colonists in Virginia in 1609 and the Mayflower Pilgrims at Plymouth to help celebrate the first Thanksgiving in 1623.

Then began more than three centuries of attempts to grow the fragile Old World wine grape, the Vinifera, in the East, all of them failing miserably. In 1619, Lord Delaware brought vines to Virginia from France and also French *vignerons* to tend them and to make the wine. The Virginia colonial assembly passed a law in 1623 requiring that every householder plant ten vines, and from 1651 to 1693 offered the colonists prizes for wine production, with no winners. In 1632, Governor John Winthrop of Massachusetts was granted Governor's Island in Boston Harbor on which to plant wine grapes. In 1643, Queen Christina of Sweden ordered John Printz, the governor of New Sweden, to encourage grape planting, and in 1662 Lord Baltimore tried unsuccessfully to grow them in Maryland. William Penn brought French and Spanish vines to plant near Philadelphia in 1683. Later plantings in Florida, Georgia, South Carolina, Rhode Island, and New York, and those of Jefferson at Monticello after 1773, also failed. The European vines took root and sometimes yielded small quantities of wine, but soon lost their leaves and died. The cold eastern winters were blamed, but what chiefly did the killing were plant diseases and insect pests, to which the wild vines that grow in these areas are immune. Had the colonists possessed the resistant varieties and modern chemical sprays which now enable Vinifera and its relatives to grow in many eastern states, wine in this country would have had a very different history. Indeed, if the early attempts to grow wine grapes had succeeded, America probably never would have come to Prohibition. Without good wine as a moderate daily beverage, the colonists and their descendants drank hard apple cider, then applejack and rum, and finally adopted whiskey as the national drink.

Wild grapes were still the principal source of American wines when in 1769*, six years before the American Revolution, Padre Serra is said to have brought Vinifera cuttings to California from Mexico when he founded Mission San Diego. If he actually planted them on his arrival, the date of the first California vintage could have been 1773. For the next sixty years, the only wine made in California was that fermented by the Franciscan friars at their chain of missions, mostly for the Mass, and for their own use on the table and as medicine.

• 3 •

The beginning of commercial winegrowing in this country dates from the time of the Revolution (1775–1783), when the first domesticated native wine grape was introduced in the East and came under regular cultivation. It was the red Alexander, later miscalled the Cape grape, a foxy Labrusca seedling (possibly an accidental cross with Vinifera). John Alexander, the gardener to Lieutenant Governor John Penn, found it growing near the Schuylkill River in the vicinity of Philadelphia, and planted it in Penn's garden. The hardy Alexander withstood the cold winters and the vine pests that had killed the delicate European plants. Of the ten Alexander vines that grew in his Virginia garden, President Jefferson wrote prophetically in 1809 that

it will be well to push the culture of this grape without losing time and efforts in the search of foreign vines which it will take centuries to adapt to our soil and climate.

Jefferson's advice was heeded: The first extensive vineyards in

---

*But the Mission grape, a Vinifera variety, was grown earlier for winemaking at the Franciscan missions in New Mexico; see Chapter 20. And the date when the grape was introduced to California is still a subject of dispute. Some say it was planted first at Mission San Juan Capistrano in 1779.

Pennsylvania, Ohio, and Indiana were planted with the Alexander in the early 1800s. (To answer the perennial question of "which was first," Pennsylvania can claim this country's earliest commercial venture in winegrowing—at York, near the Susquehanna River, where Thomas Eichelberger began growing grapes for wine about 1818.) During the next half-century, scores of native varieties better than the Alexander were found or bred by nurserymen and grape breeders. The pink Catawba was introduced in 1823 by Major John Adlum of Washington, D.C.; the blue Isabella of South Carolina by William Prince of Flushing, New York, about 1816; the purple Concord in 1854 by Ephraim Wales Bull of Massachusetts, and the green Elvira by Jacob Rommel of Missouri in 1870, to mention only a few.

Planting of the domesticated native grapes spread through much of the East and Midwest, encouraged by the Federal and state governments. By 1840, winegrowing ventures had begun in Alabama, Missouri, Maryland, New York, and North Carolina, in addition to the states already named. Some, especially that of Nicholas Longworth at Cincinnati, prospered greatly. Others, such as those of the Kentucky Vineyard Society in that state, ended in failure. Ohio, the leading wine-producing state of the Union in the 1850s, was surpassed in the 1860s by Missouri. By 1880, when the Department of Agriculture published a special report on the progress of grape culture and wine production in the nation, winegrowing enterprises were also shown to be flourishing in Georgia, Illinois, Iowa, Kansas, Michigan, Mississippi, New Jersey, New Mexico, New York, Tennessee, Virginia, and West Virginia.

• 4 •

In the meantime, California had come into the picture. When the Franciscan missions were secularized in the 1830s, a few commercial vineyards were planted at Los Angeles. After the Gold Rush of 1849, many of the newcomers turned from digging for precious metal to pressing liquid gold from grapes. News of their profits made from wine quickly spread, and an epidemic of vine fever swept the state. The California Legislature, to stimulate the new industry, offered a four-year exemption from taxes for all new vineyards planted. Vines soon dotted hills and valleys through much of the 700-mile-long state.

California was boomed abroad as a new paradise discovered for the vine, a land of sunshine where grapes easily reached full ripeness every year. Experts came from France to investigate. In 1862, they reported in the French viticultural journal *Revue Viticole*, that, indeed, California was one American region "capable of entering competition with the wines of Europe . . . in the distant future."

Better Vinifera grapes than the Mission variety, which Padre Serra had brought from Mexico, were imported early from France and Germany. By 1856, one California vintner was already shipping his wines to England, Germany, Russia, Australia, and China, and the state's wines soon began winning medals for quality at international exhibitions.

But the vine-planting boom in California soon created a surplus. In 1867, grapes were sold there for as little as two dollars a ton and wine for ten cents a gallon. Then, in 1869, the first transcontinental railroad was completed. It opened a quick route for wine shipments to the cities of the East and Midwest. California, already producing more wine than any of the eastern states, invaded their markets across the continent.

• 5 •

The eastern markets in the late 1860s and 1870s were controlled by the Ohio, Missouri, and New York producers, and they bitterly opposed the imports from California. Vincent Carosso, in his scholarly history of *The California Wine Industry*, records that the eastern vintners accused the California shippers of selling their wines under counterfeit French and German labels (which was often true) and of putting California labels on eastern wines. Later, Carosso states, the easterners' tactics changed, and merchants in New York and Boston put California labels on the worst adulterated European and blended wines, while selling the best lots from California as European. Spoiled, doctored, and falsely labeled wines were widely sold.

A national pure wine law was urgently needed, and that intensified the East-West struggle. California wanted such a law to prohibit the addition of sugar in winemaking. This the easterners opposed, because in vineyard regions with short, rainy growing seasons—such as Germany, northern France, and the eastern and midwestern states of this country—grapes often fail to develop enough sugar of their own to make wines with the necessary minimum alcoholic content, and also their juice is excessively tart. Such wines need to have sugar added during fermentation and to have their acidity lowered. But California, with its long, dry, sunny growing season, has more than enough sugar in its grapes and often not enough acidity; and since 1887 the state has prohibited any sweetening of its standard wine types except with fresh or condensed grape juice.

When the easterners protested that a Federal law against sugar in winemaking would put them out of business, a California vintner infuriated them with an invitation "to move their wineries to California's sunny clime, where pure wine can be made from the juice of grapes alone." The battle raged from the 1800s until the limited use of sugar was recognized by an act of Congress in 1894. Meanwhile, some of the eastern wineries had begun their present practice of buying neutral California wines in bulk to blend with their own and to soften their pronounced Labrusca and Scuppernong flavors. The East-West schism over sugar recurred following the repeal of Prohibition, but was healed after the Second World War, when both sides agreed on rules, since applied by the Federal Government, on the use of sugar by the vintners outside California. The leading eastern vintners have always supported legal restrictions to prevent the few unscrupulous operators from using sugar and water to stretch the number of gallons obtainable from each ton of grapes.

Before 1900, winegrowing was a full-grown, proud American industry. The brands of leading California, New York, Ohio, Missouri, and New Jersey wineries were competing with European vintages on many of the best restaurant wine lists. California wines in barrels were being exported regularly to England, Germany, Canada, Mexico, Central America, Australia, and the Orient, in direct competition with the wines of Europe. (It has been claimed but never substantiated that some went to France and returned to this country under French labels.) From the three dozen medals and four honorable mentions which American wines received at the Paris Exposition of 1900*, it is evident that their quality was excellent by international standards. I have tasted pre-Prohibition American wines that I would describe as great.

*The award winners were, from California: C. A. Baldwin, Cupertino; Ben Lomond Wine Co., Santa Cruz; Beringer Brothers, St. Helena; California Wine Association, San Francisco; California Winery, Sacramento; Chaix & Bernard, Oakville; Cuesta Francisco, no address given; Germain Wine Co., Los Angeles; Theodore Gier Co., Oakland; Grierson, Oldham & Co., San Francisco; Gundlach-Bundschu Wine Co., Sonoma; Secondo Guasti, Los Angeles; J. O'B. Gunn, Windsor; Charles Hammond, Upper Lake; Hastings Estate, Angwin; Richard Heney, Jr., Cupertino; Italian Swiss Agricultural Colony, Asti; W. S. Keyes, Liparita Vineyard, Angwin; Pierre Klein, Mountain View; Paul Masson, Saratoga; William Palmtag, Hollister; Repsold Company, Napa; Sierra Madre Vintage Co., Lamanda; Julius Paul Smith, Livermore; Southern California Wine Co., Los Angeles; Leland Stanford's Vineyard, Vina; To Kalon Wine Co., Oakville; H. J. Woolacutt, Los Angeles. From Florida: San Luis Vineyard, Tallahassee. From New Jersey: H. T. Dewey & Sons, Egg Harbor. From New York: Brotherhood Wine Co., Washingtonville; Empire State Wine Co., Penn Yan; Germania Wine Cellars, Hammondsport; Pleasant Valley Wine Co., Rheims; Urbana Wine Co., Urbana. From North Carolina: Garrett & Co., Weldon. From Ohio: Engels & Krudwig Wine Co. and M. Hommel, both of Sandusky. From Virginia: Monticello Wine Co., Charlottesville. From Washington, D. C.: Ch. Xander.

• 6 •

But while the industry was reaching maturity during the nine-teenth century, the cancer which was to destroy it was already eating away at its vitals. Actually, it took the Drys a hundred years to terrorize and lobby Americans into accepting National Prohibition in 1920. Although the early temperance advocates aimed only at hard liquor and favored "light wine, beer, and happiness," even the first American dry law, Indiana's 1816 prohibition against Sunday sale, made no exception for wine. As early as the 1830s, thousands of children were signing the pledge to abstain forever from all forms of alcohol, "the subtle poison of the devil." By the 1840s, the wineries' markets began drying up, as scores of towns and counties voted themselves dry in New York, Michigan, Indiana, Georgia, Ohio, New Hampshire, and Iowa. But even while thousands of pulpits thundered that to drink anything alcoholic meant eternal damnation, the wine men could not believe that their business was threatened. For they, too, opposed the drinking of whiskey. Professor George Husmann, the pioneer of scientific winegrowing in Missouri, innocently predicted in 1866 that soon

wine, the most wholesome and purest of all stimulating drinks, will be within the reach of the common laborer and take the place of the noxious and poisonous liquors which are now the curse of so many of our laboring men and have blighted the happiness of so many homes.

Then whole states began going dry—Kansas in 1880, Iowa two years later, followed by Georgia, Oklahoma, Mississippi, North Carolina, Tennessee, West Virginia, and Virginia. Some of these states allowed the making of wine to continue for sale elsewhere, but this did not help their vintners. Barred from selling their wines locally, and unable to compete elsewhere with the wines from California, many of them closed their doors. The ruins of their great stone cellars still can be seen in many parts of the Bible Belt, but most of their vineyards were allowed to die.

The vintners in the "wet" states still could not see their approaching doom, because occasional shortages of wine made their business seem good. What caused the shortages was the phylloxera vine pest, which between 1860 and 1900 destroyed vast portions of the vineyards of Europe and California in the most destructive plant-disease epidemic of all time. And meanwhile the Drys were at work, busily brainwashing the nation against alcohol in any form. They demanded that mention of wine be removed from school and college texts, even including the Greek and Roman classics. At their insistence medicinal wines were dropped from the United States Pharmacopeia. They published books attempting to prove that the wine praised in the Bible was really unfermented grape juice. The Kansas State Horticultural Society printed the praises of fresh grapes as food, proclaiming that

to the glory of Kansas, 99½ per cent of this luscious fruit which grows freely throughout the state, too good to be made a chief source of the degradation of the race, is used without fermentation.

By 1914, when the First World War broke out in Europe, thirty-three American states had gone dry. Then, having instilled in the nation the mass guilt feeling about alcohol that now seems incredible to most people born since the 1930s, the Drys put over Wartime Prohibition in 1919, followed by the Eighteenth Amendment and the Volstead National Prohibition Act in 1920.

• 7 •

What happened next was totally unexpected. At first, the gloomy winegrowers began ripping out their vineyards, but soon they were wishing they hadn't. For the Drys had overlooked, or else failed to understand, an obscure provision of the Volstead Act—Section 29, which dealt with the home production of fruit juices. Originally placed in the law to placate the Virginia apple farmers, Section 29 permitted a householder to make "nonintoxicating cider and fruit juices exclusively for use in his home" to the extent of 200 gallons yearly. In 1920 began the peddling of "juice grapes"* to home winemakers and bootleggers from pushcarts in New York and from trucks in Boston and other cities. Suddenly, grape prices at the vineyards leaped from ten dollars a ton to the unheard-of figure of one hundred dollars, and this started a feverish new rush of vine-planting across the nation. Soon more "nonintoxicating" wine was being made in America's basements each year than the commercial wineries had ever made before. Prohibition had brought the growers a bonanza.

The California grape growers, grown wealthy overnight, had only one gripe—a shortage of refrigerator cars—which they bitterly blamed on the railroads. Prosperity in the vineyard areas lasted exactly five years. Then, in 1925, the beleaguered railroads obliged by abruptly ending the car shortage. With plenty of refrigerator cars, too much fruit was shipped, and when it rotted at the eastern terminals waiting for buyers who already had enough, the bottom dropped out of the grape market. From the collapse in 1925, ex-

*To blot out memory of the Bacchic role of vineyards, the Department of Agriculture changed "wine grapes" in its statistical crop reports to the euphemism "juice grapes."

cept during the Second World War, California suffered from a chronic surplus of grapes until 1971.

More than a hundred wineries in California and New York and some dozens in New Jersey, Ohio, and Missouri survived the dry laws. Throughout Prohibition, they legally made sacramental wines and champagnes for the clergy, medicinal wines for sale by druggists on doctors' prescriptions, medicated wine tonics which required no prescription, salted wines for cooking (salted to make them undrinkable), and grape juice both fresh and condensed as a concentrate. Medicinal wine tonic became a popular tipple, because buyers soon learned its secret; when refrigerated, the horrible-tasting medicaments settled to the bottom of the bottle, leaving a drinkable wine. Of the sacramental wines, the greatest volume was sold through rabbis, because the Jewish faith requires the religious use of wine in the home. Anybody could call himself a rabbi and get a permit to buy wine legally, merely by presenting a list of his congregation. Millions of all faiths and of no faith became members of fake synagogues, some without their knowledge when the lists were copied from telephone directories. (My next-door neighbor in San Francisco bought port and sherry at four dollars a gallon from a rabbi whose synagogue was a hall bedroom, which he called "Congregation L'Chayim.")

• 8 •

Some of the wineries profited richly from their sales of tonics and sacramental wines, but after the grape market collapse, the vineyardists remained in a desperate state of depression. California vineyard land that had jumped in price from $200 to $2500 an acre in 1923 sold for $250 an acre in 1926, when some farmers offered their bankers deeds to their land to pay their debts. For a time, the grape industry looked to grape concentrate for salvation. Grape juice in kegs and also packages of pressed grapes called "wine bricks" were being sold to some home winemakers. With each keg or package came a yeast pill to start fermentation and a printed warning not to use it "because if you do, this will turn into wine, which would be illegal."

Captain Paul Garrett, of Virginia Dare fame, had a brilliant new idea. Why not sell concentrated grape juice in cans, together with complete winemaking and bottling "service" right in the buyer's home, and thus make wine available to everyone? And still more brilliant, why not let President Herbert Hoover's new farm relief program finance the scheme, since nobody needed relief more then the bankrupt grape industry? In 1929, Garrett led the largest surviving wineries of California into a giant combine with his New

York wineries, called Fruit Industries, Inc. Mrs. Mabel Walker Willebrandt, the star of the attorney general's enforcement staff in Washington, D.C., was hired by the combine to avert any clashes with the Prohibition law. Fruit Industries got millions in loans from Hoover's Federal Farm Board to "salvage the grape surplus" by making it into grape concentrate. In 1931, the concentrate, called "Vine-Glo" (in a naming contest among grape growers, this name won over "Merri-Cal"), was advertised for sale throughout the nation. Full-page newspaper ads announced "Home delivery—guaranteed consumer satisfaction—Port, Virginia Dare, Muscatel, Tokay, Sauterne, Riesling, Claret, Burgundy—It's Legal!" Some of the wines expertly made from the Vine-Glo syrup were of surprisingly good quality. But when the Drys got a glimpse of the Vine-Glo ads and learned that "home delivery" meant winemaking service in the home, they were furious. They stormed Washington with protests. Soon the telephone rang at the Fruit Industries office in San Francisco. An official voice from Washington ordered: "Quit! Now, today, as of this minute!" The California Vineyardists Association pleaded for reversal, but to no avail. The Association denounced the Hoover administration for "betraying the grape industry," and Vine-Glo died on the vine.

In 1932, as the dry era neared its close, a bill introduced in Congress brought new hope to the growers. It aimed to legalize light wine and beer without waiting for Repeal. Eleven percent by volume was proposed as the permissible alcoholic content for wine, and 3.2 percent alcohol by weight for beer, on the ground that beverages of these strengths would be "nonintoxicating." Hoping to speed the bill's passage—but without consulting the winegrowers—Senator William Gibbs McAdoo of California proposed a compromise: make 3.2 percent the figure for both wine and beer. To the wine people's disgust, the bill as thus amended was promptly passed. A few vintners actually diluted some wine to 3.2 percent and sold it—a watery, unappealing fluid which they scornfully christened "McAdoo wine."

• 9 •

The end of Prohibition on December 5, 1933, found the remnants of the wine industry mostly in ruins after thirteen dry years. Almost the only fine, aged wines available were held by the few altar-wine producers for the Catholic clergy, who have always demanded quality in the wines they use to celebrate the Mass. Speculators, expecting quick profits, reopened many old cellars, some with casks moldy from long disuse. Wines hastily made in October and already half-spoiled flooded the country during that frenzied December. Their contents still fermenting, bottles blew up on thousands of store shelves and in windows, creating an odorous reputation for all products of the grape. In California, several million gallons of wine were condemned by the State Department of Public Health as unfit to drink and were either distilled into alcohol, turned into vinegar, or destroyed. Sound wines, too, spoiled after leaving the wineries, because restaurateurs and storekeepers, unaware that table and sparkling wines are perishable, stored the bottles standing up, allowing the corks to dry out and the wines to become acetic or oxidized.

Although the Eighteenth Amendment was dead, vast areas of the nation remained legally dry under state and local Prohibition laws.* Dry-minded state legislatures imposed high taxes on wine, treating it as merely another form of liquor. In most of the states, exorbitant license fees and burdensome regulations prevented farmers from starting wineries to sell their grapes in the form of wine. Seventeen states established state or municipal monopoly liquor stores, the forbidding kinds of outlets which discourage housewives from venturing inside to shop for wine. These stores usually offer only skimpy assortments, and consumers cannot order wines mailed to them from other states, because the postal laws still prohibit the shipment of any alcoholic beverage by parcel post.

· 10 ·

A whole generation of maturing Americans, grown accustomed to bathtub gin and moonshine, were ignorant of wine, a foreign-seeming beverage which to them tasted sour—as many of the early shipments were. For most of the table wines made shortly after Repeal were poor in quality, and many were undrinkable. Some of their defects could have been corrected, but the main trouble was a lack of grapes suitable to make good dry table wines. Prohibition had left the nation with a vast acreage of vineyards growing the wrong grapes. During the "juice grape" boom of the 1920s, many California growers had grafted over their fine Riesling, Pinot, and Cabernet vines, whose tiny, thin-skinned grapes brought them only $50 a ton, to such coarse, thick-skinned varieties as the Alicante Bouschet, which brought $100 a ton at the vineyards because it shipped and sold well. (The Alicante also had red juice, and bootleggers could make 700 gallons of "dago

*State prohibition was not repealed by Kansas until 1948; Oklahoma remained dry until 1959, and Mississippi until 1966. Even as recently as 1970, local Prohibition laws in 32 states still barred the sale of wine in 589 of the nation's 3078 counties and in hundreds more towns and school districts, representing 10 percent of the nation's area and 6 percent of the population.

red" from a single ton by adding sugar and water.) In the eastern states, too, the best native wine-grape varieties had been largely replaced by the hardy Concord, which is good for fresh grape juice but when fermented dry makes harsh, foxy-tasting table wines. The foreign-born, who had continued drinking wine with their meals throughout Prohibition, rejected the new commercial wines, preferring to go on buying grapes and making their own.

And to make matters worse, a flood of awesome books and articles, written by dilettantes strutting their knowledge, warned Americans that rigid rules must be observed in serving wines— only certain types with certain foods, in certain glasses, and at certain specific temperatures. Rather than risk committing social blunders, millions avoided serving wine in their homes at all. Except for sometimes sampling the cheap red wines served with spaghetti in Italian restaurants, and buying occasional bottles of sherry or port, most native-born buyers of alcoholic beverages stuck to beer and hard liquor.

As a result, there was little demand at Repeal for the dry, light (usually 12 percent) table wines, which are the principal wine types of the world because they are used almost entirely with food. One group of wines sold well—the dessert wines—port, sherry, tokay, and muscatel. At that time, these dessert wines were classed legally as "fortified" because they were strengthened with brandy to 20 percent alcoholic content. Because the federal tax on wine is only a fraction of the tax on liquor, "fortified wine" was the cheapest intoxicant available, and much of it was drunk by the derelicts called "winos" on the skid rows of the nation. This situation created grave trouble for the wineries, as will be seen presently. Before Prohibition, table wines had outsold dessert wines in the United States by as much as three to one. But in 1935, the California wineries were shipping three gallons of dessert wines to one of table wines, and the wineries of Arkansas, Michigan, and Washington made the dessert or "fortified" types almost exclusively.

Such were the appalling legacies that Prohibition left in its wake. The once-proud American wine industry, which before 1900 had exported its wines around the world and won prizes at international competitions, was reborn in ruins. It was making the wrong kinds of wine from the wrong kinds of grapes for the wrong kind of consumers in a whiskey-drinking nation with guilt feelings about imbibing in general and a confused attitude toward wine in particular. Some of the vintners doubted that winegrowing would ever recover as a respected, economically sound industry. When a ruinous glut of the grape and wine markets developed after the 1935 vintage, many a grape grower, mourning the bonanza of the early "juice grape" shipping days, openly regretted the repeal of the dry law.

• 11 •

Would the Government, which had destroyed the industry, help to restore it? Some members of President Franklin D. Roosevelt's administration thought it should. There was ample precedent for Federal assistance; the Department of Agriculture had encouraged winegrowing for more than a century, operating experimental vineyards and breeding wine grapes until Prohibition intervened. As late as 1880, the only Federal census statistics of state-by-state grape production were given in gallons of wine made, because the chief purpose of planting vineyards was to grow wine. This was always the case in other countries; nine tenths of the world's grapes are grown for wine. Shipping of fresh grapes as a dessert fruit was unimportant until refrigerated freight cars were adapted for fruit shipments about 1887, and the raisin industry remained small until the 1890s.

Promptly at Repeal, Eleanor Roosevelt began serving American wines in the White House, restoring the custom that had prevailed until "Lemonade Lucy," the wife of President Rutherford B. Hayes, stopped it in 1877.

Dr. Rexford Guy Tugwell, a member of Roosevelt's famed "Brain Trust," made elaborate plans to restore winegrowing as a nationwide industry. Tugwell, who then was the assistant secretary of agriculture, even favored exempting wine and beer from taxation in order to hold down the consumption of hard liquor. In 1933 he sent the Agriculture Department's Dr. Charles A. Magoon to Europe to collect the newest wine yeast cultures. At Tugwell's direction, two complete model wineries were built, one at the Government's giant agricultural research center in Beltsville, Maryland, and the other at the Meridian, Mississippi, research station which served the southeastern states. Both wineries were fully equipped with crushers, presses, underground vats, and there was a brandy still at Beltsville.

But neither model winery ever crushed a grape. Congressman Clarence Cannon of Missouri, the perennial chairman of the House Appropriations Committee, was a lifelong Prohibitionist, and when word reached him of what Tugwell was doing, the project was doomed. "No Federal money shall go to any fermentation industry!" Cannon thundered, and he threatened to block the entire Department of Agriculture appropriation unless the wine work was suppressed forthwith. Cannon prevailed. The model wineries were stripped of their equipment, which was sold as government surplus.* During the next thirty years, "wine" was a word the Department's scientists feared to utter, and they would look around furtively before even mentioning "juice." It therefore deserves mention that when Representative Cannon died in May 1964, two Federal wine-quality research projects were promptly approved in Washington, D.C., and the work quickly got under way in the Agriculture Department's regional research laboratory at Albany, California, and at the Geneva Experiment Station in New York State.

• 12 •

A shortage of trained winemakers plagued the wineries at Repeal. Old-timers with better jobs elsewhere were reluctant to return to the cellars. Partially spoiled wines were doctored by chemists, who only made them worse. But back in 1880, by an act of the Legislature, the University of California had established a special department to conduct wine research and to teach winemaking at its Berkeley campus. And fortunately, this fifty-three-year-old wine school was still intact. It had continued through Prohibition under the innocent title of "the fruit products laboratory," concocting nonalcoholic grape drinks and grape jellies and teaching students the scientific processing of other fruits. Professors Frederic T. Bioletti and William Vere Cruess quickly switched their courses back to winemaking, and soon were graduating classes of enologists to man the wineries. The University launched new programs of wine research and grape-breeding, took over the Federal Government's neglected vineyard in Napa County, established an experimental winery and brandy distillery at its Davis campus, and developed intensive new instruction in vineyard and winery operation.

Except in New York, where Professor Ulysses Prentiss Hedrick resumed his wine-grape-breeding work at the Geneva Station in 1934, the other grape states did little or nothing at Repeal to help their winegrowers or to improve their vineyards.

In Maryland, however, an amateur winemaker and newspaperman named Philip Wagner began about 1935 to plant a different kind of wine grape which was destined to change the taste of many American wines during the next few decades. Until then,

---

*The Beltsville winery now houses a seed and nut laboratory and is called the West Building. How it came to be built is a legend still told and retold there. The winery at Meridian stood empty, its original purpose a whispered secret, until the station there was closed in 1965. On a visit several years ago to the Hallcrest Vineyard near Felton, California, I watched a shiny little crusher-stemmer receiving Cabernet Sauvignon grapes and learned that it came from the Government's model winery at Beltsville, the winery that never crushed a grape.

virtually all of the wine grown outside of California had been made of native American grape varieties with their distinctive, usually foxy flavors. Wagner imported and planted the French hybrids, the nonfoxy crosses of Vinifera with indigenous American grapes, and proved that with the hardiness inherited from their native parents, they could thrive where the delicate Old World grapes had failed. These new grape varieties spread during the 1940s to vineyards in New York and Ohio; and by the 1970s, wines without the slightest trace of foxiness were being made from the hybrids in no less than twenty states. Wagner, the amateur, had spread the hybrids almost as far as the legendary Johnny Appleseed once spread the apple tree.

· 13 ·

About this time, another journalist, wine writer Frank Musselman Schoonmaker, started still another trend that has influenced viniana profoundly in this country. Having entered the importing business in New York City following Repeal, Schoonmaker in 1939 added to his import line an assortment of the best California, Ohio, and New York State wines he could find, having them bottled by the wineries as Schoonmaker Selections. As an importer, he refused to call his American wines sauterne, rhine wine, chablis, or burgundy, the European type names they generally had borne before Prohibition. Instead Schoonmaker gave them varietal labels, naming each wine for the grape variety from which it was principally made. Varietal labels were not new, because wines called Cabernet, Riesling, Zinfandel, Catawba, Delaware, and Scuppernong had been on the market before the turn of the century. But Schoonmaker introduced additional grape names the wine-buying public had never heard of: Chardonnay, Pinot Blanc, Grey Riesling, Sémillon, Gamay, Pinot Noir, Grenache Rosé, Niagara, Elvira, Moore's Diamond. His wine selections were excellent; their strange names suggested rare quality and provided topics for conversation. These were extra values for which connoisseurs, until then the buyers of imports almost exclusively, were ready to pay. When other vintners saw Schoonmaker's American "varietals" beginning to sell at premium prices in the best stores and restaurants, they lost little time in following suit. Varietal labels soon became the mark of the costliest American wines. Then, of course, more grape names began appearing on labels, and the "varietal" wine list grew during the next two decades to include Barbera, Chenin Blanc, Folle Blanche, Gewürztraminer, Green Hungarian, Petite Sirah, Pinot Saint George, Sylvaner, and dozens more.

An ironic twist developed when European vintners, recognizing a good thing, began in the 1960s to imitate the new American labels. Until then, only a few European wines—the Alsatian, some Italian, and the muscatels—had used any varietal names. But now, for the first time, there began appearing, on American store shelves, wines from France and Spain newly christened "Pinot Noir," "Chardonnay," and "Cabernet Sauvignon," mostly at low prices and of doubtful authenticity in most cases.

Amidst the chaos at Prohibition's end, a group of old-line California winegrowers organized the Wine Institute and set out to rehabilitate their industry. In 1934, they obtained reissuance of the state's minimum wine quality standards. They worked with the eastern producers toward national standards, which were issued by the Federal Government two years later.

The Wine Institute's founders believed that by producing sound, inexpensive table wine and by educating the public to drink it daily with food, they could wean America from whiskey and gin and make this a wine-drinking country. Their models were France and Italy, whose yearly wine consumption approximates thirty gallons per capita and consists almost entirely of table wine. This had always been the goal of such historic figures as Jefferson, Longworth, and Husmann, and of California's winegrowing senators, Leland Stanford and George Hearst.

In 1938, the Wine Institute persuaded the state's wineries to tax themselves for a nationwide educational campaign to spread the gospel of wine as the beverage of temperate, civilized dining. To administer the program, they created the Wine Advisory Board under supervision of the State Department of Agriculture. Advertisements, articles, booklets, and leaflets by the millions urged Americans to glamorize their dinners with wine and to use it in cooking.

Wine use grew. Consumption of commercial wine in the United States rose from 33 million gallons in 1934 to almost 90 million in 1940, nearly all of it American-grown. The 1940 volume amounted to eight tenths of a gallon per capita, compared to a mere half gallon in the highest pre-Prohibition year. But while the advertisements preached the use of light table wine with food, more than two thirds of the total consumed—almost all of the increase—was of the port-sherry-muscatel group, the 20 percent dessert or "fortified" wines. Table wine, on which the industry's future depended, was still its stepchild. Many of the growers became convinced that the Advisory Board's efforts to promote table wine were a waste of their money, that Americans could never be taught to drink wine with meals. If this country would ever consume as much table wine as dessert wine, they said, it would represent the millenium.

The misuse of dessert wine by the "winos" endangered the legal and social status of wine following Repeal. What made it worse was the word "fortified," invented by the British to describe sweet wines preserved by the 200-year-old process of adding brandy to arrest fermentation. Unfortunately, the American wine regulations in 1936 had copied those of England, and included this frightening nine-letter word as the legal designation for dessert wines. As a result, "fortified wine" began to be blamed for the miseries of the depraved alcoholics who drank it because it was cheap. Many people, to avoid associating themselves with "winos," even banned the 20 percent wines from their homes. Soon laws to tax "fortified wine" out of existence or to prohibit its sale entirely were proposed in several state legislatures. The legislators had no objection to port, sherry, tokay, or muscatel, overlooking the fact that they contained brandy, but they imagined that any wine called "fortified" must pack some mysterious power. In 1938, the vintners decided to get rid of the word, and they persuaded the Government to ban it from all labels and advertisements. But the thought of dessert wine as "fortified" stuck in the public mind. In 1951, Treasury officials recommended to the House Ways and Means Committee that the Federal tax rates on wines be tripled on the ground that such wine was competing unfairly with high-taxed whiskey. A bill containing the new rates was promptly voted by the Committee. It was a body blow to the wine industry. At stake were the keys to its very existence: the historic tax advantage of wine over liquor and beer; the classification of wine as an article of food, and the treatment of winegrowing as an agricultural pursuit separate from the distilling and brewing industries. Alarm spread through the vineyard areas, and growers from all of the grape states besieged Washington with protests. Amendments to the tax bill in the Senate Finance Committee provided for smaller increases, resulting in the present rates of 17 cents per gallon on table wines and 67 cents on dessert wines. But to get the last mention of "fortified" erased from Federal regulations required an act of Congress, the wine law of 1954.

• 14 •

The gains in wine consumption were interrupted during the Second World War, because almost three fourths of the raisin grapes previously used by the California wineries were diverted for use as food, and wine was in short supply. Also during the war, the whiskey distillers invaded the wine industry. What caused the invasion was the Government's order converting liquor distilleries to the production of alcohol for war uses (an order which included the wineries' brandy stills). The distillers' only purpose in buying wineries was to provide their sales forces with something besides scarce liquor to sell during the war. But wine benefited from the distiller invasion, because the liquor firms supplied sorely needed capital for winery improvements, and they taught this country's winegrowers valuable lessons about packaging their products attractively. Only a dozen of the many hundreds of wine companies were actually acquired by the big whiskey firms; and when the war ended, most of the wineries were sold back to the growers.

At the conflict's end, wineries were rebuilt and re-equipped, and the planting of better grapes was accelerated. The number of wineries shrank, however, as many small growers gave up or were absorbed by the large firms. Of some 1300 bonded wineries operating in 16 states in 1936, only 271 were left—but in 20 states—by 1960.

In 1946, the University of California released the first new varieties created in its grape-breeding program at Davis. Two of these, Ruby Cabernet and Emerald Riesling, made such good table wines that their planting since has spread throughout California and to several other countries. Meanwhile, too, Philip Wagner's French hybrid grapes had begun appearing in the New York and Ohio vineyards.

Winemaking, regarded for centuries as an art rather than a science, then began to benefit from modern research. Knowledge of the chemistry of grapes and wine advanced more in the decades following the Second World War than in the preceding two thousand years. The American vintners, in the process of rebuilding, with a new breed of technically trained winemakers, took advantage of the new knowledge, while most producers in the Old World were satisfied to continue making wine by rule of thumb as in the past. During the 1950s, the University of California at Davis became the world's leading center of viticultural and enological research. Winegrowers in other countries started sending their sons to Davis to be trained, and their governments invited experts of the Davis faculty to come and advise them on ways to improve their wines. The American Society of Enologists was founded at Davis in 1950. With its annual technical conferences and its quarterly *American Journal of Enology and Viticulture*, the Society attracted an international membership and became the leading organization of the winemaking profession in the world.

• 15 •

The quality of American wines improved after the war. Some of the wineries had replaced the coarse shipping-grape varieties in their vineyards with superior wine grapes. By 1956, the twenty-third year after Repeal, the California producers of premium wines felt they were ready to challenge the wines of Europe. They set up comparative tastings in cities across the country, pitting the best California vintages against their most famous Old World rivals. Bottles from France, Germany, Italy, Spain, Portugal, and California were bought at random from store shelves, the prices of the imports averaging double those of their native counterparts. Dealers and consumers were invited to come and taste the wines "blind," i.e., from numbered glasses; the bottle labels were hidden. Nearly 1500 tasters came to sixty-eight such tastings in three years. They sampled the wines and wrote their preferences on secret ballots. When the votes were counted, the results astonished even the Californians: California outscored Europe on champagnes, red table wines, and sherries, while the European white table wines, rosés, and ports were preferred over California's; and in the total point scores, California came out slightly ahead.

Only California wines could be thus compared directly with those from Europe, because both are made of the same Vinifera grape varieties. Eastern wines, being made of the foxy native grapes and as yet to a limited extent from French hybrids, could not. But California's monopoly of fine Vinifera wines was about to end. For while the "blind" tastings were going on, a new chapter in American wine history was opening near the town of Hammondsport in the Finger Lakes district of New York State. There, after three centuries during which repeated attempts to grow Vinifera grapes in the East had failed miserably, a Russian-born German emigré named Dr. Konstantin Frank had planted a vineyard of such Old World grapes as Riesling and Chardonnay, and his wines were thriving in the New York climate. In 1957, their first crop was made into wine, and with each successive vintage these vines have confounded the viticultural experts who had predicted they soon must die in the frigid winters.

· 16 ·

By the mid-1950s, average yearly wine use in the United States had risen to 145 million gallons, and per capita consumption was approaching nine tenths of a gallon. Of this total, California supplied 119 million gallons, 22 other states produced about 19 million, and 7 million were imports from Europe. New kinds of wine were beginning to court the beer-and-cola palates of Americans: the sweet, Concord-flavored kosher type; the soft red "vinos," successors to the old, astringent "dago red"; new semisweet versions of rosé; white and red table wines with slight carbonation;

and the flood of 20 percent "special natural" flavored wines with such coined names as Thunderbird and Silver Satin. But two thirds of the total still was high-alcohol dessert wine, the same proportion as before the war.

Despite the crazy quilt of different state laws, wine distribution improved. The leading California and New York premium producers began teaching restaurant, hotel, and club staffs, wherever the laws permitted, how to store table wines properly and how to sell them with meals. People who had never bought wine before sampled it in these establishments and began serving it to guests in their homes. But of all the developments during this decade, none did more to advance the use of wine in America than the vast improvement of the mass-produced, inexpensive California table wines, made possible by the enormous recent advances in grape-growing and winemaking technology. In the past most of these low-priced wines had been shipped across the country in tank cars to more than a thousand local bottlers, who sold them, not always in sound condition, under a multitude of local brands. But now, the largest California mass producers switched to bottling their own wines, and launched multimillion-dollar advertising campaigns on television to make their brands known. This, for the first time, brought reliably palatable, branded table wines in convenient jugs within the reach of millions of households at prices low enough for everyday use. By 1960 fewer than 200 local bottlers remained in business. These were mostly old-time vintners who always had maintained the quality of the wines sold under their names.

• 17 •

The war had brought changes in popular tastes for food and drink. Millions of young Americans of both sexes, after military sojourns in the wine countries overseas, came home with a liking for continental cuisine and its liquid accompaniment, table wine. Postwar touring, spurred by bargain air fares, lured still more Americans to Europe, and they, too, returned with a new appreciation of wine. At home, people with new affluence and leisure took up gourmet cookery, and publishers noted the steady sales growth of books on wines and international cuisine. Wine tastings became popular as a new kind of social event in homes and at club and charity functions. Millions discovered wine as a symbol of status and culture. When college extension courses in wine appreciation were first offered for a fee, the classes were quickly oversubscribed by people thirsty for vinous knowledge.

Attitudes toward drinking were changing. As population shifted from rural areas to the cities, the old Bible Belt view of all imbibing as sinful began to fade. Dry counties in the "local option" states voted wet in increasing numbers, sending the WCTU forces down to ignominious defeat, and new movements were organized to repeal the remaining "blue laws" against the sale of liquor on Sundays. Women's magazines for half a century had refused to print advertisements for alcoholic beverages, but now solicited ads for wine and beer. Housewives, who had always left liquor purchasing to their husbands as an exclusive prerogative of males, began buying the wine to serve with the family dinner.

• 18 •

What the grape growers a generation earlier had called "the millenium"—when the nation would drink as much table wine as dessert wine—came in 1968. Table wine, the industry's stepchild, had doubled in consumption volume, and champagnes, which are table wines with bubbles, had more than trebled in only ten years. Millions of Americans were adding dry table wines to their daily meals, while dessert wine consumption remained virtually unchanged. A few of the states with government-monopoly liquor stores began amending their laws to let table wines be sold in grocery stores. By 1972, total U.S. wine consumption had soared to nearly 340 million gallons, over a gallon and a half per capita, three times the rate before Prohibition, and these figures appeared certain to double again in ten more years. There were forecasts that wine use might reach three, five, even ten gallons per capita, that the country eventually could consume a billion gallons per year.

These developments set off "the wine revolution," with reverberations across the continent and to wine countries around the world. Abruptly the whole national pattern of grape-growing was reversed. To supply the better grapes required to make table wines, new vineyards were needed; California's surplus raisin and table grapes and the East's leftover Concords would no longer do. Several state legislatures, despite Prohibitionist opposition, voted appropriations for wine-grape research. A wave of vine-planting unparalleled in world history spread across the United States. Entirely new winegrowing districts were discovered and were planted with thousands of acres in California and in the Yakima Valley of Washington. Winegrowing returned to the Sacramento Valley and to the old Sierra foothill gold-mining regions; to Pennsylvania, Indiana, and to the area around Hermann in Missouri; to the Willamette Valley of Oregon, and to the Ohio River Valley near Cincinnati, where Nicholas Longworth had made a famous

Sparkling Catawba more than a century ago. The planting of Scuppernong grapes for wine was revived in the Carolinas and Georgia. New York and Michigan expanded their acreage of Labrusca and of Philip Wagner's French hybrids, and new plantings of Dr. Frank's unexpectedly successful Vinifera appeared in Maryland and other eastern states. The vintners of Arkansas switched their attention from dessert wines to table wines and champagnes. New wineries opened for business in Oregon, Washington, Maryland, Michigan, Indiana, Idaho, New York, and for the first time in memory, in New Hampshire, Oklahoma, and Vermont.

Entirely new kinds of wine made their appearance: the low-alcohol, flavored "pop" or "mod" wines and new versions of the pinkish champagne called Cold Duck. Light wines made of apples, pears, and strawberries became competitors of beer for the favor of American youth.

Wine suddenly became Big Business in America. Giant corporations in other fields, led by the returning whiskey distillers, snapped up control of famous old family wineries. Food-processing, brewing, tobacco, and oil companies, some of them multinational conglomerates, invested millions in the booming United States table wine industry. Several even bought up vineyards and wineries in Europe, South America, and Australia to help supply this country's growing thirst. Thousands of investors and speculators scrambled to buy shares of winery stock issues. Immense new, ultramodern wineries were built, with research laboratories, mechanical grape harvesters, computerized processing and bottling equipment, to turn out steadily increasing volumes of the best standardized wines in the world.

Yet in another direction at the same time, American wine was becoming increasingly a romantic little business, as adventurous new pioneers of winegrowing started tiny new vineyards and built mini-wineries to produce handmade wines for the future in localities where this was done a century ago and in many others where wine was never grown before.

But most important, because a nation's wines inevitably are judged by the very best it produces, was the fact that American premium wines had surpassed in quality those produced in the pre-Prohibition past. They again were challenging, both at home and in export markets abroad, the finest wines produced in the rest of the world.

In the fourth decade since the rebirth of winegrowing in America, the nation was at last becoming the "Vineland" which Leif Ericson had named it a thousand years earlier. An entirely new chapter in the remarkable four-century history of wine in America had begun.

3

Scuppernong Country—
The Original American Wine

IN THE southeastern states, and nowhere else in the world, there grows a grape so fragrant that the early navigators, approaching the coast in September, detected its rich scent long before they made landfall. It is the Scuppernong, from which southerners have been making wine for almost four centuries to drink with their corn pone, fish muddle, and cake. This was the first, the original American wine.

The greenish-bronze Scuppernong and its many-hued relatives of the *Vitis rotundifolia* or Muscadine family are unlike any other grapes. They grow not in bunches but in clusters, each berry as large and rotund as a cherry or a marble. They are seldom picked; instead, men walk beneath the vines, beating the canes with tobacco sticks, causing the ripe grapes to drop onto sheets or hammocks laid on the ground. As you drive through Scuppernong country, almost every farm you see has its single vine, a dense, tangled mass behind the house, as much a part of the scene as the tobacco barn. A single Scuppernong vine may cover a whole acre and produce, even without cultivation, a ton of fruit yielding five barrels of wine.

The juice of Scuppernong, if fermented dry, makes an amber, strong-tasting, intriguing though usually somewhat bitter wine. But when the wine is sweetened, as winemakers in Scuppernong country have always done, it becomes an exotic nectar reminiscent of fresh plums, with a musky aroma and taste entirely its own. The flavor of Scuppernong is so pronounced that if its wine is blended with Concord, the Scuppernong character will overwhelm and hide the foxy Concord taste. It was to such a blend of Scuppernong and Concord, with California wine added, that the late Captain Paul Garrett gave the name Virginia Dare, and it was the best-selling wine in the United States during the two decades before Prohibition.

• 2 •

If you travel the Atlantic Coast Line Highway in North Carolina and wish to visit a modern Scuppernong vineyard, look up Raymond Hartsfield, whose place is eight miles northeast of Holly Ridge in Onslow County. When I was last there, he had twenty-five acres of Muscadine vines neatly trained on overhead arbors, with one perfectly flowered (male) vine for each nine vines with pistillate (female) blossoms. Hartsfield gets eight tons to the acre, but he has lost two entire crops in recent years to the hurricanes that roar in at harvest season from the Atlantic; this part of the coast is known as Hurricane Alley.

Hartsfield once operated the only winery in North Carolina, the Onslow Wine Cellar. He closed it in 1968 to devote his full time to raising grapes, which he ships to a winery in Virginia. North Carolina had thirteen wineries back in 1947, when Hartsfield and

Scuppernong Country

🍇 MUSCADINES   🍇 BUNCH GRAPES

his father first planted vines on their former tobacco fields. In the following year, Burke and Catawba Counties voted dry, putting several of the wineries out of business, and the rest, fearing that the entire state might follow, closed their cellars one by one. The grape growers began destroying their vineyards, but the Hartsfields started enlarging theirs, for they had heard that the demand for Scuppernong wine was rising—not in the Prohibitionist-dominated South, but in the northern wet states.

In 1961, Richards Wine Cellars in Virginia, the principal producer of Scuppernong wine, offered Carolina farmers five-year contracts to grow Muscadines at two hundred dollars a ton and also offered to provide them with vines to plant. A vineyard-planting boom started in North Carolina, where farmers' income from flue-cured tobacco was declining. Members of the New River Grape Growers Association set out many vineyards in Onslow, Moore, Jones, Robeson, and Lenoir counties.

Although Muscadine grapes can be eaten fresh or made into juice, jam, or jelly, the purpose of the plantings was to produce grapes for wine. In 1965, the North Carolina Legislature, convinced that the state's winegrowing industry was about to be reborn, voted a $166,000 appropriation for Muscadine grape and wine research and for grower education. At the State University in Raleigh, Dr. William Nesbitt started breeding new Muscadine varieties especially suited for winemaking, soon adding tests of bunch grapes suited for North Carolina climates. Dr. Dan Carroll set up an experimental winery in the Food Science Department to develop new types of Muscadine table wine. James A. Graham, the state director of agriculture, predicted that "North Carolina Scuppernong will someday win a place among the distinctive wines of the world."

Grape acreage in the state jumped from less than 400 acres in 1966 to more than 2200 acres in 1972. New varieties of Muscadines, self-fertile and more vigorous than Scuppernong, were introduced. They now come in all colors, jet black, red, freckled, and in pearl hues as well as in the traditional bronze. (This pre-presents a problem in wine labeling, for the Muscadines have such names as Mish, Hunt, Creek, Thomas, Higgins, Tarheel, Magnolia, Noble, and Carlos, while the only name northern consumers know for Muscadine wine is Scuppernong. The recent trend, which makes sense, has been to label any wine made predominantly from Muscadines as Scuppernong.)

• 3 •

Although Muscadines thrive in the humid Coastal Plain and Piedmont Plateau areas of all the southeastern states, North Carolina claims Scuppernong as its own. The first account of these grapes occurs in the logbook of Giovanni da Verrazano, the Florentine navigator who in 1524 explored the Cape Fear River Valley for France. He reported "many vines growing naturally there" and that "without all doubt they would yield excellent wines." Amadas and Barlow, sent by Sir Walter Raleigh to explore the Carolina coast from Roanoke Island in 1584, described a land "so full of grapes as the very beating and surge of the sea overflowed them . . . In all the world, the like abundance is not to be found."

Legend credits Raleigh with discovering the Scuppernong grape on Roanoke Island and introducing it elsewhere. This accounts for the fame of the so-called "Mother Vine," once called the Walter Raleigh vine, which is one of the tourist attractions at Manteo on the historic island near the site of Raleigh's Lost Colony. The vine has a trunk almost two feet thick, is said to be at least three hundred years old, and still produces grapes. With a few neighboring vines, it supplied the Mother Vineyard Winery, which operated at Manteo until 1954.

Scuppernong was named for a town, which was named for a river, which was named for a tree. "Ascopo" was the Algonquin Indian name for the sweet bay tree. "Ascuponung," meaning place of the Ascopo, appeared on old maps of North Carolina as the name of the river in Washington County, near Albemarle Sound. Later maps spelled it Cuscoponung, then Cusponung, next Scuponung and Scupuning, until by 1800 the spelling of the river had become Scuppernong. The grape, however, was merely called the White Grape until James Blount of the town of Scuppernong took the census of Washington County in 1810 and reported 1368 gallons of wine made there in "this small but very interesting branch of our infant manufactures." An article in the Raleigh (North Carolina) *Star* for January 11, 1811, commenting on Blount's report, was the first to call it "The Scuppernong Grape." Eight years later, Nathaniel Macon, a member of Congress, sent samples of Scuppernong, through Governor Barbour of North Carolina as an intermediary, to Thomas Jefferson, who complained because brandy had been added to the wine. The *American Farmer* for October 1, 1819, related that

Many farmers near Fayetteville in North Carolina have for years past drank excellent wine of their own making from the native grape . . . Wine is made along the Cape Fear River from Fayetteville to the Sea, a distance of near seventy miles, and the farmers use it as freely as cider is used in New England. It is common for a farmer to make eight or ten barrels of wine annually for his own use, and many sell considerable quantities.

How widespread early winegrowing was in North Carolina is evidenced by the place names that remain on its road maps and railroad stations, such as Tokay, Medoc, Cognac, Niagara, Vina Vista, and Catawba. The late Professor Carlos Williams, the Raleigh horticulturist, told me that the Pettigrew State Park in Washington County was originally the Pettigrew Vineyard and the site of a winery. The *American Wine Press* for March 1, 1897, mentions the 1200-acre Niagara Vineyard sixty miles south of Raleigh, and contains an advertisement of Colonel Wharton Green's Tokay Vineyard, three miles north of Fayetteville, and of his 100,000-gallon winery. Other North Carolina wineries, before and since Prohibition, had such addresses as Conover, Eagle Springs, Gibson, Louisburg, Murphy, Peachland, Samarcand, Tryon, Warrenton, Willard, and Wilmington.

· 4 ·

The fabulous Captain Paul Garrett, who became a billionaire selling wine with the Scuppernong flavor, was a North Carolinian. He was the dean of American vintners when I knew him in the early '30s, a tall, portly, forceful man with a deep voice and a soft southern accent. His title of "captain" was not military, but was bestowed by his employes, who also called him "the boss."

He was born in 1863, the third year of the Civil War, on the Edgecombe County farm of his father, country doctor Francis Marion Garrett. In 1865, his father and his wealthy uncle, Charles Garrett, purchased North Carolina's first commercial winery, the Medoc Vineyard, established in 1835 by Sidney Weller near Enfield in neighboring Halifax County. Weller, a northerner, had made a fortune growing mulberries, had lost it in the silk business, then planted vines among his mulberry trees, and, although an ardent Prohibitionist, had become wealthy again by making and selling wine.

At the age of fourteen, Paul quit military prep school and went to live with his uncle, who ran the winery, to learn the wine business. He worked in the vineyard, bought grapes from growers in neighboring counties, made the wine, loaded barrels on wagons, and taught Sunday school in the village of Ringwood. At twenty-one, when his uncle died, he became a salesman for the Garrett winery. He traveled through Arkansas, Tennessee, and Texas with a vial of Scuppernong wine in his pocket, inviting saloonkeepers to taste and to buy it for sale in competition with whiskey. In 1900, when he was thirty-seven, he contracted to sell the winery's entire output, but when his commissions mounted, the winery's new proprietor refused to deliver. Paul then established his own winery, first at Littleton, then at Chockoyotte, near Weldon, calling it Garrett & Company.

In the next nineteen years, Paul Garrett built a nationwide wine empire. He started by outbidding other wineries for Scuppernong grapes, buying all he could find. He began blending the juice with New York and California wines, but kept the Scuppernong flavor predominant. He called Scuppernong "the finest wine in the world," but saw drawbacks in its name: other vintners could use it on spurious wines; it was well known in the South, but the name meant nothing to northerners. Garrett also knew it was garbled from an Indian word, and he tried spelling it "Escapernong." He objected, too, to labeling American wines after European types as "sauternes" or "burgundy." Seeking a name that no one else could copy, he tried calling his white wine "Minnehaha" and his red "Pocahontas." Then he had a better idea: Because Scuppernong was the first American wine, he named it for the first child born of English parents in America—Virginia Dare—and Virginia Dare white and red became known to almost everybody in the nation.

By 1903 Garrett had five wineries in North Carolina, the largest one at Aberdeen, and vineyards on Dare Island and at Plymouth. But mounting Prohibitionist strength in the state threatened his wineries, so he established a larger plant at Norfolk in neighboring Virginia. When North Carolina went dry in 1908, he had to rush the juice from his Aberdeen cellar to Norfolk before fermentation could set in and make it illegal. Nine years later, Virginia, too, had gone dry, and Garrett moved permanently to New York State. By 1913, he had established vineyards and wineries at Penn Yan, Canandaigua, and Hammondsport in the Finger Lakes District and also the Mission Vineyard and Winery at Cucamonga in Southern California. When Wartime Prohibition began in 1919, he had seventeen plants processing grape juice or wine in North Carolina, Virginia, Ohio, Missouri, New York, and California, with a total capacity of ten million gallons.

Garrett could have retired a billionaire, but refusing to believe that Prohibition could last, he sought ways to hold his empire together until Repeal. He first sold dealcoholized Virginia Dare wine, which buyers spiked with alcohol, but its popularity soon waned. Then he lost a million dollars promoting a cola-flavored grape drink called Satenet, and another million on a venture in the flavoring extract business. He recouped with his Virginia Dare wine tonic, and then with grape concentrate for home winemaking. Then there was his ill-fated "Vine-Glo" venture, described in Chapter 2. Meanwhile he crusaded for modification of the Volstead Act to permit the sale of light wine, which he called "the antitoxin of alcoholism." If table wine could be sold as food, free of taxes like other farm products, he said, the winegrowing industry could furnish employment to eight million Americans.

When Repeal arrived in 1933, Garrett was the only vintner ready again to sell his wine in every wet state. Virginia Dare white and red were displayed in every wine store, and millions hummed the first* singing commercial ever broadcast for wine, "Say it again . . . Virginia Dare."

The enthusiastic Captain ranged through the South in the early 1930s, urging more planting of Scuppernong vineyards. He enlisted the help of Harry L. Hopkins and the Federal Rural Resettlement Administration. It was arranged that Scuppernong vines, five acres per family, would provide the chief cash crop for resettled farmers in Georgia and South Carolina, the cash crop second to tung oil trees in Florida, and the crop second to strawberries in Louisiana. In North Carolina, sufficient vines were propagated to set out four thousand acres. At Garrett's prompting, a grape growers' co-operative was organized to start a winery in Virginia.

But few new vineyards were planted. Dry Congressmen forbade Harry Hopkins to make grapes the basis for the economy of any Rural Resettlement projects. Besides, Garrett's campaign was forty years too early. Not enough markets were open for wine as yet; much of the nation and most of the South, in particular, were still legally dry.

Scuppernong grapes continued to be scarce, and Virginia Dare gradually lost its unique flavor. As Garrett was compelled to rely more on his California vineyards for grapes, Virginia Dare became more and more a bland-tasting California wine.

In his sixty-second year as a vintner, still preaching "American wines for Americans," Captain Garrett fell ill of pneumonia in New York City, and on March 18, 1940, he died at the age of seventy-six. His family life had been tragic, three of his four sons dying as infants. When his fourth son, Charles, died in 1930 at the age of sixteen, the Captain built in his memory a great chapel on Bluff Point overlooking Keuka Lake in New York State, an architectual gem in the woods, which he deeded to the Rochester Diocese of the Episcopal Church. There the Captain and his wife are buried with their sons. Garrett's wine empire went out of existence, but his Scuppernong blend called Virginia Dare and his idea of building an American wine industry have survived.

---

*But not the first advertisement ever sung for wine, because French champagne firms during the nineteenth century regularly paid performers in the music halls of England to sing such songs as "Champagne Charlie," which advertised Moët et Chandon, and "Clicquot, the Wine for Me."

• 5 •

Scuppernong and its Muscadine relatives are the principal grapes grown in North Carolina because the climate of the Coastal Plain is too humid for bunch grapes. Catawba, Concord, and other Labrusca varieties grow at higher elevations on the Piedmont Plateau, especially in the thermal belt that extends northeastward from Tryon in Polk County. The Catawba grape, incidentally, gets its name from the Catawba River in Buncombe County, where it is said to have been discovered in 1802.

Hobbyists who prefer Old World wine types have been successful since the 1960s in growing French hybrid and Vinifera wine grapes in the Piedmont. A group of such hobbyists have incorporated as the Sauratown Mountain Vineyards and are planning to build a 10,000-gallon winery in 1973. Their three-acre vineyard of hybrids is on Hall Road in wet Stokes County, six miles north of Rural Hall. "We intend to make traditional dry wines of aged, château-bottled quality," says Anthony H. Payne, president of the group, which consists of four businessmen, two physicians, and their wives. Mr. Payne says, however, that the initial products of their winery will be dry Muscadine table wines of the new types that Dr. Dan Carroll has developed in the State University laboratory at Raleigh.

Another new North Carolina winery is planned by Dr. L. Rosser Littleton, a physician and hobbyist winegrower whose Maréchal Vineyard is near Mount Airy in neighboring Surry County. His vineyard consisted of French hybrids until 1969, when he planted sixteen Vinifera varieties, including White Riesling and Cabernet Sauvignon. His Vinifera are doing well, and he plans to bond his winery when his first Vinifera wines are ready to be bottled.

• 6 •

The southern Bible Belt was described by the late Will Rogers as those states where citizens "stagger to the polls to vote dry." These are the last tottering strongholds of the professional Prohibitionists and their political allies, the moonshiners of the Blue Ridge and Great Smoky Mountains. As late as 1970, almost half of the counties in the South still were legally dry (three fifths in Alabama, nearly four fifths in Georgia and Tennessee) and wine, where available, was burdened with exorbitant taxes or variously restricted in sale. This, and the drinking customs—Coca-Cola in the morning, as traditional as the Englishman's afternoon tea, and corn liquor with branch water as the beverage of hospitality—help to explain why little table wine heretofore has been drunk in the South. It is changing gradually now, however, because with the influx of industry thousands of families have moved in from the northern states where the use of dry table wines is becoming customary. Per capita wine consumption in the South has more than doubled in ten years, and more dry counties are voting wet. Wine-growing is reviving in those southern states where the political strength of the Drys is waning, but it lags in those states where they are still strong.

• 7 •

South Carolina, although legally wet, is a case in point. It has two thousand acres of vineyards and led the southern states in grape-growing until North Carolina experienced its recent Muscadine-planting boom. But much of South Carolina's 6000-ton grape crop is shipped fresh or as unfermented juice to wineries in New York, New Jersey, Virginia, and Georgia, and the state's promotional literature makes no mention of wine.

Among the scrub pines in the Sand Hills country near Patrick in Chesterfield County is the largest single vineyard in the South, three hundred acres neatly planted with Muscadine and Labrusca grape varieties and with dewberries for blackberry wine. Adjoining the vineyard is the only winery in South Carolina, Tenner Brothers. It is an unprepossessing concrete structure, recently increased in capacity to a million gallons by a battery of outdoor wine tanks of stainless steel, and is not open to visitors; it is absentee-owned. Sal, Al, and Lukie Tenner, former Charleston tire dealers, entered the wine and restaurant business at Charlotte, North Carolina, in 1935, then established the winery at Patrick in 1953 when South Carolina granted them a preferential tax on wine made from South Carolina grapes and berries. The tax on their wine was 45 cents a gallon compared to $1.08 on wines from outside the state. Several years later the Tenner Brothers had financial difficulties, and in 1966 they sold out to Mack Sands's companies, which operate the Richards winery in Virginia and the Canandaigua winery in New York State.

On Richard Leizear's Oakview Farm at Woodruff in Spartanburg County, there is a grape-juice plant that resembles a winery. Leizear decorates his office with champagne bottles, but he does no fermenting; he is a teetotaler. The grapes for wine are only stemmed, crushed, and pumped with their pomace into plastic-lined drums, then frozen to await shipment to a winery in New Jersey.

A South Carolina Grape Festival is celebrated each August at York, sponsored by the York County Grape Growers Association and the York Junior Chamber of Commerce. The festival features are a queen contest and a parade, but the program contains nothing about wine. York County grape growers own two new mechanical harvesters, which work especially well in Scuppernong vineyards. The growers have also talked of building a winery, but since Mack Sands has increased to $325 per ton the price he pays them for Scuppernongs, the winery proposal seems to have died.

The South Carolina Agricultural Experiment Station at Clemson University has a three-acre experimental vineyard, but the University has no wine research program. However, Horticulture Professor Harold J. Sefick, who has been breeding grapes at Clemson for twenty years, happens to have a hobby interest in winemaking. Of necessity, he conducts his wine experiments at home.

South Carolina's best wines, says Professor Sefick, are made by an amateur named Eugene Charles. Since 1948, on thirteen acres around his home near the little city of Seneca in the Piedmont, Mr. Charles has been growing French hybrid and Labrusca grapes and has made wine scientifically, reporting his results regularly to other oenothusiasts throughout the South.

Although the Drys have kept South Carolina's winegrowing history a secret, they have neglected to change the state map. It still shows the town of Bordeaux (originally New Bordeaux), named for the most famous wine city of France. New Bordeaux was founded by French Huguenot emigrés, who in 1764 were granted 30,000 acres by the British government to found a grape and wine industry along the upper Savannah River.

In ampelographies you will find that three of the most successful native American wine grapes originated in South Carolina: the Isabella about 1816, the Lenoir in 1829, and the Herbemont, grown by Nicholas Herbemont of Columbia in the 1820s.

Old-time residents of Abbeville, in the South Carolina Piedmont, still remember Dr. Joseph Togno's Montevino vineyard and winery; the physician's rock house, built in 1859, is a landmark of the town. The City of Aiken, near the Savannah River nuclear bomb plant, was famous in the 1860s for a claret made there by Benson and Merrier's Winery from Isabella grapes. The Aiken Vinegrowing Society published in 1858 an essay on winegrowing in the South in which the author, A. de Caradeuc, advised farmers to grow grapes in addition to their cotton, sugar, and rice:

A few leisure days in the winter, of which there are so many, and a few hours in the grassy season, devoted to one or two acres of his hitherto poorest and most worthless land, will insure him a handsome income, and a pleasant beverage more wholesome and agreeable than Peach Mobby or Persimmon Beer, and more conducive to his and his children's morals than Whiskey, that bane of our country, which it will finally drive out of use.

• 8 •

General James E. Oglethorpe, the founder of Georgia in 1733, required the first settlers to plant grapes as well as other farm products for shipment to England. Although Oglethorpe prohibited drinking in the colony, there is evidence that wine was made during the General's time. The first commercial winegrower in Georgia probably was Thomas McCall, whose vineyard was planted in Laurens County on the Oconee River before 1823. The *Southern Cultivator* in December 1858 referred to Charles Axt of Crawfordville in Taliaferro County as "one of the most successful vintners of the South." By 1880, when the United States Department of Agriculture made its study of grape and wine production, Georgia was the sixth largest winegrowing state in the nation, producing 903,244 gallons from 2991 acres of vineyards, almost double the gallonage made in New York State in that year. The leading Georgia winegrowing counties were Bibb, Chatham, Fulton, Houston, Pulaski, and Randolph. Wild Scuppernong was the chief grape used, but the Norton, a red bunch grape, was reported making the best Georgia wine. In the 1890s, the Georgia Vineyard Company at Tallapoosa in Haralson County was making fifty thousand gallons of wine and juice annually, and forty families in a Hungarian settlement nearby were making wines that sold at fancy prices in New York. All of this ended, however, when the state went dry in 1907.

Atlanta has a million-gallon winery, the Monarch Wine Company of Georgia, the largest maker of peach wine in the world. It began in 1936, when Georgia repealed its prohibition law, and when Governor Eugene Talmadge was looking for a way to dispose of the state's peach surplus. Word of the Governor's search reached Charles Gilsten, who happened to be in Atlanta on a selling trip for Leo Star's Monarch Winery of New York. Gilsten, a native Atlantan and former newsboy, went to see Talmadge and made him a proposition: if the state would let Georgia table and dessert wines be taxed at twenty and fifty cents a gallon respectively, compared to a dollar and two dollars a gallon on out-of-state wines, Monarch would open a winery. The Governor accepted, the tax legislation was passed, and Gilsten, independent of the New York firm, opened the largest winery in the South.* Besides wines from peaches and berries, he made grape wines from Muscadines, Concord, and other varieties grown in Georgia, adding grape concentrate and high-proof brandy from California. When Georgia farmers objected to the use of California brandy,

---

*The tax rates have since risen to 40¢, $1, $1.50, and $2.50 a gallon respectively.

Monarch built its own distillery in Crawford County and now makes its high-proof brandy from Georgia fruits.

Georgia, unlike South Carolina, encourages wine research. Experimental Muscadine wines and champagnes have been made in the University of Georgia Food Science Department at Athens, and new Muscadine varieties have been bred in the horticultural research station at Experiment, south of Atlanta.

The planting of Muscadines is booming in Georgia, has more than doubled from two hundred acres in 1969 to five hundred in 1972. It may reach four thousand acres and even replace some of the state's famed peach orchards by 1976, says the noted Georgia grape breeder, Dr. Byard O. Fry. The farmers plant Muscadines because the new varieties yield almost ten tons per acre, bring high prices, are inexpensive to cultivate and easy to harvest mechanically. They are grown to make wine, but not for many Georgians to drink. Most are shipped to Virginia, New Jersey, and New York to be made into wine for consumption in the North.

• 9 •

When the British admiral, Sir John Hawkins, relieved the starving French Huguenots at Fort Caroline in Florida in 1565, he found they had "twenty hogshead of wine made from the native grapes." Since the grapes could only have been Muscadines, that Florida Scuppernong, made four centuries ago, was the original American wine.

In Florida, as in the other colonies, there were attempts to grow Vinifera grapes brought from Europe, with the same disappointing results. After the Civil War, immigrants to Florida from the North brought their favorite Labrusca grapes, such as Concord, Niagara, Worden, and Ives. Extensive plantings were made around Orlando, and by 1894 there were five hundred acres in Orange County alone, but by 1900 most of these vineyards had died. Then came the Prohibition-era grape boom of the 1920s. Nearly five thousand acres of new vineyards were planted in Lake, Orange, and Putnam Counties, this time mainly of the Munson hybrid varieties from Texas. A decade later, most of these vines, too, had succumbed to "the grape decline" (the Pierce's disease virus), which attacks most bunch grapes in Florida. After each of these debacles, there remained only the native Muscadines.

Florida Scuppernong is still being made at the Bartels Winery in Pensacola, the only one of the state's few small wineries that makes wine out of grapes. (Others in recent years have made orange, berry, and honey wines.) Bartels Winery is in the cellar of Bartels Restaurant, which specializes in fried-chicken dinners and sells its homemade Scuppernong, Muscadine, and Blackberry wines with meals at fifty cents a glass and in bottles and cases to take home. Diners are always invited downstairs to see how the wines are made. Bartels is a family operation, begun in 1937. Ralph Weaver, Sr., is the winemaker, Ralph, Jr., is the chemist, and the second son, Kenneth, is in charge of the vineyards, which consist of three acres north of Pensacola and thirty more acres at Lillian and Elberta, Alabama, on the other side of Perdido Bay. Their recent plantings are of new bunch-grape varieties that are immune to Pierce's disease, bred by University of Florida horticulturists at the Watermelon and Grape Investigations Laboratory near Leesburg.

New Florida vineyards are being planted with the virus-resistant bunch grapes in Jefferson and Lake Counties, and two small wineries are being planned.

"I believe there are possibilities for wine production in Florida, perhaps eventually on a large scale," says Dr. Loren H. Stover, the horticulturist who developed the Florida bunch grapes, which are named Stover, Norris, Blue Lake, and Lake Emerald. Dr. John A. Mortensen, who took charge of the grape-breeding program when Dr. Stover retired, agrees, and thinks central and northern Florida also can grow French hybrid wine varieties if they are grafted on suitable resistant rootstocks. Another breeding project is at Alachua, where Dr. Robert Dunstan, who supplied Philip Wagner with some of his first hybrids, has crossed Vinifera and other bunch grapes with Muscadines in an effort to develop additional resistant varieties.

• 10 •

Mississippi, which repealed its state prohibition law in 1966, has produced wine in the past and is likely to do so again. The *Southern Cultivator*, in March 1875, described the Scuppernong wine made by J. M. Taylor of Rienzi, Alcorn County, Mississippi, as "nonpareil, a great gift of the gods to the Sunny South." Dr. Dunbar Rowland's *History of Mississippi* records that wines from twenty Mississippi counties were exhibited in 1885 at the World Industrial and Cotton Exposition in New Orleans. There were thirty-one wineries in Holly Springs, Enterprise, Forest, Meridian, Waynesboro, Carthage, Oxford, and Pontotoc until the state went dry in 1908.

It is therefore not surprising that with Mississippians now drinking a million gallons of wine each year, a Committee to Promote Winery Legislation has been formed with the object of getting wineries started in the state. Leaders in the effort are William

G. Bodker of Jackson, an amateur winemaker who has a vineyard of Niagara, Delaware, and Muscadines in the foothills of the Yazoo Delta; Hamilton Allen, who grows Muscadines and makes wine at his home near Port Gibson in Claiborne County; and John Bagwell, who teaches school in Tennessee and grows Muscadines, Niagara, and Delaware grapes at Bruce in Calhoun County.

In 1968, the State Research and Development Board made a survey of the winegrowing potential in Mississippi. The survey described the Muscadine-breeding work at State College and told how wineries in other states are paying increasingly higher prices for Muscadines.

The main obstacle to commercial winemaking in Mississippi is a provision of the state law that fixes the minimum winery license fee at $1800 per year. Mr. Bodker's committee is now enlisting the help of farm organizations and legislators to get the minimum fee reduced.

• 11 •

Tennessee, too, was once a winegrowing state. A Catawba wine from the Willowbeck Vineyard, near Wartrace in New Bedford County, won first prize at the 1857 State Fair in Nashville and at the Louisville National Fair in competition with wines from northern states. The Chattanooga *Times* in 1880 reported there were "150 acres around Chattanooga within a radius of five miles entirely devoted to grape culture" and that "nearly every cultivated field between Rossville and the railroad tunnel has a vineyard of some size." Hobbyist winegrowers in Tennessee are now attempting to revive the winegrowing industry of their state. Their leader is Judge William O. Beach of Clarksville, who tends his half-acre vineyard of Labrusca, Vinifera, and hybrids and makes fine table wine and champagne whenever he isn't presiding over the Montgomery County criminal court. He has interested Governor Winfield Dunn in his idea that wine grapes might supplement the declining income of Tennessee tobacco growers. State legislators are studying a survey, made by University of Tennessee horticulturist Donald B. Williams, of Tennessee vineyards and of the winegrowing industries in Pennsylvania and New York.

• 12 •

In Louisiana, Jesuit priests made wine for altar use as early as 1750, before wine grapes were brought to California. Most of the wine made since in the Bayou State, however, has come from fruits other than grapes. There were many wineries in Louisiana before Prohibition, and several were started after Repeal in 1933, fermenting the oranges of Plaquemines Parish. Only one winery is left, at Independence in eastern Louisiana, and its main product is strawberry wine.

Scuppernong and other Muscadine grapes grow wild in parts of all of the states mentioned in this chapter. It is evident that if, in years to come, Americans show a liking for wines with the Muscadine flavor, there will be many more wineries in the South.

4

The Middle Atlantic States

WINE touring in eastern America can be both a fascinating and a puzzling experience. Why is it, you may wonder, that Virginia, with less than two hundred acres of vineyards, has five wineries turning out two million gallons of wine yearly, while Pennsylvania, with more than nine thousand acres planted to grapes, has only four small wineries making a twentieth as much wine as Virginia, and little New Jersey has ten producing wineries making four million gallons? And how does it happen that vines from a seven-acre vineyard in Maryland have revolutionized the planting of wine grapes in hundreds of localities in the United States and Canada? To unravel these paradoxes, one needs to know some of the wine history of these states, their wet-dry politics, and the widely different taste preferences for wine that are emerging in America.

• 2 •

Virginia, as we have seen, was the first of the colonies to cultivate grapes for wine. The attempts to grow Vinifera, which began in 1619 under Lord Delaware, continued in Virginia for almost two centuries. Some of the vineyards succeeded in producing quantities of wine before plant diseases and insect pests killed the European vines. About 1716, historian Robert Beverley won a wager of seven hundred guineas from his neighbors by producing seven hundred gallons in a single vintage from his three-acre vineyard at Beverley Park in King and Queen County. But Beverley apparently made the wine from native wild grapes, which he cultivated together with his few French vines. The only Virginia wines of any note in the eighteenth century were the red and white Rapidan, made by a colony of Germans who settled on the Rapidan River in Spotsylvania County after 1770. George Washington planted a garden vineyard at Mount Vernon, but there is no record of his having made any wine, although he made cider and distilled considerable quantities of applejack. In 1773, Dr. Filippo Mazzei of Tuscany brought Italian winegrowers with ten thousand European vine cuttings in a chartered ship to establish winegrowing in Virginia. Most of Mazzei's cuttings were planted at Monticello, the estate of Thomas Jefferson, in what is now Albemarle County. For thirty years Jefferson continued trying to grow Vinifera, even importing some of his vines directly from Château d'Yquem, and he is said once to have even imported some French soil. An advocate of wine as a temperate beverage, he hoped to establish grape growing as an American industry, and while minister to France from 1785 to 1789, he made his own scientific studies of viticulture and winemaking. Jefferson finally admitted his failure with Vinifera when he recommended in 1809 that native vines, such as the Alexander, be planted instead.

In 1835, Dr. D. N. Norton of Richmond produced a domesticated native blue grape that made Virginia claret wine famous during the latter half of the nineteenth century. The Norton was virtually a Virginia monopoly, because this grape variety is difficult to ripen in regions north of the Potomac. Following the Civil War, winegrowing based on the Norton and other native grapes spread through the Piedmont and Blue Ridge regions. The Virginia Winegrowers Association had branches in Albemarle, Norfolk, Warren, and Fairfax, the leading grape-growing counties. The Monticello Wine Company at Charlottesville became so noted for its Norton Claret, which won a gold medal at Vienna in 1873 and a silver medal at Paris in 1878, that the city was called "the capital of the Virginia wine belt." The company's Delaware, Catawba, Hock, Norton Port, Virginia Sherry, and grape brandy, as well as the Claret, were sold throughout the East.

Virginia's wine production totaled 232,479 gallons by 1880, making it the eleventh largest wine-producing state in the Union. But during the next few decades, cities, counties, and whole states were going dry. Competition from California wine was increasing. The markets for Virginia wines began to shrink. Grape prices declined, growers neglected their vineyards, and the vines soon died. When Virginia passed its state prohibition law in 1914, few vineyards of any size remained in the state.

A move to revive the Virginia wine industry was started by Captain Paul Garrett when National Prohibition ended in 1933. Garrett praised "the noble Virginia Claret," and Professor Ulysses P. Hedrick, the great New York viticulturist, described the Norton as "the best red wine grape grown in the Eastern States . . . best when grown in the soil and climate of central Virginia." A few of the old wineries reopened, and in 1934 the Monticello

Grape Growers Co-operative Association was formed at Charlottesville with Bernard Peyton Chamberlain, an amateur wine-grower and author of a wine book, as its president. Extensive plantings of grapes in the Piedmont counties were planned, but they never materialized; only a few thousand gallons of claret were made by the association. Again, some new vineyards were planted after the Second World War, but lacking a market for their grapes, they were soon abandoned. When Professor George D. Oberle, who had organized the new wine-grape testing program at New York's Geneva Experiment Station, joined the Virginia Polytechnic Institute College of Agriculture at Blacksburg in 1948, he found nine wineries still bonded to operate in the state. But three were just then going out of business, and most of the others seemed likely to follow.

Dr. Oberle still maintains a grape-breeding program at Blacksburg and believes that Virginia again will grow fine table wines in the future, but of new hybrid grapes rather than of Norton. Several oenothusiasts have recently planted French-hybrid vineyards in the northern Piedmont and are planning to establish small château-type wineries. One of them, Willard Scott of Radio Station WRC, also grows Vinifera varieties in his vineyard near Paris in Fauquier County. In eastern Virginia too there are small plantings of the hybrids, such as Robert Hutton's Shooters Hill Vineyard in the Rosemont section of Alexandria, which is only eight miles from Washington. Test plots of new Muscadine varieties have been planted lately in the Tidewater area west of Norfolk, where Scuppernongs grow wild on many farms.

• 3 •

Of the five wineries now operating in Virginia, there is just one that makes and sells only wine of its own grapes. It is unknown to most Virginians. On an arm of the Roanoke River at Clarksville in Mecklenburg County, John June Lewis, a Negro veteran of the First World War, has a ten-acre vineyard of hybrids and Labrusca wine varieties and makes table wines in his immaculate little (5000 gallons) Woburn Winery for sale to his neighbors. Lewis learned the art of winegrowing as a boy from the owner of the nearby plantation where his mother was born a slave. He learned still more in 1919 during his year with the U.S. Army of Occupation among the vineyards of the Rhine Valley. Returning home, he got a job in the lumber business and saved enough money to buy a farm. When Prohibition was repealed in 1933, he began planting grapes, and by 1940 had a large enough crop to open his own winery. Unfortunately, I was unable while in Virginia to visit the

Woburn Winery, but Dr. Oberle has been there and assures me that the wines are carefully made with yeast cultures from California, and are sound.

• 4 •

On Pocahontas Street in historic Petersburg is the 2-million-gallon Richard's Wine Cellar, the biggest winery in Virginia. The other large cellars in the state make mostly apple and berry wines. Richard's owner, Mordecai E. (Mack) Sands, has deliberately re-traced the footsteps of Captain Paul Garrett since opening this winery in 1951. The principal Richard's product is sweet Scuppernong wine. Like Garrett, he has persuaded farmers throughout the South to plant thousands of acres with Scuppernong, and has acquired Muscadine vineyards of his own. But why make Scuppernong wine in Virginia when the grapes are grown in states farther south? Sands won't say, but it may be remembered that Garrett, too, established a winery in Virginia to avoid the hazards of prohibition elections in the Dry-dominated South.

Born in Brooklyn in 1898, Sands entered the wine business in 1932 as a partner of Joey Applebaum in Geffen Industries, a small Long Island City winery which turned out millions of gallons during the early years following Repeal. Many of today's Federal wine regulations are said to have been aimed at reducing Geffen Industries' copious output from relatively few tons of fresh grapes. After Applebaum retired wealthy in 1945, Sands established a winery at Canandaigua, New York, where Garrett had had one of his many plants. Then, leaving his son, Marvin Sands, in charge at Canandaigua, Mack Sands moved to Virginia to open the Richard's winery, which he named for his infant grandson. In 1956, he bought the Mother Vineyard Winery at Manteo, North Carolina, moved it to Petersburg, and adopted the Mother Vineyard name for his Scuppernong wine. Later he added the Tenner Brothers vineyard and winery at Patrick, South Carolina. Now, with their wineries in three eastern states, the Sandses, father and son, have become the biggest vintners in the East. Their sweet pink Labrusca-flavored (20 percent) Richard's Wild Irish Rose, made at Canandaigua, is the largest-selling wine of its kind.

But for Mack Sands to become the successor to Garrett, one thing remained: to recover the Virginia Dare name. Following the Captain's death in 1940, Garrett & Company had moved to Cucamonga in California, then twice had been merged with California wineries. Ownership of the Virginia Dare brand meanwhile had passed to the Guild Wine Company of Lodi, California. Sands finally contracted with the Guild Company for a franchise to use the name. In 1967, Virginia Dare wines came back on the market. But only the white Virginia Dare has the Scuppernong flavor, because the Sandses use the same Virginia Dare brand name on a "complete line" of generic, Labrusca, and blackberry wine types, all bottled at Canandaigua.

• 5 •

West Virginia, too, once had its own wine industry, and since the Second World War there have been proposals to resurrect it as a means of relieving unemployment in chronically depressed Appalachia. Wine was made in the Kanawha River Valley near Charleston as early as 1826, when Nicholas Longworth was just beginning to plant Catawba along the Ohio River at Cincinnati. In that year, the Charleston *Western Courier* told of a dinner in the city at which toasts were drunk in a local wine of "excellent quality." Still to be seen in the hills behind Dunbar, near Charleston, are the vaulted stone cellars of the Friend Brothers' Winery, built into a hillside that was lined with hundreds of acres of vines long before the Civil War. Scarcity of labor during the war forced the Dunbar winery to close about 1864. The report of the commissioner of agriculture to President Lincoln for the year 1863 described vineyards and wineries extending along the river as far north as Wheeling. It mentions one vineyard on Zane's Island that produced 500 gallons to the acre. The West Virginia wine industry staged a comeback after the Civil War, and eleven counties were still reporting wine production as late as 1880.

In 1966 there was a proposal to plant wine grapes again in the Kanawha River Valley. It was to be part of an Office of Economic Opportunity program, similar to Captain Garrett's Rural Resettlement project in the South thirty years earlier. West Virginia agricultural economists vetoed the proposal because there appeared to be little demand for wine in the state. Perhaps it will be revived now, because since the sale of table wine in food stores was legalized in 1972, wine use in West Virginia has jumped 17 percent.

• 6 •

In Maryland, the seventeenth-century plantings of Vinifera apparently survived longer than in Virginia. Professor Hedrick, in his scholarly historical writings on grapes of the East, relates that from 300 acres of vines planted at St. Mary's by Lord Baltimore in 1662, considerable quantities of wine were made and sold, and that some of it was compared to the best French burgundies.

The state legislature in 1828 incorporated a Maryland Society for Promoting the Culture of the Vine, empowering it to establish vineyards and to produce wine "for the purpose of introducing into the State of Maryland, and into our country generally, the extensive cultivation of the vine."

A Marylander of this period, Major John Adlum, gave America the Catawba grape. Adlum, a soldier of the Revolution, a judge, and a surveyor, settled after the war on Pierce's Mill Road, near Georgetown, and for many years experimented in winegrowing and other horticultural research. His estate of 200 acres, which he named "The Vineyard," is now a part of Rock Creek Park in Washington, D.C. In 1823 Adlum wrote *A Memoir on the Cultivation of the Vine in America and the Best Mode of Making Wine*, the first book on winegrowing to be published in this country. In it he relates his unsuccessful attempts to grow foreign vines and his subsequent success in making acceptable wines from indigenous grapes.

Adlum found the Catawba growing beside an inn operated by a Mrs. Scholl at Clarksburg in Montgomery County, Maryland. Mrs. Scholl's father appears to have acquired the grape directly from North Carolina, where it is said to have been found growing wild in 1802. One version credits a Senator Davy with bringing the vines to his friends in Maryland as gifts for their gardens. Adlum took cuttings from Mrs. Scholl's vines and planted them in his vineyard. The wine he made from their grapes was better than any he had made before. He first named the wine "Tokay" and sent samples to all the members of Congress. He also sent Thomas Jefferson a sample with one of his red wines. A letter from Jefferson to Adlum on April 11, 1823, reads:

I received the two bottles of wine you were so kind as to send me. The first, called Tokay, is a truly fine wine, of high flavor, and, as you assure me, there was not a drop of brandy in it; I may say it is a wine of good body of its own. The second bottle, a red wine, I tried when I had good judges at the table. We agreed it was a wine one might always drink with satisfaction, but of no particular excellence.

Adlum renamed the grape Catawba, which is evidence that he was aware of its North Carolina origin. He supplied cuttings to Nicholas Longworth, who planted them at Cincinnati and made the grape and its wine world famous. Longworth later offered a reward of five hundred dollars to anyone who could find a better native variety than the Catawba. A quarter-century later he wrote that "its equal has not yet been found." Adlum said, in a letter to Longworth, that

In bringing this grape into public notice, I have rendered my country a greater service than I would have done, had I paid off the National Debt.

· 7 ·

Because in the mid-1930s a home winemaker in Baltimore disliked the Labrusca flavor of a wine he made from native grapes, the course of winegrowing in much of North America has been altered significantly during the past few decades. Failing to grow in Maryland the Vinifera grapes he preferred, this amateur introduced to this country the French-American hybrid varieties that are now planted extensively for winemaking in most states east of the Rockies and in both eastern and western Canada.

The amateur was Philip Marshall Wagner, an editorial writer for the Baltimore *Evening Sun*. Born in 1904 at New Haven, he grew up in Ann Arbor, Michigan, where his father was a professor of Romance languages at the university. His parents drank wine with their meals at home, and Philip developed the taste of a connoisseur. When he joined the *Sun* in 1930, the eleventh year of Prohibition, his liking for wine led him to make it at home in partnership with a next-door neighbor. Finding it easier to make bad wine than good, he began reading French texts on viniculture. Soon he had written a text in English, *American Wines and How to Make Them*, as a service to fellow amateurs.

Wagner had begun by buying grapes from California to make his wine, but when Prohibition was ending in 1933, his favorite varieties, Zinfandel and Carignane, were not being shipped to the East; the reopened wineries were using them in California. He then made a vintage out of the eastern Delaware grape, but being accustomed only to Vinifera wines, he had no liking for its Labrusca taste. Wondering what else he could use to make his wine, he happened to read about the hybrid vines that were being grown in France. He ordered a supply from Bordeaux, found others already in some American collections, and planted at Baltimore all he could get. By 1936 Wagner had made some wines from the hybrids that convinced him it was possible to grow, east of the Rocky Mountains, "wines that taste like wine."

He began writing articles and revised his book to tell others about the French hybrids. Then, people came asking to buy vines from him, and he soon found himself in the nursery business.

More vines planted meant more grapes harvested from his vineyard—more than enough grapes to make the two hundred gallons per year the Government permits a householder to produce free of tax. So the Wagners, Philip and his wife Jocelyn, built a winery. Then, when the winery, bonded in 1945, was full, the quantity of wine was more than they could drink, and the excess had to be sold. Wagner made his first sales to Baltimore restaurants, delivering the wines himself on the way to his office each morning. When he was too busy, having by then become editor of both the *Sun* papers, Jocelyn made the deliveries; and both Wagners came to know the tradesmen's entrances of most hotels, restaurants, and clubs in Baltimore.

It was not long before connoisseurs in New York and Washington learned that entirely new kinds of American wines were being made in Maryland. More orders for wine than the Wagners could fill came from stores and hotels throughout the East. Making only eight thousand gallons per year, they could have sold twenty times as much. But they decided not to try, and they turned over their wine sales to a Washington wholesaler.

"Boordy Vineyard, J. & P. Wagner, Props." consists of a little wood-and-stucco, French-type winery and seven hillside acres beside the Wagners' colonial farmhouse in Riderwood, one of Baltimore's more exclusive northern suburbs. Boordy Vineyard is difficult for a stranger to find, which is just as well, because visitors are received by appointment only. What does "Boordy" mean? "Nothing," reply the Wagners, "except a small Maryland vineyard and its delightful products."

The Wagners' wines are four, each vintage-labeled: the regular white, which is fresh and delicate; another white named Boordy-blümchen, made from some of the newer French hybrids; the rosé, soft and fruity; and the red, in which Philip finds a resemblance to some of the Loire Valley reds of France. He does not regard any of the Boordy Vineyard wines as great, because they usually are best when drunk young. However, I have tasted at the winery some vintages that had developed an appreciable bouquet after several years of age in the bottle.

Tall and lanky, with a mop of wavy graying hair, Philip Wagner looks more like an editor or a New England college professor than a grape farmer and winemaker. He is noted as a taster, has made many trips to Europe, and has served twice on wine juries in California. In tasting Boordy wines, however, Philip defers to *la vigneronne*, Jocelyn, who, he says, has a palate "as accurate as a barometer." In 1964 he retired from the *Sun* to devote most of his time to the vineyard, but has continued to write a syndicated twice-a-week newspaper column on public affairs. He also keeps updating his books; his first is now in the sixth printing of its fifth edition. The output of the Boordy nursery, enlarged by planting on neighbors' lands, is completely sold out a year before the vines are ready. The Wagners have supplied vines to all of the principal eastern and midwestern wineries, to the multiplying numbers of amateur growers in every state except Hawaii, and to research stations in several states and in Guatemala, Venezuela, and the Congo.

In 1968, the Wagners and little Boordy Vineyard suddenly became part of the grape and wine industries of two much more important winegrowing states—New York and Washington—through a "pooling of resources" with the big Seneca Foods Corporation of Dundee, Westfield, and Williamson, New York, and of Prosser, Washington. But at Riderwood, Boordy Vineyard and its wines remain unchanged, and—between their flights in the Seneca plane to supervise its wine operations in other states—the colonial farmhouse beside the cellar is still the Wagners' home for as long as they decide to stay.

• 8 •

Wagner and his hybrids have made possible most of the small winegrowing ventures that have started up in several eastern states since the Second World War. Several of these are in Maryland. It was also Wagner who convinced officials of his state to set its $50-per-year license fee for farmers who produce wine from Maryland-grown grapes. The figure is reasonable, compared to the exorbitant license fees charged in other states, but the Maryland law has a grievous flaw. It doesn't allow the Maryland winery to sell its wine except to licensed distributors and retailers. Few small wineries can operate profitably unless they can sell their ouptut directly to consumers.

Thirty miles northwest of Baltimore, at New Windsor in Carroll County, is the little Cároli Vineyard, the home and avocation of Dr. Charles Southward Singleton, professor of humanistic studies at Johns Hopkins University. Dr. Singleton began planting the French hybrids in 1952 to make wine for his own consumption. Then, finding that the quality of his wine would be better if he made it in larger lots, he planted more vines and bonded his barn as a winery. During the 1960s, Cároli's estate-bottled white, rosé, and red table wines achieved local fame in Carroll County and in Baltimore. Dr. Singleton now has discontinued selling his wines and maintains an experimental vineyard of Vinifera grapes.

Another Johns Hopkins savant has Maryland's newest bonded winery, the Montbray Wine Cellars. It is near Westminster in Silver Run Valley, a quiet, idyllic depression in the undulating hills ten miles north of Westminster, only two miles from the Pennsylvania border. Dr. G. Hamilton Mowbray, a researcher in psychology, discovered the fascination of wine while studying for his doctorate at Cambridge University in England. Returning to Maryland to do research in the sensory processes at the University's world-famed Applied Physics Laboratory, he began growing French hybrid grapes in collaboration with Dr. Singleton.

But a visit to Hammondsport, New York, in 1958 convinced Dr. Mowbray that Konstantin Frank is right about Vinifera for the East and that the Old World grapes, if given the proper rootstocks and spray-protection from vine pests, should grow as well in Maryland as Wagner's French hybrids do. As soon as he could get vines, he planted thirty each of Chardonnay, White Riesling, Pinot Noir, and Muscat Ottonel. They survived a series of winter freezes and thrived so well that he sold his home, because there was not enough land, bought a hundred-acre tract at Silver Run, moved his vines there, and planted additional Chardonnay and Riesling, to which he since has added Pinot Noir. His thousand-gallon winery (named for a Norman ancestor) is in an old German-style barn, the underground portion of which he has insulated to maintain an average temperature of fifty-five degrees throughout the year. The first five Montbray wines, placed on sale in 1968 at a Westminster store and in two Baltimore outlets, were white, rosé, and red table wines made of hybrids, and included two varietals, Seyve-Villard White and Ravat Red. But with the first vintage from his Chardonnay, White Riesling, and Pinot Noir vines now starting to age in his cellar, Dr. Mowbray is also making history by preparing to market the first Vinifera wines to be made commercially in Maryland since the seventeenth century.

Several other Maryland vineyards are noncommercial, including urban planner Albert Copp's planting near Baltimore and Johns Hopkins administrator Robert Dickmann's Trigonne Vineyard, principally of hybrids, at Silver Spring.

· 9 ·

New Jersey, despite its small size, is the fourth state in the nation in volume of wine production, exceeded only by California, New York, and Illinois. Although most of the wine now is made from grapes grown elsewhere, some of the Garden State's historic vineyards and wineries are well worth visiting, especially those which offer tasting and cellar tours.

One is the House of Renault, with its million-gallon winery and three hundred acres of vineyard on Bremer Avenue near Egg Harbor City, a southern New Jersey town that got its name from the nests of sea birds found by early Swedish fishermen along the nearby inlets from the sea. The firm of L. N. Renault & Sons has grown grapes and made wine here for more than a century. Louis Nicholas Renault came to the United States from France before the Civil War to represent the ancient champagne house of the Duke of Montebello at Rheims. Deciding to settle and make champagne in this country, he studied locations in both East and West, and was most impressed with the vineyards already thriving around Egg Harbor in Atlantic County. In 1864, he bought land for the present Renault vineyard, and by 1870 had introduced his New Jersey Champagne.

Renault and neighboring wineries won prizes for their wines at the Centennial Exposition at Philadelphia in 1876, and Egg Harbor soon became known as "the wine city." During the seventies and eighties, leading citizens and officials of Philadelphia came each year to the wine-tasting receptions held for them by the Egg Harbor vintners.

Louis Renault died in 1913 at the age of ninety-one and was succeeded by his son Felix. In 1919, John D'Agostino bought the company and operated it under a government permit through the fourteen years of Prohibition. His chief product was Renault Wine Tonic, which had an alcoholic content of 22 percent and was sold in virtually every drugstore in the nation. After Repeal, he acquired two old California wineries, Montebello at St. Helena and St. George at Fresno, and brought their wines in tank cars to Egg Harbor City for blending and bottling. His Charmat-process champagnes, mostly blends of California with New Jersey Labrusca wine, were sold nationwide. They were advertised by giant images of Renault bottles, which for many years lined highway roadsides in Massachusetts, Florida, and California.

When D'Agostino was killed in a car crash in 1948, his sister Maria took charge of Renault. Having a talent for design, Miss D'Agostino, an auburn-haired, five-foot-tall dynamo, transformed the old winery into a showplace. She built a gift shop and a luxurious, château-style hospitality house for visitors, hundreds of whom now come daily from the resorts and beaches of Atlantic City, which is only eighteen miles away. In 1966 she added a museum that displays only one item—wineglasses. These are not ordinary glasses. On thirty-five trips to Europe, Miss D'Agostino assembled hundreds of masterpieces of wineglass art, made for kings, queens, and merchant princes since the Middle Ages. But decoration and glass-collecting were only her avocations, for her principal interest was in the winery. It was also her home; the lady boss and her nonagenarian mother lived in an apartment upstairs from the gift shop, and Mother D'Agostino kept an eye on the winery visitors from her rocking chair in the corner of the shop. They continued living there, between trips to Florida, when Renault was sold in 1970 to the Universal Foods Corporation, a Milwaukee food-specialty house.

The early-day Egg Harbor winegrowers, such as Renault and Hiram Dewey & Sons, grew a grape named Noah, which originated at Nauvoo in Illinois but thrived best in the mild climate and sandy, chalky soils of southern New Jersey. The Noah imparted a characteristic dry, tart, faintly foxy flavor to their white wines that no other eastern wine district could match. When the phylloxera aphid was devastating the vineyards of Europe in the 1870s, Noah vines were imported from America and planted extensively in France, and Noah is the only American grape variety still grown there to make wine. In 1972, the Renault winery did something it probably should have done a century ago. It introduced a wine advertised as "new, dry and different," labeled "New Jersey State Noah White Varietal Dinner Wine."

Another New Jersey winery worth visiting for its tour and tasting is the 100,000-gallon Gross Highland cellar at Absecon, just north of Atlantic City. It makes champagnes and red and white table wines, principally of grapes from its own vineyard of thirty-two acres. Most of the wines have the Labrusca taste from such varieties as Fredonia, Clinton, Ives, and Noah. John Gross, a winemaker from Germany, opened this winery in 1934. It is now managed for his widow by Bernard J. D'Arcy, the French champagne expert who earlier served with some of the largest wineries in California.

Atlantic County has four more wineries: John Schuster & Son and the Egg Harbor Winery at Egg Harbor City; the Tomasello Winery at Hammonton, with a fifty-acre vineyard that dates back to 1888, and David Krumm's winery at Linwood with six acres, all that remained, when I was there in 1966, of the fifty acres his grandfather planted before the turn of the century. Residential growth and rising land taxes in the coastal area near Linwood have long threatened the survival of the vineyards there. Also in the path of urbanization was the Jacob Lee Winery's twenty-five-acre vineyard at Bordentown, southeast of Trenton.

· 10 ·

In Cumberland County, New Jersey, there is a town named Vineland—but for its vineyards, not for its wines. It was founded as a bone-dry community in the early 1860s by a real estate developer named Charles K. Landis. To Vineland there came in 1868 a man who fanatically hated wine, a dentist named Thomas B. Welch. It was here that Welch started the fresh grape juice industry, which led to the planting of Concord grapes across the United States—and a century later to the development of the kosher type of wine.

Dr. Welch, the Communion steward of his Methodist church, happened to read of Louis Pasteur's studies of the fermentation of wine, published in France in 1866. This suggested to Welch a way to improve the decoction of raisins steeped in water which Prohibitionist ministers of the time used for Communion in place of wine. Experimenting in his kitchen at Vineland, he succeeded in sterilizing the sweet juice of New Jersey grapes, and by 1870 had begun a small business with his son Charles, also a dentist, selling "Dr. Welch's Unfermented Wine" for church use. Later, when sales of the product spread from churches to drug stores and groceries, the name was changed to "Dr. Welch's Grape Juice."

In the '80s and '90s, grape rot attacked many New Jersey vineyards, and the Welch Company, needing more grapes, moved in 1896 to Watkins Glen in the Finger Lakes District of New York. A year later, the Doctors Welch built a processing plant at Westfield in the Chautauqua Grape Belt. During the next half century, a chain of Welch plants, which are now owned by the National Grape Co-operative (also called Welch Foods), spread to Pensylvania, Michigan, Arkansas, and to the State of Washington.

What the wine-hating Doctors Welch never knew, because they died in 1903 and 1926, was that a half-century after the father's death the Welch Grape Juice Company would start making a fermented Welch wine.

• 11 •

How can little New Jersey, with less than a thousand acres of vineyards, produce more than four million gallons of wine annually? The answer is partly that some New Jersey wine is from other fruits, apples in particular. Since 1851, except during Prohibition, the oldest distiller in this country has been operating the old-fashioned Laird and Company applejack distillery at Scobeyville in Monmouth County. The firm was founded here in 1780 and has operated additional plants at North Garden, Virginia, and Lyons, New York, making apple wine and the distilled liquor that once was called "New Jersey Lightning." Another answer is in such wineries as Nathan Paszamant's big Monte Carlo Wine Industries plant at New Brunswick, which makes great quantities of wine of all kinds, still and sparkling—but from grapes, juice, and concentrate that are shipped here from other states as far distant as South Carolina and California.

Yet New Jersey's Director of Agriculture, Philip Alampi, says there are areas in the agricultural southern half of the state that could be profitably planted to wine grapes. Harold Applegate, who has a home vineyard of Vinifera at Cranbury, four miles east of Princeton, says rising prices of land and corresponding tax increases are driving farmers off the land in that area. But the biggest area of idle land in the entire New York metropolitan complex is located in southern New Jersey. It is the Pine Barrens, 620 desolate square miles of pine and scrub oak, inhabited principally by deer, foxes, rabbits, and quail, and as yet untouched by urbanization. Although the Pine Barren soils are considered too thin and sandy for farming, a part of the Renault vineyard is at the southern edge of the Barrens and produces healthy grape crops. Neither Rutgers, the State University, nor its Cooperative Extension Service has yet conducted any grape-growing tests in New Jersey, as their counterparts are beginning to do in many other states.

• 12 •

Pennsylvania, where commercial winegrowing began, now ranks fifth in the nation in grape production (after California, New York, Washington, and Michigan), harvesting 50,000 tons yearly from more than 9000 acres of vineyards. But until now, only a small fraction of this tonnage has been produced for wine. Almost all of the grapes have been Concords, grown for fresh grape juice. Since the repeal of Prohibition, Pennsylvania has supplied some of its grapes to wineries in neighboring states, but until recently produced no wine of its own.

Now, because a new Pennsylvania law encourages winegrowing, wine grapes are being planted in the northwestern and southeastern parts of the state. There now are four Pennsylvania wineries, and a dozen more are being planned.

The Keystone State has a strange wine history. William Penn attempted to establish a Pennsylvania wine industry, bringing French and Spanish vines to Philadelphia in 1683. "The consequence," he predicted, "will be as good as any European countries of the same latitude do yield." Penn's attempt to start a vineyard failed, but the Penn Colony's interpreter, Conrad Weiser, succeeded. Weiser's vineyard, near Womelsdorf in the Tulpehocken Valley, where his home is now a state park, regularly supplied Riesling vines to the governor of Virginia during the 1750s, according to his diaries.

As mentioned earlier, it was near Philadelphia that the first domesticated native wine grape was discovered, by John Alexander, at the time of the Revolution.

In 1793, a Frenchman, Peter Legaux, founded a company to cultivate grapes at Spring Mill, on the north bank of the Schuylkill near the present Philadelphia suburb of Conshohocken. Alexander's was the only grape that survived. Legaux claimed it was one of the Vinifera varieties he had imported from the Cape of Good Hope, and he named it the Cape or Constantia grape.

Others called it the Cape, Black Madeira, Schuylkill Muscadell, and eventually the Alexander. From the Spring Mill Vineyard, the Alexander spread throughout Pennsylvania, and to Ohio, Virginia, Kentucky, and Indiana during the early part of the nineteenth century.

Thomas Eichelberger, an enterprising German who planted Alexander grapes about 1818 between York and the Susquehanna River, was America's first commercial vintner, according to Professor Hedrick. York became an early center of grape culture. There also were vineyards along the Schuylkill from Reading to the Germantown section of Philadelphia, where in 1830 Edward H. Bonsall had a winery and a vineyard of Alexander, Isabella, and Catawba.

But the Pittsburgh area, west of the Alleghenies, soon outdistanced the eastern part of the state in wine production. Grape planting began here as early as 1793, when Colonel George Morgan, a friend of Benjamin Franklin, started a vineyard at Morganza, Washington County. It was "Father" George Rapp, the leader of the communistic theocracy known as the Harmony Society, who made the Pittsburgh district known for its wines. Rapp, the son of a grape grower of Württemberg, came to Pennsylvania in 1803, seeking land on which to settle his followers. He bought 5000 acres on Connoquenessing Creek in Butler County, brought two hundred families of Rappists in three shiploads from Germany in 1804, and built the town of Harmony. The colonists planted ten acres of Old World grapevines and also produced silk, but because the vines died, they abandoned the place in 1814 and established New Harmony in the Wabash Valley of Indiana.

In 1824, the Harmonists returned to the Pittsburgh area, and on 3000 acres along the Ohio River, eighteen miles north of the city, they built another town and named it Economy. Here they again planted vineyards, apparently of native grapes, and established several industries, including a winery and a distillery. Economy became famous for its wines, woolens, and other products. The colony declined after Rapp's death in 1847, but its industries, including winegrowing, continued.

Evidently more vineyards were planted in the vicinity, because in the Patent Office report for 1855, Victor Scriba of Pittsburgh described forty to fifty acres of vines, principally Catawba, growing on hillsides facing the Allegheny, Monongahela, and Ohio Rivers. He wrote that "the wine made from the Catawba, as well as from the Isabella grapes, is good and praiseworthy, and sells from one to two dollars a gallon."

In 1880, when the special census of United States wine production was made, Allegheny County led the state in wine production with 45,000 gallons, compared to a total of 13,000 gallons made in Adams, Bucks, Cumberland, Lancaster, and Northumberland Counties in southeastern Pennsylvania.

Winemaking around Pittsburgh continued at least until 1900. *The American Wine Press and Mineral Water News*, in its issue for November of that year, refers to the claret, Riesling, and Catawba wine still being produced by the Economy Wine Vaults.

But one of "Father" Rapp's teachings, in addition to sobriety and simple living, was celibacy; and by 1905 few of the Harmonists remained, victims to their own virtue; and the Society was dissolved. In 1912, Economy was renamed Ambridge. Two city blocks of the old Economy buildings have been preserved by the state at Ambridge, including dwellings, shops, granary, Rapp's thirty-five-room Great House, and the Music Hall, in the cellar of which are the colony's wine storage vaults.

A third Pennsylvania vineyard district was established in the middle of the last century in Erie County, along the shore of Lake Erie. At North East, a town strangely named because it is in the far northwestern corner of the state, the South Shore Wine Company began making wine in 1863 from Isabella and Catawba grapes. The winery building, with its cavernous cellars, still stands and is now used as a restaurant. Thirty years later, Concord grapes began replacing wine varieties in the district because Americans were learning to drink bottled grape juice, which had been introduced to the public by Dr. Charles Welch at the 1893 Chicago World's Fair. In 1900 the Welch Company established at North East the world's biggest grape juice plant. Although a few Erie County wineries continued operating until Prohibition in 1920, Concord grapes have been the county's chief farm crop ever since.

• 13 •

When Prohibition was repealed in 1933, scores of wineries reopened in New York, New Jersey, and Ohio, but not in Pennsylvania. For the Keystone State had adopted a beverage control system purposely designed to discourage the purchase of liquor or wine. It created a gigantic state liquor monopoly, the Pennsylvania Liquor Control Board, which operates the some seven hundred liquor stores in the state.

Nobody but an amateur would have wanted to start a winery under this system, for wine could only be sold through the state-operated stores. But there was one such amateur. Philadelphia businessman Melvin S. Gordon, while vacationing in Europe in the mid-1950s, had toured vineyards and become interested in fine wines. On his return home he began reading books about grapes and started making wine in his kitchen. He then bought a farm at Birchrunville, a crossroads in Chester County eight miles west of Valley Forge, added a tractor, several barrels, a grape crusher, and a hand-bottling machine, and planted some French hybrid vines he got from Philip Wagner at Baltimore. His vines produced well, and in 1963 he bonded the tiny Conestoga Vineyard winery, the first to be established in Pennsylvania in this century.

Something went wrong with Gordon's 1963 vintage, and he poured it down the drain. When the 1964 vintage was ready, he offered it to the Liquor Control Board. He was waiting for the Board to buy it when I paid him a visit in 1966. I tasted wines from several of his barrels. A white, made of Seibel 4986 (a variety now called Rayon d'Or), had a fresh, fruity flavor reminiscent of Sylvaner and was the best wine made of a French hybrid that I sampled during that entire trip. Gordon, however, preferred his red, a full-flavored blend of several hybrids in which the Maréchal Foch variety predominated. But Gordon couldn't serve me any of his wines at lunch. In order to drink his own wine, he would have had to buy it at a state store.

A year later, the Liquor Board started selling Gordon's wines. Word that wines were actually being grown in Pennsylvania reached the state's leading restaurateurs, and some of them placed orders for them with the Board. Conestoga wines were soon added to the wine lists of famed Coventry Forge Inn, Original Bookbinders, Kimberton Country House, and a score of other three-star establishments. Gordon can no longer keep up with the demand for his wines, for his vineyard is only ten acres.

• 14 •

Meanwhile, other amateur winemakers far north in Erie County had a better idea. One was Douglas P. Moorhead, who while a soldier stationed in Germany in 1957 had visited vineyards on the Rhine and tasted wines of the White (Johannisberg) Riesling grape. A graduate in pomology from Pennsylvania State University and the son of an Erie County Concord grower, Moorhead resolved that when he returned to America, he would plant the true Riesling in his family's vineyard at Moorheadville. He obtained vines of Riesling and other Vinifera from Dr. Konstantin Frank and also some French hybrids from Philip Wagner. He began making wines in the family cellar and discussed them with other amateur winemakers who often bought grapes from his father. One of these was William Konnerth of Erie, a former newspaper reporter and a true wine enthusiast. In 1960 Moorhead and Konnerth organized the Erie County Wine Club with fifteen fellow home winemakers. Before long they had a waiting list of others wanting to join. Because winemaking equipment for amateurs was difficult to buy, the two young men made joint purchases for the club. This soon became a business, which they named Presque Isle Wine Cellars to express their hope of some-day starting a winery. The firm grew rapidly and now furnishes thousands of home winemakers throughout the country with grapes, juice, winemaking equipment and supplies, including a $1.25 booklet on winemaking by Konnerth that is one of the best you can buy.

Moorhead's Vinifera and hybrid plantings thrived in the mean-time. He became convinced that Erie County, with its 194-day growing season, has the best climate for high-quality white table wines and champagnes in the East, equaled only by the Lake Erie Islands. Neighboring growers became interested and made trial plantings of both groups of wine grapes. A committee of growers was formed in 1967 to consider starting wineries in the county. State Secretary of Agriculture Leland H. Bull became interested and allocated state funds to Pennsylvania State University's ex-periment station at North East for a study of wine-grape growing.

The growers' committee found that for wineries to operate pro-fitably, the Pennsylvania law would have to be changed, that farmer wineries should be permitted to sell their wines to the public and to restaurants without going through the Control Board. In 1967, a bill was introduced in the legislature, seeking to permit Pennsylvania winegrowers to sell at their winery premises table wines of their own production from Pennsylvania grapes. The Liquor Control Board opposed the bill, insisting that only the state monopoly stores should be allowed to sell wine. Its power-ful opposition kept the measure dormant for a year. But on the last day of the next legislative session, in August 1968, the farmers and their supporters succeeded in bringing the bill to a vote. It passed both houses, 171 to 13 and 36 to 9.

The new law permits sales of Pennsylvania table wine to any-one by wineries which produce not more than 50,000 gallons per year (amended a year later to 100,000). Within weeks of their victory, growers were planning to build two wineries at North East. Moorhead and Konnerth built and bonded their 10,000-gal-lon Presque Isle Winery, in a wooded area on Highway 20, three miles west of North East, in time to crush the 1969 vintage. At this writing, I have just tasted a sample of their 1969 Riesling and find it comparable to a young Rheingau—fragrant, well balanced, with the true White Riesling character, yet with a distinct personality of its own. I look forward to tasting their other wines, which include Chardonnay, Seyval Blanc, and six red, white, and pink blends of other grapes.

Also in 1969, a group of growers headed by George Luke, Blair McCord, and George Sceiford finished building Erie County's second winery, named Penn-Shore Vineyards, with a capacity of 135,000 gallons, on Highway 5, two miles west of North East, and began producing seven estate-bottled table wines and the first Pennsylvania champagne. North East has become a mecca for wine lovers, for both Presque Isle and Penn-Shore invite visitors and offer tasting and winery tours daily except on weekends.

The state's fourth winery was bonded in 1972 on the newly planted Pequea Valley Vineyard of French hybrids on Rawlinsville Road, ten miles south of Lancaster in the Amish country, one of the areas where wine was grown in the 1880s. Grapes for the first vintage were purchased from vineyards in Erie County.

Pennsylvania's "limited winery" law is attracting the interest of growers in a dozen other states, including Idaho and Mississippi. It has already been copied by Indiana, with the result that that state now has two wineries.

5

Ohio, Once the Premier Wine State

THE RISE and decline of Ohio wines could supply compelling material for a historical novel, because the Ohio wine star has risen not once, but twice, each time only to fall; and now it is rising again. Scores of new vineyards and five new wineries producing new kinds of wine have sprung up since 1967 in southern Ohio, where the state's wine industry began more than a century and a half ago.

This could also make an epic movie, with such characters as wine-millionaire Nicholas Longworth, poet and connoisseur Henry Wadsworth Longfellow, and Ohio's colorful winegrowers of today. And if filmed in such settings as the storied Ohio River, the ancient wine caves beneath Cincinnati and Sandusky, and the vine-clad islands of Lake Erie, the plot could weave war, intrigue, politics, and Prohibition-era gunplay without veering a grape's-width from actual history.

• 2 •

Nicholas Longworth*, the five-foot-one "crazy Jerseyman," came to Cincinnati from Newark in 1803 at the age of twenty-one with little more than the clothes on his back. It was the year Ohio became a state. He studied law for six months, established a lucrative practice, invested in land in the mushrooming town, and became the wealthiest man in Ohio. Winegrowing then was just beginning along the riverbanks at Cincinnati. It became Longworth's hobby. He also saw that drunkenness decreased in direct proportion to the use of light table wines, and he decided that by producing such wines he could woo Americans away from hard liquor.

In 1823, Longworth planted a vineyard on Bald Hill, overlooking

*The great-grandfather of the Nicholas Longworth who was Speaker of the House during the Coolidge administrations, and who was the son-in-law of President Theodore Roosevelt.

the Ohio River in the part of Cincinnati known as Tusculum. The site is now the city's Frederick H. Alms Memorial Park, in which some of the old vine roots still grow. He imported thousands of vines from Europe, but they died, so he made his first wine from the native Alexander and Isabella. Then he heard of a "wonder grape," the Catawba, grown by Major John Adlum of Georgetown, and in 1825 he obtained Catawba cuttings from Adlum. Three years later, when Longworth tasted the first Catawba wine pressed from his grapes, he quit his law practice and gave his full attention to winegrowing. By 1842 he was cultivating 1200 acres of vineyards at Tusculum, in the Delhi Hills, and on the present site of Eden Park, and began making America's first champagne.

Longworth's white Catawba wine and his champagne, which he called Sparkling Catawba, were sold throughout the East and even in faraway California. They were so successful that California winegrowers began planting Catawba grapes and attempted to copy the sensational Ohio wines. Longworth once accused New York hotels of substituting French champagnes for his, which he sold them at the then fancy price of twelve dollars a case. His fame reached England. A writer for the *Illustrated London News* in 1858 described the still Catawba as "a finer wine of the hock species and flavour than any hock that comes from the Rhine," and declared that "the Sparkling Catawba, of the pure, unadulterated juice of the odoriferous Catawba grape, transcends the Champagne of France."

But a more lasting tribute was the "Ode to Catawba Wine" by Longfellow, which begins:

> Very good in its way
> Is the Verzenay,
> Or the Sillery soft and creamy;
> But Catawba wine
> Has a taste more divine,
> More dulcet, delicious, and dreamy.

Some say the gift of a few bottles from Longworth inspired Longfellow to write the poem at his Cambridge home in 1854. But it is evident to anyone who reads all eleven stanzas that the bard had actually visited Cincinnati and had learned from Longworth about the many American grape varieties named in the "Ode," including the grape that "grows by the Beautiful River."

• 3 •

Ohio was the premier wine state by 1859, producing nearly 570,000 gallons yearly, more than a third of the national total, twice as much as California. Cincinnati was "the queen of the

West"; the Ohio was "the Rhine of America." There were 3000 acres of vineyards along the river between Cincinnati and Ripley, forty miles upstream, and a large acreage under vines across the river in Kentucky.

But just as Cincinnati's wine star reached its zenith, a plague began to spread through its vineyards. The violet-hued skins of the Catawba grapes were turning black, and many of the berries were found to be hollow shells. A cobwebby growth wilted the leaves and stems, and the vines began to die. Black rot and oïdium (powdery mildew) wrought this destruction at a time when modern preventive sprays were still unknown.

Longworth had half a million bottles in the caves beneath his two Cincinnati "wine houses" in 1860, but was running short of grapes to produce more wine. His dream fading, the little man in his latter years grew absent-minded; he carried numerous papers in his hat and a memorandum sheet pinned to his coat sleeve. When he died in 1863, two years after the outbreak of the Civil War, his business was divided among his heirs, and it was abandoned a few years later, for most of the vineyards were dead. Not less than 10,000 acres of vines in southwestern Ohio were obliterated by the "vine sickness" during the late '50s and '60s, and only a few were replaced. Cincinnati wines were virtually a thing of the past.

• 4 •

In the meantime another part of Ohio, two hundred miles north of Cincinnati, was achieving prominence as a winegrowing district. Grape planting had begun as early as 1836 along the shore of Lake Erie and on the islands that extend toward the Canadian border. Here the lake-tempered breezes kept the vines free of disease. In the decade after 1860, at least 7000 acres of vineyards were planted in northern Ohio, from Toledo to beyond Cleveland, some by growers who migrated from Cincinnati. In 1870, a half-million-gallon winery on Middle Bass Island claimed to be the largest in the nation, and the Lenk winery at Toledo turned out 400,000 gallons in that year. By 1900 several of the Sandusky wineries had won medals for their wines at judgings in this country and in Paris and Rome. The comeback of Ohio wines was complete.

• 5 •

Then, in 1920, came Prohibition, and the Ohio wine industry collapsed for the second time. During the dry years, several of the state's vintners continued to operate by government permit, making small quantities of sacramental and medicinal wines. Others made wines without official sanction, and when Federal food and drug officers approached some of the Lake Erie Islands to inspect the vines for spray residues, they were driven away by shotgun blasts.

Grape acreage along the lake again increased during the 1920s to supply home winemakers and bootleggers. At this time, however, most of the Ohio vineyards switched from wine grapes to Concords because of the expanding market for fresh grape juice. But the wineries around Sandusky maintained their vineyards of Catawba and other wine grapes, and at Repeal in 1933 they were ready to cash in on the boom demand they expected for wines. Richer in historic background than most of the New York wineries, with the best grape-growing climate in the East, and with wines distinctly different from those of California, they had the best opportunity to install their brands again on the best hotel and restaurant wine lists of the East and Midwest. But the Sandusky vintners let the opportunity at Repeal slip through their fingers. Instead of concentrating on selling their quality wines and champagnes, they tried to compete for volume sales with the low-priced wines shipped to local bottlers in tank cars from California. The Ohio wineries even tried unsuccessfully to get their legislature to levy a dollar-a-gallon tax on wines from outside the state. Meanwhile the vintners of New York's Finger Lakes District seized the chance that Ohio had muffed, and Finger Lakes champagnes became the chief sparkling wines sold in the United States. In 1937, there were 161 wineries in Ohio. By 1967, there were twenty-five left, only fifteen making wine from Ohio grapes.

• 6 •

Yet for today's wine tourist, no other district in America offers historic vineyards and colorful wineries in settings as uniquely spectacular as those that still operate along the shore and on the islands of Lake Erie.

From Sandusky eastward to the Pennsylvania border, a ten-mile-wide strip of land facing Lake Erie is dotted with vineyards, though many are now threatened by urbanization. West of Cleveland, which has several large bonded cellars, are two producing wineries. One is on Allan Klingshirn's ten-acre vineyard at Avon Lake. The other, at the Cleveland suburb of Westlake, is the 80,000-gallon Dover Vineyard winery. It was established in 1934 by eighteen grape growers in Cuyahoga and Lorain Counties, but is now owned by Andrew Somogyi, a winemaker who came here from Hungary following the 1956 revolution. The winery is under the same roof as the Dover Chalet restaurant, and diners there are sometimes permitted to watch how the wines are made.

East of Cleveland, there are small wineries at Wickliffe and Willoughby, and Geneva has two wineries, Chalet De Bonne, which is new, and the Cohodas Vineyard. Morris Cohodas formerly grew only Concords on his fifty acres, but since sending his son Alvin to the University of California at Davis to be trained for a winemaking career, Cohodas has replanted the vineyard gradually to Catawba. This is the main Concord area; nine tenths of the grapes are now harvested mechanically.

Sandusky, which succeeded Cincinnati as the wine capital of Ohio, is a venerable lakefront city with strange diagonal thoroughfares. When Longworth's vineyards at Cincinnati died, the Catawba found its adopted home here, as local maps with such landmarks as Catawba Point, Catawba Island, and Catawba Road testify. Sandusky, situated midway between Cleveland and Toledo, is now the center of a miles-long strip of summer resorts and beaches that is billed, with the neighboring islands, as "Lake Erie Vacationland." Near the city's straggling waterfront stand several century-old wineries, some of whose wine caves are tunneled beneath the streets. The Engels & Krudwig cellar on East Water Street, founded in 1863 and once famed for its Diedesheimer and Laubenheimer vintages, is still bonded, but E & K wines have not been marketed for many years. Nearby is the John G. Dorn winery, which began in 1872 with Longworth's original casks, but closed in 1957. On Clinton Street stood the great cellar of Michel Hommel, whose 1889 champagne won him medals at Chicago's Columbian World Exposition in 1893 and at the Paris Exposition of 1900, but it was closed in 1967 and destroyed by fire soon afterward. The only winery operating in the city is Meier's Sandusky cellar on Campbell Street, which ferments grapes from the islands and from the lakeshore vineyards to the east.

There still are two active wineries at Venice, four miles west of Sandusky. One is William Steuk's small cellar beside the four acres that remain of his grandfather's vineyard, which dates from 1855. Steuk produces Sparkling Catawba and an assortment of table wines "for sentimental reasons," he says, and sells them on the premises. The other Venice winery adjoins the thirty-five-acre Mantey Vineyard on Bardshar Road. Paul Mantey, whose grandfather began making wine in 1880 for the German immigrant families around Sandusky, operates the cellar by himself and makes fourteen different wines, including a dry Catawba and a semidry Baco Rosé.

Paul Mantey's brother, Norman, has his own winery five miles away on the peninsula called Catawba Island, across Sandusky Bay. Norman, a balding veteran of World War II guerrilla fighting in the swamps of Bougainville, must be the busiest vintner in Ohio, for he performs at three jobs. First, he runs his Mon Ami Champagne Company in a handsome limestone cellar built about 1872. Second, he sells the output of both his own and his brother's winery by flying his single-engined plane each week to call on wine wholesalers in cities throughout Ohio. His third job is at night, when he runs the Mon Ami restaurant upstairs from the winery and serves steaks, sauerkraut balls, and Mon Ami wines by the glass and by the bottle. With its picturesque vaulted underground cellar, the Mon Ami winery could become a showplace for the wine industry of the Sandusky area if the proprietor didn't work at so hectic a pace. He has no time to show the vaults to visitors.

• 7 •

Jutting above the surface of Lake Erie, between Sandusky and the Canadian boundary that bisects the lake, is the cluster of little, oddly shaped islands that long grew Ohio's finest wines. The Lake Erie Islands are a viticultural curiosity: being warmed in late autumn by the surrounding waters, they enjoy the longest grape-growing season in the northeastern United States. The grapes here are harvested as much as six weeks after the vintage ends on the mainland. In the winter, the lake freezes over, so solidly that automobiles can cross to the islands, and even this benefits the vineyards, because the cold air in spring delays the buds from opening until the danger of spring frosts has passed.

From Sandusky and nearby Port Clinton, ferryboats serve the islets, except when the lake freezes over, and they carry most of the grape harvest to the mainland.

In all the world there is no transportation system quite like the islands' air service. Hopping from island to island and to Port Clinton daily throughout the year are three relics of the early age of aviation, the 1928 vintage Ford tri-motors famed as the "Tin Geese." Only eleven of these lumbering, corrugated-metal planes are known still to exist. Ralph Dietrich's Island Airlines is fortunate to own its little fleet, because modern planes of this size cannot use the island airstrips. Flipping between islets only one to eleven miles apart, they carry the islanders' children to and from high school on the mainland, and they also deliver groceries, coal, pianos, and island wines.

Kelley's Island, the largest on the United States side of the lake, was planted with grapes by 1846, and here the first winery north of Cincinnati was built five years later. By 1880 its vineyards covered 750 acres and supported five wineries. Because Kelley's is the closest of the group to the mainland, summer cottages, camps, and beach clubs have supplanted all but one of its vineyards. Winegrowing is now almost entirely confined to the three Bass Islands, so named for the fishing on the reefs along their shores.

South Bass, now more often called Put-in-Bay, is the most famous because of its War of 1812 history and the lofty Peace Monument that stands at the entrace to its bay. It was from here that Commodore Oliver Hazard Perry sailed to meet the British fleet on September 12, 1813, and here he put in after the battle to send his memorable dispatch of victory: "We have met the enemy and they are ours—two ships, two brigs, one schooner, and one sloop." In earlier days, when paddlewheel steamers brought vacationists from Cleveland and Toledo, there were palatial hotels on this island. A streetcar line once ran from the steamer dock to the sprawling Victory Hotel, since destroyed by a great fire.

There are still vineyards on both sides of quaint Put-in-Bay village, but with tourism now the principal industry, only one winery, the Heineman Cellar, remains active. Norman Heineman, born on the island, and his son Louis till the twenty-acre vineyard that Norman's father planted after coming here in 1883 from the winegrowing region of Baden in Germany. In 1897, a year after the winery was built, workmen digging a well on the property stumbled into a huge cave of green crystal stalactites. The Heinemans charge tourists a fee to visit the cave, and a tour of the winery is included. They make eight kinds of table wine, including a dry white Catawba and a peculiar blend of Catawba and Concord, containing 15 percent alcohol, that they call "Sweet Belle." The wines are sold by the glass or bottle, and some of the visitors like them well enough to order shipments made by the case to their homes on the mainland.

From South Bass it is only a rowboat ride to pistol-shaped, three-mile-long Middle Bass Island and its chief landmark, the Lonz Winery, a frowning medieval-style castle on the lakeshore. To the yachting fraternity of the entire Great Lakes region, this winery with its nearby harbor has been a haven for bacchanalian festivity since the repeal of Prohibition. Island-born George Lonz, a bubbling, droll, Falstaffian host, sold his champagne by the bottle, rented guests the glasses in which to drink it, and often played the violin to entertain them. When Lonz died in 1969 he was succeeded by roly-poly Lorito Lazarony, who came from the Hommel cellar in Sandusky. Lazarony still makes Lonz's excellent Isle de Fleurs Champagne and Lake Erie Island table wines, tours guests through the underground cellars, and still rents them the glasses in which to drink the champagne. The visitors on a summer afternoon number as many as two thousand, brought by planes and by a fleet of up to one hundred and fifty boats.

The forty-five-acre vineyard adjoining the winery dates from 1862, when it was planted by Andrew Wehrle from Alsace. He also built the original winery, but it has been replaced twice following disastrous fires. It was Lonz who in 1942 built its turrets and battlements, once aptly described as "a mason's caprice."

From the Lonz castle it is an easy walk to the other winery on Middle Bass. It is owned by the Bretz family. Leslie Bretz, born here on Christmas Day in 1893, inherited the little cellar from his grandfather, Joseph Miller from Baden, who built it in 1865. Florence Bretz, a coastguardsman's daughter, came here from the mainland during the twenties to teach in the island grammar school, and married Leslie a year later. With one of their three sons, Walter, they make bottle-fermented champagne and sparkling burgundy, Catawba, Delaware, and claret wines, and an unfermented Concord juice, using only the grapes from their twenty-two-acre vineyard. Tourists buy their entire output. Leslie Bretz doubts whether the islands' thin layer of topsoil, gradually becoming thinner on South Bass, can continue supporting vines for many more years.

But on bell-shaped Isle St. George, which most charts show as North Bass Island, they think differently. "Of course this topsoil is thin," says Henry O. Sonneman, who owns most of this island, and whose Meier's Wine Cellars of Cincinnati and Sandusky is Ohio's largest wine producer. "Vines have been growing here since 1844, and they'll still be producing the best grapes in America a century from now." These islands, Sonneman explains, are mounds of limestone rising from the bottom of Lake Erie, the shallowest of the Great Lakes. The soil is cultivated to a depth of only two inches, but the limestone underneath is crisscrossed by fissures and caves, through which the water circulates, and to which the roots of the vines readily penetrate. Sometimes the limestone must be blasted with dynamite in order to plant more vines.

Isle St. George is only a mile long and covers 700-odd acres. Its highest point is scarcely fourteen feet above the lake level. It is eighteen miles from the mainland, a mile and a half from the international boundary. Some of the twelve families who live on the island are descendants of the earliest winegrowers. There is a one-room grammar school, but the older children fly daily to and from Port Clinton High School, occasionally staying overnight on

the mainland when their aerial school bus is grounded by fog or
storm. There are no stores on the island, but a telephone call via
the inter-island cable can bring an air taxi in less time than you
can get a taxi in your city. TV reception is of the best, and there is
year-round fishing, because when the lake freezes over, its surface
becomes dotted with wooden shanties, outfitted with stoves inside,
for anglers who come from far and near to fish through holes in
the ice.

Sonneman bought the Isle St. George vineyards in 1941 and expanded them to cover half the island. He grows Catawba, Delaware, and French hybrids, and has also experimented successfully with Vinifera varieties. He harvests a thousand tons yearly
on the island, mainly with the new mechanical harvesting
machines, and crushes the grapes at a press house near the boat
dock. The fresh must (unfermented juice) is then carried in fiberglass tanks by ferry to his Sandusky cellar, where the wine is
made and transported by stainless steel tank trucks to his
Cincinnati winery for aging and bottling.

• 8 •

Henry Sonneman is a stocky little man with a contagious grin
and a limp. He was born in 1904 on his parents' farm outside Cincinnati and learned grape growing from his father, who had a
small vineyard supplying grapes to home winemakers. In 1928
Sonneman bought the seventy-year-old Meier's Grape Juice Company, where he had been employed washing bottles and cleaning
tanks while attending night classes at the University of Cincinnati.
Bavarian immigrant John Meier's Catawba vineyard, planted in
Longworth's time, was long gone; the company's grapes came
from Kelley's Island. When Sonneman became the boss, he made
"Meier's Unfermented Catawba Grape Juice" popular throughout
this country and Canada.

At Repeal he began making wine, but his little juice plant
couldn't compete with the big Sandusky, New York, and California
wineries. Sonneman felt that Ohio should produce distinctively
different Ohio wines and sell them at premium prices, and decided
to do it himself.

He did it by acquiring the Isle St. George vineyards and the
cellar at Sandusky, but kept his main winery at Silverton, ten miles
from the center of Cincinnati. He since has built its capacity to
two million gallons and now ships Meier's wines, champagnes and
Catawba juice to forty states and two foreign countries. The winery
has a *weinstube* and wine garden, where thousands come each year
to tour the cellar and to dine on sherry-flavored soup, pizza, sand-

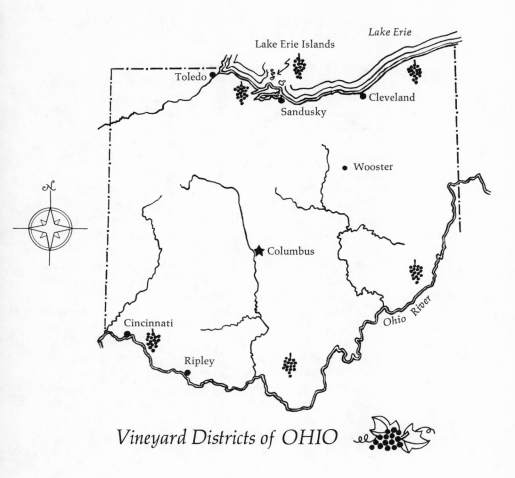

Vineyard Districts of OHIO

wiches, and Meierburgers with Meier's wines and champagnes. Meier's Catawba and sun-baked cream sherry were the only Ohio wines that were recommended on the 1966 State Department wine list.

• 9 •

It was Sonneman who sparked the revival of the wine industry in southern Ohio. After the Second World War, he began touring the world's vineyards, visiting every winegrowing area in Europe, Australia, Africa, and the Americas. From each trip he returned more convinced that Ohio could once again regain its laurels as a premium winegrowing state. He began talking with growers, bankers, and state officials about the need to replant Ohio's almost four thousand acres of Concord vineyards with wine grapes. He showed them that to supply his wineries, he was buying wine grapes and juice from Missouri, Michigan, Kentucky, and New York.

In particular, he pointed out that modern viticultural technology could make vines grow again along the Ohio River, where Longworth's vineyards had once flourished, and where farmers were now facing a tobacco surplus. Winegrowing, he said, could help solve the problems of economically depressed Appalachia.

At Sonneman's urging, state horticulturists in 1960 planted several wine-grape varieties in the new experimental substation at Ripley on the Ohio River. The vines thrived. The State Department of Development then made a study which showed a potential grape-growing belt with at least 175 frost-free days per year along a 250-mile stretch of the Ohio River. It suggested that twenty southern Ohio counties, from Cincinnati to Marietta, might grow wine grapes profitably. In 1964, at a farmers' meeting in Ripley, Ohio Governor James Rhodes heard the study report. Waving a wine bottle over his head, he declared: "We can grow as fine grapes and wines here as anywhere in the world."

Dr. Garth Cahoon, from Utah State University, was assigned in 1965 to plant demonstration vineyards of wine grapes on farms along the northern bank of the Ohio. At the state's main research center in Wooster, Dr. James Gallander from Oregon State University set up a wine laboratory. Someone questioned whether Dr. Cahoon would lead a winegrowing project, since he is a member of the ultra-dry Mormon Church. Cahoon replied that the original Mormons used wine for Communion before their successors switched to water, and that the Mormons' prophet, Joseph Smith, in the *Doctrine of Covenants*, had specified "wine, yea, pure juice of the grape," though with the proviso that "it is made new among you."

In the following spring, eleven more demonstration vineyards were planted in river counties as far east as Marietta. The state supplied the vines and the farmers furnished the land, equipment, and labor. There was great excitement; history was being made. Dr. Cahoon predicted vineyard yields of six tons per acre, and the event was recorded on television, radio, and in newspaper interviews.

Then Wistar and Ursula Marting, who had one of the state's experimental plantings on their Tarula Farm at Clarksville, planted a commercial vineyard of their own and began building a winery. By 1968 the Martings were selling their first French hybrid, Catawba, and Niagara wines at the farm and to stores and restaurants in nearby cities. Next, Sonneman's son and daughter,

Jack and Janet, planted thirty-five acres of hybrids near New Richmond in Clermont County, the Château Jac Jan Vineyard; and Merrill Bodine started a vineyard and winery at Cardington. Kenneth and Jim Schuchter planted forty acres of hybrids on their truck farm two miles west of Morrow and remodeled their cattle barn into the Valley Vineyards Winery. Charles McIntosh has since opened a winery at his vineyard near Bethel. Park Gast and Gene Dilger have planted fourteen acres of hybrids at Lebanon and are turning the old Bruckmann Brewery in Cincinnati into the Gast and Dilger Winery. Additional farmers have bought vines and planted wine grapes as far west as Indiana.

At this writing I have just tasted the first wines, vintage 1970, from the Château Jac Jan Vineyard. The Ohio Valley Chablis White Table Wine is flawless and rather resembles a good white Châteauneuf-du-Pape. The Château Jac Jan Red has excellent color, a pleasing winy aroma, and a soft but distinctive dry flavor; it is a wine with a premium future. The Sonneman family has now acquired three hundred more acres, to be planted with the same varieties, Seibels and Seyve-Villards, Baco Noir and Chelois.

The revival of the southern Ohio wine industry was celebrated in October 1971 with a wine festival at Morrow. Seven thousand people came to the three-day celebration, which featured a wine queen, a Grape Bowl football game, wine exhibits with tasting, and tours of the Valley Vineyards Winery. The Morrow of Tomorrow Committee has since voted to make the festival an annual event in the first week of October.

What more could a novelist ask for an ending? Ohio winegrowing has returned to the cradle from which it sprung. Lush vineyards again are yielding fine Ohio wines on the hillsides along Longfellow's "Beautiful River." More than a century after Nicholas Longworth's death, his dream of creating an American Rhineland is coming true.

6

New York, Champion of the East

A MENTION of New York State wines usually brings, from the average consumer of California or European wines, a remark about "that foxy taste." Vintners of New York and other eastern states abhor the word "foxy," and in deference to them I normally say "Labrusca" instead. But "foxy" is in the dictionaries and ampelographies, and it is the word commonly used to describe the fruity flavor of the Vitis Labrusca grapes—such as Concord, Catawba, Delaware, Niagara, Dutchess, and Ives—from which most New York wines are made.

However, not all wines containing Labrusca grapes are perceptibly foxy, for the Labrusca taste is readily softened, by blending with wines of neutral flavors, to a point at which only a hint of fruity fragrance remains. There is no Labrusca taste at all in the new eastern wine types that are made entirely from the French-American hybrid grapes, nor in New York sherries, from which it is removed by a heat-and-oxygen process; nor in those New York muscatels which are made from the Canada Muscat grape. And now that Dr. Konstantin Frank has shown that Vinifera grapes, too, can be grown there successfully, New York is beginning to challenge both California and Europe with small quantities of Old World wine types made from the true *cépages nobles*, such as White (Johannisberg) Riesling and Chardonnay.

But if the Labrusca flavor has been a handicap to the New York wineries, it certainly is not evident in the steady rate at which they have increased their share of the American market for wines. Between 1955 and 1970, vintners of the Empire State trebled their total wine production and more than quintupled their output of champagne. In an average year, New York now produces about twenty-one million gallons of wine and is thereby second to California, which makes ten times as much. Of the twenty-one million gallons, more than a fourth, or over five million, is champagne— a third as much of this bubbly wine as California makes. New York State's best wines are its champagnes, white table, and dessert types. Its typical dry reds leave something to be desired, but are improving steadily with the increased planting and use of the new French hybrid grapes in their blends. By 1971, the hybrids represented almost 3000 of the 36,000 acres of vines growing in New York State.

New York has four principal vineyard districts, each with distinctive wines and colorful wineries. Of its thirty-nine producing wineries, twelve are in the Finger Lakes district in the west-central

Principal Vineyard Districts of NEW YORK

part of the state; seven are in the Hudson River Valley, only an hour or two from Manhattan; three are in Chautauqua County, in the far western corner bordering Lake Erie, and one is in Niagara County, only seven miles from Niagara Falls. The other sixteen, located in and around New York and other cities, handle grapes, juices, and wines that are shipped in from the vineyard areas and from other states. During the 1960s more than a million gallons of California wines were shipped annually to New York State for blending purposes, in addition to California neutral brandy used in producing New York dessert wines.

Less than two fifths of the state's 150,000-ton average annual grape crop is used by New York wineries. The rest is used in fresh Concord grape juice, jelly, or jam, or is eaten fresh. A partial explanation is found in the peculiar history of winegrowing in New York. Prohibitionist influence during the past century accounts for the predominance of the Concord grape and for New York's strange beverage control laws, which discourage the establishment of additional wineries and actually discourage the purchase of wine.

• 2 •

New York was one of the first states to cultivate grapes, but was one of the last in the East to develop a wine industry. Vineyards were planted on Manhattan Island more than three hundred years ago, when Peter Stuyvesant was governor of New Netherland between 1647 and 1664. Stuyvesant sternly regulated the sale of liquor, but he favored the use of wine. He even authored an ordinance requiring that sailors on the high seas be provided with a daily ration of wine to protect their health. His successor, the first English governor of New York, Richard Nicolls, granted a monopoly to one Paulus Richards to plant a vineyard on Long Island. The French Protestants who settled in Ulster County on the Hudson after 1667 tried unsuccessfully to grow European grapes, but they then cultivated wild grapes to make wine for use in their homes. The healthy crops from their vines so impressed Governor Nicolls' successor that he expressed the belief, in a letter to the Lords of Trade in London, that the New York colony alone could produce enough wine to supply all the dominions of the Crown. In 1750, William Prince established the Linnaean Gardens at Flushing on Long Island, and from there the Isabella wine grape of South Carolina was introduced throughout the East after 1816. Vines grew in New York City as late as 1846, when the horticulturist, Alden Spooner, published a book on winemaking. Spooner described the wine he made at his own vineyard in

Brooklyn, and mentioned other vineyards thriving there, on Manhattan, and at Southampton and New Utrecht on Long Island.*

In 1818, a Baptist deacon, Elijah Fay, planted the first vineyard in what is now the Chautauqua Grape Belt along Lake Erie in western New York State and eastern Pennsylvania. Near the present village of Brocton in Chautauqua County, he set out wild vines which he had brought from New England. Because the wild grapes were harsh and excessively foxy, he replaced them in 1824 with Isabella and Catawba, and in 1830 Deacon Fay made ten gallons of wine. But it was not until 1859, when wineries were already operating along the lakeshore in Ohio, that the first of several "wine houses" around Brocton was built by the Deacon's son, Joseph Fay.

But the temperance movement, born in 1808 at Moreau in Saratoga County, was beginning to spread. By 1835 the state temperance society was advocating total abstinence from alcoholic beverages in any form. From New York State the temperance movement evolved into the nationwide crusade that brought about National Prohibition in 1920. In 1845, the Drys got a law passed prohibiting the public sale of liquor in New York State, but it was repealed two years later. They scored again in 1855, obtaining the passage of another state prohibition law, but it was declared unconstitutional.

Chautauqua County, where the Fays lived, was one of the centers of the dry crusade. It was also where the Concord grape variety was introduced—not for winemaking, because dry wine made from Concord is harsh—but as a table grape. The temperance crusaders, with psalm-singing fervor, exhorted farmers of the Chautauqua district to produce grapes, not wine. It was dry influence, as much as the later development of the grape juice industry by the ardent Prohibitionist Dr. Welch, that caused the Chautauqua-Erie Grape Belt to become a fresh-grape district instead of a wine center. This three-county district now produces more than half of the New York State grape crop, and although wine-grape varieties have lately been introduced, nine tenths of the vines here still are Concords.

Winemaking began tardily in the Finger Lakes district, too. The Finger Lakes wineries credit the start of their industry to the Reverend William Bostwick, an Episcopal minister, who in 1829 brought Catawba and Isabella vine shoots from the Hudson River Valley and planted them in the rectory garden of his new church at Hammondsport on Keuka Lake. He gave cuttings to his parish-

*There still are some small vineyards in the eastern part of Long Island, growing both Labrusca and Vinifera grapes for table use and for wine. The largest is two acres at Cutchogue, between Great Peconic Bay and the Sound.

ioners, and soon there were vines in most gardens in the neighborhood. In 1850, at South Pulteney, four miles up the lake from Hammondsport, Andrew Reisinger, a vinedresser from Germany, planted a vineyard in which he introduced pruning and cultivation, operations unheard of before in the region. But it was not until 1860 that the commercial production of wine began in the area, with the building of the Pleasant Valley Winery near Hammondsport. This was concurrent with the death of the Cincinnati wine industry, then three decades old, from the vine disease that killed Nicholas Longworth's vineyards along the Ohio River. The Pleasant Valley Winery began by hiring champagne makers from Cincinnati. Other wineries began springing up around Hammondsport, and this created interest in wine-grape growing here at a time when the Concord variety was taking over in the Chautauqua region. Today, although the Finger Lakes district still produces only a third of the state's total grape crop, almost half of its vineyards are planted to wine varieties.

The oldest wine district in New York State is the Hudson River Valley. The first commercial winery there opened in 1839, two decades before those at Brocton and Hammondsport.

In the Niagara district, grape growing began about 1840, but as in the Finger Lakes region, there is no record of wine being made commercially there before 1860.

The foregoing explains why, in the extensive report on wine production in the United States which E.M. Erskine, secretary of the British Legation in Washington, prepared for his government in 1859, New York State's infant wine industry was not even mentioned. Erskine gave enthusiastic descriptions of winegrowing in Ohio, Missouri, Indiana, Illinois, Pennsylvania, Kentucky, Tennessee, Arkansas, the Carolinas, and California. His omission of New York could scarcely have been inadvertent.

The Finger Lakes wine industry expanded rapidly after the Civil War and this soon became the chief wine-producing region of New York State. An influx of German and Swiss immigrants, many of them from wine districts, helped to improve vineyard practices. As wineries were built along the lakes, their wines began winning medals for quality in Paris, Vienna, and Brussels, and the vintners proclaimed their district "the Rhine and Epernay of America." In 1882, the Geneva Experiment Station was founded, and it began a program of grape breeding and vineyard improvement. New York wines grew steadily better, and by the turn of the century such New York brands as Great Western were listed by restaurants and hotels across the country. I have in my files a copy of the menu of a banquet held at the Waldorf-Astoria Hotel by the American Winegrowers Association in February

1916. Of three dozen wines on the list for this dinner, eleven were from the Finger Lakes and Hudson Valley districts of New York, fifteen were from California, three from New Jersey, and one from Ohio.

When Wartime Prohibition began in 1919, most of the New York wineries were forced to close. Yet the ruin wrought in the industry was less complete than in California. Several of the New York vintners managed to survive the dry years by switching to the production of grape juice. Most of it was sold in kegs with labels that said: "Caution — Do not add yeast or admit air or the contents will ferment." This, of course, is what the buyers proceeded to do.

With their highly-flavored Labrusca grapes, New York vintners also developed superior bottled grape juices, jams, and jellies- products which California, because it grows the relatively bland Vinifera grape varieties, has never been able to match. A few of the New York wineries also obtained government permits to continue making wine and champagne for sacramental, tonic, and cooking uses. When Captain Paul Garrett in 1929 organized Fruit Industries, the giant grape-concentrate combine headquartered in California, Garrett's own Finger Lakes and Brooklyn wineries were the only ones in New York State to join. The chief Finger Lakes vintners, having remained independent with their own production and sales organizations, were thus better prepared to resume full-scale wine production and sale, when Prohibition ended in 1933, than were most of their California competitors.

• 3 •

In the latter years of the dry era, when early repeal of the Prohibition Amendment was anticipated, public officials in most of the states set to work writing laws and regulations intended to control the sale of liquor within their borders as soon as it would become legal. Each state devised a different system that reflected the attitude of its legislators toward drinking. In New York, Prohibitionist influence was still strong, and it was strongest in the upstate counties that controlled the legislature at Albany. In consequence, the New York law that was written and became effective in 1933 was aimed at restricting the production and consumption of liquor—and it lumped wine with hard liquor. It discouraged the establishment of wineries by setting exorbitant annual license and filing fees. Farmers, who would have opened small wineries to sell their grapes in fermented form to their neighbors, could not afford to pay the fees. (The minimum New York winery license is $635, plus other fees and bond requirements making the total cost more than $1000 per year. Included is $250 for the privilege of sale at the winery, without which few small wine-growers can exist.)

Worse, the law restricted to liquor stores the sale of wine for home consumption, while it allowed food stores to sell beer. The State Liquor Authority at first issued some 1700 liquor store licenses to serve all of New York's sixty-two counties. These licenses promptly skyrocketed in value, to such a point that one retailer in New York City sold the key to his store for $60,000 more than the value of his stock. Then the store owners, to protect their monopoly on the sale of wine and liquor by the package, organized strong associations and established a well-financed lobby in Albany. For nearly four decades, this lobby has defeated every bill introduced in the legislature to let food stores sell wine. Liquor stores in the state now number about 5000, but housewives don't shop in liquor stores for the main ingredients of family meals. And to make the stores especially uninviting, a provision of the law prohibits them from stocking anything except sealed packages of liquor and wine—not even soda, lemon juice, cigarettes, or nuts, let alone such household merchandise as wine glassware. The buying of wine for its principal use—that of a daily mealtime beverage, the natural accompaniment of food—is thus discouraged by the New York law, as effectively as it is discouraged by the state monopoly stores in Pennsylvania and other monopoly states.

7

The Finger Lakes Wineries

Fᴵᵛᴱ ʟᴬᴿᴳᴱ Finger Lakes District wineries—Pleasant Valley, Taylor, Gold Seal, Widmer's, and Canandaigua Industries—produce three fourths of the wine made in New York State. The Taylors, who also own Pleasant Valley, are the number one wine family of the East and the third largest producers of bottle-fermented champagnes in the world, next to Henkell in Germany and Moët et Chandon in France. This chapter describes these principal Finger Lakes wineries and some of their interesting neighbors, and probes the controversy over the kinds of grapes to be grown for eastern wines in future decades—the native Labrusca, the French-American hybrids, or the Old World Vinifera wine-bearing family.

• 2 •

The Finger Lakes—Canandaigua, Keuka, Seneca, Cayuga, Owasco, Skaneateles, and half a dozen others—are so long, narrow, and parallel in their north-south direction that the Indians thought them the imprint of the hands of the Great Spirit. Scooped out by glacial action ages ago, these deep blue lakes make the eleven counties of the district a spectacularly scenic vacationland. Among its chief attractions are the picturesque vineyards and wineries, most of which offer cellar tours and tasting hospitality to visitors.

As in other vineyard regions that border bodies of water, the Finger Lakes temper the extremes of temperature along their shores and thereby protect the grapevines from the killing frosts of spring and fall. The growing season here, though it averages only 135 to 150 days, a third shorter than in California, is usually dry and warm enough to allow the grapes to ripen. In this respect, nearly every year in the Finger Lakes District is a vintage year—the envy of European winegrowers.

93

The snowy winters, however, average several degrees colder than in Germany and France. Winter temperatures sometimes drop to eighteen or twenty degrees below zero*, and protracted freezes in some years have damaged the vines. There already is snow on the ground when the pruning is under way in December, following the first fall freeze.

The first vine shoots appear in May, followed by leaves and by the tiny flower clusters. When the grapes begin to ripen in late August, robins and starlings descend on the vineyards to peck at the fruit. Then the bird-bangers set up their fearful clatter to frighten the birds away. These gas-operated mechanical noise-makers let go a shotgunlike blast every 45 to 60 seconds, the times varying so that the feathered thieves don't become accustomed to regular intervals of the noise. The bird-bangers are more effective than the scarecrows, stuffed owls, and fake snakes the growers have used in the past.

By the second week of September, the early-ripening varieties are juicy and sweet, and you can smell the grapes when you approach the Finger Lakes. Now the vintage season begins, usually lasting through the fourth week of October. Hundreds of area residents and townspeople formerly did the picking, but mechanical harvesting machines, which appeared in the region for the first time in 1968, have now supplanted most of the human vintagers. Each machine harvests an acre an hour and does the work of forty pairs of human hands. Straddling a row of vines, the robot slaps the wires on which the canes are trained, shaking the grapes off their stems onto a conveyor, which discharges them into plastic-lined boxes on a trailer moving alongside.

Grapes can be grown on the rocky, steep and rolling hillsides near any of the lakes, but at present the vineyards are concentrated along Lakes Canandaigua, Keuka, Seneca, and Cayuga in Steuben, Yates, Schuyler, Seneca, and Ontario Counties. Keuka, known as "The Crooked Lake" because of its irregular Y shape, has vines along its hillsides all the way from Hammondsport at its southern end to Branchport and Penn Yan at the northwestern and northeastern tips. Between the two forks of Keuka, lofty Bluff Point with its Paul Garrett chapel extends twelve miles into the lake and is gracefully draped with vines. In early days excursion steamers plied the larger lakes, and once, during a rate war between rival steamship companies, vacationists could travel seventeen miles on Keuka from Hammondsport to Penn Yan for a ten-cent fare. Now highways border the shores, and the lakes

*Nine degrees below zero was the lowest temperature recorded at Geisenheim in Germany's Rheingau during the first half of this century, while nine above zero was the minimum on the Moselle at Trier.

serve for such sports as boating, swimming, and fishing, but not for skating, for the lakes seldom freeze over.

• 3 •

In the quiet, pleasant town of Hammondsport, the birthplace of pioneer aviator Glenn Curtiss, winemaking is the principal industry. Each September, the local Episcopal Church holds a public Sunday service in a vineyard overlooking Keuka Lake to bless the grape harvest.

Driving southwest from the town, the first big winery you see is the oldest in the district, the Pleasant Valley Wine Company, home of Great Western wines and champagnes. It is named for the narrow valley through which the inlet to Keuka Lake flows. Above a tree-shaded archway that leads into the original underground wine vault is a stone plate carved with the names of Charles Davenport Champlin and his farmer neighbors who founded the company in 1860. Today the cool vault, walled with hand-cut native stone, serves as a unique tasting room for the thousands of visitors who annually tour the three-million-gallon winery and sample its products. Here the first New York State champagne was made when the Civil War ended in 1865. Joseph Masson, trained in France and hired by Champlin from the M. Werk champagne cellars in Cincinnati, made it and called it Sparkling Catawba as Nicholas Longworth did. Two years later the wine was entered in the Paris Exposition, and though the fruity Labrusca taste was strange to the European judges, they gave it an honorable mention award. Joseph Masson was joined at Hammondsport by his brother Jules, who had been superintendent of the Longworth Wine House at Cincinnati until the grape sickness obliterated the vineyards there. In 1870, the Masson brothers served a new sparkling blend of Delaware and Catawba to a meeting of the Pleasant Valley Grape Growers Association. Presiding at the meeting was famed horticulturist Colonel Marshall Wilder of Boston, who on tasting the wine exclaimed: "Truly, this will be the great champagne of the West!" By "West," Wilder explained, he meant "our entire continent," the New World. His remark gave Great Western champagne its name, strange though it seems for a product of New York State.

In 1873 at the Vienna Exposition, Great Western became the first American champagne to win a gold medal in Europe, and it later gathered additional prizes at Brussels, Philadelphia, and Paris. For half a century before Prohibition, this champagne "from Rheims, New York" was the leading sparkling wine made in this country. "Rheims" was the name of a post office in the winery;

and though the office was closed long ago, the old address still appeared on the company's letterhead until 1970. Rheims is also the name of the winery's station on the eight-mile-long, single-track Bath & Hammondsport Railroad, built by the company's owners in 1872 to haul their wine and brandy to market. The B. & H., still operating profitably today, is famous for its nickname, "The Champagne Trail," and also for its slogan, "Not as long as the others but just as wide."

When Prohibition came, Pleasant Valley was one of the few wineries to keep open because it held a Government permit to make wines for sacramental use. This permit, however, did not include the winery's principal product, champagne, because officials of the Prohibition Bureau insisted that champagne was not a wine. Pleasant Valley's chief owners, Malburn and Charles Champlin, grandsons of the founder, filed suit against the Government. Rather than fight the suit, the Bureau granted them special permission to sell champagne to the clergy. For two years the Champlins enjoyed a rich monopoly as the only winery privileged to supply bubbly to servants of the Lord. But then other vintners made a fuss, and the Government again yielded, permitting competitors' sacramental wines to sparkle, too. Pleasant Valley's business then dwindled, but the company still managed to survive, by selling grape juice to home winemakers, until Repeal. When Charles Champlin died in 1950, Pleasant Valley stock was sold to eastern financiers.

For many years past, the owners of the neighboring Taylor Winery had had their eyes on Great Western, and in 1961 the Taylor family saw a chance to buy its stock. They acquired a controlling interest and made the production and sale of Great Western wines an independent division of Taylor.

The late Greyton Taylor and his son Walter (of whom more presently) took charge of the Pleasant Valley winery and began adding "varietals" to its list of "generic" table wines. The first three "varietals" were Delaware and Diamond, named for white Labrusca grape varieties, and Isabella, a Labrusca rosé. In 1964, Pleasant Valley made history by introducing the first Finger Lakes wines made entirely of the new French-American hybrid grapes. The company then began changing its generically named table wines to "varietals" named for the increasing proportions of the many-numbered French grapes in their blends. "Aurora" was added to the label of medium-sweet Great Western Sauterne. The burgundy, which is almost dry, became "Baco Noir," and the claret, which is lighter-bodied, became "Chelois" (with a back label giving an anglicized pronunciation: "Shell-oy"). The plan is that when consumers eventually learn these varietal names, the old generic names can be dropped. Aurora is the new name coined for Seibel 9110, Chelois is Seibel 10878, and Baco is the hybrid that lately has improved the flavor of many New York State burgundies. In addition to these, I have tasted at Pleasant Valley an experimental white wine of the Seyval Blanc grape, Seyve-Villard 5276. Its rich, full flavor was reminiscent of Chardonnay.

• 4 •

Walk a scant hundred yards from the Great Western cellars and you reach the Taylor winery. By acquiring the Pleasant Valley Company in 1961, Taylor became legally, as well as in fact, New York's "Bonded Winery No. 1." With its capacity of fifteen million gallons, Taylor is now the largest American winery outside of California.

When I first visited Hammondsport in the late 1930s, Taylor consisted of just four buildings, the main one a four-story mansard-roofed structure with vaults cut back into the stone hillside. This quaint pre-Prohibition edifice now serves as a visitor reception center and office building, for it is now flanked by a complex of three dozen new above-ground processing and aging cellars and warehouses covering some fifty acres. Taylor is an ultramodern winery, with batteries of pneumatic presses and rows of epoxy-lined steel tanks holding 100,000 gallons each, in sharp contrast to the smaller, old-fashioned redwood and oak casks that are still required for the aging of its wines. Everything here has a gleaming look; pumps, valves, tanks are bright and spic and span. Shining miles of stainless-steel and pyrex-glass pipes carry Taylor wines through laboratory-controlled, precisely timed processes and finally to high-speed bottling machines, after which they are cased for shipment around the world. The traditional method of clarifying bottle-fermented champagnes has recently been mechanized by introduction of the transfer process, in which the champagnes are filtered instead of being disgorged by hand.

Taylor dates from 1880, when Walter Taylor, a master cooper, came to Hammondsport with his bride to make barrels for the thriving wineries. The young couple settled on a seven-acre vineyard, and two years later bought a seventy-acre farm on Bully Hill, north of town. Taylor planted half of it to Ives and Delaware, the grapes then most in demand for red and white wines. He had worked with his father, George Taylor, before his marriage, and he now brought his father and mother to the farm. They made table wines and sold them in barrels to dealers in New York City. Three sons and two daughters were born to Walter and Addie Taylor between 1883 and 1903. All five grew up in the business and helped it grow until salesmen, selling Taylor wine in bottles and barrels, were covering territories in several states before the First World War.

In 1919, when Wartime Prohibition began, most of the Hammondsport wineries closed their doors, but the Taylors decided to go into the grape juice business instead. The four-story, mansard-roofed Columbia Winery, built in 1886, was one of those for sale, and the Taylors bought it and moved there from Bully Hill. During the dry era they sold fresh and concentrated grape juice to home winemakers and food distributors in the northeastern states. When the Taylors saw the end of Prohibition was ahead, they began modernizing the winery. At Repeal their wines were among the first on the market and they began their climb to leadership in the East. On taking over the Pleasant Valley winery, the Taylor Wine Company "went public," the first major American winery to put its stock on the open market, and it now has stockholders throughout the United States.

Counting lands owned by members of the family, Taylor and Pleasant Valley control 800 acres of vineyards, the crops of which are supplemented by grapes purchased from 300 other growers cultivating some 5000 acres. Their French hybrid varieties, first planted in the 1950s, are a steadily increasing part of the two wineries' grape supply.

A few years ago I asked the late Fred Taylor, the eldest brother, whether any planting of Vinifera varieties was being planned. His reply was "No—why should we try to do in New York State what they do so easily in California? The wines we grow are different from those of California and Europe, and ours please the American taste."

Until Fred and Greyton Taylor died in 1968 and 1970 respectively, the management of Taylor was a family clan. The company is still headed by George A. Lawrence, the husband of Flora Taylor's daughter, Mary Lucy Keeler. Clarence W. Taylor, the second brother, still oversees the physical plant at Hammondsport and knows the location of every nut and bolt in the winery. Seaton "Zeke" Mendall, the Taylor vineyard consultant, was married to the late Rosalie Zimmer, the daughter of Lucy Taylor Zimmer. But being a Taylor is not essential to a career with the company. The outstanding example is Russell B. Douglas, the vice president of marketing and a company director, whose sales-planning genius is credited with making Taylor the largest-selling wine brand at its price level in the United States.

"Uncomplicated wines," port, sherry, sauterne, rhine, burgundy, claret, rosé, champagnes, sparkling burgundy, and vermouths have long been the mainstays of the Taylor line. The once-strong

Labrusca flavor of Taylor table wines has become gradually less pronounced as the lately planted vineyards have yielded increased supplies of French hybrid grapes. Taylor Sauterne still retains its distinct grapy flavor of Delaware and Catawba, but the champagnes and the still rosé have only a hint of Labrusca fragrance. There are now three Taylor wines with proprietary names: Lake Country Red, White, and Pink. All three are blends with the French-American grapes, but have enough Labrusca character to make them distinctly different from California wines.

• 5 •

On Bully Hill Road, a mile and a half north of Hammondsport, are the 60,000-gallon Bully Hill winery, the Greyton H. Taylor Wine Museum, the Winemaker's Shop, and an airstrip on the hilltop, from which the Taylor company plane flies the firm's executives to sales meetings in eastern and midwestern cities. All of these are recent innovations by artistic, intense young Walter Stephen Taylor, the grandson of Taylor's founder. But Walter is a rebel against the Taylor Company and was exiled from its wineries in 1970 for publicly criticizing some of the ways big eastern vintners make their wines.

Before he joined the Pleasant Valley winery as his father's assistant in the 1950s, Walter adopted among his hobbies a study of Taylor family history. Inspired by the wine museums he saw on a trip through Europe, he resolved to start the first such museum in America and perpetuate the memory of his forebears. He began by buying back his grandfather's homestead and original winery from the man to whom they were sold forty years before. Walter then collected, from attics, antique shops, and junkyards, relics of the more than fifty wineries which once had operated around the Finger Lakes—vineyard implements, coopers' tools, wine pumps, presses, bottles, old wine advertisements, and early books about wine. One of his prize exhibits was an ancient brandy still, a reminder that the pre-Prohibition wineries here also made and sold brandy. The collection was installed in the old wooden winery, and it opened to the public in 1967 with a provisional charter from the New York Education Department. Open daily from May through October, the museum receives thousands of visitors.

Walter next opened the Winemaker's Shop next door to the museum, selling grape juice, winemaking equipment and supplies to amateur enologists. Meanwhile, he wrote *Home Winemaker's Handbook* (New York: Harper & Row) with Winemaker Richard P. Vine as co-author, and he illustrated the book himself.

Meanwhile, Walter converted his grandfather's horse barn,

adjoining the museum, into the Bully Hill winery. There he and Geisenheim-trained winemaker Hermann Wiemer produce nine estate-bottled, vintage-dated table wines that are sold at the winery and across the United States. Three are French-American "varietals," Baco Noir, Aurora Blanc, and Seyval Blanc; three are "varietals" of the native Delaware, Diamond, and Ives; the rest are hybrid and hybrid-Labrusca blends called Bully Hill Red, White, and Rosé. The 1971 Bully Hill Red, which I tasted recently, was a blend of seven French-American grapes and resembled a young Bordeaux claret. Walter has also acquired the old Argus winery on Middle Road and plans to make Walter Taylor champagnes there.

Walter's rebellion, which abruptly ended his association with Great Western wines, was climaxed by a too well publicized speech he made to a wholesalers' convention in San Francisco, in which he denounced the big New York wineries for using as much as a fourth blend of California wines in wines they label as "New York State." He also criticized the eastern practice of ameliorating wines with sugar and water to reduce their acidity and to balance the musts. Although these methods are legal and are considered necessary in the East—and Walter sugars his wines, too—he continues his campaign, to the annoyance of his neighbors, by using "Wine without Water" as his advertising slogan for Bully Hill wines.

• 6 •

Four miles up West Lake Road (Route 54A) from Hammondsport is venerable Gold Seal, the most imposing stone winery in the East. Founded in 1865 as the Urbana Wine Company, it is the second oldest in the district and looks its age, with its many stories under nineteenth-century gabled roofs crowned by lines of dormer windows and a pair of steeples. Only the highway and a narrow line of trees separate the winery from the waters of Keuka Lake, where steamers docked in early days to bring supplies and to load champagne. On the steep slopes above the winery is the company's original vineyard, expanded to 500 acres in recent years. This is the home of nationally distributed Gold Seal, Henri Marchant, and Charles Fournier wines and champagnes.

When the surrender of General Lee at Appomatox Courthouse was ending the Civil War in the spring of 1865, a group of Hammondsport merchants and Urbana Township farmers, following the example of Charles Champlin and his neighbors at Pleasant Valley, organized the Urbana Company to build the winery, and to make champagne. Their product was first called "Imperial," but in 1887 was renamed "Gold Seal." The firm prospered, under the successive leadership of Clark Bell, D. M. Hildreth, and Walter Hildreth, for half a century before Prohibition. During the thirteen-year dry era, when it was headed by Corning newspaper publisher and former Congressman Edwin Stewart Underhill* and his son, it made sacramental and medicinal wines as the Gold Seal Products Company. At Repeal in 1933 the firm name was changed back to Urbana. In 1957, during a two-year association with Louis Benoist of Almadén in California, the company became Gold Seal Vineyards, Inc. In 1959 control was purchased by a group of eastern investors headed by Paul Schlem and Arthur Brody, who have interests in industrial catering in the New York City area.

In the first full century of operation, wine production at Gold Seal Vineyards was headed by only four men, all of French heritage. The first was Charles Le Breton, hired from the Roederer champagne cellars of Rheims. Jules Crance, from Moët et Chandon at Épernay, served from 1871 to 1923, and was succeeded by his son, Eugene. In 1934, President Edward Stewart Underhill, Jr., of Urbana asked Charles Fournier, the chief winemaker of Veuve Clicquot Ponsardin at Rheims, to recommend someone who could restore Gold Seal to its pre-Prohibition greatness. Fournier took the job himself, came to Hammondsport as Urbana production manager, brought his own champagne yeast culture from Veuve Clicquot, and became an American citizen.

Educated at the University of Paris and at French and Swiss wine schools, Fournier had seen the planting of the improved French hybrid grapes spreading in those countries. In 1936, while Philip Wagner was getting started with the hybrids in Maryland, Fournier introduced the Seibel 1000 and Ravat 6 varieties to Hammondsport. He introduced his own champagne blend, Charles Fournier Brut, to the American market in 1943, and it scored an immediate success. In 1950, for the first time in the history of the California State Fair at Sacramento, eastern and foreign wines were invited to be judged in open competition with those produced in California. Charles Fournier New York State Champagne was awarded the only gold medal—an event so discomfiting to the California vintners that no out-of-state wines were invited to their State Fair again.

In 1953, Fournier hired Dr. Konstantin Frank to start a nursery of Vinifera grapes at Urbana. The story of Dr. Frank and of his association with Fournier is told in the following section, but it

---

*Of the same Underhill family whose members pioneered commercial grape growing in the Hudson Valley. All were descendants of Captain John Underhill, who came from England in the seventeenth century.

should be pointed out here that the first Vinifera wines produced commercially in the East came from Fournier at Gold Seal. I was one of those present at the Winter 1961 dinner of the San Francisco Wine and Food Society in historic Jack's Restaurant when Gold Seal New York State 1959 Chardonnay and Johannisberg Riesling were served for the first time in the West. To the several California vintners in attendance that memorable night, it was a shock to realize that their long-acknowledged monopoly on the production of fine Vinifera wines in North America might at last be at an end.

Tall, lean, bespectacled Charles Fournier, who in appearance and speech resembles a foreign diplomat more than a vintner, retired in 1967 at the age of sixty-five, but continues visiting the winery daily as a consultant and as the honorary lifetime president of Gold Seal.

Gold Seal wines are still produced by French-trained enologists. The technical director is Guy Devaux from the Societé Marne et Champagne of Epernay, and the winemaker is Didier Bretonnière from Montpellier.

The best-selling table wine, of the seemingly endless list Gold Seal makes, is Catawba Pink, a medium-sweet Labrusca-flavored rosé. But the company's finest are its vintage-dated Chardonnays, the Fournier Brut Champagne that won the gold medal in California, and Fournier Chablis Nature. The Chablis Nature is a blend of Chardonnay and several French hybrids and has a delicate fruity fragrance scarcely recognizable as Labrusca and only in the aftertaste. Since Fournier's retirement, his Riesling Spätlese has been made in occasional years when "the noble mold" (*Botrytis cinerea*, which grows naturally in the Hammondsport district) has contributed its character to the grapes. In other years, the Rieslings become part of Gold Seal's Rhine Wine blend.

· 7 ·

On Middle Road, a short drive from the Gold Seal Vineyard brings you to the small winery, the all-Vinifera vineyard, and the one-story red brick house of Dr. Konstantin Frank. A sturdy, proud, assertive man, he is the Russian-born German scientist who, after countless others had failed for three centuries, has shown dramatically that the Old World grape, the Vinifera, can be grown in eastern America. He is also the most controversial figure in the eastern wine industry, because he publicly condemns the French-American hybrid grapes which the other wineries are planting in preference to Vinifera.

Konstantin Frank was born in the Ukraine on July 4, 1899, the fourth of ten children of a farmer whose crops included grapes. He fought in the White Russian army, studied agriculture at the polytechnic institute of Odessa, organized collective farms in southern Ukraine for the Communists, then completed his studies, taught viticulture and enology, and did grape research at the local agricultural institute. During the German occupation, he became director of the institute. When the Second World War ended, he went to Austria and Bavaria and managed farm properties for the Americans.

In 1951, at the age of fifty-two, Dr. Frank emigrated with his wife and three children to America, arriving in New York with forty dollars, unable to speak English. He got a job washing dishes at an Automat restaurant and saved enough to buy a one-way ticket to the nearest grape research station—the New York State Experiment Station at Geneva. There he described his Russian experience and applied for work on grapes. But instead, he says bitterly, "they let me hoe blueberries," and for two years he did only menial work.

Seeing the Finger Lakes growers planting the new French hybrids, he inquired why Vinifera were not being planted instead. The winters are too cold here, he was told; the delicate European varieties were likely to die when the ground froze. Having grown Vinifera himself in Russia—"where the temperature goes to forty below, where we had to bury the entire vine in winter, where when we spit, it froze before it hit the ground"—Dr. Frank vehemently disagreed. He argued that the Old World grapes planted in the East during past centuries could not have died from cold, that rather they were killed by diseases and pests; and these, he pointed out, modern science now had ways to control.

His argument came to the attention of Charles Fournier. Gold Seal's president, too, had known frigid winters in Europe, and had seen Chardonnay and Pinot Noir thriving at Rheims and Epernay, seven degrees of latitude farther north than Hammondsport, after winters when temperatures in the French Champagne district fell below zero. Fournier realized that the emigré scientist might be right, and in 1953 hired him as a consultant for Gold Seal Vineyards.

Dr. Frank told Fournier what his research in Russia had shown: that what were needed in climates where the ground froze in winter were hardy roots onto which the Vinifera vines could be grafted—roots that would ripen the wood of the vine before the first winter freeze. To search for such roots, the two men set out on a tour of the Northeast countryside. In the garden of a convent at Québec in Canada, they found Pinot vines growing and were told that they yielded wine, in that stern climate, in one year out of three. From the monk in charge of the garden, they obtained some of his roots. Back at Gold Seal, they began grafting—to the Canadian roots and some of their local ones—Riesling, Chardonnay, Gewürztraminer, and Cabernet Sauvignon vines they obtained from the University of California vineyard at Davis.

During the next five years, thousands of experimental grafts were made and planted. In February 1957 came the critical test: temperatures on the lake slopes plummeted to twenty-five degrees below zero. Some of the hardiest Labrusca vines, Dutchess and Isabella in particular, were frozen and bore no grapes that year. On some of the Concord, Delaware, and Catawba vines, a tenth to a third of the buds were killed. But on the first Riesling and Chardonnay vines that had been grafted on hardy roots, fewer than a tenth of the buds showed any damage. And when vintage time came in the fall of that year, these vines at Gold Seal produced ripe grapes at a rate that promised crops of three to four tons per acre.

Fournier needed no further convincing, but began planting the noble Vinifera vines as fast as he could get enough rootstocks on which to graft them. He already had seventy acres of them when I was there in 1966, but since then Gold Seal has used his plantings mostly for blending with the company's other wine types.

Dr. Frank, triumphant, bought a tract of land nearby and started planting a vineyard of his own. When the first commercial New York State Vinifera wines, made at Gold Seal, were introduced in 1961, Dr. Frank proclaimed it "the second discovery of America," his own contribution to the nation of which he had become a citizen. He built his own winery, named it Vinifera Wine Cellars, and put his own wines on the market in 1965. He since has increased the winery's capacity to 60,000 gallons and his vineyard to seventy-eight acres, and has imported from Russia and Germany cold-resistant strains of additional Vinifera grape varieties. A son-in-law, Walter Volz, now manages the vineyard, and Dr. Frank's son, Willibald, markets the wines.

Everyone who has tasted the Vinifera wines of Hammondsport has praised them highly. Dr. Frank's Trockenbeerenauslese 1961 has been served in the White House and in the executive mansion at Albany. When first introduced, it was priced in stores at forty-five dollars a bottle and outsold equivalent German wines that cost a third less. His Chardonnay, which I tasted at the winery, was equal to the best French white burgundies, and his four-year-old Pinot Noir had the nose of a ten-year-old wine.

But none of the big Finger Lakes wineries except Gold Seal has been willing to plant any commercial acreage of Dr. Frank's Vinifera. He blames the Geneva Experiment Station, which has pronounced the Vinifera varieties "marginal," less hardy than the French hybrids, too risky to be cultivated by anyone except an expert, and not recommended for large-scale commercial planting in New York State.

This enrages Dr. Frank, who incidentally seems to enjoy a fight. He insists that the Vinifera require no more care than the hybrids and claims that they ripen better at Hammondsport than in Germany or France. "The Genevians say the growers must be experts to grow these grapes here," he fumes. "The poor Italian and Russian peasants with their shovels can do it, but the American farmer with his push-button tools cannot. It is unbelievable that the hybrids, prohibited everywhere except in France and the United States, not good enough for poor Italian or even poor Russian peasants, can be called good enough for the Americans, the most prosperous people in the world."

Answering Dr. Frank's attacks, the Geneva Station still recommends the hybrids, but concedes in its publications that his Riesling wines are "comparable to those of Germany," that his Chardonnay and Pinot Noir "stand with the finest French burgundies," and that "there is undoubtedly a place for a certain percentage of these superb connoisseurs' wines."

Charles Fournier, the man in the middle of the controversy, is a close friend of Dr. Frank, whom he calls "Kotja," but has avoided taking either side. When Fournier told me that Gold Seal would continue to grow Vinifera, he explained: "It is still a young experiment. We feel safer with the hybrids, but we love the Vinifera wines." Fournier believes the future of Vinifera in the East depends on the wine-buying public, that if we are willing to pay the prices for fine eastern wines that we pay for prestige European labels, the eastern vintners will find it profitable to plant the *cépages nobles* and to produce superlative wines of their types.

• 8 •

At the head of Seneca Lake are the city of Geneva and the big State Agricultural Experiment Station, where a stepped-up program of grape and wine research has been under way since 1962.

It was at the Geneva Station, founded in 1882 and associated with Cornell University, that famed horticulturist Ulysses Prentiss Hedrick and his colleagues crossbred and tamed many American wild vines and developed some of the varieties now used in making eastern wines. Dr. Hedrick, born in 1870 in a log cabin in Iowa, came to Geneva in 1905 via agricultural colleges in Michigan, Utah, and Oregon. A prolific writer, he was the great chronicler of grapes in America and is chiefly remembered for his monumental book on *Grapes of New York* (1908). Winegrowing was Hedrick's chief interest, and when Prohibition put a stop to his winemaking research, he saved the Geneva Station's best grapes for himself and had his chauffeur take them home and make them into wine for him. Hedrick espoused the homely art of fermentation and wrote two books of advice to home winemakers and amateur vineyardists. He was also the first—long before Dr. Frank—to prove that it is possible to grow Vinifera in the East. "We know now how to control the insects and fungi that attack them," he wrote in 1945 in his *Grapes and Wines from Home Vineyards*. Hedrick, however, found it necessary to cover his Vinifera vines with earth before each winter to keep them from freezing. (But, at Hammondsport, Dr. Frank contends that the Vinifera varieties Hedrick tested at Geneva did not include the cold-resistant strains of the noble grapes grown in northern Europe. Dr. Frank only hills up the earth to protect his vines at the point where they are grafted, the same winter protection given to grafted hybrid vines.)

When Repeal came in 1933, Prohibitionist influence was still strong at Albany, and a request by Cornell University for a state appropriation of $50,000 for wine research at Geneva was flatly turned down. Although wine work at the station was taboo, Professors Richard Wellington and George D. Oberle organized a grape-testing and wine quality improvement program with New York and Canadian wineries, in whose cellars their experimental wines were made. When Dr. Oberle moved to Virginia in 1948, and Dr. Hedrick died three years later, Professor John Einset and others carried on this program. During the next decade, as winegrowing grew in importance and the Drys' political strength waned, the repeated requests by Cornell for wine research funds won support and a state appropriation was finally approved in 1962. Federal purse strings, too, were unloosed two years later at the death of fanatical dry Congressman Clarence Cannon, and "wine" was no longer a word the Geneva professors feared to pronounce. Cornell went so far as to publish a bulletin on home winemaking, authored by Dr. Willard B. Robinson—the first of its kind to come from any American university.

Although New York State has no separate college department of viticulture and enology, such as that at the University of California, the Cornell staffs at Ithaca and Geneva believe the training they now provide students in the sciences of grape-growing and winemaking is adequate for the fast-growing industry. In addition to undergraduate courses at Cornell in viticulture, plant physiology, entomology, plant pathology, chemistry, and food fermentations, there is advanced instruction in viticulture, microbiology, and chemistry at Geneva, where graduate and post-doctoral students work in wine research projects. Cornell also provides extension teaching in viticulture, and its grape-breeding program, emphasizing the hybrids, has been expanded far beyond its proportions in Hedrick's time.

A faculty group of winemakers at Cornell, who call themselves the Ithaca Oenological Union, were among the organizers in 1967 of the American Wine Society, which has its national headquarters at the home of Emeritus Professor of Chemistry Albert W. Laubengayer there.

• 9 •

Naples, at the south end of Canandaigua Lake in Ontario County, has been the home of Widmer's wines since their first vintage in 1888. Widmer's Wine Cellars, with its capacity of three million gallons, is the only winery in Naples Valley and is its chief industry and tourist attraction. During the 1960s the population of Naples village was swelled each September from its normal 1200 to ten times that number by visitors to its colorful three-day grape festival, but the event was canceled after 1970; the village could no longer handle the crowds.

Yankees of English and Scottish origin were the first settlers in this valley. Presumably it was they who named it incongruously for Naples in Italy, for surely the German and German-Swiss immigrants who arrived in the mid-nineteenth century would have named it the Rhine Valley, which it more nearly resembles, and from which many of them came. Most local histories credit the founding of the Naples grape industry to the German vinedresser, Andrew Reisinger, who came here from the Hammondsport district in 1852, although Edward A. McKay, an attorney of Naples village, had planted a vineyard of Isabella grapes four years before. It was also a German, Hiram Maxfield, the leading banker of Naples, who built the first winery here in 1861.

Maxfield's wines and champagne were already well established when in 1882 John Jacob Widmer came to Naples with his family from the Swiss village of Scherz. Jacob wanted to go into the wine business, but there already were several wineries around Naples, and banker-vintner Maxfield, to discourage more competition, refused to lend Widmer any money. Jacob succeeded, however, in getting a thousand-dollar loan from the rival Granby bank. He bought and cleared a tract of land, and planted grapes on its western slope to get the morning sun. By day, Jacob and his wife Lisette toiled in the vineyard, and by night they built their home with a stone-walled basement, in which they made their first wine. By 1910 their business had grown to such a point that they could afford to send their youngest son, Will, to the Royal Wine School of Germany at Geisenheim. There Will was trained in Old World viniculture and wine lore, which the company and its products still reflect today.

During Prohibition, the rival Maxfield Cellars closed down, but the Widmers kept going by making grape juice, nonalcoholic wine jellies and wine sauce. At Repeal in 1933, Widmer's and Maxfield's both resumed making wine, but Widmer's was already far ahead. Then President Will Widmer bought out and absorbed the competitor whose founder, half a century earlier, had refused John Jacob Widmer a loan.

While at the Geisenheim wine school, Will Widmer had learned that when Riesling grapes are left late on the vines in autumn, they grow sweeter and richer, and that sometimes a beneficent mold grows on them, causing them to shrivel and to develop an unusual flavor and aroma. He also learned that wines made from such grapes bring premium prices when labeled "Auslese" (selected picking), still higher prices when called "Spätlese" (late picking), and astronomical prices when labeled "Trockenbeeren-auslese" (dried-berry-selection). The kindly mold is *Botrytis cinerea*, called *Edelfäule* in Germany and *pourriture noble* in France. In the fall of 1939, Widmer went walking through his vineyard after the harvest. On some of the leftover white grapes he saw a gray mold developing, and he decided it must be the *Edelfäule*. He picked all the graying berries he could find, fermented their juice, and ended up with eleven gallons of Spätlese wine. The grape variety wasn't the true Riesling, the noble member of the Vinifera family, but the Labrusca variety known as Missouri Riesling, planted by his father many years before. Dr. Hedrick's books state that the Missouri Riesling was bred about 1860 by Nicholas Grein of Hermann, Missouri, by crossing Taylor, a *Vitis riparia* seedling, with a Labrusca variety. But to Will Widmer, the wine tasted like Riesling, and "Widmer's New York State Riesling" is what he called it, and what its label still says—in some years with "Auslese" or "Spätlese" added—to this day. Will Widmer always insisted that Hedrick's books were wrong, that Missouri Riesling must have been at least a relative of the true White Riesling, or that at least its Labrusca parent must have had some Vinifera blood.

The samples of Widmer Riesling Spätlese that I have tasted have indeed resembled good semidry German Rhine wines, and to my surprise, as I have tasted other wines of Missouri Rieslings, the Widmer versions have had no noticeable Labrusca taste.

When in 1939 author-importer Frank Schoonmaker was looking for American "varietal" wines to sell with his line of imports, his nationwide tasting tour took him to Naples. He found Widmer's, like the other eastern wineries, selling most of its wines as sauterne, burgundy, rhine, port, and sherry, but Will Widmer also had some unblended wines of Elvira and Delaware. Beginning in 1941, Schoonmaker introduced the eastern wine-buying public to Canandaigua Lake Elvira and Delaware, and with them an assortment of "varietal" wines made from Widmer's other grapes: Niagara, Salem, Dutchess, Vergennes, Moore's Diamond, and Isabella. Widmer's thus became the first New York State winery to specialize in "varietal" wines. During the next three decades Niagara became the best seller among the company's long list of wines. The samples of Widmer's Lake Niagara I have tasted have shown me why. To my taste it has been the ideal blend of the grapy Labrusca flavor in a tart, medium-sweet white wine.

Widmer's has been different in several additional ways. One is its use of vintage labeling, which the other Finger Lakes wineries formerly avoided because they preferred to blend together wines of different years. I once tasted at the winery an eleven-year-old Widmerheimer which was remarkably fresh for a white table wine of that age and which, though made of native grapes, had no perceptible Labrusca taste. This was also true of an eleven-year-old port, which, I was amazed to learn, was made entirely of Concord grapes. Eastern winemakers claim the foxiness disappears from Labrusca wines if they are aerated by storage for several years in small casks.

Widmer's chief trademark is its "cellar on the roof." The first thing you notice as you drive up the valley toward the winery is the main cellar roof covered with barrels—some twelve thousand of them in tiers four deep—enough to cover several acres. In these barrels, exposed to summer heat and winter snow, the sherries are aged for four years before blending in a solera-like system. I have seen sherries aged outdoors this way in Ohio, California, Mexico, and South America (in Uruguay, it is done in glass jugs), but never in the vast quantity exposed at Widmer.

Also, in this winery, instead of fermenting the grapes in the few hectically rushed weeks of the vintage season, the fresh juice is stored in refrigerated tanks to be fermented at various times throughout the year. Some enologists think that this practice, begun by Will Widmer in the early days following Repeal (because he was short of space in the winery), will become general in the industry in the future, and I already have seen it in other cellars in New York and Illinois.

In 1961, control of Widmer's was purchased by Rochester

financiers George and Walter Todd, who brought in as president of the company a professional manager named Ernest Reveal. Will Widmer continued in a consulting capacity until his death in 1968. Two years later, Widmer's was sold to the R. T. French Company, the Rochester producer of mustard and spices which in turn is owned by Reckitt & Coleman, the London spice and food products firm which also has wine interests in Europe and Australia. Reveal has started Widmer's producing its own champagne and has introduced three new Widmer proprietary table wines, French hybrid–Labrusca blends named Naples Valley Red, White, and Pink.

Then Widmer's, in 1970, after testing Vinifera vines to see how they would grow at Naples, became the first New York State vintner since Captain Paul Garrett to cross the continent and plant its own vineyard in California. In a million-dollar venture, it purchased and planted nearly 500 acres in the Alexander Valley of Sonoma County with such red wine varieties as Cabernet Sauvignon and Pinot Noir. By 1974 Widmer's expects to build a winery on its California vineyard and to be selling both its New York and California wines nationally under the Widmer's name.

• 10 •

Visitors to these Finger Lakes wineries are hospitably received. The cellar tours offered are interesting, and each ends with a glass of wine, except for youngsters, who get grape juice. But it is well to remember, in planning a trip to the lakes, to inquire first when the wineries will be open. In years past, the biggest ones have been closed on holidays and Sundays (because of the peculiar New York hours allotted for drinking). Most have closed on Saturdays, too, and Taylor and Widmer are shut down completely during the last two full weeks of July. At the height of the tourist season, winery-visiting is so popular that people who miss the last afternoon tour of a cellar have been known to stay overnight in the district to join the first tour in the morning. Wines can now be purchased at most of the wineries, but some of them, respectful of the powerful associations of New York liquor store owners, will sell only sample packages of half a dozen bottles to visitors, advising those who wish larger quantities to make such purchases at retail stores.

• 11 •

In the city of Canandaigua, at the opposite end of the lake from Naples, is the second largest Finger Lakes District winery, Canandaigua Industries. Its sprawling plant offers no visitor tours, nor is it surrounded by vineyards. It is the main New York winery of Mack and Marvin Sands, who also own Richard's Cellars in Virginia and Tenner Brothers vineyard and winery in South Carolina.

Back in 1954, Marvin Sands was operating Canandaigua as a bulk wine plant when he and his sales manager, Robert Meenan, had a bright thought. What occurred to them was that pink wines might sell in greater volume in this country if their French name—*vin rosé*, which Americans have difficulty pronouncing—were changed to simply "rose." This gave them the idea for what since has become one of the largest selling wines in the nation—their Richard's Wild Irish Rose. Pink, sweet, Labrusca-flavored (and named for Marvin's eldest son, Richard), it comes in both 20 percent and 14 percent versions, and the latter is a grapy, quite pleasant rosé. They now bottle many of their wines, but have continued their bulk wine business, shipping kosher, other Labrusca, and fruit wines in tank cars from coast to coast. They have also purchased the old Putnam or Hammondsport winery in Hammondsport to make their own champagnes.

Meanwhile, Mack Sands pursues his dream of emulating the late Captain Garrett by making Virginia Dare wine at Canandaigua, where Garrett had one of his many wineries. Garrett's idea was to blend the wines of East and West, and this the Sandses also do, advertising their Virginia Dare as "the best of California and New York State blended in a single wine." But they have ignored one of the keys to Garrett's original success, which was to make the name mean only an individual, distinctive wine with the Scuppernong wine of the South as part of its blend. Instead, Virginia Dare now represents a "complete line" of generic types, from sauterne and burgundy to port and sherry. Only two of the "line," Virginia Dare White and Rosé, contain some Scuppernong wine. And whether the white closely resembles the wine Captain Garrett served me in 1934, I cannot, after half a lifetime, be sure.

• 12 •

One winery in the Finger Lakes District uses no Finger Lakes grapes, but turns out only wines it makes from French hybrid grapes brought from the Chautauqua-Erie Grape Belt a hundred miles to the west. It is the Boordy Vineyards winery in Penn Yan at the northern end of Lake Keuka. (Penn Yan sounds like an Indian name, but it stands for Pennsylvanians and Yankees, the earliest settlers of this area.)

The reader will recall that in Chapter 4 we discussed the original small Boordy Vineyard winery, built at Riderwood, Maryland, by journalist Philip Wagner and his wife; and that Wagner introduced the French hybrid grapes to America because he disliked the Labrusca taste. It was mentioned that in 1968 the Wagners and little Boordy Vineyard suddenly became part of the grape and wine industries of New York and Washington State.

That spring someone presented a gift of the Wagners' French hybrid wines to Arthur Wolcott, the president of the Seneca Foods Corporation at Dundee, New York, a big processor of applesauce and fresh grape juice. On tasting Boordy Red and discovering its resemblance to Old World wines, Wolcott flew down to see the Wagners in Maryland. He told them he had long been interested in winemaking, and he proposed to "pool the resources" of Seneca and the Wagners to produce Boordy Vineyard wines in three states for nationwide sale. Wolcott with the Wagners could do it, because Seneca has processing plants in Dundee and Penn Yan in the Finger Lakes district, at Williamson in Wayne County, at Westfield in Chautauqua County, and at Prosser in the Yakima Valley of Washington.

The Wagners accepted, with the proviso that the Boordy wines of Maryland, made at their home vineyard outside Baltimore, would remain unchanged.

The first three Boordy New York State vintages were made from Chautauqua Grape Belt French hybrid grapes at a Seneca juice plant in Westfield, and were bottled under the Boordy Vineyards label, which was changed to read "Produced and bottled at Westfield, New York." The Westfield winery was moved in 1970 to another Seneca plant at Penn Yan (which once was Garrett's Penn Yan winery), but the grapes again came from Chautauqua and neighboring counties. Seneca meanwhile built a third Boordy Vineyard winery at its Prosser, Washington, juice plant. It made both Vinifera and hybrid wines there in 1971, labeling them "Produced and bottled at Prosser, Washington." And Wolcott now plans to build an entirely new New York Boordy winery, complete with champagne cellars, visitor tours, and tasting room, in his headquarters city of Dundee, fifteen miles south of Penn Yan.

Wagner's idea calls for the three regional Boordy Vineyards wineries to produce three distinctly different groups of vintage-dated wines, with labels that name the regions where they are grown—in the French manner—rather than the grapes from which they are made. Although some of the first Vinifera wines from Boordy of Washington State were sold as Pinot Noir, Cabernet, and Chardonnay, the rest—which bore no vintage dates—were labeled "Pinard," the French soldiers' slang word for ordinary wine.

One more Finger Lakes winery that is especially interesting to visit is at the O-Neh-Da Vineyard, hidden among the hills beside Hemlock Lake in Livingston County. This is the only Church-owned winery outside of California, the property of a missionary order, the Society of the Divine Word. Its old-fashioned cellar, with two underground levels, is small, compared to the Catholic wineries in California, holding only 150,000 gallons. Its wines, made of Labrusca grapes, are excellent, and the Brothers from nearby St. Bernard's Seminary, who help to sell them, extend a warm welcome to visitors.

O-Neh-Da Vineyard was founded in 1872 by Bishop Bernard McQuaid, the first Catholic bishop of Rochester, who said, "We can retire to the peaceful slopes of Hemlock Lake and in the cultivation of the grapes help priests to say Mass with wine that is wine." For half a century before Prohibition, O-Neh-Da made only altar wines. The winery was closed during the dry era, and only twenty acres of the vineyard were left when it reopened in 1936. Its rehabilitation was entrusted to the German-born winemaker, Leo Goering, who came in that year from the famed Geisenheim Institute. By 1972 the vines again covered more than a hundred acres, and enough wine was being produced to supply the clergy throughout the East, as well as selling to liquor stores in the Rochester-Buffalo-Elmira area. Since 1968 the property has been leased by the Society to the Cribari Vineyards of Fresno, California, which makes and sells altar wines nationally, but nothing in the winery has been changed. Albert Cribari and office manager Bob Haywood now show visitors through the cellars on weekdays and invite them to taste the wines.

Leo Goering's favorite among the O-Neh-Da wines is his haut sauterne, a blend of Elvira, Missouri Riesling, and Niagara. The other whites include a "varietal" Missouri Riesling, a Delaware, and dry sauterne. The reds are Iona and burgundy, and the rest are sherry, tokay, angelica, muscatel, and port. All are produced in accordance with the church canon law specifications for altar use, without the addition of sugar except in the form of grape juice or concentrate. Goering has also made experimental plantings of French hybrids, White Riesling, Chardonnay, and Gewürztraminer, with cuttings supplied by Charles Fournier. He harvested the first of these crops in 1971.

Hemlock is one of "the little Finger Lakes." (O-Neh-Da is the Seneca Indian word for hemlock.) The vineyard's post office address is Conesus, but it is reached by a roundabout route through Livonia Center or Hemlock, the nearest villages. On the way, a visit to the Divine Word Seminary and its lovely grottoes is alone worth the trip.

8

Chautauqua, Niagara, and the Hudson Valley

THE Chautauqua-Erie Grape Belt, the sixty-mile-long stretch of New York's Lake Erie shore which the fanatical Prohibitionists, Doctors Thomas and Charles Welch, made famous as "the grape juice capital of the world," has also become a winegrowing district.

Three wineries, two of them established during the 1960s, have started the planting of wine grapes in the district, where for generations most of the grapes grown have been Concords for fresh use and for juice. The curious fact is that while the Finger Lakes were becoming the chief winemaking district of the East at the end of the nineteenth century, temperance crusaders were persuading Chautauqua Belt farmers not to plant the grapes used for wine, but to plant Concords instead. Now, with the soaring national demand for table wines, the wineries in the Finger Lakes and other parts of New York State are depending on the Chautauqua Belt vineyards to furnish a large part of their wine-grape supply.

This is the district which the late Professor Ulysses Hedrick called, because of its climate, "the second most important viticultural section in eastern America, next to the Finger Lakes." In grape production, however, it is first, because its 21,000 acres of vines, of which fully an eighth are now wine-grape varieties, produce more than half of the state's total annual harvest. Almost a hundred of the new mechanical harvesting machines now operate here, picking more than four fifths of the grape crop.

The Grape Belt is narrow, extending inland from Lake Erie only three to sixteen miles, because grapes grow only in those sections where lake breezes protect the vines from spring and fall frosts. In New York State, the Belt extends from Erie County southwestward to the Pennsylvania border. The Chautauqua County shore section, one of the most productive, is now threatened by urbanization, which worries the Chautauqua farmers because they have nowhere else to go.

• 2 •

It was near Brocton in Chautauqua County that Baptist Deacon Elijah Fay founded the grape industry of western New York and northwestern Pennsylvania, when he planted his vineyard of wild grapes in 1818. At Brocton the first winery in the area was built in 1859 by Deacon Fay's son Joseph, with two partners, Garrett Ryckman and Rufus Haywood. Additional wineries soon started up nearby: the Wine House of Thomas Quigley in 1862, the South Shore Wine Company across the Pennsylvania line a year later, the Empire Vineyards winery of Ralph D. Fuller in 1867, and the Jonas Martin cellar, on the foundation of which St. Patrick's Church in Brocton now stands.

Brocton is also where the bearded mystic, Thomas Lake Harris, built a winery in 1867 to make his "Brotherhood" wines, which he claimed were "infused with the divine aura, potentialized in the joy spirit." The strange story of Harris centers around his utopian "Brotherhood of the New Life" and his semicommunistic colonies in three states. Relics of his Brocton colony, which he named "The Use," can still be seen near the lakeshore. Harris's great house on West Lake Road is now the residence of business-man Douglas Hayes. The ground floor of the winery, on Peerless Street, serves a family as a garage and chicken coop, but the underground cellar is still intact. Mrs. Prudence Work, editor of the Brocton *Beacon*, has found the ruins of at least six more nine-teenth-century wineries between Brocton and nearby Portland.

While the Chautauqua Belt wineries thrived during the 1870s, using Delaware, Catawba, and Isabella grapes, Ephraim Bull's new Concord grape variety was introduced to the district. With the Concord, a table-grape industry began to develop. At the same time, the dry crusade, which had begun in the eastern part of the state, was spreading westward. It found its strongest footholds in two Chautauqua County villages, Jamestown and Fredonia. At Fredonia, in 1873, Mrs. Esther McNeil organized the first unit of the Woman's Christian Temperance Union. Her WCTU ladies, denouncing the local wineries for the sin of allowing grapes to ferment, exhorted all God-fearing farmers to plant the Concord in place of the Delaware and Catawba, because the Concord was tolerated as a fresh eating grape, while the Delaware and Catawba were grown only to make wine.

During the 1880s, table grapes sold well in the eastern cities, and Concord planting reached boom proportions. Chautauqua

County merchants, doctors, and lawyers, everyone who could shake loose a down payment, bought farms and set out more Concord vineyards. Two factories were built just to make the baskets in which the grapes were shipped for sale. Concord production swelled to such a point during the 1890s that much of the crop remained unsold. The bottom then dropped out of the market, and many who had invested their last dollars were ruined.

In 1897, attracted by the surplus of cheap Concords, there came to Chautauqua County the ardent dry dentists, the Doctors Welch, who had started the grape juice industry. Only a year earlier they had moved their juice-pressing operation from Vineland, New Jersey, to Watkins Glen in the Finger Lakes District. The Watkins Glen operation was successful, but they chose a new site at Westfield, eight miles southwest of Brocton, and built there the world's first large grape juice plant. The Welches were then launching the first advertising campaign for their product; renamed only seven years earlier, it was now "grape juice" instead of "unfermented wine." Dr. Charles Welch gave up his dental practice when he moved to Westfield, and became its most prominent citizen. Old residents still remember him for his shock of white hair, his flowing artist-style ties, the autos in which he raced between the plant and the vineyards, and the high-toned restaurant he opened at the Welch plant, where Concord grape juice was always served, but never any wine or liquor. It became a tradition in the county that Dr. Welch personally would start each grape-picking season by issuing a ten-minute blast of the Westfield plant's steam whistle. By 1913, when Secretary of State William Jennings Bryan shocked the diplomatic world by serving Welch's Grape Juice instead of wine to the British ambassador at a state dinner in Washington, an entire Welch Block had been constructed in Westfield.

Wartime Prohibition forced the local wineries to close, but the vineyardists still prospered, selling their surplus grapes to home winemakers and bootleggers in the cities. Local boosters then established an annual grape festival at Brocton. Notable for the absence of any mention of Bacchus, it celebrated instead the memory of Deacon Fay and praised only the fresh Concord grape and its pasteurized juice. By the end of the 1920s, the fact that the county had once produced wine was almost forgotten.

At Repeal, in 1933, two small wineries were opened in the district. One was at Fredonia. The other, at Brocton, was primarily a grape juice plant that began making wine as a sideline. Its proprietor was the financial wizard, Jacob Merrill (Jack) Kaplan, once known as "the Boston molasses king." In 1945, Kaplan bought control of the Welch Grape Juice Company from a Tennessee banking syndicate, which had acquired it after the death of Dr. Charles Welch in 1926. And at the Brocton plant in 1950, Kaplan put the Welch Company into the wine business—a development at which the Doctors Welch, father and son, must have revolved many times in their graves. This was when the new kosher wine type, in which extra sweetening makes the Concord flavor pleasant to taste in a wine, was setting sensational sales records in every state where wine was sold. Wineries across the country were buying Concord grapes or juice and rushing into production with their own versions of the sweet kosher wine. Kaplan's idea was that by giving his version the Welch name, which signified the Concord flavor to millions, he could outsell the kosher leaders, Manischewitz and Mogen David. But his "Welch's Refreshment Wine" failed to sell, perhaps because its label didn't say it was kosher. And in 1959 the Welch Company, which Kaplan meanwhile had sold to the National Grape Co-operative Association, abruptly discontinued making wine.

• 3 •

In 1960, a young agricultural expert named Fred Johnson came home to Westfield, his birthplace, after a ten-year stay in South America. He surveyed the seventy-year-old Concord vineyard his father had left him, studied the trends in local agriculture, and concluded that the long-range future of the Chautauqua Grape Belt lay not in producing more Welch's Grape Juice nor in supplying the kosher wineries, but in growing distinctive dry table wines.

He began ripping out his Concord vines and replanting most of his 125 acres with wine grapes—French hybrids, Delaware, and Ives. In what had been the farm's cold storage house for apples, he installed casks and a crusher, and in 1961 he started the Frederick S. Johnson Vineyards Winery, the first to open in the area in twenty-eight years, and began making the Chautauqua district's first estate-bottled wines.

Johnson, a torpedo-bomber pilot in the Pacific during the Second World War, was not a stranger to winemaking. As a boy, he had helped his father make wine at home from Delaware and Catawba grapes, and at Cornell he had been trained in horticulture and chemistry. After the war, as a specialist in tropical agriculture, he had worked on pineapples for Dole in Hawaii, then had set up Nelson Rockefeller's plantations in Venezuela and Ecuador. Exposed during his travels to the wines of many countries, he was amazed that Chautauqua had not become an important wine district long ago.

His 75,000-gallon winery uses only part of his grapes; the rest are sold fresh. His "Johnson Estate" labels, which he designed himself, picture his vineyard and the 145-year-old brick house in which he was born. His seven wines, which have won a consumer following in New York and three surrounding states, are Seyval Blanc, Delaware, Dry White, Rhine, Rosé, Dry Red, and Vin Rouge. Johnson sees the district's future in such wines as his dry Rhine, which is mainly Aurora (Seibel 5279) with enough Delaware to give it fragrance without a recognizable Labrusca taste. Vineyard and winery tours and tasting are offered visitors six days a week from June through August at the Johnson winery on West Main Road.

• 4 •

Fourteen miles from Westfield, on the other side of Brocton, is Fredonia, which orator Chauncey Depew once called "the most beautiful village in New York State." In Depew's time, guidebooks listed as Fredonia's chief landmark the drinking-water fountain erected in memory of WCTU pioneer Esther McNeil. The fountain still gushes forth the drink of temperance in Lafayette Park in the center of town, but guidebooks nowadays ignore the lady, and instead list as a tourist attraction the Fredonia Products Company winery on Water Street, because it offers free cellar tours and wine tasting on weekdays (and if especially arranged, on weekends as well). This is the winery that Leo Star's Manischewitz wine built from a few small tanks in the year of Repeal to its present capacity of a million and a half gallons, not counting its additional new plant and bottling cellar at nearby Dunkirk. The Fredonia winery is operated by a galaxy of Leo Star's nephews, and makes kosher, Concord, and fruit wines under five of its own brands, which can be tasted in its Winston Treasure Room. But its principal product is fresh grape juice, which it ships in giant refrigerated tank trucks to Brooklyn to be made into Manischewitz wines.

In 1964 the Fredonia firm, which had long used local Concords and had never had to grow its own grapes, began planting 500 acres of wine grapes—Delawares, Catawbas, and French hybrids—in mostly virgin land west of the town.

• 5 •

When table-wine consumption in the United States reached unprecedented levels in the mid-1960s, wineries as distant as Ohio and Illinois reached into the Chautauqua Belt to buy more grapes. In 1967, the Mogen David Wine Corporation of Chicago, which had bought most of its grapes in Michigan, Pennsylvania, and Ohio, decided to begin growing its own around Westfield and to open its own winery there. It was a case of the winery going to the vineyard.

Mogen David acquired 500 acres of Chautauqua vineyard land and a grape juice plant, which it turned into a winery, with two more plants for wine storage. It now has a total capacity of two million gallons at Westfield. And though Mogen David is the world's biggest maker of kosher Concord wine, its new plantings include French hybrids (Maréchal Foch and Seyve-Villard 5247) and experimental plots of Vinifera varieties such as Cabernet Sauvignon, Pinot Noir, White Riesling, and Chardonnay. Next to the Welch Company, Mogen David is now the biggest single user of Chautauqua grapes.

• 6 •

Dry influence in the Grape Belt is not yet dead. A history of the county's grape industry, published serially in a county newspaper, scrupulously avoids any mention of wine. The Chautauqua County Historical Museum in Westfield still contains no mementos of the early-day wineries. And wine is still illegal at Chautauqua, the famous century-old summer center of religion, education, music and recreation on Chautauqua Lake. This is not surprising, for Chautauqua is where the WCTU really began. There, in 1873, Mrs. McNeil's furious females laid the detailed plans for the national organization that was formed at Cleveland a year later, the plans that ultimately brought about National Prohibition. To this day, the owners of homes at Chautauqua hold their property on a condition, to which they have subscribed in writing, that if any "intoxicating liquor" is ever used on their premises, their land, houses, and all the contents are automatically forfeited to the Chautauqua Institution.

But the local view of wine is changing fast. When, for example, the Silver Creek Chamber of Commerce held its fifth annual Festival of Grapes in that Grape Belt town in September 1972, it accepted an advertisement in its printed program from the Fredonia Winery and another from a local liquor dealer. But in the principal festival events—the parade, the crowning of the queen, the festival ball, and the baking contest—there still was no mention of the district's fast-growing wine industry.

• 7 •

New York's third most important winegrowing district is Niagara County, with some 1800 acres of vineyards and with more wine-grape varieties being planted each year.

The county has only one winery, the Niagara Falls Wine Cellar. Opened in 1972, it is on US Route 104 a mile and a half east of Lewiston and only seven miles from Niagara Falls. Already offering a winery tour with tasting, it is an extra attraction for the millions of visitors who come from everywhere to gaze at the awesome Falls.

Viticulturally as well as geologically, the Niagara district is unique. It consists of the Niagara Peninsula, only twenty-five to thirty miles in width, that separates Lake Erie from Lake Ontario. Through the peninsula flows the Niagara River, rushing over the falls and down its deep gorge, spilling the waters of Lakes Erie, Superior, Michigan, and Huron into Lake Ontario. The inland seas on both sides of the peninsula moderate its climate, making the plains that face Lake Ontario a land of peach and cherry orchards and vineyards. On the Canadian side of the river, which is the international border, virtually the entire grape and wine industry of eastern Canada is situated, with twelve times the vineyard acreage on the New York side. There are spots where the Canadian and New York vineyards, separated by the river, are less than two miles apart.

The winter climate is milder, with fewer days recording below-zero temperatures, than in any of the other grape districts of New York. An eighteen-year study by the Geneva Experiment Station, published in 1968, showed that Lewiston, Westfield, and Long Island are best suited for the cold-tender grape varieties such as Vinifera (of which Niagara has several acres) that make the finest wines.

A single winery operated at Lewiston from 1933 to 1970, specializing in champagnes. It was Château Gay, opened at Repeal by the Canadian firm which owns the Château Gai winery near the Canadian city of Niagara Falls. Bought in 1937 by Dr. Hector Carveth, it prospered until it was moved to an ornate new building in 1966. Four years later the wine company went bankrupt, all the winery equipment was dismantled and sold, and the building was offered for sale.

An appropriately named young winemaker, Richard P. Vine, who had just quit his job at the Pleasant Valley winery to plant a vineyard in Indiana, heard about the sale. With an equally young wine-buff partner named Edward Moulton, Vine bought the empty building in 1971 and named it the Niagara Falls Wine Cellar. In less than a year they re-equipped it with casks and machinery, bought their first grapes in the Chautauqua Belt, and offered ten wines for sale.

Vine, with eleven years' experience under the late Greyton Taylor at Pleasant Valley, is an accomplished winemaker. He expects within the next few years to produce in Niagara County the best wines yet made in New York State, including champagne. Vine has his own ideas about wine. He is opposed to most American wine labeling and intends to call his sparkling wine "Blanc de Blancs," not champagne. His first Niagara Falls Wine Cellar wines all have varietal names: Seyval Blanc, Aurora Blanc, Delaware, and Dutchess among the whites, with a Chardonnay that is still being aged in cask; a rosé named Pink Catawba, and reds named Maréchal Foch, Chelois, and Cascade.

Winegrowing in Niagara County began before the Civil War. County Historian Clarence O. Lewis has found records showing that a winery operated at Lockport during the 1860s and that it had vineyards on both sides of the town. It was at Lockport, in 1868, that the Niagara grape variety, sometimes called the white Concord, was created by crossing Concord with a vine called Cassady. A Niagara-growing boom followed and lasted until the 1890s, when too many grapes were produced, the market collapsed, and many vineyards were uprooted.

A new grape-planting rush in Niagara County began in the late 1960s, and Viticultural Extension Specialist Trenholm D. Jordan has issued a warning to farmers against planting vines unless they are certain of a market for their grapes; he worries that the market collapse of the 1890s may occur again.

• 8 •

The Hudson River Valley, with seven wineries and some 1200 acres of vineyards, is the oldest winegrowing district in the United States. Wine has been made continuously in this historic valley for at least three centuries, since French Protestant refugees settled at New Paltz in Ulster County in 1677. When their plantings of European vines failed, the Frenchmen made wine of the native wild grapes until such domesticated varieties as the Isabella became available early in the nineteenth century.

The first large commercial vineyard in the valley was planted with the Isabella about 1829 on Croton Point, the peninsula that is now Westchester County's Croton Point Park, on the east shore of the Hudson thirty-five miles north of New York City. No marker or plaque exists to tell the thousands who now enjoy picnicking at the park that this was once their state's most famous vineyard. Campers who take shelter in the great cavern hollowed out of the hillside are unaware that it originally served as the aging vault for Croton Point wines.

Dr. Richard T. Underhill, the bachelor physician who planted vines there, was so enthusiastic about grape culture that he abandoned his medical practice in the city to give the vineyard his full time. He was also the first American advocate of the Grape Cure, the diet of fresh grapes then popular in Europe, where it was believed to prevent dyspepsia, liver ailments, and a long list of other diseases. Dr. Underhill first sold his grapes fresh, but later established a winery on the peninsula. His Croton Point wines were offered in New York City during the 1860s as "the pure product of the grape, neither drugged, liquored, nor watered, recommended by leading physicians in all cases where a stimulant of a bracing character is required." Members of the Underhill family were prominent in the New York wine industry for several more decades.

• 9 •

The oldest active winery in the United States is at Washingtonville, several miles from the river in Orange County. It is the Brotherhood Corporation winery, established in 1839. Its ancient caves, which resemble those beneath old wineries in Europe, are the largest wine storage tunnels I have found in North America. They are well worth visiting, though some of the capacious vaults are empty, and the great vineyards which once covered this part of the valley are no more. The last vines were uprooted in 1960 to enlarge the winery's parking lot, where a fifty-cent charge is made for parking in the afternoons.

Situated only fifty-one miles from New York City, the Brotherhood winery now specializes in selling its wines at retail to visitors, of whom more than 300,000 come each year for free tours of its caves and to sample the wines (also free) from paper cups. Two dozen hosts deliver impressive one-hour lectures on the romance and the making of wine and on its uses in cooking. Merry evening parties are held in the cellars for the Brotherhood of Wine Tasters, loyal customers who sometimes use professional-type scorecards to rate the Brotherhood wines. I found their quality adequate, typical products of the Delaware, Catawba, and other Labrusca grapes the company buys in the Hudson Valley, Chautauqua, and Niagara districts. Of the twenty types the company sells, the best were the brut champagne, the sparkling burgundy, and the sauterne, in which the Labrusca taste was least pronounced.

I went to Washingtonville expecting to unravel there the early history of Brotherhood wines and their connection with the fabulous Thomas Lake Harris, whose utopian Brotherhood of the New Life gave the wines their name. My research in California had shown that Harris's religious, semicommunistic Brotherhood had first made wine in the Hudson Valley before it moved to Brocton, then to the Fountain Grove Vineyard in Santa Rosa, California. I therefore assumed that it was at the Brotherhood winery that Harris's winemaking began. Imagine my disappointment when Columbia-trained Francis Llado Farrell, who has owned the

Brotherhood winery since 1948, told me he had never heard of such a person as Thomas Lake Harris, nor of his Brotherhood religious cult either!

Since that visit, the mystery has been cleared up by further research, by studying the numerous books that have been written about the fantastic career of Harris, and by Farrell's wife Eloise, who has investigated the local historical sources.

The founder of this Brotherhood winery was not the English-born Harris, but Jean Jaques from France, who settled at Washingtonville in 1816. Jaques, a shoemaker, was the first to plant grapes in Orange County, soon after Dr. Underhill started his vineyard at Croton Point. In 1838, Jaques sent his first grapes to market and received for them only thirteen cents a pound, so he decided in the following year to make his crop into wine. He sold some to the First Presbyterian Church, of which he was an elder. For many years thereafter, Jaques had a prospering trade in sacramental wines, which kept the Brotherhood winery open during Prohibition. It still enjoys a lucrative clerical trade.

Harris's Brotherhood of the New Life first made wine during the 1860s, not at Washingtonville, but at his third colony, which was at Amenia in the Hudson Valley. (His first two colonies were at Mountain Cove, West Virginia, and at Wassaic, New York.) Winegrowing was the Amenia colony's industry. It kept the disciples busy while angels dictated the sermons and celestial poems that Harris claimed came to him when he was in a trance. He preached that his wines had divine and miraculous powers, "the finer electro-vinous spirit of the collective body of the grape," and that therefore they brought joy without alcoholic intoxication.

There were bizarre occult and sexual practices in his colonies, including "celibate marriage," Harris dictating where wives and husbands were to sleep, usually apart. Harris was the patriarch, wielding absolute power and holding the devout members' personal fortunes. His disciples included many wealthy people, including Laurence Oliphant, the renowned British author and former Parliament member, and Lady Maria Oliphant, his mother. It was with Lady Oliphant's jewels that Harris purchased the larger tract at Brocton, to which the colony moved from Amenia in 1867. Eight years later Harris abandoned his heaven at Brocton to found his new one at the Fountain Grove Vineyard in California; the colony at Brocton fell apart soon after he left. Harris ruled at Fountain Grove until 1892, when, embroiled in lawsuits and scandals about free love, he suddenly left Fountain Grove in charge of his samurai Japanese secretary, Baron Kanaye Nagasawa, and sailed for England. He lived there for a time, and died in New York in 1906.

Meanwhile, Brotherhood wines and Brotherhood Grand Monarque Champagne were being sold throughout the United States and even in Europe and Africa. The Brotherhood Wine Company had its own five-story building at Washington and Spring Streets in New York City and boasted of vineyards at Washingtonville and at Hammondsport in the Finger Lakes.

But how could Harris, in trouble with his disciples at Amenia, at Brocton, then in California, have possibly built this vast wine business, and what was its connection with his Brotherhood of the New Life?

The answer, it turns out, was a pair of enterprising New York wine merchants—Jesse and Edward R. Emerson, father and son. During the 1870s, the Emersons bought the wine from Harris's Brotherhood colony at Brocton, and also bought some wine from Jaques, blended them together, and sold the blend, with Harris's blessing, under his Brotherhood name. Then in 1885, Harris having left for California, and John Jaques and two of his sons having died, the surviving Jaques son, Charles, sold the Washingtonville winery to the Emersons. They promptly changed its name from Blooming Grove, which Jaques had called it, to Brotherhood.

· 10 ·

There are no million-gallon wineries in the Hudson Valley such as those in the Finger Lakes. The Brotherhood cellars hold a quarter-million gallons; the Royal Wine Corporation at Milton and the Marlboro Industries winery at Marlboro, which specialize in kosher wines, and the Hudson Valley winery at Highland, are of comparable size. Mandia at Clintondale, whose owner claims to have been the first to bottle Cold Duck, is much smaller, though it turns out ample quantities of champagne.

But because of the valley's proximity to New York City, there are more hobbyist winegrowers in this locality than anywhere else in New York State. Only two have thus far bonded their cellars to sell their wines, but others, such as Tom Clarke with his Vinifera vineyard at Marlboro, tell me they would do so if the state would reduce its extortionate winery license fees.

· 11 ·

One of the best-known small winegrowing estates in eastern America is the seventy-eight-acre High Tor Vineyard near New City, twenty-eight miles from Manhattan. It was planted in 1951 by playwright Everett Crosby.

From his boyhood in California, Crosby had cherished a dream of someday becoming a winegrower. When he came to New York he planted a grapevine on the terrace of his penthouse apartment in the city, and when he moved to West Nyack in Rockland County, he planted vines around his house there. In 1949 he bought an old farm atop High Tor, the craggy mountain about which Maxwell Anderson wrote his prize-winning play of that name, and finally planted his dream vineyard there. Crosby's High Tor wines, introduced in 1954, were the first in New York State to be made entirely of French hybrids. They were praised by connoisseurs and were featured on the wine lists of prestigious New York restaurants and clubs. The samples I tasted at the winery when I was last in the Hudson Valley were evidence that they deserved their fame. His four-year-old Rockland Red was rich in tannin, perfectly balanced, and had developed a bottle bouquet; his white was dry and fragrant, and the rosé was as fine as any pink wine made of Vinifera grapes.

After lavishing care on his vineyard for twenty-three years, Crosby sold High Tor in 1971 to a younger oenothusiast named Richard Voigt, who owns the Peppermill Restaurants in Connecticut. Voigt's winemaker is an Episcopalian priest named Father Thomas Lee Hayes, but Crosby continues as their consultant and is teaching them the art. I have known many clerical winemakers in the Catholic Church–owned wineries, but Father Hayes is the first American enologist to wear the robes of the Episcopal faith.

· 12 ·

The newest and most charming small winery in New York State is Benmarl Vineyard, which is perched on a hill above Route 9W, overlooking the Hudson at Marlboro in Ulster County.

From his five-year stay in Europe following the Second World War, when he became a member of Burgundy's Confrérie des Chevaliers du Tastevin, the noted illustrator Mark Miller wanted to become a winegrower. He found the site in 1956, the original fifty-acre vineyard where in 1867 Andrew J. Caywood developed the Dutchess grape, one of the best of the white Labrusca varieties. Miller found some of the ancient vines still growing on the property and the crumbling ruin of a century-old winery nearby. Records of the town of Marlboro dating from the 1700s are decorated with its symbol, a bunch of grapes. He named the estate Benmarl; ben is early Gaelic for hill, marl describes its slaty soil.

Miller planted a dozen acres with French hybrid vines and a half-acre with Chardonnay. Before building his winery, he organized fellow wine lovers into a unique kind of co-operative. Members of the Benmarl Societé des Vignerons bought vinerights of two vines each, which entitled each *vigneron* to the Droit du

Seigneur, an invitation to help with the harvest, and a dozen bottles of personally labeled wine.

After two years as a co-operative, the 5000-gallon Benmarl Vineyards winery was bonded in 1971. Its wines have since been added to the wine lists of several nearby restaurants and stocked in some of New York's leading stores.

The winery is a family operation of Mark, whose sculptures adorn the grounds, his wife Dene, who designed the rustic building, and their sons Eric and Kim. Benmarl welcomes visitors on weekdays and Saturday afternoons and offers seven wines for sale: estate-bottled, vintage-dated Seyval Blanc, Blanc Domaine, Rouge Domaine, Baco Noir, Rosé Domaine, Cuvée du Vigneron, and Chardonnay.

• 13 •

On a lofty bluff overlooking the Hudson near Highland, there is a 200-acre Italian winegrowing estate, so nearly perfect in its setting of vines on rolling hills that it might have been transplanted in one piece from the hills of Tuscany. In the middle of the vineyard, clustered around the manor house and garden, are stone winery buildings and the homes of families of vineyard workers, some of whom have lived here all their lives.

This is the Hudson Valley Wine Company, established by Alexander Bolognesi from Bologna after he retired from a Wall Street banking career in 1907. It still produces the same estate-bottled Labrusca wines and champagnes that the Bolognesi family did, though it has been owned since 1969 by Monsieur Henri Wines, the New York City wine importers, who in turn were purchased three years later by PepsiCo, Inc. of New York.

When I first visited the estate, Bolognesi's widow, Valentina, maintained a firm rule against visitors to the winery. The Monsieur Henri owners, however, saw it as the Hudson Valley's perfect tourist attraction. They established winery tours and tastings six days weekly from mid-April to late October and a Saturday evening champagne tour by reservation, and offered the use of the manor house for group luncheons and dinners. The only flaw is a three-dollar charge for parking, but the tour is well worth it. Hudson Valley still has the same Italian winemaker, Sam Williams, who was born on the estate; his father was the Bolognesis' vineyard manager. The vineyard is entirely of wine-grape varieties, Delaware, Catawba, Iona, Bacchus, and some recently added French hybrids. To reach the estate, take the New York Thruway to New Paltz, go west on route 299, and turn south on Highway 9W past the Mid-Hudson Bridge.

9

The Vine Grows in New England

I N THEIR book on *American Wines,* published in 1941, Frank Schoonmaker and Tom Marvel speculated that if the American colonies had undertaken from the start to cultivate the hardy native grapes, instead of attempting in vain to grow the delicate Old World varieties, a winegrowing industry would have developed in the stern climates of the New England states as it did elsewhere in the East. They went on to declare that if given the right conditions, such a development eventually would be "inevitable."

The "inevitable" apparently is coming to pass. Farmers and horticulturists are discovering that some parts of New England are as climatically suited for grape growing as are some of the present viticultural areas of other eastern states. And although winegrowing there is still in a pioneering stage, there already are some commercial wines being produced in New Hampshire, causing great excitement among farmers there and in two neighboring states.

• 2 •

The history of winegrowing in New England goes back two centuries, but has been obscured by time and by dry attitudes in American agriculture, which focused attention on grapes rather than on wine. That grapes grow abundantly, both wild and under cultivation, in this part of America is shown by the names given in colonial times to such places as Martha's Vineyard,* the twenty-mile-long island off the Massachusetts coast, and to the island town called Vineyard Haven. Nantucket Island also was once noted for its grapes.

*Historians have found no trace of any "Martha" for whom the island might have been named. Current opinion is that the name is a corruption of "Martin," referring to a friend of either the discoverer, Bartholomew Gosnold, or of the first proprietor, Thomas Mayhew.

The great seal of the State of Connecticut is a picture of three grapevines bearing fruit, symbolizing one of the agricultural activities of the early settlers. During the seventeenth century a large planting of European vines was made at the mouth of the Piscataqua River near the present site of Portsmouth, New Hampshire, and presumably it failed. But an early Massachusetts vineyard, the one planted by Governor John Winthrop on Governor's Island in Boston Harbor (which is now part of Logan International Airport), apparently produced grapes for a time. The payment Governor Winthrop undertook to make for the island in 1632—a hogshead of wine per year—was actually made by him and his heirs in the form of wine (sometimes of apples), until Adam Winthrop made a cash settlement in 1683.

Grape growing in Massachusetts during the nineteenth century is described by Alden Spooner in his book about winemaking, published in 1846. "Great quantities of grapes are raised in and about Boston," Spooner wrote, "but we do not know of any large vineyards for wine. Men of wealth raise foreign varieties in hot houses, and the finest grapes I have ever seen were at horticultural exhibitions in that city."

New England's principal contribution to American viticulture was the Concord grape, named for the historic town in Massachusetts whence it came—the principal grape now grown in the eastern, midwestern, and northwestern states. Its originator, Ephraim Wales Bull, became interested in grape growing as a boy, when his father had a vineyard at Bullville in the Hudson River Valley of New York. As a young man, employed as a goldbeater in Boston, Bull raised grapes in his garden on Fayette Street in that city, and on a larger scale when he moved in 1836 to Concord, where he also made his own wine. There, in 1843, trying to find a hardier dark grape than the Isabella, he sowed the seeds of numerous whole grapes that he picked from the local wild Labrusca vines. Among the seedlings that sprouted, one of the hardiest and most prolific yielded, in 1849, the purple, foxy-flavored grape he named the Concord. Bull propagated the vine from cuttings, and in 1854 he offered the Concord to nurseries at five dollars per vine. But the nurserymen propagated the vine themselves, and Bull earned little from the countless millions of its progeny that were planted throughout the nation. He became embittered, and died a poor man in Concord's Home for the Aged in 1895. Bull's tombstone records his resentment against commercial nurseries in these words: "He sowed, but others reaped." One of the historic shrines of Concord is Bull's Grapevine Cottage on Lexington Road, next door to the Wayside, which once was the home of his friend, Nathaniel Hawthorne. Visitors there are told that a massive grapevine beside the cottage, still bearing abundant crops each season, is Bull's original Concord vine.

I have found only one record of commercial winegrowing in New England during the nineteenth century. It is a letter published in the *American Wine Press and Mineral Water News* for August 1900. The writer, one Albert Bernard of Meriden, Connecticut, described Meriden as a wine-producing locality at that time. In particular, he mentioned a "Coe Farm" southwest of Meriden as having cultivated Concord and Worden grapes for wine between 1894 and 1897, and as having produced "a superior claret" that was sold in Hartford and in New York City.

• 3 •

Connecticut now has a number of small vineyards, mostly planted by amateur winemakers who commute from their offices in New York. The best-known is Thomas R. Clarke, who has a half-acre of Chardonnay adjoining his home at New Canaan, forty-five miles from the city. Clarke says southern Connecticut, near Long Island Sound, has one of the best climates in the East in which to grow Vinifera grapes, but with land growing scarce near his home, he has expanded by planting another vineyard in the Hudson Valley of New York. In 1963, wine merchant Ciro Buonocore of North Haven planted several acres of French hybrids there and made a Connecticut wine for several years, but failed to interest the state's agricultural authorities in his idea that grapes might replace tobacco as a Connecticut farm crop. The newest vineyard in the state is on the outskirts of Norwalk, beside Elmer and Don Singewald's liquor store. It consists of a few hybrid vines they planted as an experiment, but Don Singewald hopes to plant several thousand more vines and produce Connecticut wines for sale in the store.

• 4 •

The first winery in New Hampshire is the almost incredible achievement of John J. Canepa and his wife Lucille. They have launched a successful and expanding winegrowing industry in the center of the Granite State, where so far as is known, nobody has ever grown wine before.

The Canepas moved to Laconia, New Hampshire, from New York in 1958 because John was offered a job as pharmacist in the Laconia Clinic. They made their new home in a cottage on Governor's Island in nearby Lake Winnipesaukee, where they had spent several summer vacations. On walks on the island roads during that autumn, they noticed the profuse growth of the wild winter grapevine, which, pruned only by wintry gales, climbs sixty feet high in the pine trees. They picked some of the grapes, found them almost as sweet as the famous syrup the New Hampshire farmers obtain from the sap of their maple trees; and the Canepas' dream of becoming winegrowers was born. John had known wine since childhood, when his Italian-born father crushed grapes each autumn in the family garage and served the fermented juice, diluted with water, to his children. As a pharmacist, John knew chemistry, and he had learned some wine technology from the part-time job he had held during his senior year at Columbia University, analyzing samples for a wine importer. The Canepas decided it would be fun to try, in a region where grapes grew wild, to grow them under cultivation for wine.

They began searching for literature on viticulture. They visited the state university at Durham, learned that Belknap County had exactly twelve grapevines, and that the only variety recommended for this climate was the Beta, which makes a harsh, almost undrinkable wine. Undiscouraged, they sent for the book called *General Viticulture* by California's Professor Albert Winkler, and devoured its contents. Winkler's tabulation of summer temperatures in the world's chief winegrowing regions gave the Canepas a clue. They obtained records of weather at Laconia for twenty years and discovered that heat summation during their normal 150-day growing season measured higher than in Germany's Rhineland and was almost equal to that of the Champagne region of France. On weekends and days off from the clinic, the Canepas searched the fields and mountains and found many spots with southern exposure, sheltered from the cold northwest winds, with microclimates tempered by the nearby lakes. Next, they began visiting and studying the techniques of successful winegrowers in such other eastern states as Pennsylvania, Maryland, and New York. They meanwhile selected vines of American and French hybrid grape varieties that might mature in New Hampshire and survive the Laconia winters, which dip to fifteen and twenty degrees below zero.

In the spring of 1965, John planted 800 vines on three test sites, Lucille helping to dig the holes. When the buds sprouted green shoots, the Canepas chased the deer away. The vines showed good summer growth. University horticulturists and agricultural officials showed some interest, but stayed on the sidelines, skeptical.

The winter of 1965–66 was severe, and some of the vines died, but when most of them leafed out well in the following spring, excitement spread through the neighborhood. Blueberry farmers Marshall Hodsdon and Gordon Bean decided to plant an acre of grapes each. County Agent Horace Ballard and Horticulture Professor C. A. "Kelly" Langer came from the university to see what was going on. They found the Canepas already planting a thousand more vines. Word of what was happening reached New York City, and a wine merchant there wrote the Canepas, offering to sell any wine they might produce. That summer and autumn, there began a pilgrimage to Laconia of professional experts who wanted to see for themselves the improbable sight of wine grapes growing in New Hampshire. Tom Marvel came with his wife, and pointed out that Laconia is in the same latitude as New York's famous Finger Lakes. Next came professors from the Geneva, New York, research station, followed by Seaton Mendall, the chief of viticulture for the Taylor wineries of New York, and each of them offered advice. In 1967, the French hybrid vines yielded a thousand pounds of grapes, and the procession of visitors swelled, with Ernest Reveal, the president of Widmer's Wine Cellars from Naples, New York, scores of New Hampshire farmers, and more professors from the state university. Pictures of the Canepas and their visitors appeared on the front page of the Laconia *Citizen*, and the *Sunday News* at Manchester devoted a full picture page to the state's future wine industry. The Boston Sunday *Globe* photographed the Canepas' vineyard with the caption, "Soon, Yankee Wine." The Grape Growers Association of New Hampshire was organized with Canepa as chairman.

After the 1968 vintage, when their vineyard yielded three tons of grapes testing 18 to 20 percent in sugar content, the Canepas bought a 150-acre farm on Cotton Hill near Belmont, increased their plantings to twenty-five acres, and began building and equipping a modern winery, the White Mountain Vineyards of New Hampshire, on Durrell Mountain Road, just off Route 107. The cellar was finished and bonded in time to ferment all six tons of the 1969 vintage.

In 1970, only five years after the planting of their first vines, Canepa estate-bottled Foch* New Hampshire Burgundy and Lakes Region Dry White Dinner Wine went on sale in the state monopoly liquor stores and in a dozen New Hampshire restaurants.

The White Mountain Vineyards Winery has since been enlarged to 50,000 gallons, John has quit his job at the clinic, has added an apple wine which he ships to stores in neighboring states, and is preparing to make the first New Hampshire champagne. Forty farmers around the New Hampshire lakes have planted nearly 100 acres of vines, four more have started vineyards in Vermont, and three are planting French hybrids for the Canepas in central and southern Maine.

*"Foch" refers to the French hybrid grape variety called Marèchal Foch, which is a cross of American *Vitis riparia* grapes with Burgundy's noble Gamay and Pinot Noir.

· 5 ·

Vermont has reduced its state license fee for wineries from $3000 to $150 per year, and the Green Mountain State, too, now has its first winery, at Danby, where Frank and Mitsuko Jedlicka are making apple and honey wines. They expect to use Vermont grapes when new vineyards along the lakes in the west start to produce.

And in Maine, the Department of Economic Development has undertaken a study of the feasibility of starting a wine industry to ferment blueberries, apples, and grapes.

Now Canepa is working with other growers to get an amendment to the New Hampshire law, like the one adopted in Pennsylvania, to let him sell his wine direct to consumers and restaurants instead of through the state monopoly stores. He expects to win because neighboring Vermont, which is also a monopoly state, recently showed the way by permitting table wines to be sold in food stores.

· 6 ·

This chapter had already gone to my publishers when I learned that Massachusetts, too, has a new vineyard and winery, established in 1971. In the center of Martha's Vineyard island, electronics engineer George Mathiesen and his wife Catherine have planted ten acres with White Riesling, Chardonnay, Cabernet Sauvignon, Pinot Noir, and Gamay Beaujolais and have built the 15,000-gallon Chicama Vineyard winery. The Mathiesens, home winemakers from California, bought their vines from Dr. Konstantin Frank at Hammondsport, New York, and from the Mirassou Vineyard in California. They made their first few gallons of Massachusetts Johannisberg Riesling in 1972. The vineyard is near West Tisbury, on Stoney Hill Road. Chicama is a local Indian name.

10

Wines of Some Mid-Continent States

At Hermann, Missouri, in 1866, the year after the Civil War, Professor George Husmann penned his first book, *The Native Grape and the Manufacture of American Wines.*

"The nation is affected with grape fever," he wrote. "I firmly believe that this continent is destined to be the greatest wine-producing country in the world. America will be, from the Atlantic to the Pacific, one smiling and happy Wineland, where each laborer shall sit under his own vine, and none will be too poor to enjoy the purest and most wholesome of all stimulants, good, cheap, native wine."

In that year Missouri surpassed Ohio as the second largest winegrowing state of the Union, and the grape-planting fever was spreading through such neighboring states as Iowa, Kansas, and Illinois.

But local prohibition laws and vine diseases were also spreading while Husmann wrote his book. Too many grapes were being planted for the wineries to absorb, and the prices paid for grapes declined. Vineyards became neglected, were attacked by plant pests, and were abandoned to die. Husmann, professor of horticulture at the University of Missouri, abandoned his home state in 1881 to become a winemaker in California's Napa Valley. He had discovered in a single visit during that summer how ideal the conditions were for winegrowing there.

National Prohibition in 1920 closed all of the mid-continent wineries except two monasteries which continued producing altar wines. A few dozen commercial wineries reopened in 1933, but much of the area was still legally dry, and there was little demand for any wine except the cheapest dessert types. Eighteen states between the Appalachians and the Rockies (not counting Michigan) have produced less than three percent of American wine since Repeal.

Yet all of these states are natural grape-growing country; Labrusca grapes flourish in tens of thousands of midwestern gardens, and more vine species grow wild here than anywhere else on earth. Most of the wine produced in the world today comes from vineyards grafted to, or crossed by hybridizing with, native midwestern vines.

• 2 •

More than a century since Husmann wrote his book, millions of Americans, including midwesterners, have begun buying table wines for mealtime use, and now there is grape fever in Missouri again. New vineyards have been planted and old ones are expanding in a dozen Missouri counties. Five wineries have been bonded in Missouri within the past few years, giving the state a total of eight.

Professor Husmann's hometown, the picture-book Missouri River hamlet of Hermann, is one of the places where it is happening. For the first time in half a century, wine is flowing from the huge, turreted Stone Hill Winery, which Michael Poeschel from Germany began building in 1847 at the south edge of town. It once held more than a million gallons and was the second largest in the nation. Its wines, such as Hermannsberger, Starkenberger, and Black Pearl, won eight gold medals at world's fairs between 1873 and 1904. When Prohibition closed the winery, Ottmar Stark ordered all of its vineyards destroyed, virtually ruining the economy of the town. The great Stone Hill cellars then were used to cultivate mushrooms, producing sixty-five tons of the fungi per year.

In 1965, farmer James Held, whose ancestors came to Hermann 128 years earlier, saw that table wines were becoming popular in Missouri. He arranged to move into the second floor of the old winery with his wife Betty Ann and their four children. The Helds installed antique casks and his grandfather's wooden roller-crusher in one of the underground vaults and made a thousand gallons of Catawba wine. Their first wine sold so well that they since have cleared the mushroom beds out of the other seven vaults and now turn out 60,000 gallons per year of Missouri Riesling, Catawba, Niagara, Virginia Seedling, burgundy, rosé, and sauterne. Held has doubled to twenty acres his vineyard of Cynthiana, Catawba, and French hybrid vines on the Gasconade River hills, and he also has several neighboring farmers growing grapes for him. Stone Hill now offers wine tasting and a tour of its cellars for a dollar, and has opened its own wine museum.

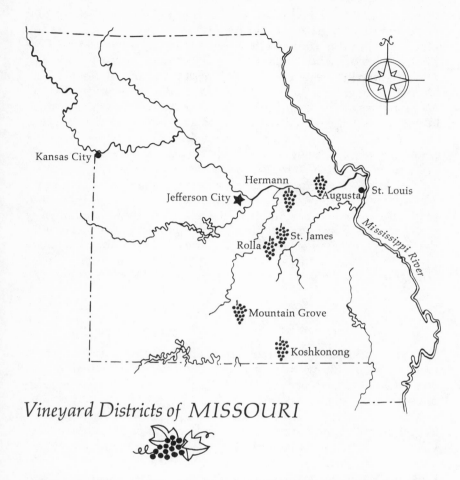

Kansas City

Jefferson City

Hermann

Augusta   St. Louis

Rolla   St. James

Mississippi River

Mountain Grove

Koshkonong

Vineyard Districts of MISSOURI

Wine has been part of the flavor of Hermann since grapes were first planted there by Jacob Fugger in 1843. Many of its citizens, including the Helds, rear their children by "the Hermann formula: the first year wine, the second year wine and sauerkraut." The revival of Hermann's "days of wine and glory" is now celebrated on the third weekend of each May with German bands, folk dancing, knackwurst, and a house tour of "Little Germany."

• 3 •

Another historic Missouri winery was reopened in 1968 at Augusta, a town of German heritage on the Missouri River bluffs thirty miles west of St. Louis. The proprietor is young accountant Lucian Dressel, who became enamored of wine during his travels in Europe. On completing his studies at Harvard and Columbia, he recognized the trend to wine-drinking in America and decided to become a winegrower. Touring with his wife Eva, he found the place at Augusta where there were eleven wineries before Prohibition. An old brick cellar with underground storage vaults was for sale; it had been converted into an apartment house. The Dressels bought the place and discovered it was originally the Mount Pleasant Vineyard winery of Friedrich Muench, a famous Lutheran minister and hybridizer of grapes, who once wrote a book on wine in German, its title in English, *School for American Grape Culture*. The winery was built by Muench in 1881, and his prize-winning wines were known from coast to coast.

The Dressels have replanted a dozen acres of the Mount Pleasant Vineyard with French hybrids, Virginia Seedling, and with an experimental patch of Vinifera, including Johannisberg Riesling and Chardonnay. They plan eventually to specialize in the wines of whichever grape varieties grow best. They have opened a tasting room and are selling mostly their estate-bottled, vintage-dated "Emigré" table wines made of the French-American grapes.

· 4 ·

Wine grapes are being planted again in the part of Missouri's Ozark Plateau known as Big Prairie, where the principal grapes grown now are Concords for the Welch co-operative's grape juice plant at Springdale, Arkansas.

Near St. James, where the Ozark Grape Festival is held each September, Concord-grower William B. Stoltz began adding wine varieties in 1965 to his seventy-acre vineyard three miles northeast of town. He planted mainly such Labrusca types as Missouri Riesling, Catawba, and Delaware, but also some French and New York State hybrids. In 1968 he opened the 5000-gallon Stoltz Vineyard Winery and introduced several native Ozark table wines, which he named for his grapes, and also an "Old-Fashioned Missouri Sweet Grape Wine." Stoltz soon found that many people in the area especially liked those of his wines with the least Labrusca flavor. He now has planted more French hybrids and has expanded his winery to 10,000 gallons.

· 5 ·

A second winery opened at St. James in 1970 and began producing the only champagne made wholly of Missouri grapes. It is James and Patricia Hofherr's St. James Winery, on the access road beside Interstate Highway 44.

Hofherr holds a degree in microbiology from the University of Texas. He had five years' winemaking experience with the Bardenheier winery at St. Louis before coming to St. James and also made champagne for a year at the Post Winery in Altus, Arkansas. He chose the Big Prairie section as the place for his winery because most of Missouri's 2500 acres of vineyards are there.

The St. James Winery holds 20,000 gallons and is new from the ground up, with an inviting rustic tasting and sales room. Hofherr makes three bottle-fermented sparkling wines, a brut and a pink champagne and an almost-dry Cold Duck. I found the pink the best of the three. His table wines range from Rhine and Niagara through a list of six other Labrusca types, and he also makes apple and berry wines. But he has one interesting French hybrid dry red called Cascade, which has no foxy flavor and would please most drinkers of Bordeaux wine. He intends soon to plant his own vineyard of Vinifera varieties, which he thinks will grow well in the Ozarks, but for his champagne *cuvées* he prefers the grapy flavors of Catawba and Delaware.

• 6 •

The newest winery in Missouri is Dr. Axel Norman Arneson's Peaceful Bend Vineyard cellar on the Meramec River near Steelville, a few miles southeast of St. James. It is a two-story wooden structure with a Dutch barn-style roof, built with earth on three sides of the cellar, and was bonded in 1972.

Dr. Arneson, professor of clinical obstetrics and gynecology at Washington University School of Medicine in St. Louis, first learned about winemaking by helping his father ferment grapes for their home use in Texas during Prohibition. His travels in later years through Europe so stimulated his interest in viticulture that in 1951 he purchased some French hybrid vines from Philip Wagner and planted them on his Missouri farm.

Dr. Arneson makes only two dry table wines, each a blend of several hybrids. His red is named Meramec for the river and the white is called Courtois, the name of the township and of a nearby Ozark mountain stream. The doctor is fascinated with the history of Missouri viniculture and is writing a book that traces Professor Husmann's career. The Peaceful Bend Vineyard is on Highway M, originally named Peaceful Bend Road for the deep bend the river takes at the doctor's farm.

• 7 •

Another sign that winegrowing is coming back in Missouri is that the state's biggest vintner, Bardenheier's Wine Cellars of St.

Louis, which mainly blends and bottles California wines for sale in thirty midwestern states, has become a Missouri winegrower, too, and is preparing to make its own local champagne.

The Bardenheier Brothers, John, Joseph, Carl, and George, whose grandfather founded the firm in 1873, noticed in the mid-1960s that Ohio and New York wineries were buying most of the Catawba grapes that grow around the Missouri Fruit Experiment Station at Mountain Grove. They decided to enlarge their St. Louis cellar and to begin making some wines of their own. "Our state's wine industry is reviving," said brother Carl, who was trained in enology at the University of California, "and we're going to be part of it."

In 1970, the Bardenheiers planted their first vineyard, fifty acres of native and French hybrid varieties, on the big Lost River Ranch of Ott Coelln at Koshkonong on US Highway 63 in southern Missouri. This is the area, six miles from the Arkansas border, where Michael Brand, the founder of nearby Brandsville, began producing Ozark Maid wines in 1887. The land reverted to cattle grazing when Brand closed his winery in 1904.

The success of the Bardenheiers' first planting was celebrated in 1972 when the vineyard was blessed in a ceremony which I think was unprecedented, for it was conducted jointly by a Methodist minister and a Catholic priest.

· 8 ·

The revival of Missouri winegrowing is of little interest, however, to the proprietor of the state's smallest winery, Wepprich's at St. Charles, on the Missouri River, twenty miles northwest of St. Louis. Emil Wepprich has no place to expand. The winery is in the basement of his home, next door to his Wepprich's Wine Gardens, a bit of old Germany where waltzes fill the air on moonlit evenings. When his grandfather founded the winery in 1859 it was surrounded by hillside vineyards, but Wepprich sold the land a century later to developers, who uprooted the vines, and he since has bought his grapes in the upriver counties. The Gardens' wine card lists thirty selections, but he says three out of four patrons demand the foxy, semisweet "Wepprich's Own Concord," the only wine he still makes, a thousand or so gallons a year.

· 9 ·

Irvin Brucker, a St. Louis oenothusiast, has spent half a lifetime gathering the history of Missouri winegrowing and once published some of it in a mimeographed publication he called *The*

Wine Press, but he has enough left to fill a fascinating book.

The first Missouri wine was made in 1823 from wild grapes by the French Jesuit priests who founded the St. Stanislaus Seminary at Florissant, now a St. Louis suburb. They later planted vineyards around the Seminary, which sold both sacramental and commercial Florissant Valley wines in the St. Louis area for more than a century. When the winery at Florissant closed in 1960 for lack of labor, it was the oldest in this country, having produced wine continuously for 147 years. The Seminary's vineyard was uprooted, except that Brother Eilert, who had tended it for most of his life, kept the best half-acre and continued making wine as his hobby. When Lucian Dressel was buying equipment for his Mount Pleasant Vineyard winery, he found the ancient casks at Florissant being broken up for firewood, and rescued them for his winery at Augusta.

There were wineries in forty-eight Missouri counties before Prohibition. Bluffton, Boonville, Cape Girardeaux, Hannibal, Owensville, and Stanton were some of the addresses on famous Missouri wine labels. In the Kansas City area, the town of Independence, with Shaffer's Winery and Lohse's Native Wine Garden, was known for its wine long before Missourians came to know Harry Truman. A history of Newton County records that in 1867 grape-breeder Hermann Jaeger of Neosho advised French viticulturists to graft their phylloxera-devastated vineyards onto wild Ozark vine roots. He shipped them seventeen carloads of rootings and later was awarded the Cross of the French Legion of Honor.

St. Louis was the nation's chief early center of wine study and research and was also the home of Missouri's most famous winery. The story of Cook's Imperial Champagne Cellar is one of the strangest in the annals of this country's wines. The cellar is still in existence, a stone-arched maze four levels deep beneath an entire city block on Cass Avenue—but it is now a vinegar plant. Built in 1832 by the Missouri Wine Company, it was purchased in 1859 by Chicago connoisseur and political leader Isaac Cook, who made its Missouri champagne famous. Reopened after Prohibition by new owners as the American Wine Company, it was headed by Alsace-born Adolf Heck, Sr., the father of the Heck brothers who now own the Korbel vineyard in California. Heck was uncomfortably short of capital until a little-known Swiss firm invested in Cook's stock in 1939. Five years later, during the Second World War, Government investigators tracing Nazi investments in this country discovered that the secret owner of the Missouri winery was Hitler's foreign minister, ex-champagne salesman Joachim von Ribbentrop. The American Wine Company was seized by the

Government and was sold several times until it became part of the Schenley liquor empire in 1946, the same year von Ribbentrop was hanged for his war crimes. Since 1954 Cook's champagnes have been made as Heck, Sr., made them—from California wines with eastern Catawba in the blend—but at the Roma winery in Fresno, which is now owned by the Guild Company of Lodi.

Missouri's greatest contribution to the wine industry was the work of Professor Husmann. Like Jaeger, he shipped millions of phylloxera-resistant vines from Missouri to re-establish the dying vineyards of Europe. He established at St. Louis *The Grape Culturist*, one of the earliest American periodicals on viticulture, and wrote two books after the one quoted from at the beginning of this chapter. On moving to California, Husmann helped to overcome the phylloxera plague there. He made prize-winning wines for the Talcoa Vineyard of Napa and the Oak Glen Vineyard of Chiles Valley until he died in 1902.

• 10 •

Winegrowing is also reviving with great excitement in Indiana, where it flourished more than 150 years ago.

When in 1971 the Indiana Legislature enacted a virtual copy of Pennsylvania's new law permitting "limited wineries," two wineries prepared to open in the Hoosier State and plans got under way to build several more.

Indiana's first new winery is the 12,000-gallon Treaty Line Wine Cellars on the Whitewater River, four miles northeast of Liberty in the southeastern part of the state. It opened less than four months after the law was passed, with Lieutenant Governor Richard Volz ceremonially pressing the first grapes and proclaiming it the start of a new Indiana industry.

The Treaty Line winery and vineyard is an undertaking of Dr. Donald MacDaniel, a Connersville optometrist, with eight associates, including three more doctors. In their first year they planted twenty acres of French hybrids, soon to be increased to ninety, and installed winery equipment from France and Italy in their winery, which is a rebuilt pre–Civil War barn. In the following summer their first six table wines went on sale to crowds of visitors in a rustic *weinstube* built beside the cellars. "Treaty Line" refers to the nearby boundary, set in 1795 by Revolutionary War General "Mad Anthony" Wayne, which opened the Indiana Territory to settlers. The winery is on the Brownsville Road, which takes off from Indiana Route 44 between Liberty and Connersville.

Seven miles north of Bloomington on Highway 37 is the Oliver

Vineyard winery, opened in 1972 by Professor William Oliver, a member of the University of Indiana Law School faculty. Professor Oliver's eighteen-acre vineyard of hybrids, which he began planting in 1966 and is expanding to ninety acres, supplied the first Baco Noir grapes pressed at the Treaty Line Cellars. Both wineries are buying additional grapes in southwestern Ohio until their new Indiana vineyards come into bearing.

Dr. MacDaniel and Professor Oliver both began growing French hybrid grapes and making wine in their homes as hobbyists. When they heard about the revival of winegrowing along the Ohio River near Cincinnati, they decided that Indiana, with its similar climate, should follow Ohio's example. Together they obtained passage of the Indiana winery law, which allows wineries under 50,000 gallons to sell their products to consumers as well as to restaurants and stores.

There is another winegrowing project bordering Lake Michigan in northwestern Indiana, where old Concord vineyards supply grapes to the processors in adjoining Michigan. Carl Banholzer, after selling his interest in Michigan's new Tabor Hill Winery, planted eighteen acres of hybrids and Vinifera in Laporte County, near the Michigan border, and announced plans to plant more and to build a winery there.

A fourth project, to plant vines and open a winery at Vevay on the Ohio River, was interrupted when former Hammondsport winemaker Richard P. Vine, who was leading it, moved instead to the Niagara Wine Cellars at Lewiston, New York. Others are studying Vevay as a future winegrowing district, and Vine says he hopes eventually to plant vines there.

• 11 •

But winegrowing isn't new to Indiana. It is at least six years older than the state.

The first Indiana vineyards were planted about 1810 at Vevay, Switzerland County, where you still can see some of the hillside terraces on which they grew. Vevay celebrates its vinous history with its mid-August Swiss Wine Festival, begun in 1968, with Swiss bands, a carnival, quilting bees, and with *steintossen* (stone-tossing) and grape-stomping contests. The stomping contestants jump barefoot on grapes (brought from Ohio) in wooden tubs fitted with spigots. The winners are those who press the most juice through the spigots into jars.

In 1796, the year after Washington delivered his Farewell Address, Jean Jacques Dufour left his father's vineyard at Vevey (the French spelling) in Switzerland with an ambitious plan to found a Swiss winegrowing colony in America. He organized the Kentucky Vineyard Society and in 1801 planted Swiss vines along the Kentucky River twenty-five miles from Lexington. His Kentucky vineyards were attacked by phylloxera and died. Dufour then bought the present site of Vevay and named it for his Swiss home. Here he planted the grape variety which Peter Legaux of Philadelphia had falsely named "the Cape grape," really a Labrusca, the Alexander. Legaux's fake turned out to be Dufour's good fortune, for the hardy Alexander flourished at Vevay, where any European grape would have perished. At Vevay, Dufour wrote one of the first American books about winegrowing, *The American Vine Dresser's Guide*. It was published in 1826, a few months before he died.

Thomas Jefferson and Secretary of State Henry Clay approved of Vevay wine, and Clay once had a dozen bottles sent to him, to be served to some distinguished visitors. When he opened the bottles he found all twelve filled with whiskey, substituted by his son James, who must have liked the wine.

When Nicholas Longworth introduced the Catawba to Ohio, the Indiana winegrowers switched their plantings to that "wonder grape." By 1880 Indiana was producing 100,000 gallons of wine yearly and selling much of it in Cincinnati. But by then the rot which had killed Longworth's vines had spread to such Indiana vineyard centers as Vevay and Connersville. Grape production in the Hoosier State reached an all-time high in 1911, when its crop totaled 11,000 tons. It declined during and after Prohibition, until by 1954 only 900 tons were produced.

· 12 ·

Northern Kentucky, across the Ohio River from Cincinnati, shared the southern Ohio grape boom in Longworth's time, but the only Kentucky winery of which I have found any record was at the Trappist Abbey of Gethsemani in Nelson County, about fifty miles south of Louisville. Trappist monks from France planted vines on the hillsides when they established the Abbey in 1848. They produced altar wine for almost a century, but they discontinued the winery in 1940 and abandoned most of its vineyard. "Something like a shift in climate took place here, and the grapes were frozen almost every spring, whilst apple crops were the exception," Brother Edward of the Abbey explains. Besides, he admits, "The wine we did produce in days more favorable was never of high quality."

Now, with the new boom in winegrowing across the Ohio River, farmers in northern Kentucky are planting French hybrids and

Labrusca grapes, which they sell to the wineries in southern Ohio. One of them, William Schwerin at Alexandria, returned from a trip through Europe with the idea that Vinifera vines, too, can be grown in this part of Kentucky. He and his son have grafted Cabernet Sauvignon vines from California on French hybrid roots, have already harvested several crops, and have made the first experimental lots of Kentucky Cabernet Sauvignon wine.

The Schwerins would like to establish their own winery, but they must wait until the day when the State of Kentucky will reduce its exorbitant $1500 annual winery license fee, which is far too high for any small winegrower to pay.

• 13 •

Illinois is the third state in the nation in wine production, making six million gallons per year. But as will be seen in a later chapter on the kosher wine producers, almost all of it is made by the giant Mogen David Wine Corporation in Chicago from grapes grown in Michigan, Missouri, Pennsylvania, and New York. Yet the Prairie State once had many winegrowers, and it has two of the most interesting small wineries in the Midwest.

On the Mississippi River at the far western edge of the state is a winery that has grown its own grapes for more than a century. Few people in Chicago or Springfield know it exists. Fred Baxter's Gem City Vineland vineyard and winery at Nauvoo produces only two wines from its grapes, a red Concord and a sauterne, though Baxter is preparing to add a rosé.

The cellars and the 120-acre vineyard date from 1857, eight years after Baxter's English great-grandfather came to Nauvoo with Etienne Cabet's French communistic Icarian sect. Members of the Baxter family are glad to show you the winery with its original steam-operated wine press and century-old casks. But the Illinois beverage law won't let them sell you their wine or even offer you a taste. This peculiar law is the reason there aren't many more vineyards and wineries in Illinois.

Old Nauvoo is especially worth visiting for its strange history, its restored homes of the original Mormons, the caves of its old wineries, and for the annual Wedding of Wine and Cheese, an ancient French ceremony that is part of the Nauvoo Grape Festival on the weekend before Labor Day. In the wedding pageant, written by the Benedictine Sisters of St. Mary's Academy in Nauvoo, the bride places the wine on a barrel which symbolizes the altar; the groom places the cheese beside it, and the magistrate encircles both articles with a wooden barrel hoop, which symbolizes the wedding ring.

Nauvoo was founded by the first Mormons, led by their founder, Prophet Joseph Smith. They fled here from western Missouri in 1836 and drained malarial swamps to build their temple and the city, "Nauvoo the Beautiful," which then was ten times the size of Chicago. Political quarrels with non-Mormons led to riots, and in 1844 a raging mob in Carthage shot and killed Joseph Smith and his brother Hyrum; and two years later the temple was burned to the ground. To escape further persecution, the Mormons in 1846 abandoned Nauvoo, leaving it a virtual ghost town, and began their epic wagon journey into Utah, led by Brigham Young. To Nauvoo five years later came Cabet and his Icarians, who moved into the empty Mormon homes. The Icarian brand of communism failed to work, and Cabet abandoned his utopia, leaving many of his flock behind. Meanwhile, winegrowing became the leading industry of Nauvoo, John Tanner from Berne in Switzerland having planted the first vineyard in 1847.

The winery Alois Rheinberger from Lichtenstein founded in 1850 now serves as Nauvoo's Historical Museum. Memorabilia on display show that Rheinberger's wines became famous and were known as late as the nineties in such faraway places as St. Paul and New York. In the museum cellar you will see his press and other winemaking implements, and the huge stone he used as a weight on his press is on the lawn nearby. An acre of Rheinberger's vineyard still bears grapes in the Nauvoo State Park. The extent of pre-Prohibition winemaking at Nauvoo can be estimated by counting the dozens of vaulted wine caves that honeycomb the hills along the river shore.

When Prohibition emptied the Nauvoo wineries, it was found that the wine caves had just the proper temperature and degree of moisture for the culture of blue cheese. This was the birth of Nauvoo's cheese industry, now celebrated by the Wedding of Wine and Cheese.

• 14 •

Forty miles southwest of Chicago, near the town of Monee, an ancient Illinois Central railroad station stands in a thirty-acre rolling vineyard of French hybrid, Delaware, and Catawba vines, which are interspersed with rows of White Riesling and Chardonnay. Beneath the quaint old station is a model 12,000-gallon wine cellar that produces bottle-fermented champagne.

This is the Thompson Vineyard and Winery, owned by Dr. John E. Thompson, a nutritionist and former instructor in physiology at the Illinois Institute of Technology, who also owns the adjoining 3000 acres of Thompson Farms. Dr. Thompson has operated the vineyard and winery as a hobby since he bought it from Bern Ramey and Joseph Allen in 1970.

Ramey, a champagne maker from Ohio's Lake Erie Islands, a graduate of the University of California–Davis wine school, and a lecturer and writer on wines in Chicago, planted the vineyard in 1963 because he wanted to prove that wine as fine as any can be grown in Illinois. He proved it by making in 1966 a brut champagne, which I tasted at the winery with Chicago *Tribune* writer Ruth Ellen Church, that was as fine as any produced in the United States.

But inspecting the vineyard one morning in the spring of 1968, Ramey discovered strange streaks on the leaves of the vines. The leaf edges resembled the teeth of a saw—unmistakable symptoms of injury by the weed-killer used on adjoining cornfields, known as 2,4-D. Ramey & Allen Champagne was already on the market and winning connoisseur favor in Illinois, but soon half of the vines were stunted back to year-old size. Part of the vineyard was ploughed under and the model winery was closed. "It cost us a quarter of a million dollars to learn that grapes cannot be grown in corn country," Ramey says.

Dr. Thompson has since restored and expanded the vineyard, neighboring farmers having promised him to spray no more with 2,4-D. His new champagne, named Père Marquette for the Jesuit priest who explored the Midwest, went on sale in 1972 and is to be followed by a series of French hybrid and Vinifera table wines. Ramey now travels between California and European vineyards as the boss of import sales for Browne Vintners, but visits Monee each year to see how his Illinois vineyard grows.

• 15 •

The 2,4-D weed-killer has also damaged Baxter's vines at Nauvoo, but it has done far more damage in the century-old winegrowing districts of Iowa and Kansas.

Yes, you read correctly: Kansas, the home of Carry Nation, had a well-established wine industry until the state was voted dry in 1880. The Prohibitionists expunged its history from the archives, but the evidence remains in the shells of venerable Kansas wineries, underground cellars walled with stone, which you still can see along the rivers in the eastern part of the state. One of the oldest, three miles northwest of Wathena, was built in 1872 by Emanuel Madinger, who compared the vineyards along the west bank of the Missouri to those of his native Württemberg in the Rhineland. The 1880 census shows that 226,249 gallons of wine were produced in that year by vineyards in Doniphan, Labette,

Wyandotte, Leavenworth, and thirty-eight other Kansas counties. When the state went dry, Concords replaced wine grapes in Kansas. This pleased the Dry-dominated State Horticultural Society, which in a 1901 publication referred to grapes as "a fruit too good to be made a chief source of the degradation of the race."

Some grapes still grow in eastern Kansas, but Professor Erwin Abmeyer, superintendent of the state's Northeast Experiment Fields at Wathena, says that even his test plots have been damaged by 2,4–D and that many of the old vineyards have been removed. "I see little hope for their revival," he says, "as long as the use of 2,4–D and 2,3,5–T continues."

• 16 •

As for Iowa, with 2,4–D killing more vines each year, little is left of the state's once-important wine industry except scattered vineyards around Council Bluffs and near Keokuk, and the quaint little wineries of the Amana Colonies.

The Amanas and their wines are something out of another world. The colonies are seven Old World villages on the banks of the Iowa River ten miles north of Interstate 80, eighteen miles southwest of Cedar Rapids. An eighteenth-century German communistic and religious sect called The Community of True Inspiration came here in 1854 from Ebenezer, New York, purchased 25,000 acres of virgin prairie, and built a utopia named Amana, a biblical word meaning "remain true." Three more colonies, Middle, West, and South Amana, were built two miles apart, an hour's travel by ox team. High and Upper South Amana were added in between, and the small town of Homestead was purchased outright.

Communism survived here for almost three generations. Everything was owned by the Amana Society; the members worked without pay in the mills, shops, and fields and had their meals together in communal kitchens. But in 1932 the Depression threatened them with bankruptcy, and communism was forsaken for capitalism. The colonists became stockholders of a corporation which paid them wages, and capitalism worked: one of the colonies' several industries, Amana Refrigeration, has become the biggest maker of home freezers in the world.

The five tiny Amana wineries make Piestengel and grape wines in the basements of the owners' homes. Piestengel is rhubarb wine; the word means pie stalk in German. It comes both dry and sweet, white and pink, and usually doesn't taste of rhubarb; it has a flavor of its own. Nine tenths of Amana wine is sold to tourists, who taste and buy it in the cellars and drink it in the local restaurants. The tourists are happy to pay six dollars a gallon for the Amana product—double the price of many standard wines—because, in the rest of Iowa, wine to take home can only be bought in the state monopoly liquor stores. A special section of the Iowa law, adopted when Prohibition was repealed, allows the native wineries to sell their homemade wines to anyone, but they are not sold in the state stores. Most Amana wines are labeled "other than standard wine" because to reach their usual 16 percent alcoholic content more sugar must be added than Federal wine regulations allow.

In the old days each Amana colony had its communal winery, which provided each family with a daily allowance of wine. Workers in the fields received an extra portion at three each afternoon. "Our village winery was under our church," recalls Friedrich Ackerman, who owns the South Amana Winery. "But our elders ordered all the barrels emptied when Prohibition became the law in 1920, and the wine ran in the ditches for hours." The vineyards were abandoned during the 1920s, and when the wineries reopened at Repeal, they got their grapes from a vineyard near Fort Madison on the Mississippi. Then the Fort Madison vineyard was ruined by 2,4–D, and most of the grapes since have come from Fred Baxter's vineyard across the river at Nauvoo.

One Amana winery has its own vineyard because Ramon and Bette Goerler, who own the Old Wine Cellar Winery, believe they should grow their own grapes as their forebears did. Goerler, a Navy veteran and a graduate of the University of Iowa, planted the vineyard in 1966, six acres of Fredonia, Concord, and Beta grapes a mile north of town.

In 1880, when the national census of winegrowing was taken, Iowa produced 334,970 gallons of wine, thirteen times as much as the 26,000 gallons the state produces today.

Some of the best-known Iowa wines came from the hundred-acre White Elk Vineyard of Hiram Barney near Keokuk. An 1879 article in *The American Wine and Grape Grower* said that Barney's wines "have some reputation in the East but are better known in the West and South." White Elk wines bore varietal labels such as Catawba, Ives, Norton's Virginia, Delaware, and Clinton, and were described as "the pure juice of the grapes whose names they bear."

Nebraska, across the Missouri River from Council Bluffs, also had many wineries in the 1880s, principally around Omaha, Plattsmouth, and Nebraska City in Cass, Nemaha, and Sarby Counties. The vineyard of Julius Pitts, who had a winery near Plattsmouth, is reported as still producing grapes today.

• 17 •

Near Caney in southern Oklahoma, nine poor families settled in surplus government house trailers on a 160-acre tract of virgin land during the spring of 1972 and planted thirty acres of French hybrids as the start of a Federal project to make welfare recipients self-sufficient by growing grapes for wine. They were the first of 300 families who were to plant vineyards of twelve acres each, which officials estimated would earn $7000 a year per family when their crops would be harvested after four years.

This is the plan that Captain Paul Garrett and Harry Hopkins proposed in Georgia forty years earlier, only to be frustrated by the Drys in Congress, and the same that was proposed for West Virginia in 1966 and vetoed by state officials there.

When Oklahoma Office of Economic Opportunity director Rex Sparger planned the project, he first considered starting the welfare families on rabbit or catfish farms. When he announced the decision to have them grow wine grapes instead, several thousand families applied to join.

French hybrids from New York State and Canada were chosen for planting, on the advice of Oklahoma State University horticulturists and of Professor John Einset, who came to Oklahoma as a consultant from the Geneva Experiment Station of New York. Sparger reports two groups of Oklahomans are interested in starting wineries as soon as enough wine grapes are produced.

Oklahoma already has a winery, opened in 1971 at Okarche, forty miles northwest of Oklahoma City, but its owner, Peter Schwarz, buys his grapes from Tontitown in Arkansas, 230 miles away, because his land at Okarche is unsuited for grapes. Schwarz makes a sweet and a sweeter Concord wine and sells all he makes at the winery, which is on a country road a mile east of town.

Professor Herman A. Hinrichs of the University at Stillwater says grapes are a dependable crop in Oklahoma. He has tested many wine varieties and has seen them grown successfully by wine hobbyists in several parts of the state.

• 18 •

When I tell my friends in the East and West that good table wines and champagnes are now being made in Arkansas, they are amazed and some are openly skeptical, because few Americans, even former Arkansans, have ever associated Arkansas with the gentle art of appreciating wines. Yet it is true that in this part of the changing South, new vineyards of wine-grape varieties have been spreading through the Ozark backwoods, and that four

Vineyard Districts of
ARKANSAS

of the state's ten wineries are now concentrating on the production of table wines for mealtime use. Two of them have begun making Arkansas champagnes.

Most of this is taking place around a little town called Altus in the Ozark plateau region in the northwestern part of the state. Near the outskirts of Altus a narrow road that winds up St. Mary's Mountain through the woods has been named Champagne Boulevard. About a mile up the road, in a wide clearing at the summit, stands a wine cellar that resembles a Swiss chalet. Nearby are clusters of wine tanks of fiberglass and stainless steel. These are the Wiederkehr Wine Cellars, which with its capacity of 1,500,000 gallons is the largest and most modern winery in the Southwest. Adjoining is a two-story replica of an Alpine inn with a tasting room, gift shop, and a Swiss Wein Keller Restaurant which serves such dishes as quiche Lorraine and poulet rôti au vin blanc.

Here, in August of each year, the Altus Grape Festival is celebrated for the benefit of nearby St. Mary's Church, with pageantry, music, vineyard workers wearing *lederhosen*, pretty girls in bright Swiss peasant frocks, and with a King Bacchus crowning the festival queen. At the edge of the clearing the Wiederkehr vineyards begin. Symmetrical rows of grapevines stretch across the sandy plateau that slopes toward the wide Arkansas River Valley—325 acres planted to French hybrids, Delaware, Campbell's Early, Cynthiana, the best red-wine grape of the Ozarks, and a forty-five-acre patch of young Johannisberg Riesling and Chardonnay.

The settlers of Arkansas made wine more than a century ago from the Scuppernong grapes that grow wild through most of the state, but the frontiersmen generally preferred moonshine whiskey to wine. Between 1879 and 1900, Swiss, German, and Italian immigrants settled in the Ozark plateau country and began cultivating American bunch grapes. They made wine for their own use, then opened small wineries to make it for sale. Prohibition closed the wineries and brought to Arkansas scouts of the Welch Company, looking for new lands to grow more Concords for Welch grape juice and jelly. In 1923, a Welch plant was built at Springdale and a boom in Concord-planting ensued. Vineyard acreage in Arkansas expanded to 9000 acres by 1925, almost four times the 2400 acres there now.

During the Depression, Arkansas faced a grape surplus, so at the repeal of Prohibition in 1933 the state legislature voted to revive the wineries. This was done by taxing wines from outside the state seventy-five cents a gallon and letting Arkansas wines pay only a five-cent tax. More than a hundred wineries sprang up in Arkansas, but the chief product they turned out was 20 percent "sneaky pete," made from surplus Concords as a cheap intoxicant for hillbillies. This brought a reaction; many Arkansas counties voted themselves dry, closing the wineries. By 1957 only sixteen were left.

Though by then most of the grapes grown were Concords, the Swiss and German growers whose families had settled at Altus about 1880 still grew the native wine grapes. One of these was Herman Wiederkehr, who made table wines, the kinds his father, John Andrew Wiederkehr from Weinfeld in Switzerland, had always served at home. Herman and Mary Weiderkehr worried that Franklin County might vote dry at any time and close their little winery. Seeing no future in wine, they sent their five sons to college to study for other professions. But their youngest son, Alcuin, coming home on his vacations from Notre Dame and the University of Arkansas Law School, kept saying he wanted to be a winegrower. When a new Arkansas law was passed to let a winery continue operating even if its county went dry, Alcuin quit law school, went to the University of California at Davis to study viticulture and enology, and was joined there by his older brother Leo. Alcuin had a chance to go to Europe as an exchange student in 1962. He requested France, and was sent to Bordeaux. He worked in the vineyards, helped in the vintage, and after ten months came home filled with new ideas. He began planting the French hybrid grapes he had seen used to make French wines, and added an experimental plot of Vinifera vines from Dr. Konstantin Frank. During the next five years the two brothers enlarged the Wiederkehr vineyards and built the family winery to twenty times its original size.

By 1965, Alcuin was campaigning for a bill that would allow the state's restaurants to sell Arkansas table wine with meals. The bill wasn't expected to pass, but Alcuin arranged to have half-bottles of Wiederkehr table wines served at the Governor's Ball. The ladies present approved of the samples, especially when cherubic, curly-headed young Alcuin danced with them, and some took home the bottles as souvenirs. The next morning the bill passed the Senate, and when the restaurants in eleven cities began offering wine with dinners, table wine sales in Arkansas quadrupled in a few months.

Wiederkehr wines and champagnes resemble the principal wines of the northeastern states. The assortment is complete, ranging through all the generic and varietal eastern table and dessert wine types, and includes such specialties as Cynthiana, Edelweiss, Alpine Rosé, Vin Blanc Sec, and Vin Rosé Sec. At the winery a few years ago I tasted from the cask a dry Cynthiana that had sufficient tannin and body to develop bouquet with age. Perhaps such a Cynthiana, if given bottle-age, eventually will win recognition beyond Arkansas as the state's most distinctive wine. But Alcuin Wiederkehr says he hopes someday to compete against European and California wines with Arkansas Johannisberg Riesling and Chardonnay.

• 19 •

At the bottom of St. Mary's Mountain, with a Swiss chalet front like Wiederkehr's, is the 400,000-gallon Post Winery. The Wiederkehrs and the Posts, who are cousins, turn out the lion's share of the million gallons now produced in Arkansas, and both now sell some of their wines in neighboring states.

Five-foot-five Mathew J. Post, who is the mayor of Altus, insists that his winery is a year older than the Wiederkehrs' because his great-grandfather, Jacob Post from Bavaria, founded it in 1880. Like his uphill neighbors, Post welcomes visitors, inviting them to tour his attractive cellar and to taste his assortment of wines, which include a really admirable dry champagne with the character of the best French hybrid grapes. With the rising demand for dry and semidry table wines in Arkansas, he has added twenty-five acres of the hybrids to his 160 acres of vines.

Adjoining Mathew Post's winery is the smaller Mount Bethel Cellar, operated by his brother Eugene. The younger Post has been making table wines since the restaurant bill became law. Henry Sax, with his 5000-gallon winery at Altus, added French hybrids to his vineyard when his son began studying horticulture at the University of Arkansas. At Paris, south of Altus, Robert and Bette Kay Cowie, who opened their small winery in 1967, make only three products, Cynthiana, Campbell's Early, and Ives red table wines. The two wineries at Center Ridge, the Heckmanns at Harrisburg, and Freyaldenhoven's at Morrillton, make both table and dessert types.

There no longer are any wineries among the Concord vineyards around Tontitown in the northwestern corner of Arkansas, but Italian residents of the community still celebrate their annual grape festival. It honors the memory of Father Pietro Bandini, who was sent from Italy in 1897 to investigate the condition of Italian immigrants in America. Finding a half-starved, malaria-ridden colony on Lake Chicot in the southeastern Arkansas cotton country, he bought a tract of several hundred acres in Washington County and moved the families there. He started them planting grapes as they had always done in Italy.

• 20 •

Texas has only one winery, though it once had more. On the palm-lined road between Del Rio, the county seat of Val Verde County, and the bridge across the Rio Grande to the Mexican city of Ciudad Acuña in Chihuahua, stands the two-story adobe brick Val Verde Winery of Louis Qualia, bordering his fourteen acres of vineyard.

Qualia's parents came from Milan in 1883, planted vines and fruit trees, irrigated them by building a canal from a spring nearby, and began making wine for sale. Louis, born there in 1897, built his present 7000-gallon winery in 1920, but immediately closed it because that was the year National Prohibition began. He reopened it in 1936, when Texas repealed its dry law, and has kept it going since as a matter of family pride. It is Del Rio's oldest industry.

He bottles three kinds of table wine under his Felipe del Rio brand, named for the spring that irrigates his vineyard. The dry and the sweet red are made of the native Lenoir grape, which is called Black Spanish in Texas. The sweet amber is mainly a blend of Herbemont and Lenoir. He sells all he can make, a few thousand gallons per year, to local residents and tourists who come to the winery. When one of his three sons undertook in 1967 to carry on the wine business, Qualia planted additional vines at another vineyard thirty miles south in the Quemado Valley.

Viticultural authorities have long praised Texas as a natural home of the grape because of its profuse growth of wild Mustang vines. At Denison in northern Texas, from 1880 to 1910, noted grape breeder Thomas Volney Munson developed many new native grapes for eating, not for wine, and most of his records have been lost. His son, Will, wrote in 1923 that all thirteen climatic districts of Texas can grow grapes commercially. Professors at the State Agricultural Experiment Station near Montague have done some grape research, but they are forbidden by a state law to do any work involving wine.

For several years such Texas farmers as Norman Willms of Los Fresnos in the lower Rio Grande Valley have conducted independent experiments, attempting to develop grape varieties that would support wineries in their areas. Willms, who raises cotton and grain sorghum, has crossed more than 300 different grapes with the red Mustang, but none of his crosses has done as well as Qualia's Lenoir variety. He has hopes, however, for some of the new grapes that have been developed in Florida. Meanwhile, Willms makes wine for his own use by adding water and sugar to the acidulous juice of the wild Mustang. He says people love his red Mustang wine.

• 21 •

In the other mid-continent states, except for the berry and cherry wines that are made commercially by the three small wineries in Wisconsin, winegrowing is only an avocation of true oenothusiasts. There are a few of them even in Minnesota, where the Agricultural Extension Service recommends that anyone planting grapevines should bury them in the fall to protect them from the freezing winters. One is Dr. Donald White, horticulturist of the state university, who makes wine out of the French hybrid grapes he grows at his home on White Bear Lake. Others are John F. Kistner, a research chemist, and John A. Heideman, a mathematician, who have planted hybrids on the Mississippi River between Stillwater and Red Wing.

11

Wines of Michigan

Although Michigan ranks fourth among the states in grape-growing and sixth in wine production, our connoisseur writers almost never write anything about Michigan wines. Yet I have tasted many Michigan wines and found them all clean and sound, and a few that I would rate as excellent. The fruit belt of Michigan is as capable, climatically speaking, of producing fine wines as most of the other viticultural districts east of the Rockies, including even the justly famous Finger Lakes region of New York. But until very recently, the Michigan wineries never tried.

Michigan's southwestern counties, behind the towering sand dunes of the Lake Michigan shore and extending east and north to Kalamazoo, are one of the great fruit-producing sections of the earth. The deep lake waters, which rarely freeze over, yield warmth for the vineyards and orchards in winter, and cool winds from the lake in spring usually retard the buds from opening until danger of killing frosts has passed.

This is grape, apple, blueberry, and peppermint country. Paw Paw, the seat of Van Buren County, is the vineyard center. At the end of September, when Paw Paw holds its week-long grape festival, you can sniff the fragrance of the grapes as you approach the town. In past years, tourists driving through on festival days were stopped at the main street intersection and handed baskets of freshly picked Concords. More than ten thousand acres in Van Buren, Berrien, Kalamazoo, and Allegan Counties are planted to grapes, mostly picked by the new mechanical harvester machines since 1968. All but a few hundred acres are Concords, because four fifths of Michigan's grape crop is used for juice and jelly or is sold fresh for table use. The other fifth goes into wine.

Six of the state's eight producing wineries are in the southwestern corner of the state. Some of them welcome visitors, and the trip from Lansing, Ann Arbor, Detroit, or from Chicago (which is nearer) is well worthwhile.

• 2 •

The wineries of Michigan are still young. There were no famous wineries with castlelike cellars in the state before Prohibition, such as those in Ohio, Missouri, and New York. But actually, the growing of fruit, including grapes, began in southern Michigan in the mid-nineteenth century. By 1880, when the national wine-growing census was taken, there were 2266 acres of vineyards in the state, and Michigan wine production in that year was 62,361 gallons valued at $75,617. At that time more wine was made in southeastern Michigan, along the Lake Erie shore, than on the Lake Michigan side. Philip Wagner, who grew up at Ann Arbor, recalls that before Prohibition there were many small wineries operated by German farmers in Monroe and Muskegon counties.

What started the massive vineyard plantings in southwestern Michigan was the grape juice boom. When the Welch Grape Juice Company, with its newly built plant at Westfield, New York, began about 1900 to buy Concords from neighboring states, the planting of Concords began in Van Buren and Berrien Counties.

The old Michigan wineries were closed by Wartime Prohibition

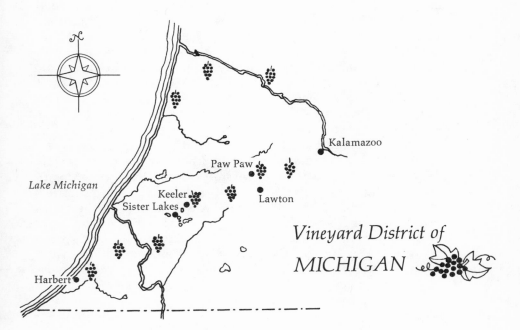

in 1919, but the Michigan grape boom continued, for in that year Welch established its own grape juice plant at Lawton, near Paw Paw. Then a huge demand developed throughout the nation for grapes for bootleg and homemade wine, an opportunity in which the Michigan vineyardists shared.

Still another outlet opened for Michigan grapes during the 1920s: four new wineries sprang up in the Canadian town of Windsor, across the river from Detroit. Much of their "exported" wine, consigned to distant countries, traveled only as far as the Michigan and Ohio shores.

Next came the Great Depression, and with it Repeal in 1933— and the market for grapes collapsed. The price of Michigan Concords fell to as low as ten dollars a ton. Fifteen wineries began operating in the Detroit area, including two that were moved, complete with crushers and casks, across the river from Canada. Soon there was a surplus of wine as well as of grapes, because Michigan wines, made of the foxy Concord, could not compete with those coming from other states and from abroad.

Michigan's grape-growing industry was in serious trouble. One of the Canadian vintners from Windsor, the late Major Maurice R. Twomey, proposed a remedy: reserve the Michigan wine market for Michigan wines. Twomey, who had established the La Salle winery at Farmington, designed the peculiar Michigan wine law, which levies a tax of 50 cents a gallon on table wines from outside the state but taxes Michigan wines only 4 cents, provided they are made at least 75 percent of Michigan-grown grapes for which the winery has paid the grower at least $100* a ton. The remaining 25 percent of the grapes is allowed to come from outside the state, and arrives principally in tank cars from California. Principal author of the law was William C. Geagley, the chief chemist of the Michigan Department of Agriculture, a man with rigid ideas of his own about wine. One of Geagley's ideas was that all wines over 16 percent in alcoholic content should be classified as hard liquor, and this was written into the Michigan law in 1937. Geagley thereby created in Michigan an entirely new class of wine previously unknown in America—16 percent "light" ports and "light" sherries. The sale of standard ports and sherries, which range from 17 to 20 percent, was restricted to the state-operated liquor stores, while the "light" versions were freely sold in Michigan food stores along with the 12 percent table and sparkling wines. Wineries in California, New York, and Ohio were thereby compelled to begin making these 16 percent dessert wine

*Originally $55 a ton in 1937.

types—which are sold nowhere else—in order to compete with the Michigan wineries.*

For two decades, prospering with their protective state tax, Michigan wineries made no attempt to compete with out-of-state premium wines. But when, after the Second World War, some of their customers discovered they preferred dry table wines to the peculiar local products, the Michigan producers saw their sales beginning to shrink. From the four-fifths share of the Michigan wine market they had enjoyed before the war, their share dropped by 1965 to less than a third. The Michigan vintners began paying new attention to the making of dry table wines and champagnes. Their trade association, the Michigan Wine Institute, started meetings between the winemakers and the scientists of Michigan State University, at which the wines were tasted and criticized. Some of the Michigan vintners then took a leaf from the successful experience of New York State wineries and began calling attention to their better wines by labeling them "Michigan" instead of merely "American."

• 3 •

How greatly some Michigan wines have improved was apparent when I visited the Bronte vineyard and winery at Keeler, twelve miles south of Paw Paw. I tasted there a dry red, proudly labeled "Sister Lakes District Premium Michigan Baco Noir," that was equal to most of the burgundies now made of this French hybrid grape in the East. It had enough of the powerful Baco aroma to give the wine character, and in addition it had developed, from aging in cask and bottle, the bouquet that distinguishes fine from ordinary red wines. Particularly good, too, with their slight fragrance of Labrusca, were the Bronte Rhine wine—a blend of Delaware, Elvira, and a Seibel hybrid with Sylvaner—and the company's bulk-process champagne.

The Bronte firm started in May 1933, six months before Repeal, in the old Columbia brewery building on Riopelle Street in Detroit. Its first product was 3.2 percent wine, which had just been legalized together with 3.2 percent beer. To make this curious potion, full-strength wine was diluted to 3.2 percent alcoholic content with water and a fluid extract of the South American beverage herb called *maté* which tastes somewhat like tea. "Bronte," the name of the extract, was chosen as the company's name.

The chief owner of Bronte is Dr. Theodore Wozniak, a retired Detroit dentist with a lifetime interest in wine. Not satisfied to

*But this also taught California vintners a valuable lesson; see the discussion of minimum alcoholic content standards on page 422.

continue making all kinds of wine out of Concord grapes, Wozniak in 1943 bought a farm and began planting wine varieties. On 200 acres in the Sister Lakes district near Keeler, there is now a fifty-acre block of Baco in addition to white Seibel varieties, Catawba, Delaware, Ives, Fredonia, Niagara, Ontario, Van Buren, and the Vineland (Canadian) hybrid called Veeport. The million-gallon Bronte winery was built beside the vineyard and was equipped with cooperage from the company's Detroit cellar and from one of Al Capone's breweries at Kankakee, Illinois. Wozniak recruited two expert winemakers. The first was Angelo Spinazze, a graduate of Italy's Conegliano viticultural school, who had been making wine for Major Twomey at Windsor. Later, John Dohrow, one of the pioneers of bulk-process champagne making in America, came to Keeler from the Mon Ami winery near Sandusky, Ohio. Bronte claims it was the first in Michigan to make champagne (in 1946) and the first in the world (in 1964) to bottle the sparkling wine called "Cold Duck." Bronte welcomes visitors to a tour of its winery on weekdays and invites them to sample wines in its new tasting room. Its wines can be purchased on the premises by the case.

Biggest vintner in the state is Michigan Wineries, Inc., with 2,500,000 gallons' capacity in its two wineries, one at Paw Paw and the other at Lawton. A farmer and banker, the late John Turner, founded the firm in 1938. His son-in-law, James K. Warner, and members of the Turner family own five hundred acres of vineyards and buy grapes from four hundred other growers. Besides its still wines, the company makes champagnes, still and carbonated grape juices, grape concentrate, fruit and berry wines, and grape essence, the methyl anthranilate ester extracted from Concord grapes, which is used to impart the pungent Labrusca flavor to grape drinks. Its Hungarian-born winemaker emeritus, John Treuhaft, believes that Michigan grapes can make as good wines as any in the East, and thinks his 1967 Delaware—the first Michigan wine to be labeled with a vintage date—is proof of this. Treuhaft's young successor, Nathan Stackhouse, who was trained at the University of California at Davis, goes farther. "Michigan's climate for winegrowing is better than California's," he says, "because California weather in some respects is too good for grapes."

Treuhaft, trained in Austria and Germany before he came to this country in 1936, was also for some years the winemaker for the nearby Frontenac winery. Frontenac welcomes visitors and has its own retail wine store. When I was there the manager was John Corsi, the former Detroit importer who started the Bronte winery with Dr. Wozniak. Corsi's favorite wine was a dry Concord which he called Vino da Pasto. The company was acquired in 1967 by the American Distilling Company of Pekin, Illinois, and its capacity has since been doubled to 500,000 gallons.

A third winery in Paw Paw is St. Julian, owned by Eugene and Robert Meconi. Their father, Mariano Meconi, arrived in Canada from Italy during the early 1900s. In 1921, he quit his job in a Canadian brewery to start the Meconi Wine Cellars in Windsor, Ontario. In 1934, after Repeal, he moved it with all its equipment to Detroit; then five years later established the present cellar in Paw Paw. It is named for the patron saint of his birthplace, the village of Falaria near Rome. The best St. Julian wines I tasted were the rosé and the champagne. Both were medium dry, with a barely perceptible Labrusca flavor.

At Harbert in southwestern Berrien County, near the shore of the lake, is William Lett Ruttledge's Molly Pitcher winery. Its surroundings and interior are unusually attractive, so much so that I found the local Episcopal Church holding its Sunday services, baptisms and christenings in Ruttledge's office, which was equipped with an electric organ. Ruttledge, a slender, white-haired food faddist, was born in County Galway, Ireland. He was a graduate in engineering when he came to America in 1908. When Prohibition was repealed, he was manufacturing pumps in Detroit. At the advice of his uncle, a Dublin wine and tea merchant, he quit the pump business and started a winery. At first he made only port wine, because port was the favorite wine in Ireland. But nobody in Michigan seemed to want his port, so he now makes twenty-seven different wines. Ruttledge is the only vintner I know who praises the Concord as a grape for winemaking. "When I first tasted Concords, I couldn't stand their flavor," he says, "but then I became accustomed to it, and I realized that once you develop a taste for Concord, any other wine seems insipid. Moreover, the fact that Concord is one grape that California cannot grow makes it the right grape for Michigan."

• 4 •

In July 1972, the first new winery to start in Michigan in a quarter of a century opened for business near Baroda in Berrien County. It is the little (15,000-gallon) Tabor Hill Vineyard Wine Cellar, a young family's premium-wine operation that produces estate-bottled, vintage-dated French hybrid and Vinifera table wines and has begun also making champagne.

Two couples, the Leonard Olsons and the Carl Banholzers, were home winemakers in Chicago in the early 1960s when they read about Dr. Konstantin Frank's success in growing Vinifera wine grapes in the New York Finger Lakes region. They wondered whether such grapes could also be grown in the Midwest. They studied climatic records, traveled the lake region looking for possible vineyard sites, and watched the Ramey & Allen Vineyard develop west of Chicago. When they found a farm for sale on the south slope of the hill called Mount Tabor, six miles from Lake Michigan, they decided it should be better for winegrowing than either the Finger Lakes or Illinois. The land was purchased in 1965 and the planting of vines begun two years later. They crushed their first grapes with their feet while their winery was being built.

Tabor Hill Vineyard covered fifteen acres, including new plantings, when its first wines went on sale. Labeled "Berrien County Michigan" were the 1971 Seyval Blanc, Cuvée Blanc, Baco Noir, Cuvée Rouge, a Vidal hybrid wine called Trebbiano, and several cases of Johannisberg Riesling and Chardonnay. The champagne wasn't yet bottled, but was promised for the 1972 Christmas season. If the quality of the 1969 vintage Chardonnay and champagne I tasted are any indication, the 1971s should be premium wines.

Olson has bought out the Banholzers, has quit his job as a steel salesman, and has moved to Tabor Hill with his family. He expects, by making the rustic château a showplace and offering daily tasting and cellar tours, to sell most of his wines at retail to connoisseurs. Tabor Hill Road is easily reached from nearby midwestern cities, and Chicago is only an hour's freeway drive away.

• 5 •

Michigan's chief contribution to the wine world is Cold Duck, the bubbly pink wine that exploded from Detroit during the 1960s to revolutionize festive drinking halfway around the world. Its story is as bizarre as its name.

In Germany early in this century—authorities disagree on just when—partygoers who saved the contents of open wine bottles by pouring them together after a celebration, called the mixtures *kalte ende*(cold end), a German phrase for leftovers. Because *ende* sounds like *Ente* (duck in German), the term for leftover wine became *kalte Ente;* it was a German pun. Kalte Ente became the name of a popular drink in Germany. It is usually made there of white wine and *schaumwein* (champagne), flavored with a spiral of lemon rind and sugar, and is served either in a punch bowl or by the glass.

Back in the 1930s, Detroit restaurateur Harold Borgman, on a wine-buying trip in Germany, tasted Kalte Ente, and on returning home introduced it as a bar drink in his restaurant, the Pontchartrain Wine Cellars. He made it by mixing a New York State champagne and a California sparkling burgundy. It was Borgman who translated the name into English—the duck you don't eat, but drink. It became locally famous.

Two Detroit vintners, both Pontchartrain patrons, claim to have originated the idea of putting Cold Duck into bottles. Bob Wozniak, whose father heads the Bronte winery, says he first thought of it in 1963. But, at the same time, Detroit importer William O'Connor gave the Mandia winery of Clintondale, New York, an order to make and bottle the mixture for him.

The name and taste of the concoction tickled the celebration bone of Americans. Within months, vintners in other states followed with their own versions, inevitably with duck wings on the labels. The Internal Revenue Service officially recognized the product as a blend of champagne and sparkling burgundy, requiring that the label specify bulk process if the champagne is made that way.

Because the first Cold Ducks were made of eastern Labrusca grapes, the big California wineries found it necessary to import vast quantities of Concord juice from the State of Washington to make their versions taste the same. Other California producers found their Cold Ducks sold as well or better without Labrusca grapes, so long as the wines were made new, fresh, foamy, and sweet.

Cold Duck had only begun to fly. In 1970 its production spread to Canada, then to faraway Australia, and finally reached Europe. French vintners began shipping French Cold Duck to this country, followed by Cold Ducks from Italy and from Germany. The bubbly pink drink was also introduced in France, its name translated there to *Canard Froid Froid.* In America, the brewing industry responded with a Malt Duck, while vintners created a Cold Hawk, a Blueberry Duck, a Strawberry Duck, and a carbonated mixture of white wine and cranberry juice called Cold Turkey.

Now I hear that bottled Cold Duck may not have originated in Michigan after all, that German vintners have been selling white Kalte Ente in bottles since before the Korean war, and that they have a red version called Turkenblut. There is also a story that attributes the original *kalte Ente* pun to the famous German diplomat, Franz von Papen, at a dinner given by Kaiser Wilhelm II.

But perhaps this is merely history, for vintners now report that Cold Duck sales in the United States have slumped ominously since the celebration of the New Year in 1972. One of my champagne producer friends, who never got around to producing a Cold Duck of his own, is gleefully predicting it may even become a dead duck erelong.

12

California—Paradise for the Vine

MUCH OF what has been written since Repeal about California wines stresses the industry's colorful history, such as the fact that the Spanish mission fathers brought wine grapes here from Mexico two centuries ago, as though that were the reason this state has nine tenths of this country's vineyard acres and produces four fifths of American wine.

The real reason, seldom mentioned and therefore not understood, was best expressed almost a century ago by Professor George Husmann, explaining why he abandoned his post as professor of horticulture at the University of Missouri to become a winegrower in California:

A visit to this shore, in the summer of 1881, convinced me that this was the true home of the grape, and that California . . . was destined to be the vine land of the world . . . We have the finest climate in the world and can always make a good product even in the most unfavorable seasons. We can raise grapes and make wine cheaper than any other nation or climate. We have the world for a market. We can satisfy every taste.

Husmann, of course, did not dwell on the spring frost disasters that strike California vineyard districts at least once in each decade, nor on the constant hazards of vine diseases, pests, or sunburn, which keep vineyardists from enjoying a carefree life in California or anywhere else.

Yet it is true that it is easier to raise Vinifera grapes in the fabulous climates of California than in any other part of the globe. The Old World grape varieties will grow and ripen anywhere there is water and good soil in the Golden State, except at frigid mountain elevations and on the foggiest portions of the northern seacoast. California's long, warm, normally rainless growing seasons, its mild winters, and its low humidity which discourages

Vineyard Districts
of CALIFORNIA

most vine pests, make it a paradise for the Vinifera vine. Only one percent of the earth's surface has weather that resembles—but for growing Vinifera grapes scarcely equals—that of the great viticultural districts of California. Yet few of the state's present generation of winegrowers realize how fortunate they are, or how great their wines can be. Few of them are aware that their climates are the secret envy of the winegrowers of Europe.

California has not only one, but so wide an assortment of such climates, that within its borders there are produced, year after year, wines of all the traditional types grown in the leading wine countries of the world—and with no need to add cane sugar to the juice of the grape, the practice that is common elsewhere in North America and in the famous winelands of Europe.

The ranges of these climates, which are evident when you glance at the state map, help to explain the wide differences you find in the qualities and prices of California wines. The light-yielding, delicate, costly grape varieties which make the finest table wines (such as the Rieslings, the Pinots, and Cabernet Sauvignon) develop their highest flavors when grown in the valleys near the coast, where the sunny days are cooled by ocean breezes and fogs. The University of California classes these premium table wine districts, in the order of the coolness of their climates, as Regions I, II, and III.* The northern San Joaquin Valley, farther inland, is much warmer in summer and is classed as Region IV; vineyards there yield more tons to the acre. This district produces many excellent wine grapes and includes Lodi, where the famous Flame Tokay table grape grows. In the still hotter central and southern San Joaquin Valley—Region V— the vineyards are chiefly of table and raisin varieties, especially the Thompson Seedless. They yield tremendous crops, which are used for wine and brandy as well as for sale as fresh and dried fruit. In the past, most of the wines made in Region V were the sweet dessert types, but

---

*In 1938, Professors Albert Winkler and Maynard Amerine classified the climates of California vineyard districts into five regions by their average daily temperatures during the growing season (April through October) and compared them to the wine districts of Europe. They measured "degree-days," the number of days when temperatures exceed 50° F. For example, when the temperature for a day averaged 70°, it was expressed as "20 degree-days." Region I means 2500 degree-days or less and includes Geisenheim (1709) and Trier (1730) in Germany, Beaune (2400) in the French Burgundy region, and Sonoma (2360) and Oakville (2300) in the coolest parts of the Sonoma and Napa Valleys. Region II means 2500 to 3000 degree-days and includes Bordeaux (2519), the Italian Piedmont region (2980), and most parts of the Napa and Sonoma Valleys. Region III means 3000 to 3500 degree-days and includes the Livermore Valley in California and Tuscany in Italy. Region IV, 3500 to 4000 degree-days, covers central Spain, areas from Lodi to Ceres in the northern part of the San Joaquin Valley, Davis in Yolo County, and Cucamonga in Southern California. Over 4000 degree-days is Region V and includes the central and southern San Joaquin Valley and the Sacramento Valley.

the production of table wines is fast increasing there now; vast acreages in the hot valley have lately been planted with grapes for table wines. The Cucamonga district, east of Los Angeles, has a Region IV climate and produces mainly inexpensive wine grapes for all types of wine. Finally, there is the Coachella Valley near Salton Sea in the southeastern corner of the State, where, in almost furnacelike heat, great irrigated vineyards supply ripe grapes for fresh table use as early as May and June to bring high prices in the eastern markets for fresh fruit.

In sunny California, grapes develop higher sugar content than in the sun-starved northern wine districts of Europe, but their acidity (tartness) is usually not as high. This is why, in "blind" tastings—the popular social game in which you try to distinguish one wine from another by smell and taste—the easiest way to tell California wines and champagnes from those of Europe is to mark those with higher acidity as European; the California samples are likely to be softer, less tart.

Even the cooler California districts may be too warm and sunny for some of the noble Old World wine-grape varieties, in particular Germany's White (Johannisberg) Riesling and Burgundy's Pinot Noir. Though the Riesling and Pinot Noir ripen early with high sugar contents and make consistently fine wines in California, their wines have not yet achieved the greatness they attain in their cloudy Old World homelands, where these grapes barely ripen by the end of the season. Perhaps California's climate is too ideal. Wines, like people, seem to be more interesting, to have greater depth and complexity of character, if they have to struggle to reach maturity.

Another characteristic of California weather—low humidity—normally prevents the growth of the "noble mold" (*Botrytis cinerea*) that grows on ripe grapes in Europe and gives unique flavors to French sauternes and to Germany's rare Trockenbeerenauslese wines.

These few differences between the finest European and California table wines are easy to recognize in "blind" sampling. But if the wines you are tasting are red Bordeaux or white burgundy types, and the California and French samples are both made of the same grape varieties, grown in the best climates (and have been stored in the same kind of oak barrels), they will be more difficult to tell apart. For the grapes that make these latter two wine types develop ideal acidity in balance with their sugar content in the California coastal districts and make some of the finest wines in the world.

Still another difference between California and European table wines—which you cannot detect by taste—is in alcoholic strength, which is also the result of climate. Because it is the grape sugar that fermentation turns into alcohol, California table wines are usually one to three points higher than their European counterparts in percentage of alcohol by volume. The Riesling in Germany, for example, seldom makes wines of more than 9 or 10 percent; in California its wines usually reach twelve. Perhaps grape-growing locations will yet be found in California with climates in which this grape can develop the zestful yet delicate flavor it attains in the vineyards of the Moselle and Rheingau.

What European growers envy most about California weather is that the grapes ripen sufficiently every year to make sound wine without chaptalization—the addition of cane sugar to their juice (see Chapter 26). This is why it is often said (and as often challenged) that "every year is a vintage year in California." Of course, the truth of this statement depends on what is meant by "a vintage year."

In the European fine-wine districts, which are subject to cold and rainy weather during their growing-seasons, the grapes ripen fully in the occasional years when they receive sufficient sunshine; in their normal years it is necessary to add sugar to the musts. The purpose of vintage labels on European wines therefore is to enable buyers to choose the wines of the "vintage" (good) years— to avoid buying the mediocre or the bad. In sunny California no such purpose is served by vintage labels. Here, about once in a decade, abnormally early autumn rains result in lower-than-normal grape sugars; but even then, the sugar levels are sufficient to make sound wines. The three worst-weather autumn seasons in California vintners' recent memory, 1948, 1957, and 1972, would have been considered "vintage years" in Europe, for in each of those seasons lovely natural wines were made.

Of course, the wines from individual California vineyards vary in flavor and quality from year to year as the weather and the grapes inevitably vary. But here again, the point is that sound wines are produced every year from the juice of the grape alone. In the European sense, the claim that "every year is a vintage year in California" is therefore literally true.

• 2 •

Some of the highlights of California's wine history were reviewed in Chapter 2, and the colorful stories of individual California districts and vintners are contained in the regional chapters that follow. But the overall story of California wines before, during, and since Prohibition has not yet been clearly told.

While wines were made first at the Franciscan missions, the

chain of church settlements established from San Diego to Sonoma between 1769 and 1823, the wines the padres made could not have been very good. The inferior Vinifera grape they introduced—the Mission variety—impeded the development of fine wine in California for almost a century.* Most writers dwell at length on how this grape was grown by the Jesuits in Baja California and was brought north by the great Franciscan friar, Junípero Serra. Yet the Mission grape, also called the Criolla, had been grown throughout the two preceding centuries in mainland Mexico.

The well-annotated histories of early California wines by Herbert B. Leggett, Irving McKee, and Vincent Carosso tell the fantastic story of Agoston Haraszthy, the Hungarian "count" or "colonel" (he was neither), and credit him with introducing the better Vinifera varieties from Europe to California between 1851 and 1862. But Haraszthy was not the first to do this, nor was he the first to introduce the Zinfandel grape to America. As a later chapter on "varietal grapes" will show, the Zinfandel was already here when Haraszthy left Hungary for the United States.

Because the Prohibitionists labored for years in California, as elsewhere, to erase the history of wine in America, its role in building the economy of the Golden State—more important than the mining of gold—is seldom if ever mentioned in the school books. Grapes, mostly used by wineries, are California's most important fruit crop. Many people who now bear the names of great pioneer California families—in agriculture, government, banking, publishing, education, and industry—may not know that their forebears were prominent winegrowers, who contributed to the character of the state's wines of today.

Vineyards were flourishing and wine was being made at nearly all of the twenty-one Spanish missions by the second decade of the nineteenth century. The chief exception was Mission Dolores at foggy, chilly San Francisco, where the padres used grapes they obtained from Missions Santa Clara and San José.

When commercial viniculture began at Los Angeles in the 1830s, at the time the Mexican government secularized the missions and caused most of them to be abandoned, there were 100,000 vines on the site of the present City of the Angels. An early writer, Alexander Forbes, was already telling America and Europe that California offered "a wide and promising field for the cultivation of the grape in all varieties."

---

*Although it is of the Vinifera species, no counterpart of the Mission grape has ever been found in Europe. Ampelographers say it probably grew from a seed brought from Spain to Mexico in the time of the *conquistadores*.

The first commercial winegrower of note in California, Jean Louis Vignes (appropriately named; *vigne* is French for vine), was so successful at his El Aliso Vineyard in Los Angeles that in 1834 he sent to France for eight of his relatives to join him, for he believed that this land was destined to rival "la belle France" in both the quantity and quality of its wines, including champagnes. It was Vignes, not Haraszthy, who was the first to bring European wine-grape cuttings to California, having them sent in the early 1830s to Boston and then brought around Cape Horn to Los Angeles.

How swiftly winegrowing spread through the state is evident from the fact that, before the discovery of gold on the American River in 1848, there already were vineyards as far north as Santa Clara, Alameda, Contra Costa, Sacramento, Yolo, Sonoma, and Napa Counties. The Gold Rush brought the first wine boom in the 1850s; many of the newcomers found winemaking a surer road to riches than the trail to the mines. When the California Legislature in 1859 exempted new vineyards from taxation, grape-planting fever reached epidemic proportions. By 1863 there were twelve million vines in the state, most of them planted in the preceding half-dozen years.

Glowing descriptions of California's marvelous winegrowing climate were published abroad before the Civil War. The French viticultural journal, *Revue Viticole,* reported in a series of articles between 1859 and 1862 what French viticultural experts found in a survey of the state: that California has a climate that makes it capable someday of "becoming a serious competitor" to France in the production of fine wine. This may help to explain why France, to this day, still refuses to admit any regular commercial shipments of California wine, although it imports wine in vast quantities from almost everywhere else. (Praise California wine to a proud Frenchman and see him scowl!)

• 3 •

Leggett brings out another characteristic of the California industry: its periodic wine-price declines, its recurring cycles of boom and bust. The first bust was recorded in 1858 and 1859 at Los Angeles, where wine was so plentiful and some of it so poorly made that the value of vineyard land suddenly dropped by half, and wine was difficult to sell at fifty cents a gallon. "But the bubble wasn't broken," Leggett comments, "it had merely shrunk temporarily."

Much of the early-day California wine was obviously bad, and a great deal of it was sold under counterfeit European labels. However, the wine that Vignes and his nephews made was good enough by 1860 to be sold under their own name in New York; and a San Francisco firm of vintners, Kohler & Frohling, was regularly shipping its bulk wines to England, Germany, Russia, Japan, China, and South America as early as 1856. Some improvement in the quality of California wines was evidenced during the 1860s and 70s. This is generally credited to the spectacular "Count" Haraszthy, to his expedition to Europe in 1861 for vine cuttings, and to his voluminous writings about viniculture. Later chapters will show, however, that there were many other viniculturists, principally from Europe and more experienced than the "Count," who imported their own foreign vines and who were making good wines from superior grapes before he made any from his.

The second wine-market bust came in 1876. Although the world economic depression of the 1870s had begun three years earlier, grape-planting in California had continued without a letup, from 30 million vines in 1873 to 43 million by 1876. When the break came, grape prices plunged to two dollars a ton, wine to 10 cents a gallon, and brandy to 37 cents. Barnyard animals were turned into the vineyards to dispose of the grapes. Many vineyardists uprooted their vines and planted fruit trees instead. But those winegrowers who survived the crash planted better grape varieties and improved the quality of their wines. With the help of late spring frosts in 1879, which reduced that year's grape crop by a third, the industry prospered again by 1880.

During the early 1880s, the devastation of European vineyards by the phylloxera vine louse was at its height, and the resulting shortage of French wines helped the California growers to sell theirs at a profit. What they did not know—and had failed to realize even when the destructive vine pest was positively identified on vines at Sonoma in 1873—was that the plague was killing their own vineyards at the same time.

· 4 ·

It was the phylloxera—when it spread statewide and threatened to destroy the entire California industry—that influenced the legislature, by the act of 1880, to establish a State Board of Viticultural Commissioners, and also a department for viticultural research and instruction in the University of California. Although there was bitter rivalry between the Commissioners and the University, which led to the abolition of the Viticultural Commission in 1894,* the spread of phylloxera was finally checked. It was

---

*A Board of Viticultural Commissioners was established again by the legislature in 1913, and it continued until Prohibition.

controlled by the same means as in France—by grafting the Old World vines onto phylloxera-resistant native American roots. The roots which saved the California vineyards came principally from Missouri, but were actually imported from France. Californians first tried to use the roots of the local wild vine, Vitis californica, then learned the French were having success with the midwestern roots and began ordering theirs from France.

Two men are credited with eventually stopping the havoc wrought by phylloxera in the state. One was Professor Husmann, the erstwhile Missourian. The other was Eugene Waldemar Hilgard, professor and later dean of agriculture at the University of California. Born at Belleville, Illinois, where his German-born father grew grapes, Hilgard experimented with viticulture in Mississippi and Michigan before coming to California in 1875. Working first on the phylloxera problem, he planted a vineyard on the Berkeley campus, where the Life Sciences Building now stands, and a wine cellar near old South Hall. (The University vineyard was bitterly protested by the Livermore winegrowers, who feared the wind might carry the phylloxera pest over the Berkeley hills to them.)

Hilgard made important contributions to wine improvement in the state. At a time when some of the small vintners were still having their grapes trodden by Chinese coolies and Indians, he called for the building of large, modern wineries that could be operated scientifically. He advocated the slow fermentation of wines at controlled low temperatures. He was the first to point out the sole defect in California's climate, that when grapes are left on the vines until their sugar content is at its peak, their acidity drops too low—thus challenging the European idea, in which the California growers believed, that every additional day of sunshine is so much gain to the quality of wine. He urged that the grapes be harvested early, when their acid is in balance with their sugar, because "what is true in the cloudy climate of Europe is not necessarily true in California." He also opposed over-cropping (letting vines bear too heavy crops), which lowers the quality of the grapes and wines. These are lessons that many California growers have only now begun to learn.

Abhorring drunkenness, and himself a user of light red wines with his meals, Hilgard also advocated that the alcoholic content of California table wines should be kept low. In this he was opposed by Charles Wetmore of the Cresta Blanca Vineyard, the executive officer of the Viticultural Commission, who favored fermenting them to 15 percent strength. Hilgard's assistant and successor, Professor Frederic T. Bioletti, was the first to divide California into viticultural districts by their climates—the coastal counties for table wines and the interior valleys for dessert types.

• 5 •

The prosperity of the winegrowers lasted until 1886, when a bumper grape crop, the result of still more plantings, brought on the third California wine bust. This time bulk-wine prices sank to 6 and 8 cents a gallon. In 1889, Publisher William Randolph Hearst, whose father, Senator George Hearst, owned a vineyard in Sonoma County, published in his San Francisco *Examiner* a call for "all patriotic citizens to do all in their power to assist in placing the business of winemaking, which is of such vast importance to the state, on the best and firmest basis."

Most of the published replies to Hearst urged the planting of fewer grapes, the drying of more raisins, and the distilling of more brandy—remedies for overproduction that were still being attempted seven decades later. But Professor Hilgard's reply to Hearst was that the best remedy would be expert winemaking and longer aging to improve the quality of the wines.

Quality did improve. Although the bulk wines that went begging may not have been very good, there were in California, by 1890, at least a hundred great winegrowing estates owned by some of the wealthiest families of the state, who produced fine wines for pride rather than for profit alone, and who won medals for them in international competitions. Glimpses of the glamour and wealth of these nineteenth-century winegrowers can be had in Frona Eunice Wait's *Wines and Vines of California*, published at San Francisco in 1889, with its descriptions of such opulent estates as Captain Gustav Niebaum's Inglenook Vineyard at Rutherford, "Lucky" Baldwin's Santa Anita Ranch, Senator Hearst's Madrone Vineyard near Agua Caliente, Tiburcio Parrott's "Miravalle" in the Napa Valley, and the Warm Springs Vineyard of Josiah Stanford, brother of the governor and senator, who had his own great vineyard at Vina in the Sacramento Valley.

It is not generally realized that many of these pre-Prohibition wines were great. During the 1920s and 30s, I tasted numerous California wines of the 1914, 1915, and 1916 vintages. The long-lived Cabernets and Zinfandels, in particular, and also some of the dessert wines, were superb. I have a few of these venerable bottles in my cellar, given to me by heirs to the collections of departed connoisseurs, and I find an occasional one still good after half a century.

• 6 •

The third depression in the California wine industry lasted

from 1886 to the mid-90s. In 1892, when Zinfandel grapes were selling at San Francisco for ten dollars a ton and Missions, if they could find buyers, at half that price, a brilliant British accountant named Percy T. Morgan had arrived in that city with two dollars in his pocket. He registered at the Palace Hotel and soon enlisted some prosperous clients, including the old vintner firm of S. Lachman & Company. Within two years, the persuasive Morgan convinced his client and six other big wine firms to form the California Wine Association. The CWA grew to giant size, operating as many as sixty-four California wineries. Another such group, the Winemakers Corporation, was formed at about the same time. The CWA and the Corporation stabilized prices by bringing grape and bulk-wine supplies under their control. Meanwhile, the grape crop was being reduced by the continuing ravages of phylloxera, and still further by the severe spring frost of 1896, which helped to bring the third wine bust to an end.

The San Francisco earthquake and fire of 1906 destroyed 15 million gallons of the CWA's inventory and gutted all but one of its several cellars in the city. Morgan then built, on the shore of San Francisco Bay near Richmond, what was at that time the largest winery in the world, which he named Winehaven. From Winehaven, with its own pier for ocean vessels, the CWA shipped California wines, in bottles under its "Calwa" label and in barrels under its "Big Tree" brand, to most countries of the world.

By 1911 an oversupply of grapes broke the wine market for the fourth time, and Morgan retired to his mansion in the Los Altos Hills. Most of Winehaven's vast wine stores eventually were shipped to Britain and Germany, which could not pay for them during the Great Depression; also, an entire cargo was lost in a North Sea shipwreck. Winehaven was not finally emptied of its wine until 1937. The huge, fortresslike red brick structure and its small city of workmen's homes still stand as a monument to Percy Morgan; they are now part of a naval fuel depot.

• 7 •

The tragic developments in California at the start of Prohibition were briefly reviewed in Chapter 2: the initial uprooting of vineyards, the short-lived boom in "juice grapes," the unfortunate grafting-over from delicate fine-wine grapes to coarse varieties that shipped well, and the grape market bust in 1925 when too many grapes were shipped east. In 1927, halfway through the Prohibition period, California vineyards covered 635,000 acres, an all-time high and much of it surplus, a third more acres than today.* The California Vineyardists Association, formed the year before, employed a "czar" for the industry, who promised to find new uses for the grape surplus. Herbert Hoover, then Secretary of Commerce, had picked a railroad expert, Donald D. Conn, for the job. Conn's ideas for new products, such as grape candy, grape salad, grape pie, and raisinade, failed to sell any fruit. And fresh California grape juice, made from the bland-tasting Vinifera varieties, could not compete with the more flavorful Concord juice from other states.

A law proposed at that time to prohibit further planting of vines was ruled unconstitutional. Farmers then were offered five dollars per acre to uproot their vines, but only a few of them did. This was when Captain Paul Garrett formed Fruit Industries, with Donald Conn as its head, to salvage the grape surplus by selling it as concentrate for home winemaking—only to have its "Vine-Glo" advertisements suppressed by the Hoover Administration in 1931 under pressure from the Drys. In 1930, the Federal Farm Board and California banks lent nearly 25 million dollars to convert surplus grapes into raisins and grape concentrate, and to limit shipments of fresh grapes to eastern markets. Almost half a million tons were thus diverted from the marketing channels in that year. This staved off bankruptcy for the grape growers, and the short crop of 1931 kept them in business until the wineries, anticipating Repeal, bought and crushed extra quantities of grapes in 1932 and 1933.

The California vintners flooded the nation with wine at Repeal in December of 1933, then found they had far too much left. Almost overnight, more than seven hundred wineries had been bonded in the state, many of them by bootleggers to whom the Government granted amnesty, conditioned on their payment of Federal taxes on their stocks. Much of their wine had soured and was later condemned by the State Department of Public Health. The California industry remained in a depressed condition as severe as that during the latter Prohibition years.

At the end of the dry era, wine in California was sold principally in bulk, as was still the custom in the European wine countries at that time. The bulk wines were sold in "barrel houses." The typical "barrel house" was a liquor store with a rack holding from six to a dozen barrels with spigots, from which buyers who weren't too fastidious about vinegar and flies could

---

*Vineyards in the 1920s produced fewer tons per acre than now. Yields have increased enormously in recent years. The 1927 crop from 635,000 acres totaled 2.2 million tons, compared to almost 4 million tons produced from only 486,000 acres in 1965.

fill their own gallon jugs or demijohns for a few dimes per gallon. Chain food stores refused to stock any wines at all until the "barrel houses" were outlawed several years later.

Most California wines were shipped in tank cars to bottlers in other states, and, when inexpertly handled before bottling, were of poor quality when sold. The nation's connoisseurs failed to appreciate the few—bottled in California by the handful of premium-quality producers who had survived Prohibition—that were fine.

• 8 •

During the first five post-Repeal years, overly bountiful sunshine presented the California vineyardists with three bumper grape crops and two of moderate size, far more than the struggling wineries, the raisin packers, and the fresh-grape shippers could absorb. Each spring the growers prayed that frost might come to reduce the yield (naturally, of their neighbors' vineyards, not their own), but their prayers were in vain. The curse of Prohibition was replaced by the curse of plenty, which was more to be feared than frost.

In the fifth Repeal year, the situation was so desperate, with a record grape crop of 2,531,000 tons, half of it surplus, that an "artificial frost"—the Grape Prorate of 1938—was voted under a California farm law. That emergency measure required every vineyardist to convert 45 percent of his harvested grape crop into brandy and to hold it off the market for at least two years.

The grape growers in the coast counties bitterly opposed the Prorate. They maintained that the surplus existed in the hot San Joaquin Valley, not in the cool districts near the coast. Their leaders in the Wine Institute backed an opposite kind of plan, the Wine Advisory Board consumer-education program.* Voted in the same year as the Prorate, the wine-education program was unpopular with some of the larger wineries, several of whom fought for several years in the courts to avoid paying the assessment that supports the Board. They could not believe that wine would ever become popular in the whiskey, beer, and cola drink-

---

*The Wine Institute was incorporated in 1934 as the successor to the Grape Growers League (1932) and the Wine Producers Association (1933). The Marketing Order for Wine, assented to by two thirds of the California wineries in 1938, created the Wine Advisory Board as an instrumentality of the State Department of Agriculture. The Marketing Order, renewable every three years, levies assessments—of 1 cent and 1½ cents on each gallon of California table and dessert wines shipped to market—which support the Board's program. The Board contracts with the Wine Institute to perform most of the educational and market-expansion work.

ing United States. Renewals of the Board program were almost defeated twice, but each time the old table-wine producers, who believed that Americans someday would learn to drink table wine with meals, produced enough votes to keep it alive.

The 1938 Prorate was a success as an emergency surplus-control measure. Half a million tons of that season's grapes were converted into brandy under the Prorate—and this later turned out to have been fortunate in another way, as we shall see. But the coast counties winegrowers meanwhile pushed a bill through the legislature specifying that no such program could ever apply to their grapes again.

The year following the Prorate brought still another disastrously heavy crop. The resulting 1939 wine glut forced twenty large San Joaquin Valley wineries into a conglomerate called "Central California Wineries Inc." Intended to keep surplus bulk wine off the market and thereby to bolster grape and wine prices, the CCW merger nearly got the wine industry and cooperating bankers indicted under the Federal antitrust laws. The refusal by the grand jury at San Francisco to vote that indictment was one of the few defeats in the legal career of a certain bright young lawyer in the antitrust division. He was Joseph Alioto, who three decades later became the mayor of the city.

Then came the Second World War, which suddenly cut off the supplies of European wines and diverted raisin grapes for food. This temporarily ended the surplus. The war years were a period of wine shortages, high prices, and frenzied prosperity for the growers and vintners. But when the conflict ended, the grape surplus was back to haunt them—and the wine market crashed in 1947.

Artificial frosts in new forms were tried again. A state marketing order for wine processors kept some of the surplus wine off the market between 1949 and 1952 by limiting the quantity which each winery was allowed to sell in bulk during specified periods. At the same time, a "marketing order for grape stabilization" was adopted to raise millions for the purchase and diversion of surplus grapes from normal marketing channels. Nature, however, obliged with natural frosts that reduced the 1949 and 1950 crops, and the stabilization funds were given back to the wineries. Again, in 1961, a new artificial frost was voted, this time under Federal auspices. It diverted almost 40 million gallons of surplus Central Valley dessert wine into industrial alcohol, and functioned for two years, but was defeated by another grower vote in 1963. Attempts during the next several years to hatch new surplus-control plans met with failure.

· 9 ·

Of what did the surplus consist? Not of wine grapes; California has been short of wine grapes since before Prohibition. It consisted of the heavy crops of raisin- and table-grape varieties grown in the hot San Joaquin Valley—grapes which could also be used to make low-priced dessert wines and brandy. The chief raisin variety, the Thompson Seedless, was widely planted by the valley vineyardists after Repeal because it had three outlets. It could be sold in July as a fresh table grape, or laid on trays between the vine rows in August to be sun-dried as a raisin, or if market prices for table grapes and raisins proved unattractive during the summer, the Thompson crop could be left on the vines until October and sold to the wineries. Table grapes such as the Flame Tokay, Malaga, and Emperor were widely planted, too, because they had two outlets: whatever part of their crops the growers could not sell to be eaten fresh did not need to go to waste; the leftover grapes were delivered to the wineries for crushing.

Thus the valley wineries became victims of the viticultural calendar, serving as the salvage receptacle for the leftover three-way Thompsons and two-way table grapes. Some grower-owned wineries in the valley existed solely to salvage the table-grape culls. Better grapes, needed to make better wines, remained scarce. Growers in the valley saw no reason to plant wine-grape varieties, which have only one use—to make wine.

The planting of three-way Thompsons and two-way table grapes, easy to grow and dispose of, doubled in the San Joaquin Valley after the Second World War. By the mid-1960s the acreage of Thompson vines in the valley amounted to almost half of the grape acreage in the state, and the valley's table grape acreage represented almost a sixth. California's annual grape harvest was averaging more than three million tons, and less than a fifth of it consisted of wine grapes. The valley's wine industry was dominated by leaders of the raisin and table grape industries, some of whom owned wineries but who seldom drank any wine themselves; they regarded it as a drink for skid row. It was they who dictated the artificial frost programs, which treated wine as a by-product of grapes. They argued that grape growing is a single industry of three segments—fresh, dried, and crushed—and that the wineries, coming last, must salvage the vast surplus tonnage in order to prevent waste. This made economic sense of a sort, and economists, bankers, and government agencies readily agreed. The fact they ignored was that the salvage outlet was using half of the valley's grape crop.

To make matters worse, the per capita consumption of fresh grapes by Americans had declined by half since the war, and of raisins by a sixth. People also drank less of the low-priced dessert wines, the chief types theretofore made in the valley, thus adding to the huge surplus of grapes, worsening the depressed state of the valley's viticultural industry.

· 10 ·

Prosperity had come to the coast-counties vineyards by the mid-60s because Americans since the war had been learning to drink table wines, especially those with the varietal names of coast-counties grapes. Soon there was a shortage of such premium wine grapes as the Rieslings, the Pinots, and Cabernet.

At the same time, urban sprawl was gobbling up old vineyards in the districts close to San Francisco Bay. The California climate that favors vines also attracts people, and the best vineyard land is also the best for housing tracts, the worst destroyers of vines. The state's population had jumped from 6 million at Repeal in 1933 to 15 million by 1960 and rose to 20 million in 1970, a rate of growth that could mean 38 million or even 40 million by the year 2000. To save the coast-counties vineyards, a state law in the 1960s provided for the creation of agricultural preserves—known as "green belts"—in which land is taxed on its value for farming, not at the higher rates charged for homes. The agricultural-preserve law came too late to save some of the vineyards. Fortunately, however, a few of the coast vintners found new climatically favored lands in sparsely settled areas outside the path of population growth and moved their vineyards there—a dramatic development described in the chapters on those areas.

· 11 ·

But also since the Second World War, California vintners, including those in the San Joaquin Valley, had gotten around to doing some of the things that Professor Hilgard had advised seven decades earlier. They were modernizing their wineries, outfitting them with refrigeration and new equipment of the latest scientific designs. The new generation of enologists, taught in the University of California's wine school at Davis and at the new Department of Viticulture and Enology at Fresno State University, brought scientific new cellar treatments to the ancient art of making wine.

In addition to dessert wines—their chief product—the valley wineries had always produced some dry and semisweet table wines, but those had averaged poor in quality and had been used primarily for blending with coast-counties wines. Gradually, the valley table wines began to improve, and became at least reliably palatable and sound. In the 1960s, the valley vintners finally learned to make acceptable table wines out of their raisin- and table-grape varieties. They achieved this by adopting early harvesting and low-temperature fermentation, which Hilgard had advocated in vain. For such grapes as Flame Tokay, Thompson Seedless, and Emperor are, after all, members of the Vinifera (wine-bearing) family, and their juices when expertly handled can be made into clean, though bland-flavored table wines and even into champagnes, at remarkably low cost. (This helps to explain some of the extremely low-priced, yet quite palatable California table and sparkling wines found on the market in recent years; there is Tokay or Thompson juice in many of the whites and even in some of the rosés and reds.)

· 12 ·

A different vineyard product—brandy—emerged after the Second World War to provide a home for some of the San Joaquin Valley grapes. In a way never expected, it turned out that the bitterly fought 1938 Prorate had been a boon, after all. By forcing the production and aging of vast quantities of brandy in that year, the Prorate had launched the California brandy industry on its way. During the war, emigré experts trained in brandy-blending in Europe had surveyed and tasted the Prorate stocks. From the best of them, these experts had blended a new type of beverage brandy, lighter than the cognacs and armagnacs of France and different in bouquet. At the war's end, new-type distilleries were designed to make this distinctive brandy. So popular did it become that brandy consumption in the United States quadrupled between the war and 1970; three-fourths was this new California type. These European experts made still another notable discovery: that the Thompson Seedless, if harvested when its sugar-acid ratio is in balance, is an excellent basic grape for brandy. By 1969, an eighth of the valley grape harvest—320,000 tons, mostly of surplus Thompsons—was distilled to make sixteen million wine gallons of the new type of brandy that Americans have shown they prefer.

· 13 ·

Then came another remarkable development—the introduction of "pop" or "mod" wines. When in 1955 the Government first authorized "special natural wines" to contain natural pure flavors without paying an extra excise tax, the San Joaquin Valley wineries introduced a wide assortment of new flavored wines with exotic coined names. The first of these were mostly of 20 percent alcoholic content, and they sold well, but they mainly succeeded in reducing the wineries' sales of their sherries, ports, tokays, and muscatels. Three years later, the Congress voted to allow "still" grape wines to contain carbon dioxide gas up to seven pounds pressure per square inch—enough to produce a slight "pop" when the bottle is opened—also without paying any additional tax. It then occurred to the makers of flavored wines that there might be some Americans who would like low-alcohol wines with flavors of other fruits besides grapes, also carbonated with seven pounds of "pop." When these apple, strawberry, and tropical fruit types hit the market in the late 1960s and early 70s, they scored an overnight success.

Suddenly the remainder of the surplus Thompson crop, which had depressed the valley's vineyard industry for two decades, was no more. For there is no better grape than the bland-tasting Thompson to blend with the exotic fruit flavors of the "pop" or "mod" wines, which by 1971 accounted for almost a tenth of all the wine consumed that year in the United States!

· 14 ·

When the consumption of table wines outstripped dessert wines in 1968 and set off the "wine revolution," it caught both the California grape growers and the vintners by surprise. In 1849 the cry was "gold," now the cry was "wine grapes." The planting rush started in the coast counties, regions I, II, and III, but it soon became evident that the coast cannot produce enough, that the hot interior valley henceforth must supply most of the table wines. Soon much of the San Joaquin's agriculture was in ferment, shifting from table grapes, raisins, cotton, peaches, and oranges, to grow "varietal" grapes for table wines instead.

In 1971 came startling news from the University: Dr. Harold Olmo had bred for hot climates a dozen new red-grape hybrids which—planted in the San Joaquin Valley—had made experimental wines described by some tasters as equal to most coast-counties Cabernet Sauvignons. The new vines had yielded eleven tons per acre at Fresno, almost double what the true Cabernet produces in cooler climates. I tasted wines, made from these grapes at Fresno State University, that had traces of Cabernet character and were superior to most reds heretofore grown in the valley. The first of these grapes, a cross of Cabernet Sauvignon with Grenache and Carignane called "Variety 12" or "Carnelian" was ready to be introduced for general planting in 1973.

Equally sensational, for the valley, were the University's newest experiments in hot-climate winegrowing. The scientists showed that by retraining vines on trellises to let the leaves shade the grapes from the scorching valley sun, ripening of the fruit could be slowed, the sugar content increased without lowering the acidity, and the flavor thereby enhanced. Another experiment was still more exciting—the evaporation cooling of grapes by intermittent sprinkling—vineyard climate control! Trials of this kind of sprinkling suggested that farmers in the sizzling interior valley might someday create their own mountain-vineyard climates and produce wines as fine as those grown in the cooler parts of the state. If these measures can produce such results in the Central Valley, California conceivably will have enough potential vineyard land—despite the alarming population growth along the coast—to produce literally billions of gallons of fine table wines per year, more than the total output of France, Italy, Spain, or Portugal.

Another advance in California, though of a different kind, was the amendment of the state standards for dessert wines in 1971. The amendment permits California sherries to be bottled at 17 percent alcohol content, which improves their flavor, instead of at the old California minimum standard of 19½ percent, and allows port and other dessert wines to be shipped at 18 percent. At the same time, sherries made in the state improved still further when the submerged-culture flor process, invented in Canada, was coming into general use. Premium wineries' port wines, too, were getting better, because they had begun planting some of the better port-grape varieties, such as Tinta Madeira, Tinta Cão, Souzão, and Touriga. This suggested that the recent steady decline in the popularity of the traditional California dessert wine types might soon be reversed.

· 15 ·

By 1972, there were eighteen times more acres of Chardonnay in the state than thirteen years earlier, eleven times more of Johannisberg Riesling, nine times more of Pinot Noir, sixteen times more of Cabernet Sauvignon, seventy-four times more of Barbera, and comparable increases in the acreages of dozens of other fine wine-grape varieties that have been scarce in California until now. As these young vines gradually come into bearing, enough fine wines are being made to prove to additional millions of buyers the vinous greatness that can be achieved in this paradise for the vine. This is why the former sneers at California wines by visiting dilettante writers have just recently, and somewhat abruptly, been changing to praise.

Still lacking in the state, however, are enough wines with sufficient age to compete directly with the rare treasures in great cellars of the world—wines with great bouquet from years spent mellowing in cask and bottle. This lack, too, is being corrected, thanks to an action by the California Legislature in 1970. The amended law now permits a vintner's inventory of wines and brandies to be taxed by county assessors only once, in the month of March following the vintage, and to be aged for as many more years as the vintner may choose, without paying this tax again.

· 16 ·

And when the explosive gains in table-wine sales began in the late 1960s, out-of-state investors suddenly became interested in winegrowing, which they had long ignored as an unstable business. In 1967, National Distillers, which had owned three California wineries during the Second World War but had sold them after the conflict, returned to winegrowing, buying the Almadén Vineyards and pouring millions into their expansion. In 1969, Heublein, the Connecticut company which two decades earlier had introduced Americans to vodka, bought control of the giant United Vintners group of farmer-owned wineries, and also purchased Beaulieu Vineyard, one of the top-rated Napa Valley producers. By 1970, fully 60 percent of the state's entire wine output was controlled by just two companies—Heublein and the giant of the industry, the Gallo wineries. Other multimillion-dollar companies, visioning table wine as an American growth industry in its earliest stages, began trying to buy out famous coast counties wineries. Nestlé of Switzerland purchased Beringer Brothers of St. Helena in 1970. And you will recall that Widmer's of Naples, the third largest of the big New York Finger Lakes wineries, startled its neighbors by invading California, starting its own vineyard, and preparing to build a winery in Sonoma County.

In the rush to get in on the table-wine bonanza, new owners reopened a dozen old cellars that had been closed and gathering cobwebs for decades, and two dozen new wineries were opened in various parts of the state. Eighty-two thousand new acres of wine grapes, mostly of premium varieties, were planted in California between 1970 and 1972, including 37,000 acres in 1972 alone. Meanwhile many old-time vineyardists, who remember the industry's past boom-and-bust history, were issuing stern warnings against the grape-planting and winery-building spree.

Recalling that Americans have never been wine-drinkers, they foresaw the danger of eventually creating a grape and wine surplus again.

· 17 ·

The California vineyard and wine scene visible to the tourist is also changing markedly each year. The new mechanical harvesting machines, given their first trials here in 1968, already are picking some of the raisin and wine grapes and are expected to be picking four fifths of the state's entire grape crop by 1980. (European winegrowers, facing labor shortages, are experimenting with the grape-picking robots, too.) Winemakers say mechanical harvesting, because it is speedy, will result in better wines, because hand-picking in the vineyards is slow and can be done only by day. The robots can harvest by night, picking the grapes when they are cool and fresh, and precisely when they reach ideal ripeness. This presages the future crushing of the grapes in the vineyard, by a crusher mounted on the harvester, the juice protected by a blanket of carbon dioxide gas until it reaches the winery. The prospect is that we may see wineries of the future receiving no whole grapes at all, but only the newly-crushed grapes, called must.

Subterranean wine cellars, usually damp and moldy, became passé years ago, when vintners learned to build insulated, spotlessly clean cellars above the ground. Stainless- and epoxy-lined steel tanks have begun replacing redwood and concrete vats for the fermenting and storage of wine. Now you see many wineries with no roofs at all: batteries of steel tanks that stand exposed to the sun while temperature-controlled water circulates inside their shells and keeps the wine as cool as though it were underground.

Though grape-growing and winemaking will become increasingly mechanized and automated in years to come, in California and other states, vineyards will always be beautiful, and some wines will still need to be aged in wooden casks to become truly fine. The romance of the wine districts will always be part of the flavors of their wines.

· 18 ·

To the visitor who would explore the California wine country, the puzzle is where to begin, for more than 12,000 vineyards and almost 300 wineries and brandy distilleries dot the countryside in 43 of the state's 48 counties, and they cover 535,000 acres or more than 800 square miles.

But a tour is well worth undertaking, and it can start almost anywhere, for more than a hundred of the wineries welcome visitors to taste their wines, and an equal number in addition can be visited by appointment made in advance. In fact, wine-touring, with tasting, has become one of California's chief visitor attractions, vying with redwood forests, Spanish missions, and Disneyland for the tourist trade.

There are wineries of every description: charming ivy-clad castles; grape-processing plants with steel storage tanks that resemble oil refinery tank farms; family-sized vineyards that specialize in delivering wine by the jug to their customers' doorsteps; estates of gentlemen farmers who grow wine only as an avocation; Church-owned cellars alongside monasteries; and also, scores of tasting rooms, which, though related to wineries, operate mainly at city and highway locations to sell their wines to the public.

Though representative California wines are now available in all of the fifty states and increasing numbers of foreign countries, the only way to get acquainted with the full assortment is to go where the wines are produced. The rarest vintages still seldom leave the state. Made in small quantities, they usually are snapped up by California connoisseurs. Many of the small wineries sell their entire output at their cellar doors or to their mailing lists of loyal customers throughout the state. Few attempt to ship their wines to other states, most of which have burdensome tax and licensing requirements that are relics of Prohibition. And United States postal law on this subject, another such relic, does not allow a winegrower to send you even a single bottle of his wine through the mails; you can only use parcel delivery or express.

Californians themselves drink a sixth of the wine produced in their state. Not only because they are Californians; seven out of ten of them were born somewhere else and discovered wine after they arrived. The main reason for California's high wine consumption, more than three gallons per capita per year including imports, is that the state's laws recognize wine as food and allow it to be sold freely in all kinds of stores and at the lowest state excise tax rates in the nation—1 cent per gallon on table wine, 2 cents on dessert types, 24 cents on champagnes.

If you wish to cover all of the California wine districts, to meet the vintners in person and sample their products at the cellars, the trip will take at least a month. Since two million tourists each year now visit the wineries, some of which haven't enough of the finest and oldest wines to serve the crowds, you should plan your tour with enough time to search for the best.

13

Sonoma, Mendocino, and Lake

HEADING toward the north coast wine country from San Francisco, you cross the Golden Gate Bridge and drive first through suburban Marin County, which had scores of vineyards before Prohibition but saw the last of them replaced by housing tracts after the Second World War. Marin red wines were deficient in color and alcohol because they were made mainly from Zinfandel, the wrong grape for the county's cool climate.

At Ignacio in northern Marin, you turn inland on the Black Point Cutoff, cross the Petaluma River into southern Sonoma County, then follow Highways 121 and 12 into Sonoma Valley, which Jack London named the Valley of the Moon.

You begin to see vineyards here because the weather becomes warmer as you travel north. The lower part of the valley, only seven miles from San Pablo Bay, is Region I in the classification of wine districts by climate (page 164). A few miles farther, as the valley narrows between the Sonoma and Mayacamas ridges of the Coast Range, it becomes Region II, and farther on, Region III.

Highway 12 leads to the picturesque Spanish pueblo of Sonoma and to the restored Mission San Francisco Solano de Sonoma (founded 1823), the northernmost of the Franciscan mission chain, and to the valley's several wineries, of which Buena Vista, Sebastiani, and Hanzell are the best known.

Sonoma Mission is where winegrowing north of San Francisco began. When the mission was abandoned by order of the Mexican Government in 1834, the provincial *comandante*, General Mariano Guadalupe Vallejo, took over its vineyard, planted more vines on his own extensive lands, and became Sonoma's first commercial winegrower. At his home, Lachryma Montis, northwest of the town plaza, you can see the awards his vintage 1857 Sonoma Red and Sonoma White wines received at the 1858 California State

Fair. Vallejo's example soon was followed by his brother-in-law, Jacob Leese, and by many others, including Emil Dresel and Jacob Gundlach, experienced winemakers from Germany.

In 1856 came the spectacular "Count" Agoston Haraszthy, attracted by the success of the Sonoma winegrowers. Haraszthy, a political exile from Hungary, was a promotional genius of many interests, among which was a passion for raising grapes. He had tried and failed to grow them in Wisconsin, where he founded the town of Haraszthy (now Sauk City) before migrating to California in 1848. He imported European vines to San Diego, where he speculated in farming and was elected sheriff. Settling later in San Francisco, he planted European vines near Mission Dolores, where they failed to ripen because of the summer fogs. He then moved them to a location near the Crystal Springs Lakes in adjoining San Mateo County, where they failed again.

On his 1856 visit to Sonoma, Haraszthy found the vines there thriving, and promptly bought the vineyard originally established by General Vallejo's brother, Salvador. The "Count" transplanted his vines again, this time to Sonoma. He built a palatial Pompeian villa on a knoll, surrounded it with formal gardens and fountains, and named it Buena Vista. He wrote pamphlets extolling California's winegrowing climate and sold cuttings of his imported vines to farmers throughout the state. In 1861, he got himself appointed by Governor John G. Downey to visit Europe to study winegrowing and to import more grape varieties. From this trip he brought back 100,000 vines of some 300 varieties (for which the state failed to pay him) and material for his book *Grape Culture, Wines, and Wine Making*. For these exploits he became known as "the father of modern California viticulture."

Two years after his return from Europe, with financial backing from San Francisco banker William Ralston, Haraszthy organized the Buena Vista Vinicultural Society. Two sandstone wineries were built, with tunnels extending into the hillside. The "Count" became General Vallejo's rival in the State Fair wine competitions, but Vallejo had employed a French winemaker, a Dr. Faure, and usually won more medals than Haraszthy. The rivalry was friendly; Haraszthy's sons, Arpad and Attila, had married two of the General's daughters.

Haraszthy had sent Arpad to France to learn champagne making in the Moët et Chandon cellars at Épernay, but Arpad's attempts to make champagne at Sonoma were failures. And financially, so was the Buena Vista Society, even when its champagne was finally perfected by a French expert; the San Francisco *Alta California* described it as "the largest winegrowing estate in the world, and also the most unprofitable." At length, banker Ralston refused to supply any more capital. Haraszthy was accused of extravagance and was deposed as head of the Society in 1866. In disgust, the "Count" left for Nicaragua and a new adventure, to establish a sugar cane plantation and make rum for the export trade. In 1869 he disappeared. On his plantation was a stream infested with alligators. It is believed that he tried to cross it on a tree limb, and fell.

During the 1870s, the phylloxera vine louse invaded Buena Vista and neighboring vineyards. By then, Arpad Haraszthy had moved to San Francisco and become a wine merchant, later acquiring the Orleans Vineyard in Yolo County.

The aging tunnels of Buena Vista collapsed during the earthquake of 1906. The vineyards were virtually gone, and the wineries had been closed. During Prohibition the Haraszthy story was forgotten.

• 2 •

At an auction held in Sacramento in 1941, San Francisco newsman Frank Bartholomew bought a 435-acre tract of Sonoma land that he had never seen, intending to build a country home. Coming to inspect his purchase, he found on the property two abandoned stone buildings that might once have been wineries. Nobody in the neighborhood could tell him what they were. Thinking that I might know their history, Bart asked me to come to Sonoma and look them over. When I told him the strange Haraszthy story and that he had bought historic Buena Vista, he was amazed.

Journalist Bartholomew perceived what such a story might be worth in prestige if, as a winery owner, he could bring back Buena Vista wines. That, in the following decade, is what he and his wife Antonia did. They reopened the tunnels, replanted the vineyard, employed expert help to produce premium Buena Vista wines, and by retelling the spectacular Haraszthy story made them nationally known.

Buena Vista, beautifully situated in a grove of majestic eucalyptus trees, welcomes visitors and invites you to taste its wines, of which there now are twenty-two types. The best, year after year, have been the cask-numbered Cabernet Sauvignon, the Zinfandel, a "Haraszthy Cabinet" Chardonnay, and a luscious Sylvaner named Vine Brook. Also pleasing to drink is the Green Hungarian, made from a grape that other vintners used only for blending until the Bartholomews, liking the name, made it popular as a "varietal" white wine. Recent additions are four champagnes, which are given their secondary fermentation in Buena Vista bottles by Hanns Kornell at St. Helena. The best are an estate-grown champagne brut—called Sparkling Sonoma Pinot Chardonnay—and a Sparkling Cabernet Rosé.

The Bartholomews succeeded where Haraszthy had failed; they made Buena Vista pay. Bartholomew, now the board chairman of United Press International, sold the wine business in 1968 to Vernon Underwood of Young's Market Company of Los Angeles, retaining the home and the adjoining vineyard. The new owner has purchased a 600-acre tract in the southeastern corner of Sonoma Valley, has planted more vineyards, and plans to build another winery there.

• 3 •

The revival of Sonoma's wine industry is celebrated by its annual vintage festival during the last weekend of September with pageants, nostalgic costume parades, and the ceremonial blessing of the grapes. These events are held around such landmarks as the Mission, the historic structures around the Plaza, and the Bear Flag Monument where in 1846 California was proclaimed a republic free of Mexican rule.

Among the more conspicuous Sonoma landmarks are those named Sebastiani, for the founder of the town's principal winery. These include the Sebastiani Theater, Sebastiani Hotel, Sebastiani Dance Hall, Sebastiani Cannery, Sebastiani Bowling Alley, Sebastiani Skating Rink, Sebastiani Motel, and the Sebastiani Bus Depot. In fact, the late Samuele Sebastiani is said to have once offered the city fathers a fabulous sum if they would rename Sonoma for him.

His son August, who now owns the Sebastiani Winery at Spain and Fourth Streets, tells how his father arrived in Somona in 1896 from Tuscany, saved enough money while making cobblestones for San Francisco streets to buy the old Milani winery in 1904, outlasted Prohibition by making sacramental and tonic wines, and became Sonoma's leading citizen, building some of its streets and giving it a parochial school.

August Sebastiani wears striped bib overalls around the winery as his father did, though since some visitors began commenting, he now has them tailor-made. Since taking over the winery in 1934, he has transformed it from an anonymous bulk wine operation to one of California's leading producers of varietally labeled table wines. With his son Samuel, he has replanted a corner of the original mission land with such varieties as Cabernet Sauvignon, Barbera, and Pinot Noir, and has persuaded neighboring growers, from whom he buys most of his grapes, to do the same.

August Sebastiani entered the premium wine field by winning prizes with his Barbera, a deep-flavored, well-aged, dry yet fruity red wine. He since has added bin-numbered and vintage-dated lots of the top "varietals" to his list of some two dozen other wines. His 2-million-gallon winery is bigger than he needs to make the wines sold under the Sebastiani name. The extra capacity is used to make and bottle varietally labeled wines that bear the brands of wineries in less climatically favored parts of the state. If the bottling address at the bottom of a Cabernet Sauvignon or Pinot Noir label from an interior valley winery reads "Sonoma," the wine probably was made by Sebastiani.

• 4 •

On a private road up a hillside just north of Sonoma there is a tiny jewel of a winery, a millionaire's plaything that is unique in the world of wine. On sixteen acres of beautifully terraced vines stands a partial copy of the Clos de Vougeot château in Burgundy, with a miniature model winery inside. The vineyard is called Hanzell (Zell for the late financier and United States Ambassador to Italy, James D. Zellerbach, who had it planted in 1952, and Han for Hana, his wife.) Mrs. Mary Schaw Day, who owns Hanzell now, has preserved the name and also the price of its Chardonnay and Pinot Noir, six dollars a bottle, which is precisely what Zellerbach found they cost him to produce. The small output is snapped up each year by buyers who prize Hanzell wines as superb rarities, which they are.

What Zellerbach never knew, as he died in 1963, was that one of his expensive whims would lead to the solution of a century-old winemaking mystery and would cause scores of America's leading vintners to make an important change in the flavor of their wines.

While living in Europe during the 1940s, Zellerbach had developed a liking for the Montrachet and Romanée Conti wines of Burgundy's Côte d'Or. He conceived the idea of attempting to grow identical wines on his 200-acre Sonoma estate. While home on a visit, he invited the viticultural experts of the University of California at Davis to tell him how this might be achieved.

He followed every costly, specific detail of their advice, except one. Instead of American white oak barrels, customarily used to age wines in this country, he insisted on ordering from France the wooden-hooped oak barrels, called *pièces*, that he had seen in the cellars of Burgundy; he liked their primitive look.

When the first Hanzell wine, the 1956 Chardonnay, was ready, he had his winemaker, Ralph Bradford Webb, send him a quantity in Rome. Zellerbach submitted it to European experts to taste.

They identified it as a white burgundy, but couldn't decide from which Côte d'Or vineyard it came.

California vintners tasted Hanzell wines and recognized their French flavor. It was the elusive flavor certain French wines possess, often described as their "complexity." American researchers had tried for years to explain it, attributing it to peculiarities of French climate or soil. Now its source was known: the barrels Zellerbach had bought in France. California wineries began buying similar barrels from coopers in Beaune and Bordeaux. Their wines, too, acquired that elusive "complex" taste.

But why should French barrels make a difference? Aren't all oak barrels the same? The explanation was found in forestry libraries: Different species of oak trees grow on the European and American continents. European oaks, usually referred to by French coopers as Limousin, Nevers, Austrian, or Yugoslavian according to the localities where they grow, have a varietal vanilla-like fragrance markedly different from that of American white oaks*—a fragrance that the wood imparts to the wine.

Now that wineries here have filled whole cellars with European barrels, some have decided they prefer American oak after all. A little Limousin or Nevers oak flavor in a Chardonnay or a Pinot Noir is desirable, they say, but too much hides the aroma of the grape and can even ruin a fine wine. "It gives me splinters in my esophagus," said one of my connoisseur friends recently, describing a Chardonnay that had spent too much time in European oak.

• 5 •

There were more than a hundred wineries around Sonoma in the last century, when the hills on both sides of the valley were clad with vines. Sonoma Valley wines rivaled those of the Napa Valley, the more famous neighbor to the east. Among the most celebrated vineyards were the Gundlach & Bundschu Rhinefarm at Vineburg, Captain J. H. Drummond's Dunfillan Vineyard north of Sonoma, the nearby Madrone Vineyard of United States Senator George Hearst,** Charles Kunde's Wildwood Vineyard

---

*Native American white oaks, from which most barrels for wine and liquor aging are made, are chiefly of the species *Quercus alba, Q. Lyrata, Q. prinus,* and *Q. bicolor.* The main oak species grown in Europe for wine or brandy barrels are *Quercus robur* and *Q. sessilis.* Suppliers of cooperage say these species do not grow in this country, except perhaps in some northeastern states.

**The multimillionaire mine owner and newspaper publisher, the father of William Randolph Hearst. The Senator bought the Madrone Vineyard in 1885, planted it with the finest Bordeaux varieties, and was proud to serve his own wines and brandy to his guests in the national capital. At his death in 1891 his widow, Phoebe Apperson Hearst, sold the winery to the California Wine Association.

near Kenwood, and Kohler & Frohling's Tokay Vineyard at Ellen, which is now part of the Jack London State Park.

During Prohibition, the lower Sonoma Valley became a summer playground for sporting types from San Francisco because it is close to the city. Great vineyards were chopped up into small holdings, while the vineyard estates of wealthy San Franciscans in the Napa Valley remained more or less intact. After Repeal, the several wineries that reopened in Sonoma Valley sold jug wines to passersby or in bulk to the bigger wineries.

Now, since the table wine boom of the 1960s, winegrowing in the valley is coming back to life. Towle Bundschu has replanted the Rhinefarm, where his forebears, the Gundlachs and Bundschus, once produced their famous Bacchus wines. Robert and Fred Kunde have enlarged and replanted their grandfather's Wildwood Vineyard, which again stretches into the eastern hills. Gino Zepponi and Norman de Leuze have added Cabernet Sauvignon, Pinot Noir, and White Riesling to the old Zepponi vineyard at Sonoma and have opened the new ZD winery, a small premium wine enterprise on Burndale Road near Vineburg. North of Glen Ellen, young Allen Ferrara and Robert Magnani have revived the stone Lamoine winery with its underground cellars that date from 1886, have renamed it the Grand Cru Vineyard, and have opened a tasting room. At Kenwood, equally young John Sheela, Martin and Michael Lee have bought the old Pagani winery, named it the Kenwood Vineyard, and invite visitors to taste their new wines.

But the closeness of Sonoma Valley to San Francisco and other nearby cities poses a new threat to the vineyards—urban sprawl. The county is threatening to convert winding Highway 12 into a four-lane expressway, which would cut off part of the Kenwood Vineyard and encourage the building of more housing tracts, drive-ins, and hotdog stands. The young Sonoma winegrowers are fighting the project, following a successful example set by their Napa neighbors, of which more later.

• 6 •

When you leave the upper Sonoma Valley and travel west and north, you will see few vineyards until you pass Santa Rosa, the bustling county seat. Before Prohibition, there were vineyards on the hills of southwestern Sonoma County between Penngrove and Petaluma, and there was a winery in Petaluma city. On the Petaluma River shore near Lakeville, United States Senator James G. Fair, for whom San Francisco's Fairmont Hotel is named, had a large vineyard, winery, and brandy distillery, which the present owner has converted into a summer home.

Some of the greatest California wines before and after Prohibition came from the famous Fountain Grove Vineyard, which stood on a hillside four miles north of Santa Rosa. It was to Fountain Grove that the mystical prophet, Thomas Lake Harris, moved his Brotherhood of the New Life in 1875 from Brocton, New York. Among the disciples who came with Harris to his new California heaven were the Missouri viticulturist, Dr. John W. Hyde, and the Japanese prince, Baron Kanaye Nagasawa. While the Fountain Grove Press poured forth Harris's pamphlets, sermons, and hymns, Dr. Hyde and his pupil, Nagasawa, planted four hundred acres with Pinot Noir, Cabernet, and Zinfandel. By the early 1880s Harris was shipping Fountain Grove wines, "potentialized with the electro-vinous spirit of joy," across the United States and as far as his old headquarters in England. Involved in new scandals about free love practices at his utopia, Harris departed suddenly for England in 1892. Nagasawa was left in charge and became Fountain Grove's owner when Harris died in 1906. The Baron was noted as a wine judge and for his knowledge of viniculture, acquired from Dr. Hyde and their mutual friend, Luther Burbank, the Santa Rosa botanical wizard. Nagasawa maintained the vineyard and was preparing to reopen the winery at the repeal of Prohibition, when he died. His estate hired an incompetent winemaker, and the first post-Repeal Fountain Grove wines were moldy and sour. Then mining magnate Errol MacBoyle bought the estate, partly to acquire the Baron's collection of samurai swords and Japanese art, and partly to impress his millionaire friends with his own private brand of champagne. MacBoyle hired two winemakers, emigrés from Germany, Kurt Opper and his cousin, Hanns Kornell. During the 1940s Opper restored Fountain Grove to greatness. His 1945 champagne, Johannisberg Riesling, and his Pinot Noir were the finest made that year in the state. But after MacBoyle's death in 1949, his widow Glendolyn remarried and let the vineyard fall into neglect. Opper then quit to join the Paul Masson Vineyard at Saratoga, and in 1951 Fountain Grove was closed for good.

• 7 •

In the Santa Rosa Valley, homes and shopping centers compete with vineyards for space. But to the west, between Forestville and Sebastopol, prune orchards and even some of Sonoma County's famous Gravenstein apple orchards have been displaced by new vineyards since vintners began paying record prices for coast counties' grapes.

Near Trenton, eight miles northwest of Santa Rosa, is the 2-million-gallon Martini & Prati Winery, a group of old wooden and concrete cellars, one of which dates from 1881. Elmo Martini and Edward Prati, descendants of old Sonoma winegrowing families, make mainly bulk table wines for other California wineries. When the Fountain Grove winery closed, they bought its famous label and used it to introduce their own bottled wines, which are sold in their tasting room and in Bay Area stores.

In an old cottage in Trenton village is Sonoma County's smallest winery, bonded in 1969. Veteran Western Airlines pilot Joseph Swan, an amateur winemaker, has replanted part of the adjoining ten-acre Zinfandel vineyard with Pinot Noir and Chardonnay. Swan and his wife plan to make the Joseph Swan Vineyard their business when the age limit for airline pilots requires him to retire from flying in 1974.

Trenton is at the lower end of the Russian River Valley, so named because Russian fur hunters from Alaska settled on the Sonoma coast in 1812 and remained there for thirty years. The Russian River rises some 200 miles farther north in Mendocino County and flows almost due south between parallel ridges of the Coast Range. In prehistoric times the river emptied into San Francisco Bay until upheavals of the earth forced it to cut a new channel westward through the coastal hills to the sea.

Most Sonoma County wine now comes from the two dozen wineries and some 15,000 acres of vineyards scattered through this valley and its series of tributary valleys with local names.

• 8 •

On the left bank of the Russian River, two miles east of Guerneville and just past the woodsy summer resort colony of Rio Nido, is the Korbel champagne cellar with its quaint Norman tower, which once housed a brandy still.

Korbel is now owned by the Heck brothers. Adolf, Paul, and Ben Heck have known winemaking since boyhood, when their father, who came from Strasbourg, managed the Cook's Imperial champagne vaults in St. Louis. Adolf, after a course at the Geisenheim Institute in Germany, served as Cook's champagne maker for nine years. When the Government seized the American Wine Company in 1944 because of its Nazi ownership, he moved to the Sweet Valley winery in Sandusky, and for six years made Ohio champagne.

In 1951, Adolf came to California to succeed General John R. Deane as president of the Italian Swiss Colony, and Paul managed the Colony's Sonoma County winery at Asti. Then came the opportunity the Heck brothers had been waiting for: Anton (Tony)

Korbel, less interested in champagne than in judging dog shows, was offering the Korbel vineyards and winery for sale. The brothers bought it, Paul took charge of the vineyards, Ben became the sales manager, and Adolf, with his champagne-making experience in Germany, Missouri, and Ohio, became the president and winemaker of Korbel.

The winery dates from 1886, when the Korbel brothers, natives of Bohemia, gave up lumbering along the Russian River. They planted vines where they had cut down a grove of redwoods, and built the cellar with bricks they baked in a homemade kiln. They made only still wines and brandy until 1896, when they were joined by an expert winemaker named Franz Hazek from Prague. Hazek brought choice vine cuttings from Europe and made a dry sparkling wine called Grand Pacific to compete with Arpad Haraszthy's "Eclipse" and the champagne of Paul Masson. The Korbels renamed the wine Korbel Brut and followed it with a Korbel Sec and a sparkling burgundy named Korbel Rouge. Hazek's successor was another Czech named John Hanuska, who so jealously guarded his secret *cuvées* that nobody was allowed to enter the winery in his absence, not even the Korbels.

When the Hecks bought Korbel, they enlarged the vineyard to 450 acres and expanded the winery by buying the nearby Santa Nella cellar. They added three more champagnes: Korbel Extra Dry, Korbel Rosé, which is semidry, Korbel Natural, which is bone-dry; an assortment of table and dessert wines; and a brandy that is blended for them at Lodi.

Visitors to Korbel are given tours of the cellars and shown how champagnes are made. The Hecks advertise that theirs are "fermented in *this* bottle," a slap at competitors who use the modern transfer method of disgorging (removing the sediment formed by fermentation). They have invented a machine that riddles (shakes) thousands of bottles at once and disgorges them automatically.

The Korbel tasting room is an old railroad depot which Tony Korbel bought for five dollars from the Northwestern Pacific in 1935. There you can buy, besides the advertised Korbel products, less expensive wines under the Heck Bros. and Santa Nella labels, not available anywhere else.

• 9 •

Climatically, the Russian River Valley equals the Sonoma and Napa Valleys as a potential premium wine district, with summer temperatures ranging from Region I to Region III. But except at Korbel and the Italian Swiss Colony, this valley until now has produced mostly ordinary grapes and bulk wines because those were what the winegrowers here knew how to produce and sell.

The wine boom that began in the 1960s is swiftly changing this. Big and small investors are scrambling to start new premium vineyards and wineries, and the valley shows a dramatic contrast between the old and the new.

In the village of Windsor, eight miles north of Santa Rosa, the 250,000-gallon Sonoma County Co-operative Winery still ferments the grapes of its farmer members into bulk wine that is shipped in tank trucks to the Gallo Winery at Modesto. The building is a relic of the past, the last of the statewide chain of wineries established by Kohler & Frohling, the greatest of early California wine firms, established in 1853 at Los Angeles by Charles Kohler and John Frohling, musicians from Germany. The company at one time owned wineries at Glen Ellen and in the Sacramento and San Joaquin Valleys, wine depots in New York, in the Montgomery Block of San Francisco, and in the basement of the Los Angeles City Hall, and shipped California bulk wines to Europe, South America, the Orient, and Australia. In 1894, Kohler & Frohling was absorbed by the California Wine Association, which operated the Windsor cellar until Prohibition. The Co-op was organized in 1935 to provide a home for its members' crops.

On the Old Redwood Highway three miles northwest of the Co-op is the 2-million-gallon Windsor Vineyard Winery, a striking example of what is new. Built in 1970, the Windsor Winery is shaped like a cross with four metal-roofed wings rising from the vineyard level to a high center structure that contains a tasting room, a rooftop promenade, and offices; a French chef cooks luncheons and dinners by reservation for visiting groups of connoisseurs. On the north side is a landscaped amphitheater where benefit concerts, operas, and ballet performances are held.

The Windsor Winery, or rather Tiburon Vintners which owns it, is a ten-year creation of a professional dancer who likes to make wine and an advertising man who saw the first sparks of the table wine explosion.

In 1960, when Rodney Duane Strong was thirty-three, he disbanded his Rod Strong Dance Quartet after performing on Broadway and at the Lido in Paris, "because I didn't want to be an old dancer." His grandparents had been winegrowers in Germany and he had caught the wine bug during his terpsichorean tours of Europe. In a century-old railroad men's boardinghouse on the waterfront of Tiburon, across the bay from San Francisco, Strong began bottling and selling bulk wine under the Tiburon Vintners name. Four years later he was joined by New Yorker Peter Friedman, who had an idea that many more people would buy wine if a winery would print their names on "personalized labels" on the bottles, with such legends as "Bottled Expressly for Tom and Mary Jones."

Friedman's idea proved a sensational salesmaker, so they leased the old Monte Carlo vineyard and winery near the Co-op at Windsor. Strong started making wines to supplement those they bought from other wineries. Mrs. Strong, the willowy blonde former Charlotte Winson of *Guys and Dolls*, turned a farm cottage into their first tasting room.

Tiburon Vintners acquired land for more vineyards while the table wine boom was still getting started. When the new winery was built, the firm "went public" to finance the new vineyards. Friedman says that by 1973 the company will have 2700 acres in twelve Russian River Valley vineyards, more than any other winery north of San Francisco Bay, each vineyard planted exclusively with either White Riesling, Chardonnay, Cabernet Sauvignon, or Pinot Noir. Thus far Windsor's fourteen table wines and its new bottle-fermented champagne have been sold directly to consumers by mail in California and at the winery. They are now being introduced through stores and restaurants outside California under a new Sonoma Vineyards label, and special vintages under a Rodney Strong label are due to follow.

On a 200-acre vineyard a mile north of Windsor is the million-gallon Foppiano Winery, which dates from 1898. Louis Foppiano switched during the 1960s from shipping bulk sauterne and burgundy in tank cars to eastern bottlers to begin supplying "varietal" wines to other California wineries. He also opened a retail store and tasting room at the winery and has discovered that visiting connoisseurs are willing to pay a dollar a bottle more for Foppiano Cabernet and Pinot Noir than for his burgundy made of Zinfandel.

Two miles southeast of Healdsburg, the Cambiaso family have been making sauterne and burgundy from Burger, Carignane, and Zinfandel since Giovanni and Maria Cambiaso built the winery on their hillside vineyard in 1934. When during the 1960s a famous Napa Valley winery began buying their burgundy for blending with its own high-priced Cabernet, the Cambiasos' son and daughters began ripping out their Carignane vines and replacing them with Cabernet Sauvignon. When I was last there, they were preparing a Cabernet Sauvignon of their own for sale in their tasting room.

On Dry Creek Road northwest of Healdsburg, the 800,000-gallon Frei Brothers winery, like the Sonoma Co-op, produces all the wine from its 300-acre vineyard in bulk for the Gallo Winery of Modesto.

The Simi Winery, on the Old Redwood Highway north of

Healdsburg, has been transformed into a producer of top-grade vintage wines since Russell Green of Los Angeles took it over in 1970. The imposing stone cellar was built in 1876 by San Francisco wine dealers Giuseppe and Pietro Simi, who named it Montepulciano for their birthplace in the mountains of central Italy. It produced bulk wine before and following Prohibition, except during the Second World War wine shortage, when an English winemaker named Remington took charge and bottled some prize-winning table and dessert wines and bulk-process champagnes. Montepulciano was too tongue-twisting a name, so the wines were sold under the Hotel Del Monte label, then eventually were renamed Simi.

Green, the former president of the Signal Oil Company, bought the Simi Winery to provide a home for the grapes he had begun planting twelve years earlier around his summer home in the nearby Alexander Valley. He recruited German-trained winemaker Robert Stemmler, who had worked at the Charles Krug and Inglenook wineries, replaced the Simis' ancient tanks and crusher with stainless steel equipment and new French oak barrels, and built a new tasting room out of the staves of the obsolete redwood tanks. Within a year, Green put his 1970 premium-quality table wines on sale at the winery and in California stores. With the winery came a stock of table wines, ports, and champagnes bottled by Remington, with vintage dates of the late 1930s and early 1940s. Most of it was spoiled, but Green salvaged some rarities, including some excellent ports and a red wine labeled Carignane with so powerful a bouquet that Green says he may continue producing Carignane despite its reputation as one of the commonest of red wine grapes. With the winery, Green also acquired the services of Giuseppe Simi's octogenarian daughter, Isabelle Simi Haigh, who enjoys telling her family's history as she presides over the new Simi tasting room.

The Alexander Valley on Highway 128, two miles east of the Simi Winery, was mostly prune orchard and grazing land when Green planted the first few rows of vines at his summer place in 1958. Now he has 500 acres in vines. The Alexander Valley has become the most concentrated area of premium wine-grape plantings in Sonoma County. Widmer's Wine Cellars of New York State purchased 500 acres of prune orchard near Green's property in 1969, has replaced the trees with Cabernet Sauvignon and Pinot Noir under permanent overhead sprinklers for frost protection, and is preparing to build a winery there. Between the Widmer vineyard and the Russian River are two of the Windsor Winery's new vineyards, also under set sprinklers, planted entirely with Cabernet Sauvignon. There is another big new vineyard nearby, said to be owned by an unidentified new company with eastern financing that plans soon to build a premium winery there.

The sprinklers and wind machines that Sonoma grape growers are buying to protect their vines from frost damage are something new. In past years of grape surpluses such things could not be afforded, but the high prices now paid for scarce grape varieties make the investments worthwhile. Some vineyardists have even hired helicopters to be flown over their vineyards on frosty spring nights to blow the cold air away.

Also new are the mechanical grape-harvesting machines, which are already common in the Concord vineyards of the east, but less widely used in California because Vinifera grapes are more difficult than Concords to pick. Russell Green owns the first mechanical harvester in Sonoma County, and says it works as well as hand-picking does.

One of the first northern Sonoma wineries to begin changing from bulk to premium bottled wines was that of the Pedroncelli Brothers, a mile west of Geyserville on Canyon Road. John and James Pedroncelli took over their father's hillside vineyard and small wooden cellar in 1955, when John completed a short course in enology at the University of California. In the following year, the brothers bottled three of their wines and entered them in the California State Fair wine competition. To their surprise, all three won medal awards, silvers for their burgundy and rosé and bronze for their Zinfandel. This attracted the notice of Bordeaux-born San Francisco wine merchant and importer Henry Vandervoort, who was looking for a new supply of California bulk table wines good enough to bottle for his restaurant customers under their private labels. The Pedroncelli wines bottled by Vandervoort sold well, so the brothers began bottling more under their own name. When Vandervoort saw that the Pedroncellis were making their rosé entirely out of Zinfandel, he suggested they give it a varietal name. In 1958 it became California's first Zinfandel Rosé. Five years later, they made a cask of Cabernet Sauvignon so outstanding that Vandervoort had them set it aside for extra aging and bottle it under two-inch corks with his own label as "An Importer's Choice." The Pedroncellis found that finer wines are easier to sell, and have doubled their father's original sixty acres with such classic varieties as Cabernet Sauvignon and Pinot Noir. They have added extra cellar space for aging, Limousin oak casks, and a tasting room, and continue winning awards each year at the Pomona Fair.

Three new wineries have started in the Healdsburg-Geyserville area. East of Highway 101, vineyard owner Leo Trentadue has begun bottling table wines with labels that display the number "32," which is trentadue in Italian. On a hilltop overlooking the Dry Creek Valley five miles northwest of Healdsburg, David Stare is building a miniature replica of a Médoc château. A graduate of Harvard, where his father heads the nutrition department, David has home-winemaking experience and has taken an enology course at the University of California. On another hilltop northwest of Geyserville, electrical engineer Keith Nelson is building a small winery named Viña Vista for the view it commands of the Russian River Valley. Before Prohibition this was the site of the Trusendi Winery, whose owner may have named the approach to the winery, Chianti Road.

Overlooking Highway 101 a mile north of Geyserville is the million-gallon old Geyser Peak Winery, purchased in 1972 by the Joseph Schlitz Brewing Company of Milwaukee, which plans to convert it into a showplace with landscaped grounds and a tasting room. Reopened after Repeal by Dante and William Bagnani, Geyser Peak made only wine vinegar, which they sold under their Four Monks brand. For years a pixyish sign facing the road read: "Sorry—no retail sales—we drink it all." But when the wine boom began in the 1960s, the Bagnanis began producing wine for other wineries. Dante Bagnani says Schlitz, making its debut in the wine business, plans to enlarge the 110-acre vineyard and to specialize in premium wines.

Bulk wine is still produced by most of the wineries in northern Sonoma County. The Seghesio family, who have wineries at Cloverdale and Healdsburg, have replanted half of their 300 acres with superior grape varieties and now supply "varietal" wines in tank trucks to premium producers outside the county. The Nervo winery, two miles south of Geyserville, sells to other wineries, but also offers bottled "varietals," including a Zinfandel that the proprietors claim to have aged in redwood tanks for twenty years. The Rege winery, three miles south of Cloverdale, makes jug wines for restaurants and the family trade in San Francisco.

• 10 •

The Italian Swiss Colony at Asti, four miles southeast of Cloverdale, is huge, historic, and unique. More people visit this winery— 400,000 a year—than any other in the world, because it borders the main tourist route between the Pacific Northwest and California, US 101, and signs for miles beckon them to stop. Costumed guides show crowds daily through its 8-million-gallon forest of redwood and steel tanks, then usher them into the big Swiss chalet tasting hall to sample the vast assortment of wines now sold under the Italian Swiss name.

Its early history is that of a philanthropic farming venture, started by San Francisco grocer-turned-banker Andrea Sbarboro in 1880 to settle penniless Italian and Swiss immigrant farmers on land where they could support themselves by growing grapes. Each worker would be given board, room, and wine for his daily use and would be paid monthly wages of thirty-five dollars, but five dollars would be deducted each month for the purchase of stock in the Colony, which would make him an independent vineyard owner in twenty-five years. Vines were planted, and the place was named Asti for the resemblance of the hills to those around Asti and Canelli in the Italian Piedmont. The colonists, however, refused to allow the deduction from their wages; they preferred dollars in hand to independence in the future. Sbarboro accepted defeat, and the Colony became a private vineyard venture.

A winery was built in 1887, but the first vintage turned to vinegar. Sbarboro then persuaded one of the Colony's original supporters, San Francisco druggist Pietro C. Rossi, to take charge. A graduate in pharmacy of the University of Turin, Rossi knew the principles of winemaking, and under him the Colony prospered for two decades. Before the turn of the century Asti wines were winning medals for excellence in Europe and America and were being shipped in barrels to Europe, South America, China, and Japan. The Colony acquired more vineyards and wineries at nearby Fulton and Sebastopol, at Clayton in Contra Costa County, and at Madera, Kingsburg, and Lemoore in the San Joaquin Valley.

During a price war in 1897, Rossi kept surplus Sonoma wine off the market by building at Asti what was then the world's biggest underground wine tank. Made of concrete, it held 300,000 gallons. Its completion before the vintage was celebrated with dancing inside the tank to the music of a military band. The tank is still in use today.

Sbarboro and Rossi erected elegant villas for their families and entertained famous personages from around the world. In 1907, the Colony built its famous "church shaped like a wine barrel," the El Carmelo Chapel, on land donated by the Archbishop of San Francisco. When Rossi's twin sons, Edmund and Robert, won their science degrees at the University of California, the family celebrated with a trip through Europe. While in France, Pietro Rossi met champagne maker Charles Jadeau of Saumur and persuaded him to come to Asti. Two years later, Jadeau's Golden State Extra Dry Champagne won the grand prix at the Turin international exposition.

Tipo Chianti red and white, bottled in raffia-covered Italian *fiaschi*, were the Colony's most popular wines, but the Italian Government objected to an American wine being called chianti. In 1910 the Colony renamed the wines "Tipo Red" and "Tipo White," not to please Italy, but to stop other wineries from calling their wines "Tipo." This four-letter word in Italian means "type" or "imitation," but in one of the quirks of wine nomenclature, it has become the American name for any wine in a chianti flask. The original Tipo Red was a tannic, long-lived wine unlike Italian chiantis, which are softened by blending white grapes with red. The 1914 Tipo, which was served at a Wine and Food Society banquet in the San Francisco Stock Exchange Club in 1936, was one of the best pre-Prohibition California wines.

Pietro Rossi was killed in a horse and buggy accident in 1911. Two years later, the Italian Swiss Colony was taken over by the California Wine Association. In 1920 came the next disaster, Prohibition. Sbarboro had fought the Drys to the last. His solution for intemperance was to encourage the drinking of wine instead of hard liquor. Chronic drunkards, he said, should be jailed for thirty days and given dry wine with their meals, and if not cured should be given the same treatment for sixty days more. His disparagement of liquor so annoyed some whiskey distillers that they attempted a boycott of the Colony's wines.

During Prohibition Edmund and Robert Rossi with vineyard superintendent Enrico Prati bought back the Colony from the CWA and supplied grapes, juice, and concentrate to home winemakers until Repeal. The Rossi twins foresaw the failure of Prohibition, and it was they who in 1932 led the old-time California winegrowers in forming the Grape Growers League, which became the Wine Institute two years later.

During the years before the Second World War, the Italian Swiss Colony under the Rossis became the third largest wine company in the nation, with its La Paloma Winery near Fresno using the surplus grapes of Joseph Di Giorgio's vast vineyards in the San Joaquin Valley. When the whiskey distillers invaded the wine industry during the war, National Distillers bought the Colony and added another winery, Shewan-Jones, at Lodi. Thence came the French-sounding name, Lejon, for the Colony's brandy and champagnes; Lejon is a contraction of the name of Lee Jones, the kindly, crusty former revenue inspector who founded Shewan-Jones.

When the Rossi Brothers retired, Edmund became the manager of the Wine Advisory Board and guided its national program of wine education until 1960. And winemaking at Asti is still guided by a pair of Rossis: Edmund, Jr., is in charge of quality control and Robert, Jr., is in charge of production.

The story of the Colony's purchase by Louis Petri and then by Heublein, and of the appearance of its strange new "pop" or "mod" wines, which are made at Madera, will be told later. The huge winery at Asti now bottles mostly brandies and makes only the superior "private stock" Italian Swiss wines. It also again makes Tipo, which has regained some of its old-time flavor, but more for sentimental reasons than for sales, because at today's cost of labor the hand-wrapped Tipo bottle costs more than the wine inside.

• 11 •

Three miles beyond Cloverdale, still following the Russian River, you enter Mendocino, northernmost of the coastal wine counties, where lumbering is still the principal industry. Like northern Sonoma, Mendocino formerly produced mainly bulk table wines, but with the accelerated planting of superior grape varieties since the 1960s, it has become one of the premium wine districts of the state.

There were more than seven thousand acres of vines in the county in 1972, a third more than in 1960, and there was talk of planting several thousand acres more. Most of the vineyards are in the Ukiah, Redwood, McDowell, and Feliz Creek valleys, where the climate is Region III, but newer plantings have sprouted west of the mountains around Boonville and Philo in the Anderson Valley along the Navarro River, which is classed as Region I. There is a new Johannisberg Riesling vineyard at Hearst, on the Eel River east of Willits, and test plots have been planted in the Potter Valley and as far north as Round Valley, near Covelo.

Mendocino has six wineries, of which the best known is the Parducci Wine Cellar with its attractive tasting room, situated west of the 101 freeway three miles north of Ukiah. Adolph Parducci opened this winery at the repeal of Prohibition, selling most of his wine to the roadside trade and shipping the rest in tank trucks to vintners in the San Joaquin Valley. In 1946, his sons, John and George, ventured to enter the State Fair competition with a fresh, fruity dry white wine of French Colombard. It was awarded a silver medal, and mail orders for Parducci wines began coming from Bay Area gourmets. When the sons took over the business, they began replanting the family vineyard with premium varieties, planted more in the Talmage district, and embarked on a long-range program of aging and vintage-dating Parducci red wines. The best I have tasted here thus far are the 1969 Cabernet Sauvignon and a remarkably robust Pinot Noir. Bottled without fining or filtering, these wines require decanting, but they are developing excellent bouquet.

Across the freeway from Parducci, on Brush Street, is a pre-Prohibition winery built by the French-American Wine Company in 1910 and still in operation. Later owners during the dry era produced a famous grape concentrate for home winemaking, called "Caligrapo." At Repeal this was the Ukiah winery of the California Grape Products Company and produced an excellent claret, Victor Mendocino Zinfandel, that was popular in New York City. In the 1940s the winery was owned for a time by Garrett of New York State, whose name is still displayed on the building. Now the Italian Swiss Colony crushes its Mendocino grapes there and transports the must in tank trucks to Asti to become part of the Colony's best table wine blends.

On State Street, north of Ukiah, is the home winery and tasting room of the Cresta Blanca Wine Company, one of California's most historic and famous premium wine producers.

The 1,500,000-gallon winery was originally built by the Mendocino Growers Co-operative in 1946, then became the Mendocino winery of the Guild of Lodi and for a decade produced the best of the Guild's assortment of table wines.

When the Guild in 1971 purchased the famous Cresta Blanca name from Schenley Distillers, the original Cresta Blanca winery at Livermore had been closed for several years. Though owned by the Guild, Cresta Blanca then was made a separate company, and the Ukiah cellar became its principal winery, producing a dozen premium table wines from Mendocino, Sonoma, and Napa County grapes. Displayed in the tasting room is the complete Cresta Blanca assortment of table, dessert wines, and champagnes.

Also on State Street, adjoining the freeway where Highway 20 takes off north of Calpella, is Mendocino County's newest winery, built in 1972 by the Weibel family of Alameda County to process the grapes from their recently-acquired 250 acres of Mendocino and Sonoma vineyards. A tasting room is also being built there, in which the dozens of Weibel wines and champagnes will be displayed.

In a secluded western arm of nearby Redwood Valley, reached by Uva Drive and Bel Arbres Road, is the Fetzer Vineyards winery. Five buildings of a homemade château design stand in a park-like setting of lovely vineyards against the spectacular backdrop of heavily wooded Black Hill. Visitors are welcome, but there is no tasting room.

Bernard and Kathleen Fetzer bought the property in 1957, a two-mile-long ranch with vines a century old. They moved into the biggest building, an early-day stagecoach stop, with their five daughters and six sons, their future vineyard and winery staff. Taught winegrowing in his youth by his father and German grandfather, who had a Labrusca vineyard in Lancaster County, Nebraska, Fetzer replanted 150 acres with premium varieties, principally Cabernet Sauvignon, Sémillon, and Sauvignon Blanc. He sold his first crops to amateur winemakers, shipping both grapes and juice by air freight as far as the Atlantic Coast. Meanwhile, he built the winery and equipped it with temperature-controlled stainless steel fermenters, bottling equipment from Germany, and 200 Nevers oak casks from Bordeaux. It was finished in time to ferment the 1968 vintage. The first Fetzer Vineyard wines had too much European oak flavor, but this was corrected during the next few years. Each bottle, "100% varietal," is proudly labeled "Mendocino" because, Fetzer says, "this county has the best climate in California and our wines eventually will put Napa County in second place."

Near Philo in the Anderson Valley, nine miles from the Pacific Ocean, a tiny sign facing Highway 128 reads "Husch Vineyards." Wilton (Tony) Husch quit his job as a city planner in San Francisco and came here in 1968 with his wife Gretchen, to escape from the troubled metropolis. Undecided at first about what to do with the land around their cottage, Husch heard that people in the vicinity were planting grapes to capitalize on the wine boom. He began reading books on viticulture, got vines and advice from several leading winegrowers, and planted twenty acres with the premium varieties recommended for the valley's Region I climate. In 1971 he bonded the first winery in the valley and made eleven barrels of better-than-average Chardonnay and Gewürztraminer. Gretchen Husch designed the Husch Vineyards label, and the wines were offered for sale in 1972. "We came here to escape," says young Tony Husch, "but we were just lucky. At the very height of the wine boom, we landed in the best future premium wine district in the United States."

A year after the Husches, equally young Deron and Paula Edmeades bonded a farm building that had housed an apple-drier on the nearby thirty-two-acre vineyard planted in 1963 by the late Dr. Donald Edmeades of Pasadena, and crushed their first vintage of Anderson Valley Chardonnay, Gewürztraminer, and Cabernet Sauvignon. They plan to plant more vines and build a winery with a tasting room when their production reaches 10,000 gallons.

• 12 •

The wine awakening of America has revived vine-planting in neighboring Lake County, which has a glamorous but long-forgotten winegrowing past. From less than 300 acres in 1965, vineyards in this county multiplied to 1000 acres by 1972, and were expected to double again in another year, while a group of farmers laid plans to build a winery and to promote Lake County wines.

Back in 1891, Lake County had seven wineries and 1000 acres of vines. Among the county's famous winegrowers were California's first chief justice, Serranus Clinton Hastings, who owned the Carsonia Vineyard and Champagne Cellars at Upper Lake; Colonel Charles Mifflin Hammond, whose Ma Tel Vineyard at Nice on Clear Lake produced wines that won awards at the Paris Exposition in 1900, and the English actress, Lily Langtry, who brought a *vigneron* from Bordeaux to tend her vineyard near Middletown and bottled wines with her portrait on the labels, but was prevented from selling them when Prohibition came in 1920.

At Repeal in 1933, only 600 acres of vines, mostly Zinfandels, remained in the county, and the grapes were being sold to the wineries in neighboring Mendocino, Napa, and Sonoma.

The new Lake County vineyards are principally of Cabernet Sauvignon, which does well in the valleys surrounding nineteen-mile-long Clear Lake at 1320-foot elevation and around lofty Mount Konocti, where the climate ranges from Region II to Region IV. Patches of vineyard extend south beyond Middletown and almost to the border of Napa County, which will be explored in the next chapter.

Professor Albert Winkler, the University of California viticulturist, searching for potential new premium grape districts, has found climates favorable for winegrowing in eastern Humboldt County, around Alderport and Blocksburg. Dr. Winkler suggests that "a real adventurer might find it interesting" to plant vines on some of the slopes near the Hoopa Indian Reservation around Weitchpec, the steelhead fishermen's paradise on the upper Klamath River.

Someday the north coast wine district may stretch northward beyond Mendocino and Lake Counties for another hundred miles.

14

Napa, the Winiest County

NAPA COUNTY, separated from Sonoma on the west by a spur of the Mayacamas mountain range, is the winiest county in the United States. It has fifty-three bonded wine cellars and 16,000 acres of vineyards, almost as many as Sonoma, which is twice Napa's size.

The Napa Valley, where most of the county's vineyards and wineries are, is only one to five miles in width and thirty-five miles long. Outside the town centers, this valley is an almost unbroken expanse of grapevines, a scene that is idyllic and unique.

Visitors come here from all over the world. Highway 29, which traverses the valley, is known as "The Wine Road," and it merits the name. On one eleven-mile stretch there are ten wineries, almost one per mile, which welcome the public to tour their cellars and taste their wines. Tourists' cars on the road are bumper-to-bumper on an average weekend. The visitors listen to the lectures the winery guides give, sip the samples offered afterward, and make purchases of the wines they like best. Some of the guests make a day of it, moving from one winery to the next and the next, until the tasting rooms close at four in the afternoon. (Fifteen Napa wineries now offer tasting; ten receive visitors by appointment only; the rest are mostly production or storage cellars closed to the public.)

The fame of Napa wines is spreading, in gourmet publications, in travel magazines, in the new wine books, on select wine lists. But except for the motorized crowds, this is really a repetition of their history, for Napa wines first became famous almost a century ago.

• 2 •

The Napa River, Napa County, and Napa city are named for

the Napa Indians, one of the so-called Digger tribes who once lived there. "Napa" is said to mean "plenty" or "homeland," but some early records say it was originally the Indians' word for fish, which abounded then in the streams and supplemented their diet of roots, seeds, grasshoppers, and worms.

Some five thousand Indians inhabited the county before white settlers came from Sonoma during the 1830s. Forty years later, smallpox and bloody wars with the newcomers had reduced the Indians' numbers to scarcely a score. The wholesale slaughter of the Indians is commemorated in the grisly name that was given in 1839 to the Rancho Carne Humana land grant south of Calistoga. *Carne humana* is Spanish for human flesh.

From Sonoma, the first settlers brought the Mission grape to Napa. In 1836, George Calvert Yount, the North Carolinian trapper and explorer, built his fortified log blockhouse two miles north of present-day Yountville and two years later planted Mission vines he brought from the Sonoma vineyard of General Mariano Vallejo. Yount's first vintage could have been in 1841. There is additional evidence that wine was being made at several locations in Napa County during the 1840s, but the earliest records available show Yount producing 200 gallons annually by 1844. Planting of the better imported European grape varieties was begun about 1852 by William and Simpson Thompson on their Suscol land grant south of Napa city. In 1859, Samuel Brannan, the ex-Mormon millionaire of San Francisco, purchased three square miles at Calistoga and began planting choice cuttings he had collected on a tour through Europe.

Robert Louis Stevenson, honeymooning in the valley and writing his *Silverado Squatters* in 1880, described the Napa vintners' search for the best vineyard sites: "One corner of land after another is tried with one kind of grape after another," he wrote. "This is a failure; that is better; a third best. So, bit by bit, they grope about for their Clos Vougeot and Lafite . . . and the wine is bottled poetry."

By the late 1800s there were 4000 acres of vines and 142 wineries in Napa County. In Napa city, the rivershore was lined with wineries, such as the Uncle Sam and Napa Valley cellars, from which wine was barged to San Francisco, much of it for shipment around Cape Horn to Atlantic ports. Connoisseurs in New York and San Francisco were already serving wines from the To Kalon Vineyard of Henry Crabb near Oakville, from the Inglenook Vineyard of Captain Niebaum at Rutherford, and from the vineyards of Charles Krug and Jacob Schram at St. Helena and Calistoga, to mention a few.

Napa vineyards covered 18,000 acres in 1891. Since then, like a magic green carpet, they have shrunk dramatically and spread repeatedly in response to alternating plagues and booms.

The phylloxera plague, which had begun a decade earlier, devastated all but 3000 acres before 1900, but during the following decade nearly half of the dead vineyards were replanted with vines grafted on resistant roots.

Napa again had almost 10,000 acres in 1920, when an even worse plague—Prohibition—struck. It did not destroy the vineyards, but economics compelled the growers to graft over their Cabernet, Pinot, and Riesling vines to the coarse varieties that were preferred by the buyers of grapes shipped east for homemade and bootleg wines. Repeal in 1933 was a disappointment to the Napa winegrowers, too, because it brought little demand for their dry table wines. There still were only 11,500 acres of vines in the county by 1965.

Then the wine boom reached its height, and vines began to spread throughout the valley again. As vintners raised their offers for "varietal" grapes, growers grafted back their vineyards from shipping varieties to the noble Cabernets, Rieslings, and Pinots. The growers started buying sprinkler systems and $6000 wind machines to guard their vines from frostbite on chilly spring nights. You now see more of these huge fans in the Napa Valley than in any other vineyard district in the world. When disastrous frosts hit the coast counties in late April of 1970, the wind machines throbbed and smudge pots burned all night—much to the annoyance of those valley residents who do not grow grapes—and saved half of the crop. The least loss, incidentally, was in those vineyards protected by sprinklers, which kept the vines coated with a protective film of ice.

As the planting fever reached a climax in the late '60s, scores of Napa prune orchards were ripped out and replaced with wine grapes. New vineyards also sprang up in the mountains west and east of the valley, on slopes that had been bare of vines since the phylloxera epidemic eighty years before. Half a dozen pre-Prohibition Napa wineries meanwhile were refurbished and reopened for business. Nine entirely new wineries were built in the county between 1970 and 1972, and at least five more are in the planning stage. Giant conglomerates began buying up the old established Napa wineries, but many of them, enjoying their new-found prosperity and proud of their family histories, turned down multimillion-dollar offers to sell.

Vineyard plantings in Napa County may reach 25,000 acres in another few years. But that is all the space left in the county with the soil, drainage, and climatic conditions considered suitable for the commercial cultivation of wine grapes.

A bitter struggle has raged in recent years to protect this open space from urban sprawl, which already has wiped out many fine vineyards in the other counties neighboring San Francisco Bay. When in 1968 the Napa Board of Supervisors blocked the sub-dividers' bulldozers by enacting a minimum twenty-acre agricultural preserve zoning law,* the land-development interests challenged the law in the courts. The Supervisors also compelled the state highway division to reroute a projected new freeway that would have cut a six-lane swath through the valley's main vineyard areas. While these battles drag on, alarmed conservationists have come up with an idea to save the vineyards if all other measures fail. They hope to persuade the Federal Government to designate the Bay Area grape-growing districts as a National Vineyard, like the National Parks.

· 3 ·

To get acquainted with Napa wines, you should tour the vineyards along the side roads and in the hills as well as those along the highway before you join the crowds in the tasting rooms. You will find that Napa, like Sonoma and Mendocino, has several climatically different winegrowing districts.

A striking example is the Carneros ("sheep" in Spanish) district, through which you pass when driving east from Sonoma on Highway 12-121. You enter the Napa Valley at its lower end. The vineyards here are close to San Pablo Bay. Because the Carneros is cooled in summer by winds and fogs from the salty bay, it is called the burgundy district of Napa County; its climate is rated as "low Region I." Such burgundian grape varieties as Chardonnay and Pinot Noir are said to develop higher flavors here—at least one more point of acidity in balance with their sugar content when ripe—than when grown farther up the valley. Vintners whose main vineyards are in those warmer areas have acquired lands in this district to grow these two grape varieties in particular. On the other hand, Cabernet Sauvignon, a Bordeaux variety, fails to ripen fully in some of the Carneros vineyards except in unusually warm years, although when it does reach full ripeness here, it makes a superlative wine.

There is only one active winery in the Carneros, the old cellar

---

*Under this Napa County law, no house may now be erected in the main vineyard areas on any parcel of land smaller than twenty acres. Another measure that is helping to protect the vineyards is the state's 1965 Land Conservation Act. Under the state law, landowners who pledge to use their property only for agriculture for at least ten years can have it taxed on its value for farmland instead of at its higher value for business or for subdivisions. This is called "greenbelting the land."

on the Garetto vineyard, now owned by Beringer, on Buchli Road. Before Prohibition there were many others, the greatest of which was Judge John Stanly's La Loma Winery on Stanly Lane. Another famous winery was the stone castle that can be seen from the highway, in the spectacular vineyard to the left with its lake and modernistic sculptures. It is now the baronial residence of art collector Rene di Rosa, who replanted the century-old vineyard in 1961.

Different climates are also found in the uplands, where temperatures vary with the altitude and with the angle of exposure of each slope to the sun. The upland growers will tell you that certain grape varieties, Riesling in particular, develop higher aromas and more delicate balance in mountain vineyards than when grown on the valley floor. Before you continue up the valley, a side trip into the hills to explore this aspect will be worth your while.

• 4 •

Redwood Road, at the north end of Napa city, takes off in a northwesterly direction through a thickly wooded canyon into the hills. In a six-mile drive of many turns, you climb a thousand feet and reach a lovely, undulating mountain meadow that is carpeted with almost a hundred and fifty acres of vines.

Side by side in this vineyard stand the imposing mission-style monastery of the Christian Brothers,* an ivy-clad stone winery, a wooden tasting room with a "Visitors Welcome" sign, and a modest brick office building that faces the road.

The monastery is the Novitiate of Mont La Salle, where young men are trained to join this worldwide Catholic teaching order, founded in France in 1680 by Saint Jean Baptiste de la Salle. The old winery is one of five the Brothers own; it is where they have made their table wines. The brick building is the corporate headquarters of their Mont La Salle Vineyards, which, the Brothers want you to know, is a taxpaying concern like any other commercial vintner.

The Brothers are now the largest producers of Napa grapes and wines, and also of California brandy and premium-priced California dessert wines. Remembering that winemaking monks in the monasteries of Europe advanced the art and science of the vintager through the Middle Ages, it is of historical interest that the Christian Brothers of California are now the largest Church-owned producer of wine in the world.

---

*Officially, Fratres Scholarum Christianarum (the initials F.S.C. follow the members' names) or Brothers of the Christian Schools.

Though the Brothers are educators, not priests, they take vows similar to those taken by priests and wear much the same clerical garb, including black ankle-length robes. Three members who live at the Napa monastery supervise the vineyards and wineries. Brother U. Gregory, who was Hubert Schiefelbein when he gave up a successful business career to join the order, has been the president since his predecessor, Brother John, died in 1963. His assistant is Brother Frederick Portillo. The cellarmaster and vice president is courtly Brother Timothy, whose picture you see in the magazine ads. Brother Tim was graduated from the Brothers' high school in Los Angeles as Anthony Diener, then taught chemistry before coming to Mont La Salle in 1936. He is famous for his collection of a thousand corkscrews and for his part in creating the Brothers' exhibit, entitled "Five Hundred Years of Wine in the Arts," which will be housed in their wine museum, opening in 1973 at Beach and Hyde streets in San Francisco.

In their upland vineyard, its northeasterly slope exposed to the morning sun, the Brothers grow the grapes for their two estate-bottled wines—the pale gold, pleasingly fragrant Chardonnay and the deep-flavored red Pinot Saint George.

Counting their altar wines, which are sold only to the clergy, the Brothers make some fifty different products, ranging from burgundy and brandy through nearly the entire list of generic and "varietal" table, dessert, and sparkling wine types. Many of them are distinctive, especially the Château La Salle, a sweet but non-cloying light table wine made principally of the Muscat Canelli or Frontignan grape; it is the best-known wine of its type in the world. The Brothers use no vintage labels, preferring to blend together the wines of different years, which contributes to quality and makes it possible to maintain uniformity from bottle to bottle. Some of their wines, produced in small quantities, have *cuvée* numbers on their labels, because these may vary from batch to batch.

The Christian Brothers began making wine in 1882 at their original novitiate in Martinez, first for their table and altar use, then for sale. The city of Martinez began growing up around the novitiate, so they decided to move, and in 1931 bought the Napa upland site. The vineyard there was originally planted by one H. Hudemann about 1864, later was owned by Rudolf Jordan of the pre-Prohibition wine firm of A. Repsold, then was purchased and replanted by Oakland vintner Theodore Gier, who built the stone cellar in 1906.

When the building of the new novitiate began in the depression year of 1932, the western schools of the Christian Brothers were in imminent danger of going bankrupt, their property heavily mortgaged. Their creditors suggested that the Brothers' altar wine business, which had continued during the dry years, should go commercial, now that the repeal of Prohibition appeared imminent. The Brothers agreed, and began to pray for Repeal.

The winemaking job at the Napa winery was given to stalwart young Brother John, who before he joined the order was Stanley (Biff) Hoffman of Oregon gridiron fame. Brother John's first act was to enroll at the University of California in Berkeley for a crash course in enology under Professor William V. Cruess. Returning to the winery, he managed to put some reasonably sound wines on the market in San Francisco by the end of 1934. He next sent his younger brother, John Hoffman, to the Davis campus for more advanced training, and then made John his winemaker, a job John still holds. ("Brother John's brother John is on the 'phone," my secretary used to say.)

In 1937, the astute Brother John teamed with the Europe-trained wine merchants, Alfred Fromm and Franz Sichel, to launch the wines on the national market. The name on the Brothers' wine labels was then changed from Mont La Salle, which is still used on their altar wines, to "The Christian Brothers"—which many buyers still mistake as meaning some brothers named Christian.

In 1940, the Brothers' brandy blend made its debut. Since then, as their sales grew, they have added several more vineyards in the Napa Valley, making a total of 1400 acres in the county, and 1000 more in the San Joaquin Valley. They also added four more wineries, two of them at St. Helena and one each at Reedley and Fresno. By 1972 their wines were known throughout the nation and were being exported commercially to thirty-four countries around the world, and their brandy to thirteen. They now have an additional brandy, named "XO Rare Reserve," which resembles French cognac because it contains 50 percent potstill brandy aged in wood for ten years.

• 5 •

From Mont La Salle, if you are an adventurous driver and have telephoned ahead for an appointment, climb another thousand feet via tortuous Mount Veeder and Lokoya Roads to the spectacular Mayacamas Vineyard, the highest in Napa County. The forty acres of terraced vines cling to the upper slopes of 2600-foot Veeder Mountain, an extinct volcano. At this elevation, far above the valley fogs, the grapes ripen with high acidity a week earlier than elsewhere in the county. In an average winter the vineyard is blanketed with snow.

In the volcanic crater stands a three-story cellar of native stone, built by John Henry Fischer from Stuttgart in 1889. This is the kind of place that lures amateurs who dream of owning a winery and growing great wines. In 1941, just such amateurs, British-born chemist J. F. M. (Jack) Taylor and his American wife Mary purchased Mayacamas. The Taylors replanted the abandoned vineyard, fenced it against the deer who ate the first shoots, and then fought off the grape-stealing birds. They reopened the old winery, and a succession of winemakers made them some wines, of which the best, to my taste, was an occasional lot of Cabernet. To help keep the enterprise going, some 500 customers bought stock in Mayacamas at ten dollars a share, which entitled them to buy the wines at a discount. Handsomely labeled, the wines eventually acquired top-level distribution in several states. The Taylors devoted three decades to their labor of love, and then began looking for someone else to carry on.

A young San Francisco investment banker educated at Stanford, Robert Travers, had caught the wine bug about 1963 when he began reading wine literature. He visited wineries, studied viticultural texts, took three short courses in enology at Davis, and then spent six months touring the vineyards of Europe and South America before deciding to make the break. In 1968, he shed his Brooks Brothers suit for Levi's and took a job working in the Heitz winery to gain experience, searching meanwhile for a vineyard site. A year later, with six limited partners, Travers purchased Mayacamas. He bought out all the little stockholders, and moved with his wife and baby into the old still house beside the winery on the mountain.

Travers has reduced the list of Mayacamas wines from seventeen to eight, and is specializing in four vintage-dated "varietals" that he makes himself—Cabernet Sauvignon, Chardonnay, Chenin Blanc, and Zinfandel Rosé.

• 6 •

As you head north from Napa on The Wine Road up the valley, the change in climate along the route is noticeable in summer. As far north as Oakville it may be cool, for that area is in Region I. From Oakville to St. Helena, the weather gets warmer, averaging in Region II. As you approach Calistoga, summer days are still warmer, and that part of the valley is classed as Region III.

After leaving Napa, the first large vineyard on the right is Oak Knoll, planted by Joseph Osborn in the early 1850s. A later owner was J. Clark Fawver, who called it the Eschcol Vineyard, which may have been its original name. The place now belongs to Eugene Trefethen, the executive vice president of Kaiser Industries. He has replanted the vineyard and is studying plans for a future winery there.

Beyond Oak Knoll, on the site of an old dairy, is a new vineyard of Pinot Noir and Chardonnay owned by Llords & Elwood, an Alameda County firm. Richard Elwood says his firm plans soon to move all its operations to Napa because it is the only county in which vineyards are protected by a zoning law.

At Yountville village, three miles north of Elwood's, the big brick Groezinger winery and distillery have been transformed into a tourist shopping complex named "Vintage 1870." That was the year when Gottlieb Groezinger from Württemberg began building the structures and planting his great vineyard nearby. The Groezinger cellar stood idle through Prohibition and until the wine shortage during the Second World War, when wine was made there for a few seasons. Now Robert Ellsworth, "The Compleat Winemaker," uses part of the cellar for a retail wine shop and for his home-winemaking equipment business. During the vintage season, he also sells fresh grapes to amateur vintners at thirty-nine to sixty-four cents a pound, either pressing the grapes on the spot or shipping them refrigerated to any part of the United States. He has bonded one end of the building and makes wine while the amateurs watch, using the same equipment he sells to them. Beside the bonded area, Ellsworth's wife, Phoebe, makes wine labels in a little print shop which she calls "The Vintage Press."

Three miles past Yountville is an abandoned great stone cellar a half mile to the left. Captain John Benson built it during the 1880s; the label on his wines showed a little girl sleeping in a hammock and the slogan "Without a Care." The adjoining great vineyard, west of Oakville, was once the famous To Kalon, founded by Henry Crabb in 1868 but now divided among several owners.

Nearby, on the Oakville Grade Road, is the state-owned vineyard where the University of California tests new grape varieties for suitability to the Napa climate. Many such experimental vineyards were maintained by the Federal Department of Agriculture in several grape-growing states before Prohibition. All were abandoned during the dry era except the ones at Oakville and Fresno. The former was deeded to the University in 1940.

In Oakville village, there is a stucco-fronted winery on the right that dates from 1877. Originally it was the Nouveau Médoc Vineyard cellar of Brun & Chaix, who were refugees from the troubles in France following the Franco-Prussian war. Jean Adolph Brun knew winemaking, and his partner, Jean Chaix, was experienced in growing grapes. They bought a small vineyard on Howell Mountain, east of St. Helena, and built their cellar on the flat at

Oakville, close to the railroad. By 1889 their vineyards covered 115 acres; their Nouveau Médoc sweetish red wine was the favorite in New Orleans, and their whites were popular in California and the East. But Brun died young, and in 1913 Chaix and his widow sold the property. The buyer was the California Wine Association, which in turn sold to the Covick Company, makers of sacramental wines during Prohibition. In 1940 the cellar was sold at auction to the Napa Wine Company of Louis Stralla. He sold it six years later for a quarter-million to the Cella Vineyards of Fresno. Now United Vintners crushes and ferments the grapes there for Inglenook table wines.

Next door is another old winery, with a new sign that says "Oakville Vineyards." This is a premium wine enterprise launched in 1969 by a group of connoisseurs headed by Wilfred E. van Loben Sels of Carmel. Built in 1892 as the Madonna Winery, the cellar was used after Repeal to make bulk wine and brandy by the Bartolucci brothers, from whom Oakville Vineyards has purchased the buildings and nearly 300 acres of vineyards nearby. The new winemaker is Peter Karl Heinz Becker, who had his own winery in Germany before coming to this country to manage Almadén's Cienega Vineyard winery near Hollister, where he stayed for eleven years. The new proprietors have converted the still house, which borders Oakville Cross-Road, into a handsome tasting room.

· 7 ·

On the left just past Oakville is the Robert Mondavi Winery, which crushed its first vintage in 1966 before the attractive mission-style building was half finished. It has been growing ever since, stainless steel tanks for new wines going up faster than walls could be erected to conceal them from the highway. Starting without vineyards of their own, Bob Mondavi and his son Michael have acquired 800 acres, of which half are already planted with premium grape varieties.

They planned their winery to accommodate visitors, are getting them at the rate of 1500 per week and are selling them a tenth of the winery's output. There are three tasting rooms, an art exhibit, and interior and lawn space for visiting groups to hold concerts and plays, with tastings provided during the intermissions. Robert Mondavi wines are distributed through wine merchants in some three dozen states with the help of Sick's Rainier Brewing Company of Seattle, which owns half of the enterprise as an investment in diversification.

This was one of the first California wineries to make extensive use of European oak barrels and casks for aging its wines after they are fermented in the stainless steel tanks. Several of the Mondavi wines are therefore reminiscent of their Old World counterparts. Thus far eleven types, all vintage-dated "varietals," have been introduced: two different Sauvignon Blancs, the drier one named Fumé Blanc because it resembles the French Pouilly-Fumé from the Loire; Chardonnay, Chenin Blanc, Riesling, Johannisberg Riesling, Traminer, Cabernet, Pinot Noir, Gamay, and Gamay Rosé.

In September 1972 at the Buena Vista Vineyard near Sonoma, eleven of California's leading winegrowers participated in a "blind" tasting of their own Cabernets, which were purchased for the occasion from retail stores, to determine whose wine was currently the finest. When the scores of all eleven wines were tallied, Robert Mondavi's Cabernet Sauvignon 1969 led all the rest.

• 8 •

Next on the route is the hamlet of Rutherford, the home of two famous wineries with similar ownership but contrasting histories and competing managements—Inglenook and Beaulieu.

When the Finnish sea captain, Gustave Ferdinand Niebaum (originally Nybom), had made his fortune in the Alaska fur-sealing trade, he wanted to build a ship. But his wife did not share his love of the sea, so he adopted winegrowing as a hobby instead. In 1879 he bought a young vineyard named Inglenook from one W. C. Watson and retained the name, which suggests a pleasant nook by a fireside. Niebaum replanted the place with vines he imported from the best wine districts of Europe. He then built the three-story Gothic winery of stone, now covered with ivy, at the end of Niebaum Lane. It was finished in 1887, when the captain was forty-five.

Niebaum's aim was to grow wines as fine as any in the world, regardless of expense or financial gain. He often said that the only wines on which he ever made a profit were those he gave to his friends. A perfectionist, he wore white cotton gloves when he inspected his cellars, and woe betide the employees if his gloves became soiled. His sample room was a gustatory chapel with tinted Dutch glass windows and antiquities worthy of a European museum. He also made brandy, but becoming offended one day by the manner in which a revenue agent inspected his distillery, the captain ordered it to be torn down the following morning.

Frona Eunice Wait, writing in 1889, described Inglenook as the

California equivalent of Schloss Johannisberg in Germany or of Châteaux Lafite and d'Yquem in France. In that year Niebaum achieved his goal when Inglenook wines won quality awards at the Paris Exposition. They continued to do so until his death in 1908 at the age of sixty-six. Twelve years later came Prohibition, and the winery was closed.

At Repeal in 1933, Niebaum's widow Suzanne entrusted the reopening of Inglenook to Carl Bundschu of the great pre-Prohibition wine firm of Gundlach & Bundschu. Six years later, Mrs. Niebaum's grandnephew, John Daniel, Jr., took charge. Captain Niebaum had never allowed the Inglenook brand to appear on any bottles except his best. Bundschu and Daniel were enjoined by Mrs. Niebaum to conduct the business the same way. They seldom made any profit for Inglenook, but they restored it to the eminence it had reached in the captain's day.

In 1939, the San Francisco Wine & Food Society held a dinner in tribute to Inglenook, at the Palace Hotel. Among the wines served were four relics supplied by Daniel from the family cellar: Inglenook Sauterne 1907, Riesling 1910, Pinot Noir 1892, and Napa Valley Red 1884. Those ancient vintages, though frail and varying from bottle to bottle, gave us proof of the great longevity of Napa Valley wines. The Pinot Noir, which had been recorked in 1912, was exquisitely delicate, rich in bouquet, magnificent. That evening we also drank up the last few bottles of Niebaum's brandy, *circa* 1885.

It was that dinner which caused me to choose the Cabernet of Inglenook to start my own cellar collection of Napa Valley reds, which now includes every vintage bottled since 1938. Two years are missing, because the entire '45 and '47 vintages of Cabernet were sold in bulk; John Daniel didn't consider them fine enough to bear the Inglenook name. The Cabernets of the early 1940s required ten to eleven years of aging in wood and glass to develop great bouquet, and some of them have retained it for almost thirty years. I wasn't surprised when a case of the 1941 vintage brought twenty dollars a bottle at the 1969 Heublein auction in Chicago.

Daniel was one of the first premium vintners to adopt (in 1940) varietal instead of generic labels for most of his table wines. The exception was his rosé, first made in 1935, which he named Navalle for the creek that curves through the Niebaum estate.

Under Daniel, Inglenook carried on the Niebaum tradition for twenty-five years. It therefore was a shock to the lovers of its wines and of antiquity to learn in 1964 that the old winery had been sold to the giant United Vintners wine firm—even though John Daniel stayed on. He continued to live in the great Niebaum house, which is uphill from the cellars. He retained and enlarged

the family vineyards, and he continued as a member of the Inglenook tasting panel until his death in 1970. Why did he sell the
winery? He never gave his friends a reason, but Daniel, unlike
the Rothschilds of Europe, had no sons to carry on.

The same twelve estate-bottled, vintage-dated Inglenook
"varietals" and Navalle Rosé are still being made, as well as the
"cask selection" vintages of Cabernet, Pinot Noir, and Chardonnay. My favorite winemaker, George Deuer, retired when Inglenook was sold and has now been succeeded by Ernest Digardi. A
new, modern bottling house has been built beside the old cellar,
and no wine has been made at Inglenook since the crushing and
fermentation were moved to Oakville. The "estate" represented
by the "estate bottled" label has been enlarged to include 1500
more Napa Valley acres owned by Bruno Solari and other members of the Allied Grape Growers co-operative, of which United
Vintners is the marketing arm. Five generic and "varietal" coast
counties "district wines" have been added under an Inglenook
Vintage label that is priced a fourth lower than the estate-bottled
line, plus five less-expensive Inglenook "Navalle" wines that may
come from anywhere in northern California. The two San Joaquin
Valley dessert wines that Inglenook used to blend and age have
been increased to five, and an Inglenook Champagne has been
introduced, with the champagnizing done by the Hanns Kornell
cellar at St. Helena. Inglenook wines, formerly sold in only seventeen states, have attained national distribution since Heublein
bought control of United Vintners in 1968 and quadrupled its
budgets for advertising.

To those of us who are sentimental about old Inglenook, there
may be some comfort in what Daniel's immediate successor as
manager, Lelio N. (Bob) Bianchini, told me the year after the take-
over—that Inglenook operations were showing a profit for the
first time in many years.

• 9 •

In 1883, while Captain Niebaum was building the great Inglenook winery, a stocky little twenty-six-year-old Frenchman,
Georges de Latour from Périgord, arrived in San Francisco to seek
his fortune. During a try at gold-mining in the Sierra foothills,
he lost what little money he had. Then, because his family in
France had made wine and he had learned chemistry at the École
Centrale in Paris, he took himself to the north coast wine country.
He traveled by horse and wagon among the wineries, buying the
sediment and crust (argols) from their wine tanks to make cream
of tartar, which he sold to be made into baking powder. For six-

teen years he built up his cream of tartar business at Healdsburg in Sonoma County, but meanwhile planned to become a wine-grower. In 1899, when Inglenook wines were already famed at home and abroad, de Latour bought an orchard and wheatfield immediately north of Inglenook. His wife Fernande named it Beaulieu, "beautiful place." He went to France, brought back vines of the best French varieties to plant on his land, and opened his first small winery. Several years later he acquired additional vineyards at Oakville and on the east side of the valley along the Silverado Trail. In 1915 he bought the Seneca Ewer winery across the road from his home vineyard, enlarged its stone cellar, and made it the main Beaulieu winery.

When Inglenook, its owner long dead, was closed down at the beginning of Prohibition, de Latour kept Beaulieu open, for he held the approbation of San Francisco Archbishop Patrick Riordan as a supplier of altar wines, which were legal, to the Catholic Church. He prospered during the dry years, building a nation-wide business in altar wines, which Beaulieu still enjoys today. At Repeal he was one of the few vintners ready to supply fine, fully aged California wines to the connoisseur trade. In the wine judg-ing at the Golden Gate International Exposition in 1939, his Beaulieu Burgundy (which he made of Cabernet Sauvignon grapes) was chosen above a hundred other entries to receive the grand prize for red wines.

At the home vineyard, de Latour and his wife—a stately, gra-cious *grande dame*—added wings to their rambling country house, planted formal gardens studded with fountains and statuary, and made Beaulieu the most famous estate in the Napa Valley. They dispensed hospitality to San Francisco high society and enter-tained such illustrious personages as President Herbert Hoover, Sir Winston Churchill, and visiting nobility. They made annual visits to France, which was how it happened that their daughter, Helene, was married in 1924 to the Marquis Galcerand de Pins, himself a winegrower at his ancestral estate, the Château de Monbrun in Gascony.

George de Latour was said to be the colorful central character of the best-selling novel of 1942, *The Cup and the Sword*, which fifteen years later became the feature movie *This Earth Is Mine*. I can confirm this because, after his death in 1940, I furnished the back-ground material to the author, Alice Tisdale Hobart; and she re-warded me by making me a recognizable character (Galen Ritter, the ex-newspaperman) in the book. The French winegrower hero of the story, Jean-Philippe Rambeau, portrayed in the movie by Claude Rains, bore only basic resemblance to de Latour because Mrs. Hobart took pains to alter his picture sufficiently—by giving him wineries in both the San Joaquin and Napa Valleys—to avoid the possibility of a lawsuit. (I was disappointed by the novel, however, for the author put all of her dramatic writing into her fictional scenes and none into the single episode that was true—the climax to de Latour's career—the greatest funeral held in San Francisco in that decade, at which four archbishops presided.)

Georges de Latour was a great judge of wine and also of winemakers. When his enologist, Professor Leon Bonnet, retired in 1937, de Latour and the Marquis de Pins traveled to France to find a successor. At the Institut National Agronomique in Paris, they asked Professor Paul Marsais to recommend a man. Marsais had a Russian assistant, a research enologist named André Tchelistcheff, who might be right for the job. Tchelistcheff was hired and arrived at Rutherford in time for the 1938 vintage.

In bringing Tchelistcheff to California, de Latour did as much for the state's wines in general—and later for the wines of northern Mexico and of the State of Washington—as for the wines of Beaulieu. Tchelistcheff was born in Moscow in 1901, the son of a law professor, and was educated in Czechoslovakia after serving in the czarist and White Russian armies. This intense little man was thirty-seven when he left France. He brought to California the latest findings of French enological and viticultural research.

When Tchelistcheff first tasted Napa wines, he decided that Cabernet Sauvignon grown in this climate was destined to become one of the great wines of the world. He persuaded de Latour to build a separate cellar to age Beaulieu Cabernet in oak barrels for at least two years. When the Cabernet from the new cellar was bottle-ripe, he matured it for another two years in glass. Released the year after the founder's death, it was named "Georges de Latour Private Reserve." It was the 1936 vintage and was priced at a dollar and a half. (At this writing, the ten-year-old Private Reserve brings fourteen dollars a bottle in the few stores that have any in stock. The three-year-old can be bought at the Beaulieu tasting room in Rutherford for $5.25, but there is a limit of two bottles per buyer. BV Private Reserve Cabernet has become the single most-praised and most sought-after American wine.)

For years Tchelistcheff urged the Beaulieu owners to concentrate on producing only Cabernet Sauvignon or at most one or two other fine wines—to discontinue selling their dozens of different types. "With thirty wines to take care of," he argued, "I am producing little starlets when I should produce only great stars." But like other medium-sized American wineries which try to sell their brands nationally, Beaulieu had to continue offering "a complete line." BV still sells both generic and "varietal" table wines, five dessert wines purchased in the San Joaquin Valley and aged at Rutherford, and since 1955 has offered an assortment of champagnes. Its best buys, in my opinion, are the second-grade Cabernet and the Burgundy, priced about half and less than half respectively as much as the Private Reserve. BV also produces one dessert wine of its own, Muscat Frontignan, from this choicest of Muscat grapes, which de Latour planted in his vineyard on the Silverado Trail.

About 1960, Tchelistcheff tasted a Pinot Noir made by Louis Martini from grapes grown in the cool Carneros district, and found it finer than Beaulieu's. He persuaded Madame de Pins to let him plant a Beaulieu vineyard in the Carneros. It is vineyard number five, 140 acres of Pinot Noir and Chardonnay, planted in 1963. If you compare Tchelistcheff's 1966 (Rutherford) Pinot Noir and Chardonnay with his 1967 (Carneros) wines, you will find that he was right.

Besides managing the BV vineyards and winery, Tchelistcheff for fifteen years maintained his own enological laboratory in St. Helena and served as consultant to other Napa and Sonoma wineries. He tutored several young enologists at those wineries who since have made some of the finest post-Repeal California wines. One of those he trained was his son Dmitri, who since has produced some of the finest wines thus far made in Mexico. André Tchelistcheff himself has guided the Washington State wine industry in its first concerted effort to produce premium European-type table wines.

In 1969 the admirers of Napa wines, still perturbed over the sale of Inglenook four years earlier, got another shock when Beaulieu and four of its five vineyards were sold to the mammoth Heublein liquor, wine, and beer firm. "Another Winery Swallowed by the Giants!" the newspaper headline read. The sale was not made through Allied Grape Growers and United Vintners as in Inglenook's case, but to Heublein direct.

"It's a terrible wrench," said the Marquise de Pins, who had succeeded her late mother as Beaulieu president, "but circumstances force changes; it's more practical for a big organization to operate in these times." However, the de Pins' and their daughter, Dagmar Sullivan, have kept the Beaulieu estate, which is de Latour's original Cabernet vineyard. They are selling the grapes to Heublein, but a small winery stands on the old vineyard, and there is a de Latour grandson, Walter Sullivan III, who someday may be interested in following his ancestor's steps.

Despite the change in ownership, Tchelistcheff, now in his seventies, remains as consultant on Beaulieu vineyards and wines, as enthusiastic as ever about making each vintage better than those before. At the 1970 meeting of the American Society of

Enologists, his pupils and the rest of the nation's wine industry joined to pay him tribute as "the winemaker's winemaker," presenting him with the annual A.S.E. merit award.

Although Inglenook and Beaulieu both are now Heublein companies, they are competitors like Cadillac and Oldsmobile, managed by separate Heublein divisions. Inglenook is the top brand of United Vintners, which also owns Italian Swiss Colony and the numerous Petri brands. Beaulieu wines are sold by the division which sells most of the Heublein imports. People at first wondered which of the two would be featured as Heublein's best California wine. The Beaulieu wines, bringing higher prices, seem already to be winning the competition. United Vintners recently answered this with full-page magazine ads for Inglenook, saying: "Our only competitor . . . is us."

• 10 •

A mile past Beaulieu, land has just been cleared for the Franciscan Vineyards winery, another addition to Napa Valley's "Winery Row." Charles Dilling, the son of a leading San Francisco wine merchant, plans to build there a mission-style cellar with a bell tower, reflecting pool, and tasting room, to open in fall of 1973.

As you approach St. Helena, a sign at the right invites you to the Heitz Cellar tasting room. It is worth a stop, but be sure to save time for a later visit to the Heitz family's winery and vineyard two miles to the east.

On the left is the big Napa Valley Co-operative Winery, which makes wine out of Napa grapes for Gallo and sends it all, except what the grower members bottle to drink themselves, in tank trucks to Modesto. The Co-op cellar is two wineries in one, for it was built around a much older stone winery that once belonged to Oakland vintner Theodore Gier.

Next door to the Co-op is the Sutter Home Winery, which warrants a pause to taste California's only Chinato, the sweet quinined apéritif wine much favored in Italy. The firm was founded on Howell Mountain in 1890 by John Sutter, a cousin of the Captain Sutter of Sutter's Fort fame, but was moved in 1906 and has been owned by the Trinchero family since 1947. Bob Trinchero also makes several kinds of table wine, including an excellent Zinfandel, a light Moscato Canelli, and a sweet rosé from some Mission grapes that he found growing in an old vineyard west of Plymouth in Amador County.

• 11 •

Across the road from Sutter Home, there is a 2-million-gallon concrete cellar with a new tasting room and a modest sign facing the highway, that says "Louis M. Martini Winery." Few know the true story of its famous founder and his wines.

Louis Michael Martini was born in 1887 in the seaport of Pietra Ligure on the Italian Riviera, the son of a shoemaker. When Louis was thirteen, he crossed the Atlantic in the steerage to join his father, Agostino, who had emigrated six years before and started a shellfish business in San Francisco. During his teens, Louis dug clams on the bay mud flats, gathered mussels from the piers, and gill-netted striped bass on one of his father's gaff-rigged fishing boats. In the earthquake year of 1906, his father started a back-yard winery near Hunter's Point because the clam population in the south bay was dying from pollution. The whole first vintage turned out spoiled, so Louis, then nineteen, was sent to Italy to learn how to make wine. After eight months in the Alba enology school, he came home in time to make the 1907 vintage, which didn't spoil. Louis peddled the wine, together with mussels and clams, to the San Francisco fish markets and then sold wine from door to door in the Italian North Beach district. He later made wine at a vineyard his father rented between Pleasanton and Suñol in Alameda County, then in successive seasons was the winemaker at the Bradford Winery in Thornton and the Guasti Vineyard near Cucamonga. Early in the Prohibition era, as a partner in the former Italian Swiss Colony winery at Kingsburg, Fresno County, he made a grape concentrate called "Forbidden Fruit," a name which appealed to the nation's home winemakers. At Repeal he switched to making bulk wine and shipped it across the country in tank cars to eastern wineries.

I remember my first meeting with Louis Martini because he would never let me forget it. It was in 1935 at the Hotel Senator in Sacramento, where we were attending a hearing on wine taxes. This fiery, blue-eyed, square-jawed ex-fisherman always loved to argue. I have heard him say, in order to heat up a discussion, "I don't agree with you—and if you agree with me, I'll change my mind!" That evening in Sacramento he said to me, "Five years from now, mark my words, I'll be making the best dry wines in California." I judged him then as either a boaster or a dreamer, for how could a San Joaquin Valley bulk wine maker fulfill so absurd a promise?

What I didn't know was that Martini a few years earlier had bought a St. Helena vineyard, had built a new winery there, and had begun quietly amassing a hoard of fine, aged table and dessert wines, not a drop of which would be released until all were bottled and ready.

In 1940, Martini sold his Kingsburg plant to the Central California Wineries merger, moved with his family to St. Helena, and put his whole line of aged wines on the market at once. At that time when fine California wines were scarce, their quality created a sensation. He became famous overnight as one of the coast counties premium table-wine producers. For decades afterward, Martini reminded me each time we met, "What did I tell you that night at the Hotel Senator in Sacramento?"

One of the wines he introduced in 1940 was his Moscato Amabile. It is still sold, but only at the winery. At 10 percent alcohol it is so delicate that it must be kept refrigerated until served. When I first asked Martini how he made it, he said it was a secret; but years later he said it was an accident. At Kingsburg, in 1928, he found several barrels of Muscat of Alexandria juice that had lain in a corner of the winery all winter because his fermenting tanks were full. In spring, when the juice was tasted, Martini expected it to be spoiled, but instead it sparkled like champagne. He couldn't remember what else had been put in those barrels, but kept experimenting until another batch, fermented for four years in a cold room, turned out the same as the original. Moscato Amabile has yet to be duplicated in this country. However, Cyril Ray describes in his *Wines of Italy* a semi-sparkling 8 percent Muscat wine called Moscatello, made in Liguria and favored there for family picnics.

On Martini's second Napa vineyard, situated near the hills south of St. Helena, there is a handsome stone winery that dates from 1883. This was where he amassed his secret stock of fine wines during the 1930s, and beside it he built his home. In 1937, he bought the 300-acre Mount Pisgah Vineyard on the Sonoma County side of the Mayacamas range, a thousand feet above Agua Caliente, and renamed it Monte Rosso for its red volcanic soil. With half of his grapes coming from Sonoma, he could not call his wines "Napa" so he used the appellation "mountain" instead. He kept adding vineyards: a part of the Stanly Carneros property in 1942, 200 acres on the Russian River below Healdsburg in 1962, more Carneros acreage two years later, and in 1970 he planted 15 acres in 900-foot-high Chiles Valley, five miles east of St. Helena, making almost 900 acres in all.

In 1960, at the age of seventy-three, Louis relinquished the presidency of his firm to his son, six-foot-four Louis Peter Martini, who had studied enology and viticulture at the University's Berkeley and Davis campuses. But Louis the elder was still the boss, one of the last few pre-Prohibition winemakers still active in California. Louis Peter lives with his wife Elizabeth and three of their children on the old Edge Hill Vineyard, founded in 1870 by the pioneer Indian fighter, General E. D. Keyes. Their home has two-foot-thick walls, for it was once the Edge Hill winery. Their eldest son, Michael, has studied viticulture at Davis and expects to join the winery when he completes his service with the Air Force in Germany.

The Martinis sell thirty table and four dessert wines. Eleven of the table wines are old private reserve and special selection lots sold only at the winery. The "varietals" are all vintage-dated and bring higher prices than the generic types. Outstanding are the old Cabernets, Pinot Noirs, and Zinfandels, and the Private Reserve Gewürztraminer, which is drier and spicier than most on the market. Martini's is the only winery that makes a "varietal" wine of Folle Blanche, a white grape grown in the Monte Rosso Vineyard. I once congratulated old Louis on having planted Folle Blanche, a grape the University doesn't recommend for California, but which he makes into a lovely dry, crisp wine resembling chablis. "I didn't plant it," he replied; "it was growing there when I bought the vineyard."

• 12 •

Next door to Martini is the handsome South St. Helena Cellar of the Christian Brothers. Built in 1965 to store bottled wines, it is already being enlarged as the beginning of a winery complex more immense than anything the valley has ever seen. New crushers and presses have been installed, and the Brothers henceforth will make most of their wines here. In the next four years they plan a circular complex of new champagne cellars, warehouses, offices, tasting rooms, catering kitchens, and a tourist facility to accommodate millions of visitors.

The old town of St. Helena has fourteen bonded wineries within the city limits and also a considerable acreage of vineyards, which unfortunately are not protected by the county zoning law. Although most of the city's 3000 population are concerned in some way with winegrowing, there are many who oppose the drinking of wine. They are the Seventh Day Adventists, whose big St. Helena Sanitarium frowns down on the vineyards from the hill east of town; they also oppose the consumption of tea, coffee, and meat.

The St. Helena Library contains the only public wine library in the United States. It is supported by the Napa Valley Wine Library Association, which anyone may join for five dollars a year, and which conducts periodic wine tastings and wine appreciation courses, the latter taught by the local winemakers.

On the main street is the Sunny St. Helena Winery, a co-operative of twenty-five growers headed by Charles Forni, which produces bulk wine for the Charles Krug Winery. Many venerable stone buildings on the side streets are pre-Prohibition wineries, since remodeled to house small business ventures. Several historic wine cellars in the neighborhood have been converted into attractive homes.

· 13 ·

From St. Helena, a half-hour climb of Spring Mountain Road affords glimpses of some once-famous mountain vineyards, now being replanted because of the soaring demand for fine table wines. The elegant old estate at the left, where the hill begins, was Tiburcio Parrott's "Miravalle." A half mile further, a narrow private road through forests of oaks and redwoods leads to the great La Perla Vineyard, which is one of the most spectacular in the world. Literally miles of valleys and hills, rising to 1500 feet elevation, are contoured or terraced and carpeted with vines. Charles Lemme from Germany built the stone La Perla winery in the 1870s. His successor was Claus Schilling of the San Francisco family of dealers in wine, spice, coffee, and tea. Now La Perla is owned by realtor-vineyardist Jerome Draper, whose son, Jerome, Jr., expects to reopen the winery when the replanted vines, all of premium varieties, reach full production by 1975.

A mile beyond the La Perla entrance, also on a private road, is Château Chevalier. With its Victorian exterior, twin steeples and stained-glass windows, this is one of the loveliest old stone cellars in the United States. Two San Francisco oenothusiasts, Gregory Bissonette and James E. Frew, bought the property in 1969, replanted the hundred-plus steep acres with the noble vines, started making wine from purchased grapes in 1972, and hoped to market the first Johannisberg Riesling from their vineyard within another two years.

On Langtry Lane, above the La Perla Vinyard, Fritz Maytag of the Newton, Iowa family owns the hundred-acre York Creek Vineyard, which once was part of La Perla. But Maytag is busy running the Anchor Steam Beer Brewery in San Francisco, delivers his grapes to the Napa Co-operative, and does not plan to make his own wine.

Still higher on the mountain, at almost two thousand feet elevation, Fred Aves and his son Russell have built the handsome stone Yverdon winery, which has quatrefoil stained-glass windows, Tudor arches, and the first hillside tunnels dug in Napa County during this century. Aves, a Los Angeles manufacturer of auto supplies, began making wine in his bathtub in 1962, planted vines around his home in Beverly Glen, then sold his factory because he was bored and wanted to become a winegrower. Father and son have cut and laid every stone of the winery by hand, have bought casks and barrels from Italy and have assembled them themselves. They have planted vines on the mountain, but made their first wine in 1971 from grapes they grow near Calistoga. Yverdon is the name of the village in Switzerland where Aves's grandparents were winegrowers.

Another new mountain winery is the Lyncrest Vineyards, bonded in 1972 on an old vineyard at the west end of White Sulphur Springs Road. It is owned by San Francisco management consultant Richard K. Lynn and seven partners. They plan to produce only Chardonnay, Johannisberg Riesling, and Pinot Noir.

• 14 •

Just beyond the business district of St. Helena is the Beringer Brothers winery, with its picturesque Rhine House, gardens, and maze of wine-aging tunnels dug a thousand feet into the limestone hillside almost a century ago—a tourist attraction that brings hordes of visitors throughout the year.

The title of "oldest Napa winegrower" belongs to this winery because it has never closed since it was built in 1876 and has produced wine in every vintage since 1879, including the Prohibition years when it made sacramental wines.

Jacob and Frederick Beringer came to the United States from Mainz on the Rhine, where Jacob began his winemaking career. From 1872 to 1878, Jacob worked at the nearby Charles Krug winery while the Beringer cellars and vineyards were being established. Frederick then joined him and built the Rhine House, the elegant seventeen-room mansion with carved oak panels and slate roof, which stands beside the winery.

A duplicate of the Rhine House was built by their uphill neighbor, Tiburcio Parrott. Parrott grew grapes for the Beringers on his great estate, which he called "Miravalle" for its view of the valley. He also made his own wines, and the late Almond R. Morrow once told me that a Miravalle claret called "Margaux" was the greatest California wine produced before Prohibition.

After the Beringer brothers died, the descendants of Jacob bought the shares held by the widow and children of "Uncle Fritz" who sold the Rhine House and moved away. Jacob's son, Charles Tiburcio Beringer, let the quality of the wines decline, but was succeeded by his nephew Otto, who improved them and bought back the Rhine House from absentee owners, transforming it into a colorful visitor center and tasting hall. Otto also rediscovered an old Beringer wine called Barenblut ("bear's blood"), a pleasing blend of Grignolino and Pinot Noir.

In 1970, President Gerard J. Gogniat of Nestlé, the multinational Swiss maker of chocolate, Nescafé, and a hundred other food products, decided to enter the fast-growing wine business in the United States. He bought Beringer and its 700 acres of vineyards at St. Helena, Yountville, Knights Valley, and in the Carneros district, where it has the old Garetto winery. The new winemaster of Beringer is Myron Nightingale, the famed creator of Cresta Blanca Premier Sémillon.

· 15 ·

Next door to Beringer is the most prodigious structure in this part of the valley, the Greystone cellar of the Christian Brothers. Millions have toured its cavernous tunnels, which hold two and a half million gallons of aging wine, have watched in fascination how the Brothers' champagnes are made upstairs, have exclaimed over Brother Tim's corkscrew collection on display, and have sampled the Brothers' wines on the main floor. Also fascinating is the history of the colossal building, which when it was built in 1889, was the largest stone winery in the world. During the 1880s, the small Napa winegrowers could not afford to age their wines and had to sell them in bulk to San Francisco wine merchants at ruinously low prices, for no bank would accept wine as collateral for loans. William Bourn, the wealthy young owner of two Napa vineyards, of San Francisco's Spring Valley Water Company, and of sundry mines, conceived of an altruistic scheme. He offered to build this winery to make wine of the growers' grapes, to age the wine, and to lend them ten cents a gallon until it could be sold. When Greystone was opened, however, the phylloxera vine plague had caused a shortage of wine, and the building became a white elephant. It had a procession of owners during the next half century: Charles Carpy, the California Wine Association, Bisceglia Brothers, Central California Wineries, Roma, and Cresta Blanca. The low point in its history was in the Depression year of 1931, when Bisceglia bought it at auction for ten thousand dollars. By 1945, the Christian Brothers needed extra space in which to age their growing stocks of table wines, and rented part of Greystone from Roma. Five years later they bought it, and when Brother John decided in 1955 to begin making champagnes, that department was installed on the third floor. In the cornerstone of the building, according to an early issue of the St. Helena *Star*, there repose, among other historic objects, bottles of Charles Krug and Bourn & Wise wines of the 1884 to 1877 vintages, and a bottle of 1883 Beringer Brandy.

• 16 •

In the competition to be called "the oldest," the Charles Krug winery, across the road from Greystone, cites the date of 1861 when the Prussian emigré for whom it is named built his first winery there. However, only one stone wall of that winery remains, and credit for the many good and fine wines now made there belongs not to Krug, but to the Italian family named Mondavi, who have owned the site since 1943.

Krug was one of the pioneer winegrowers in the valley, but he was not the first. George Yount and several others preceded him by as much as twenty years. Charles (né Karl) Krug came to the United States in 1847, taught for a year in a free-thinkers' school in Philadelphia, returned to Germany and was imprisoned for participating in a revolt against the reactionary parliament, then came back to the United States and became editor of the first German newspaper on the Pacific Coast, published in Oakland. In 1854 he tried farming for several months near "Count" Haraszthy's failing vineyard in San Mateo County, next worked briefly in the San Francisco Mint, then followed Haraszthy to Sonoma, learned winemaking from the "Count" and General Vallejo, and planted a vineyard there. In 1860, the year Abraham Lincoln was elected President, Krug sold his Sonoma vineyard, moved to St. Helena, and married Vallejo's grandniece, Caroline, the daughter of Dr. Edward T. Bale. Her dowry was the land on which he planted vines and erected the original winery in the following year.

During the next two decades, Krug became "the wine king of Napa Valley" and a prominent member of the first State Viticultural Commission. His wines and brandy were sold in the East, in Mexico, Germany, and England. Then phylloxera destroyed most of his vineyard, and Krug's estate was in debt when he died in 1892. A nephew ran the winery until Prohibition, when the then owners, the Moffitt family of bankers and paper merchants, closed it down.

At Repeal, the cellar was leased to Louis Stralla's Napa Wine Company until Stralla moved to the old Brun & Chaix place at Oakville in 1940. The Moffitts meanwhile declined to sell the estate, hoping to find a buyer who could reestablish the earlier prestige of its wines.

In Lodi, one day in 1935, when Robert and Peter Mondavi were home from their studies at Stanford, their father asked them what kind of careers, if any, they had in mind after college. Cesare Mondavi, who had come to America from Italy twenty-seven years before, had a grape shipping business in Lodi and Fresno and had begun making bulk wine at the Acampo Winery at Repeal. When the boys replied that they would like to get into the wine business, Cesare advised them that the future lay in table wines and that the Napa Valley was the place to go.

After graduation, both sons were taught enology by University of California scientists. To start them off, Cesare bought the Sunny St. Helena Winery in 1937. When the chance came six years later to buy the Krug estate for $75,000, the Sunny St. Helena and Acampo wineries were sold.

When C. Mondavi & Sons took over at Krug, bulk wine shipped in tank cars to regional bottlers was the mainstay of their business. To rehabilitate the hundred-acre vineyard, to develop a stock of fine wines, and to introduce a new generation to the name of the long-dead Charles Krug, should have taken many years. But the Mondavis wisely kept their bulk wine business and bottled only their finest wines under the Krug name. Within five years they were winning medals at the State Fair. They opened a tasting room, held lawn tastings, invited visitors to hold picnics (by reservation) on the estate, and published a newsletter named *Bottles and Bins*, which has now been going for more than twenty years. Their August Moon Concerts began in 1965.

The Mondavi and "CK" names on wine labels are a puzzle to the public today. At the Krug winery, the Mondavis have sold their ordinary wines labeled "CK" and "Napa Vista," under the private brands of wholesale buyers, and in bulk. (In recent years of wine shortages sales of bulk and Napa Vista were curtailed.) In 1966, in a family tiff, Robert, the elder Mondavi brother, suddenly quit as manager of the company and started his own Robert Mondavi Winery, described earlier. Peter, the winemaker at Krug, replied by introducing additional wine brands called "Mondavi Vintage" and "Mondavi Vineyards," priced above the "CK" line. But Bob continues as one of the owners and directors of C. Mondavi & Sons and he still lives on the Krug estate. The family still gathers for the holidays at the home of the mother, Mrs. Rosa Mondavi, who has been president of the firm since Cesare died in 1959. Two daughters, Mrs. Helen Ventura and Mrs. Mary Westbrook, and John Alioto, the son of San Francisco Mayor Joseph Alioto, are also directors. Columnist Herb Caen in the San Francisco *Chronicle* reported in 1972 that the directors, by a four-to-three vote, had turned down an offer of $30 million by the Schlitz brewery to buy them out.

At last count, the company was selling under the Charles Krug brand ten generically and sixteen varietally labeled wines, plus a "vintage select" Cabernet Sauvignon when available. The sales of the regular Cabernet, Chardonnay, and Pinot Noir were being rationed to the trade.

The C. Mondavi & Sons or Charles Krug winery has a capacity of some four million gallons, not counting the contract-production at the Sunny St. Helena Winery or the wines the firm owns but has in storage at wineries outside of Napa County. With a new vineyard planted in 1971 in the Carneros district, the firm and members of the family have some eight hundred acres in vines.

• 17 •

Continuing north on The Wine Road past Krug, the winery on the right, with the steel tanks in front, is the former St. Helena Co-operative, now added to the chain of United Vintners-Heublein wine-processing plants.

Beyond the old co-op, the century-old Victorian house at the left, with the acre of vines in front, has a miniature model winery in its cellar. Michael Robbins, an Annapolis graduate engineer and lawyer from Iowa, saw the house during a business visit to the valley in 1963, bought and rebuilt it, and moved in with his wife Shirley and their two young sons. He took winemaking lessons from his neighbors and from Consultant Brad Webb, and made his first wine in 1968. Two years later he planted a twenty-acre vineyard west of Oakville and began building a stone winery behind the house. "Coming from Iowa, we discovered a new world of wine here," he explains. "We hope someday to make the best Chardonnay and Cabernet in the world." Robbins's Spring Mountain Chardonnay and Sauvignon Blanc were released in 1970 and were excellent. His first Cabernet Sauvignon, a blend of 1968 and 1969, just released, shows promise of equaling the best in the Napa Valley of either year.

Next on the right is Freemark Abbey, the moss-covered stone cellar with the candle and gourmet shops upstairs. The building dates from 1895 and was never a monastery, but was named by a group of former owners who combined syllables from their names. The basement, which is entered from the rear, was re-activated as a modern winery in 1967. The new proprietors are seven Napa grape growers who aim to produce small lots of premium table wines from the finest grapes in their vineyards. The chief partner is Charles Carpy, whose Bordeaux-born grandfather owned the Uncle Sam Cellars in Napa city in 1887 and was the largest shareholder in the California Wine Association when it was formed in 1894. If the second Freemark Abbey Cabernet Sauvignon, the 1968, is a fair example, the others to come will be superb. Blended with 3.14 percent of Merlot and aged for precisely the right amount of time in Nevers oak barrels, it is the first California red wine I have thus far tasted that I might have mistaken for a good vintage of Château Margaux.

· 18 ·

About a mile beyond Freemark Abbey there is an unmarked private road on the left. If you have made an appointment with Fred and Eleanor McCrea, you may climb almost two miles up the dirt road and visit their Stony Hill Vineyard. The vines rise almost a thousand feet above the valley and cover some thirty-eight acres of rocky soil, which explains the name. The three wines made here—Chardonnay, Gewürztraminer, and in some years a White Riesling—are so prized by connoisseurs that most of the supply is sold before it is ready to be shipped.

The McCreas' story is an example of what dedicated, meticulous amateur winegrowers can achieve. It has inspired many others to try, and some to succeed. Looking for a place on which to build a summer house, they bought their Napa hillside in 1943, then wondered what to do with the extra space. Neighbors said it would be good for only goats or grapes, so they chose grapes. McCrea, a San Francisco executive of the McCann-Erickson advertising agency, knew nothing about winegrowing, but he knew whom to consult. He asked the University experts what to plant, and they advised Chardonnay. The McCreas first practiced winemaking in their home, and threw their first batch away. Then, guided by friendly Napa vintners, they had their winery built and equipped by 1951. Four years later, they entered their one-year-old Chardonnay in the State Fair at Sacramento and it was awarded a silver medal. In 1960, they entered the two-year-old Chardonnay. It got the gold medal, the highest prize in the state.

The Stony Hill winery is tiny, consisting of several dozen oak barrels, some of which were recently acquired from France, holding five thousand gallons when full. The McCreas sell most of their grapes to neighboring vintners. Each September, when their wines have had a year or two of bottle age, they draft a letter to a small mailing list stating which wines are ready for sale. If your order is sent in promptly, it is likely to be filled, but it is wiser to order a year ahead.

• 19 •

On Larkmead Lane, a quarter mile off The Wine Road, are the champagne cellars of Hanns Kornell, where he makes his excellent "Third Generation" sparkling wines and also the champagnes that several other wineries sell as their own.

The Larkmead Vineyard has been famous since the 1880s, when it was owned by Mrs. Lillie Hitchcock Coit. She was known then as a sort of mascot to the San Francisco Fire Department because of her passion for running to fires, but she is remembered now as the donor of Coit Tower on that city's Telegraph Hill. Another owner before Prohibition was the Felix Salmina family from Switzerland, who after Repeal made a great wine from the true Petit Sirah or Shiraz grape. A succession of proprietors followed, including National Distillers, Bruno Solari, and the Larkmead Co-operative, until Kornell took over in 1958.

Kornell is a stocky little man of incredible stamina and energy. He is more of a legend than his winery. In 1915, at the age of four, he was picking grapes in his grandfather's vineyard at Lublinitz in Germany. At five, he was already cleaning bottles in the cellar. During his school years his father taught him the art of tasting. At graduation he was sent to the Geisenheim enological institute, then worked in wineries in France, Italy, and England. When he was ready in 1939 to take over the family vineyard, the gathering war clouds warned him to go to America. With two dollars in his wallet, he started hitchhiking from New York to California. He worked first as a laborer, then briefly at the old Los Amigos Winery, and next at the Fountain Grove Vineyard, where he was succeeded by his cousin Kurt Opper. In 1942, Kornell went to Covington, Kentucky, to work for the Gibson Wine Company. There he made the first Kentucky champagne (out of California wine) in 1942. Three years later, on a visit to the American Wine Company cellars in St. Louis, whom should I find three stories underground making Cook's Imperial Champagne, but Hanns Kornell? After the American Wine Company was sold to Schenley, Kornell returned to California in 1952, leased the rundown former Tribuno winery at Sonoma, and made his own champagne. Bottling and riddling by night and selling by day, he saved enough in six years to buy Larkmead, and moved to St. Helena. In that same year, he married Marielousie Rossini, whose grandfather planted the first Souverain Vineyard seventy-two years before.

At the Kornell Champagne Cellars you are shown every step in the making of bottle-fermented champagne. Your amiable guide most likely will be the indefatigable owner himself, for he still works fourteen hours a day. Besides the numerous champagnes he makes for other wineries, he makes six kinds—his best—under his own name. He also sells an assortment of eight still wines that he selects from other wineries.

· 20 ·

Five miles north of St. Helena, a small sign at the left of the highway reads "Schramsberg Champagne Cellars—Founded 1862." A narrow road from there winds nearly a mile up the southern slope of Mount Diamond through a thicket of redwoods, buckeyes, and madrones. In a wide clearing at the end is the scene that Robert Louis Stevenson described in *Silverado Squatters*, the same house with its broad verandas where RLS and his bride were entertained in 1880 by Jacob and Annie Schram, and the five underground cellars "dug deep in the hillside like a bandit's cave."

Schram (originally Schramm) arrived in America from the Rhineland in 1842, became an itinerant barber, and stopped in San Francisco long enough to get married. When he reached Napa in 1862, Charles Krug had begun building his winery on the valley floor two years before. Schram had saved enough money to buy a mountainside of his own. While Annie supervised the planting of their vines, Schram continued tramping from farm to farm with his razor and shears. Eighteen years later, Stevenson found Schramsberg "the picture of prosperity." Schramsberger Hock, Golden Chasselas, and Burgundy of Refosco had already won a place on such wine lists as the Palace Hotel's in San Francisco and the Carlton Club's in London.

When Schram died in 1904, his son Herman took over and made wine until Prohibition, when he sold the estate for a summer home. Following Repeal there were two brief revivals, the first by Joseph Gargano's California Champagne Company in 1940, the second in 1951 by the Douglas Pringles. Pringle, a flamboyant interior decorator, revived the Schramsberg label and made rather poor champagnes for a few years. The winery was closed again, and Pringle killed himself in 1960.

Meanwhile, a Stanford and Harvard Business School graduate named Jack L. Davies had joined the San Francisco Wine and Food Society and had developed a taste for fine wines. In 1961 he invested in a Cabernet-planting venture with Martin Ray in Santa Clara County, then sold his interest after a dispute with that controversial vintner; but Davies's fascination with winegrowing increased. In 1965, he formed a corporation with fourteen fellow wine lovers and bought Schramsberg from Pringle's former wife, Mrs. Louis de Laveaga Cebrian. He quit his job as a management consultant, moved with his wife, Jamie Louise, and their three children into the ninety-year-old Schram house on the mountain, and set out to make the world's finest champagne.

The next seven years were difficult at Schramsberg. The cob-webbed, long-neglected tunnels were cleared and the earth floors paved; the old vineyard was torn out and replanted with Char-donnay and Pinot Noir. Grapes were purchased from nearby hillsides in 1966, but the new crusher broke down on the first day; and with a ton of Chardonnays left, Jamie took off her shoes and finished the crushing the age-old way. Davies hired the best professional help, enlisting as consultants Dmitri Tchelistcheff from the Santo Tomás winery in Mexico and Dmitri's father, André Tchelistcheff of Beaulieu. The first two-year-old Blanc de Blancs champagne was released in 1968, followed by a spar-kling pink Cuvée de Gamay. A Blanc de Noir champagne made in 1967 from Pinot Noir and Chardonnay was offered in 1971. Davies succeeded in getting the wines stocked by a limited number of prestige wine shops around the country, including one in Washington, D.C. He then told his partners they might hope for sufficient sales to turn the corner financially in another year or two.

In February 1972, Schramsberg Champagne became world-famous overnight. President Richard M. Nixon had flown an American champagne to Peking to serve at his historic, globally-televised banquet for Red Chinese Premier Chou Enlai. On the day of the banquet a Washington newspaper columnist identified the shipment as thirteen cases of Schramsberg, Nixon's favorite champagne. Press, TV, and radio spread the name, Davies's story, and the fame of Napa Valley wine.

It may be some time before the supply of Schramsberg Cham-pagne can catch up with the worldwide demand.

• 21 •

The Sterling Vineyard, across The Wine Road from Schrams-berg, is an impressive sight with its 400 acres of thriving young vines of Cabernet Sauvignon, Merlot, Gamay Beaujolais, Zin-fandel, Chardonnay, Chenin and Sauvignon Blanc. Still more impressive is the revolutionary design of the new winery this company has built on a hilltop beyond the vineyard—an edifice like a Mediterranean monastery that dominates its part of the valley, with an aerial tramway to transport visitors from the vineyard to the lofty cellars and tasting hall.

Sterling is the biggest new winegrowing venture in Napa County, an investment of some six million dollars in the future market for premium table wines. It was begun in 1964 by the three owners of Sterling International, the San Francisco paper products firm. They are Peter Newton, a former London journalist and officer in the British Army, Yale-educated former Navy fighter pilot Michael P. W. Stone, and Martin Waterfield. The winemaker is Richard Forman, who earned his master's degree at UC Davis in 1968.

A temporary winery, intended eventually to become a warehouse, was built in 1968 in the vineyard, just south of Dunaweal Lane. The first wine, the 1969 Chardonnay, was bottled in the following spring, and was excellent except that the flavor of the new European oak barrels in which it was stored was too pronounced. The 1969 Merlot, which I tasted from a French barrel, closely resembled many of the clarets I have tasted from casks in the *chais* of the Médoc.

When the spectacular hilltop winery is finished in 1973, visitors will have a dramatic view of the entire valley winescape and of towering Mount St. Helena. Also planned for the future are concerts and operas in a natural amphitheater at the base of the hill.

• 22 •

A mile and a half farther north is Calistoga, the city that began in 1859 as the personal empire and obsession of the fabulous Sam Brannan. He is said to have named Calistoga by a slip of his tongue, saying: "I'll make this place the Calistoga of Sarafornia."

So spectacular were Brannan's other exploits that his role as a major Napa winegrower of the 1860s appears to have been forgotten. Little of his story can be learned in Calistoga, which is a sleepy tourist town with numerous bathhouses situated around the founder's hot mineral springs. To recall his memory there are only a side street named Brannan, a plaque, and two small, faded wooden buildings.

One must dig into libraries elsewhere to read the fantastic story of that wandering printer from the Ohio vineyard center of Painesville, who joined the original Mormons, brought two hundred of them to San Francisco by sea, founded that city's first newspaper, led the Vigilantes, quarreled with Brigham Young, and then abandoned the Mormon faith.

California's first millionaire, Brannan bought 2000 acres to found Calistoga around its natural mudpots and geysers, spent millions planting the 125,000 vines that he personally brought from Europe, and built a winery, brandy distillery, hotels, race-track, and luxury baths. Brannan's Calistoga empire collapsed after his divorce in 1870. He soon lost his fortune, and in 1889 died penniless near Escondido in the arms of an Indian squaw.

• 23 •

Two miles north of Calistoga, hidden in a grove a few hundred yards from Tubbs Lane, there is an historic winery, newly reactivated, named Château Montelena. Its facade of many arches, pilasters, parapets, and towers is an architectural curio, reminiscent of some nineteenth-century Italian palace. It was built of native stone in 1882 by cordage manufacturer Alfred L. Tubbs, the patriarch of a noted San Francisco family, and has often been compared to Château Lafite. Tubbs, with Charles Krug and other winery owners, organized the Napa Valley Wine Company in 1883 to sell their wines and those of independent vineyardists to the retail trade. Eleven years later, the company became part of the California Wine Association.

A grandson, Chapin Tubbs, made wine here for a few years following Repeal. In 1947, a Chinese engineer bought the property, made the upper story of the winery his home, and built the Oriental Water Gardens, a five-acre lake with three islands, arched bridges, and an authentic five-ton Chinese junk in the center.

Then in 1960 Lee and Helen Paschich, dedicated home wine-makers living in Marin County, bought a farm on Pickett Road near Calistoga, replanted an old vineyard there, and eight years later bought the Tubbs place, winery, water gardens, and all. Paschich moved his home and wood-fabric factory from Marin to the winery, installed new casks and crusher, and in 1969 made his first commercial wines, Chardonnay and Cabernet Sauvignon. With two new associates, he now has replanted ninety acres of the original Tubbs vineyard, and expects to put Château Montelena wines on the market and open the winery to the public when the new vines come into bearing.

• 24 •

Beyond Tubbs Lane, Highway 29 climbs the foothills of Mount St. Helena and heads for Lake County. It is time to turn back down the Napa Valley, this time taking the east-side highway, the Silverado Trail.

The first winery to be seen is the new Cuvaison Cellar, built in 1970 just south of Dunaweal Lane. In April of that year, a pair of oenothusiast scientists from Santa Clara, physicist Dr. Thomas

Cottrell and engineer Thomas Parkhill, bought a nearby thirty-five-acre vineyard of Gamay and Pinot Noir. A few weeks later, the valley suffered the worst frost in five decades, but enough grapes were harvested to make their 1970 vintage. *"Cuvaison,"* Dr. Cottrell explains, "is the French word for the fermenting of red wines on the skins of the grapes." Within a year, the partners had built a tiny tasting room and were already selling their first 1970 vintage wines.

• 25 •

Taplin Road, on the left a few minutes' drive past Pope Street, takes you to the winery and vineyard of Joseph and Alice Heitz. An appointment is worth making in advance, for their wines are among the finest in Napa County.

In 1944, after two years in a midwestern college, Airman Joe Heitz was chief of a night-fighter ground crew at the field near the Italian Swiss Colony winery outside Fresno. Dale Mills, the winemaker there, put Joe to work in the cellar by day, and discovered that he had an exceptionally keen palate. Mills advised him, on his discharge from the Air Force, to enroll at Davis and study enology. Heitz did so and won his master's degree in 1949. For ten years he worked at Beaulieu and other wineries, then taught enology at Fresno State College for four years. In 1961, married and with three children, Heitz decided to start his own wine business.

He bought Leon Brendel's "Only One" Grignolino vineyard on The Wine Road south of St. Helena, the site of the Heitz tasting room today. The orange-pink Grignolino wine he made there could not support his family, but Heitz has the rare ability to select lots from other wineries that will improve with blending and aging. The quality of these Heitz selections, of his Grignolino, and of wines he made from purchased grapes, attracted connoisseurs to the little old winery. Five-foot-tall Alice Heitz developed a mailing list and sent periodic letters to their customers, announcing each new Heitz selection.

Soon a larger winery was needed, and in 1965 Heitz found the place in a small valley at the end of Taplin Road. On the property was an empty seventy-year-old winery building and an old house. He equipped the cellar with a new crusher, stainless steel fermenters, and racks of French oak casks, some of them from the Hanzell Vineyard, while Alice made the ancient house livable. In the next few years he planted the best part of the valley with Chardonnay and Pinot Noir.

Although Heitz wines are sold mostly to those on Alice's mailing list and at the highway tasting room, leading restaurants and wine merchants feature some of the rarities. A recent offering on the mailing list, which will give you an idea, ranged from the Grignolino Rosé at $3 a bottle to the 1965 Cabernet Sauvignon at $7.50, and a lot of just 260 bottles of "Alicia," a sweet white wine made in 1967 of overripe Chardonnay spiced with Gewürztraminer, at $27.50 each.

• 26 •

A mile or so south of Taplin Road, a sign on the left marks a private road that leads a half-mile uphill from Silverado Trail to the new Souverain winery, built in 1972 because the old one on Howell Mountain was no longer able to supply the demand for its premium wines.

Souverain was founded in 1943 by J. Leland Stewart. Looking for a country home near the coast when he retired from business in Fresno, Stewart bought and restored the old Rossini vineyard of thirty acres, 1100 feet high on Howell Mountain, the eastern rim of Napa Valley. He learned winemaking from the valley vintners, eventually produced some of the best Johannisberg Riesling and Cabernet Sauvignon in the county, and gradually enlarged his cellar to 100,000 gallons. In 1945 Stewart was the first vintner to produce a "varietal" Green Hungarian wine. He also duplicated the Sherry Sack blend created by the late Robert Mayock in the old Los Amigos winery at Mission San José. His latest creation is a dry Chenin Blanc, which he has named "Pineau Souverain" to distinguish it from the usually semidry wines of this grape variety.

When Stewart again retired in 1970, wealthy Oakville vineyardist Fred Holmes and a group of fellow investors bought Souverain, and built the handsome new Souverain winery off Silverado Trail. A real estate developer plans to surround the winery with vineyard estates that are a new concept in wine-country living, with wooded bridle paths and common areas planted to vines. The plans also call for an inn and a restaurant nearby. Souverain is now partly owned by the Pillsbury Company.

The old Souverain cellar and home vineyard on Howell Mountain has been purchased by Tom and Linda Burgess from Poughkeepsie, New York, who have renamed it the Burgess Cellars. Tom, a retired airplane pilot, plans to live at the winery and operate as Stewart did, inviting visitors but offering no tasting.

• 27 •

From Silverado Trail just south of new Souverain, Highway

128 to the east leads to two more Napa wineries. Opposite Lake Hennessy, a steep private road at the right leads to the hundred-acre hilltop vineyard and spectacular new winery of former Los Angeles capitalist Donn Chappellet. The cellar, a triangular pyramid designed by Santa Rosa structural engineer Richard Keith, has rust-colored metal roofs. Chappellet's enologist is red-bearded Philip Togni, who has worked in Algerian, French, Chilean, and California wineries and holds diplomas from Mont-pellier and Bordeaux. Four wines are made there, Chenin Blanc, White Riesling, Chardonnay, and a Cabernet with Merlot in the blend.

Four miles farther east on Highway 128 is the hilltop winery of Jim and Rosemarie Nichelini. It is an old-fashioned roadside cellar, built in 1890 by Jim's grandfather, Anton Nichelini from Switzerland. Open to the public on weekends, it is a cheery place. Visitors are invited to sample the wines on the terrace, which Rosemarie calls "the only outdoor tasting room in California." There's no space for tasting inside the small cellar, which is crowded with casks and barrels. Sometimes Jim plays his accordion for the visitors.

Several red and white wines are made, but the Nichelini specialties are Chenin Blanc and Sauvignon Vert. The wines are inexpensive and are stocked in a few Bay Area restaurants and stores, although a good part is sold to people passing the winery en route to and from Lake Berryessa nearby. The fifty-acre Nichelini vineyard is a mile beyond the winery in Chiles Valley, where the Kentucky trapper, Colonel Joseph Chiles, was the first winegrower during the 1860s.

The climate of Chiles Valley, nine hundred feet high, has attracted the interest of vintners who are looking for more Napa land suitable for vines. The first to plant extensively there is the younger Louis Martini, whose land is three miles north of Nichelini's. For many years, Chiles Valley was considered too warm for the premium wine grapes, because the hills there turn brown in summer; the locality "looks warm." But Martini took thermograph readings for four years before he began planting and discovered that the temperatures are those of "low Region II." Cool, fresh afternoon winds are apparently the cause. There are also some experimental plantings in Pope Valley, a few miles to the northwest, and an old winery there was reopened in 1972.

· 28 ·

There are three new Napa Valley wineries still to be seen off the Silverado Trail. Two miles west, off Galleron Road, Roy

Raymond and his sons, members of the Beringer family, have planted a new ninety-acre vineyard under sprinklers and are building a small family winery. On Conn Creek Road, which takes off from Route 128 southwest of Silverado Trail, veteran vineyardist Charles Wagner has built the small Caymus Vineyard winery (named for the Caymus Spanish land grant) to make estate-bottled wines of his best grape varieties.

A mile south of Yountville Cross Road, a country lane leads off eastward from Silverado Trail toward the historic Stag's Leap Hotel, built in 1883 by Horace Chase and said to have been named by him for a legendary elk. The Carl Doumani family, wine buffs from Los Angeles, have torn off the third story of the hotel to make their home in the lower two floors. They have replanted half of the hundred-acre vineyard and are building their new winery near the ruins of Chase's stone cellar. Their winemaker is John Henderson, formerly of Souverain.

· 29 ·

When I first wrote a draft of this Napa chapter a few years ago, before the wine boom brought the recent great changes in the Napa wine scene, my closing sentence stated that this winiest county in America must someday be delimited for wine-labeling purposes, as are Bordeaux, Burgundy, the Rhineland, and hundreds of other famous wine districts in the Old World. Furthermore, the preceding pages have shown that not only the county, but the many Napa wine districts with their differing climates or microclimates and soils must someday be recognized as producing wines with distinctive characteristics of their own.

By coincidence just at press time, fourteen of the winegrowers mentioned in this chapter, led by Robert Mondavi, have formed a Napa Valley Appellation Council to seek a means of defining their viticultural area by law or regulation. What has prompted their move is the new Federal regulation which permits wines made from grapes grown in one viticultural area but vinified in another area to be labeled with the name of the area where the grapes were grown. The Napa Appellation Council opposes this use of Napa-grown grapes, and goes farther. The Council members would like a regulation that would require wines with varietal names, labeled with the name of Napa, to be made 100 percent from Napa grapes and at least 75 percent from the grape varieties named on the labels.

In 1973, the Moët et Chandon champagne firm of France bought 800 acres in Napa County to grow its own California sparkling wine. Though a Moët subsidiary makes champaña in Argentina, the California name won't be "champagne."

15

Alameda, Contra Costa, and Solano

ALIFORNIA's new "green belt" laws, enacted to preserve farmlands from urbanization, have given a new lease on life to the few vineyards that remain in Alameda, Contra Costa, and Solano Counties, east of San Francisco Bay. Although forecasts of population growth envision the East Bay cities soon expanding into a virtual megalopolis, some of the historic vineyards in their environs are being replanted in response to today's unprecedented table wine boom.

One can see this happening by visiting the Livermore Valley, which is reached by the MacArthur Freeway (Interstate 580) from the San Francisco–Oakland Bay Bridge, less than an hour's drive. It doesn't look like a valley, for it is an almost flat basin, fourteen miles long, between the low grassy foothills of the Diablo and Hamilton mountain ranges. Beyond the Altamont Hills, only seventeen miles farther east, lies the hot San Joaquin Valley. But the climate of Livermore is Region III, like the upper Napa Valley and northern Sonoma County, because sunny days in Livermore are followed by evening breezes from the Bay.

Most California wine literature describes Livermore as a white wine district. Some writers state flatly that its climate and gravelly soil are unsuited for the growing of red wine grapes. Though the only Livermore wines that have attained national fame are white, the reason is neither climate nor soil, as we'll see presently, and you will find the red wines grown here quite as good as the whites.

Once primarily a vineyard and livestock center, the City of Livermore has multiplied seven times in size since the University of California built the Lawrence Radiation Laboratory in 1952. Nuclear and electronic industries have followed the big "Rad Lab," and subdivisions to house new residents have crowded out many farms. One of the biggest vineyards has become a housing tract of 5000 people and five schools.

During the 1960s mounting real estate values were threatening to tax out of existence Livermore's two principal vineyards—Wente and Concannon—which are two miles southeast of the city on Tesla Road. Members of the third generations of these two old winegrowing families, each with growing sons, pondered whether to sell out and move. In 1968 they decided to stay. By signing ten-year contracts with the county under the new legislation they dedicated their vineyards as "green belts" or agricultural preserves, which are taxable only on their highest value as farms.

• 2 •

The Concannon Vineyard of 300 acres, on the left of Livermore Avenue, has a brick-fronted, old-fashioned winery that is filled to the rafters with oak and redwood wine-aging casks of miscellaneous sizes. It has no separate tasting room. Visitors are invited into the cellar to taste the Concannon wines. The present generation of owners, Joseph Concannon, Jr., and his winemaker brother Jim, like it that way.

Founder of the winery was their grandfather, James Concannon, who emigrated from Ireland in 1865 at the age of eighteen. He landed in Maine and worked his way up from bellhop to management of a hotel, going to night school meanwhile. Ten years later he was traveling the west coast from San Francisco selling a new invention—rubber stamps—which were quite the rage before typewriters came into general use. His travels took him as far as Mexico City. There the resourceful Concannon got a franchise from Dictator Porfirio Díaz to set up the capital's first street-cleaning system, promptly selling it at a profit to a French syndicate. Back in San Francisco, he learned from Archbishop Joseph Alemany that money could also be made by producing altar wines for the Catholic Church. In 1883 Concannon bought a farm in the Livermore Valley and planted vines imported from France, which others were beginning to plant there at that time. With his vineyard started, he needed capital to develop his winery. He returned to Mexico and got another concession from President Díaz—to introduce French wine grapes to that country, where only the inferior Criolla or Mission grape had been grown until then. Between 1889 and 1904, Concannon shipped several million vine cuttings from Livermore to haciendas throughout the southern republic. For what happened to the Mexican vineyards, see page 373 in my chapter on Mexico. Concannon returned to Livermore and died there in 1911.

Altar wines were the Concannon winery's main products. Altar wines also kept the winery going through the thirteen years of Prohibition, when the founder's son, Captain Joseph Concannon, was in charge. Every five years for the rest of his life, "Captain Joe" expressed his appreciation by sending a gift barrel of his finest Muscat de Frontignan to the Pope in Rome.

Altar wines, sold mostly to the Catholic clergy, are still a fourth of the Concannon Vineyard's business today. This helps explain why most of its wines are white. A red wine would stain the purificator napkin with which the priest wipes the chalice during Mass.

Even so, the best wine that Captain Concannon made was not white. His St. Julien, a wonderfully smooth, flavorful claret blend, was my favorite California dinner wine during the first few years after Repeal. But in 1936, the new Federal labeling regulations issued from Washington contained a provision specifically prohibiting use of the St. Julien name except on wines from that Bordeaux commune. This so angered "Captain Joe" that he withdrew his St. Julien from the market, and he never made that blend again.

Today another red is the best-seller among the fourteen Concannon table and dessert wines, which are sold in some two dozen states. It is a dry, medium-bodied "varietal" of the Petit Sirah grape that grows beside the winery. Also grown in the family vineyard and considerably finer, to my taste, is the vintage-dated limited bottling of Concannon Cabernet Sauvignon.

• 3 •

The Wente winery is at the right a half mile beyond Concannon and is more than twice as big, because Wente table wines (the only types it makes) are sold in all fifty states. The winery and its separate tasting room are new and ultramodern, having been built in the late 1960s when the old facilities proved too small.

Carl Heinrich Wente came from Hanover to this country in 1880, learned winemaking from Charles Krug in the Napa Valley, then moved to Livermore and in 1883 acquired an interest in the fifty-acre vineyard planted four years earlier by Dr. George Bernard. Wente expanded his holdings and soon was cultivating a total of 300 acres.

He had three sons. The oldest, Carl F. Wente, was advised by his father to study bookkeeping, got a job as a bank messenger, and forty-five years later became president of the worldwide Bank of America. The second son, Ernest, preferred farming, was sent to the College of Agriculture at Davis, and on graduation took charge of the vineyards. The youngest son, Herman, studied enology at the University in Berkeley and became a winemaker, one of the greatest California has yet known.

Like the Concannons, the Wentes specialized in white wines, though for a different reason: In the old days bulk red wines, sold inter-winery, brought producers as little as ten cents a gallon, while bulk whites seldom sold for less than fifty cents. The Wentes see no reason to change their specialties now.

Before Prohibition, the Wentes sold their entire output in bulk, much of it to the Napa & Sonoma Wine Company of San Francisco, of which they were part owners, and some to Oakland vintner Theodore Gier. During the dry era they made altar wine in bulk for Georges de Latour of Beaulieu, but sold most of their grapes fresh.

In 1934, the year following Repeal, they bottled some wines for the first time, calling them "Valle de Oro"; the name of Wente wasn't yet known outside of Livermore. Then in 1939, Valle de Oro Sauvignon Blanc won the grand prize for white wines at San Francisco's Golden Gate International Exposition. This brought importer Frank Schoonmaker from New York, looking for California wines to introduce nationally with his import line. The first he chose were the Wentes' Sauvignon Blanc, Sémillon, Grey Riesling, Pinot Blanc, Ugni Blanc, and a light-bodied red named Mourastel. Though the labels called them "Schoonmaker Selections," the name of the Wentes was shown as the producer and became known in the East and Midwest.

Herman Wente died in 1961 and Ernest's son, Karl, became the head of the firm. Two years later, when there was no more space to expand at Livermore, the Wentes planted a 300-acre vineyard of white and red grapes near Greenfield in the Salinas Valley of Monterey County.

The Wentes always had made a red wine for their own use, and had sold a burgundy after Repeal. During the 1960s they introduced annual vintages of Pinot Noir and Gamay Beaujolais. (The Mourastel was discontinued during the Second World War.) The Wentes also make, entirely from grapes they grow at Livermore, a Zinfandel that American Airlines considers so fine that it buys the entire vintage for exclusive service on its planes. The Zinfandel is not available anywhere else.

Ugni Blanc was never popular because of its hard-to-pronounce name and was withdrawn from the market, but reappeared in 1967 in a blend with Chenin Blanc under a new name: Wente Blanc de Blancs. Semidry and fruity, the Blanc de Blancs has become popular nationwide. Wente wines come in fifth and tenth sizes and in magnums for some varieties, but also available at the winery are two Valle de Oro wines in half-gallon jugs. Priced a third to a sixth as much as Wente wines, these are best buys. The jug white is so popular that people drive to the winery from the Bay Area to load their cars with it in case lots.

• 4 •

The loveliest and most historic vineyard in the valley is Cresta Blanca. To get there from Livermore Avenue, take Wente Street (there is also a Concannon Boulevard), Marina Boulevard, and Arroyo Road. The million-gallon Cresta Blanca winery, with its great tunnels bored into the hillside, is used only for wine storage now, but even to see it from the exterior is worth the extra drive.

Cresta Blanca was founded by journalist Charles Wetmore. A reporter for San Francisco newspapers, he became interested in wine and went to France in 1879 to report on the Paris Exposition for the California Vinicultural Society. He then wrote a series of sensational articles, declaring that 95 percent of French wine imported to the United States was adulterated *vin ordinaire*. He denounced San Francisco restaurateurs for featuring European wines while selling the best California wines under counterfeit French labels or as their "house" wines with no labels at all. Wetmore's articles helped to get the State Board of Viticultural Commissioners established by an act of the Legislature in 1880. Wetmore became the Board's executive officer and then decided to become a winegrower himself. He bought 480 acres of Livermore pasture land for $200 in gold coin, set out his vineyard, and named it Cresta Blanca for the white-crested cliff above. Wetmore then learned that the wife of Louis Mel, the French-born owner of the El Mocho Vineyard, was a friend of the Marquis de Lur-Saluces, the proprietor of world-famed Château d'Yquem near Bordeaux. Armed with a letter from Madame Mel, Wetmore went again to France and obtained from the Marquis cuttings of the three grape varieties that make the Yquem blend—Sémillon, Sauvignon Blanc, and Muscadelle Bordelais.

Wetmore divided the Yquem cuttings between his vineyard and that of Louis Mel, who later sold El Mocho to the Wentes. In Wetmore's vineyard, the vines from France produced wines that won two gold medals for Cresta Blanca in the Paris Exposition of 1889.

During the 1940s, a successor to the Marquis de Lur-Saluces visited Livermore "to see how my children are doing." On tasting a sample of Herman Wente's Sauvignon Blanc, the Marquis told Herman that no Bordeaux vintner had ever made a wine of such quality from that grape alone—that it was impossible in the Bordeaux climate.

Perhaps the direct importation of vines from Yquem explains why, through the years, I have found Livermore Sauvignon Blancs richer and spicier in flavor than those made from this grape grown elsewhere in California. The Livermore producers, however, insist the reason is their climate and in particular their gravelly soil, which holds the heat after the summer sun goes down. I recall tasting a Sauvignon Blanc made by Herman Wente that was magnificent at the age of twenty years.

Cresta Blanca wines with such names as Sauterne Souvenir and Médoc Souvenir were nationally famous before Prohibition. They again were at the top rank of California wines after Repeal, when the vineyard was owned by Wetmore's younger brother, Clarence, and later by his chief salesman, Lucien B. Johnson.

In 1941, during the wartime liquor shortage, Schenley whiskey king Lewis Rosenstiel bought Cresta Blanca from Johnson. This enabled Rosenstiel to advertise on radio, from which his liquor brands were barred by the broadcasting industry code. In 1942 he produced the first advertising program for a wine brand to be aired on a national network. It introduced the first singing commercial for a California wine: "C-R-E-S-T-A" in rising notes and "B-L-A-N-C-A" going down the scale, then the two words repeated in the same notes and followed by the pop of a cork. Rosenstiel introduced the first California sherries to be priced higher than Spanish imports, Cresta Blanca Dry Watch and Triple Cream. But when wines came under wartime price controls, he used the Cresta Blanca label to sell enormous quantities of other wines—something wine merchants remembered when the war ended; his competitors wouldn't let them forget.

History was again made at Cresta Blanca in 1956, when winemaker Myron Nightingale and University enologists produced there the first French-style sauterne ever made commercially outside of Bordeaux. They did it by spraying Sémillon and Sauvignon grapes in the winery with spores of *Botrytis cinerea*, the "noble mold" which grows naturally on late-harvested grapes in the Sauternes district of Bordeaux.* Rosenstiel named the wine Premier Sémillon, priced it six dollars a bottle, and in 1961

---

*The Botrytis mold grows in California vineyards, too, but not enough to produce the botrytized flavor because California's climate is too dry. In 1969 the Wentes found the mold on White Riesling grapes in their Arroyo Seco Vineyard in the Salinas Valley. They left the grapes to ripen for three extra weeks, and sold the resulting wine as a *Spätlese* Riesling. The wine was lovely, but I couldn't taste any botrytized flavor. California vineyards have been fogged artifically to encourage botrytis to grow, but the experiments have excited little interest thus far.

unveiled it at a nationally publicized San Francisco tasting. In a speech later inserted in the *Congressional Record*, Senator Tom Kuchel hailed Premier Sémillon as "this product that has broken a European monopoly in one of the gourmet treasures of the world."

Premier Sémillon wasn't enough to restore Cresta Blanca to its prewar prestige. In 1965 the winery was closed to the public and winemaker Nightingale and his wines were shipped to Schenley's big Roma winery at Fresno. When, six years later, Schenley sold the Cresta Blanca name to the Guild Wine Company of Lodi, Nightingale quit to join the Beringer winery in the Napa Valley. No more Premier Sémillon was made after the 1966 vintage. I have one bottle left in my cellar.

Cresta Blanca wines have now come back on the market from a winery in Mendocino County, and the famous Cresta commercial is returning to the air.

• 5 •

North of the Cresta Blanca vineyard, the name "Olivina" appears on the arch over an imposing stone gate at the intersection of Arroyo and Wetmore roads. Julius Paul Smith of "20-Mule-Team Borax" fame founded Olivina and planted vines there in 1881. The Olivina Vineyard was killed by phylloxera long ago, and except for the crumbling shell of the winery, the fields are bare. No trace remains of such other early Livermore winegrowing estates as Alexander Duval's Château Bellevue on Vallecitos Road, nor of the Chauché & Bon winery on Stanley Boulevard, nor of the vineyard Theodore Gier named Giersburg, four miles south of town.

But if you drive west along Vineyard Avenue toward Pleasanton, you will see new vines planted in old vineyards, such as the Oakdale or Hagemann Vineyard of 200 acres, which is under lease to Almadén. Other wineries now compete to buy the grapes of the adjoining Ruby Hill Vineyard, planted by John Crellin in 1883 and named for the red knoll on which its handsome brick and stone winery stands. Ernest Ferrario bought the Crellin estate early in the Prohibition era, reopened the winery at Repeal, and produced excellent wines, including the best Malvasia Bianca then made in the state. With no sons to carry on his business, Ferrario quit making wine during the mid-1960s, and now stores wines made by other wineries.

In the City of Pleasanton, a half block north of Main Street, is the million-gallon Villa Armando or Loretto Winery, which has changed with the times. It was built in 1902 by Frank Garatti and except during Prohibition when it was closed, made mostly bulk wine until 1962. Then Brooklyn wine merchant Anthony Scotto bought it to produce the peculiar wines his Italian customers along the eastern seaboard preferred, the kinds they made themselves during Prohibition from San Joaquin Valley grapes. One was a 16 percent sweetish earthy red called Vino Rustico. Another, made of Muscat grapes from Delano, was called Orobianco. By 1970, Scotto found that people's tastes were changing, and added a dry Sémillon from Livermore grapes and a fairly good dry blend of Sonoma and Lodi Zinfandels. A year later, he hired a Romanian refugee professor of winemaking named Petre Bulumac, bought a vineyard in Lodi, built a tasting room in front of the winery, and now makes such vintage-dated table wines as Pinot Blanc, Chenin Blanc, and Pinot Noir.

• 6 •

Five miles south of Pleasanton (via Suñol Boulevard and Interstate Highway 680) there is an old Alameda County winegrowing district that awaits replanting with premium wine grapes. At the left just past Scott's Corner, there is a patch of old vineyard. This is the Suñol Valley, which can never become urbanized because it is part of San Francisco's municipal water system. In 1969 the city granted Almadén Vineyards a forty-year lease on almost a thousand acres there and in the nearby San Antonio Valley. Almadén later chose to plant instead in Monterey County, and other coast counties winegrowers have opened negotiations to use the land.

The vineyards of Alameda County declined from 7,000 acres in 1900 to less than 2,000 acres in 1972, but will be increased by more than half when the area around Suñol is planted with vines. At least 3,000 more acres of this San Francisco–owned watershed are considered suitable for vineyards. If all are planted, Alameda County will produce more fine wine in the future than it ever did in the past.

• 7 •

Many other parts of the county, including Niles and the present cities of San Lorenzo, Hayward, and Alameda, were winegrowing districts a century ago. But the Mission San José district is older still.

Four miles south of Suñol, the Mission Boulevard exit from the freeway leads to the Mission San José de Guadalupe, founded in 1797. There the Franciscan Fathers planted the first vineyards in Alameda County, a quarter century before those at Sonoma.

From the mission the padres at Mission Dolores in San Francisco obtained the grapes to make their wines for the Mass. And from there the English seaman Robert Livermore obtained the vines that he was the first to plant, during the 1840s, in the valley that bears his name. Among early-day wineries near the mission were Joseph Palmer's Peak Vineyard, planted in 1852 with vines imported from Europe; the Los Amigos Vineyard of Grau & Werner, Conrad Weller's Willow Glen Vineyard, and Linda Vista, the vineyard and wine cellars of Charles McIver. Bigger than any of the Livermore vineyards was the 1000-acre tract which Juan Gallegos, a former Costa Rican coffee planter, owned around the Mission in the 1880s. The million-gallon Gallegos winery and distillery, two miles west at Irvington, was damaged by the earthquake of 1906 and had to be destroyed.

• 8 •

Four miles south of the mission, a spring of hot water gushing from a hillside was visited by early Spanish California ladies who found it a convenient place to wash their linens. The place was named Rancho Agua Caliente, the Warm Springs Ranch. Clement Colombet from France built a stone winery there about 1850 and later built the Warm Springs Hotel around the springs. It was the most fashionable suburban spa around San Francisco until it was wrecked by the earthquake of 1868.

In the following year came Leland Stanford, the railroad builder, California governor, and United States senator, who bought a square mile around the springs. He cultivated a hundred acres of vines and made 50,000 gallons of wine per year. He later gave the place to his brother Josiah, who tripled its size and added a brandy distillery. Had the property not been occupied by his brother's prospering wine business, the Senator might have built Stanford University there rather than at his Palo Alto horse farm. Josiah Stanford's son inherited the property and made 250,000 gallons of wine per year until phylloxera destroyed the Warm Springs vineyard during the 1890s. Meanwhile another earthquake shut off the springs.

In 1945, half a century later, Rudolf Weibel, the proprietor of the Weibel Champagne Cellar in San Francisco, went looking around the Bay Area for land on which to plant a vineyard of his own. Weibel had arrived nine years earlier from Switzerland with his son Fred and had prospered making champagne under other vintners' brands. He bought the abandoned vineyard at Warm Springs, patched the old buildings, and replanted the vines. Weibel had never heard of Stanford or of the winery's history. He didn't learn it until a year later, when he came to consult me about his new labels, and I happened to tell him the Stanford story.

At Warm Springs, the Weibels continued making champagnes for other vintners, using the Charmat process, but fermented their best in bottles under their own name. They added table and dessert wines and a citrus-and-herb-flavored apéritif wine Rudolf had made in Switzerland, named Tangor.

When Rudolf Weibel died in 1971, a new city named Fremont had grown up around Warm Springs, embracing the mission and several surrounding towns. Fred Weibel then bought vineyards in Mendocino and Sonoma Counties and built a new Weibel winery at Ukiah. He plans to stay at Warm Springs, keeping his Chardonnay vineyard and making his champagnes there.

The Weibel winery on Stanford Avenue, four miles south of the mission, gets thousands of visitors per month because it is near both the 680 and 17 freeways. The visitors are received in an adobe-style "hacienda" tasting room, where champagne is now dispensed on tap by a new patented invention. On weekdays, a girl from the winery office takes them on a tour of the old brick buildings, then around the sherry *soleras* and stainless steel tanks the Weibels and another vintner have added. Between the cellars and the vineyard is a pergola for picnics and a bandstand for concerts.

Among the three dozen wines labeled "Weibel," I have tasted some that were outstanding, but have found the Chardonnay Brut Champagne and the Dry Bin Sherry to be the best.

The winery still makes champagnes for other vintners and uses so many hundreds of different labels that it has its own printing plant. To tell whether a champagne comes from Weibel, look for the address on the bottom of the label, which may read either Warm Springs, Fremont, or Mission San José.

• 9 •

One winery inside another is Llords & Elwood, which has its main bonded winery in a corner of Weibel's property.

For two decades after Repeal, Julius Hugh (Mike) Elwood owned the Llords & Elwood chain of prestigious liquor stores in Los Angeles. He stocked the private wine cellars of such Hollywood luminaries as Charlie Chaplin, Ronald Reagan, and Gloria Swanson almost exclusively with European wines. American wines lacked age and glamour and were not expensive enough. Then in 1953 Elwood and his wife took their first trip through the vineyards of Europe. He came back convinced that California wines could excel imports if someone would just give them enough aging and care. He decided that he was the one to do it, sold his stores, and became a vintner.

With his own ideas of how wines should taste, Elwood created his own blends. He bought grapes and wines and leased space in three wineries, two in San Jose for crushing and barrel-aging and part of Weibel for bottling. He also gave his wines beguiling names, such as Castle Magic Riesling, Velvet Hill Pinot Noir, Ancient Proverb Port, and Dry Wit Sherry; and retained the name of a liquor store once named Llord's "because it sounds better than Elwood alone." His wines, introduced in 1961, regularly win over costly imports in blind tastings because he has chosen and finished them well.

Until recently, Elwood had not tried grape-growing, but that has changed. As previously mentioned, Mike's son Richard, now the head of the company, planted the Llords & Elwood Vineyard in Napa County in 1970 and is preparing to build a winery there.

• 10 •

The smallest Alameda winery is a one-man operation in the rear of a store on busy San Pablo Avenue in Albany, north of Berkeley. After studying enology and making wine at home for fifteen years, journalist Davis Bynum quit his job on the San Francisco *Chronicle* in 1965 to start the Bynum Winery. He bought his grapes in the coast counties and made such good table wines that they soon attracted a Bay Area following of connoisseurs. Sometimes, before buying a batch of Cabernet grapes, he would sell futures on the wine, deliverable when bottled three years later. The front of the store serves as his tasting room and is stocked with home-winemaking supplies for sale to amateur vintners. Bynum is also a humorist and a teacher. To spoof big wineries' advertising, he sells his leftover red wines in gallon jugs labeled "Bynum's Barefoot Burgundy." He likes to teach winemaking, and sometimes lets his students help him during the vintage season, charging them a fee for the privilege. He recently added a dry mead (honey wine) to his assortment, and now has a vineyard of his own, twenty-six acres near Rutherford in the Napa Valley.

• 11 •

Contra Costa County had 6000 acres of vineyards and twenty-seven wineries and was one of California's finest winegrowing districts before Prohibition. Dr. John Marsh, the first physician in the county and its first winegrower, was producing wine as early as 1846 on his great ranch south of Brentwood. Another physician,

Dr. John Strentzel from Poland, planted vines in the Alhambra Valley during the 1850s. He was succeeded by his son-in-law, the great naturalist John Muir. The Muir House, beside Highway 4 two miles south of Martinez, is now a national historic site, and includes a half acre of Muir's Vineyard, replanted in 1969.

Another Contra Costa winegrower was the educator John Swett. The wines from his Hill Girt Vineyard, which he planted during the 1880s, regularly won prizes at the State Fair. His son Frank continued making wine there until Prohibition. Grapes still grow on the Hill Girt Farm on Alhambra Avenue, but they are Concords, planted during the dry years.

In 1891, such major vintners as the Italian Swiss Colony and Theodore Gier had wineries in the Clayton Valley, and the Brookside Winery in the Ygnacio Valley was operated by the California Wine Assocation. In Martinez were the original novitiate and vineyard of the Christian Brothers, where they began making wine in 1882.

At Repeal, Joseph E. (Joe) Digardi reopened the winery in the Vine Hill district south of Martinez which his father had founded half a century before. Digardi sent two of his sons to Davis and by the 1940s the wines they helped him make were winning awards at the State Fair. When his Diablo Valley Gamay won a gold medal in 1948, he sold most of it to Frank Schoonmaker for six dollars a case. Later, at the Mayflower Hotel in Washington, Digardi ordered a bottle of his Gamay. It cost him three dollars. The Digardi vineyard is gone, ruined by smog from the oil refineries, but son Francis Digardi continues operating the winery with grapes from other coast counties. His brother Ernest is in charge of production at the United Vintners wineries in the Napa Valley.

Hidden beyond a hill a half mile west of Digardi is the small Conrad Viano Winery on Morello Avenue, still making wine from its own grapes. Connoisseurs who know its location buy its wines by the case, especially the Zinfandel and Cabernet Sauvignon. All of the reds are aged in oak for three to six years and binned for at least six months. Viano's son Clement is a graduate of the enology school at Davis and wants to stay in the wine business. The Vianos have dedicated their vineyard as an agricultural preserve and have expanded it to 125 acres. There are more vineyards in the far eastern corner of the county, where the climate is Region IV. Their grapes are usually shipped fresh to eastern markets.

• 12 •

Solano is another county where the "green belt" laws have

saved a few vineyards from urban sprawl. Before Prohibition there were 2000 acres of vines and a dozen wineries in Green Valley, Suisun Valley, and around Rockville, Cordelia, Fairfield, and Vacaville. Only 700 acres are left, and two wineries still in operation. The almost century old Mangels Vineyard on Highway 80 at Cordelia still produces grapes, but is in the path of encroaching subdivisions, and the million-gallon Solano Winery, once operated by the Italian Swiss Colony, has been closed since the Second World War.

Near Mankas Corner is the Wooden Valley Winery of Mario Lanza (no relative of the late singer, whose real name was Cocozza). It is a busy place, patronized by families from the huge Travis Air Force Base a few miles away.

Only Frank Cadenasso, whose winery and vineyard are just east of the Interstate 80 freeway at Fairfield, still makes wine mostly of grapes that he grows himself. His wines, especially the Pinot Noir and Zinfandel, are excellent and so reasonably priced that some of my friends travel from San Francisco to the winery to buy them by the case. Frank's father planted his first vineyard in Green Valley in 1906, moved to Fairfield and planted another, sold it to the county as a hospital site, then planted the present vineyard, his third, across the road from the hospital, in 1926.

Since then Fairfield has more than trebled in population, and Cadenasso is planning another move. "I ought to sell out and quit," he says, "but after starving for years when people wouldn't buy good wine at a decent price, I'm finally making a living for my family and starting to enjoy it." Instead of quitting, he has bought a hundred more acres in Green Valley, has planted more grapes, and has dedicated his land as an agricultural preserve. He intends to move his winery to his new vineyard across the freeway.

"Don't write off Solano County as a wine district yet," Cadenasso adds. "I know of at least one more new vineyard planted and green-belted near Vacaville, and we may have more before long."

16

Santa Clara and Other Central Coast Counties

T HE COUNTIES north and east of the Golden Gate, described in the three preceding chapters, are publicized nowadays as "California's fine wine country." Yet there is fully as much to interest the visitor—famous wineries, great vineyards, and fine wines—in the coast counties situated south of the Bay. In fact, the visitor who travels south instead of north from San Francisco may get a clearer concept of the past, present, and future of premium California wines.

Viticulture is changing more dramatically in this central coast region than anywhere else in America. Because of exploding population around the Bay, the old vineyards in the upper Santa Clara Valley are fast being paved over for housing tracts and shopping centers. The historic showplace wineries remain, but the grape is retreating southward to less-populated areas, including some where vines were not grown commercially before. For example, a single new district, the Salinas Valley of Monterey County, is likely soon to match Napa and Sonoma Counties in vineyard acreage and may even surpass both in "fine wine country" importance.

Climatically, as the California map shows, the same ocean breezes and fogs which cool the sunny valleys of the northern Coast Range Mountains perform the same beneficent function for the valleys of these mountain ranges extending south from San Francisco through San Mateo, Santa Clara, Santa Cruz, San Benito, and San Luis Obispo Counties—a distance of more than two hundred miles. Summer temperatures in most of this area range from Region I to Region III, the best for growing grapes for superior table wines and champagnes. The new central coast vineyards are therefore equal in climate to the old ones they replace, and they are already greater in size.

• 2 •

The best route south from San Francisco is the scenic Interstate 280 freeway. It passes first through what was once a high-quality winegrowing area in now-urbanized San Mateo County. At the south end of San Andreas Lake is the site where "Count" Haraszthy planted his ill-fated San Mateo County vineyard in 1854. The hills farther south, beyond the Crystal Springs Reservoirs, have warmer weather, and were dotted with vineyards before Prohibition. Emmett Rixford's La Questa Vineyard at Woodside, planted in 1883, grew some of the most prized of all California Cabernets. His elegant winery was closed by the dry law, was operated again by his sons for a few years after Repeal, and has since been converted into a residence. Another handsome cellar, at Menlo Park, once belonged to Governor Leland Stanford. It now houses a bank in the Stanford Shopping Center.

San Mateo land is too costly now for commercial vineyards, but the county has many avocational winegrowers, and two of them have bonded their cellars. When home-winemakers Robert and Polly Mullen built their new house on Kings Mountain Road in Woodside in 1961, they did so primarily to provide a twenty-five-foot-square winery downstairs. They have a patch of Pinot Noir and Chardonnay vines beside their house, and they buy the Cabernet grapes produced on the three remaining acres of the La Questa Vineyard. The Mullens' 2000-gallon cellar is enough to supply themselves, the friends and neighbors who attend their spring wine tastings, and the Village Church, which uses their Woodside Vineyard wines for Communion. Occasionally a few bottles are available for sale to callers (by appointment on weekends only).

The other San Mateo winery is the Nepenthe Cellar of George and Yvonne Burtness in nearby Portola Valley. Burtness dug the cellar with pick and shovel beneath their ranch-style home in 1967. He cultivates two thirds of an acre of Cabernet, Pinot Noir, and Chardonnay, but buys additional grapes from nearby vineyards and makes enough wine to keep a stock in the Portola Valley liquor store. He recently made a Cabernet Sauvignon, neither fined nor filtered, which had more of that grape's powerful flavor than any commercial wine I have ever tasted from either California or Bordeaux.

• 3 •

Santa Clara is the oldest of the northern California wine districts and was one of the best. The Franciscan Fathers planted grapes at Mission Santa Clara de Asis soon after its founding in 1777. This was almost half a century before Sonoma Mission (1823), from which winegrowing spread north of the Bay. Mission records show the Santa Clara padres producing twenty barrels of wine annually by 1827 and supplying some of it thereafter to Mission Dolores at San Francisco. They also gave vine cuttings to neighboring rancheros, who made their own wine. By mid-century there were half a dozen commercial winegrowers around Santa Clara and its satellite pueblo of San José. Many of them were French, and the Gallic influence was evident in the character of the top Santa Clara wines. By 1854 one of the French *vignerons*, Antoine Delmas, was already importing superior wine-grape varieties from his homeland and replacing his Mission vines.

After the Civil War, winegrowing spread south through the Santa Clara Valley, then east and west into the foothills of the Diablo and Santa Cruz mountain ranges, and became the county's main industry. Names on San Jose maps recall such early vine-yardists as Captain Elisha Stevens, Isaac Branham, and James Lick (the millionaire donor of Lick Observatory), whose winery was on the Santa Clara–Alviso Road. Another was retired Union Army General Henry M. Naglee (Naglee Street was named for him), who made fine wines but became most famous for his prize-winning brandy. Phylloxera attacked the Santa Clara vineyards during the 1890s, but they were saved by grafting to resistant American roots brought back from France. By the turn of the century, Santa Clara County had more than a hundred wineries and 8500 acres of vines, more than in Napa County and almost as many as in Sonoma.

Prohibition failed to kill the vineyards. Grapes brought high prices when shipped east for basement winemaking, and a few local wineries continued making sacramental and tonic wines, so the farmers planted still more grapes. Prune-growing meanwhile had become a rival industry, but there were still nearly 8000 acres of vines in 1933. When the dry law was repealed in that year, sixty-four Santa Clara wineries reopened for business.

Then came the great westward migration, sparked by the Second World War. Millions of new California residents had to be housed. Chambers of commerce advertised the climatic advantages of the area south of the Bay, and subdivisions began invading the prime farmland on the valley floor. When land values soared, the vineyards were taxed more as real estate than their crops were worth, and one by one the grape growers were forced to sell. Of the 8000 acres that were producing grapes in this county in 1948, three-fourths had disappeared by 1970. In two decades of wild urban growth, the upper part of the valley, the onetime "garden of the world," was transformed into a sprawling Los Angeles of the North, and then came the smog. Why didn't Santa Clara preserve its vineyards, fresh air, and open space, as Napa has thus far? The chambers of commerce did their work too well.

· 4 ·

But there still are some lovely vineyards tucked away in the nearby hills. The loveliest is Paul Masson's renowned "vineyard in the sky," perched two thousand feet high in the Santa Cruz Mountains above Saratoga. On steep slopes the venerable Pinot, Cabernet, and Riesling vines are still mostly cultivated by hand. The sparse crops of grapes they yield are still crushed in the venerable three-story stone Mountain Winery, which is State Historical Landmark No. 733. But the fine old oak casks inside mainly store ports and sherries, made elsewhere and sent here for long aging. The main Paul Masson vineyards and producing winery are now in the Salinas Valley of Monterey County.

The vine-clad hillsides form a natural amphitheater in front of the stately Mountain Winery, with its twelfth-century Romanesque portal, brought around Cape Horn from Spain. In this dramatic setting the famous, often-televised Music at the Vineyards concerts have been held on summer weekends since 1958. Noted artists perform melodic masterworks, chilled Paul Masson Brut Champagne is served at the intermissions, and Bay Area music lovers reserve months ahead for the concert tickets, which benefit colleges' music scholarship funds. The vineyard terrace, with its magnificent view of the valley below, is often loaned to connoisseur groups for catered luncheons and dinners. Otherwise the gates to the precipitous road up the mountain are kept closed.

On the valley floor in Saratoga are the Paul Masson Champagne Cellars, built in 1959, one of the most spectacular winery structures in the world. On a spiral ramp leading from the rotunda, a 153-foot-long mosaic mural depicts the history of wine from ancient times. Almost 200,000 visitors climb the ramp each year. At the top, tour hosts meet and conduct them on an elevated gallery through the temperature-controlled cellars, where each step in champagne making, wine aging and bottling is viewed and explained. The circuit ends in the tasting hall, where the guests sample their choices among the company's thirty-nine different wines and six of its champagnes.

Several of the wines here are Paul Masson originals with proprietary names. An international favorite is Emerald Dry, which I can best describe as the kind of wine the growers on the Moselle strive to produce but can't in Germany's rigorous climate (though I love their failures!). Emerald Dry is named for the Emerald Riesling grape, which is the principal variety used in its uniquely flavorful, fresh-tasting blend. An original Paul Masson red called Rubion has an aged-claret flavor and bouquet, yet is soft and light and is even pleasant served chilled. Baroque is a much richer red, resembling some of the better Rhone wines, with a powerful bouquet from the old cask-aged red wines in its blend. Among Masson's other specialties are its new Pinnacles Selection of higher-priced "varietal" table wines and its old dessert wine rarities, which come in heart-shaped, numbered bottles. Another is Blanc de Pinot Brut Champagne, the first to be made in the United States from the traditional French *cuvée* of all three Pinot grapes—Pinot Noir, Chardonnay, and Pinot Blanc.

The colorful story of Paul Masson Vineyards parallels that of Santa Clara wines. In 1852, two years after California became a state, Etienne Thée, a *vigneron* from Bordeaux, planted vines along Guadalupe Creek, five miles east of present-day Los Gatos. Thée was succeeded by his son-in-law, Charles Lefranc, and the latter by his son-in-law, Paul Masson. Since these and subsequent owners have produced wine continuously since Thée's vineyard first bore grapes, the present Paul Masson Vineyards is California's oldest winegrower.

Born in 1859 near Beaune in Burgundy, Paul Masson came to California at the age of nineteen. The phylloxera vine plague had devastated the vineyard on the Côte d'Or where his family had made wine for three centuries, and glowing descriptions of California's fabulous climate had already drawn many French winegrowers here. Young Masson first enrolled to study science at the University of the Pacific, which then was located in Santa Clara. While there he became acquainted with his compatriot Charles Lefranc, and soon became Lefranc's employee. In 1884 Masson went to France, brought back champagne-making equipment and French experts to install it, and began making champagne for Lefranc. Four years later, he married his employer's daughter, Louise, and the firm became Lefranc & Masson. In 1892 he bought the interest of Lefranc's son Henry and founded his own Paul Masson Champagne Company. His champagnes won numerous awards, including the grand prize at the Louisiana Purchase Exposition of 1904. But Masson was always proudest of the honorable mention an all-French jury gave them at the Paris Exposition of 1900.

In 1896, Masson began planting the mountain vineyard, which he called La Cresta, and nine years later started building the Mountain Winery. When the 1906 earthquake destroyed St.

Patrick's Church in San Jose, he bought its ancient portal and erected it as part of the winery facade.

Masson, the broad-shouldered, jovial Burgundian, was both a noted epicure and a flamboyant host. His lavish entertainments of San Francisco society and of such theatrical luminaries as singer Anna Held and Charlie Chaplin are legend, but local historians disagree on where they took place. The chief controversy concerns which bathtub he used to give Miss Held her famous champagne bath in 1917—the tub in his château at the mountain vineyard or the one in his Los Gatos villa.* Robert Balzer, his latest biographer, says it must have been at La Cresta because at Los Gatos Mrs. Masson wouldn't have permitted such goings-on.

During the early Prohibition years Masson continued to prosper because he held the first government permit to make medicinal champagne, sold by druggists on doctors' prescriptions. But one night in 1929, an armed hijacking gang, posing as Federal prohibition agents, raided his mountain winery, and in four truckloads emptied it of wine. At the approach of Repeal in 1933, Masson sold the Los Gatos winery, but continued making champagne in a San Jose cellar for three more years. By then he was seventy-seven years old, a widower with an unmarried daughter. He sold out and retired, and four years later he died.

A stockbroker turned realtor named Martin Ray bought Masson's mountain domain in 1936. In that year the expert winemaker at the Jesuit Fathers' Novitiate of Los Gatos winery, Brother Oliver Goulet, had quit his job and the priestly order to get married. Goulet went to work for Ray, and the Paul Masson wines that Goulet made continued winning medals as before.

In the war year of 1942, when the big liquor distillers were buying up California wineries, the House of Seagram bought Paul Masson from Ray. After the war, the late Seagram whiskey king, Samuel Bronfman, foresaw the enormous potential growth of winegrowing in America, and while his competitors in the liquor business got rid of their wineries, Bronfman kept a silent (majority) interest in Masson. When the present wine boom exploded and the other distillers rushed back into the wine business, Seagram (which also owns many European and Latin American wineries) took over Paul Masson marketing in 1971 and combined it with Browne Vintners, its worldwide wine-importing firm.

Seagram's partners in Paul Masson Vineyards were Alfred Fromm, the late Franz Sichel, and Otto E. Meyer, emigrés from Germany, where their families had owned wine firms for genera-

*A more likely version, attributed to an old vineyard worker on the mountain, is that no bathtub was used, that Masson merely shook up a magnum of unchilled champagne, held his thumb over the mouth, and sprayed the lady with the foam.

tions. Fromm, a graduate of the great Geisenheim wine school, also heads Fromm and Sichel, the worldwide marketer of the Christian Brothers' wines and brandy. Otto Meyer, trained from boyhood in his grandfather's winery at Bingen on the Rhine, has been in charge of Masson production since 1945. In that quarter of a century, the company has increased its vineyards to more than 5000 acres and its wine-aging capacity to 12 million gallons, divided between the Mountain Winery, the Champagne Cellars in Saratoga, and the Pinnacles Vineyard cellar in Monterey County. In 1960, Masson became the first American winegrower to establish an export department and to pioneer foreign markets for bottled California wines. "We decided," Meyer explained, "that our wines, like our opera stars, must go abroad to enhance their reputation in order to become fully appreciated at home." Within a decade, Masson wines had established commercial distribution in some fifty countries around the world, including England, Germany, Italy, Belgium, Switzerland, Australia, the Philippines, and Japan.

Meyer, endowed with a phenomenally keen sense of smell, is also the company's chief taster. He heads a tasting team that once included the great Kurt Opper and Hans Hyba from Germany and which now stars California-trained Leo Berti, Guy Baldwin, Thomas Leong, E. J. Lowe, Joseph Stillman, and Edward Friedrich from Germany. Before he joined Masson, Meyer was the creator of the unique California brandy blend that in this country far outsells the cognacs of France. A Masson full-page magazine ad in 1971 pictured him in close-up profile with the fitting caption, "The secret of our brandy is Otto Meyer's nose."

Paul Masson and the Christian Brothers are the only leading California premium producers who refuse to use any vintage labels. They prefer to blend young wines for freshness with old wines for bouquet and to keep the blend uniform from bottle to bottle, each wine ready to drink.

· 5 ·

There are more vineyards and several more wineries scattered through the rugged mountains west of Saratoga. Atop Mount Eden, north of the Masson mountain vineyard, Martin Ray cultivates a hundred acres owned by himself and various investors. Ray preaches that his are the only fine American wines, prices them astronomically, and does not welcome visitors except by appointment made far in advance.

On Montebello Road, a mile beyond the Stevens Creek Reservoir, Josephine and Anita Pichetti live beside the old-country vineyard and winery they inherited from their husbands, who were brothers. Their cellar is still bonded, but they now sell their grapes and haven't made any wine since 1963.

Three miles of steep curves beyond the Pichetti Vineyard, Montebello Road climbs a ridge of towering Black Mountain and reaches an elevation of 2600 feet. There is the Ridge Vineyard, a small winegrowing enterprise owned by six families of wine enthusiasts. It began in 1960, when a talented home winemaker named David Bennion interested three of his fellow scientists at the Stanford Research Institute in renovating an old vineyard and a ramshackle wooden cellar on the mountain to make wine for themselves and for sale to their friends. With their wives and children, the partners climbed the Montebello grade on weekends to tend the vineyard, to which a previous owner had added several acres of Cabernet and Chardonnay. In autumn the families had great fun picking and crushing the grapes, and later everyone helped to bottle the wines.

Bennion soon found wine more exciting than electronics research, and quit his Stanford job in 1968 to become the group's full-time winemaker. To keep the business going, he also imported and bottled an assortment of French and Portuguese wines, and, by holding frequent tastings, developed a connoisseur clientele. Then he and two of his original partners, Hewitt Crane and Charles Rosen, were joined by three more, Stanford Professor Carl Djerassi, pharmaceutical manufacturer Alejandro Zaffaroni, and Los Angeles industrialist Richard Foster. They planted more Cabernet and Chardonnay, added some Merlot, bought the Zinfandel crops of the nearby Schwabacher and Pichetti vineyards, and purchased a ten-acre patch of choice white grapes in Santa Cruz County. In 1970, with an additional winemaker, Paul Draper, they moved their equipment and wines uphill to a better cellar, the old stone Montebello Winery, which Dr. Osea Perrone had closed thirty-three years before.* Ridge Vineyard (the label name) wines are aged in small casks and are seldom fined or filtered; it is usually advisable to decant the reds. The best I have tasted thus far are its vintage Zinfandels.

• 6 •

Los Gatos, on Highway 17, is the home of a historic winery. High above that city, against a spectacular backdrop of hilltop vineyard, stands the Sacred Heart Novitiate, established in 1888 to train young men, enrolled as novices, for membership in the

---

*The Montebello name then was acquired by a St. Helena winery, which since has changed hands twice. "Montebello" wines now come from a winery in northern Sonoma County.

Jesuit Order as Priests or as Brothers. Beside the imposing build-ing is the Novitiate of Los Gatos Winery, which during all those years has produced wines in accordance with the canon law of the Catholic Church, the sale of wine helping to support the Or-der's educational work.

Father Louis Franklin manages the winery and Father James Ransford and Brother Lee Williams supervise the winemaking, helped by eight Brothers and eight lay employees. The previous winemaker was Father Thomas Dutton Terry, who became presi-dent of the University of Santa Clara; he is the only winemaker-college president in this country, if not in the world. Father Henri Charvet manages the Novitiate's six hundred acres of vineyards in Santa Clara, San Benito, and Stanislaus Counties.

The training of novices was moved in 1967 to a new seminary at Montecito in Southern California, and the old Novitiate was turned into a Jesuit residence. Each autumn, however, the novices return to help harvest the grapes. The oldest vineyard, the one behind the winery, has shrunk in recent years, and a larger one near Almadén has been sold and chopped up into housing tracts. But the Novitiate still grows grapes around the old Jesuit Alma College on Bear Creek Road, and its new vineyards north of San Juan Bautista and near Modesto supply more grapes than the win-ery used before.

Until recent years, four fifths of the Novitiate output consisted of altar wines with such names as L'Admirable, Villa Joseph, Guadalupe, and Vin Doré. The rest was sold commercially, labeled "Novitiate Jesuit Wines," and included Cabernet, Pinot Blanc, Château Novitiate, Flor Sherry, Angelica, and Black Muscat. Best known to connoisseurs was the Black Muscat, one of the few fine red muscatels in the world.

Unlike the Christian Brothers, who have built their well-ad-vertised wine and brandy business nationwide, the Jesuit Fathers long de-emphasized their commercial wines. Until recently they could only be bought in Los Gatos and in the few cities where there were distributors of Novitiate altar wines. Now this is chang-ing. The capacity of the Novitiate winery, now 750,000 gallons, is being doubled. More wines (Chenin Blanc, Pinot Noir) have been added. The Fathers are now planning an advertising program, and they say they may soon start making brandy and champagne. A public tasting room has been opened in one of the moss-covered cellar tunnels, is now kept open daily except Sunday, and wine tours with Brother Thomas Koller are offered on Tuesday and Friday afternoons.

In the past, several Church-owned wineries carried on the monastic tradition of winegrowing in the United States. Another

Jesuit winery, the Villa Maria Vineyard on Stevens Creek Road southwest of Cupertino, was operated by the University of Santa Clara until 1938. The only ones left are the Novitiate, the Christian Brothers, and the O-Neh-Da Vineyard and winery in upstate New York.

• 7 •

Bear Creek Road, where the Novitiate has its vineyards around Alma College, extends into Santa Cruz County and reaches an altitude of 2000 feet. At that height, two miles past the county line, Dr. David Bruce, whose medical practice is in San Jose, lives with his wife Carol and their four children and pursues his avocation of growing fine wines. When the Bruces bought this hilltop in 1961, there was a century-old farmhouse on the property and traces of a former vineyard. While the doctor terraced the land and planted Chardonnay, White Riesling, Pinot Noir, and Cabernet, Carol supervised the building of a new home. He studied texts on viticulture and enology, practiced making wine in small quantities, then bonded a temporary winery in 1964, and three years later put David Bruce wines on sale in a few San Jose stores. Since then he has built a two-story concrete-block cellar with modern equipment, some of it of his own design, has bought another vineyard, and has won a reputation with several unique table wines, which he sells at three to twenty dollars a bottle, mostly to California connoisseurs who order them by mail. The best I have tasted are his Chardonnays and Zinfandels, but the most unusual is a wine he had not planned to make. During the first vintage in his temporary winery, he discovered he had more red grapes than his aging-casks could hold, so he fermented the white juice of his Zinfandel grapes without the skins, bottled the wine young, and named it "Zinfandel Blanc de Noir." It developed with a full Zinfandel aroma, but it has an orange tinge. He since has also made a white wine of Pinot Noir. Although Dr. Bruce specializes in vintage wines of the high-priced noble varieties, he hopes also someday to "bring the mountain-grown Zinfandel to the place it deserves in the world of fine wines."

• 8 •

Santa Cruz was a famous wine county before Prohibition, when thirty-nine wineries cultivated 1600 acres of vineyards between Ben Lomond, Boulder Creek, Corralitos, Felton, Glenwood, and Soquel. Less than 200 acres are left; many old vineyards have been replanted with Christmas trees, which are easier to cultivate than wines. After Repeal, the best-known Santa Cruz wines came from lawyer Chaffee Hall's Hallcrest Vineyard near Felton. He closed the winery before he died in 1969, and his choice Riesling and Cabernet grapes now go to the Concannon winery at Livermore.

There are four bonded wineries in the county besides Bruce. The oldest and biggest is Martinelli at Watsonville, which dates from 1868, but it makes only hard apple cider, light apple wines, and nonalcoholic sparkling cider and apple juice from local fruit. Vincent Locatelli's small vineyard, adjoining the Lockheed missile plant near Eagle Rock, was planted in 1902. Locatelli, a former county supervisor, makes only one wine, a claret, which he sells to weekend visitors.

Electronic engineer Dan Wheeler's tiny Nicasio Vineyard winery is in a hand-hewn cave in the mountains six miles north of Soquel. It began as a home winemaker's hobby in 1952, when he dug the cave; he bonded it three years later. For several years Wheeler flew daily to his own hilltop airfield from his business in Palo Alto, but one day he missed the airstrip and landed in the trees beside his cabin. He cultivates an acre of Pinot Noir, buys the rest of his grapes, makes several distinctive table wines and champagnes, and sells them to his mailing list of customers in California and neighboring states.

The 100,000-gallon Bargetto Winery in Soquel is the only one in the county with a public tasting room. Visitors are welcomed daily to tour the cellar and sample the wines. Lawrence and Ralph Bargetto took over the winery from their father in 1964 and converted it to a premium wine operation. For several years they bought their grapes from various Santa Cruz vineyards, including one near Glenwood owned by Alfred Hitchcock of movie-thriller fame. In 1970, Santa Cruz grapes were in such demand by wineries that the Bargettos began planting their own vineyards on patches of farmland in hills behind Soquel. They also have begun making mead and fruit wines from local honey, apricots, peaches, and plums.

· 9 ·

Returning to Santa Clara County, only one winery is left in the Guadalupe Creek district east of Los Gatos, where there were a dozen a few decades ago. Hedged in by the new housing tracts along Blossom Hill Road is the huge, sprawling home winery of Almadén Vineyards. This is where Almadén gets its founding date of 1852, which it shares with Paul Masson; for it was there in that year that Etienne Thée planted his vineyard, where he was succeeded by son-in-law Charles Lefranc and by Lefranc's son-in-law, Masson.

Only thirty acres of the once-great vineyard remain, serving mainly to separate the winery from the surrounding homes. The original small adobe-and-brick cellar and the lovely Lefranc-Masson villa and French gardens have been preserved. They are surrounded now by bustling modern cellars, in which Almadén wines are finished and bottled and where the company's champagnes are made. Its producing wineries are now in San Benito County, and its 8000 acres of vineyards are there and in Alameda and Monterey Counties.

Almadén no longer invites visitors to its wineries, but its wines can be sampled in its two attractive tasting rooms, one on the Plaza in old San Juan Bautista and the other on Pacheco Pass Road, Highway 152. To taste them all would be an undertaking, for at last count there were more than fifty, including a Blanc Fumé and a red Grenache named Grenoir that were added in 1972. Almadén's champagnes range from the expensive *cuvée*-dated Blanc de Blancs Brut to its moderately priced "Le Domaine" sparkling wines, and its table wines run the whole gamut from fine "estate-bottled," vintage dated "varietals" to the good, inexpensive "mountain red" and "mountain white" generic types.

The first wines named Almadén* were introduced by Henry Lefranc before the turn of the century. The name again appeared on labels at Repeal in 1933, when Charles Jones and his associates reopened the old winery and for a few years sold wines they called "Almadén Maison Blanc" and "Almadén Maison Rouge."

In 1941, San Francisco socialite Louis Benoist, then president of the Lawrence Warehouse Company, bought the property as a place to entertain his weekend guests. He persuaded a great chef, Madame Louise Savin, to close her nearby restaurant and take charge of the kitchen at Almadén.

Benoist started looking for someone to tell him what to do with his winery. Learning that the importer and wine-writer Frank Schoonmaker was having success selling premium California wines in New York, Benoist placed a call for him there. That day Schoonmaker happened to be in San Francisco, where he had a wine shop on Maiden Lane. He became the wine advisor to Benoist, and has been advising Almadén owners, writing their wine labels, and editing their "News from the Vineyards" ever since.

Schoonmaker also found a winemaker for Benoist; he knew that Oliver Goulet was having a disagreement with Martin Ray. Goulet went to work for Almadén and made fine wines there until his death in 1962. His assistant, Albert Huntsinger, from the Napa

*For the old quicksilver mine in the hills. Almadén means "mine" in Spanish.

Valley Co-op winery via Charles Krug, has been Almadén's wine-master since then.

One day soon after the purchase, inspecting the old vineyard with Benoist and Goulet, Schoonmaker noticed some Grenache grapes, which Goulet said were being used to make port wine. Schoonmaker asked him why they weren't used to make rosé, as in France's Rhone district of Tavel. Goulet's puzzled answer was: "What's rosé?" Six months later, Almadén started the pink-wine vogue in the United States by launching its first Grenache Rosé. And with its fresh varietal aroma and intriguing puckery taste, Grenache Rosé is still the company's best-selling wine.

Benoist bought and planted more vineyards in the Santa Clara Valley and in the Santa Cruz Mountains. During the Second World War Almadén Champagne and Rosé became nationally known. But when the wine market crashed following the war, the firm began to lose money. Benoist then worked out a merger with the Madrone Vineyards of Eugene Selvage, boss of the Lucky Lager Brewery. They couldn't agree on what to name the merged firm, so it became "Almadén-Madrone." The merger lasted until 1950, when Selvage's Canadian backers suddenly ordered Madrone closed down. Almadén again became independent, with a new manager, Hans Peter Jurgens, who had headed Madrone.

Then suburban subdivisionitis began to bite chunks out of Almadén's 900 Santa Clara and Santa Cruz acres, and Benoist saw his vineyards there were doomed. In 1954 the company began acquiring land in San Benito County and started planting there four years later. When the new vines came into bearing, all but a few dozen acres of the historic vineyard near Los Gatos gave way to a housing tract named "Almadén Estates."

In 1967, when Louis and Kay Benoist owned seven houses, two airplanes, and a 110-foot yacht named *Le Voyageur*, something went wrong between Benoist and his Lawrence Warehouse Company. The Benoists suddenly sold their yacht and their Aptos beach house, and Almadén was offered for sale. The wineries and vineyards were snapped up for $14 million by National Distillers, which had owned three California wineries during the Second World War but had sold them all when the conflict ended. Under the new ownership, Almadén keeps expanding, has added new vineyards in Monterey and San Benito Counties, and has plans to double its wine output by 1975.

· 10 ·

Across the Santa Clara Valley, in the Evergreen district on the slope of Mount Hamilton, the Mirassou Vineyard invites visitors to tour its winery and to sample the wines in its new tasting room. The Mirassou family, winegrowers there for five generations, is one of the oldest in the wine industry, but its name is one of the newest on labels in retail stores.

In 1858, ancestor Pierre Pellier brought cuttings of vines and prunes from France by sailing ship, each twig carefully placed in a sliced potato to protect it from drying out during the six-month voyage around Cape Horn. He delivered them to his brother's Pellier Nursery in San Jose; then three years later planted his own vineyard in the Evergreen district and built a cellar to age his wines. Pellier's son-in-law, Pierre Mirassou, succeeded him, followed by his son, Peter Mirassou, and then by his sons, Edmund and Norbert. They have been joined now by their four sons and a son-in-law, who are rearing a sixth generation.

Edmund and Norbert, who own the winery, made only bulk wines for sale to other producers until 1942, when they had a few labels printed in order to sell a few bottled wines to their neighbors. Then they entered a few wines in the State Fair judgings, and when they received gold and silver medals, connoisseurs began coming to the winery to buy. Meanwhile, the boys of the fifth generation were growing up, getting experience working in the vineyards and winery. Then, in 1966, that fifth generation formed a marketing company, took over the sales, and introduced bottled Mirassou wines to the nationwide premium trade. While these things were happening, the Mirassou vineyards were spreading far beyond the Santa Clara Valley. Their new plantings, which now give them a total of a thousand acres, are in the Salinas Valley of Monterey County. The sixteen Mirassou "varietals," "generics," and champagnes, all vintage-dated and labeled as to their Santa Clara or Monterey vineyard origin, are now among the finest produced in the United States.

• 11 •

In the Evergreen Valley two miles southeast of Mirassou, there is a relic of the glamorous past of Santa Clara wines. The stately million-gallon William Wehner winery, built in the 1880s with four cupolas on its roof, is still producing wines. But of its great vineyard, which once covered 1200 acres, only 500 acres are left. Since 1959, an adult community development named "The Villages" has been biting off chunks of the vineyard, and the remaining vines are doomed to go when the community expands to full size. Meanwhile, Anthony Cribari has leased the vineyard and winery and produces wine in bulk for several premium producers. Before the Second World War the House of Cribari, founded by

Anthony's father in 1904, owned thousands of acres in the Santa Clara Valley and operated famous wineries at Madrone, Fresno, and New York City. But the "Famiglia Cribari" name on wine labels was given up in a merger many years ago and now appears only on Guild wines bottled at Lodi.

· 12 ·

South of the Evergreen district, there are no more wineries until Morgan Hill, fifteen miles from San Jose. The old Cribari and Madrone vineyards at the north end of Morgan Hill are gone, and the massive wood-and-brick cellar on the highway, where their wines were made for two decades, was demolished in 1967. A small wooden building that remains there serves now as the Richert winery tasting room. When Walter Richert, a veteran enologist who once was editor of the *Wine Review*, started his own winery in the Cribari-Madrone cellar in 1953, he planned that his sons would carry it on someday. So, although his boys were still of preschool age, Richert optimistically named his business "Richert & Sons." His hopes were fulfilled when Robert and Scott Richert finished college and joined him in his present winery, which is two miles west of the highway. The Richerts specialize in blending and aging choice sherries and ports and in making apricot and berry wines.

An old wine district that is just now beginning to be invaded by housing tracts extends from Morgan Hill south to beyond Gilroy. Before Prohibition, the small farmers there sold their wines in bulk to the old California Wine Association, which had wineries at Evergreen, Los Gatos, and Gilroy. At Repeal, these winegrowers again sold in bulk to big wineries, but some of them developed a business of delivering wine in jugs each week to Italian stores and restaurants and to the doorsteps of wine-drinking families, much as the dairies deliver milk.

One of the latter is the Emilio Guglielmo Winery, on Main Avenue two miles east of Morgan Hill. Before and during World War II, Guglielmo's Cavalcade Burgundy in gallon jugs at $1.50 was one of the best wine buys in San Francisco. His son, George, took over after the war, modernized and expanded the winery, opened a tasting room next door to this home, and added "Emile's Reserve" wines in bottles at seventy cents a fifth. Then, new kinds of buyers began asking him if he didn't have some finer wines. George obliged them by adding Pinot Noir and Cabernet, bought from another winery, at a dollar a bottle more. From his own vineyards he makes only sauterne, burgundy, and Grignolino rosé, which are still bargains at the higher prices he gets for them now.

Doorstep delivery of chablis and burgundy in jugs is still part of the business of Edward Pedrizetti, who has a small winery and a sixty-acre vineyard on San Pedro Avenue, a mile southeast of Guglielmo. But Pedrizetti is beginning to have other ideas. When his wife Phyllis opened a tasting room on the highway in 1969, he discovered many people want to pay more for wines with fancier names. He has planted more "varietal" grapes and has begun bottling his Barbera, Cabernet, and Pinot Blanc separately instead of blending them in his burgundy and chablis. He has added vintage dates and "estate bottled" to some of his labels and now gets twice as much for these wines as for those in jugs with generic names. The Pedrizettis, recognizing that population growth threatens the farms in this part of the valley, put their vineyard into an agricultural preserve in 1969.

Numerous billboards along Highway 101 invite tourists to stop at the San Martin Winery's tasting room, which is four miles south of Morgan Hill. It does a thriving business, also selling glassware and other wine-related merchandise. Visitors are offered a series of wines for tasting in one-ounce glasses, each preceded by a lecture. The 2-million-gallon brick winery, built in 1892, is across the railroad tracks from the tasting room and is not open to visitors. San Martin is the only big winery in the southern Santa Clara Valley and the only one whose wines are distributed nationally. It is owned by the several sons, grandsons, and in-laws of Bruno Filice, who came from Cosenza in southern Italy and settled in the valley during the 1880s. The Filices have 800 acres of vineyards in the hills east and west of Gilroy, replanted with premium varieties in recent years, and, like Pedrizetti, are putting some of their land into agricultural preserves. "Other winegrowers have abandoned this valley," says San Martin Manager Michael Filice, "but we're planning to stay." The Filices sell forty-six different wines under their San Martin and Castlewood labels, including bottle-fermented and Charmat-process champagnes, numerous still and sparkling fruit wines, and a Malvasia Spumante, which resembles Asti Spumante, northern Italy's fine muscat-flavored champagne. All can be sampled at their tasting rooms on Highways 101 and 152 and in San Francisco, San Jose, and Monterey.

Gilroy is known as the nation's garlic capital, and the pungent aroma from the dehydrators east of the city is sometimes quite pronounced. But west of town on Highway 152, the road to Hecker Pass, there is a different aroma in autumn—the heady smell of fermenting wine. Clustered in two verdant, scenic valleys there are seven wineries surrounded by vineyards of their own. In past years, mostly bulk wines were grown here by the Italian-born

Gilroy vintners for sale to larger wineries or in jugs, demijohns, or barrels to the family and roadside trade. Now some of the owners' sons have taken over, and since Americans discovered wine in the '60s, have begun replanting the vineyards with the grape varieties that make premium wines. People from San Jose and the bay cities come here looking for wine bargains, in such numbers that four of the Gilroy vintners have opened public tasting rooms. Peter Scagliotti was the first to post billboards on Highway 152 to attract tourists to his Live Oaks Winery. This inspired Angelo Bertero and his sons, whose winery is directly across the road, to do the same. Then Mario and Ernest Fortino took over the old Cassa vineyard and winery and offered wine tasting, too. In 1971, home-winemaker Tom Kruse and his wife Sue bought and bonded an old winery between Bertero and Fortino, acquired thirty acres of vineyards, opened the Thomas Kruse Winery, and began producing Grignolino and several other "varietal" rosés for sale to passersby. As a sideline, Tom teaches courses in home winemaking and the appreciation of wine.

The Louis Bonesio winery, across the hill in the well-named Uvas Valley (*uvas* is Spanish for grapes) has gone ahead of its neighbors and has begun selling its top estate-bottled "varietal" wines to the connoisseur and restaurant trade. When Louis Bonesio, Jr., finished a stint in the navy, he persuaded his family to begin replanting part of their 140 acres with Chardonnay, Malvasia Bianca, Cabernet Sauvignon, and Pinot Noir. The Bonesios still deliver their jug wines to householder customers spread between King City and San Francisco, but in their tasting room they now feature their "varietals," which include two unusual reds, Malvasia Nera and Mataro.

Two other Gilroy wineries, Conrotto and Giretti, have taken down their "wine for sale" signs, but still supply their old customers with country-style wine by the barrel, demijohn or jug.

Other vineyards are located three miles east of Gilroy on Highway 152. Near where the highway joins Ferguson Road are the new plantings of the San Martin winery and Paul Masson's 300-acre San Ysidro Vineyard, planted under direction of University viticulturists in 1948. It contains, among other varieties, the first commercial plantings of Dr. Harold Olmo's original wine-grape creations, Emerald Riesling and Ruby Cabernet.

• 13 •

From San Juan Bautista, a half hour's drive south of Gilroy, the San Benito Valley extends southeastward between the Diablo and Gavilán (Hawk) mountain ranges for some sixty miles. To this sparsely populated valley, outside the path of urban sprawl, came Louis Benoist of Almadén in 1954, seeking land to replace his doomed vineyards in the Santa Clara Valley. The northern part of San Benito County is one of the oldest winegrowing districts in the state. The Franciscan friars who founded Mission San Juan Bautista in 1797 planted vines in the mission garden to make wine for the Mass. A half century later, Théophile Vaché established the first commercial vineyard in the Cienega Valley, eight miles southeast of the mission, and hauled his wine to market in a puncheon on wheels drawn by oxen. By the 1880s, there were 400 acres of vines in San Benito County, and wines made at Cienega by William Palmtag, the mayor of Hollister, were winning medals in Europe. Palmtag's successor was Dr. Harold Ohrwall of San Francisco, who was joined in 1908 by Professor Frederic Bioletti of viticultural fame. During Prohibition, the San Benito wineries closed, but more vineyards were planted to supply grapes to the home-winemaking trade. There were 2000 acres of vines and eight bonded wineries in the county at Repeal in 1933. Edwin Valliant then owned the Palmtag winery, and during the late 1930s he made some of the best Rieslings in the state. He sold out to a subsidiary of the Hiram Walker distillers during the Second World War.

When Benoist came to San Benito County, he first leased and later purchased the Cienega winery and vineyard. In 1958 he began planting lands near Paicines, thirteen miles farther south, and soon afterward built a brandy distillery and a second winery there. By 1967, when he sold Almadén to National Distillers, his San Benito vineyards covered almost 4500 acres, which then was the largest planting of premium-variety grapes under a single ownership in the world.

It is worth a trip through the valley to see these spectacular vineyards, five square miles of rolling hills carpeted with vines. They are watered by permanent overhead sprinklers, fed through hundreds of miles of underground plastic pipe. The sprinklers also protect the vines from frost; when temperatures drop to freezing, they switch on automatically to insulate the vines with a protective coating of ice. Fifty electronic scarecrows, loudspeakers on towers, frighten off grape-eating birds by broadcasting their tape-recorded calls of distress.

Almadén's Cienega Valley cellar is world-famous as "the walking winery." Palmtag unwittingly built the old cellar precisely astride the San Andreas earthquake fault, the most active earthquake belt in the United States; the halves of the winery move a half inch farther apart each year. Seismologists come from many countries to observe the deep cleft in the cement floor because it keeps widening with each tremor of the earth. Although the winery is not open to visitors, you can stop and see the cleft in a concrete drain outside the building. In 1960, a comparatively mild temblor jolted a redwood tank off balance, and eight thousand gallons of wine were lost through its loosened staves.

There is another amazing sight across the road: a single roof covers four acres of barrels and tanks of aging wines. Almadén makes only red wines at Cienega; the whites are made at the Paicines winery; the company's sherry *soleras* are also there. Almadén brandy is distilled in the San Joaquin Valley and is blended and bottled by National Distillers at Cincinnati, Ohio.

· 14 ·

Across the Gavilán Mountains from the San Benito Valley, the Salinas Valley stretches southeastward through Monterey County for some eighty miles. To the west are the rugged Santa Lucia Mountains, which rise abruptly from the Pacific shore twenty-five miles away. The valley is mostly a level plain ten to twenty miles wide, from which side valleys climb into the foothills on both sides.

A viticultural revolution has taken place in the area since 1962. Long known as the "Salad Bowl of the World" for its vast plantings of iceberg lettuce and celery, the Salinas Valley has become, in a single decade, the "wine bowl" instead—the newest and potentially the most important premium winegrowing district in North America.

During the century when pioneer vintners were establishing the vineyards around San Francisco Bay, the Salinas Valley was considered a poor place to grow grapes. Of four hundred acres of vines in Monterey County during Prohibition, more than half were abandoned after Repeal. The chief reason was scant rainfall, only ten inches annually, half of the minimum required for adequate vineyard yields. And the strong wind that sweeps unimpeded up the valley from Monterey Bay each afternoon from May to November was regarded as injurious to vines.

Consequently, when Professors Winkler and Amerine at the University published their analyses of California climates, begun in 1935, their findings about the Salinas Valley went unnoticed. One of their findings was that growing-season temperatures in the north-central part of this valley are the same as in the most-favored north coast districts, Region I and Region II.

Twenty-five years later, as cities began closing in on the Santa Clara vineyards, the Mirassou brothers and their Paul Masson neighbors began an urgent search for other areas in which to plant vines. They first surveyed Sonoma County, and the Sierra foothills next, but neither offered sufficient flat open space. Then they noticed the old Winkler-Amerine figures on summer temperatures in the Salinas Valley, and decided to investigate there for themselves. They discovered that the sparse Salinas rainfall was actually no problem, for through this remarkable valley flows the Salinas River, the greatest underground stream in America. Plentiful water, pumped from only a hundred feet below the parched surface, already supplied artificial rain for the lettuce crops; it could do the same for grapevines. And they saw that the afternoon gales could not damage the grapes if the vine rows were simply planted parallel to the wind. In fact, the wind is the key to the Salinas climate; it keeps the valley cool. They found still another advantage: vines planted on fertile benchlands above the valley floor would be virtually immune from damage by frost. And of perhaps greatest importance, this area, situated far from the fast-growing cities to the north and south, seemed safe for many years from urban sprawl.

In a multimillion-dollar gamble, these two vintners in 1957 bought 1300 acres in the valley between Soledad and Greenfield, and in 1962 began planting vines in what for grapes was virgin soil. The Mirassous set out 300 acres on the west side near the now-restored Mission Nuestra Señora de la Soledad. On the east side along Metz Road, Masson planted 1000 acres and named it the Pinnacles Vineyard for the Pinnacles National Monument, the area of lofty crags and weird caves in the Gavilán range nearby. A year later, the Wente Brothers of Livermore followed, choosing 300 acres near the Arroyo Seco, southwest of the Mirassous. Normally, four years would have elapsed before the results of the gamble could be known. By the third year, however, the grapes showed such promise that Masson began building a winery on its Pinnacles Vineyard and started sending its grapes there from Santa Clara to be crushed.

The 1966 vintage proved that Winkler and Amerine were right. The Mirassou and Masson vineyards in that year harvested Gewürztraminers that made wines richer in spicy Gewürz fragrance, better balanced, and more delicious than any Traminers from Alsace. Masson in 1966 made a Johannisberg Riesling from its Pinnacles Vineyard grapes that excelled any in the Santa Clara Valley. And if I were still judging wines at the California State Fair, I would vote gold medals now for the Mirassous' 1966 "First Monterey Harvest" Pinot Noir and Cabernet Sauvignon (their labels now distinguish between their Santa Clara and Monterey wines) and for the *Spätlese* Riesling the Wente Brothers grew in their Monterey vineyard in 1969.

A historic luncheon was held among the casks in Masson's new Pinnacles winery in October of 1966. It was a gathering of wine industry and Monterey County civic leaders to honor Professors Winkler and Amerine. Toasts were drunk to their health and to their achievement, "the world's first fine wine district established as the direct result of scientific temperature research."

In the next few years, vineyard planting in the Salinas Valley multiplied no less than seven times. Masson first added 4000 acres around Greenfield and Soledad. Mirassou planted 600 acres on its San Vicente Ranch. Almadén followed in 1970, buying 2500 acres of grazing and vegetable land below King City and San Lucas, and started planting in the same year. Still others chose the areas around Gonzales and Chualar, north of Soledad, and some planted as far south as Bradley, near where Monterey County ends.

But this is only the beginning, says Edmund Mirassou. "If the demand for coast counties wine and champagne continues growing at its present rate, vineyards in the Salinas Valley can reach a hundred thousand acres by the end of this century—more than all the vineyards of Napa, Sonoma, Mendocino, and the other coast counties combined!"

• 15 •

There is only one more winery in Monterey County thus far. It is nine steep miles and two thousand feet above the Salinas Valley on the Chalone bench of the Gavilán Mountains. The thirty-five-acre Chalone Vineyard is almost a century old, but yields sparse crops because moisture is so scarce at that elevation that water must be hauled up the mountain in tank trucks. The grapes it does produce are of such quality that Wente and Almadén paid high prices for them long before the "varietals" became scarce. In 1966, Davis-trained Richard Graff built a small winery on the vineyard, and he has since produced there some table wines and champagnes that bring extra-premium prices, such as nine dollars a bottle for his Chalone Vineyard Pinot Noir.

The Mirassous and Wentes, with their wineries a hundred miles distant from their Salinas Valley vineyards, faced a problem of keeping their grapes perfectly fresh during the long trip. The Mirassous solved it in 1969 by adding to one of their new mechanical-harvesting machines a grape-crusher-stemmer and a tank of carbon dioxide gas. The crushed grapes, protected from air by a blanket of CO_2, then traveled in a cooled and pressurized tank truck to their winery near San José. The resulting wine was later compared in blind tastings—and found superior—to wine made from the same grapes picked that day by hand.

• 16 •

San Luis Obispo County, where the Salinas River begins, is an old winegrowing district that is becoming important again. Since the 1960s, when Americans developed a taste for table wines, vineyard acreage in this county has jumped from seven hundred to a thousand acres. "This is only the beginning," says County Farm Advisor John Foott. "We have at least thirty thousand acres suitable for wine grapes, in districts with climates ranging from Region I to Region IV."

At Templeton, an hour's drive south of San Lucas, old vineyards line both sides of Highway 101. This area has long been noted for its Zinfandel grapes, which north coast wineries buy for use in their blends. There are three small wineries near Templeton, and two of them are among the oldest in the state. Because of their location, about halfway between San Francisco and Los Angeles, their wines have been sold mostly to the local and tourist trade and have seldom been tasted by connoisseurs.

The Rotta Winery on Vineyard Road dates from 1856, when a French farmer named Adolph Siot planted the first grapes in this locality. The Pesenti Winery, Rotta's neighbor, has only been in business since Repeal. The York Mountain Winery, eight miles west on the road to Cambria, was built in 1882, and became briefly famous sixty years later by making wine from the Zinfandel grapes grown by a world-renowned neighbor named Ignace Paderewski. This happened because that musician-statesman, incapacitated by an arthritis attack during a concert tour in 1913, was advised to go to Paso Robles for the mud baths and found the baths relieved his pain. Paderewski returned often for treatments, fell in love with the district, planted an orchard and vineyard west of Paso Robles, and once considered starting a winery of his own. He sold some of his grapes to the York Brothers, who later won medals with wines said to have been made from his Zinfandels. Paderewski's vineyard, which he named San Ignacio, was still producing grapes when he died in 1941, but later became neglected and has since been removed.

The York Mountain Winery has a new owner, who has begun making the first San Luis Obispo County champagne. He is veteran enologist Max Goldman, who after forty years of wine making in California and New York, bought the winery in 1970 from the founder's grandson, Wilfred York. Goldman is replanting the rundown vineyard with Chardonnay, Pinot Noir, and Cabernet, but also with some Zinfandel to continue supplying the wine that won medals for the York Brothers in Paderewski's day, and has begun making champagne.

On Peachy Canyon Road in the hills above Paso Robles, Dr. Stanley Hoffman has just opened the Hoffman Mountain Ranch winery on his forty acres of Chardonnay, Sylvaner, Cabernet Sauvignon, and Pinot Noir.

San Luis Obispo County vineyards now extend from west of Paso Robles, to an entirely new and promising district around Shandon in the Cholame Hills, sixteen miles to the east. This doesn't include a still newer and much larger area now being planted, between Nipomo and Santa Maria. But that district extends much farther south into Santa Barbara county, and is therefore described in the following chapter.

17

Southern California

A<small>T THIS</small> writing, the winegrowing scene in Southern California, where the state's great vineyard industry was born two centuries ago, is in a process of dramatic change.

A dozen venerable wineries are still turning out the unique wines which the region has produced for generations, but their vineyards are being decimated by smog and urban sprawl from nearby cities, where population is growing faster than anywhere else in the United States. Yet at the same time, entirely new Southern California vineyards are springing up on virgin lands outside the path of population growth, where the air is still clean and the climates have been found superior to those of the old southern districts for the growing of premium wines.

• 2 •

The Franciscan Fathers brought Vinifera vines to their Southern California missions from Mexico after the founding of San Diego Mission in 1769. Vineyards were set out at each of the missions. The padres made wine mainly for the Mass and for their own table use, but they also sold some of their wine and their *aguardiente* (brandy) to the early Spanish and American settlers. Their biggest wineries were at the San Gabriel and San Fernando Missions in present-day Los Angeles County. By 1821, San Gabriel, with three wine presses, was producing 400 barrels of wine and half that many of brandy each year. You can still see, behind that restored mission, the adobe building with its stone floor and sump where the Indians once crushed the grapes with their feet.

Within a few decades, vineyards were thriving where some of today's great southern cities stand. Vignes Street in downtown Los Angeles commemorates California's first professional winegrower, Jean Louis Vignes from Bordeaux. Aliso Street is where, by 1833, Vignes had imported European vines to his El Aliso Vineyard, which was entered through a grape arbor a quarter-mile long. Boyle Heights recalls Andrew Boyle from County Galway, whose thirty-acre vineyard flourished in 1860 below the cliff on which his brick home stood. The first mayor of Los Angeles, Benjamin Davis Wilson, for whom Mount Wilson is named, won fame for the white wines from his Lake Vineyard, established near San Gabriel in 1852. Thirty-five years later, Wilson's son-in-law, J. de Barth Shorb, was boasting that his San Gabriel Winery, with a capacity of 15 million gallons, was the largest in the world. At Santa Anita Race Track in nearby Arcadia the fabulous Elias (Lucky) Baldwin produced medal-winning wines and brandies on his 1200-acre vineyard, which was described in the 1880s as "a second Garden of Eden, bewildering in its beauty." Baldwin's gingerbread mansion still stands as a historical monument. Anaheim in neighboring Orange County, the home today of Disneyland and the baseball Angels, began in 1857 as a utopian winegrowing colony of German immigrants. Anaheim was one of the leading wine districts of the state until 1884, when the vines were suddenly destroyed by a mysterious disease (the Anaheim or Pierce's disease, now known to be caused by a virus). Other parts of Orange County had wineries and 1,000 acres of vineyards as late as 1900. There were fifteen acres left in 1972.

There were 5000 acres of vines and forty-nine wineries in Los Angeles County at the beginning of the Second World War. Then came the flood of new population to the Los Angeles basin, and the vines soon were virtually gone. The last big vineyard, at John McClure's Burbank Winery above San Fernando Boulevard, was bulldozed in 1947 to make room for a subdivision.

Three bonded cellars still operate in metropolitan Los Angeles, but two are new and they all use grapes grown outside the county. The San Antonio Winery, on downtown Lamar Street, dates from 1917 and preserves its old-time atmosphere. In 1970, photographer Sam Pierson and rocket engineer Leslie Navé rented a former dry goods store on San Fernando Road, bought grapes from San Luis Obispo County, and opened the first winery bonded in Los Angeles since 1917. A short time later a group of physicians bonded the Academy of Cellarmasters winery on an estate at Malibu, a private hobbyist enterprise. The Old Mill Winery in Whittier, President Richard Nixon's hometown, was just shutting down when I was there, because its grape supply at Cucamonga was gone.

San Diego County has a few hundred acres of vineyards left in the once-famous Escondido district, and there are some small new plantings of wine grapes southeast of Escondido around Alpine.

• 3 •

The Cucamonga Valley, forty-five miles east of Los Angeles, has grown the bulk of Southern California wine during the present century. The vineyard area extends from Ontario east to Fontana and from the base of the San Gabriel Mountains southward to the Jurupa Hills in Riverside County. The climate, though tempered by winds from the ocean, is as warm as the northern San Joaquin Valley and is classed as Region IV.

Tiburcio Tapia planted the first vines in San Bernardino County on his Cucamonga Rancho in 1838. When the railroad arrived forty years later, others began growing grapes along the streams in the rich foothills north of Cucamonga and between Redlands and Banning in southern San Bernardino and northwestern Riverside County.

But nobody thought of planting vines or anything else in the vast flat, sandy waste in between—the Cucamonga desert—until Secondo Guasti came. Guasti arrived in Los Angeles in 1878 from the Italian Piedmont via Mexico, an unschooled, penniless youth. He shoveled coal in the freight yards, cooked in a restaurant, married the owner's daughter, and saved enough to start a small Los Angeles winery and to buy a vineyard in West Glendale. On occasional visits to the Cucamonga Valley, he noticed that the winter floods from the mountains flowed only as far as the desert and there disappeared. It occurred to Guasti that there might be water beneath the desert sand. One day he found a scraggly vine growing in the parched waste. Borrowing a shovel, he dug to find its root. Legend says that he discovered moisture after digging down twenty-four feet. Back in Los Angeles in 1900, Guasti organized the Italian Vineyard Company, selling shares to his countrymen. He bought eight square miles of the Cucamonga desert, built fences against rabbits, and planted a hundred varieties of grapes. He brought whole families from Italy to till the land and built an Italian town—which he named Guasti—with its own school, inn, general store, fire house, post office, and a church as lovely as those in the Italian countryside. Others planted in the desert, and more wineries were built. In 1911, Captain Paul Garrett acquired his 2000 acres at Cucamonga to grow grapes for Virginia Dare wine. By 1917, Guasti was advertising the IVC vineyard as "four thousand acres, the largest in the world." San Bernardino County had 20,000 acres of vineyards, more than in Sonoma and twice as many as in Napa County—when Prohibition came in 1920.

During the early dry years, instead of pulling out their vines, the Cucamonga growers reaped a bonanza by shipping their grapes fresh across the country to the eastern bootleg and home-winemaking trade. The Guasti winery switched to making the legal sacramental and kosher wines. Then Captain Garrett, at his Mission Vineyard and Winery in Cucamonga, created Virginia Dare Wine Tonic by adding beef extract, pepsin, and iron to port and sherry, which made the concoction salable under the dry law. Guasti and the big Padre winery followed with their own wine tonic brands. When in 1929 Captain Garrett formed the Fruit Industries merger of old wineries to produce "Vine-Glo" grape concentrate, the Italian Vineyard Company was one of the first to join. By then Secondo Guasti had died. Much of the nation's supply of "Vine-Glo" was made at Guasti during the latter Prohibition years.

• 4 •

At Repeal in 1933, the Cucamonga district wineries had an opportunity to interest the connoisseur trade in at least three distinctive local wines. The late great wine judge, Almond R. Morrow, rated Cucamonga port the finest in the state. Cucamonga Zinfandel and Grignolino, grown in the district's unique climate and soil, are unusually soft to the palate, yet possess pronounced flavors and aromas unlike any other red table wines. Home winemakers in the East long paid premium prices for Cucamonga Zinfandel grapes because of their distinctive, almost cheesy taste. Because of it, some Northern California winemakers refuse to use Cucamonga wine in their blends. But the Cucamonga vintners, instead of capitalizing on the unique character of their grapes, ignored the connoisseur trade and tried to compete with the San Joaquin Valley wineries for the Los Angeles mass market in cheap wines. There was one brief attempt before the Second World War to sell Cucamonga wines as something different. Nicola Giulii, Guasti's brother-in-law, took the Italian Vineyard Company out of Fruit Industries in 1940 and advertised IVC wines as "better because they are made from non-irrigated grapes." Few people were impressed, however, because the IVC wines were low in price. Whatever the reason, Cucamonga wines have been sold at bargain prices during most of the years since Repeal. The reds some of the wineries were still selling at 69 to 80 cents at bottle in 1972 were the best wine bargains in the United States.

• 5 •

When Henry Kaiser built his huge steel plant among the vines at Fontana in 1942, an industrial and housing boom began spreading eastward from Los Angeles. When the military flying field adjoining Guasti was expanded after the war to become Ontario International Airport, it displaced hundreds of acres of vineyards. Still more acres were bulldozed during the 1960s to make room for the adjoining Holiday Inn and for the mammoth new Ontario Motor Speedway.

Meanwhile smog, already withering the leaves of southern citrus groves and even threatening to kill the Ponderosa pines in the San Gabriel Mountains, began to affect the Cucamonga vineyards, too. What smog does to grapevines was strikingly shown by University experimenters who in 1968 built plastic greenhouses around patches of vines at Cucamonga and filtered the air inside. The vines left exposed to smog yielded only half as many grapes, with only four fifths of the sugar content, as the grapes grown in filtered air.

The Crop Reporting Service listed San Bernardino County as having 12,728 acres of vineyards in 1972. This was almost a fifteenth of the state's total acreage of wine grapes, but it showed a drop of 7686 acres in only seven years—the toll taken by befouled air and urban sprawl. At the very peak of the nationwide boom in table wine use, when vineyards were expanding at a record rate elsewhere in the state, the exact reverse was happening in the Cucamonga district.

On a recent visit to Southern California, after an absence of four years, I witnessed the Cucamonga district's rapid decline. As my plane circled the Ontario Airport, I looked down on the familiar expanse of vineyards, still stretching north, south, and east for miles. But on landing and stopping to inspect the vines, I found large blocks no longer pruned, and many placarded with "for sale" signs.

Five Cucamonga wineries had been shut down since my previous visit. When I had called in 1967 at the Original Cucamonga Winery, the Accomazzo cousins, Arthur and Edmund, were enlarging their 600 acres with new plantings of Ruby Cabernet. In 1971, however, they were dismantling their winery; they were selling their grapes and would make their wines somewhere else. I next visited the Fontana Winery on Arrow Boulevard and found it closed. One of the partners, Andrew Tudor, had moved to Grandview in the Yakima Valley of Washington to raise grapes and open a winery there. "Washington is the only place to go now," Martin Tudor, his brother, said.

John Ellena's big Regina Winery at Etiwanda was being stripped of its champagne-making equipment. Its famous Lilliputian horses, stabled in small oak wine casks, had been sold to a real estate developer. Heublein's United Vintners had bought and closed the Regina Winery and henceforth would make only wine vinegar there.

But some of the other local wineries appeared as busy as in the past. The 4-million-gallon former Vai Brothers or Padre Winery on Eighth Street in Cucamonga was doing a brisk new kind of business, making wine and champagne cocktails and "pop" wines, including an extra-low-alcohol type named Touch o'Wine, as well as Cesare, San Gabriel, and nine other brands of champagne. This was the leading Southern California winery before the Second World War, when colorful James L. (Padre Jim) Vai was making, from Cucamonga Burger grapes, one of the better champagnes in the state. His nephew, Cesare, operated the winery as the Cucamonga Vineyard Company following Padre Jim's death in 1961. The great Padre vineyards are no more, and the Padre and Vai Brothers brand names have been sold.

A mile south of the Vai cellar, Louis Romolo was still caring for his small vineyard and selling his wines in jugs at the cellar door. Near the freeway in Fontana, Louis Cherpin was selling his wines locally as in the past, but had also added a line of private-label table wines for Los Angeles restaurants. Bernard Galleano's vineyard on Wineville Avenue in Mira Loma (which originally was named Wineville when the big Charles Stern vineyard was established there) had shrunk in half to 400 acres, but he meanwhile had enlarged his tasting room and put up billboards on Highway 60 to attract more visitors. On a previous visit, Galleano had begun making a "varietal" rosé of the Mission grape, but had changed it now to a red vino type, Mission Vino Rosso. Joseph Filippi's Winery on Jurupa Avenue had expanded and had added six retail wine-tasting branches in neighboring counties to sell his wines. The former Thomas cellar in the center of Cucamonga, which some say is the oldest winery building in the state, had become Filippi's biggest branch.

• 6 •

Old Guasti, the wine town in the desert, appeared little changed by the passage of years. The massive stone winery buildings, the workers' dwellings, the Louisa Guasti School, the post office, the store, and the lovely San Secondo d'Asti Church seemed much the same as I remembered them from earlier times. Secondo Guasti's baronial residence, with its luxuriant tropical gardens, was empty now, as were the old distillery and the fermenting room.

But there was bustling new activity around two of the buildings.

The main aging cellar, with its three-foot-thick walls, had been occupied since 1957 by the Brookside Vineyard Company, controlled by the French family Biane, who are Philo, his sons Michael and Pierre, and Philo's nephew, André. The adjoining cooper shop, converted into a Brookside tasting room, was crowded with visitors, who overflowed onto a picnic area under the trees. Preparations were under way for a harvest festival in October, when there would be a ceremonial blessing of the grapes following High Mass in the church, and folk dancing afterward on the winery grounds. Since moving to Guasti, the Bianes had added thirty Brookside and Brookside-Mills winery branches to sell, in their unique winery-to-consumer operation, their eighty different Assumption Abbey, Brookside, Vaché, Biane, and Vins de Biane Frères wines. The two newest branches are in Arizona, one at Tempe-Phoenix and the other in Tucson.

In a corner of the aging cellar, the Bianes had opened a Brookside wine museum. Some of the exhibits told how things had changed at Guasti since the founder's time. During the wartime wine shortage, Horace Lanza of Delano bought the Italian Vineyard Company to get control of the huge Guasti grape crop. In 1945 the heirs of Captain Garrett bought Guasti from Lanza, transferred the Garrett winemaking operation there from New York, and changed Virginia Dare into a California wine. When the Garrett company was liquidated in 1961, its business was sold to Alta Vineyards of Fresno, but the Guasti vineyards were sold to Los Angeles oilman and real estate developer Edwin Pauley, who leased them back to the Alta interests. Then Alta was merged with Guild wines of Lodi, which licensed Canandaigua Industries of New York to revive Garrett's Virginia Dare as an eastern wine.

Other exhibits in the Brookside wine museum traced California wine history made by the forebears of the Bianes. Théophile Vaché from France started a wine business at Monterey in 1832 and pioneered winegrowing in the Cienega Valley of San Benito County about 1849. His nephews, Adolphe, Emile, and Théophile, moved to Southern California and established the Brookside winery near Redlands in 1883. The late Marius Biane came from Gascony in 1892, served the Vachés as their winemaker, and married Adolphe's daughter, Marcelline. Marius Biane moved to Cucamonga in 1916 to make wine for Captain Garrett and acquired his own vineyards there. His sons, Philo and the late François, succeeded him, making wine for Fruit Industries, Secondo Guasti, Captain Garrett, and the Cucamonga Growers Co-op Winery. In 1952, Philo Biane took the Cucamonga Co-op out of Fruit Industries and reestablished the Brookside Vineyard Company near Cucamonga. Five years later he bought the Guasti cellar and moved Brookside headquarters there. Winemaking at Guasti had ceased after Guild took over the Garrett cellar and converted it into a warehouse for Guild wines. Brookside wines were made at the old Cucamonga Pioneer Winery until Brookside bought the 4-million-gallon Gallo bulk winery on Arrow Boulevard in 1972.

Brookside–Mills Cellar table wines could still be bought for ninety-five cents a bottle in 1972, but the "varietal" Assumption Abbey table wines, frequent medal winners at the Pomona Fair, were priced as high as $2.70. Brookside's oldest and best red table wine, Dido Noir, was priced the same as the varietal reds. Full-bodied, fruity in flavor, and with an impressive bouquet, Dido was a blend of Cucamonga Ruby Cabernet with Carignane grapes grown on one of the few vineyards left in the old Escondido district of San Diego; Escondido inspired its name. (The Assumption Abbey brand is used on Brookside altar and commercial wines by an arrangement made in 1956 with the Benedictine monks at that abbey in Richardton, North Dakota.)

• 7 •

My chief purpose on the trip just described was not to visit the Cucamonga vineyards, but to see two entirely new Southern California districts where there were extensive new plantings of wine grapes. Philo Biane had consented to show me the new Rancho California wine district at Temecula in southwestern Riverside County.

On the sixty-mile drive from Guasti on Highway 395 to Temecula, Philo explained why he thinks Southern California will still produce wines for many more years. "When Ed Pauley bought the land at Guasti," he said, "I knew the Cucamonga vineyards wouldn't last many more years. We're dedicating our several hundred Cucamonga acres as an agricultural preserve, but that's only for ten years. As early as nineteen fifty-nine I began searching for new places to grow grapes. I even planted test plots in two Arizona counties and helped to build the Arizona winery at Glendale, which never made any wine. Now we've found a district climatically better than Cucamonga, and out of the smog. It's safe from urbanization, too far from Los Angeles and San Diego for commuting, and safe from vacation crowds who prefer the coast. There will be five thousand acres producing wine grapes within the next several years and then we'll build a winery here."

At Temecula I saw Rancho California, a unique planned community of ranches built since 1965 by the mammoth Kaiser-Aetna land development combine. On sixty square miles of rolling land east of the highway, there were country homes, a man-made lake, livestock farms, avocado and citrus groves, with another seventy square miles to the west held in reserve. On a mesa designated for tree crops and vines, there were almost a thousand acres of sprinkler-irrigated vineyards, most of them planted only a year before, but including many three-year-old vines and a test plot six years old. The plantings were mostly premium varieties such as Cabernet Sauvignon, Gamay Beaujolais, White Riesling, and Chenin Blanc. At Cucamonga the main varieties had always been Zinfandel, Mission, Grenache, Palomino, and Mataro. The temperature at Temecula that day was eighty-two degrees; back at Guasti it was ninety-five. Rancho California is Region III; Cucamonga is Region IV. Cooling westerly winds come to Temecula from the ocean through Santa Margarita Pass. In the past this was range land, too arid for grape-growing, but 500-foot-deep wells provide enough water for the farm acreage thus far developed.

Besides the Bianes' new vineyards, there were several others with newer owners. One hundred-acre tract belonged to Ely Callaway, the president of Burlington Industries of New York. Another of 150 acres was owned by Los Angeles radio station owner John Poole. Rancho California was offering ready-made forty-acre and larger vineyards with expert care provided—an entirely new and novel phase of the winegrowing boom.

I have recently sampled the first three wines from the Bianes' plantings at Rancho California. They tasted like North Coast wines.

• 8 •

The other new Southern California vineyard district is 120 miles northwest of Los Angeles in northern Santa Barbara and southern San Luis Obispo Counties.

Both of these counties, as well as nearby Ventura, were important wine producers in the past, as evidenced by the various "Vineyard Roads" you still see on their maps. What is now downtown Santa Barbara was dotted with vineyards a century ago. Santa Cruz Island, thirty miles off the coast at Santa Barbara, was renowned before Prohibition for the prize-winning wines grown there by the late San Francisco importer and hardware merchant, Justinian Caire. His heirs again made wine there for a short time following Repeal, but the island winery was destroyed by fire and and the vineyard was torn out. The Santa Ynez Valley in west-central Santa Barbara County also was once a winegrowing district, and a new forty-acre vineyard was planted there in 1971. And Santa Barbara again has a producing winery, established on Anacapa Street in 1962 by wine-buff architect Pierre Lafond. He uses Santa Barbara and San Luis Obispo grapes and berries to make several creditable wines.

But the new Santa Barbara–San Luis Obispo grape district is on virgin land in a sparsely populated area where nobody had ever tried to grow grapes before. It consists of a twenty-mile-long belt of foothill land, inland from Santa Maria, on the slopes of the Sierra Madre and San Rafael mountain ranges. What is significant is the district's climate, cooled by ocean fog and by the Santa Maria wind. Its growing-season temperatures are Region I, said by the University to be the best for the top-rated table wine and champagne grapes.

A hundred acres of Cabernet Sauvignon, Johannisberg Riesling, Sauvignon Blanc, Sylvaner, and Chardonnay were planted under permanent sprinklers in 1964 near the juncture of Tepusquet Creek and the Sisquoc River, twelve miles southeast of Santa Maria. The first grapes were made into wine three years later at the Mont La Salle winery of the Christian Brothers in Napa County. Justin Meyer, the former Brother Justin, said the wines were of superior quality.

This interested the owners of two great ranches nearby. One is the 36,000-acre Rancho Sisquoc, owned by a descendant of the early mining tycoon, James Flood. Even larger is the Suey Ranch of the Newhall Land and Farm Company, just northeast of Santa Maria. Test plantings of vines were made on both ranches in 1970. Two years later, vineyards in the immediate area totaled almost a thousand acres. H. W. (Bill) Collins, who planted the first vineyard at Tepusquet Creek, tells me there is sufficient frost-free land and enough water to provide 10,000 more acres in the Santa Maria area and make it "another Napa Valley."

If the Rancho California and Santa Maria vineyards both live up to their present promise, wines from these two new Southern California districts will rank among America's best in years to come.

18

Lodi, Sacramento, the Foothills, and Davis

WHEN people say "Lodi" (pronounced *low-dye*), they mean the fifty-square-mile expanse of flat, extremely fertile vineyards which completely encircle that city at the edge of the Sacramento-San Joaquin River Delta in northern San Joaquin County, California.

Along a six-mile stretch of Highway 50-99, which bisects the town of Lodi, are fifteen bonded wineries which store some 40 million gallons of wine. Five of them have public tasting rooms and highway billboards inviting travelers to stop and sample their wines. The leading industry of Lodi is the production of grapes, wine, and brandy distilled from wine. The most elaborate vintage celebration in the United States is the Lodi Grape Festival and National Wine Show, held in mid-September with grape exhibits, tastings, and a spectacular Sunday parade.

The Lodi district is viticulturally unique. Grapevines grow to enormous size in its deep sandy-loam soil, washed down from the mountains for centuries. Many vines around Lodi are eight feet tall and have trunks as large around as trees. Summer days in San Joaquin County are less torrid than in the main Central Valley; the county's climate is Region IV. At Lodi, however, the vines are further cooled at night by moist westerly winds from the nearby Delta with its thousand miles of tidewater rivers, bays, and sloughs. This is why the Flame Tokay table grape develops its flaming red color, which attracts buyers in the fresh fruit markets, only in the Lodi district. Lodi produces 98 percent of the Flame Tokays in the nation. Nineteen thousand acres are planted to Tokays and 14,000 to wine grapes. Most of the latter are Zinfandels and Carignanes, two wine varieties of which Lodi grows more than any other district in the state.

A tenth of California's wine output is made in Lodi. But you seldom can tell from labels which wines are Lodi-grown, because fleets of tank trucks bring millions of gallons from elsewhere to be bottled there, and other trucks take Lodi grapes and wines to wineries in other districts, which use them in their blends. In the past, the Lodi wineries produced mostly sherry and port. The chamber of commerce once sought to publicize Lodi as "America's Sherryland," and even got Federal recognition of Lodi as a delimited district for wine labeling purposes. The "wine revolution" since the late '60s has compelled the wineries to switch to making mostly table wines.

• 2 •

Grape growing in San Joaquin County began in 1850 at Stockton, twelve miles south of Lodi, when Captain Charles Weber founded that city and planted Mission vines in his garden. Eight years later, a gold miner from Massachusetts, George West, planted vines he got from Captain Weber and began building his El Pinal Winery on West Lane, two miles north of Stockton. By the end of the Civil War, West had one of the greatest vineyards in California. In later years he and his son Frank owned vineyards and wineries in Fresno, Madera, and Kings Counties and shipped wines and brandy to their own sales depot in New York.

Lodi was watermelon and grain country during that time. Vineyards were already established in the Sierra foothills and the rest of the Central Valley, but there were only scattered grape plantings at Lodi until Tokays were planted at the turn of the century. Then the eastern fruit auctions, supplied by trains of new refrigerator cars, made cross-country shipping of fresh grapes profitable. In two decades Lodi, with its brilliant red Tokays, became the most prosperous grape district in the United States. At Stockton, where Tokays ripened as elsewhere with only a dull buckskin color, the vineyards were attacked by phylloxera and died.

The first few wineries around Lodi were built after 1900, using the local wine grapes and providing a home for leftover Tokays. When Prohibition came in 1920, some of the wine grapes were shipped east for home winemaking and the rest were used to make grape juice, concentrate, and sacramental and tonic wines. Huge tonnages of surplus Tokays were left to rot on the vines.

In 1933, as Repeal approached, the growers expected the new demand for wine to make them rich. But in that vintage season, only five Lodi wineries were ready to crush any grapes. When the wineries, flooded with grapes, offered the growers only twelve dollars a ton, then seven dollars, and in a subsequent rainy season only five dollars, the angry growers decided to build wineries of their own. Twelve farmer-co-operative cellars were opened around Lodi during the next few years, and growers' groups built a dozen more co-op wineries in other parts of the state. The co-op wineries banded together in two Lodi-based marketing organizations to sell their wines.

One was Fruit Industries, the combine that had made "Vine-Glo" concentrate for home winemaking during Prohibition. The other, started in 1937 by the late Lawrence K. Marshall with a nucleus of two new Lodi co-ops, was California Wine Sales, which later became the Wine Growers Guild and the Guild Wineries & Distilleries of today.

Fruit Industries, managed by Walter E. Taylor of Lodi, became the post-Repeal giant of the wine industry, bigger than the California Wine Association of pre-Prohibition days. In 1950, Fruit Industries, with eleven wineries throughout the state, changed its name to California Wine Association and adopted "Eleven Cellars" as its chief brand name. The choice of that name soon proved embarrassing, because one by one the member wineries began dropping out of the group. CWA's "Eleven Cellars" have now dwindled to one at Delano.

The Guild in 1962 combined with a Fresno merger of old commercial wine firms (Alta Vineyards, A. Mattei, Cameo Vineyards, B. Cribari & Sons, Garrett). It then bought the wineries of its co-op members and became a single co-op owned by its grower members throughout the state. In 1970, the Guild bought Schenley's Roma and Cresta Blanca wineries at Fresno, Kingsburg, and Delano and increased its membership to 750 growers. Already owning six wineries—three at Lodi, one at Ukiah, two at Fresno—the Guild thereby increased its total to nine. With its total capacity of 50 million gallons, the Guild is now the third largest vintner in the nation.

Most of the wine labeled with Lodi as the bottling address comes from the Guild's blending, bottling, and champagne-making winery at the northeast edge of town. There, too, is the Guild's big Winemaster Hospitality House and restaurant, where hundreds of tourists stop daily to taste the wines and to be conducted on cellar tours.

Of the Guild's fifty-seven different wines, brandies, and Charmat-process champagnes (not counting the assortment from its Cresta Blanca subsidiary), the most interesting and by far the best-seller is a red table wine called Vino da Tavola, with a label that resembles a red-and-white-checkered tablecloth.

One night in 1949, three sales executives of the Guild, dining in an Italian restaurant in Chicago, were discussing the main problem of the wine industry—why most native Americans were rejecting dry red wines as "sour." Then they noticed that most of the people at tables around them were drinking dry red wine with Italian food. This gave them an idea: why not sweeten dry red wine with a little port and sell it with a label like the restaurant's tablecloth and with an Italian name? Then and there they designed the label and chose the name, Vino da Tavola, which in Italian means "wine on the table." Back in Lodi, they challenged Guild Winemaster Lawrence Quaccia to blend a wine to fit the name. He did it with Lodi Zinfandel, a touch of port, and a wood-aged Mendocino Carignane, a coast counties wine "to give it life," he said. Other wineries had made sweetened "vinos" before, but lively red Tavola with its tablecloth label quickly outstripped them all in sales. In the years since, it has taught millions of Americans to enjoy red wine with their meals. "What wine is served in the French Embassy in Washington, D.C.?" read a Guild magazine advertisement in 1969. It pictured General Charles de Gaulle hiding a jug with a checkered label and saying, "I'll never tell." The French Government protested indignantly to our State Department, but to no avail, for the Frenchmen at the Embassy had indeed been consuming Tavola by the case.

A half-mile south of the Guild is the 4-million-gallon East-Side Winery, so named because it is on the east side of town. This is the only local co-op that bottles most of its wine. Eighty Lodi families, led by Jacob Kurtz and his neighbors, the Mettlers, Preszlers, and Handels, joined in East-Side in 1934. Most of its members, and many in other Lodi co-ops, are descendants of German families who migrated to Russia in the time of Catherine the Great, then three generations later to the Dakotas, and finally to Lodi around the turn of this century. In front of the winery office stands "Das Weinhaus," a 50,000-gallon redwood wine tank converted into an attractive tasting room. On display inside are some of the hundreds of medals awarded to East-Side's Royal Host wines while Herman Ehlers was the winemaker, a job from which he retired in 1970 after thirty-seven years.

Ehlers and a few other East-Side members were among the first to plant in Lodi, during the 1950s, small acreages of superior grape varieties for table wines. Though East-Side still makes its popular-priced Gold Bell wines, it now offers half a dozen "select premium" varietally labeled table wines under its Royal Host brand. The best I have tasted recently was a Grey Riesling that equaled most coast counties wines made of that grape. Also of premium quality were the Ruby Cabernet, Emerald Riesling, Chenin Blanc, Dry Sémillon, and a semidry white made of the University's new grape variety named Gold. In recent years East-Side has installed stainless steel tanks, small oak casks for aging, and the special cooling equipment needed—and until now lacking in most Lodi wineries—to protect delicate table wines. East-Side's other specialties are its Royal Host brandies, one of which a Sonoma winery advertises under its own name and sells at a higher price.

Across the road from East-Side is the old Roma winery, a relic of Lodi wines of the past. The massive brick building is now a cookie factory, but wine is still stored there for various vintners who rent the use of its great concrete tanks. It was here, when Prohibition ended, that the Cella brothers, Battista and Lorenzo, began expanding their Roma Wine Company into the biggest commercial producer of California wines of the early post-Repeal years. On the roof of the winery, Roma wines were once "solarized"—an advertising gimmick that consisted of pumping them through glass tubing exposed to the sun—which did the wines harm instead of good. Roma's radio slogan was "Don't drink it, sip it," first broadcast by Art Linkletter from the Wine Temple at the San Francisco 1939 world's fair. When the co-op wineries were built during the 1930s to crush most of the local grapes, the Cellas abandoned their Lodi home and moved to the present Roma winery in Fresno.

On Turner Road, across the highway from Roma, is a warehouse that once was the Shewan-Jones winery, which made the best Lodi table wines at the time of Repeal. There a great winemaker named Elbert McSherry Brown and his then assistant, Herman Ehlers, made Tokay and Burger juice into a sweet sauterne which Shewan-Jones sold as "Château Yquem." When the Federal Government in 1936 outlawed "Château Yquem" labels on American wines, owner Lee Jones created a French-sounding word out of his own Welsh name, and made the wine nationally famous as "Château Lejon."

Northwest of Lodi is the million-gallon Acampo winery in the village of that name. Its owner, Dino Barengo, makes three dozen different table and dessert wines. He sells them mostly from his tasting room, except his May wine (woodruff-flavored, white), which is sold throughout the United States. His main brick cellar was originally a granary. At Repeal a group of grape growers and shippers headed by Cesare Mondavi bought it and turned it into a winery. Barengo, who like Herman Ehlers was trained in winemaking by Elbert Brown, had been hired as Acampo's winemaker three years before. He became Acampo's owner after the Mondavis sold it to buy Krug. Barengo in 1949 was the first Lodi winemaker to make a wine of Ruby Cabernet. He now grows this grape exclusively in his own vineyard, while he buys the rest of his grapes.

A Sacramento importer in 1968 happened to taste an old Barengo blend of Ruby Cabernet. He persuaded Barengo to store some of it in French oak barrels. In a few months the Ruby Cabernet tasted like an unusually fine red Bordeaux. The importer bought that entire bottling and sold it at a higher price than most of his imports from Bordeaux. In connoisseur circles, however, Barengo is best known for his flavorful wine vinegar, which he ages in a *solera* like those in the sherry *bodegas* of Spain. His old association with the Mondavis has continued; much of his production in recent years has been under contract for them.

Beside the Coloma tasting room at the north end of Lodi is a busy winery that doesn't make any wine. It is operated by the Wine-Art company, supervised by veteran Lodi winemaker Wallace H. Pohle. This winery crushes grapes but doesn't ferment the juice. Instead, it extracts the water by a vacuum process and turns out grape concentrate for the American and Canadian home winemaking trade. Strange to say, there are some vineyardists around Lodi who are Prohibitionists and refuse to sell their grapes to wineries. They are glad, however, to sell them to Wine-Art, even though they know its product eventually will be made into wine. Wine-Art was founded at Vancouver, B.C., in 1959 by a home winemaker named Stanley Anderson. Pohle, after twoscore years of winemaking in Lodi, went to Canada in 1961 to build two wineries in British Columbia. There he became acquainted with Anderson, who then was selling his Canadian customers grape concentrate from Spain and Greece. Pohle said he could make better concentrate from California grapes. With Anderson and others he founded Wine-Art of America in 1968, installed new concentrating equipment in the old Da Roza Winery, and now supplies its product to 108 Wine-Art stores in this country and Canada.

The 4-million-gallon Cherokee co-op winery on Woodbridge Road was sold in 1972 to a new company called Pop Wines, Inc., which renamed it Montcalm Vintners and plans to make table and sparkling wines out of the Cherokee members' grapes.

Other wineries in the Lodi district include Bear Creek and Del Rio, the two original members of the Guild; the old Community co-op, which was the first of CWA's "Eleven Cellars" but is now owned by Heublein's United Vintners; the Rio Vista Winery, once operated by the Sebastianis of Sonoma; the Woodbridge and Lodi independent co-ops; and the Liberty Winery, which has produced wine for Gallo in recent years. The former Lockeford co-op, in the northeastern corner of the district, is now an independent producer of Charmat champagnes, assorted wines, and brandy, and has its own tasting room on the Lockeford-Stockton highway.

• 3 •

The Flame Tokay is an oval, thick-skinned, fleshy grape with three seeds. It was introduced to this country a century ago from Algeria, where it is known as the Ahmeur bou Ahmeur. It has nothing to do with the medium-sweet, pinkish-red California dessert wine type called Tokay, which can be made from any grape. It is usually a blend of sherry and port. Neither the grape nor the wine is any way related to the Tokay or Tokai wines of Hungary, which are traditionally made of a grape called Furmint that is grown only experimentally in the United States. I know of only one "varietal" Tokay wine; the East-Side Winery makes it entirely of that grape and labels it Flame Tokay. J. Walter Fleming, the first manager of the Lockeford Winery, once named a brandy "Lodi Tokay" and sold Tokay table wine to producers of sparkling wines, who made it into a champagne.

When Jim Kissler, a graduate of the University's wine school at Davis, became San Joaquin County's farm advisor in 1967, he began trying to persuade Lodi growers to change from Tokays to the "varietal" grapes for table wines, such as Grey Riesling and Ruby Cabernet. Carl Mettler, an East-Side director, donated two acres for test plantings. The tests showed that several of the "varietals" are well suited to the Lodi climate and soil. Kissler's efforts have had moderate success. By 1972, San Joaquin County had 2264 acres of Chenin Blanc, Grey Riesling, Emerald Riesling, and French Colombard, much of it planted during the few preceding years. But these are white grapes. Of Ruby Cabernet—the variety that has made the best Lodi table wine—the entire county still had less than two hundred acres. The farmers are reluctant to plant more Ruby Cabernet because the stem of its cluster is especially tough; vineyard workers have to be paid extra to pick the grapes.

Despite the rising costs of growing grapes to be eaten fresh—which can't be harvested by machine—and the declining sale of fresh fruit in general, Lodi growers have kept replanting Tokays. "Why should we change?" one of them recently asked, "when our wineries have won all those medals at the fairs with wines made of Tokay?" What they ignore is that the medal-winning wines weren't made of ordinary Tokays. To make good table wine, this grape must be harvested when its acidity is high, when its sugar content tests only 18 to 19 on the Balling or Brix scale, instead of the customary 22. The wineries have only recently recognized this, by agreeing to pay growers the same price per ton for 19-Balling Tokays as for those fully ripe at 22. (And a similar change has occurred in the case of the Thompson Seedless; the wineries now pay the same price for "early Tokays" and "early Thompsons" as for fully ripe grapes.)

Kissler has been more successful in getting "varietal" grapes planted outside the Tokay district. One new planting, under permanent sprinklers, is on 1100 acres of virgin land around Forest Lake, eight miles northwest of Lodi. Others are on Mandeville and McDonald Islands, fifteen miles west in the great San Joaquin River Delta. The islands are below sea level, protected by levees from flooding; they are the Netherlands of the West. Their soil is mostly inflammable peat; there used to be signs along the levee roads warning motorists that "This land will burn!" But the soils at higher elevations on the islands are not peat and have lately been proved suitable for vines. Kissler finds the islands' climate cooler and the grapes grown there of such quality that he foresees an entirely new table wine district of 3000 acres developing in the Delta in future years.

• 4 •

The Sacramento Valley, which stretches northwest from Lodi and the Delta region for almost 200 miles, is older in winegrowing than the San Joaquin. Before Prohibition there were scores of wineries and nearly 40,000 acres of vineyards in the nine Sacramento Valley counties. By 1970 only four wineries and less than 500 acres were left. The valley is interesting historically, and recent new plantings of grapes indicate that it may soon be important in winegrowing again.

In 1842, Captain John Augustus Sutter, the Swiss adventurer turned empire builder, began distilling brandy out of wild grapes in his fort at Sacramento, which he named New Helvetia. Ruined instead of enriched by the discovery of gold in 1848 at his Coloma sawmill, Sutter gave up his fort and moved to his 600-acre Hock Farm on the Feather River in Sutter County eight miles south of Yuba City. There he planted a vineyard with cuttings he imported from Europe. Sutter's vineyard helped support him until he left California in 1866 for Washington, D.C., where he died fourteen years later.

Sutter County is also where farmer William Thompson of Yuba City in 1872 introduced the English hothouse grape he named Thompson's Seedless, which became the most widely planted variety in California.

Neighboring Butte County's wine industry was founded in 1847 by Captain Sutter's aide-de-camp, General John Bidwell, on his ranch at Chico. Twenty-one years later Bidwell married a fanatical Prohibitionist. Before the wedding he emptied his winery, uprooted his wine grapes, planted table and raisin grapes instead, and in 1892 he became the Prohibition Party's candidate for President of the United States. At the turn of the century, Butte County still had five wineries and 1000 acres in grapes. In 1970 it had about fifty acres, mostly scattered among fruit orchards and olive groves, and only one winery, the retail wine cellar of the Ghianda family on their old hilltop vineyard at Thermalito, a suburb of Oroville.

In Yuba County, which borders Sutter and Butte, winegrowing was begun in 1855 by Charles Covillaud from Cognac, who planted grapes at Simpson's Crossing, a mile north of Marysville, the city Covillaud named for his wife, the former Mary Murphy. Within five years the county had four more wineries and 800 acres of vines, which expanded by 1930 to a thousand acres, but then were gradually replaced by orchards of peaches and prunes.

In Tehama County, Peter Lassen, the Danish pioneer for whom volcanic Mount Lassen is named, planted the upper Sacramento Valley's first acre of Mission vines in 1846. This was at Vina, on the east bank of the river twenty miles north of Chico. At Lassen's death seven years later, Henry Gerke from Germany enlarged the vineyard and built a 100,000-gallon winery. Gerke made brandy as well as wine and is said to have shipped some to Europe.

Then came wealthy California ex-Governor Leland Stanford, who bought the Vina property from Gerke in 1881. Stanford expanded the vineyard to 5000 acres, making it then the largest in the world. He built there the costliest winery in the state to hold 2 million gallons of wine, and brought expert winemakers from France.

Stanford had two altruistic objectives in winegrowing: to prove that California could produce finer wines than those of Europe, and to combat drunkenness in America by mass-producing good table wines and promoting their temperate mealtime use. But though successful in his other careers as lawyer, merchant, railroad builder, and breeder of champion racehorses, Stanford made a series of grievous winegrowing mistakes.

His first error was in turning over his original vineyard in Alameda County to his brother Josiah, because that coastal district would have been ideal for his purposes. His second was in choosing Vina and in planting there such varieties as Zinfandel, which in the hot Sacramento Valley in the days before refrigeration could make only poor table wines. When Stanford's first Vina vintage was ready in 1886, he saw his mistake; the wines had an objectionable earthy taste. He then switched to making only dessert wines and brandy and Stanford became the largest distiller of brandy in the world. Barges brought his product in barrels down the then-navigable Sacramento River from Red Bluff to be loaded on ships for New York. His brandy was excellent, if the one I tasted at a Wine and Food Society dinner at the time of Repeal was a fair example. Having learned his lesson about climate, Stanford succeeded in growing some fine table wines in a third vineyard, which he purchased in 1888 at Menlo Park in San Mateo County. But he did not live to taste them; he died in 1893. All that remains of his third winegrowing venture is the winery building, which stands in the Stanford Shopping Center and has been converted into a bank.

At his death, the great Vina estate with its winery and distillery were bequeathed to Stanford University at Palo Alto, which he had founded eight years earlier in memory of his only son, who had died in Italy at the age of fifteen. The sale of wine and brandy helped support the University for a time. But Palo Alto was a wineless community, for Stanford had made still another mistake: The deed to land he had bought to expand the campus contained a proviso that no alcoholic beverage could ever be sold there. (Downtown Palo Alto remained dry until 1970, when a court declared the eighty-year-old proviso void.) Also, Stanford's wife Jane was a teetotaler, violently opposed to wine except for medicinal use. She disrupted the University's management of its beverage business until she was mysteriously murdered by poisoning in 1905. Drys attacked the Stanford trustees for letting alcoholic drinks support the University. When a fire damaged the winery in 1915, the trustees ordered the vineyards uprooted and sold the land in parcels for farms. The winery land and buildings were purchased in 1955 by Trappist monks from Kentucky as the site for their monastery, Our Lady of New Clairvaux.

In Stanford's time, Tehama County had two dozen wineries and 10,000 acres in grapes. There were vineyards as far up the valley as Redding in Shasta County, which counted 400 acres of grapes in 1890. But Sacramento County had the most.

Sacramento Sheriff Benjamin Bugbey grew wines at Folsom that won medals at the 1863 State Fair. In 1889 there were twenty-four wineries between Sacramento, Mormon Island on the American River, Folsom, and Galt. The old Mormon Island wineries are now inundated by Folsom Lake. The Natoma Vineyard south of Folsom covered nearly 2000 acres. The California Winery on R Street in Sacramento was four decades old when Prohibition in 1920 forced it to close.

Why did 40,000 acres of vines disappear from the Sacramento Valley, while almost 300,000 acres were being planted in the southern San Joaquin Valley counties of Fresno, Tulare, and

Kern—since both of these districts have Region V climates? Urbanization was the chief reason in Sacramento County, where 12,000 acres dwindled to a few hundred after the Second World War. Eight old Sacramento wineries had reopened at Repeal in 1933, but five closed when their vineyards were swallowed by nearby towns. Without grapes to crush, the Frasinetti Winery, south of Florin, and the Mills Winery on Folsom Boulevard have become retail outlets, the latter with numerous branches. Only the million-gallon Gibson Winery at Elk Grove continues producing, but it makes only wines of berries and fruits other than grapes, which can be sampled at its new tasting room on Highway 50 nearby. Gibson is now owned by the Sanger Winery of Fresno County and bottles grape wines shipped from Sanger.

In the upper Sacramento Valley there was another reason. When Prohibition shut down the wineries, the grapes that remained were mostly sun-dried for raisins, which can be ruined by early autumn rains. The raisin-growing industry soon became concentrated around arid Fresno, where in most years the grapes can be dried before the rain comes.

But now, with grapes for table wines in unprecedented demand, winegrowing in the Sacramento Valley is being revived. After half a century, Stanford's Vina Vineyard is again growing grapes for wine. In 1965, west of the old winery, Jerome Dobson of Chico planted seventy-five acres of Emerald Riesling, French Colombard, Ruby Cabernet, Chenin Blanc, and Gamay. The first three are high-acid varieties, which if harvested early and properly handled can make good table wines in Region V. Dobson's grapes now go from Vina to the United Vintners' wineries at Lodi and Escalon. He is already thinking of building a winery.

More than 2000 acres of vines, all of wine grape varieties, have been planted since 1969 in Butte, Colusa, Glenn, Sacramento, and Yuba Counties. In 1972 an old dairy plant on the main street of Chico was converted into the Butte Creek Vineyards winery and crushed its first vintage of grapes grown near Orland in Glenn County.

· 5 ·

New vineyards and wineries are also springing up in the historic Mother Lode gold-mining country of the Sierra foothills in response to the table wine boom. Five wineries, four of them new since 1967, are operating in Amador, El Dorado, and Tuolumne Counties, and more are being planned.

Frederick Merrill has reopened the pre-Prohibition Torre

Winery at Amador City. In Tuolumne County, Jerrell Butler and sons have built a winery on Longaway Road two miles southwest of Twain Harte. In the mining ghost town of Columbia, Spencer Hoffman has opened a winery in an old theater building. Uphill from the gold-discovery town of Coloma in El Dorado County, high school teacher John Hempt, the grandson of winegrowers in his native Yugoslavia, has planted eight acres of Cabernet Sauvignon and White Riesling and has built the 5000-gallon Gold Hill Winery beside his home. He bought the grapes to make his first wines, and introduced his first estate-bottled Johannisberg Riesling in 1972.

The D'Agostini Winery, in the Shenandoah Valley eight miles northeast of Plymouth in Amador County, dates from 1856, when Adam Uhlinger from Switzerland quarried rock from the local hillside to build the cellar walls. Enrico D'Agostini bought the place from Uhlinger in 1911 and made wine until Prohibition. He was succeeded by his four sons, who enlarged the vineyard to 125 acres. After Repeal they made mostly old-fashioned sauterne and burgundy, but since the boom in premium wines they have added a creditable estate-bottled Zinfandel.

There will be many more wineries in the Sierra foothill counties, to judge by the scores of test plots of premium grapes being planted lately all the way from the Scott River in Siskiyou County to the Coulterville and Darrah areas in Mariposa County, 300 miles south. Samples made at the University from grapes grown in Amador, Placer, and El Dorado Counties show that wines of coast-counties quality can be grown in the Mother Lode.

The Sierra foothills have a winegrowing history as old as the state. In Gold Rush days many miners planted vines around their diggings and turned to producing wine. El Dorado County alone had more vineyards in 1860 than either Sonoma or Napa. By 1890, more than a hundred wineries were operating at such locations as Nevada City, Colfax, Lincoln, Penryn, Auburn, Placerville, Coloma, Shingle Springs, Ione, Volcano, Jackson, San Andreas, Sonora, Columbia, and Jamestown. When Prohibition closed the last of the wineries, grape-growing gradually moved to the hot valley regions, where irrigated vineyards yield heavier crops.

Today the foothill counties do not interest the big vintners, because available tracts in the rolling hills are too small for mass cultivation, and there is danger of frosts. There is sufficient land in relatively frost-free areas, however, for vineyards of moderate size and small winegrowing estates. Viticulturists predict that those who pick Mother Lode locations with good air drainage, such as the D'Agostinis' Shenandoah Valley, will produce fine wines profitably in years to come.

• 6 •

In pre-Prohibition times Yolo County, situated between Sacramento and Napa, had 2000 acres of vineyards and more than fifty wineries, scattered from Woodland to Winters, Madison, and Capay. The largest was the Orleans Vineyard of Arpad Haraszthy & Company, three miles west of Esparto, with its winery four stories high. Another was on a farm at Davisville, where Jerome Davis, a member of the Bear Flag rebellion, had settled about 1852. Yolo vineyards increased to 4000 acres during Prohibition, then dwindled after Repeal, when grape-growing in the Sacramento Valley declined.

Davisville, fourteen miles west of Sacramento, was renamed Davis when the University of California bought the Davis ranch in 1906 and opened a practical farming school with a beginning class of forty, including Ernest Wente of Livermore. Since then, the farm has become a university of 18,000 students in forty-five departments, including a complete medical school. It now covers six square miles on both sides of Freeway 80, is by far the largest of the nine UC campuses, and even has its own airport, from which Davis experts fly to the University's experiment stations and the other campuses where agricultural courses are taught.

Davis still has a winery and 140 acres of vineyard. They are parts of the University's Department of Viticulture and Enology. Some forty men and women full-time students, half of them from foreign countries, are enrolled in the dozen grape, wine, and brandy courses and in many research projects. More than 400 students in other fields take the introductory enology course. Short courses are also offered periodically for those professionally engaged in growing grapes or making wine. The demand for Davis graduates to man wineries in the United States and abroad is four times as great as the school can fill.

In the two-semester general viticulture course, each student plants vines in a practice vineyard, cultivates, fertilizes, prunes, and thins them, and harvests the fruits for fresh use, for raisins, and for wine. Each three-term enology student makes red, white, pink, and sparkling wines, performing each step from crushing through fermentation, racking, aging, finishing, stabilization, and bottling to the analysis and tasting of the final product. Many also take the brandy-distilling course. What they make, however, cannot be drunk or taken from the department buildings. More than 100,000 research samples made since 1935 are stored in the temperature-controlled cellar under the Enology Building, where the winery and distillery are. The rest goes down the drain.

The University is still doing the same job the legislature assigned it in 1880, when Professor Hilgard began his work at Berkeley.

Hilgard in 1889 hired as his cellar foreman Frederic Bioletti, an Englishman with an Italian name, who had worked in California and South African wineries, and who eventually succeeded Hilgard in charge of the work on wine. Among those trained by Bioletti were William Vere Cruess, who became the world's most renowned food scientist of his time, and Texas-born Albert Julius Winkler, who attained equal viticultural fame. Cruess in turn taught winemaking to several of his graduate students, especially one named Maynard Alexander Joslyn. At the repeal of Prohibition, this group around Bioletti, with two French-born professors, Edmund H. Twight and Leon O. Bonnet, trained most of the winemakers who since have rebuilt the quality of the state's wines.

In 1933, Bioletti chose from among his graduates a tall, blond, green-thumbed young geneticist named Harold Paul Olmo and gave him a lifetime project—to breed better grapes for the unique climates of California. Olmo became the Burbank of the grape. He planted seedlings of old varieties to develop new ones and crossed old varieties to combine their best characteristics in new hybrid grapes. Then from tens of thousands of vines, he chose the best producers, made wines from their grapes, aged and evaluated the wines. The few dozen best vines were replanted in different climates and soils, repeating the whole process until from among the dozens, a promising new variety was chosen. In 1946, Olmo introduced his first successful wine varieties, Ruby Cabernet and Emerald Riesling*, and four new table grapes. Twelve years later, he brought out five more new wine grapes and five more table varieties. To create and complete the testing of a single new wine grape takes him fifteen to eighteen years. And that is only the beginning, for the rest depends on the vineyardist, then on the vintner, and finally on the people who will buy the wine.

Olmo also found time to travel to other grape-growing countries. He traced the routes through which the wine-bearing *Vitis vinifera* grape has been carried through the centuries, evolving its thousands of varieties in different soils and climates. He hoped someday to discover Vinifera's birthplace and the vine in its primitive state. In 1947, on a 7000-mile trek by plane, train, mule-

*Ruby Cabernet—Cabernet Sauvignon x Carignane—combines the quality of the noble Cabernet with the productivity and vigor of Carignane. Emerald Riesling is White Riesling x Muscadelle, an old French variety. Both crosses are high in acidity and flavor. They make excellent wines in Regions III and IV and acceptable wines in Region V.

back and on foot, his quest came to an end. In mud-walled villages at the border of ancient Persia and Afghanistan Olmo found the original Vinifera vine growing wild. He brought cuttings back to Davis, made them part of his breeding program, and began the ages-old evolution of the wine grape over again.

More than 100,000 different grape varieties grow in the Davis vineyard. About 1000 are the principal named varieties that are cultivated around the world. The rest are Olmo's crosses and seedlings, which he is testing for planting in the future. They cannot all be tested at Davis, where the climate is Region IV. Varieties for cooler regions are tested at the Oakville Vineyard; those for hot regions at four San Joaquin Valley locations.

Olmo has a dozen new varieties of Cabernet parentage that he has bred especially to make improved red table wines in the hot Central Valley. The first of these is being released for commercial planting in 1973. They are new crosses involving other crosses of Carignane, Cabernet Sauvignon, and Grenache. If the valley wineries make wines from them as flavorful as the University samples I have thus far tasted, these varieties may eventually replace such old California mass-production standbys as Mission, Alicante, Carignane, and even Zinfandel. Olmo also has two Cabernet descendants, better suited for cool climates, which make wines even more flavorful than Cabernet Sauvignon and which are nearly ready for release. He is testing several dozen new varieties of Chenin Blanc parentage, which show promise for improved Central Valley white wines.

Beginning back in 1935, much of the University's wine research work was shifted gradually from Berkeley to the Davis campus, where the vineyards are.

In that year Dr. Winkler, Bioletti's successor as chairman of viticulture, hired as his junior enologist at Davis a young graduate student named Maynard Andrew Amerine, who then was studying for his Ph.D. The only son of a California farming family, Amerine had grown up at Modesto, where his father raised grapes and other fruits. He had attended junior college there with Ernest and Julio Gallo, who lived a mile away. While the Gallo boys at their graduation went into the grape industry, Amerine continued his studies at Berkeley, where he received his plant-science degree.

Amerine's first task under Winkler at Davis was to make experimental wines from grapes grown in each viticultural district of the state. The several thousand wines he made became the basis of the 1938 Winkler-Amerine classification of California climates that have had such a profound effect on the Salinas Valley. Amerine later initiated scores of other research programs, ranging from studies of grape sugar-acid ratios at ripening to improved methods of analysis and organoleptic testing of wines. By 1957, when he succeeded Winkler as department chairman, his bibliography totaled 122 separate publications. Four years later, bachelor Amerine gave up the department chairmanship to gain time for travel and more research. Interested in vinicultural progress in the Soviet Union, he spent two years learning the Russian language before going to that country in 1962. Since then he has been virtually commuting to the European and Iron Curtain wine countries and has visited all the other winelands of the world. Wherever he goes, he is consulted on winegrowing problems, and other nations have invited several of his colleagues to come and advise them on the results of UC research. When Clark Kerr was president of the University, he, too, traveled abroad a good deal. "In every wine country," Dr. Kerr reported, "as soon as I mentioned that I came from California, people would ask me, 'Do you know Professor Maynard Amerine?'"

The first texts on winemaking after Repeal were published by Drs. Cruess, Joslyn, and their Berkeley colleagues in 1934. Six years later, Amerine teamed with Joslyn in writing a series of University circulars on the commercial production of wines and brandies, Amerine presenting the viticultural aspects and Joslyn the enological side. The first Amerine-Joslyn circular on table wine summarized their scientific knowledge of that subject in 143 pages. By 1951 they had published a new 397-page text covering the same ground more fully. The same book appeared in 1970 in a second edition of 997 pages—a good index to how much has been learned by California investigators about this ancient art and science of table wine production in a span of only thirty years.

At present the Department of Viticulture and Enology staff at Davis numbers forty-five, including such internationally noted research workers and professors as Chairman Harold Berg, Curtis J. Alley, James A. Cook, James F. Guymon, Mark M. Kliewer, Ralph E. Kunkee, Lloyd A. Lider, Klayton E. Nelson, Cornelius Ough, Vernon L. Singleton, Robert J. Weaver, A. Dinsmoor Webb, and Dr. Winkler, who is still doing consulting work, though he officially retired in 1963. Also at Davis are Dr. Austin Goheen, the Federal Government expert on grape virus diseases; professors in four other UC departments dealing with grapes or wine, and UC's three extension viticulturists, George M. Cooke, Amand N. Kasimatis, and Hilton B. Richardson. The Davis wine school is now larger than such famous European stations as those at Geisenheim, Montpellier, and Conegliano, but the Russian vinicultural station at Yalta is twice as large.

19

The Main San Joaquin Valley

ALL OF the vineyard districts covered in the last six chapters comprise only the top third of the California wine iceberg, so to speak. The other two thirds of the state's wine production comes from the main San Joaquin Valley, a fabulous agricultural empire in which grapes are the chief income crop and the chief wineries are the biggest in the world.

From the Delta region west of Lodi, the valley of the San Joaquin River extends southeastward more than two hundred miles. It is a trough, thirty to fifty miles wide and almost as flat as a table, between the snowcapped Sierra Nevada mountains on the east and the Coast Range on the west. A twentieth of its total surface is covered by vineyards—some 420,000 acres, almost seven hundred square miles.

The summer climate is hot, mainly Region IV toward the northern end, and becomes still hotter—Region V—in the south. No rain falls there until autumn, and what falls thereafter is sparse, averaging only fourteen inches at Stockton and less than six inches at Bakersfield. Much of the land was a dry, barren waste until a century ago, when men began building dams in the Sierra to trap the melting snows and started to dig the irrigation canals that now crisscross most of the valley. Mountain water has transformed once-parched wasteland into lush farms more fabulously productive than the delta of the Nile.

In the sizzling heat and the rich valley soil, washed down from the mountains for eons, irrigated vines yield enormous grape crops, double the average in the coast counties. Here, eight to twelve tons per acre is considered a normal harvest of the common wine-grape varieties, and seventeen tons is not unusual from an acre of overcropped Thompson Seedless vines. From this valley come all of the raisins produced in the United States, two thirds of the California table grapes that are eaten fresh, nearly all of the port, sherry, muscatel, and brandy produced in the state, and more than half—a figure now swiftly rising—of California table wines and champagnes.

Much of the San Joaquin's agriculture is conducted by corporate farmers on a gigantic scale of mechanized "agribusiness," a term coined here. Airplanes are commonly used to spray the larger vineyards. Some of the big table-grape growers employ helicopters to dry their grapes on the vines after early rains. Vineyard foremen and grape buyers travel such vast distances daily that, to keep in touch with their offices, most of them have radio-telephones in their air-conditioned cars.

Fleets of wine-tank trucks, like those used to transport milk, ply the highways night and day through the year, exchanging their vinous cargoes between wineries in the different parts of the state. Who owns or makes what in the California wine industry is increasingly difficult to figure out nowadays, but some of the answers may be found here. Don't expect to find romantic, vine-draped little château wineries with aging-tunnels, such as are seen in the coast counties; the average valley winery is merely a processing plant among the farms.

• 2 •

The main valley is reached via Highway 99 from Stockton to the Manteca-Escalon district in the southeastern corner of San Joaquin County. (We explored Lodi, with its Tokays that color red on cool nights, in the preceding chapter because Lodi differs climatically from the rest of the valley; it is a distinct viticultural district by itself.)

In the Manteca-Escalon area, chiefly wine-grape varieties are grown, especially the red Grenache, which retains some of its pronounced aroma when grown in Region IV. This district has supplied most of the Grenache grapes used by wineries in other parts of the state to make their Grenache rosés.

First on the route from Stockton is the million-gallon Sam-Jasper Winery, three miles above Manteca on the frontage road beside Highway 99. The "Sam-Jasper" name comes from Sebastiano (nicknamed Sam) Luppino and his brother-in-law, Gaspare (Jasper) Indelicato, who opened the winery in 1935. Jasper's three sons operate the business now, and they also use the name Delicato Cellar, a considerable improvement over the family name. They make mostly table wine, bottle and sell some of it in their tasting room and to stores in the Stockton area, and produce the rest in bulk for wineries in other parts of the state.

On Austin Road, off the freeway south of Manteca, is the small Bella Napoli Winery of Tony R. Hat, who was born Antonio Cappello near Naples but translated his name to its English equivalent when he came to the United States in 1899. He and his four sons own vineyards, but sell most of their grapes. The table wine they make is mostly sold at the cellar door. A third local winery, operated by Raymond and Theodore Cadlolo in the town of Escalon, holds a quarter-million gallons, also of table wine. It is offered for tasting amid the redwood tanks in the cellar, and is sold to visitors by the barrel, bottle, or case. Four miles east of Escalon, on Highway 120, Joseph Angelo Rossi operates the old Oakdale Winery. He, too, sells table wines, and also grape juice during the vintage season, to passersby. Rossi's son, Joseph, is now the winemaker of the Brotherhood winery at Washingtonville, New York. At Salida, east of Highway 99 and just north of Salida in neighboring Stanislaus County, Alfred Pirrone owns the winery his father built in 1936. He has increased its capacity to a million gallons, has built a tasting room, and has replanted the 180-acre vineyard with "varietal" grapes for table wines, which he produces mainly for Gallo of Modesto.

The winery that is especially interesting to see in this district is that of the Franzia Brothers, on Highway 120 six miles east of Manteca and five miles north of Ripon. It is an exemplar of efficient mass wine production. On the family's 1200-acre vineyard, rows of shining epoxy-lined, insulated steel tanks stand outdoors and hold 12 million gallons of wine. The several narrower ones are pressurized; they hold Charmat-process champagnes. The tanks are partially hidden from the highway by the brick and tilt-up-concrete cellars, where the wine is processed and most of it is bottled for shipment throughout California and to thirty-seven other states. The Franzias make thirty-three different wines and champagnes and bottle the same wines under seven different brands, such as Franzia, FB, Mountain Castle, Louis the Fifth, Old Château, and Grand Maison. Regardless of the brand, you can always recognize a Franzia wine by the name of Ripon in the small type at the bottom of the label, because this is the only winery that uses Ripon as its post office address.

Franzia wines are among the lowest-priced in California, selling there for as little as 69¢ and 89¢ a "fifth" bottle in 1972. They are usually young and relatively bland in taste, but I have found them reliably palatable in the past few years. You can sample them yourself (and some more costly wines that the Franzias buy from coast counties producers) in the attractive tasting room that faces the highway. You also can tour the winery if you make an appointment in advance and bring a group of friends. That the

Franzia enologists, Fernando Quaccia and his Davis-trained son Louis, are competent winemakers is evident from the twenty-six medals and honorable-mention awards that their wines received in the 1971 judging at the Los Angeles County Fair. Though it may seem incredible that such inexpensive wines can win medals for quality, the Franzias insist that all but three of their award winners came from their regular stocks.

Five Franzia Brothers and six of their sons formerly operated the vineyards and winery, with Joe, the youngest, as president of the firm. At the height of the table-wine sales explosion in 1971, three of the brothers sold their interest to eastern investors, and the company issued stock for public sale. Joe is still in charge with the second oldest brother, John, his champagne-maker son John, Jr., and Joe's two sons, Joseph S. and Fred.

The father of the family, Giuseppe, came to California from Genoa in 1892, worked for fifty cents an hour in truck gardens around San Francisco, saved enough by 1906 to establish the family vineyard, and started his winery nine years later. It was closed during Prohibition, but his sons kept up the vineyard and reopened the winery at Repeal. They sold their wine mainly in tank cars to eastern bottlers until the Second World War; then began concentrating on bottled wines, adopting the mass-production techniques introduced by the Gallos. Incidentally, the Franzia Brothers' toughest competitors are the Gallos, although Ernest Gallo is their brother-in-law.

• 3 •

Three miles toward Escalon from the Franzias is a winery almost twice as large. It was once the main Petri winery, from which in the 1950s grew the Petri–United Vintners complex of nine wineries with a tank ship, all of which in 1968 became part of the Heublein wine and liquor empire. Until just recently the sign in front read "United Vintners Inc." and "Petri Wine Co.," but the "Petri" portion has been painted out. Since the table-wine boom, the winery now makes only table wine and ships it to the United Vintners plant at Madera for bottling.

Back in 1887, when California bulk wine was eight cents a gallon, an immigrant from Tuscany named Raffaello Petri, who owned a hotel in the North Beach district of San Francisco, began selling wine as a sideline. When his son Angelo grew up, he joined his Uncle Amadeo's cigar factory, rolling fermented tobacco leaves into the twisted, double-ended, strong-tasting black Italian cheroots called Toscani. During the First World War, Marca Petri wine and Marca Petri cigars both became so popular among Italians across the country that Raffaello and a partner named Dante Foresti acquired their own vineyards and winery at Escalon.

During Prohibition, Foresti managed the vineyard and sold the grapes for home winemaking while the Petris concentrated on their cigar factory in San Francisco and later on a boot-making venture in Tennessee. At Repeal, Angelo Petri returned the family to the wine business, leasing wineries in Napa and Sonoma Counties, and then reopening the Alba winery at Escalon, all this in conjunction with the cigar company.

In 1933, Angelo's younger son, Louis, had enrolled to study medicine at St. Louis University; his parents wanted him to become a physician. But Louis was in love with Flori, the youngest daughter of Roma Winery president Battista Cella, and Flori's love letters from Lodi told him about exciting happenings in the reviving wine business. In his sophomore year Louis abruptly quit medical school, came to San Francisco, married Flori, and went to work washing barrels at seventy-five dollars a month in the cellar of the Petri cigar factory on Battery Street. In 1944, at the age of thirty-two, he became president of the Petri Wine Company.

Louis Petri, a restless young man who stuttered when excited, set out to dominate the wine industry. During the next eight years he bought the Tulare and Mission Bell wineries, and in a major coup, bought from National Distillers the Italian Swiss Colony wineries at Asti and Fresno, the Shewan-Jones winery at Lodi, and the Gambarelli & Davitto cellars at New York. Meanwhile, seeing more profit in selling wine than in making it, Petri organized the Allied Grape Growers co-operative, then sold his wineries to the co-op for $24 million, retaining their operation and the wine-marketing rights in United Vintners, which he headed as president. In 1957, he built the first wine tank ship ever to serve under the American flag, naming it the *Angelo Petri* for his father. He almost lost it one day three years later, when the ship became disabled outside the Golden Gate and drifted, rudderless, toward the beach. An SOS brought three tugs in time to tow the vessel back to port for repairs. Delivering two-and-a-half-million-gallon cargoes of bulk wine from the Port of Stockton to Atlantic Coast ports through the Panama Canal seven times a year, and bottling the two dozen United Vintners wine brands in cellars in Newark, Chicago, and California, he was selling nearly a fourth of all the wine consumed in the United States. At forty-four Louis Petri was the wine king of America.

Meanwhile, at Modesto in Stanislaus County, twelve miles south of Petri's Escalon winery, a rival—the E. & J. Gallo Winery—was beginning to challenge him for leadership in wine sales. The

Gallo Brothers had bid in 1953 to buy the Italian Swiss Colony before Petri bought it for $16 million. The duel of Gallo versus Petri for dominance in the wine industry—billed in the trade press as "the battle of the giants"—lasted for more than a decade.

When, in 1957, Petri built the first American wine tanker for $7 million, his saving in freight costs enabled him to sell his wines for ten cents less per bottle in eastern market centers than wines that were shipped east by rail. The Gallos parried by building at Modesto for $6 million the first glass factory ever owned by a winery. By making their own lightweight bottles, the Gallos could sell their wines in the East at the same price as Petri's and advertise that their wines were bottled in California.

Nine years later, Petri added the prestigious Inglenook Vineyard to his kingdom, but the Gallos stuck to their policy of making and selling only inexpensive wines.

Gallo's sales crept up on Petri's during the sixties. By 1968, Gallo was well ahead. Bruno (Larry) Solari had replaced Petri as board chairman, and in that year Heublein bought control of United Vintners for $33 million in Heublein stock. Three years later, the wine tanker *Angelo Petri* was sold. Meanwhile, Heublein joined a glass company in building a $16 million bottle factory, like Gallo's, beside its Mission Bell winery at Madera. Before long, all of its enormous volume of California wines will be bottled in California.

Louis Petri continued in the wine business as the largest single member of the Allied Growers co-op, supplying grapes from his vineyards in Napa County to the complex of wineries he once controlled. He sold his last vineyard to Heublein in 1971 and, now a multimillionaire, he concentrates on his realty and hotel investments in Hawaii and San Francisco.

• 4 •

In the Repeal year of 1933, young Ernest and Julio Gallo rented an old warehouse in Modesto, bought some new redwood tanks and a grape crusher on credit, and made their first wine. Ernest was twenty-four, Julio a year younger. While at Modesto Junior College, they had planned to start a winery whenever Prohibition ended.

During boyhood they had worked in their father's vineyard west of Modesto, and they remembered the small winery their grandfather, from Italy's Piedmont, had operated at Hanford before Prohibition. But all that the boys knew about winemaking was how their father had made wine in their basement for his own use. In the Modesto public library they luckily found two of the University's pre-Prohibition pamphlets on winemaking, and the red wine they made in 1933 turned out sound. When it was ready, Ernest boarded a plane for New York with samples, called on the wine bottlers there, and sold them the 1933 vintage in bulk. Two years later, the brothers built a small concrete winery in the southern outskirts of Modesto on the bank of Dry Creek.

I remember stopping there one day in the late 1930s. In a cramped office in front of the cellar I found young Ernest Gallo. He told me that he and his brother were only making bulk wine to get started, but that someday the Gallo name with their family crest (the rooster, for which *gallo* is the Italian word) would appear on bottles that would be sold throughout the United States. His confidence impressed me, though his chances didn't.

Today at that same location the Gallos are bottling more than a third of the wine consumed in the United States. Their Modesto winery has grown to 60 million gallons, the biggest in the world. It is almost a city by itself, with its hundreds of giant steel tanks, the biggest of which holds a million gallons; enormous bottling cellars, bottle and cap factories, research laboratories, and vast warehouses from which Gallo wines are shipped by the trainload to all fifty states. There is also, surrounded by parkland, an elegant new "contemporary-classical" administration building (now proudly pictured on some Gallo labels), where the brothers, their sons, and a son-in-law have their offices. Gallo has become Modesto's biggest industry. None of it is open to the public, though there is talk of someday building a Gallo visitor center with a tasting hall and a wine museum. There are two more Gallo wineries at Livingston and Fresno, which bring the total capacity to 175 million gallons. A score of other wineries around the state, some operating on long-term contracts, now make all or most of their wines for Gallo. Altogether, more than a hundred thousand acres of California vineyards, including almost ten thousand owned by the family, produce the grapes for the company's wines.

When the Gallo name first appeared on bottles in 1940, the brothers aimed at a specific goal: to become "the Campbell Soup Company of the wine industry," to supply the nation with reliable mass-produced wines under a single name, priced for everyday use. But their wines were not yet reliably palatable; troublesome vineyard and winery problems had to be solved. During the early 1940s, many California table wines, especially those grown in the San Joaquin Valley, still were unpleasant to drink—heavy, coarse, harsh, puckery with excessive tannin, usually oxidized, and often actually sour. In the next fifteen years the Gallos succeeded in eliminating those defects. They brought wines from Napa and Sonoma wineries to Modesto to improve the taste of their valley table-wine blends. They planted better grape varieties in their valley vineyards and became the first vintners to launch their own research program. Their staff of research enologists is now the biggest at any winery anywhere.

To get rid of unpleasant wine flavors, the Gallos did some revolutionary things. They eliminated woody and musty-wood taste by ripping out all of the wooden cooperage in their winery and replacing it with tanks of epoxy-lined steel. Some of the discarded redwood tank staves were salvaged in 1957 by their younger brother, Joe Gallo, who built a new house with them; for years afterward, the rooms of his house smelled of wine. To get rid of the mouth-puckering tannin in their press wines (red wines pressed from the pomace after fermentation), they began making Gallo wines entirely from the free-run (unpressed) juice. This inspired their radio-advertising jingle, nationally broadcast in the late 1950s: "Only the first/ squeezing of the grapes/ goes into Gallo wine." But Gallo Burgundy, when made from only free-run juice, lacked flavor; its taste was too bland. To remedy this, the Gallos then added some press wine—abandoning their "first squeezing" jingle—and in 1962 introduced the new blend as their "Hearty Burgundy," which since has been praised by visiting wine authorities as one of the better California reds. To prevent the oxidized or sherrylike taste caused when wine is exposed to sunlight, the Gallo bottle factory introduced an amber-green "flavor-guard" glass, which filters out the damaging ultraviolet rays.

Connoisseurs of the Wine & Food Society cult rarely discuss or even mention Gallo wines because they are mass-produced, closed with screw caps rather than corks, and are low in price; for example, 99¢ a "fifth" for Paisano and $1.19 for Hearty Burgundy in San Francisco in 1972. The really knowledgeable connoisseurs admit privately that Gallo table and dessert wines are remarkably good. In completely "blind" tastings, panels of experienced New York judges have scored some Gallo products above famous imports and premium-priced California wines. Obviously, however, wines at Gallo prices must be young, because to age wines for extended periods as the premium wineries are expected to do, a vintner must multiply the storage capacity of his winery for every additional year that he keeps his wines before sale.

Still lower in price are Gallo's "Red Mountain" wines (69¢ a quart locally at this writing). They once were known as the favorite wines of the hippies, who in Berkeley called themselves "the Red Mountain Tribe." The "Red Mountain" label reads "Made and Bottled by Carlo Rossi Vineyards, Modesto." But Modesto means Gallo, and Carlo (Charles) Rossi is a Gallo cousin and sales executive.

The Gallos consider their wines as good as any, regardless of price. They are irritated and amused when they hear their connoisseur friends rhapsodize over high-priced imports, in which the Gallos usually can taste flavor defects. They expressed these feelings rather snidely a few years ago in a television commerical that said: "Gallo—for the man who doesn't care *what* it costs." Ernest Gallo has his own original method of judging the quality of wine. He serves many bottles of different wines to a group of consumers, lets them pour for themselves, and keeps watch while the contents of the bottles disappear. He reasons that the wines in the bottles that are emptied soonest (and Gallo products score high by this test) must be the best. As for the screw caps on their bottles versus the corks that premium wineries and imports use, the Gallos claim the screw caps protect their wines better; that corks don't "breathe" as is generally believed, but only leak.

A family-owned corporation, Gallo is firmly ruled by Ernest as chairman and brother Julio as president. The other directors are Ernest's sons, David and Joey, Julio's son Bob, and his son-in-law, Jim Coleman. Ernest concentrates on marketing, Julio on the vineyards and wineries, but important company decisions are made only by both brothers, and they taste their wines daily together. Ernest, poker-faced behind his horn-rimmed glasses, is formidable in any business dealing, and he is cagy; those who seek interviews with him soon discover that he is interviewing them. For three decades he traveled each year through each market where his wines were on sale, calling on fifty stores a day, watching how his bottles were displayed. Though now a multimillionaire, he still makes store calls wherever he goes. Julio, a farmer and organic gardner, resembles Ernest but is more easygoing, but doesn't tell you what he is thinking, either.

The Gallos long ago achieved their original objective and then invaded wider fields. Theirs was the first American winery to introduce the new flavored wines, beginning with Thunderbird in 1957, and then the lightly-carbonated "pop" or "mod" wines, starting with Ripple in 1960. They brought out their first Charmat-process champagnes in 1966 and started selling a Gallo brandy in 1968. When they entered the glamorous champagne field, the Gallos departed from their single-brand-name idea. Their first champagne was called "Eden Roc," for the fashionable beach club at Cap d'Antibes, and a lower-priced champagne was named André. Now they are abandoning the "Eden Roc" name to simply call it Gallo Champagne.

In the mid-'60s Michigan and New York wineries came out with their sensational Cold Ducks made of Concord grapes, which do not grow well in California. The Gallos went to the State of

Washington for a supply. They now contract for the entire output of a growers' co-operative at Grandview in the Yakima Valley, which ships them Concord juice in refrigerated tank cars. The California grape industry was jolted in 1970 when the Gallos changed the appellation of origin of their port wine from "California" to "American," and tasters detected a hint of Concord flavor in the wine.

But the Gallos' most radical departure from old-fashioned wines is their enormous sales success with the new low-alcohol, slightly gassy "pop" or "mod" wines made not only of grapes, but also of apples, strawberries, and pears. Their popular Spañada is an eleven percent grape wine, flavored to resemble the Spanish wine-and-fruit punch called *sangría* (a word that relates to blood). Their Boone's Farm apple wine, labeled 11 percent, in 1970 became the largest-selling single wine of any kind in the United States. It was followed a year later by 9 percent Boone's Farm Strawberry Hill, a carbonated apple wine with strawberry flavor, and then by Wild Mountain, a 9 percent wine that tastes mainly of Concord grapes. By lowering the alcoholic content of some of their "special natural" wines to 9 percent (when the California legal minimum for standard white table wines is 10 and most table wines made in the state are labeled 12), the Gallos have invaded the enormous national market for beers. Their Ripple, originally 11 percent, now comes in three versions—Pear Ripple (white) at 10, Red at 11, and Pagan Pink (flavored with passion fruit) at 10. Evidently such wines are cutting into the sale of beer, because several breweries have responded lately by introducing fruit-flavored malt beverages. And when the Gallos popularized apple wines nationally in the 1970s, they created a stir in the world market for that ancient fruit. They imported apple concentrate from several foreign countries, and in 1972 planted their own 800-acre apple orchard near Hopeton in Merced County.

When department stores across the nation recently began soliciting youngsters to buy new T-shirts that reproduce the labels of Boone's Farm Apple, Pagan Pink Ripple, and Thunderbird, Gallo wines had achieved a kind of folk fame never equaled by Campbell Soups.

• 5 •

Winegrowing in Stanislaus County dates from 1854, when George H. Krause from the Rhineland laid out his Red Mountain Vineyard near Knight's Ferry in the foothills some twenty miles east of Modesto. Krause and his successors made good wines before Prohibition, including a sherry in my cellar that is still in fair condition. Their cellar, a tunnel cut into the stone hillside, was again operated briefly after Repeal by Modesto restaurateur Emanuel Galas, who called it the Oakdale Winery. More than a century later, the original name, "Red Mountain," was adopted by the Gallos and combined with "Carlo Rossi" as the brand for their bargain-priced wines.

As in the neighboring Manteca-Escalon district of San Joaquin County, wine grapes predominate in the vineyards around Modesto, the Stanislaus County seat. You will see more Thompson Seedless vineyards around Turlock, as you travel farther south. Modesto, incidentally, means "modest." When the site of its railroad station was chosen in 1870, rail magnate Timothy Hopkins offered to name it for his associate, William Ralston, but Ralston declined the honor. Hearing this, a Mexican companion exclaimed *"El señor es muy modesto!"* The sound of the Spanish word pleased Hopkins, who promptly marked it on the map.

But vineyardists around Modesto are not modest about the quality of their wine grapes, having planted some 4000 new acres of Chenin Blanc, French Colombard, Barbera, and Ruby Cabernet since the prices for these table wine "varietals" skyrocketed in the late 1960s. Led by Stanislaus County Farm Advisor Paul La Vine, the growers have organized a Grape Improvement Association and are trying to convince the wineries that their grapes are as good as those grown in adjoining San Joaquin County. The argument, however, is more about climate than grapes.

The growers' problem is that the University's classification in 1938 of California wine-district climates placed only three Stanislaus districts (Ceres, Hughson, and Vernalis) in Region IV. This seemed to leave Modesto, Salida, and the rest of the county in the hotter Region V. In consequence, they complain, wineries pay growers ten dollars a ton less for grapes grown at Salida or Modesto than for those across the Stanislaus River in San Joaquin County, where the Escalon-Manteca district is recognized as in Region IV. "You can throw a rock across the river from a ninety-dollar vineyard to a hundred-dollar vineyard of the same grape variety," says La Vine. He claims that a cooling wind from the Delta blows through this part of the valley each afternoon and brings down the temperature by four or five degrees. La Vine hopes to persuade the University to reclassify Stanislaus County as Region IV, hopefully even as Region III.

Growers in northern Merced County, Stanislaus' southern neighbor, claim that they, too, get that afternoon wind, and they have joined enthusiastically in La Vine's campaign. This raises the puzzling question of where Region IV really ends and Region V begins. La Vine now suggests that the Merced River is the proper boundary, which would include about half of that county's vineyards.

The University's bioclimatologist, Dr. Dewayne Gilbert, replies that the valley's climate needs further study before any such boundary can be redefined. He concedes that parts of Stanislaus and Merced may belong in Region IV, but adds that some parts of the present Region IV may yet be found to belong in Region III, or even, unhappily, in Region V.

In France and Italy, with their hundreds of district appellations of origin for wines, controversies have raged for generations over which vineyards are or are not entitled to label their wines with famous district names, which determine how much each bottle of wine is worth. Now that grape-district boundaries are becoming an issue in California, such questions have begun to be hotly argued there, too.

• 6 •

Merced County, with 14,000 acres of vines, is in the upper half of the San Joaquin Valley. Although seven tenths of its vineyards are now planted to wine grapes, this county had no wineries for almost two decades, its few small ones having closed following the Second World War. But in 1970, when the Gallos' Modesto plant reached its limit of expansion, they built a new 15-million-gallon winery on their vineyard along the south bank of the Merced River west of Livingston. A year later the winery was doubled in size, and all the grapes that formerly went to Modesto now go to Livingston to be crushed. The Gallos' Livingston vineyard covers 6500 acres, and they are expected to plant more near their apple orchard in northern Merced County, fifteen miles up the river near Hopeton.

Next to Merced is Madera County, and then Fresno, which marks the center of the valley vineyard area. Winegrowing began in this part of the valley about 1873, when Francis Eisen from Germany planted the first commercial vineyard at Fresno and built his winery two years later. Within a decade, half a dozen more wineries sprang up in the neighborhood, including the Eggers, Barton, Margherita, Mattei, and Henrietta estates. In 1880, George West & Son came south from Stockton to Minturn in Madera County and became partners with Thomas Minturn in the big Sierra Vista vineyard and winery there. Before the turn of the century, the Wests were operating additional wineries at Fresno, Selma, and at Hanford. By 1900 the Italian Swiss Colony of Asti owned a winery at Madera and had built new wineries at Kingsburg and Lemoore.

The most colorful of the pioneer valley vintners was George H. Malter, whose St. George Winery was five miles east of Fresno on Fancher Creek. Malter, born in Germany, had already made a fortune as a mining engineer when he became a winegrower in 1879. He named his vineyard Maltermoro, issued his own scrip or currency, and advertised his wines and brandy as the best in the world. One of his products was a "bathing brandy," which he recommended as a feminine beauty aid.

The early wineries in this region made mostly sweet dessert wines and brandy; their table wines were poor. For this reason, Malter's St. George Winery bought the grapes for its table wines in the cooler coastal districts and fermented them in a northern St. George cellar at Antioch in Contra Costa County.

When Eisen laid out his vineyard at Fresno, one of the grapes he planted was the Muscat of Alexandria, which makes both wine and raisins. When the Thompson Seedless was introduced from Sutter County in the 1890s, Fresno became both the sweet wine and raisin capital of the nation. In 1900, with almost 70,000 acres of vineyards producing wine, raisins, and table grapes, Fresno was the leading vineyard county in the United States, the rank it still holds.

As dry agitation reached its height in the early 1900s and Prohibition became a threat, the Fresno community preferred to publicize itself as the raisin capital. Its wine and brandy industry, under increasing attack, was not the basis of community pride. When the wineries, idle during the dry era, reopened at Repeal in 1933, and the coast-counties wine towns revived their wine festivals, Fresno continued to celebrate its annual Raisin Day. This may explain why histories of Fresno County tell only of Eisen's part in founding the raisin industry, and omit mention of his winegrowing career. And descriptions of the county's Kearney Park, seven miles west of Fresno, refer to Kearney as a leader of the raisin industry, but ignore his role as a wine industry pioneer. (M. Theo. Kearney was an eccentric man of mystery; his Fresno neighbors never learned his full name. He willed his five-thousand-acre estate, which he called Château Fresno, to the University of California, which exchanged it after his death for county land near Parlier and built its Kearney Horticultural Field Station there. At Kearney Park, which comprises the remaining 350 acres of Château Fresno, there is nothing to mark the site of the Kearney Winery, which stood near the eastern corner of the estate.)

Such bits of local history also help explain why, during three decades following Repeal, wine in the valley was treated as the salvage by-product of the raisin and table grape industries, even when the by-product was using most of the valley grapes. Related facts were the flat, earthy taste of table wines made in the valley, and that its people, including the vintners, seldom drank wine of any kind.

It was considered impossible to produce acceptable dry table wine in the hot valley climate, and with the coast counties producing more wine following Repeal than they could sell, there was no reason to try. Considerable quantities of "sauterne" and "burgundy" were nevertheless made in the valley, but were blended with table wines from the coast to make them palatable and were sold as "north coast and valley blends." Yet Almond R. Morrow, the great wine taster of the old California Wine Association, said at the time of Repeal that "excellent dry wines can be made in the valley if you know how." Professor Hilgard, too, had known how, but had failed to convince the vintners that in sunny California, unlike Europe, grapes for good table wines must be harvested early, before their sugar content becomes too high and their acidity too low.

For thirty years after Repeal, the valley wineries continued paying the grape growers a premium for each extra degree of sugar content in their fruit. Grape prices per ton were based on "22 Balling, plus or minus $1 for each sugar point above or below 22." Moreover, the big wineries delayed buying grapes until after September 20, the last day it is considered safe for growers to lay their Thompsons on trays to make raisins without risking damage from early rains. The purpose was to keep the huge annual Thompson surplus out of the wineries by forcing them onto the trays. Table wines made in the valley from grapes harvested in late October or November, sometimes as late as December, did more than Prohibition to make Americans refuse to drink wine and turn to liquor or beer.

• 7 •

The abrupt, complete flip-flop that has occurred in the San Joaquin Valley grape industry in less than a decade was partially described in Chapter 12. But not until the mid-1960s, when national consumption of table wines was about to exceed that of dessert wines, and the coast counties no longer could produce enough to supply the mounting demand, did the big valley vintners begin to realize that they were doing everything wrong. The demand for better table wines compelled them to learn the lesson of early harvesting that Hilgard had tried to teach eighty years before. Now, September instead of October has become the start of harvest season for wine in the valley, and some grapes for table wine are picked as early as the beginning of August. Now, farmers who previously grew only raisin and table grapes are rushing to plant the table-wine "varietals" that are newly in demand. For the first time in this century, people in the valley are beginning to realize that the main product of their vineyards is neither raisins nor table grapes, but wine and brandy, which now utilize two thirds of the entire California grape crop.

Equally important is the revolution taking place in winemaking, as the valley wineries adopt radically new production methods and install refrigeration and other equipment needed to produce acceptable dry table wines. "Since I began making really good dry wine," the winemaker at one of the major valley wineries confided to me recently, "I've begun drinking it with my dinner every night."

The first fine table wines to be grown, bottled, and labeled as local products in Region V came in 1962 from the little Ficklin Vineyard winery, on Avenue 7½, seven miles south of Madera.* Fourteen years earlier, the late Walter Ficklin, a wealthy farmer and wine buff, with his Davis-trained sons, Walter, Jr., and David, had built his 40,000-gallon cellar with the idea of making one superior wine. Believing that the only fine wine that could be grown in Region V would have to be either a port or a sherry, they chose port. They obtained cuttings of Tinta Madeira, Tinta Cão, Souzão, and other superior port varieties from the University, and made some of the finest ports thus far produced in the United States. But, needing some table wine for their own use, the Ficklins also planted an acre of Professor Harold Olmo's then-new hybrid Vinifera grapes for hot climates, Emerald Riesling and Ruby Cabernet. They picked these grapes in mid-August and fermented them at low temperatures. Soon their neighbors and visiting connoisseurs, who came to buy their port, were also buying all the table wine the Ficklins could produce. Introduced to San Franciscans at a gourmet banquet in the Hotel St. Francis in 1965, Ficklin Emerald Riesling 1962 was chosen by many of those present in preference to a château-bottled white Bordeaux. Their Ruby Cabernet has since proved even better than their white. The Ficklins still make only enough table wine to sell at the winery, because they are too busy supplying the mounting demand for their ports, of which there are two kinds. Their Tinta Port is a *solera* of all the vintages since 1948; the others are limited bottlings of vintage ports, obtainable only direct from the winery. Both kinds in my cellar have developed greater bouquet with each passing year.

*From 1956 to 1968, Horace Lanza's Cal-Grape winery near Delano produced and bottled small quantities of a creditable dry red table wine from the Italian Nebbiolo grape, but the Nebbiolo label gave the company's San Francisco address.

· 8 ·

Northwest of Ficklin, on Avenue 13, is the Heublein–United Vintners' 40-million-gallon Mission Bell winery. Its 120-foot-high distillery tower dominates the landscape for miles around. With its newly-added champagne cellar and bottle factory, Mission Bell is now almost as big as Gallo's Modesto plant. It is not open to visitors, either, but is worth the side trip from Madera to see from the outside.

Mission Bell has had many owners. Before Prohibition it belonged to the Italian Swiss Colony of Asti, which later was absorbed by the California Wine Association. During the dry years, it was purchased by Krikor Arakelian, the one-time melon king of California, who had become one of the biggest grape growers in the state. Arakelian, who came to America in 1895 from Armenia with five dollars in his pocket, made Mission Bell after Repeal the second-largest independent winery in the nation, then sold it in 1949 for $3¼ million to Louis Petri, who in turn sold it two years later to the Allied Grape Growers co-operative. Then came Heublein, the Hartford, Connecticut, firm that John Martin had built from a small manufacturer of "A-1" meat sauce into one of the world's largest marketers of vodka, premixed cocktails, rum, tequila, cordials, beer, and European wines.

Since buying control of United Vintners from Allied in 1968, Heublein has made Mission Bell its biggest California winery. Most of Heublein's American wines and champagnes (except Beaulieu, Inglenook, and Tipo table wines) are now bottled at Madera. The labels on the bottles, however, usually give the address as "Italian Swiss Colony, California." That is the name of a post office United Vintners established for labeling purposes at the Madera winery in 1964. (Some of the other labels that go on bottles at Mission Bell read "San Francisco," where United Vintners has its office.) The wines that come from Mission Bell include Petri, Lejon, Napa-Sonoma-Mendocino, Jacques Bonet, and such flavored and "pop" wines as Bali Hai, Key Largo, Silver Satin, Paree, Zapple (a cinnamon-flavored apple wine), and the three new Italian Swiss Colony "pop" wines named Annie Green Springs, I, Love, and You. United Vintners also owns many older names, such as G & D, Padre, Margo, Sante Fe, Greystone, and Cella, which are used to supply distributors in local markets where these brands have a consumer following. Another unique product made at Mission Bell is the water-white, unaged Petri Grappa, the only pomace brandy (called *eau de vie de marc* in France) made in the United States.

Allied Grape Growers, supplying Heublein–United Vintners

with grapes, meanwhile has become the world's biggest co-operative of vineyardists, with some 1700 members, including a growers' co-op in the Yakima Valley of Washington that ships refrigerated Concord juice to Madera for use in making the United Vintners' brands of Cold Duck.

A third Madera winery, two miles east of Mission Bell, is that of the Bisceglia family, who since they began in 1880 at San Jose have operated wineries at St. Helena and Fresno before taking over the former Yosemite Co-operative cellar, which they now occupy. Among the numerous Bisceglia products, the specialties are sparkling and still pineapple wines.

Madera County will soon have its fourth winery. It is being built on Highway 99 southeast of Madera, will hold three million gallons, and will have a tasting room.

· 9 ·

Fresno County has twenty-two wineries. They are a surprising assortment of sizes and kinds. Only a few bottle what they produce, and still fewer invite the public to visit their cellars.

Passengers on airliners approaching Fresno Airport can see three of the principal wineries strung along Clovis Avenue, north and south of the field. The clump of enormous wine tanks a mile south is Gallo's Fresno winery, which when enlarged by 1973 will surpass that company's Modesto winery as the biggest in the world. On its site in 1890, Benjamin Woodworth established his Las Palmas Vineyard, which he named for the line of palms that led to his estate. At Repeal the Cribari family of San Jose bought the old wooden cellar and continued making wine there until 1954, when Gallo bought and replaced it with tanks of steel. Each season now, this single winery crushes more than 300,000 tons of grapes.

Directly across McKinley Avenue from the airfield is the 4-million-gallon Cameo winery, built by Harry Hitzl and associates in 1938. After the Second World War it became part of the Alta Vineyards Company, which sued the city for damages when the airport was built next door, claiming that the vibrations of plane motors disturbed the aging wines (the suit was lost). When Alta merged with the Guild of Lodi in 1962, this winery became the principal Fresno cellar of the Guild.

Two miles north of the airfield is the La Paloma Winery with its handsome ivy-clad tower, built by vineyardist M. F. Tarpey in 1895. During the Second World War, National Distillers bought La Paloma and added its output to that of the Italian Swiss Colony, then sold it, with the winery at Asti, to Petri's United Vintners. All that remains to recall the Tarpey family is the adjoining Tarpey Village housing tract.

To the wine tourist, the most interesting of the big valley wineries is Roma, at Church and East Avenues in the industrial district of Fresno. The huge casks in its great air-conditioned oak cellar are among the most spectacular in the state. Since buying Roma from Schenley Distillers in 1971, the Guild Wine Company of Lodi has made many changes, and is planning to reopen the public tasting room and again to offer tours of the cellar. What is confusing is that since the sale, the bottling of all Roma wines has been moved to the Guild cellars at Lodi. The Guild now bottles at Roma its two bottle-fermented champagnes—Cresta Blanca, which once came from Livermore and is now headquartered at Ukiah, and Cook's Imperial, which originated in Missouri. Next door to Roma is the Schenley whiskey, gin, and vodka distillery, which was not included in the sale to the Guild. This is the source of this country's supply of Dubonnet apéritif wines, American rights to which are Schenley-owned.

The story of the Cella family, who once owned Roma, parallels that of the Petris. John Battista Cella and his brother Lorenzo came to the United States in 1900 from Bardi in northern Italy. They worked as waiters in a New York restaurant, then went into the wholesale grocery business. They bought their cigars and wine from Raffaello Petri and Dante Foresti, whom Battista visited on trips to California. Three years before National Prohibition began, Battista bought the old Scatena wineries at Lodi, Manteca, and Healdsburg from Foresti, and made Roma sacramental wine there through the dry era, while Lorenzo stayed in New York to handle the sales. Then, when Lodi vineyardists began building their co-op wineries, he moved from Lodi to the Santa Lucia winery at Fresno, renamed it Roma, and made his headquarters there. In 1942, the now-retired king of Schenley Distillers, Lewis Rosenstiel, bought Roma and Cresta Blanca (events I especially remember because Rosenstiel then summoned me to his summer home at Tucson to give him a complete education in wine in three days. Rosenstiel thereupon tried unsuccessfully to convert the state's vintners to his pet liquor-selling ideas). Cella soon resigned from Roma and in 1944 bought the Rusconi vineyard and winery near Wahtoke, north of Reedley, which he renamed the Cella Vineyards and expanded to 12 million gallons. Following the deaths of Battista and Lorenzo Cella, the latter's son, John B. Cella II, became the owner of the Cella Vineyards. In 1955 he joined Allied Grape Growers, sold the Wahtoke winery to Allied, which sold it to United Vintners; and John II, still the owner of the vineyards, is now United Vintners' vice president.

The oldest winery in Fresno County is probably the one at Lac-jac, between Reedley and Parlier. Since 1945 it has been the Mount Tivy or Reedley winery of the Christian Brothers of Napa; the Brothers produce and bottle their dessert wines and brandy there. Originally this was the Sanford winery, but nobody seems to know when it was built. In 1899 Lachman & Jacobi, the San Francisco wine merchants, who then were fighting the California Wine Association's attempt to monopolize the state's wine supply, bought and enlarged the Sanford cellar to a million gallons and began to make their own wine. They later were absorbed by the CWA. At Repeal, Fresno Assemblyman Lucius Powers and associates reopened the old winery and changed its name from Lacjac to Mount Tivy, for an early settler of the county. During the Second World War, Seagram bought it from an intermediate owner and at the end of the conflict sold it to the Christian Brothers. Today the great cellars and the clusters of new outdoor steel tanks hold three million gallons of aging dessert wines, and the big distillery, with its continuous and pot stills, makes the Brothers' brandies, which outsell all others in the United States. The Brothers own a thousand acres of vineyards in the vicinity, in which they grow three dozen wine-grape varieties. Included are Tinta Madeira for their port wines and the rare Muscat Canelli or Frontignan, which accounts in part for the delicacy of their Château La Salle sweet white table wine.

Two wineries in Fresno county are owned by groups of grape growers. The Sanger Winery Association, which has a two-million-gallon winery in the center of Sanger, is a co-op of 140 members. It also owns the Gibson wineries at Elk Grove, California, and Covington, Kentucky, and ships the wines from Sanger to those cellars for bottling. The 2-million-gallon Del Rey winery, on Central Avenue near Malaga, was organized in 1945 as a co-op, but in 1971 was changed to a grower-owned corporation. Built to make bulk dessert wine, Del Rey now also makes table wine, bottles some of its output, offers it for sale at the winery, and contemplates building a tasting room. This is also the head-quarters of Cribari Vineyards Company altar wines, which are marketed jointly with those made at the Church-owned O-Neh-Da Vineyard winery near Conesus, New York

At Monmouth, a crossroads on the county map between Caruthers and Selma, are several acres of stainless steel tanks and warehouses that resemble an army depot. This is the unique Vie-Del Company, headed by Jim Riddell and Massud Nury. They make more than a dozen different winy products from the grapes grown on the company's 2000 acres of vineyards, but sell only two under the Vie-Del name. One is their trio of "Wine

Chef" dealcoholized, concentrated wine flavors (Burgundy, Sauterne, and Sherry) for gourmet cookery. The other is "Wine-Craft" grape concentrate for home winemaking. It comes in various-sized cans and also in a home-winemaking kit, complete with fermentation lock, siphon hose, yeast, yeast-nutrient, bottle caps, and instructions for making four gallons of "select Burgundy wine." Another interesting item is blending-sherry, of which Vie-Del, partly owned by Seagram, is the nation's chief supplier. This is the heavy-bodied sherry that is blended with fine whiskeys, brandies, and rums, and accounts for their smooth taste. But the main product at Vie-Del is brandy. Its heady aroma can be breathed in the air at Monmouth, for almost four million gallons of it—the biggest concentration of brandy in the world—is aging in barrels in the warehouses for other producers, who have their brandy made or aged there.

In contrast to the giant valley wineries is the old-fashioned 75,000-gallon cellar of the Nonini family on their 200-acre vineyard in the Rolinda district, eight miles northwest of Fresno. When Antonio Nonini began making table wine in 1936, his principal customers were Basque sheepherders who came down from the mountains each year to have their barrels filled with his burgundy, made from his Barbera grapes. Antonio's sons, Reno, Gildo, and Geno, still make their burgundy to the sheepmen's taste. It is 14 percent in alcohol content because the Noninis wait until October to pick these grapes. Their Zinfandel and their rosé, made from Mission grapes, are somewhat easier to drink. The Noninis have built a small tasting room, where their wines are sold mostly by the bottle and jug. But now that table wine is becoming a popular mealtime drink in the valley, numerous Fresno householders have begun emulating the Basque sheepherders, buying their table wines from the Noninis in small barrels and bringing them back to be refilled at the bargain barrel price.

Also unique is the small cellar of the Nicholas Verry family, opposite the railroad tracks in the town of Parlier. The Verrys are the only American producer of retsina, the resin-flavored wine that is popular among the Greeks. The Verrys' other specialty is a light white wine they call Philery, which means "quick love" in Greek.

There are three old wineries between Selma and Kingsburg, raisin-growing centers along Highway 99. On Huntsman Avenue is Kenneth Knapp's Selma Winery, an independent producer of bulk wine. Next, on Sierra Street in Kingsburg, is the one-time Italian Swiss Colony Kingsburg cellar, which Louis Martini sold to Schenley when he moved to the Napa Valley; it is now owned by the Guild of Lodi. The one-time Muscat Co-operative Winery, a mile north of there, is now operated by Vie-Del.

The Sun-Maid Growers raisin-processing plant, on Bethel Avenue two miles northwest of Kingsburg, is the biggest of its kind in the world and is worth a visit to take the 25-minute plant tour (offered on weekdays) showing how the co-op stems, washes, and packages the sun-dried Thompson, Muscat, Sultana, and Zante currant grapes of its 2000 members. Sun-Maid was organized in 1912 and during the First World War promoted its five-cent package of raisins at candy counters with the slogan "Have you had your iron today?"—until it was stopped by the discovery that raisins contain very little iron.

For many years, any mention that grapes also make wine was taboo in promoting the sale of raisins. At Sun-Maid you are told a legend of how the Fresno raisin industry began. In 1873, the story goes, an unprecedented hot spell dried Francis Eisen's grapes on his vines before he could pick them. What is omitted from the story is that Eisen's purpose in growing grapes was to make them into wine. According to the legend, Eisen salvaged the heat-shriveled fruit by shipping it to a San Francisco grocer who, inspired by the arrival that morning of a ship from Peru, put them on sale as "Peruvian delicacies." Soon the grocer was regularly sending Eisen orders for more.

The taboo against mentioning wine was finally lifted in 1970. In that year raisin industry leaders, seeking a way to reverse the declining sale of their product, hit on the idea of taking advantage of the nationwide home-winemaking craze. The Raisin Advisory Board organized an "American Raisin Vintners Guild" and began selling, for two dollars and a boxtop from any brand of California raisins, a home-winemaking kit with equipment and instructions for fermenting raisins into "balanced, mellow, aromatic, beautiful wines." Although raisins normally make only white wine with a somewhat raisiny taste, an extra recipe in the kit explains that adding beets will change it to rosé.

· 10 ·

The Fresno area ranks next to Davis as a center of viticultural teaching and research. There are two Federal Government experimental vineyards, one at Clovis, the other on Peach Avenue in the southeastern outskirts of Fresno. On Manning Avenue near Parlier is the University of California's big Kearney Horticultural Field Station, where all kinds of vineyard problems are explored, and where Dr. Harold Olmo tests his new wine-grape hybrids for Region V. There is still another UC fruit-testing station at Five Points on the west side of the valley.

Research is combined with the teaching of grape-growing, wine-making, and raisin production at Fresno State University. Almost a third of the 600-acre campus on Shaw Avenue in northeastern Fresno is occupied by the University vineyard. Adjoining it is a 5000-gallon model winery, built in 1958 despite vehement protests by local Drys. Sixty-five students major in viticultural subjects, two thirds of them in enology. Many Fresno State graduates now manage vineyards and wineries throughout California and in two dozen foreign countries; the demand for them is greater than the school can fill.

Vincent Petrucci, an Escalon farm boy and one-time high school football coach, has headed the Fresno State viticulture program since 1947, when he got his master's degree at UC under Drs. Winkler and Olmo. Although Fresno lacks the scientific staff UC has at Davis, Petrucci has pioneered many research projects that are contributing to the improvement of valley wines. He was the first, in 1966, to attempt vineyard climate-control.

Petrucci believes wine use in the United States will treble within the next decade, and predicts that the wine grapes now being planted in the San Joaquin Valley will eventually supply most of the nation's "better than average" table wines.

In the enology course at Fresno State, each student is taught wine tasting and analysis and learns to make all of the principal types of still and sparkling wines. What troubles Petrucci is having to destroy all the wines his students make, a requirement of the Federal law that governs colleges' experimental wine cellars. "We at least ought to be allowed to sell our wines to the wineries instead of pouring it all down the drain," he says.

The University does sell the grapes that students produce as part of their viticulture course. Each student is assigned five acres to farm, and he shares in the profit when the fruit is sold. Some earn as much as several hundred dollars in a season.

In 1966, this enabled one of Petrucci's students, twenty-year-old Dale Landis, to start the first new winery built in Fresno County in more than twenty years. Dale started by buying the best wine grapes grown by his classmates, making them into wine in the tool shed behind his father's home in the Oleander district of Fresno. Then he persuaded his father, a semiretired dentist, to help him build an 8000-gallon cellar adjoining the house and to equip it with oak cooperage and refrigeration. He makes excellent Ruby Cabernet and Zinfandel, and also a pair of sherries, which he buys from the Vie-Del winery and ages in small oak barrels. He has designed an attractive Landis Winery label, on which he uses "San Joaquin Valley" instead of "California" as the appellation of origin for his wines. No other Fresno vintner has done anything like this since the 1930s, when the old Mattei winery sold a wine labeled "Mattevista Fresno Port." Dale finds that calling his wines "San Joaquin Valley" helps their sale. They are stocked as premium wines by two dozen stores and restaurants from Fresno to Los Angeles.

Fresno County has two more new wineries. When the wine boom began in the 1960s, the Noble Land & Cattle Company began planting table-wine "varietals" on parts of the 39-square-mile tract it owns southeast of Kerman. By the spring of 1971, when the vine plantings covered six square miles, a stemmer-crusher and refrigerated tanks of stainless steel were erected on a concrete slab in the vineyard. This is the kind of winery Professor Petrucci envisions for the valley in the future, a plant that converts grapes, minutes after picking, into table wines. Also of steel is the Nordsman Winery, built in 1971 by Homer Hansen and associates at Wahtoke on the east side of the valley. There is impressive contrast between these grape-processing plants and the romantic stone wineries of the past.

· 11 ·

Tulare County, with almost 70,000 acres of vines, four-fifths of them table-grape and raisin varieties, is second to Fresno in the extent of its vineyards. There are four wineries in the county.

Beside the tiny Armenian village of Yettem (Armenian for "Garden of Paradise"), on Highway 201 four miles south of Cutler, is the California Growers Winery, newly enlarged from four to six million gallons. Established in 1936 by Arpaxat (Sox) Setrakian, a leader of the raisin industry, Calgro was primarily a producer of bulk dessert wines and brandy until 1972, when under son Robert Setrakian it entered the exploding table-wine and champagne business. Since the boom in light wines began seven years earlier, the Setrakians had planted 800 new acres of such "varietal" grapes as Chenin Blanc, Emerald Riesling, Ruby Cabernet, and Barbera. Now, with new stainless steel crushers, refrigerated storage and Charmat champagne tanks, and an automatic bottling line, they are introducing a complete assortment of bottled still and sparkling wines and brandies under the Setrakian name as well as under their old "Growers" brand.

The 6-million-gallon Sierra Winery, a bulk producer on Highway 43 northeast of Tulare, also exemplifies the striking changes taking place in the valley wine industry. Back in 1904, Frank Giannini, from the Island of Elba, owned a vineyard here and made wine for himself and his friends. His favorite was a dry

wine of Aleatico, the red Muscat grape of Elba; only one California winery (Filippi of Mira Loma) makes it anymore. Giannini
had so many thirsty friends that he built a winery and began selling them his wines. After his death in 1944, his winery had various
owners until a group of vineyardists headed by Ross Bagdasarian
bought and enlarged the old cellar in 1963 to provide a home for
their grapes. Nine tenths of its output was port and sherry,
shipped in tank cars to eastern bottlers. The table wine boom has
reversed this; nine tenths of Sierra's production is now table wine,
produced for other California wineries. An important development there in 1964 was the introduction of the submerged-culture
flor sherry process. In that year Sierra became the first American
winery to make *flor* sherry by this speedy method, invented in
Canada. Winemaker Philip Posson supplies it by the tank truck
and barrel to other California producers, who are beginning to use
it in their dry sherry blends. Some send their barrels to Sierra to
be filled and kept there for aging outdoors in the warm Tulare
climate. Posson says the aging of sherry in barrels outdoors improves its flavor because it cools at night and warms during the
day.

· 12 ·

Kern County, where the San Joaquin Valley ends in the foothills of the Tehachapi Mountains, has 58,000 acres of vineyards
centered between Delano and Arvin, a sixth of this newly planted
in 1972. This is John Steinbeck country, the setting of his Pulitzer
prize-winning novel of 1940, *The Grapes of Wrath*. More than half
of the Kern acreage still is of Thompsons and table grapes, but
the stampede to plant table-wine "varietals" is changing that now.
County Farm Advisor Donald Luvisi predicts that Kern will have
80,000 acres by 1974, and that most of it will be wine grapes.
There are four big wineries in the county, and two more across the
Tulare County line at Trocha are regarded as within the Delano
district, making a total of six in the area.

At Trocha, five miles northeast of Delano, are the Delano
Growers co-op, the Cal-Grape winery, now owned by Sierra, and
the one-time Del Vista cellar, which is now the L. K. Marshall
Winery of the Guild. South of Delano is the winery of A. Perelli-
Minetti & Sons. At Edison, six miles east of Bakersfield, is the 4-
million-gallon winery of Joe Giumarra, who is the biggest fresh-
grape shipper in the United States. Eight miles farther south, at Di
Giorgio, is the 20-million-gallon Bear Mountain co-op. Bear
Mountain and Perelli-Minetti are the only ones in the district that
do any bottling and invite visitors to tour their plants. In 1972

Giumarra announced plans to develop "varietal" vineyards and to begin bottling all types of wine.

Grape growing at this end of the valley began in 1888, when the waters of the Kern River were diverted for irrigation. To Kern County in 1919 came the fabulous Giuseppe (Joseph) Di Giorgio, the Sicilian immigrant who rose from an eight-dollar-a-week clerk for a New York fruit jobber at the age of fourteen to become, at thirty-seven, the biggest grower and marketer of fresh fruits in the world.

Di Giorgio began planting grapes around Delano, where predecessors were already cultivating 7000 acres of vines. Then he went exploring farther south in a virtual desert near Arvin, then known as "the weed patch." He found underground water, bought eighteen square miles there, and began planting vineyards, which eventually covered 5600 acres. That is the vineyard district which is now Di Giorgio on state maps.

When Prohibition began in 1920 and the market for grapes boomed, bootleggers and home winemakers swarmed at the fruit auctions, which Di Giorgio controlled, for hundreds of thousands were making their own wines. Then Di Giorgio heard of a winemaker at Ukiah in Mendocino County, who was making a grape syrup called Caligrapo, which bore an inviting label: "When diluted, do not store in a warm place because it will ferment, which is against the law." Di Giorgio saw that, for home winemaking, concentrated grape juice was an improvement over fresh grapes. He went to Ukiah, brought the winemaker to Kern County in 1922, had his surplus grapes made into concentrate during the remaining Prohibition years, and at Repeal established his own wineries at Delano, at Kerman in Fresno County, and at Di Giorgio.

· 13 ·

That one-time Ukiah winemaker, Antonio Perelli-Minetti, can still be found at his own winery three miles south of Delano at the Pond Road exit from Highway 99. He is the oldest pre-Prohibition vintner still active in the state. His career is as colorful as Di Giorgio's.

He was born in 1882 at Barletta on the Adriatic coast of southern Italy, where his father owned two wineries. At nineteen, Tony was completing his studies at the Conegliano Viticultural Institute when Dr. Ollino of the Italian Swiss Colony, recruiting winemakers in Italy, persuaded the young man's father to send him to California. Perelli traveled to the Colony at Asti in 1902, made wine there, then at Livermore for the California Wine Association, and later at two Healdsburg wineries. Eight years later, Perelli went broke attempting in a partnership wine-selling venture at San Francisco to compete with the giant CWA.

Told by a visiting Mexican vintner that he could recoup his fortunes quickly in Mexico, Perelli went there in 1910 and was hired to plant a vineyard near Torreón. In his sixth year below the border, the chaos of the Mexican Revolution compelled Perelli to return to California. He since has returned many times to Mexico and has helped to build and equip some of that country's leading wineries.

Back in California, Perelli settled at Ukiah, where Di Giorgio found him making Caligrapo in 1922. When Di Giorgio brought him to Kern County, Perelli began planting his own Delano vineyard, but kept his home at Ukiah for a dozen more years. During that time he built two more Delano wineries, moving to his third and present one in 1936. Today Perelli's vineyards spread over 1200 acres on both sides of the freeway and his plant holds 14 million gallons of wine, brandy, and champagne. Visitors who apply at the office are given tours of the cellar on weekdays. Construction of a tasting room is being planned.

In 1971 the winery acquired an additional name, that of the California Wine Association. Remember that the CWA, formed in 1894, swallowed up sixty-four California wineries and controlled most of the state's wine supply until Prohibition, and that in 1929 the CWA and other old wine firms combined as Fruit Industries—the days of the "Vine-Glo" concentrate. At the height of its power in 1950, Fruit Industries resumed the name of the old California Wine Association, and counting eleven wineries among its members, introduced its Eleven Cellars brand. But then, one by one, the members dropped out, until in 1971 the Cherokee co-op winery of Lodi finally withdrew, which left Perelli-Minetti as the last of the Eleven Cellars.

This unravels several who-owns-which-wine puzzles, such as why Perelli-Minetti at Delano now bottles and sells wines bearing such old-time names as L & J (Lachman & Jacobi), Greystone (for the Christian Brothers' showplace cellar at St. Helena), F.I., Guasti, Calwa, Ambassador, and Eleven Cellars, and brandies called Aristocrat and A. R. Morrow. As the last CWA member, Perelli now owns all of these names, and more than 200 additional famous wine and brandy brands of the past.

CWA's varietally labeled table wines, under the Fino Eleven Cellars name, are produced by wineries in the coast counties. Its leading brandy is called Aristocrat. Under the A. R. Morrow name, CWA sells one of the few bottled-in-bond (100 proof) brandies made in the United States.

The vineyards, the winery with its new bottling and champagne cellars, and CWA sales are managed, respectively, by three of Perelli's sons, William, Fred, and Mario, but Tony is still the active boss.

Because he prefers the coast counties table wines, which are higher in acidity than those of the valley, he plants seedlings of those grapes he finds in his vineyards that tend to mature with high acidity late in the season. By doing this for almost thirty years, Perelli has developed half a dozen new red-wine grapes and has patented the first, which he calls "Perelli 101." It develops 1.12 acidity at 22 Balling and doesn't ripen until mid-November, sometimes not until early December. I have tasted its wine, which is full-bodied and fresh and could easily be mistaken for a north-coast wine. Perelli has planted his "101" vine on 350 of his acres and will soon be ready to put its wine on the market. Other vintners have scored sensational sales successes by introducing new "varietal" wines, only to face competition as soon as other vintners could introduce wines bearing the same varietal names. Perelli, by breeding and patenting his own new grapes, has found a way to sell wines with varietal names no other vintner can copy, that are exclusively his own.

• 14 •

The vast Di Giorgio vineyards and the big winery near the Di Giorgio post office have new owners now.

When the founder died in 1951, he owned almost fourteen square miles of vineyards, more than anyone else in the world. His nephews became the heads of the Di Giorgio Fruit Corporation; Joe had no sons. Until then, the entire output of the Di Giorgio wineries had been sold in bulk to bottlers and to other wineries. The nephews decided to try selling it in bottles. They bought the old Santa Fe, Padre, and Vai Brothers brand names, acquired bottling cellars in Los Angeles, and introduced "the Di Giorgio family of fine wines." After six years they gave that up, sold the brands to Petri's United Vintners, and returned to selling the wines in bulk. Then, because irrigation water reaching their part of the valley in Federal projects from the north was denied to single owners of more than 160 acres, they began disposing of the Di Giorgio vineyards. They sold the winery in 1966 to a new grape growers' co-operative and erased "Fruit" from their corporate name. The Di Giorgios are now big in the lumber business.

The Bear Mountain Winery, ex-Di Giorgio, is named for a nearby peak in the Greenhorn Mountains, which rise east of Bakersfield. Many of the co-op's hundred grower members have planted large blocks of their vineyards with "varietal" grapes for table wines. In 1969, Bear Mountain became the first Kern County winery to bottle its own line of wines, which now include such locally grown table wine "varietals" as Chenin Blanc, French Colombard, Ruby Cabernet, Barbera, and Grenache Rosé. It has shifted fully half of its production to table wines and has opened the first public tasting rooms in the county, one at the winery, a second beside the freeway south of Bakersfield. In 1972 the co-op was getting ready to make its first champagne.

"This is only the beginning," says Bear Mountain President Keith Nylander, who managed wineries at Fresno for sixteen years before taking charge of the winery at Di Giorgio in 1959. Nylander's production manager, Jim Lawrence, is experimenting with "varietal" grapes that are not supposed to grow in Region V— Johannisberg Riesling, Cabernet Sauvignon, Pinot Noir, and Gamay Beaujolais. Lawrence, a 1966 enology graduate from Fresno State, recently invited me to taste the first samples of his wines made from these noble grapes. I found them all better than drinkable, and the Riesling was the best of the four.

Most of the co-op's bottled wines are called "Bear Mountain," "Gold Peak," "M. Lamont," or "Mountain Gold," but some reach the market under the brands of distributors in many states, and much of the output is still sold in bulk. The bottle labels do not mention the Di Giorgio address; some give it as Arvin, which is four miles south, and others say Lamont, which is four miles to the west.

· 15 ·

The most important aspect of the wine revolution of the 1970s is the rush to plant "varietal" grapes for table wines in the San Joaquin Valley.

On the east side of the valley, where the wineries are, new vineyards are scattered all the way from Manteca to Delano. Travel south, east, and west from Bakersfield and you see many more—vines even sprouting among the oil wells. There are important new plantings in the foothills of the Tehachapi, near Wheeler Ridge; in the Cuyama Valley to the southwest; to the northwest, around Huron, Wasco, and Famoso; and at Blackwell's Corner on the eastern edge of the Coast Range. East of Arvin, on the lower slope of Bear Mountain, is a 2400-acre vineyard, planted under set sprinklers in 1971, in which the vine rows are four and a half miles long.

Equally important are the new plantings on the west side of the valley. Much of the west side still is virtually desert, not badlands in the usual sense, but contaminated with minerals, including boron. In prehistoric times this was ocean floor. To this arid wasteland in the early 1970s, the man-made river called the California Aqueduct began delivering northern water, which in the next few decades is expected to leach out the minerals and create a quarter-million to a half-million new acres of fertile farms. Since the growing of cotton, once the king of valley crops, has become less profitable in recent years, owners of west-side land, who have already contracted to buy irrigation water, are beginning to plant wine grapes.

These are the areas of immense landholdings of farming corporations, oil companies, and conglomerates, and some of them are eligible to receive the water from the California Aqueduct. The 160-acre limitation on water to single owners does not apply uniformly there because the new aqueduct is primarily a state, not wholly a Federal, project. To these big landholders, a hundred acres of new vineyard is merely a test plot. When they decide to go ahead with wine-grape planting, a test plot can expand to a thousand or even to ten thousand acres.

This arouses fear among vineyardists elsewhere who for a few years have enjoyed rising prices for their grapes. They remember too well the disastrous grape and wine gluts of the past. At the height of the grape-planting spree in the valley, warnings are already being broadcast that the supply of grapes and wine may soon equal, then overrun the skyrocketing demand.

To consumers, who find their favorite wines in short supply and rising in price nowadays, it is reassuring to know of the massive new wine-grape plantings in the valley. There is no danger of permanent shortages or of sky-high wine prices in the long-range future while hundreds of thousands of acres are still available for planting with wine grapes here.

This assures quantity, which will keep wine prices within reason, but what about quality?

Quality will depend on which grapes the valley growers plant, on the progress of current viticultural and enological research, and on the expertise of the vintners. The grape varieties that are being planted in the valley are mainly those recommended by the University as producing good table wines and champagnes in Region IV and Region V climates. The principal grapes recommended are French Colombard, Emerald Riesling, Chenin Blanc, Barbera, and Ruby Cabernet. The University strongly advises the valley growers not to plant the scarce noble varieties, the Pinots, Chardonnay, White Riesling, and Cabernet Sauvignon, which produce fine wines in the cool coast counties, Regions I, II, and III.

In hot climates, according to the University, those grapes can produce only "inferior, or at best, ordinary" wines.

Some valley vineyardists, tempted by the $625 per ton offered in 1971 for the noble grapes by coast counties vintners, have nevertheless planted them in some Region IV and Region V localities. University viticulturists have denounced this, saying those varietal names should not be thus "debased."

That the San Joaquin Valley can produce better than everyday-quality table wines and champagnes is already evident in the contents of the bottles and jugs still available at moderate prices in stores throughout the nation. The lowest in price are almost entirely valley-grown wines. But the better wines I have tasted lately at some Region IV wineries, at the tiny Ficklin and Landis wineries in Region V, and at Fresno State University from Dr. Olmo's new red-wine hybrids for Region V, are evidence that the valley can produce superior, as well as merely good wines of those types.

20

Wines of Other Western States

WHEN Dr. Konstantin Frank introduced his New York State Johannisberg Riesling and Chardonnay wines in 1965, writers of articles in national magazines heralded the news as a sensation because to them this meant that California no longer was the only state that could grow the true Vinifera wine grapes of Europe.

What none of them seemed to notice was that Vinifera grapes, unheralded, had been grown for much of this century in Washington, Oregon, Arizona, Idaho, and Utah. The reason these other western states were ignored was that in all of those years they had never produced any fine wines of European types.

Since 1970, premium quality Vinifera "varietal" wines grown in Washington and Oregon have appeared on the wine market in California, and some connoisseurs suggest that they may someday rival California's finest wines. More than 2000 new acres of the best Vinifera grape varieties have been planted lately in eastern Washington and western Oregon in the hope that the suggestion will come true. Six new wineries have been opened in the Northwest to specialize in making Vinifera wines and there are plans to build more. There is a new winery in Idaho and a rush is on to plant more grapes there.

What has caused this is the nationwide wine boom, with the consequently spiraling prices of wine grapes in California and the stampede to plant new vineyards there.

• 2 •

The State of Washington ranks third in the nation in grape production, though its record harvest of 79,400 tons in 1971 is dwarfed by New York's 200,000 tons and by California's usual 3.5 million ton crop. Washington is eighth, however, after Ohio, in the quantity of wine it produces. Only about two million gallons are produced annually because only a tenth of Washington grapes in recent years have been used to make Washington wine. Nine tenths of the state's 18,000 acres of vineyards grow Concords that are mechanically harvested and either go into fresh grape juice or are shipped as juice to California wineries to make their Cold Ducks and "pop" or "mod" wines. Most of the 7000 acres of new vineyards planted since 1968 are Concords for the California wineries. University economists predict that Washington by 1980 will displace New York as the nation's second largest grape-producing state. Before the new plantings began, there were only about 500 acres of Vinifera, mainly of common varieties. But by 1972 Vinifera acreage in Washington exceeded 1200 acres, including mostly such premium grapes as Johannisberg Riesling, Cabernet Sauvignon, and Pinot Noir.

The first grapevines in Washington were planted in 1872 by a Confederate Civil War veteran named Lambert B. Evans on Stretch Island in the southern part of Puget Sound. To the island about 1890 came Adam Eckert from the Chautauqua Grape Belt of New York. Eckert sent to New York for more vines and later bred a black Labrusca grape variety he called the Island Belle. Plantings spread to neighboring islands and to the mainland, where a village was founded and named Grapeview.

Around 1906, irrigation water from the Cascade watershed began transforming the Yakima Valley in eastern Washington from an almost rainless desert into a lush fruit-growing region. The Island Belle grape was then brought there from the western part of the state. Grape juice plants were built at Yakima, Grandview, and Prosser, and the Island Belle soon was largely displaced by the Concord grape of the East.

There are no records of any wineries operating in Washington before 1933. The only reports of early wine production were of occasional seizures of bootleg wine during the 1920s.

At Repeal, realtor Charles Somers started on Stretch Island the St. Charles Winery, the first in the state. Almost overnight, everyone in Washington with so much as a berry patch wanted to build a winery; there were forty-two in operation, including three on Stretch Island, by 1937. Others started along the Columbia River, but the largest ones were at Seattle and in the Yakima Valley.

At Sunnyside, twenty miles down the valley from Yakima, lived a farmer, lawyer, and ex-school teacher named William B. Bridgman. Born on a farm beside Jordan Creek on the Niagara Peninsula of Ontario, where his father grew Labrusca grapes, Bridgman came to Sunnyside in 1902 aboard a horse-drawn stage when the valley's principal crop still was sagebrush. He promoted the local irrigation system, was elected mayor of Sunnyside, and became one of the area's principal grape growers. At Repeal, Bridgman built a winery, but he also took time to make a study of California and European vineyards. He concluded that the Yakima Valley climate is better for winegrowing than that of central France, having more days of sunshine, and noted that its latitude (46 degrees north) is midway between the latitudes of Burgundy and Bordeaux. This convinced Bridgman that Washington could grow finer European grapes than California could. He imported many Vinifera varieties and supplied neighboring growers with cuttings from his vines. He hired a German winemaker and produced such wines as Johannisberg Riesling and Cabernet. Unfortunately, however—and I recall this because I tasted an assortment that the late Herman Wente brought from Washington during the 1940s—Bridgman's wines were poorly made, and they soon were withdrawn from sale.

Another unfortunate development was the Washington liquor control law, adopted at Repeal, which established state monopoly liquor stores, thus discouraging most people from buying table wines. Washington wineries were allowed to sell directly to taverns, which gave them an advantage over the out-of-state wineries. Prospering under their legal umbrella, the Washington vintners were content to make ordinary dessert wines such as port and sherry, mainly out of Labrusca grapes. In 1965, however, the Washington wineries saw that their protective law was about to be changed, and they persuaded the State University to start a wine research program at its Prosser Station.

In 1966, I visited the Yakima Valley and saw several vineyards of such pedigreed varieties as Cabernet Sauvignon and Pinot Noir. I was amazed to find the wineries were wasting these costly grapes, mixing them with Concord in nondescript port and burgundy blends. The only fine Vinifera wine I tasted on that trip was a Grenache rosé made by a home winemaker in Seattle. I remarked to Victor Allison, the manager of the American Wine Growers wineries, that perhaps Washington vintners might make some good Vinifera wines if they would bring someone from California to show them how. Allison asked me: "Such as who?" I mentioned a few good winemakers, including André Tchelistcheff, the great enologist of Beaulieu.

Allison persuaded Tchelistcheff to come to Washington in 1967 to discuss the state's winemaking potential. Tchelistcheff tasted most of the Washington table wines and rejected them all. But then a friend of the Seattle home winemaker whom I've mentioned let him sample a Gewürztraminer made from grapes grown in the Yakima Valley. Tchelistcheff was astounded; he pronounced it the finest Gewürztraminer yet produced in the United States. He accepted the challenge to show Washington vintners how to make fine wines.

Tchelistcheff first directed that the Vinifera vines in the American Wine Growers' vineyards be immediately pruned to reduce the crop and to achieve proper sugar-acid balance in the grapes. He returned to Washington that September, selected perfect batches of Cabernet Sauvignon, Pinot Noir, Sémillon, and Grenache, and had them fermented at controlled temperatures. He had the Cabernet stored in American white oak barrels and the Pinot Noir in new Limousin oak from France.

In 1969, I accompanied Tchelistcheff to Seattle to sample his one- and two-year-old Washington wines. We tasted separately, scoring them as unfinished wines, and then compared our notes. Tchelistcheff gave the 1967 Cabernet seventeen out of a possible twenty points, sixteen to the 1968 Sémillon, and fifteen and sixteen to the two Grenache rosés. The Pinot Noir wasn't yet ready to be tasted. I scored each Cabernet a point higher and my other scores were close to Tchelistcheff's.

A year later these wines were bottled under the American Wine Growers' Ste. Michelle label and were introduced to California. They were rated by the San Francisco Sampling Club as "challenging the quality supremacy of California varietal wines." I have since sampled the 1969 Cabernet and Sémillon from a commercial shipment and found them equal to many premium-priced California and European wines, except for a hint of oxidation in the Sémillon, apparently the fault of a loose cork.

In 1968, when Philip Wagner of Boordy Vineyard in Maryland joined the Seneca Foods Corporation as wine consultant, he flew to the Yakima Valley, where there is a big Seneca fruit-processing plant in Prosser, to survey the possibility of making wine there. When Wagner saw the Vinifera grapes growing in Washington, he brought samples of their frozen juice back to Seneca's winery in New York State and had them made into wine. The result convinced Seneca that it should turn part of its plant at Prosser into a 200,000-gallon winery. In 1972, Seneca's Prosser winery began turning out blends of Vinifera and French hybrids labeled "Boordy Vineyards 1971 Yakima Valley" Red, White, and Rosé. L. Jerome Wolcott, Jr., in charge of the winery, says "the Yakima Valley has the potential of producing some of the finest wines in the world." He plans to introduce such Washington State Boordy Vineyards "varietals" as Chardonnay, Pinot Noir, and Cabernet Sauvignon when those wines have been sufficiently aged in wood.

• 3 •

The gently-rolling Yakima Valley is situated east of the lofty

Cascades in southeastern Washington. It follows the Yakima River southeastward for some 120 miles past Ellensburg and past the fruit-growing center of Yakima, to where the Yakima joins the Columbia near Kennewick. The valley's width is about twenty miles from the Rattlesnake Hills on the north to the Horse Heaven Hills on the south, named for the bands of wild horses that roamed there in Indian days. To the northeast is the Atomic Energy Commission's vast Hanford plutonium project reservation. Most of the 15,000 acres of vineyards there—about nine tenths of the state's total grape acreage—are concentrated in the lower valley between Wapato, Sunnyside, Grandview, Prosser, and Benton City.

That part of Washington is semi-arid; rainfall ranges from six to seven and a half inches per year, but water for irrigation is plentiful. Bridgman was right about its sunshine, which provides 160 to 210 frost-free days per year. Moreover, days are longer in the northern latitude, and sunlight is least intense at the beginning and end of the growing season. By the California system of classifying climates, the lower Yakima Valley, averaging 2437 degree-days of heat units, is either Region I or low Region II. Horticulturist Walter J. Clore at the Prosser Station says "Washington is better suited for grape growing than New York State; we have milder winters, better soil, ample water, and more sun."

The Yakima's defect is low winter temperatures, which drop to seven degrees below zero in one year out of three and to twelve to twenty below in one year out of six. Cold-tender Vinifera vines such as Muscat are buried with earth after each Thanksgiving to protect them during the winter, then are uncovered in March when the soil becomes warm again. But the top Vinifera varieties at the Prosser Station have survived minus-eleven-degree temperatures without covering and have borne either partial or full crops.

Vinifera vines in the valley are grown on their own roots instead of grafting them to phylloxera-resistant rootstocks as is done in most of California and in Europe. Some of the yields at Prosser are impressive, ranging from 3.8 tons per acre for Chardonnay to 12.5 tons for Melon and 20 tons for the Foch hybrid, yet with acidity and sugar content that requires no amelioration with sugar and water.

On Hinzerland Road, five miles north of Prosser, two dozen Seattle families planted in 1972 a twenty-five-acre vineyard of Chardonnay, White Riesling, Chenin Blanc, and Cabernet Sauvignon. They are headed by school administrator Jerry Wallace and his son Mike, who is studying viticulture and enology at the UC Davis wine school. The Wallaces and their fellow stockholders plan to build the Hinzerland Vineyard winery and to be producing wine by 1977.

Nor is the valley the only part of Washington's Inland Empire that can grow Vinifera. In 1969, Vere Brummund of the Prosser Station staff, with several other investors including three in California, formed the Veredon Vineyards and planted 155 acres of thirteen Vinifera varieties on the north shore of the Columbia River across from Umatilla, Oregon. Bidders for their first small crop in 1972 included two Washington wineries and one in nearby British Columbia that now buys most of its grapes from California. The Veredon group plan soon to enlarge the vineyard to 800 acres and to have their own winery in another year.

There are at least 50,000 more acres that could grow wine grapes in the Columbia Basin, such as the Wahluke Slope, to which the Grand Coulee Dam brought irrigation water in 1968. Some say eastern Washington has space for as much as 250,000 more acres of vines. Thousands of acres of Concords and some Vinifera are being planted in the lower Snake River Valley near Pasco, and one owner there says that by 1974 he will have the largest Concord vineyard in the world. There also are trial plantings of vines in Washington's north-central apple-growing counties. But in the Puget Sound area, where the Washington grape industry began in 1872, only about 100 acres are left. Farmers along the Sound have mostly given up growing the Island Belle grape because heavy rainfall there results in erratic crops.

• 4 •

Of the eight commercial vintners in Washington, the biggest is American Wine Growers, with 2 million gallons capacity between its wineries at Seattle and Grandview in the Yakima Valley. American is a merger of the Pommerelle, National, and Italian wineries, all of which started soon after Repeal. Its six vineyards around Grandview have patches of Vinifera, principally Muscat of Alexandria. Ten acres of Grenache were planted in 1950 to improve the firm's burgundy, and several rows of Pinot Noir and Sémillon were added five years later. Some of the best Washington wines in past years have come from this company. Its best lower-priced table wines have been its Pommerelle Grenache Rosé, its burgundy, made partly of Vinifera, and a Labrusca sauterne made of Delaware and Diamond. American Wine Growers' Ste. Michelle Vinifera "varietals" are now sold in eighteen states.

The Santa Rosa Winery, which Bridgman built on Snipes Mountain at Sunnyside, is a fourth the size of American. Bridgman kept active in its management until a year before his death in 1968 at the age of ninety-one. The winery and the vineyard have had new owners since then.

A third winery in the valley is Alhambra, which is at Selah, north of Yakima. Its vineyard, forty miles down the valley at Grandview, consists of Concord, White Diamond, Island Belle, some French hybrids, and Pinot Noir. The company was founded by banker Otis Harlan at Seattle in 1935, was moved to Selah two years later, and the vineyard was purchased after the Second World War. When the St. Charles Winery closed down in 1965, Harlan bought its trademark and has kept Washington supplied with its specialties—17 percent dessert wines made without adding brandy but by the syruped fermentation method used in Ontario. Most interesting of the St. Charles wines is a red appetizer type called Caliante. It tastes like a dry port, and though made from Labrusca grapes, it has no foxy flavor.

The original St. Charles vineyard on Stretch Island is still maintained by Charles Somers's son, Bill, but he now sells the Island Belle crop on a "U-pick" basis to people who drive up from Tacoma, thirty miles away. He has transformed the winery into a maritime museum, displaying his hobby collection of old coastal steamboat days, an exhibit well worth crossing the bridge from the mainland to see.

Only one winery remains in operation of the seven that started along the Sound in the 1930s. It is Werberger's, an old-fashioned cellar of 80,000 gallons in a scenic seven-acre vineyard a mile south of the Hartstene ferry landing on Pickering Passage. The late Rudolph Werberger, a coal miner from the Sudetenland, set out the vines in 1918 with Island Belle cuttings he got from Adam Eckert. For many years, Werberger's was the only Washington winery open to the visiting public, and its wines could even be tasted when the cellarman wasn't too busy. When the law was changed in 1969, however, it specifically permitted Washington wineries to hold wine tastings and to sell wines on their premises. When I was last there, Werberger's son Bill had increased the winery's output by buying grapes from eastern Washington.

· 5 ·

The home winemaker in Seattle who made the Grenache rosé that I tasted in 1966 is Dr. Lloyd Woodburne, professor of psychology at the University of Washington in Seattle. In 1951, while at home recovering from a cold, Professor Woodburne happened to pick up a copy of Philip Wagner's first book on home winemaking. Intrigued, Woodburne telephoned his famous wine-buff colleague, Angelo Pellegrini, a professor of English, and asked, "Pelly, how difficult is this winemaking thing?"

"Easy as boiling an egg," replied Pellegrini, who makes red

wine from the Cabernet grapes he gets from his friends at the Louis Martini vineyard in California.

Woodburne bought grapes and a barrel and made a batch of Zinfandel. He and his wife managed to drink it, liberally diluted with soda water. Three years later, he bought Delaware grapes in the Yakima Valley, made white wine, and invited some of his fellow professors over to sample it. They, too, began buying grapes and became home winemakers. Soon a total of eighteen families around the campus were doing the same. Someone thought of buying a power crusher, which was installed in the Woodburnes' garage. But a lawyer member, Professor of Law Cornelius Peck, warned them not to ferment their grapes together because the Federal law permits only individual householders to make wine in their homes.

Another member, Professor Philip Church, made a study of Washington's climates and found that heat units in the lower Yakima Valley are the same as in Beaune, the center of Burgundy's Côte d'Or. In 1961, ten of the group formed a corporation, Professor Peck supplying the knowhow, and bought five acres adjoining Bridgman's vineyard at Sunnyside. They planted seven Vinifera varieties from UC Davis and added Pinot Noir vines from the American Wine Growers' vineyard. Each member was entitled to a tenth share of the grapes.

When I tasted Woodburne's rosé in 1966 and found it outstanding, I suggested that his group ought to start their own winery. A year later, with Tchelistcheff's praise of their Gewürztraminer (which came from Dr. Church's cellar), the professors took the plunge. They built a small cellar in the Seattle suburb of Kirkland and moved the crusher from the Woodburnes' garage in time for the 1967 vintage. In the following May, as the "Associated Vintners," they introduced the 1967 Riesling and Gewürztraminer in three Seattle gourmet food shops and in the new Mirabeau Restaurant. Connoisseurs heard about it and came from a hundred miles away to buy the wines. By August, all their wines were sold; there were advance orders for the reds, still aging, and for the '68 and '69 vintages as well. Four years later, with the demand for their wines still increasing, they planted twenty more acres at Sunnyside with Cabernet, Pinot Noir, Riesling, Gewürztraminer, Sémillon, and Chardonnay.

· 6 ·

In Oregon, as in Washington, Vinifera and Labrusca grapes have long flourished side by side. Also, as in eastern Washington, the planting of Vinifera grapes for wine has multiplied since the late 1960s, though on a smaller scale, from a few acres to a few hundred by 1972. Counting the new plantings, Oregon still has less than 500 acres of vines, but the proprietors of the five small new wineries that have organized the Oregon Winegrowers Association expect this to more than treble in the next few years.

The "father of the Oregon fine wine industry" is Richard Sommer, whose 15,000-gallon Hillcrest Vineyard winery ten miles northwest of Roseburg in Douglas County makes such good White Riesling that it is featured in gourmet shops and restaurants in Portland and is even sold in California.

When Sommer was studying agronomy at the University of California in Davis, he took an introductory course in viticulture taught by Professor Maynard Amerine. For six years after leaving college, Sommer worked at odd jobs, served a hitch in the army in Korea, then spent another year at the University, uncertain of what he wanted to do. Finally he made up his mind to grow grapes. Remembering what Dr. Amerine had taught, that the finest wine grapes in California are grown in the cooler vineyard districts, Sommer went where it is still cooler, to Oregon. An uncle of his lived in the Rogue River Valley and grew Vinifera table grapes, but Sommer found that locality still too warm. He went farther north, testing the grapes in each locality. At Roseburg in the Umpqua River Valley he found some Zinfandels in the eighty-year-old Doerner's Winery vineyard that tested right. In 1961 he bought a hillside farm on Elgarose Road, planted vines from the Napa Valley, and bonded his winery two years later. His wines at first were not very good because his methods and cellar equipment were faulty, but one of his White Rieslings that I tasted recently was sound and well balanced with the true Riesling aroma, evidence that the Umpqua Valley can produce fine white wine.

In the same year that Sommer bonded his winery, another Californian named Charles Coury, a climatology graduate of UC at Los Angeles, quit his job selling European wines and enrolled at Davis to learn scientific winegrowing. On winning his master's degree, Coury spent a year in France studying how wine is grown in cool climates. Then, unaware that Sommer had preceded him, Coury, too, chose Oregon as the place to grow great wines. "Roseburg is fine, but too warm for the very greatest whites, which I wanted to grow," Coury says. The locality he chose was the Tualatin Valley, an offshoot of the Willamette thirty miles west of Portland. In 1966 he moved with his wife and two teen-age sons into a century-old farmhouse on David Hill Road, three miles northwest of Forest Grove, began planting his vineyard and building his winery. In 1972 he began selling the first Charles Coury Vineyards Riesling, Gewürztraminer, and Pinot Noir.

On a rainy January day in 1962, David Lett, a new graduate of the University of Utah, was in San Francisco waiting to start training for a career in dentistry. Having nothing else to do, he visited wineries in the Napa Valley and discovered that winegrowing appealed to him more than dentistry. He enrolled for a two-year course in viticulture at Davis, spent nine months visiting the wine countries of Europe, and decided to plant in Oregon. The locality he chose was the hills between Dundee and McMinnville in Yamhill County, overlooking the Willamette Valley. He planted his Eyrie Vineyard in 1967, bonded his winery three years later, and sold his first "Oregon Spring Wine," a young Pinot Noir, in 1972.

The fourth new Oregon winegrower, Richard Erath, is another emigré from California. On a vacation trip through Oregon in 1967, he bought some of Richard Sommer's grapes, took them home, and made them into wine. Erath, an electronic engineer, then moved to Beaverton, Oregon, and bought fifty acres in the foothills of the Chehalem Mountains, eight miles north of Newberg. In 1969, when his vineyard was three years old, he bonded his Erath Vineyards Winery.

Vine fever spread in Oregon after 1968, when the state Economic Development Commission came out with a study painting "a dramatic potential" for quality wine grapes in the state. In that year school teacher Paul Bjelland started the Bjelland Vineyard winery southeast of Roseburg and organized the Oregon Winegrowers Association. Two years later he founded the first Oregon Wine Festival.

Coury has now started a nursery of new heat-treated vines from California and can scarcely fill the orders coming from excited Oregon farmers. There are new plantings in the Rogue River Valley and in the Medford-Grants Pass district, and there are reports of vineyards being planned in the Columbia Basin of northeastern Oregon. Dick Erath is developing a 125-acre vineyard near Newberg for a lumber company executive who plans to build a winery and to produce the first Oregon champagne.

Oregon has a longer history of winegrowing than Washington. Among the settlers who came to the territory in wagon trains over the Oregon Trail in the middle of the last century were some who brought vine cuttings and began raising grapes in the Willamette Valley south of Portland. Farmers at Ashland in southwestern Oregon grew Vinifera table grapes and were shipping Flame Tokays to market before the Tokay industry developed at Lodi in California. In 1880, when the special national census of winegrowing was taken, Jackson County was listed as producing 15,000 gallons of wine and two Willamette Valley counties, Clackamas and Marion, reported producing 1900 gallons. Concords were grown as far northeast as Umatilla County in the Columbia Basin.

The knoll on which Charles Coury planted his vineyard is known to his neighbors as Wine Hill because it was the site of a pre-Prohibition winery. Ernest Reuter, who came from Germany in the 1880s, made a wine there he called Klevner, one of the German names for Chardonnay. Reuter's daughter told Coury that her father's wine was awarded a silver medal at the 1904 St. Louis Exposition. Old residents recall how people would drive to Wine Hill in their buggies from Forest Grove on Sunday afternoons. When they got tipsy, their horses would find the way home, one of the advantages of the era before automobiles. Adolph Doerner built his winery at Roseburg in 1890 and made wines of both Vinifera and Labrusca grapes. Louis Herboldt grew sixty-five grape varieties at his Sweet Home Vineyard near Hillsboro, west of Portland. I remember visiting the Herboldt vineyard during the early 1940s and tasting its Zinfandel grapes. They tasted even fresher than most of the Zinfandels I have tasted in California.

Around the turn of the century Professor Frederic T. Bioletti, the California expert on viticulture, suggested that several Oregon localities seemed climatically suited for Vinifera grape varieties. But Oregon agricultural authorities were not impressed with the idea of developing the state's wine industry. With the Prohibitionist crusade then at fever pitch, they recommended grapegrowing for home gardens, not as a commercial enterprise. In fact, as late as 1965, when Sommer's vineyard had already produced its second crop of White Riesling, a circular published by Oregon State University concluded that "the American grapes, *Vitis labrusca*, are more suited (than Vinifera) to Oregon climates."

There were dozens of old farmer wineries in Oregon when Prohibition began in 1920, and the dry law did not put them completely out of business. At Repeal in 1933, the legislature made them legal by establishing a farmer's winery license of $25 per year for anyone making only light wine from fruit of his own production. From twenty-eight such small producers, selling their wines at retail, in 1937, the number dwindled, because few of their sons were interested in winemaking, until only two were left in 1972. One is Henry's Winery overlooking the Clackamas River at Oregon City, fourteen miles west of Portland. Henry is Henry Endres, Jr., whose father bonded the place in 1936. In addition to a light red Labrusca wine, he makes others of apples, berries, and rhubarb, including a loganberry type he calls "Henry's Lowball." Endres's vineyard is four acres of Concord, Worden, and Campbell's Early, all Labrusca varieties. He thinks this part of the Willamette Valley is better for berries and apples than for grapes.

The other old producer in Oregon is the 5000-gallon Redwood Winery, with an acre of Concord vines beside a rambling white farmhouse in the Portland suburb of Oak Grove. The proprietor is Dora Broetje, a pixyish spinster who hands you a glass of sweet rosé and invites you to identify the grape variety. When you fail, she shows you the bottle label, which reads "Rosé Rhubarb Wine." Miss Broetje's grandfather came to Oregon in 1883 from Belleville, Illinois, where at that time there were many Concord vineyards. He brought cuttings from Illinois and made Concord wine for two decades, being succeeded by Miss Broetje's father. When Broetje, Jr., died in 1943 his daughter took over, and she has done all the winemaking since. She had me taste a thirteen-year-old wine made of Concord. It had lost its red color and foxy taste and was surprisingly pleasant, somewhat resembling a montilla from Spain.

There are two new farmer wineries in Oregon that make their wines of berries rather than of grapes. One is on Loretta Bender's forty-acre Pioneer Homestead Ranch at Sandy near Mount Hood, where berries grow better than grapes. Mrs. Bender, who also drives the local school bus, bonded the winery in 1968 to make wine of her dozen acres of raspberries. The other is Ronald and Marjorie Vuylsteke's Oak Knoll Winery near Hillsboro, opened in 1970 in a converted dairy barn. Their main product is wine made of their surplus blackberry crop.

The biggest winery in Oregon is the 350,000-gallon Honeywood cellar at Salem, started in 1934 to make berry and currant wines. The boss of Honeywood is a Salem housewife named Mary J. Reinke, whose husband is the battalion chief of the local fire department. When she became bookkeeper for Honeywood's founder, John Wood, in 1943, he was aging his berry wines a year before sale. Taught by her Italian mother that fruit wines, like jams and jellies, are best served fresh, she persuaded Wood to begin selling the wines young, and his business improved. When Wood died in 1955, she became president of the winery. The Women's Liberation movement would approve of Mrs. Reinke, for half of her eight employees are women. Besides the berry and currant wines and a flavored berry wine she calls Turkenblut, Honeywood makes Mizpah kosher wine under the supervision of a Portland rabbi.

Can the Pacific Northwest states someday compete with California in high-quality Vinifera wines? The answer cannot be known for several years. The theory that attracted Sommer, Coury, and Lett to Oregon is that the noble grape varieties achieve their highest flavors when they have to struggle to get ripe, which purports to explain the classic wines grown in the miserable climates of the top European districts. A new study by UC Davis viticulturists supports the theory. Professors Mark Kliewer and Lloyd Lider found that temperatures lower than those prevailing in most California wine districts produce higher acidity and better color in grapes, but still enough sugar content to make good wines. Another finding in their work, which relates to the cloudy and often rainy weather in western Oregon and in some of California's coastal counties, is that low daylight intensity slows the ripening of grapes. This confirms what Professor Albert Winkler at Davis has taught for many years and stated in his textbook, *General Viticulture*: "Moderately cool weather, under which ripening proceeds slowly, is favorable for the production of dry table wines of quality."

• 7 •

Grape fever has spread from Washington and Oregon into neighboring Idaho, and the Gem State already has a winery, opened in 1971.

Idaho had wineries long before Prohibition. At the 1898 Chicago World's Fair a prize was awarded to the wine of Robert Schleisler, whose vineyard was in the Clearwater River Valley near Lewiston. J. E. Moore operated the Shaeffer Vineyards winery near Ahsahka in the early 1900s. After Repeal, Gregory Eaves had his winery near Juliaetta for several years. The chief grapes grown commercially in Idaho are Concords. Vinifera varieties are popular in home gardens, though they are injured in occasional twenty-below-zero winters.

In 1969 it appeared that table wine might be freed from the Idaho state monopoly liquor stores and allowed to be sold in food outlets. That was when grape-planting in earnest began. (The legislature voted the change in 1971.) The new plantings are still mostly Concords, but include some commercial plantings of Chardonnay, White Riesling, Aligoté, Cabernet Sauvignon, several French hybrids, and Pinot Noir.

The sole winery, named Idaho Wine and Grape Growers, was established by Peter Cook, R. Bruce Higgins, and Robert Fergason in a former food market on the main street of Troy, near the university town of Moscow in north-central Idaho. Higgins and Fergason are university staff members who recently made a feasibility study of winegrowing in the state. Their first commercial wines were made in 1971 of the Chelois hybrid grown in the Boise Valley, where most of the vineyards are, and of Zinfandel from the Yakima Valley of Washington. In October of the following

year a festival of wine and the arts was held in Troy with partici-
pation from the University of Idaho and from nearby Washington
State University.

· 8 ·

Arizona, too, grows Vinifera and is seventh among the states in
annual grape production, but its usual 14,000-ton crop from some
4500 acres consists almost entirely of table varieties such as
Thompson Seedless and Cardinal. The main vineyards are west
of Phoenix in Maricopa County, in the Salt River Valley to the
east, and in southeastern Yuma County, which borders California
and Mexico. The purpose of growing grapes in these irrigated
desert areas is that they ripen early and reach the eastern fresh
fruit markets ahead of those from the Arvin and Delano districts
of California. Arizona has no wineries. The so-called Arizona
Winery was established at Glendale in 1959 to distill leftover
grapes into wine spirits, which found their way into other states'
dessert wine production. It did not operate after 1966.

However, there are indications that Arizona will become a
winegrowing state in the future. It may already be happening,
because I hear at this writing of substantial recent shipments of
vines from California to Arizona buyers, all of top-rated premium
varieties. Philo Biane of Brookside Vineyards in California helped
make experimental plantings of wine grapes in two Arizona
counties in 1959, and he predicts that the state will develop a wine
industry within the next several years. One small wine-grape
vineyard now borders the highway between Tucson and Nogales.
During the 1960s other California vintners, notably the Gallos of
Modesto, surveyed plateau areas in Cochise County, which
borders New Mexico, and reported finding locations there climatically suited for both Labrusca and Vinifera grape varieties.

· 9 ·

New Mexico produced wine long before California did. When
the Rio Grande Valley was colonized by Spaniards early in the
seventeenth century, grapes were cultivated at the first Franciscan
missions to make wines for the Mass. The grapes apparently were
the same Mission variety that the Franciscans brought to California from Mexico more than a century later.

General Stephen Kearny reported finding viticulture well established in the Rio Grande Valley when he took possession of New
Mexico in 1846 to proclaim it a territory of the United States. W.
H. Davis in his book, El Gringo, published in 1857, described the
claret of Bernalillo as "better than that imported from France"

and added that "if there was a convenient market to induce an extensive cultivation of the grape . . . wine would become one of the staples of the country, which would be able to supply a large part of the demand in the United States instead of importing it from Europe." The census taken in 1880 listed New Mexico as fifth in the nation in wine production, making 908,500 gallons from 3150 acres of vineyards, almost double the figures shown in that year for New York State.

But the 1880 figure seems incredible to anyone who views the minuscule winegrowing industry of New Mexico today—eight little roadside wineries selling inexpensive table wines in gallon jugs. Louis Gross of Albuquerque has a 12,000-gallon cellar and a fifteen-acre vineyard at Bernalillo, and the rest of the state's wineries are smaller than his. Gross's father came from France in 1895 and made wine at Bernalillo until Prohibition. The son replanted the vineyard in 1939 and grows Black Malvoisie, Zinfandel, and some Pinot Noir. Two more wineries are at Albuquerque, two are farther up the river at Corrales and Algodones, and the rest are clustered two hundred miles south around Doña Ana, Las Cruces, and Mesilla. Wine production in New Mexico has not exceeded 15,000 gallons since the 1950s, and some of it has been made of California grapes.

New interest in winegrowing in New Mexico has developed since the nationwide table wine boom began, and Vinifera vines grow readily in the state, says New Mexico University Professor of Horticulture Darrell Sullivan. He has tested many Vinifera varieties on the experimental farm near Las Cruces, but says that low winter temperatures make it necessary to cover the vines with soil each fall. Others, such as Donald Burnham of the Tucumcari field station and hobbyist winegrower L. E. Tatreault of the University's physical science laboratory, say that New Mexico may have been growing the wrong grapes, that perhaps varieties more resistant to cold, including the French hybrids and native American grapes, should be introduced.

· 10 ·

Utah, land of the Prohibitionist Mormons, grows wine grapes as well as Labrusca varieties and has a winegrowing history that is unknown to most members of that Church. Many farmers in northern Utah grow Concords for home use and for sale. But in the Virgin River Valley of southwestern Utah, called "Dixie" for its warm summers and mild winters, there are many small vineyards of Vinifera varieties, such as Missions and Thompson Seedless, and an old three-story stone winery at Toquerville in

Washington County in which the Mormons once produced wine.

J. Walter Fleming of Lodi found the winery by chance while touring the valley some years ago. Inside he found casks and an ancient wine press that showed evidence of generations of use. Local residents told him that wine for Communion had been made there from the 1860s until about 1910. On a later visit, Fleming found the building converted to a granary; all the traces of wine-making were gone.

Knowing that devout Latter-day Saints are teetotalers and are forbidden even coffee and tea, I wrote to the Mormon church historian in Salt Lake City for further information. By return mail came explanatory excerpts from *The Doctrine and Covenants*, which contains the revelations given to Prophet Joseph Smith, the founder of Mormonism; and a mass of historical details about past winemaking in southern Utah. The Saints there made wine not only for the Holy Sacrament, but for medicine, celebrations, and for sale to the Gentiles.

The original Mormons regularly used wine—"yea, pure wine of the grape"—at their services when the Church was organized in 1830 at Fayette, New York, for the Book of Mormon is winier than the Bible. The Saints then became persecuted for their polygamous ways, and were driven from New York to Ohio, then to Missouri and Illinois. One day, Prophet Smith was on his way to buy some wine for a religious service, when he was met by a heavenly messenger. "It mattereth not what ye shall eat or what ye shall drink when ye partake of the Sacrament," the messenger told him, according to *The Doctrine and Covenants*. On this revelation, the Mormons now base their use of water instead of wine for Communion. But in so doing, they ignore the rest of the revelation, for the heavenly messenger continued: "A commandment I give unto you, that you shall not purchase wine neither strong drink of your enemies; wherefore, you shall partake of none except it is made new among you." This clearly permits Mormons to use homemade wine, provided it is new. Their Church, however, construes "new" as permitting only unfermented juice.

This was not the view of President Brigham Young, the genius who led the Mormons to Utah in 1847 following the murder of Smith and his brother Hyrum in Missouri. Brigham Young during the 1850s sent Mormon colonies from Salt Lake to southern Utah expressly to plant cotton fields, sugar-cane plantations, and vineyards. He directed them to build wine cellars and to make as much wine as they could. He named an experienced winemaker from Germany, John Naegle, to take charge of the wine industry. Mission grape cuttings, a wine press, and a brandy distillery were brought from California. Brigham Young gave specific instructions for winemaking: "First, by lightly pressing, make white wine. Then give a heavier pressing and make colored wine." He ordered that the wine be "properly graded in quality . . . then stored in oak barrels as far as possible."

He permitted the wine to be drunk for Communion, but he guarded the Saints' sobriety. This he did by ordering special drinking vessels to be made for the Sacrament—"tumblers that will hold a swallow and no more."

"If my counsel is taken," Brigham Young added, "this wine will not be drunk here but will be exported." His counsel wasn't taken. The Dixie Mormons drank the wine at their social functions and used it as an article of trade. They also paid their tithes to the Church in wine, though not of their best, which they reserved for themselves. The Tithing Office at St. George finally decreed that tithes must be paid in other produce or in cash.

Winegrowing in southern Utah reached its peak at the turn of the century, then declined because by then the Church frowned on the Mormons' drinking and because their wines couldn't compete with the better article coming from California.

Not only do wine grapes still grow in "Dixie," but an effort recently was made to revive the local winegrowing industry, apparently inspired by the national boom in table wine consumption and by the promise of irrigation from the Virgin River. Beginning in 1963, Utah State University made test plantings of thirty Vinifera varieties—including such premium wine grapes as White Riesling, Gewürztraminer, Chenin Blanc, and Pinot Noir—on the Clifford Reusch farm in Washington County. University Extension Agent Don Huber, stationed there, says the results were so promising that three farmers have planted new commercial vineyards of Thompsons. There has been talk of building a winery there, but the project has not progressed.

· 11 ·

The farthest western state, Alaska, has its first winery. Father Emet R. Engel, a septuagenarian Catholic priest, and his brother George bonded the Casa de San José Winery near Palmer in south-central Alaska in 1972.

Their product is milk wine, an opaque whitish drink fermented from powdered skim milk and cane sugar to an alcoholic content of 11 percent. "We are reviving a family tradition," says Father Engel. "Milk wine saved the lives of our ancestors in Bohemia from the Black Plague in 1383 and 1665."

21

The Kosher Winemakers

THE single best-known North American wine, sold halfway around the world and never duplicated elsewhere, is the syrupy-sweet red Concord grape type with the Hebrew word kosher on its label.

Nine tenths of its consumers have no clear idea of what kosher means, not being members of the Jewish faith, but they happen to like the wine's taste. To them, kosher—the Hebrew religious word for proper, fit, or clean—suggests that a wine or food has a pronounced flavor, as in pickles, sausages, and in the "especially sweetened" purplish-red wine with the piquant, grapy Concord taste. Though nowadays there are dozens of wines of different flavors and colors labeled kosher, the one you will find in stores throughout the United States and in hotels as distant as Japan and Australia is Manischewitz Concord Grape in the square bottle with the six-pointed Star of David on its label. It is the one that made kosher a part of the flavor-language of wine.

Dozens of wineries in this country and Canada now produce the kosher Concord type, but to call it kosher they must make it under the strict supervision of an orthodox rabbi, from the picking of the grapes to the bottling of the wine. Each such winery must use separate crushers, tanks, and bottling machinery for the wine in order for the label to bear the rabbi's *hechsher* seal.

Oddly enough, the sweet red Concord kosher type became the best-known American wine purely by happenstance. At Repeal, young Leo Star, the son of a cantor from Russian Poland, bought a few wine tanks, rented a store with a double cellar on Wooster Street in New York City, ambitiously named it the Monarch Wine Company, and began bottling bulk port and sherry from California. Leo Star had bottled kosher port and sherry during the dry years, when anybody could buy it legally by merely joining a Hebrew congregation; but that business had died together with the Eighteenth Amendment.

As a sideline after Repeal, Star also bottled a small quantity of a kosher New York State extra-sweet Concord wine called Mount Zebo, which he also had sold during Prohibition. Its only buyers, when the dry era ended, were New York orthodox Jewish families who were accustomed to using it once a year as an essential part of their Passover feast, or *Seder*, in spring.

When the Passover season of 1934 came to an end, those New York store proprietors who had stocked Mount Zebo for their customers found they had quantities of it left unsold. They told Star to take it all back because they could not sell it again until the following spring. Star took it back, and most of it spoiled. Before the 1935 Passover season, Star notified the store owners that they should order only as much Mount Zebo as they could sell—that he would accept no more returns. Again after Passover, they had leftover stock and wanted Star to take it back. He refused and waited for complaints.

To Star's amazement, instead of complaints, the stores sent him rush reorders. Their non-Jewish customers were trying the kosher wine, finding they liked the sweet Concord taste, and were coming back for more.

Star had launched the kosher wine industry, but he did not know it yet. When more reorders came, he thought the wine sold because it was kosher, so he contracted with the old firm of Manischewitz, famed for its kosher food products such as matzos, to let him use the Manischewitz name on his wine. When his "Man Oh Manischewitz What a Wine" radio commericals went on the air in 1945, he knew that the kosher wine type ("that Massachusetts wine" to many of its buyers) was here to stay.

It was also a happenstance that gave Star's biggest competitor its start. In Chicago on September 23, 1947, at 5:17 P.M., Max Cohen and Henry Marcus, owners of the Wine Corporation of America, sadly opened the drain cocks of their wine tanks and let all 40,000 gallons of their Barloma California port and sherry flow down the drain because something had gone wrong with the wine. The only stock they had left was a small quantity of their kosher sweet red Concord wine called Mogen David (Shield of David), leftover from the preceding Passover season. Until more port and sherry could arrive from California, they began promoting the sale of Mogen David to the nonJewish trade as "the wine like Grandma used to make." It soon so far outsold their Barloma wines that the company became the Mogen David Wine Corporation.

Other vintners saw the sensational sales successes of Manischewitz and Mogen David and rushed into production with their own sweet Concord wines. Gallo in California introduced one called Galloette, backed by a huge billboard advertising campaign. The big Welch company jumped into the market with its Concord Refreshment Wine. But Gallo and Welch both had ignored a key element in the semantics of thirst, that a wine's label influences its taste. Without Hebrew names and characters and the word kosher, their sweet Concord wines didn't taste the same, and they failed to sell. Other wineries in California, New York, New Jersey, Michigan, the State of Washington, and in Canada saw the light, employed local orthodox rabbis to make their Concord wines kosher, and designed labels liberally adorned with Hebrew characters and stars. Kosher wines with such names as Mazel Tov, Sholom, Mizpah, Maccabee, and Hadassim became a permanent part of their trade.

However, there seems to be a limit on how much specially sweetened red kosher Concord wine people can drink. Sales in the United States rose to ten million gallons in the 1960s but have grown relatively little since. Manischewitz and Mogen David realized that their customers' tastes were turning from sweet toward dry. They began turning out semidry and dry white and pink kosher wines, and started making kosher burgundies, sauternes, rosés, and champagnes. Manischewitz then expanded with a line of nonkosher Colonial Heritage New York State wines and began importing European Tytell wines. In 1970, the Mogen David Corporation was purchased by the Coca-Cola Bottling Company of New York, a fact of some historic Bacchic interest. In 1885, before Coca-Cola became the American temperance drink, it was French Wine Coca, a flavored wine. Mogen David has moved into nonkosher wines and into the exploding "pop wine" market with products called Cold Bear and Black Bear.

Both big kosher wine companies also grow increasing proportions of their own grapes. Mogen David now claims to be the fifth largest American vintner, with 5 million gallons in its two wineries in Chicago and its three in Westfield, New York. Monarch (Manischewitz) has grown to 3 million gallons at the Bush Terminal in Brooklyn, where it has been located since 1938.

Because kosher wines are the only sacramental wines normally sold to the public in this country, they are often used in Christian churches. I once asked the rector of the Episcopal Church in Sausalito which wine he was using for Communion. He couldn't remember the name, except that it was a sacramental wine, but he soon found the bottle for me. It was Manischewitz kosher Concord Grape.

The State of Israel, which displays the Mogen David shield on its flag, now ships kosher wines to the United States. Some of them are even labeled as Concord, though they lack the flavor of the American grape.

22

Wines of Canada

CANADA produces many good wines, including some that are excellent by other countries' standards, and also makes an assortment of unorthodox wines that are not found anywhere else. The best Canadian wines are still little known outside the Dominion, however, because their growing popularity in Canada is something new. For Canada, too, had Prohibition during most of the years when the United States were legally dry, and its rigid provincial monopoly liquor store system, set up afterward, has long discouraged the use of wine.

But Canadians returned from the Second World War and from travel abroad with a taste for table wine, and the postwar flood of immigration has brought millions of people from the wine countries of Europe, starting a swing to mealtime wines. In a single decade the country's wine consumption jumped from 10 million gallons, less than five pints per capita, to 23 million gallons, more than a gallon per capita, in 1971.* Two thirds of the total is Canadian-made, and half is of low-alcohol types. Canada's wine-growers have responded by planting new grape varieties to produce steadily improving table wines and champagnes.

• 2 •

Wineries in Canada's two vineyard districts are prohibited from offering public tours and tasting as vintners elsewhere do, because dry influence in their provincial governments is still strong. But Canadian vineyards and wineries are uniquely interesting, and visits to most of the cellars can be arranged for groups by mail or telephone, so that wine touring in Canada is well worth while.

*U.S. gallons, not British imperial gallons, which are approximately a fifth larger.

The eastern Canadian wine district—the western district is 2000 miles away beyond the Rocky Mountains—is situated on the slender arm of the Niagara Peninsula that connects southwestern Ontario to Niagara County, New York. This proximity explains why Ontario wines basically resemble those of New York State. Almost nine tenths of the vineyards of Canada, some 24,000 acres, are concentrated on that narrow strip, which extends westward from Niagara-on-the-Lake some thirty-five miles toward the city of Hamilton. Farmers call it "the Banana Belt of Canada" because the waters of Lakes Ontario and Erie, on its northern and southern shores, moderate the climate and protect the vines from winter damage and frost.

Most of the vineyards are situated below the Niagara escarpment, the 350-foot-high cliff that crosses the Peninsula north of Niagara Falls. Subdivisions and industries are now competing with farms for the most desirable land, and lately some of the vineyards have retreated up the escarpment. At first the growers were fearful that the higher elevation would expose their vines to cold north winds, but they since have found there is better protective air drainage atop the escarpment than below.

Eight of the nation's twenty-five commercial wineries are located on the Niagara Peninsula and produce nearly three fourths of all Canadian wine.

On Martindale Road outside St. Catharines, near the original Welland Canal built to carry ocean ships around the Falls, is the 1,500,000-gallon Barnes winery, the oldest in Canada, still operated by the grandsons and great-grandsons of George and Thomas Barnes, who founded it in 1873. The modern winery is built around the original stone-walled underground vaults. The 100-acre vineyard, called Barnesdale, is planted principally with such Labrusca grapes as Agawam, Catawba, Concord, and Diana, but French hybrids have been added lately to make table wines without the Labrusca taste.

Facing Dorchester Road just outside the city of Niagara Falls is Canada's biggest and second oldest winery, by a year, T. G. Bright & Company, with 9 million gallons and 1200 acres of vineyards. Lumberman Thomas Bright started the company at Toronto in 1874. He moved it sixteen years later and changed its name to Niagara Falls Wine Company, but after his death his family changed it back to Bright's. In 1933, Harry Hatch, boss of the Hiram Walker distillery, purchased Bright's and hired Dr. John Eoff from Fruit Industries in California to modernize the winery. Eoff had as his assistant a talented young French chemist named Adhemar de Chaunac.

When de Chaunac started work, Bright's was producing only

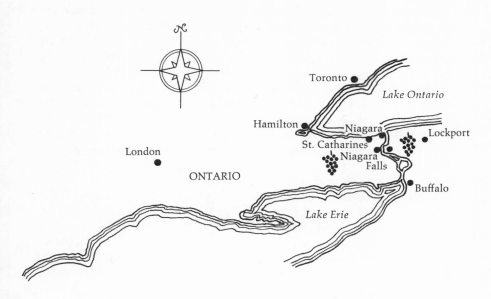

Vineyard Districts of EASTERN CANADA and Niagara County, N.Y.

ports and sherries. The young Frenchman searched the company's vineyards, which then consisted mainly of Concords, found some Delaware and Catawba grapes, filled two boxes with them, and took them home. He fermented them into a dry table wine and took it to the winery for Eoff and Hatch to taste. Hatch was so impressed that he started Bright's making its first table wines.

With the end of the war in Europe, de Chaunac in 1946 brought several dozen French hybrid varieties to Bright's from France, and with them a hundred Vinifera vines, including Chardonnay and Pinot Noir. (This, the company's chief viticulturist, George W. B. Hostetter, points out, was before Dr. Konstantin Frank, who introduced Vinifera to the eastern United States, had left Germany for New York.)

Bright's first champagne, de Chaunac's blend of hybrids and Labrusca varieties, was introduced in 1949 and in the following year it won a bronze medal at the California State Fair. A decade later, Bright's brought out Canada's first Chardonnay and a Pinot champagne made entirely from Chardonnay and Pinot Noir. The Chardonnay, which I tasted at the winery a few years ago, could have won a medal, too. There was also a Gewürztraminer, not yet on the market, that might have come from Alsace.

Two otherwise well-made Bright's wines, a claret of Chelois and a white described on its label as "extra dry," were too severely dry for even a connoisseur's taste, and I inquired why they were made that way. The explanation was that Ontario has a peculiar regulation which prohibits claret, burgundy, chianti, and any wine called "dry" on its label, from having a sugar content higher than 1 percent. Bright's other table wines were more pleasing because the bone-dry requirement does not extend to wines not labeled "dry."

De Chaunac retired in 1966 and was fittingly honored by Ontario winegrowers in 1972 when they gave his name to one of the best French hybrid red grapes, Seibel 9549. Bright's president, W. Douglas Hatch, recalls when his father, who preferred fine wines to whiskeys, asked de Chaunac to teach Douglas how to make wine: "De Chaunac started me on a ladder taking samples of wine out of the tanks and wouldn't even let me handle a saccharometer at first."

Douglas, whose brother Clifford heads Hiram Walker, is noted for his stable of thoroughbred horses and has given some of them names like Cresta Roja and Cresta Blanca, which are among Bright's many Canadian wine brands.

Also on the outskirts of Niagara Falls is the 4-million-gallon Château-Gai winery, which dates from 1890. It has no vineyards of its own, but buys its grapes from some hundreds of Niagara vine-yardists. "It is our policy," says Château-Gai President Thomas R. Comery, "to leave the highly important art of viticulture to the growers."

Comery is proud of his company's dozens of table and dessert wines, champagnes, and vermouths, and especially of having made Château-Gai the first Canadian winery to export some of its wines regularly to Great Britain, starting in 1965. The English connoisseurs who first sampled them at a tasting in London's Ontario House that spring were astonished at their quality, and even more so to learn that any wines are grown in Canada at all. Château-Gai also now exports its "Château Bon" wines to the northern tier of the United States. The winery has another historic distinction: in 1928 it was the first in North America to make champagne by the Charmat or bulk process, which was perfected in 1907 by Eugene Charmat in France. It also introduced the process to the United States when it opened the Château Gay winery across the river at Lewiston, New York.

In the village of Jordan on Highway 8, seven miles west of St.

Catharines, is the Jordan winery, founded in 1921. Adjoining the winery, on Twenty Mile Creek (named by the early settlers because of the creek mouth's distance from the Niagara frontier) is the Jordan Historical Museum of the Twenty. The winery owners established the museum to preserve the life style and relics of the Empire Loyalists who fought on the British side during the American Revolution and who migrated to Canada after the war. Jordan Wines has a larger winery at St. Catharines, making its total capacity almost 8 million gallons. President Noah Torno and his family own the company jointly with Canadian Breweries, a subsidiary of Rothman Tobacco, which in 1972 bought the share formerly owned by the Seagram interests. The best Jordan wines I tasted were its bottle-fermented champagnes, sherries, and crackling rosé, a Canadian specialty about which there is more on a later page. Jordan also makes a strange 19 percent flavored wine called Zing, which tastes almost exactly like gin. There are no small wineries in Ontario; all but one are well over a million gallons.

West of Jordan, via roads lined with vineyards, is Winona, site of the winery that was called Beau Chatel when it was built by the Imperial Tobacco Company in 1967, but which was purchased and renamed Andrés three years later by the owners of the Andrés winery in British Columbia. On the outskirts of Toronto is the Château Cartier winery, formerly called Parkdale, owned by the Labatt brewing interests. The Turner winery, which dates from 1920, is in the York section of Toronto. At London, a hundred miles farther west, is the London Winery, still operating in an area where there no longer are vineyards, but where there were many when it was founded in 1925.

During the past century there were wineries as far west as Essex County, opposite Detroit, with their vineyards on the Lake Erie shore. One of the greatest was the Vin Villa Vineyard winery on little Pelee Island, across the international boundary from the Lake Erie Islands of Ohio. Old residents tell how, when the Pelee Island Winery was moved to the mainland, its huge casks--too unwieldy to be brought to the mainland on lake boats—were emptied, floated in the lake, hitched to a tugboat, and towed ashore.

• 3 •

If your interests are in grapes or in wine research, the place to visit in Ontario is the Horticultural Experiment Station at Vineland, off the highway a mile east of Jordan village. There Ralph Crowther can show you the leading wine research laboratory in eastern America, and can introduce you to grape-breeder Oliver (Ollie) Bradt, whose Canadian hybrids are changing the character of many Canadian wines and of some New York and midwestern wines as well.

Crowther, the scientist engaged in wine research, is most noted for his invention of the Crowther-Truscott submerged-culture *flor* sherry-making process, which is revolutionizing the production of dry sherries in Canada and the United States and is even being studied by enologists in the sherry country of Spain. Others have claimed to have invented the process, including a Spanish researcher who even got a patent on it in Spain in 1968. I can testify, however, that Crowther was making his *flor* (Spanish fino-type) sherry at Vineland as far back as 1955, because I was there in July of that year and tasted his then-as-yet-unrevealed "seven-day wonder," the simple, quick way to give sherry the pungent *flor* character which old-time winemakers describe as "the bedbug taste." It takes years to develop by the method used for centuries in Spain. There, the *flor* yeast (*Saccharomyces beticus*) grows naturally as a film on the surface of the wine, but it often fails to do its job, which is how a Spanish sherry becomes an amontillado instead of a fino. Crowther started his work with *flor* yeast in 1952 because the Canadian Wine Institute asked him to try growing it on the surface of wines made from Ontario grapes.* At first, Crowther used the Spanish film-yeast method, but the yeast failed to grow on some of his wines. Then he discovered that by agitation—by circulating the *S. beticus* culture through the wine—he could make the yeast work harder and produce the *flor* taste reliably in days instead of years. The Ontario wineries were the first to use his process, and I since have tasted some excellent fino-style sherries in their cellars. Now wineries in the United States have begun adding *flor* wines, made Crowther's way, to many of their sherry blends. The flavor is improved so markedly over that of madeirized (baked) sherries that in years to come sherry with the *flor* character may become the favorite apéritif in Canada and the United States, as it is in the British Isles.

More important than sherry is Vineland's grape-breeding program, because Canadians are learning to appreciate wines without the foxy Labrusca taste. Hundreds of new, nonfoxy wine-grape varieties have been bred at the Vineland station since Ollie Bradt went to work there in 1938. When a new variety, at first designated by a number, has proved itself by several years of testing in the vineyards and wineries, the station releases it to the industry and

---

*The late Professor William V. Cruess of the University of California at Berkeley did the basic research on *flor* yeasts in 1939. It was he who taught the California and Australian wine industries the Spanish method of making *flor* sherries.

gives it a name, which in each case begins with the letter *V*. Vineland's first outstanding success was the blue grape named Veeport, released in 1961. At the laboratory I tasted experimental ports made of Veeport, ranging from one to eight years of age. California wineries should be jealous of the lovely bouquets these wines had developed. Veeport and two more Vineland varieties—Vincent for burgundy and Vinered for rosé—have now been widely planted in Canadian vineyards, and Veeport and Vincent have been introduced in some United States vineyards as well.

Vineyard improvement has become the theme of the Niagara Grape and Wine Festival, which is held at St. Catharines during the third week of each September. The festival was started in 1952 to aid tourism with its parade and other events, but its main event now is the crowning of the Grape King, who is chosen from among Ontario growers for the quality of his grape crop. When the king is selected, his vineyard gets an official visit from the prime minister of the province.

French and Canadian hybrids have replaced many of the Concord vines that once predominated in Ontario. Concords are reported down to 40 percent of the total acreage, compared to 70 percent in New York State. Mechanical grape harvesters, first used in Ontario in 1970, now pick half of the crop.

• 4 •

Winemaking began earlier in eastern Canada than in most of the United States. In the year 1636, Jesuit missionaries at Québec were making sacramental wine from the wild grapes that thrive along the St. Lawrence River.

The first commercial winery in Canada was Clair House, established in 1811 by a German ex-soldier, Corporal Johann Schiller, near the shore of Lake Ontario at Cooksville, now a suburb of Toronto. The Toronto *Leader* for July 8, 1867, records that Clair House wines were shipped to France for judging at the Paris Exposition and that the wine jury found them "pure and of excellent quality," comparing them to French *vin ordinaire*.

By the 1890s, there were 5000 acres of vines and thirteen flourishing wineries in Ontario, but meanwhile the dry crusade in the United States had spread northward into Canada, and towns were voting themselves dry.

Then in 1916 and 1917, while Canadian soldiers were away fighting in Europe, all but one of the Canadian provinces adopted Prohibition laws. Québec, with its French heritage, held out until 1919 and then forbade the sale of liquor, but allowed its people to continue buying wine and beer.

Ontario, then Canada's only wine-producing province, pro-hibited liquor and beer, but to protect its grape growers, permitted its wineries to continue making wine for local sale. Buyers had to go to the wineries to make a purchase, and by law they could buy no less than a five-gallon keg or a case at a time. The export of wine to foreign countries was also permitted, and when the United States went dry in 1920, several new Ontario wineries opened for business. Canadian wine "exports" rose to levels never reached before or since. Shipments destined ostensibly for faraway coun-tries found their way into the United States despite the American border, lake, and river patrols. Sailormen along the Canadian shore of Lake Erie still chuckle over recollections of "those one-hour trips to Cuba." When United States Prohibition was re-pealed, the "exports" of Canadian wines abruptly ceased.

By 1927, Ontario and the neighboring provinces had had enough of Prohibition, and they legalized the sale of liquor. Pro-hibition had come earlier and had ended sooner in Canada than in the United States. But it left the country's wine industry more handicapped than the industry in the United States was at Repeal, because in place of Prohibition all of the Canadian provinces established government monopoly liquor stores. One of the worst features of the stores was the requirement that each individual must buy a two-dollar annual permit in order to purchase any alcoholic beverage.

Ontario, however, allowed its wineries to continue selling their wines to consumers, and finally abolished its drinker's permit during the 1960s. It now is easier to buy wine in Ontario than any-where else in Canada, for besides the government liquor stores, there are fifty-one attractive special wine stores that are owned and operated by the Ontario wineries. They exist because while Ontario had Prohibition, there were fifty-one wineries selling wine in the province. Later, because most of the wineries were situated a day's trip from Toronto, the provincial government allowed each to stop selling at the winery and to open a store in a city instead. The big wineries promptly bought out the small ones and closed them down, because all they wanted was the store licenses. Of the eight wineries remaining in Ontario, Bright's now owns fourteen stores throughout the province, and the others have one to seven stores each, the total remaining at the original fifty-one.

· 5 ·

Canada's other winegrowing district is beyond the Rocky Mountains in the far western province of British Columbia. The story of its wines is a curious one, as the following incident will illustrate.

In March 1967, the San Francisco Wine and Food Society and the Medical Friends of Wine were planning to hold a champagne tasting. Having just returned from a research trip to the eastern states and Canada, I suggested that we invite champagne producers outside of California to participate. The committee agreed, and the invitations went out. Acceptances came from nine California wineries, from three located in Canada, three in New York State, and from one each in New Jersey, Ohio, Michigan, and Illinois. When our several hundred members and guests gathered for the event in the Rose Room of San Francisco's Palace Hotel, we faced an array of sixty-seven white, pink, and red sparkling wines—thirty-four from California and thirty-three from outside the state.

As is usual among such tasting audiences in winy San Francisco, those accustomed to California champagnes preferred them to those from the eastern states and Canada, most of which had in varying degrees the Labrusca taste of native American grapes.

But of particular interest to the members of our group were the Canadian champagnes. Typical of the tasters' responses was what "Winemaster" Henry Rubin wrote in his wine column in the San Francisco *Chronicle*: "I was pleased to note some acceptable Canadian wine." He noted that some had "strange" Labrusca flavors, and ended with: "The best one seemed to me the Richelieu De Luxe Champagne Brut of British Columbia."

Because I had visited the British Columbia wineries a few weeks before, I was able to explain to Henry Rubin why he had preferred that particular champagne. It had been made, I told him, entirely from California grapes.

In fact, British Columbia wines have been made partly, and in some years wholly, from California grapes since 1934. The labels say "Canadian champagne," "Canadian sherry," "Canadian burgundy," etc., but most of the grapes have come in refrigerated trucks from vineyards in California's San Joaquin Valley. The varieties are not California's best, but they stand the thousand-mile trip fairly well, and the wines made from them are usually sound.

• 6 •

The grape-growing district of British Columbia is the Okanagan Valley, a 120-mile-long, narrow, steep-walled stretch of farmland, lakes, and resorts between the Trepanier Plateau and the Monashee Mountains. It extends from the head of Okanagan Lake, above Vernon on Highway 97, southward across the United States border. When speaking of the Okanagan, you usually include the lower Similkameen River Valley from Keremeos and Cawston to the Washington State line near Osoyoos.

That part of British Columbia was inhabited only by Indians, fur traders, and missionaries until the introduction of placer mining brought gold prospectors after 1860. The Oblate Fathers built a mission about 1864 at a point seven miles south of the present city of Kelowna. The Fathers planted a few vines, but when farmers settled in the valley during the next few decades, they grew apples, peaches, and apricots; nobody thought of planting vineyards.

During the 1920s, the first two British Columbia wineries started operating on Vancouver Island, more than 200 miles west of the Okanagan. The wine they made was not from grapes, but from the loganberries grown north of Victoria on the island's Saanich Peninsula.

About that time a Hungarian winemaker, Dr. Eugene Rittich, visited the Okanagan Valley and thought its climate might be suitable for wine grapes. Most of the valley lies between the 49th

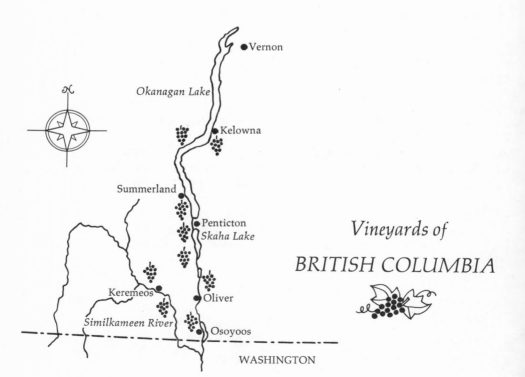

Vineyards of

BRITISH COLUMBIA

and 50th parallels of latitude, which are regarded as the northern-most limits of viticulture; Germany's Rheingau is at 50 latitude and the Champagne district of France is at 49. But the deep waters of Okanagan, Skaha, and the other lakes, dug out by prehistoric glaciers, prevent the temperature from going to extremes and give parts of the Okanagan a growing season as long as 185 days. Farm-ing is on the bench lands above the lake level, and this normally protects the plants from frost. Rainfall is only 8 to 12 inches per year, but water for irrigation is plentiful in the lakes and upland streams.

Dr. Rittich made some experimental plantings that proved him right, and he interested farmer Jesse Willard Hughes in planting a vineyard near the old Oblate Fathers Mission in 1926. Four years later, the first commercial grape wine in British Columbia was made from Hughes's grapes in the Growers' Winery at Victoria.

In 1932, the depth of the Great Depression, Okanagan Valley apples were unsalable at a cent a pound and were rotting on the ground. A Kelowna hardware-store owner named William Andrew Cecil Bennett talked about it with the Italian grocer next door, Pasquale "Cap" Capozzi, and they decided the way to sal-vage the apples was to turn them into wine. Though both are tee-totalers, they became partners and started a winery, Calona Wines Limited, with Bennett as its president. Their apple wine couldn't compete with the Growers' Winery's genuine wine made of Hughes's grapes, so in 1934 Calona started buying grapes from California. The wineries on Vancouver Island began doing the same.

For the next twenty-six years, the British Columbia wineries prospered by making "Canadian wines" almost entirely from California grapes. As wine consumption in the province grew, more B.C. wineries were built.

This was the situation when Bennett, Capozzi's former partner in the Calona winery, became Premier of British Columbia in 1952. He had sold his shares in the winery eleven years earlier when he was first elected to the B.C. parliament.

As Premier, teetotaler Bennett turned his attention to the win-eries. He decided that if they were to continue selling their wine in the British Columbia government stores, they ought to be re-quired to make it out of B.C. grapes. In 1960, he ordered his Liquor Board to establish quotas, minimum percentages of B.C. grapes which wines made in the province must contain in order to be sold. There then were only 585 acres of vineyards in the Okanagan Valley, so the quota for 1961 was set at 25 percent; but the Board announced it would go up to 50 percent in another year and to 65 percent by 1965.

A stampede to plant more vineyards in the Okanagan began. Vines were put into the ground without waiting for grape stakes. In four years the Okanagan Valley vineyards were quadrupled to almost 2400 acres.

But in December of 1964 a spell of sixteen-below-zero temperatures and forty-mile winds hit the Okanagan, freezing most of the vines to the ground. Only 334 tons of grapes were picked in the following autumn, and the Liquor Board rescinded the quota for that vintage. This explains the all-California flavor of the British Columbia champagne we tasted at San Francisco in 1966.

• 7 •

The Okanagan still has only about 2500 acres of vineyards because suitable land there is scarce. I have read, however, that some favorably situated Indian lands are now being planted with vines in the southern part of the valley near Oliver, and that some of the Indians are becoming vineyardists.

The Calona Winery was sold by the Capozzi family in 1971 to Standard Brands of Montreal, a subsidiary of Standard Brands in the United States, and its capacity has been quadrupled to 4 million gallons. You still can find rotund, cheery "Cap" Capozzi there on occasion because the winery is still run by his second son, Tom. "Cap" enjoys telling how he arrived nearly penniless from Naples in 1905 and worked his way up from a railroad section hand to become the owner of the biggest businesses in Kelowna.

Tom Capozzi is responsible for developing the best-selling red wine in British Columbia, Calona Royal Red. It is light-bodied and semisweet with characteristics of both burgundy and port, yet easier to drink than port because its sweetness is balanced by acidity and tannin. Its alcoholic strength is 15 percent, a fourth more than standard table wines, so that a normal serving can send a diner from the dinner table drunk. Calona Royal Red became so popular that the other B.C. wineries had to copy it, but they admit it contains too much alcohol for a mealtime wine. Some say the Canadian law, which provides the same tax rate for still wines between 7 and 20 percent, should include a separate tax class for wines under 14 percent, which is the dividing line between table and dessert wines for tax purposes in the United States.

South of Kelowna, on a knoll overlooking Okanagan Lake, stands one of the most attractive winery buildings in North America, a mission-style structure with a bell tower. It was named the Mission Hill winery when orchardist R. P. (Tiny) Walrod formed a company to build it in the 1960s, but Walrod died before construction began. In 1969, "Uncle Ben" Ginter, who owns three breweries and several other businesses across Canada, bought it and renamed it Uncle Ben Ginter's Gourmet Winery. His wine-maker, Joseph Raffeinen, tells me its best-selling wine is a red called Fuddle Duck.

On a hillside nearby is the loveliest vineyard in all Canada, Beau Séjour, which Jesse Hughes planted in the 1920s. The grapes are now crushed at Kelowna and the refrigerated must is shipped to the Growers' Winery at Victoria on Vancouver Island.

At Penticton, between Okanagan and Skaha Lakes thirty-nine miles south of Kelowna, is the newest winery in the valley, built in 1966 by a group of local businessmen headed by former hotel-owner Evans Lougheed. Though the Okanagan wineries cannot invite passersby to see their cellars, they are made architecturally inviting in the hope of attracting visitors in prearranged groups. It is the only way they can advertise, because Premier Bennett has prohibited all alcoholic beverage advertising in British Columbia.

Three more B.C. wineries are in Pacific Coast cities, 200 miles west of the Okanagan. Growers' at Victoria is owned by Imasco, a food and tobacco firm, and makes a complete assortment of grape and fruit wines. The best I tasted was a red called Rougelais, a name selected to express the wine's resemblance to Beaujolais. In the Vancouver industrial suburb of Westminster is Villa Wines, built in 1960 beside the Seagram distillery on Braid Street. It was partly owned by Seagram, as was Jordan of Ontario, until both were sold to Canadian Breweries in 1972. Villa wines bear a family resemblance to those of Jordan, and include an apéritif type named Zim that tastes like Jordan's Zing. The best I tasted there was a two-year-old dry red made from the Seibel 9549 grape (now renamed de Chaunac), grown in the Okanagan.

The original Andrés winery is at Port Moody, outside Van-couver. It was built in 1961, the first year of the B.C. grape quota, by Andrew Peller, a Hungarian brewmaster who had sold his brewery at Hamilton, Ontario, several years before. There is no such person as André; he is a mustachioed character Peller in-vented to use in publicizing his wines. The first winemaker at Andrés was Wallace H. Pohle of Stockton, California, who equipped the cellar with machinery from a defunct winery at Madera. Pohle disliked the Labrusca grapes which then grew al-most exclusively in the Okanagan, and talked Peller into planting French hybrids and Vinifera on forty acres near Cawston in the Similkameen. His successor, when Pohle returned to Stockton, was another Californian, Davis-trained Guy Baldwin (now at Paul Masson in California). It was Baldwin who made the champagne that was praised at our San Francisco tasting.

Scientists at the Summerland Research Station in the Okanagan, after many years of testing grape varieties, are advising growers in the area to plant French hybrids and Labrusca types. They say Okanagan winters are too cold for Vinifera, though they recommend limited commercial trials of a grape called the Okanagan Riesling. Dr. John F. Bowen of the Station says this is not the White (Johannisberg) Riesling of Germany, but a cold-hardy Hungarian variety that Dr. Rittich brought to the Okanagan.

Californians Pohle and Baldwin, having made wine in British Columbia, differ with the Summerland scientists. They say that cold-resistant Vinifera varieties should suffer no worse in Okanagan winters than the hybrids, and point out that Vinifera have been grown successfully for many years in the Yakima Valley of Washington, which is only 200 miles south and has much the same climate. "If the Okanagan growers would produce three tons per acre instead of six to sixteen tons (which the vineyards there are reported to yield)," says Baldwin, "this part of British Columbia could grow some of the best Vinifera wines in the world."

· 8 ·

Not to be confused with the Ontario and British Columbia wineries are a dozen others, all big, in such places as Truro in Nova Scotia, Scoudouc and Moncton in New Brunswick, Moose Jaw in Saskatchewan, Calgary in Alberta, Winnipeg and Gimli in Manitoba, or Québec city and Ste. Hyacinthe in Québec. It may seem strange that wine is made in these provinces because no grapes are grown commercially in any of them, though there is a small experimental vineyard in Nova Scotia.

These wineries without vineyards make and sell wines and champagnes of all types, but not from Canadian grapes. Their raw materials are either California grapes, or juice or grape concentrate (condensed juice) imported from California and from such European countries as France, Spain, Greece, and Cyprus, though a few make wines also from locally grown berries. One such winery advertises its products as "Produced from the finest European grapes, fermented and bottled in Canada." Another says it expects soon to sell some of its concentrate wine in the United States.

Concentrate wine fits the legal definition of wine in most countries, including the United States, but in grape-growing countries concentrate is used only to sweeten wines or to increase the sugar content of musts. Concentrate also has been one of the materials for homemade wines since Prohibition days, and there are wineries in some tropical Latin American countries that correspond to the strange new establishments in Canada.

The original reason such wineries were built in Canada during the 1960s was that by opening a plant in a given province and by employing local people to ferment and bottle their wines, the owners automatically got all their products listed in the province's monopoly liquor stores. Incidentally, some of these wineries are architecturally handsome, and at least one province allows them to offer tasting and cellar tours.

But as wine consumption continues setting all-time records in Canada, there is doubt of whether the Dominion has enough land with suitable climates in which to grow grapes to meet the future demand. Some of the Ontario wineries have asked the Liquor Board to let them use imported concentrate, too.

The Ontario wineries are required by the Ontario Liquor Board to make their wines exclusively from materials grown in Ontario, though this may change if Canadian wine consumption continues to soar at its present rate. There is no such requirement in the other provinces.

Searching for potential grape land in Canada, some growers have made test plantings in parts of southwestern Ontario that formerly had vineyards. An area between Lillooet and Lytton in the Fraser River Valley of British Columbia has also been considered as possibly suited for vineyards. Actually, several thousand tons of Ontario grapes are exported each year to the United States, where they are used by processors, including wineries. But Canada annually imports a dozen times as much from California for table use and to be made into wine.

• 9 •

Half of the wine made in Canada is not made in its wineries, but is fermented in the basements and kitchens of Canadian homes. Rather than buy from the government liquor stores, which among other things charge too much for wine, many people prefer to ferment their own from locally grown or California grapes or from concentrate. While this is especially true of consumers of European-immigrant backgrounds, large numbers of other Canadians who are not particularly interested in saving money have taken up winemaking as a fascinating hobby.

One of every five families in British Columbia now makes its own wine, says Stanley Anderson of Vancouver, who started the business called Wine-Art.

• 10 •

Canadian wine laws differ from those of the United States, which explains some of the unorthodox Canadian wines. Already mentioned is Canada's crackling rosé, which now comes also in red and white versions and is relatively low in price. During the 1960s this became the most popular single table wine in the country. In the United States and most of Europe, wines called crackling (or *pétillant* or *frizzante*) are expensive because they must be naturally fermented in closed containers like champagne and pay the same tax rate as champagne. Canadian crackling wines mostly get their sparkle from artificial carbonation like the "pop" or "mod" wines of the United States, and pay the same tax rate as still wines if they contain no more than an extra atmosphere of carbon dioxide. This is about 14.7 pounds of pressure per square inch, compared to almost 90 pounds in champagne.

Another Canadian specialty, permitted under a section of the law originally intended to encourage the sale of sparkling apple cider, is carbonated wine, usually sweet, that is fully as effervescent as champagne, but which contains no more than 7 percent alcohol. It is less expensive than the crackling type because it is taxed only half as much as wines over 7 percent in alcohol. Bright's started selling such a wine in beer bottles, called Winette, in 1955. Andrés in British Columbia followed in the 1960s with one called Chanté in champagne bottles, and other Canadian wineries have followed with their own versions, such as Baby Duck and Ben Ginter's Fuddle Duck.

Canadian labels do not tell you the alcoholic contents of wines, and Canadian sherries and ports range from 15 to 17 percent, compared to the United States minimum of 17 percent for sherry and 18 percent for port. Ontario wineries usually ferment their dessert wines to these alcoholic levels rather than add wine spirits as is done in the United States and Europe. This is primarily because Ontario does not allow its wineries to operate distilleries.

Nor do Canadian labels ever state vintage years; the wineries say they prefer to blend together wines of different years.

The French Government in 1964 sued the Château-Gai winery to stop it from calling its sparkling wines "champagne," and the French won the suit in 1967. But the verdict was handed down in the fiercely French province of Québec by a judge of French descent, and the Canadian wineries appealed it to English-speaking Ottawa, where they expect it to be reversed. Incidentally, bulk-process champagnes in Canada are not required to state that fact, which is mandatory in the United States.

Proprietary names for wines are becoming popular in Canada, such as Jordan's Perle Blanche for its effervescent white, and Growers' Rougelais for its best red wine. The most curious proprietary name in Canada is an example of how the hard-to-pronounce French haut sauternes type confuses people outside of France. An Ontario winery shortened the name of its sweet sauterne to "Haut," a French adjective that means high, tall, upper, or loud.

Canadian wines are seldom given more than passing mention in most wine books, and British author Hugh Johnson omitted them entirely from his most recent one, *The World Atlas of Wine*. When asked to explain, Johnson said that the one Canadian wine he had tried was the worst he had ever tasted.

The Canadian growers' indignant replies to this slur received nationwide publicity and brought many patriotic drinkers to the defense of their country's wines. With the steadily improving quality of Canada's best grapes and wines, and with table types and champagnes now making up nearly half of the wine made from Canadian grapes, they are less likely to be ignored in the future.

23

Wines of Mexico

GUIDEBOOKS to Mexico list, among the attractions that lure millions of us across our southern border each year, its archaelogical wonders, its colorful native customs, its fabulous scenery, resorts, and excellent fishing—but usually omit any mention of Mexican wines. Partly because of this, few Americans are aware that the land of the conquistadores has extensive vineyards and imposing wineries, some of them centuries older than ours, and that many Mexican wines are good and are getting steadily better.

The chief reason the wines of Mexico are little known is that the nation's wine industry, despite its ancient beginnings, is really new. Its oldest winegrowing estates have just lately been revived, replanted, and rebuilt. Most of the approximately fifty wineries in the Republic have only started operating since the 1950s. A new generation of enologists, technically trained in European and California wine schools, has taken charge of the modern cellars and is producing wines of types and qualities not made in Mexico before. A few are even being exported to California.

Why is this happening only now in an industry that began more than four hundred and fifty years ago? The answers are in Mexico's turbulent history and in its relatively recent emergence as a nation of the modern world.

· 2 ·

There already was wine in Mexico in the time of the conqueror, Hernando Cortez. As the governor of New Spain from 1521 to 1527, Cortez established mines and farms. He insisted that all ships coming from Spain to Vera Cruz should bring with them supplies of plants and seeds. In 1524, Cortez made it a rule that every Spaniard holding a *repartimiento* (a grant of land and of Indians to till the soil) must plant, annually for five years, a thou-

Ensenada

Hermosillo

Rio Grande River

Delicias

Torreón

Parras

Saltillo

Aguascalientes

San Juan del Río

Mexico City ★

Principal Vineyard
Districts of MEXICO

sand grapevines for each hundred Indians. Wine was an essential part of the Spaniards' diet and was indispensable for their priests to celebrate the Mass. Ships brought the wine in casks from Spain and the Canary Islands, but space in the ships was limited. The conquistadores first made their wine from wild grapes, then from cultivated grapes when their vineyards bore fruit. By 1554 wine-growing was well established at haciendas as far west as the present state of Michoacán. The first two commercial wineries or *bodegas vinícolas* in Mexico were established in 1593 and 1626 at Parras in Coahuila, 400 miles north of Mexico City. Both again are producing wines today.

But Spain was jealous of the New World's blossoming viniculture. The vintners of Cadiz were complaining as their shipments shrank. Philip II acted in 1595 to keep the wine trade as a Spanish monopoly; he issued an edict forbidding new plantings or replacements of vineyards in New Spain. The viceroys repeated Philip's edict during the next two centuries, and some went so far as to order that all existing vineyards be uprooted. But winemaking continued despite the edict, though without any records of the quantities made. It was from Mexico—not from Europe—that wine-growing spread during the sixteenth century to Peru, Chile, and Argentina, and during the seventeenth and eighteenth centuries to what is now the western United States.

Padre Miguel Hidalgo, the revered Father of Mexican Independence, was the only one who dared openly to defy the Spanish law. At his village of Dolores, the rebel priest taught the natives to raise grapes, which he himself pressed into wine, and the civil authorities came repeatedly to Dolores to tear up his vines. One of Father Hidalgo's aims in launching the revolution against Spain in 1810 was to end the Spanish prohibition against winegrowing in Mexico. Although the revolution finally succeeded eleven years later, Hidalgo meanwhile had been captured and shot.

Viniculture languished during the half-century of disorder that followed. Only two new wineries of any importance were established during the first seven decades of Mexican independence—the Bodegas Ferriño at Cuatro Ciénegas in Coahuila in 1860 and the Bodegas de Santo Tomás in Baja California in 1888. Most of the country's vineyards still grew the same grape variety originally introduced by the conquistadores. It was the Criolla or Mission, which is a member of the Vinifera wine-grape family, but not a very good one, because it is deficient in acidity and color. It is now thought to have grown from a seed brought from Spain in the time of Cortez.

The first step toward better Mexican wines came during the dictatorship of President Porfirio Díaz, who came to power in 1876. Díaz, the *mestizo* "strong man of Mexico," surrounded himself with young men called *científicos* and welcomed foreign capital and modern industry. In 1889, the Irish-American winegrower from Livermore, James Concannon, seeking more capital to develop his own vineyard in California, went to Mexico and convinced Díaz that viticulture in the Republic could be developed on a commercial quality basis and that he, Concannon, was the man to do it. The dictator granted him a concession to introduce better wine grapes to the country, and even assigned him a cavalry escort to impress the *hacendados* whom he would visit. From Livermore, where the better French varieties were just then being planted, Concannon shipped several million cuttings to haciendas throughout Mexico, with pamphlets in Spanish on grape cultural methods, and sent his brother Thomas along to superintend the deliveries. The biggest plantings were made at Hacienda Roque near Celaya, which was owned by the father of Díaz's daughter-in-law. By 1904 the project was completed and Concannon returned to Livermore. Díaz meanwhile assigned a young Hungarian viticulturist, the son of the Hungarian ambassador, to see to it that every state in the Republic would have at least one vineyard. With the better grape varieties from California, the Mexican wine industry started to boom.

In 1910 the boom attracted to Mexico the Italian-American winemaker Antonio Perelli-Minetti from California, seeking an opportunity to recoup the fortune he had lost in a wine venture at San Francisco. On his arrival in Mexico, Perelli was taken to Chapultepec Palace to meet the dictator, who told him about the grape plantings. Díaz encouraged Perelli to join the Mexican industry—"The sky is the limit here"—but warned him to stay out of politics, saying, "Don't let the fever of commanding get hold of you." Perelli went to work for Felipe Cárdenas of Ocampo, a brother of the former governor of Coahuila. His assignment was to plant vines on Cárdenas' Rancho El Fresno near Torreón. Perelli brought from California cuttings of Zinfandel, Petit Sirah, Malaga, and Flame Tokay and planted almost 900 acres, the largest vineyard in Mexico at that time.

Then came the Revolution of 1910, led by Francisco I. Madero, and the bloody civil war that lasted for ten years and cost a million lives. During the chaos, most of the vineyards fell into neglect and many were destroyed. Perelli stayed on at the Cárdenas rancho, guarding his young vines. To Torreón in 1913, the year President Madero was murdered, came Pancho Villa, the former bandit chieftain who had become a general of the Revolution. Perelli promptly presented Villa with a basket of grapes and pleaded for protection for the vineyard. Villa consented and assigned him a guard of three soldiers. But a year later Villa left Torreón to join General Alvaro Obregón in Sonora. Conditions then became so chaotic that Perelli quit his job in 1916 and returned to California, where he went on to make his fortune in the San Joaquin Valley.

Perelli often returned to Mexico after the Revolution, and later it was he who helped to establish some of the new wineries that are making good Mexican wines today.

After the years of conflict, the tragic remnants of Mexico's vineyards continued to shrink. Wineries that started in Baja California imported grapes from San Diego and Cucamonga to make some of their wines.* This was a period when grapes were scarce and sugar cheaper. Mexican wines were often "baptized" (watered), and they earned a poor reputation, something the present industry

*The Mexican Government is reported to have stopped this after the 1965 vintage.

would prefer to end and forget. The vintners' trade association, the Asociación Nacional de Vitivinicultores, takes the position that though their industry is actually the oldest in the Americas, it is also the youngest. Its director, Alberto Jardi Porres, says "It was not until 1939 that the Mexican wine industry began its true development with characteristics that augur its future."

• 3 •

One summer morning in 1929, a thirty-six-year-old grocery merchant of Saltillo, the capital of Coahuila, went for a drive through the nearby countryside. It was election day, and because Nazario Ortiz Garza was a candidate for governor, he had decided to spend it outside the city. Passing an old hacienda, he noticed a few abandoned grapevines that had grown to enormous size and saw that they bore a crop of luscious-looking grapes. It occurred to him that it might be worthwhile to buy the hacienda, plant more vines, and make the place his country home—which he proceeded to do after winning the election. That day's drive in the country started don Nazario's second career, which since has made him Mexico's *capitan de la vitivinicultura*, the largest producer of wine and brandy in the Republic.

The vineyard that he planted grew well. When he began making wine, he sent his second son, Mario, to the University of California at Davis to study viticulture and enology. A few years later he won another election which made him a member of the Mexican Senate. Then in 1946 President Miguel Alemán appointed him Mexico's secretary of agriculture. In that post—already owning wineries at both Saltillo and Mexico City—don Nazario traveled on government business throughout the Republic for the next six years. Wherever he went, he distributed grapevine cuttings to everyone who would agree to start a vineyard. He also bought, for his own account, 700 acres of wasteland in the State of Aguascalientes, planted most of it in vines, and there built his third winery in 1952. He went on establishing new vineyards in Coahuila, Durango, and Chihuahua, and at Torreón built his fourth winery in 1966. By then he was using, in his four plants, a fourth of the grapes grown in the nation.

• 4 •

Following the Second World War, the Mexican Government stimulated the planting of vineyards by quadrupling the tariffs on European wines and by putting quota restrictions on wine imports. The result was that French and Spanish wines cost two to ten times as much as Mexican wines.* When the supply of grapes increased, European and American companies began establishing their own plants in Mexico—such firms as Pedro Domecq, Martell Cognac, and Seagram—though primarily to make brandy rather than wine. In three decades the area planted to vineyards in Mexico multiplied fifteen times, from 4000 acres in 1939 to over 60,000 acres in 1972.

Don Nazario says that is only the beginning, that Mexico has enough unused land to multiply its grape crop five hundred times. The country's wine consumption is only about 2 million gallons a year, less than a third of a pint per capita, a twenty-fourth of the rate in the United States. If the Mexican Government would help to remove obstacles to wine use, don Nazario declares, it could be increased ten times within a few years.

One of the obstacles is that wine is still a new product to most of the Mexican people, though such table wines as rosé should go well with the highly seasoned native cuisine. Wine has three formidable competitors in Mexico: pulque, beer, and soft drinks. Pulque, the ancient Aztec drink fermented from the sap of the maguey cactus or century plant, is a whitish, cloudy liquid of about 4 to 6 percent alcohol. Millions of gallons are sold annually at farms and in the pulquerías in the cities. From special types of pulque the Mexican liquors called tequila and mezcal are distilled.

Another obstacle to wine use is that, selling so little, restaurateurs and storekeepers have not yet learned to store it properly. Consequently much of the table wine becomes partially spoiled before it is used. On my last three visits to Mexico I tasted—at the wineries—a total of 452 wines, and all but four ranged from at least drinkable to good. But of the table wines served to me in restaurants and hotels, almost two thirds had the objectionable oxidized or sherrylike taste that comes from storage in warm rooms or sunlight or with corked bottles standing upright instead of horizontal. This kind of partial spoilage occurs in other countries, too, especially in South America and in the midwestern United States, but more often in Mexico than anywhere else I have visited. The place to judge Mexican wines therefore is at the wineries, where they have not yet had an opportunity to spoil.

But the chief obstacle facing the winegrowers of Mexico is the lack of an appreciative audience. What little wine is used is bought mostly by wealthy and upper-middle-class people to serve on special occasions, for which they choose the expensive brands

*At this writing, no United States wines are admitted to Mexico; no import permits have been granted.

imported from Spain and France. Mexican wines thus suffer from snobbery—but of a kind more deeply rooted than that which still hinders American wines in the United States. The Mexican kind even has a name—*malinchismo*.* It is the attitude prevalent among the wealthy in Mexico for four and half centuries, that no native product or custom can equal its counterpart in Europe, from which civilization came to the New World.

A blow against *malinchismo* was struck by the Mexican Congress in 1965 with a law that requires all restaurants and night clubs in the Republic to offer Mexican-made wines (and Mexican cheese) on their menus. Since the restriction on imports, some of the Spanish and French wine shippers have licensed Mexican wineries to bottle their best wines under the old European brand names the *malinchistas* have favored in the past. These Mexican wines bring higher prices than the rest and cope with snobbery to some extent.

• 5 •

Mexico has eight main vineyard districts: northern Baja California, the Laguna district at the border of Coahuila and Durango, Parras and Saltillo in Coahuila, Aguascalientes, the San Juan del Río region in Querétaro, Delicias in Chihuahua, and the Hermosillo district in Sonora. Some grapes also are grown in Zacatecas, San Luis Potosí, Tlaxcala, Puebla, Guanajuato, and Hidalgo. There are wineries around Mexico City that are supplied with grapes or wines grown farther north.

Some viticultural authorities consider Mexican climates too warm for grapes because almost half of the country lies south of the Tropic of Cancer. But the central vineyards are situated on Mexico's mile-high Central Plateau, where elevation may be as important as latitude. For each thousand feet of elevation the average annual temperature decreases about three degrees, and there is a further factor: summer days are shorter than in the higher latitudes. A trouble in the high plateau region is the extreme fluctuation of day and night temperatures. On warm days in the fall the vines continue to grow under cloudless skies, making them vulnerable to freezes that sometimes follow during

---

*From Malinche, the Indian girl who, as the interpreter, mistress, and slave of Cortez, guided him up from Vera Cruz to his conquest of Montezuma's Aztec empire between 1519 and 1521. For betraying her race, according to legend, she was condemned to wander forever in tears and agony beneath the waters of Lake Texcoco by day and through the surrounding country by night. *Malinchista* became the term applied to people who show a preference for customs other than Mexican, and their snobbery became *malinchismo*.

the nights. But the main flaw is too little moisture or too much. Dry districts depend on severely limited supplies of water for irrigation. Others have too much rain during the grape-growing season.

· 6 ·

One of the water-deficient regions is Baja California. That 750-mile-long, narrow peninsula of Lower California is for the most part a forbidding, moonlike country of rugged mountains and grim deserts. Some sections receive no rain at all over a period of years, while the tropical southern tip, noted for its luxury fishing resorts, gets torrential downpours.

At San Xavier Mission near Loreto on the peninsula, the Jesuit missionary Padre Juan Ugarte introduced the Mission grape from mainland Mexico about 1697 to make altar wine. It was from Loreto that the Franciscan, Padre Junípero Serra, set out in 1769 to colonize Alta California, traveling on foot and horseback and reputedly carrying the Mission grape to San Diego.

In contrast to the rest of the barren peninsula are several temperate, fertile valleys in its far northwestern corner. The vineyards of Baja California are in five of these valleys—Santo Tomás, thirty miles south of Ensenada; Rancho Viejo, inland from Ensenada; Guadalupe, fifty miles below the California border, and the Valle Redondo and Tañama districts near Tecate, across the border from San Diego County. Rainfall there ranges from only five to eighteen inches per year, and vineyard planting is limited to the supply of underground water for irrigation. Like the coastal counties of Alta California, these valleys are cooled by ocean breezes and fogs from the Pacific, ten to thirty miles to the west. The growers call their district "the Napa Valley of Mexico."

Of the Baja California wineries, the Bodegas de Santo Tomás, with 1,500,000 gallons capacity, is the oldest and biggest. It was founded in 1888 by Francisco Andonegui, an Italian gold miner who built an adobe winery near the ruins of Santo Tomás Mission. When Andonegui was dying in the late 1920s, he sold his property to the then governor, General Abelardo Lujan Rodríguez, who owned it for forty years. Rodríguez, the revolutionary general who later became President of Mexico, was prodigiously wealthy, owning fleets of tuna and shrimp boats, canneries, factories, and some eighty other businesses, including the Caliente racetrack, which he sold in 1932. After his term as President ended in 1934, General Rodríguez moved the winery from the Santo Tomás

Valley to its present location on Avenida Miramar in the port city of Ensenada. He later planted more vineyards at Rancho Guadalupe to supplement those near the Mission.

Santo Tomás wines are now among the best in Mexico, a fact related to the improvements in its vineyards and winery since a young California winemaker named Dmitri Tchelistcheff took charge as its technical director in 1961. He is the son of André Tchelistcheff. Dmitri, born in Paris in 1930, learned winemaking from his father at Beaulieu, earned his degree in viticulture and enology at the University of California at Davis in 1953, served in the Korean war, then worked at Napa's Schramsberg Vineyard and at the Gallo Winery in Modesto. Hearing from a Mexican former UC classmate that General Rodríguez wanted a California-trained enologist, Dmitri paid Ensenada a visit and was promptly hired. He began replanting the General's vineyards with cuttings shipped from Beaulieu by his father. Of the company's 700 acres of owned or leased vineyard at the Mission and at Guadalupe, a tenth are now planted with Cabernet Sauvignon, Pinot Noir, Johannisberg Riesling, Sémillon, Chenin Blanc, Aligoté, and Chardonnay. Dmitri introduced cold fermentation of white wines, installed bins for the bottle-aging of red wines, and made flor sherry, bulk-process and bottle-fermented champagnes (the latter in ammunition tunnels dug during the Second World War), and a pot-still brandy.

The results were evident in what I tasted there. Of the whites, the best was the moselle, a very dry wine that goes particularly well with the excellent seafoods of Ensenada. The best champagne I found in Mexico was Santo Tomás Cordon Azul Brut, made mainly of Chenin Blanc. There were pleasant young red wines called San Emilion and Vino Tinto, an effervescent sweet rosé called Rosato Rubi, a semisweet Zinfandel, a creditable Chenin Blanc, and an assortment of 17 percent muscatels, ports, and sherries. But the outstanding Santo Tomás wine was a four-year-old Barbera, superior to any Barbera I have tasted in Italy. It was the best wine I tasted in Mexico, and it even is finding buyers in California, because in 1969 the Barbera and three other Santo Tomás wines became the first Mexican wines imported to this country since a few entered during the Second World War short-age.

General Rodríguez, in his great house at the end of a drive lined with palm and olive trees at the north edge of Ensenada, was too ill to visit his winery when Dmitri Tchelistcheff arrived, but the General enjoyed its improving wines until he died in 1967 at the age of seventy-eight. The vineyards and winery passed to his widow, the former Aida Sullivan of San Diego, and to his three sons, but were sold a year later to the Elias Pando wine-importing firm of Mexico City.

The Guadalupe Valley, twenty miles northeast of Ensenada, has a thousand acres of vineyards and one of the largest olive groves in the world. It was settled early in this century by a religious colony of immigrants from Russia. They are said to have lived in poverty, even robbing beehives for food, until General Rodríguez advised them to plant vineyards and to sell him their grapes. There now are two modern wineries in the valley. Productos Vinícola, built in 1957, sends its Terrasola wines and brandy in barrels to its plant in Mexico City. Jacinto Bortoluz, from the Conegliano school in Italy, makes the wines at Guadalupe, and Jules Michaud, a graduate of Bordeaux, finishes them in Mexico City. Those I tasted at both places were clean and sound. A new million-gallon winery at Guadalupe was built in 1972 by Pedro Domecq of Mexico especially to make table wines. It is situated on the vineyard owned by Estaban Ferro, who once managed the Santo Tomás winery for General Rodríguez. Ferro's own rather unattractive winery in Ensenada was making bulk wine and brandy and "Miramar" bottled table wines when I was there.

In Valle Redondo, the principal vineyard is the 125 acres owned by Conrado Perez. He built his winery in Tijuana to make his El Mirador wines and Casa Blanca brandy in 1940, when the winery was "out in the country," but booming Tijuana now surrounds the site, and the winery is not listed in the latest directory of Mexican producers.

When I was last in Baja California, another Tijuana winery was operated by the Cetto family, whose firm name is Productos de Uva. Angelo Cetto came from Italy to Guadalajara in 1923, worked as a laborer, then went north to Tijuana and began to make bulk wine. He sent his sons to college in Mexico City, and when they joined his business it began to grow. They bought the winery at Tecate established during the 1950s by José Vasquez, and began bottling wine there under the F. Chauvenet brand, then acquired vineyards at Valle Redondo, Guadalupe, and Tañama, and later another at Aguascalientes in Central Mexico, where they built their third winery in 1964. Their best wines were chianti and other *tintos* under the Valle Redondo brand.

The remaining Baja California district, Rancho Viejo, is a small valley between brush-covered hills five miles off the Ensenada-Tecate highway, not far from the old gold-mining town of El Alamo. The vineyard and winery there were established about 1940, but production has been limited by the scarcity of water for irrigation.

• 7 •

Hacienda Alamo at Saltillo, where Nazario Ortiz Garza planted his first vines, is now the headquarters of all his *viñedos* (vineyards) in four Mexican states. Though situated directly on Federal Highway 54, only three miles from the modern city, the hacienda cannot have changed much since colonial times. It is a self-contained village with its own ancient adobe church and primary school, with the homes of vineyard workers clustered around the baronial residence of Mario, don Nazario's son. Its vineyard, however, has shrunk lately to half of its original 450-acre size. Lack of water is the reason; the fast-growing city of Saltillo has first call on the supply that is pumped from local wells, which now range in depth from 600 feet to half a mile.

On Xicotencatl Street in Saltillo, near the railway station, is don Nazario's oldest winery, where his Alamo wines and Club 45 brandy are made. The best of the Alamo wines that I sampled there were the Vino Rosado, a fresh rosé with an unusual flavor reminiscent of some Italian chiantis, and the Manzanilla Alamo, a well-aged, flavorful dry sherry.

In the State of Aguascalientes, nine miles north of Aguascalientes city, is don Nazario's third winery. If you travel on the Carretera Internacional (CN 45) between El Paso and Mexico City, you cannot miss it, because his property spans the highway. On one side, a mammoth wine bottle perched atop his winery dominates the valley skyline and can be seen for miles. Across the road a rococo portal announces the entrance to his Viñedos San Marcos, which now cover some 8000 acres; San Marcos is the brand of his Aguascalientes wines. Behind the winery is an hacienda even greater than that of Alamo, again with its own church and primary school. Fifty families live there, and the hacienda has its own school bus that takes the older children to the Aguascalientes high school. The residence is also huge. In its central court in 1954, notables from throughout the Republic gathered to inaugurate the annual Fería de la Uva, which celebrates the emergence of Aguascalientes as a viticultural district. During the five grape-festival days in mid-August, there are parades and dances in the city plaza, a queen is crowned, and Aguascalientes restaurants include wine in their guests' meals.

What is most striking in Aguascalientes, when one views the thousands of acres of flourishing vineyards, the big new wineries and brandy distilleries that line the highway and byroads, is to realize that none of them existed before the Second World War. Until then, this area was largely a wasteland of nopal, maguey, and mesquite. Now it leads all the other Mexican states in vineyard acreage.

The oldest Aguascalientes winery is the Bodegas de San Ygnacio, established by Filemon Alonzo in an old woolen mill in 1948. The Bodegas de Monte Casino of Victor Manuel Castelazo was built in 1955. Among the newer plants are the Cetto family's Productos de Uva Aguascalientes cellar, built in 1964, the Industrias de la Fermentación winery of David Alonzo and son, and Vinificación y Destilación, added in 1968 to the group operated by Pedro Domecq of Mexico.

• 8 •

At Paila on the Saltillo-Torreón highway (CN 40) through southern Coahuila, you turn off on state route 35 through a valley of pecan groves and vineyards to reach Parras de la Fuente, sixteen miles to the south. Most guidebooks neglect Parras, merely mentioning it as the birthplace of the martyred president of Mexico, Francisco I. Madero. It is a lovely, unspoiled colonial town that still has horse cabs, but no tourist guides. Ringed in by mountains, it also has no television, and the art of conversation still flourishes among its friendly people.

For the wine tourist, a visit to the valley is particularly interesting, for the two oldest wineries in Mexico are there. One is the Vinícola del Marqués de Aguayo, founded in 1593 by a Spanish captain, Francisco de Urdiñola. *Parra* is the Spanish word for grapevine. Urdiñola found wild grapes growing in the valley, and he named it Santa María de las Parras, which was changed after the French invasion of 1862–67 to honor Antonio de la Fuente, a hero of that conflict.

If local historians are correct, the Parras valley was the cradle of viniculture in the Americas. They say that from here, Urdiñola sent his wines and vines to Peru, Chile, and Argentina before any vineyards existed in South America, and that he continued doing so until the Spanish authorities enforced the royal order that wine in the New World must come only from Spain. Urdiñola's great-granddaughter married a Spaniard, who through the captain's influence was given a title, and when the Marqués inherited the property, he gave it his new name.

Although this is the oldest winery on the American continent, all that remains of the original structure is the adobe wall of enologist Gianbattista Masante's office. The rest was destroyed in 1965 when new owners, the Almacénes Guajuardo merchants of Monterrey, began rebuilding it and started making wine and brandy. Masante, who comes from the school of enology at Alba

in Italy, said they had acquired land on which to plant new vineyards, and that he hoped soon to concentrate on making premium
table wines and champagnes.

Second oldest, and with its 6-million-gallon capacity one of the
most important in all Mexico, is the Bodegas de San Lorenzo of
Casa Madero. Founded in 1626 by Lorenzo Garcia, it is now
owned by eight branches of the Madero family, cousins of the late
President. There are five more wineries at Parras and the ruins of
many more, because, despite the Spanish law, every early hacienda had its own vineyard and made wine.

The Maderos have owned the bodegas since 1870. In that year,
Evaristo Madero Elizondo, a young merchant from northern
Coahuila across the border from the United States, bought Hacienda San Lorenzo and Captain Urdiñola's original property,
Hacienda Rosario. Don Evaristo traveled to Europe and brought
back superior grape varieties from Italy, Switzerland, Spain,
Portugal, and France. In Cognac he bought a brandy still, and
brought French experts to install it at Parras. By the turn of the
century, don Evaristo's wines and brandies were winning medals
at the Paris, Buffalo, and St. Louis expositions. After his death in
1911, the property passed to his sons by his second wife, although
he had the foresight to incorporate his Parras holdings. To his
sons and grandsons by his first wife he willed lands in the Laguna
district. One of these grandsons was Francisco, the idealistic
cotton planter and intellectual who started the Revolution of 1910
and became President Madero of Mexico.

In don Evaristo's time, vineyards covered 3000 acres in the
Parras Valley, but most of them were destroyed by the phylloxera
and the rest by neglect during the Revolution. The 1200 acres
replanted since, of which the Maderos own 500 acres, all are on
phylloxera-resistant roots.

Rebuilt since 1962, with its parklike entrance, striking fountain,
and beautiful church beside the cellars, Casa Madero is now one
of the handsomest wineries in the world. It is also hospitable; a
sign on the road from Paila invites you to visit the bodegas. After
you tour the cellars and the distillery with its quaint French-type
pot stills, you are served wines on the veranda of Casa Grande,
the three-century-old guest house. But one time *not* to visit Parras,
unless you have reserved accommodations months in advance,
is during its Fiesta de Uva in mid-August, the annual grape
festival which the Madero family revived in 1946 to celebrate
the three hundred and twentieth anniversary of Bodegas San
Lorenzo.

Two Madero cousins are in charge of Casa Madero's wine and

brandy production. Eduardo manages the vineyards and Benjamín is superintendent of the winery and distillery. A mobile laboratory mounted on a truck cruises through the vineyards, testing the grapes in each row of vines to determine when they are ready to be picked. A new *criadera de crianza* has been built especially for the aging of red wines in small cooperage. The winery laboratory has been equipped with the latest wine-testing instruments, such as you see in the most modern California wineries. Casa Madero's enologist, Angel Morales, a graduate of the technical institute of Monterrey, has gone twice to Davis to take the short courses in enology.

The improvements were evident in the wines. San Carlos Tinto Fino was soft, dry, well-balanced, and had more fruity aroma than I find in most Mexican wines. Morales said this and the San Lorenzo Rosado (rosé) were made from blends of Carignane, Grenache, and Cinsaut. There was a good 16 percent medium-dry sherry called Pedro Ximénez Tipo Jerez Oro Dulce, though Morales said it was made from Palomino, not Pedro Ximénez. He had also begun making a bottle-fermented champagne, Vino Espumoso blanco brut, from Ugni Blanc and the red Cinsaut grape.

Benjamín Madero, who was educated in Michigan and played guitar in the university orchestra there, says Mexican wines will continue to improve as better grape varieties are planted. He believes Parras, 5000 feet above sea level, is the best winegrowing district. He has kept temperature records there since 1953, and concludes that Parras has a Region IV climate, comparable to Lodi in California and Florence in Italy. (Dmitri Tchelistcheff says the climates of Santo Tomás and Guadalupe are between Region II and Region III, but bases his opinion on tests of his wines, not on temperature records.)

• 9 •

Two hours' drive west of Parras, clustered at the border of Durango and Coahuila, are the charming old triplet cities of Gómez Palacio, Lerdo, and Torreón, only minutes apart. Torreón, the largest, is on the Coahuila side. Around the cities, in the reclaimed Laguna district, hundreds of former cotton fields have been replanted with vineyards since Mexico's grape industry came back to life in the early 1940s. At Torreón in 1966, the Mexican Government established its first mother vineyard with stocks from Davis to propagate and supply the grape growers with virus-free vines.

The two newest wineries in La Laguna, those of Nazario Ortiz Garza and Pedro Domecq at Torreón, were designed to make brandy, into which go almost nine tenths of the grapes grown in Mexico.*

The oldest winery in the district, the Vinícola del Vergel at Gómez Palacio, also makes brandy, but devotes a third of its production to wines. Vergel was built in 1943 by one of the district's leading cotton planters, the late Luis Garza (not related to don Nazario), with equipment supplied by Antonio Perelli-Minetti. The founder's son, Santiago A. Garza, is now in charge. With its outdoor batteries of temperature-controlled tanks of Mexican-made stainless steel, Vergel resembles the modern new wineries of California. But beneath the main building is one of the most spectacular Old World underground cellars in North America. Its vaulted roof and supporting pillars are made entirely of rough marble quarried from the nearby mountains. Each of the large wine casks in the cellar bears the name of a saint.

Santiago Garza predicts that wine-drinking in Mexico will increase when enough wine-grape varieties are planted to make better table wines. The vineyards of Vergel still contain many table grapes, but Garza has added such wine varieties as Trebbiano (Ugni Blanc), Ruby Cabernet, and French Colombard. He has sent his winemaker, Valente Arellano, a graduate of Monterrey, to take the short courses in enology at Davis. His manager, Fernando Menéndez, also was trained at Monterrey and has worked at the Perelli-Minetti winery in California. Of the Vergel table wines that I sampled, the best was one then not yet on the market: a Ruby Cabernet with varietal character. Also pleasant were a dry red called Noblejo, a semidry rosé labeled Corina Rosado Seco, and a five-year-old, sun-baked amontillado sherry, which the company was then preparing to introduce.

• 10 •

At Hermosillo in the semitropical west coast state of Sonora, vineyards were planted among the orchards and cotton fields

---

*This came about partly through a quirk in the semantics of drink. The Spanish word for spirits is *aguardiente*, literally burning water. New, water-white grape brandy is *aguardiente de uva*, and aged beverage brandy is *coñac* in Spanish. But after World War II the Mexican government prohibited all *coñac* labels except on those from the Cognac district of France. The Mexican *coñac* distillers, suddenly left without a label for their product, adopted its English name, though there is no such word as brandy in the Spanish language. It turned out to have such snob appeal to Mexicans that brandy has since passed rum and tequila as the chief distilled liquor drunk in Mexico.

beginning about 1961. The grapes, however, were mostly the early-ripening table varieties, intended for shipment to the United States in competition with the early Coachella Valley crop from California. A winery was built at Hermosillo in 1965, but its principal product was brandy, not wine.

Table grapes and brandy are also the chief products of the vineyards around Ciudad Delicias and Jiménez in Chihuahua. Grape growing became important there after the Second World War, when growers found it more profitable than raising cotton. There are two wineries, both at Ciudad Delicias.

• 11 •

The southernmost vineyard district of Mexico is the valley of the Río de San Juan, 100 miles north of Mexico City. It is also the highest, 6100 feet above sea level. Though situated two degrees within the Torrid Zone, the valley successfully grows the delicate grape varieties that make superior table wines.

A mile east of the old colonial town of San Juan del Río is a handsome stone winery named Cavas de San Juan, which produces Hidalgo wines. Francisco Domenech, born in Catalonia, where his family produced vermouth, built the winery in 1958 to make both wine and brandy, but primarily table wines. As his enologist he employed Carlos Reulet, a graduate of the vinicultural school of Onde near Bordeaux and a former pilot in the Free French Air Force. Meanwhile, Domenech sent his son, Francisco Domenech T., to Davis to be trained in viticulture.

When young Francisco came home, he began replanting part of the vineyard with such varieties as Cabernet Sauvignon, Pinot Noir, Gamay, Pinot Gris, Chenin Blanc, Ugni Blanc, and Chardonnay. Since I was there, the winery has supplemented its Blanco Seco, Blanco Amabile, Rosado Seco, Clarete, and Tinto with a Cepa Pinot Noir, a Blanc de Blancs blended from Chenin Blanc and Ugni Blanc, and an assortment of Charmat-process Vinos Espumosos. (Mexico does not allow its vintners to call their sparkling wines champagne.)

Attached to each attractive Hidalgo bottle is a leaflet that lists the wines, gives directions for serving them, and extends an invitation to visit the Cavas de San Juan.

Twelve miles north of San Juan del Río, at the picturesque village of Tequisquiapan, the Martell Cognac interests of France built a brandy distillery and planted extensive vineyards in 1965. Three years later, Martell of Mexico introduced its first Mexican wine, a red table type called Lorimont.

• 12 •

Around Mexico City there are several wine and brandy establishments, and some of them can be visited by appointment.

In the suburb of Los Reyes, an eleven-mile drive on the road to Puebla, is the impressive brandy blending, aging, and bottling plant of Pedro Domecq of Mexico. In personal charge there is Pedro F. Domecq, a member of the world-famous sherry-making family of Spain. It is worth the trip to see Domecq's great brandy *soleras* and the lovely "La Sacristía," with its display of glass-fronted barrels showing the year-by-year benefits of aging brandy in oak. (Be sure to telephone for an appointment and to get driving directions before starting out.)

Domecq also produces two Mexican table wines, but no sherries, because Domecq sherries are produced only in Spain. Marcial Ibarra, who learned enology from Professor Cruess at the University of California in Berkeley and later taught it at the University of Mexico, is the technical director of Domecq brandy and wine production. One of the best Mexican red wines is Domecq's Los Reyes, produced at Ramos Arizpe. The new Domecq winery in Baja California is expected to produce additional table wine types.

At ancient Tlalnepantla, several miles north of the capital near the road toward Querétaro, are the old Bodegas Santa María of Antonio Fernandez y Cia., where David Alonzo from Spain makes assorted table and sparkling wines. This company has a new, modern winery at Aguascalientes, headed by Alonzo's son, called Industrias de la Fermentación.

Around Mexico City, too, are the modern plants of such world-famous companies as Seagram, Cinzano, and Martini & Rossi; the latter two make their vermouths there from Mexican wines.

But the busiest winery in the area is the Mexico City winery of Nazario Ortiz Garza on Avenida Mixcoac. There I tasted the three best wines from his Mexican vineyards. One, a six-year-old Tinto, bore the world-renowned brand name of the Federico Paternina firm of Haro in the Rioja district of Spain. Paternina is one of the several European vintners who have licensed Mexican wineries to use their labels on especially selected Mexican wines. Another Tinto, four years old and under don Nazario's Alamo Extra brand, was almost as good as the Paternina. Finally, there was a medium-sweet brown sherry called Jerez Solera Alamo, sun-baked in the rear of the Mexico City winery, that was one of the best sherries I tasted in all of Mexico.

• 13 •

To visit all of the Mexican vineyard districts in a single trip is impractical except by car, or preferably by private plane. Torreón, Aguascalientes, and Chihuahua are served by scheduled airlines, but at this writing Ensenada, San Juan del Río, and Saltillo are not. For private planes, arrangements can be made to use the airstrip at Parras adjoining the Casa Madero vineyards.

Wine-touring in Mexico will become increasingly interesting in the future, as the better grape varieties lately planted come into bearing and as the quality of Mexican wines continues to improve.

24

The Hobbyist Winemakers

WHILE big wineries are getting bigger in order to slake America's growing thirst for wine, little winemakers are increasing in numbers at an accelerating pace.

Small wineries that sell their own products have almost doubled in numbers since 1965, and, as more states reduce their exorbitant winery license fees, are certain to multiply in the next several years. Yet more important, in terms of millions of gallons, is the fast-growing trend toward winemaking in American homes. Both kinds of small-scale winemaking are doing as much as the commercial wineries to change the face of the nation's viticulture.

• 2 •

Home winemakers, who ferment juice only for their own use, fall into several categories, which sometimes overlap. During Prohibition, more than 30 million gallons were made annually in home basements in this country, especially by immigrant European families to whom wine was a mealtime necessity. Most of their immediate descendants, however, have given up the fermenting of grapes as too much trouble. Today's noncommercial winemakers are a new breed.

They usually start with the simple kitchen experiment of adding yeast to a crock of crushed grapes, juice, or reconstituted concentrate. Some try it once and give it up when they find they have made inferior vinegar instead. But many go on to spend hundreds and even thousands of dollars on crushers, presses, chemicals, and testing instruments, and many even to make their own champagnes.

While some who make wine regularly are merely saving money, another and more numerous category are primarily hobbyists, motivated not by economy but by their fascination with the mystique and romance of wine. They are mostly talented white collar people bitten by the wine bug, who have found in this scientific kind of handicraft a hobby of continuing interest, more esthetically satisfying than collecting coins, stamps, or books. Wine, because it keeps changing and takes months and years to mature, gives the winemaker a sense of the future that no other hobby does. The oenothusiast knows that better wine than he makes can usually be bought for little more or even less at the store.

Most devoted of the avocational winemakers are professional people, particularly physicians, engineers, chemists, college professors, accountants, artists, and writers. The doctors are the most avid of them all. Far more MDs than people of any other occupation are counted among the customers of the winemaking supply firms. Why wine especially fascinates physicians was explained in a recent book called *Vine and Scalpel* by Dr. Max Lake, who owns a vineyard in Australia. "The doctor," he wrote, "has a comfortable amount of winemaking science as part of his medical training. He must also learn to evaluate sensory impressions and cultivate mental discipline, two attributes that tend to make him a wine connoisseur."

Hundreds of home winemakers' societies have been formed across the United States because amateur enologists want others to taste and compare their wines. Their national organization, the American Wine Society, lists 1300 members and seventy-three chapters in three dozen states and publishes its own quarterly journal, called *Vintage*.

Since a new Federal ruling permits home winemakers to hold competitions with prizes for their best vintages, the lure of possibly winning championship awards is added as a motive for making one's own wine. Amateur winemakers are as proud of their achievements as flower growers, dog breeders, artists, and others who hold quality contests, perhaps even prouder, for winemaking is both an art and a science. (The first public judging of home-made wines in this country was held in August 1972, at Mason City, Iowa, as part of the North Iowa Fair. The first national judging was planned at San Francisco for February, 1973).

• 3 •

Federal law permits the home production of up to 200 gallons of wine each year without paying a tax on the product, but restricts the privilege to heads of households. It thereby prohibits winemaking by an individual living without his spouse or without dependents in the household under his control. Bachelors of both sexes have long protested this discrimination, and a bill (HR 5372) to eliminate the head-of-household restriction has been pending in Congress since 1971. A Federal regulation further classifies home winemaking as illegal unless the householder first files Form 1541 with the nearest office of the Internal Revenue Service. Though the form is free, it merely constitutes a registration or a declaration of intent to make wine—not a license or permit—and consequently not many people bother to file it. The Federal Government is not really interested in home winemaking, anyway, but only in seeing that if wine is to be sold, the requirements for permits, bonds, tax stamps, and for payment of the Federal gallonage tax are obeyed.

Another part of the regulation prohibits the amateur from transporting his homemade wine from his dwelling without Federal permission. I haven't heard of any attempt in recent years to enforce either the filing regulation or the transportation taboo. It was the prohibition on transportation that led to the Federal ruling that now permits wine to be taken to places where quality competitions are to be held. Amateur enologists' organizations complained that such contests, with judges awarding prizes for the best wines, have been held for years in England and should be permitted in the United States. (Under the ruling, special permission must be obtained for each competition the home winemaker enters.)

A conservative estimate, based on average annual interstate carlot shipments of fresh grapes from California, is that at least 7 million gallons of wine are now being made noncommercially in the United States each year. But if wines made from grape concentrate are counted, the quantity is probably closer to 10 million gallons, enough to supply a half-million amateurs with forty gallons each. And this does not include the production of those householders who ferment only dandelions, rhubarb, elderberries, blueberries, or honey (to make mead), as their grandmothers and great-grandmothers did.

A multimillion-dollar accessory industry has come into existence to supply amateur enologists with home-winemaking materials, equipment, corks, and even with labels printed with their names, such as "Chateau Smith Vin Blanc" or "Maison Jones Private Stock." Some firms offer free classes in winemaking and distribute bumper strips that say MAKE WINE NOT WAR.

Purists, of course, prefer to make their wines out of fresh grapes or juice, which can only be bought at vintage time. Grape concentrate, available year round, is more convenient for winemaking at home. The reviving use of concentrate recalls the Prohibition era a half century ago, when millions of gallons of "Vine-

Glo," "Caligrapo," and "Forbidden Fruit" concentrates were fermented to wine in American homes.

Well-made concentrate wines cannot be distinguished from ordinary commercial types, but they generally lack aroma. Experiments now in progress are attempting to extract the aromatic essences of wine grapes before the juice is concentrated. The idea is to supply home winemakers with the bottled essence to be added after the wine is made.

The Wine-Art Company, the biggest supplier, now sells plastic jugs of "varietal" concentrates of a dozen different grapes, including Cabernet Sauvignon, Pinot Noir, Johannisberg Riesling, and Zinfandel, and imports another dozen kinds of concentrate in cans from Europe, including Bordeaux, Beaujolais, and Chianti blends.

A beginner's winemaking kit, which can be bought nowadays for only a few dollars, contains a quart of concentrate, small envelopes of yeast and chemicals, fermentation locks, siphon hose, a collapsible plastic jug, and a recipe to make a single gallon (five bottles) of table wine. Bigger kits, at twelve to twenty dollars, have become such fast-selling items that Sears, Montgomery Ward, and the big Welch Company have jumped into the homemade-wine-supply business and are selling millions of dollars' worth of such materials and equipment. Their sales are especially big in areas where commercial wines are expensive because of high state wine taxes or where wines can be bought only in state monopoly stores.

Oldest of the firms that sell home-winemaking supplies, the Aetna Bottle Company of Seattle, has customers in every state in the Union, in Canada, India, Thailand, and even in Saudi Arabia. Scores of books are published for home winemakers, and also three magazines: *The Amateur Enologist* at Vancouver, B.C.; *Cellar Notes* at North East, Pennsylvania, and *The Purple Thumb* at Van Nuys, California, which also serves home brewers of beer. (Home brewing is technically illegal, however, under a change made in the Federal law in 1959; the brewing industry considers it unfair competition. Few commercial wineries oppose home winemaking because amateurs help to popularize the drinking of wine, and most of them buy as much wine as they produce.)

• 4 •

Co-operative groups of avocational winemakers take some unique forms. In an earlier chapter I told the story of Seattle's scientific amateurs, who have their own vineyard and bonded winery and are producing some of the best Washington State wines for sale.

In Illinois, twenty Chicago wine buffs have organized a Society of Viniculture and Enology and are cultivating ten vines each in a joint venture on Dr. Thompson's vineyard southwest of Chicago. They expect eventually to produce 4000 gallons per year for the members' private use.

California has an Academy of Cellarmasters, which may be a national model for similarly dedicated groups. It has a fully equipped miniature bonded winery producing wine for the members' exclusive use. It began in 1967 when several colleagues of Dr. August J. Haschka, Jr. (a Santa Monica internist) wanted to become partners in his home-winemaking hobby. Because the law limits the privilege to individual households, they incorporated the Academy and obtained the Federal and state permits and licenses required for commercial wineries. The Academy has nineteen members, fourteen of whom are doctors, two are lawyers, and three are members of other professions. Their thousand-gallon winery consists of a concrete cellar originally built as a fallout shelter and an ivy-covered guest house, which are leased to the Academy, on Dr. Haschka's Malibu estate. At harvest season, the members rent a moving van and drive to the vineyards of either Napa or San Luis Obispo County. They load the grapes into polyethylene-lined barrels, have the grapes crushed at a neighboring winery, and take the must to Malibu to be fermented, racked, and aged. The members share the work and expenses and divide each vintage, which supplies each member with several cases of excellent wine. The Academy prints its annual proceedings like any scholarly institution, and is dedicated to the advancement of enological science and art. Each November, the members and their wives relax and gather at the winery for a Roman-style Bacchanal.

• 5 •

The truest of all wine lovers are those who grow their own grapes to make their wine. Their appreciation of the final product is multiplied by the years of back-breaking labor, suffering the depredations of weather and of grape-eating birds, and waiting for their first crops. How patient they must be is evident from the three to five years it takes from the planting of a vine until it bears a usable crop. If you add at least four years for a fine red wine to mature, you see that the new winegrower is investing a decade of his life. Yet there are many who consider the rewards infinitely greater than those from the raising of other crops that one cannot drink.

Philip Wagner, whose books have encouraged thousands of amateurs to plant wine grapes, spells out the attractions. A hundred healthy vines in the lower end of a back yard, he says, will yield a vintage of sixty gallons, which supplies the grower with three hundred bottles, or almost a bottle of table wine per day through the year. (Dr. Albert Winkler calculates that a hundred vines in sunny California can produce three times as much as Wagner's figure.)

An amateur who plants more than a hundred vines can use only a little over a ton of his crop to make wine, because more would exceed the 200-gallon limit. If he makes more, he must bond his cellar and consider selling some of his wine.

Most of the small winegrowers who have bonded their cellars hope to make a profit by selling their wines. Whether they profit or lose depends on many factors, including their talent, industrious habits, business sense, and particularly on the ups and downs of the market for wine. The shortage of premium grapes that developed in the 1960s may well end by the late 1970s.

Winegrowing is like most other industries in that it costs multiple millions to start out in competition with the leaders. Yet wine is also one of the few industries in which an individual can start with a small acreage and make something in his home basement that he can sell. Better yet, of course, is to start out wealthy, with no thought of early profits, as many have done. For some there is sufficient reward in merely achieving the admired status of gentleman winegrower.

Decades ago, Herman Wente gave me some advice to pass on to the many would-be winegrowers who have come to me for guidance before entering the wine industry. The small winegrower can succeed, Herman said, only if he remains small and sells his wine at retail. Thereby he makes not only the profits (if any) of the grape grower and of the wine producer, but the profits of the wholesaler and of the retailer in addition. To my knowledge, those who have followed Herman's advice have prospered thus far.

Small winegrowers also have an advantage that Herman didn't mention. Because their output is limited, their wines become rarities, which lends them extra charm. Connoisseurs nowadays gladly pay extra prices for good wines if they are especially scarce and hard to find. Some small wineries sell all they can make, at prices considerably above those of the nationally known premium brands, by merely sending announcements to the customers on their mailing lists that their latest vintages are ready to be shipped.

There is no truth, of course, in the belief held by many wine snobs, that fine wines can only be made in small quantities. The

American wines that are now winning high praise around the world come from sizable wineries that have modern equipment and staffs of expert enologists.

Yet commercial wines need to be filtered, fined, made brilliantly clear and sufficiently stable to survive cross-country transportation and storage in excessive heat and cold while awaiting sale. The small winegrower can let his wines clarify themselves, can bottle them while they still contain grape solids that will precipitate in the bottles, and can explain this to his customers.

In particular, commercial grape growers have found it economically necessary to abandon their old hillside vineyards, which once produced their finest wines. Their tractors and mechanical harvesters cannot operate on steep terrain, and labor costs have made hand-cultivation prohibitively expensive. (This is also happening in Europe.) Only the avocational winegrower can afford to till the hillsides.

The small winegrower may not make wines that are finer than others, but what he makes will at least be excitingly different. Only he can afford to experiment in localities where grapes have not been grown before, planting new grape varieties and developing wines with new regional characteristics.

I was discussing the future of fine American wines recently with André Tchelistcheff. He pointed out that as the production of the leading vintners in Europe and America continues to grow in volume, their wines become more uniform; they have less opportunity to engage in pioneering experiments. "The apostolic mission of the future," said Tchelistcheff, "belongs to the small winegrower."

25

Some "Varietal Grapes" and Their Wines

WHEN American vintners, during three decades following Repeal, introduced almost a hundred wines newly named for grape varieties, they multiplied the delicious confusion that surrounds the subject of wine. Most of the varietal names on bottle labels and restaurant wine lists present a viticultural puzzle to most buyers of wine.

But in adopting varietal labeling, the vintners also contributed vastly to the improved quality of American wines. For by renaming their best and costliest vintages for the grapes from which they are made, the wineries gave vineyardists a profit motive to plant superior wine-grape varieties in place of the more prolific fresh-juice, raisin, and table grapes that have mainly been grown in this country until now.

If, for example, the vintners had not taught wine merchants that Chardonnay, White (Johannisberg) Riesling, Cabernet Sauvignon, and Pinot Noir make the world's finest table wines, the grape growers would not have planted the nearly thirty thousand acres of these four noble varieties that have been added to American vineyards in recent years. Buyers who have learned to recognize these varietal labels now gladly pay a dollar to three dollars more per bottle for these wines than for their old generically named equivalents—chablis, rhine wine, claret, and burgundy. And once a status-conscious American masters the pronunciation of such tongue-twisting names as Cabernet Sauvignon and Pinot Noir, he proudly orders them in stores and restaurants to display his knowledge of fine wines.

How this motivates vineyard planting is evident from the all-time-record prices some California coast counties wineries were paying growers in 1971 for some "varietal grapes": $625 per ton for Chardonnay, White Riesling, Cabernet Sauvignon, and Pinot Noir, and $325 for Sauvignon Blanc, Chenin Blanc, and Barbera, compared to the San Joaquin Valley prices of $54 per ton for Thompson Seedless and $60 for Flame Tokay.* This is why more than two-thirds of the new vineyards planted in California during that year consisted of grape varieties with whose names premium wines are most frequently labeled.

Grapes whose names appear on wine labels are commonly called "varietal grapes," although this is a redundancy, because every grape, including those that make the poorest wines, is a member of some variety, no matter how obscure its botanical parentage may be. Another foggy popular term is "varietal wines," which doesn't describe the wines, but only means that their labels tell you the grape varieties from which they are principally made. The Federal regulation requires a varietally labeled wine to contain at least 51 percent of the grape named, but says nothing about the other 49 percent, which may have an entirely different taste.

Wines sold under grape names are usually better than those labeled with the old generic names of European geographic origin. Not always, however, because a wine's quality depends also on where the vine grew, whether it was pruned to keep the crop small, when the grapes were picked, and how the vintner processed, blended, and aged the wine.

Adding to the confusion is that most grapes have many different names, by any of which the wines made from them can be called; some examples will follow a few pages hence. Many grapes are misnamed, and European vintners, now imitating the American varietal labels, are adding to the tangle with their own contradictory versions of some variety names. The result is that one needs an ampelography, which can't be found in the average library, to be guided through the wine-nomenclature maze.

• 2 •

The jumble of varietal names is now being at least partially unraveled, however, for the principal grapes grown for winemaking in the United States. Through a grape-certification program founded by the University of California in 1952, Vinifera vines certified as correctly named, and also as free of virus diseases, are now being supplied to growers and co-operating nurseries. Confusion is also being lessened among the many-numbered French hybrid grapes grown east of the Rockies.

---

*At press time, California wineries were paying growers sharply higher prices for their 1972 crops than they paid in 1971, not only for "varietal" wine grapes but also for Thompson Seedless and Flame Tokay, which were in short supply following severe spring frosts in the San Joaquin Valley.

The purpose of the California certification program was not to untangle grape nomenclature, but to supply the wine industry with disease-free vines. It was prompted by advances after the Second World War in plant pathology and vine research, which showed that most of the world's vineyards are hosts to a previously unidentified disease called the leafroll virus, which reduces vine vigor and productivity without killing the plants. Were it not for this virus, plant pathologists say, the vineyards of Europe would have more frequent vintage years than they do. One of their surprising discoveries was that the much-admired autumn coloring of vineyards is mostly caused by the leafroll virus—that the leaves of healthy vines seldom develop those spectacularly lovely shades of red!

Unfortunately, when the mad vineyard-planting spree of the late 1960s began, the supply of certified healthy, variety-true vines was not sufficient to meet the demand. Thousands of acres were recklessly planted with cuttings from diseased vines, purchased from infected vineyards and from nurseries with uncertified stocks. When this was realized in 1970, quarantines against virus-infected vines were hurriedly established in the states of Washington and Oregon.

The shortage of certified vines continued until 1971, when two new discoveries shortened the time it had been taking the California program to provide supplies of healthy vines. The first discovery was that by exposing vines to controlled heat for a period of several weeks, cuttings can be taken from them that are completely free of disease. The second was an assembly-line method of growing vines in moisture-controlled greenhouses, called "mist propagation," which makes it possible to produce a million cuttings within a single year from a single parent vine.

· 3 ·

In California for almost a century, except during Prohibition, University viticulturists have been testing wine grapes, growing more than a hundred different varieties in various parts of the state, making experimental wines of each variety and evaluating the wines. As the main result of this research, the University has listed some twoscore varieties as "acceptable" or "recommended" for planting in specific climatic regions to make wines of high quality and to earn the growers a profit.

The University strongly recommends that the four *cépages nobles* (Chardonnay, White Riesling, Cabernet Sauvignon, Pinot Noir) be grown only in the cool coast counties, Region I, II, and III. For Regions IV and V, the varieties mainly recommended are Ruby

Cabernet and Barbera for red table wines and French Colombard and Chenin Blanc (for Region IV) for whites. For port wines in warm climates the University favors such Portuguese grapes as Tinta Madeira, Touriga, and Souzão.

Most of the University's planting recommendations are being followed, but not all. We have seen how, by the late 1960s, the record high prices vintners were paying for the four noble varieties in the coast counties were tempting farmers in the hot San Joaquin Valley to begin planting them in their Region IV and V climates, where they yield grapes of lower quality but more tons per acre. This alarms the University savants because there is nothing to prevent wines from the valley being sold to the public under the four most prestigious varietal names. "It would seem wise," warns Professor Maynard Amerine in a 1971 article in *Wines & Vines*, "that these labels not be debased by using wines of varieties grown in regions that do not meet present expectations of quality." If the top varietal names are thus "debased" by the valley growers, he adds, the coast counties vintners may be compelled to start labeling all their products as "Coast Wines."

• 4 •

Is the Federal regulation too lenient in allowing a wine to bear a varietal label when it contains as little as 51 percent of the grape named? This question has been hotly argued ever since the regulation became effective in 1936. Some coast counties vineyardists in California have petitioned the state's legislature to enact a law that would raise the minimum percentage to 75 for California varietally labeled wines. Most vintners admit privately that the 51 percent requirement could well be raised to 60 or 75, but they want such a change postponed until their newly planted vineyards come into bearing to relieve the present extreme shortage of the prestige grapes. (European countries have never specified any such percentage, but the new German wine law, effective in 1970, sets a minimum of 75 per cent.)

Since any minimum over 51 percent would be an improvement, why not make it 100 percent? That would be a mistake, because most wines need blending with wines of different grapes to be at their best. No single grape variety can be relied on, year after year, to produce wines of ideal balance in every respect.

Morever, complexity of wine flavor, an elusive quality that many American wines still lack, is best attained with a blend of different grapes. The fine wines of the Champagne region of France are traditionally blends of Pinot Noir and Chardonnay, and the French appellation control permits French champagnes to contain as many as four additional grapes (Pinot Blanc, Pinot Gris, Arbanne, Petit Meslier). The finest clarets of the Médoc district of Bordeaux are always blends: Cabernet Sauvignon there is normally blended with such relatives as Cabernet Franc, Merlot, and Petit Verdot. French sauternes are always blends of Sémillon and Sauvignon Blanc, sometimes with the addition of Muscadelle. While the famous Côte d'Or red burgundies owe their greatness to Pinot Noir and the famous whites to Chardonnay, the Côte d'Or vineyards also contain appreciable acreages of Gamay Noir, Pinot Blanc, Pinot Gris, and Melon or Aligoté (which in the Loire Valley is called Muscadet). And the French appellation control permits as many as fifteen different grapes to be blended in Châteauneuf-du-Pape, the most renowned of Rhone Valley reds.

Although most wine books call Cabernet Sauvignon the chief French claret grape, that variety represents only a fraction of the red-grape acreage of Bordeaux. In the great châteaux of Saint-Émilion, for example, if you ask a *maître du chai* what percentage of Cabernet Sauvignon his wine contains, he will reply, "*Pas du Sauvignon.*" Jacquelin and Poulain, in their *Wines and Vineyards of France* (Paul Hamlyn, London, 1965), state that nine tenths of the Château Margaux vineyard is planted to Cabernet Sauvignon but that Château Lafite-Rothschild is five eighths Cabernet Sauvignon and three eighths Cabernet Franc and Merlot. On my several visits to the Médoc, few of the château proprietors of whom I inquired on this point claimed that their wines contained more than a third of Cabernet Sauvignon. In fact, if you wish a wine made 100 percent of that noblest of Bordeaux grapes, you are likely to find it only in California. (In years past, more Cabernet Sauvignon was grown in the Médoc than now. But because its wine required many years to mature, it gradually was replaced by Cabernet Franc and Merlot. However, now that Bordeaux winegrowers have learned—as California winemakers have, too—to speed the aging of their red wines by removing them from the skins before fermentation is complete, they are reported to be planting Cabernet Sauvignon again.)

• 5 •

How do you describe the varietal taste of a wine? The grapy or foxy flavor of Labrusca wines is familiar to anyone who has ever tasted grape jelly or Welch's grape juice. Also recognizable, with some practice, are wines made from the scented, aromatic, or "spicy" grapes—the Muscats, Sauvignon Blanc, and Gewürztraminer. The characteristic aromas of Grenache and Gamay Noir, which also make wines that are somewhat "spicy," are readily recognized by at least some connoisseurs. Zinfandel wines are sometimes recognizable, too, because they have an aroma subtly reminiscent of raspberry, which, however, is not often perceptible when the wines are old.

Cabernet Sauvignon wine has a powerful, astringent flavor, as distinctive, when the wine is new, as that of a stale cigar. Professor Amerine says that even when Cabernet Sauvignon is blended down to the legally allowable 51 percent, unless with Zinfandel or another grape of high flavor, the Cabernet will still dominate the blend. Its great virtue is that when its wine is properly aged in cask and in bottle, it gradually loses its astringent taste and develops a fine bouquet. California vintners used to say that Cabernet Sauvignon was undrinkable until it had been aged at least four years in wood and had undergone a malolactic fermentation. Lately, however, I have tasted some Cabernet Sauvignon samples, fermented only briefly on the skins, that were recognizable, fruity, and delicious after only two years in wood.

Most other Vinifera wines have only winy or vinous tastes, developed during vinification and aging, that are not readily identifiable when the wines are new. Chardonnay is the best example. The juice of this tiny, thin-skinned, translucent grape, which makes the greatest white burgundies and champagnes, ferments to a young wine that has no outstanding flavor. But Chardonnay is one of the few white wines that are capable of improving greatly after a year in wood and further aging in glass. Because of its ideal combination of body, delicacy, acidity, and unusually high alcoholic strength, it develops an enchanting winy bouquet. The new winegrowers who are planting Vinifera vines in the East and Midwest choose Chardonnay above other varieties because of its high quality and the high prices its wine commands, and also because it excels most other Old World grapes in its ability to survive their freezing winters. (Other whites besides Chardonnay that are likely to improve with age, but only after bottling, include White Riesling and Sauvignon Blanc.)

Dr. Amerine and Dr. Vernon Singleton, in *Wine—An Introduction for Americans* (University of California Press, 1965), offer some terms descriptive of the principal varietal flavors in Vinifera wines. They describe the taste and aroma of Cabernet Sauvignon as "green olive, herbaceous," Ruby Cabernet as "green olive, weedy, tannic," and Malbec (Cot) as "krautish, soft." They say Pinot Noir is "pepperminty" and that Gamay Beaujolais is "fruity, tart." Nebbiolo they describe as "fruity, licorice," and Tinta Madeira as "prunish, cheddar, rich." Their descriptions of Vinifera white wines mainly use such terms as "fruity," "tart," "spicy," and sometimes "floral," but the character of Chardonnay is described

as "applish" and that of Sémillon as "figs, faintly cigar-like."
Omitted from their descriptions is the flavor of European oak
barrels, which is perceptible in most French clarets and white
burgundies and nowadays in many California Chardonnays. The
University at Davis does not encourage the use of European cooperage because the oak obscures the delicate flavors contributed
by superior grapes.

• 6 •

Muscat grapes, of which there are scores of different varieties,
all of them "spicy," are a study by themselves. The one commonly
grown in California is Muscat of Alexandria, which is primarily a
raisin and table grape but nevertheless makes most of this country's muscatel. Its wines lack the delicacy of the smaller Muscat
Blanc, which is called Moscato Canelli in Italy and Muscat
Frontignan in France. Canadian and New York wineries have
made superior muscatels from the Canada Muscat, a hybrid
developed at the Geneva station in upstate New York.

The name of Muscat seems to lack appeal, however, to most
buyers of wine. For example, when the Christian Brothers in the
1940s introduced a delectable table wine called Light Sweet
Muscat, few people would buy it; but when they changed its name
to Château La Salle, it became their best-selling single wine.
Muscat wines are most delicious when they are made sweet and
low in alcohol, as are Louis Martini's Moscato Amabile at ten
percent and the Muscat champagne of Italy called Asti Spumante,
at nine. And Muscat wines are usually harsh or bitter when fermented completely dry.

There also are dark-colored Muscats, such as Aleatico, which
makes wines that are popular in Italy, and Black Hamburgh, from
which the Novitiate of Los Gatos makes its famous Black Muscat
dessert wine. A French ampelography tells an intriguing story
about the Black Hamburgh grape. It once was widely grown in
France, but when the phylloxera vine louse devastated the French
vineyards, the Black Hamburgh disappeared. Many years later, a
Frenchman visiting a hothouse in England noticed a beautiful
black grape named Venn's Seedling and brought it to France,
where it was identified as the long-lost grape. The only thing
wrong with the story is that the Black Hamburgh was never lost;
it has been grown continuously under its own name for more
than a century in graperies in the eastern United States.

• 7 •

A somewhat similar story is told of the plump, oval-shaped

Thompson Seedless, the most widely planted grape in California.

Its origin is something of a mystery. Some say it is the Sultanina or Sultanieh of Persia. Others identify it with the Oval Kishmish or Chekirdeksiz of Turkey, the Ak-Kishmish of Russia, or the Sultana of Australia. Sultana in California, however, is a different grape, also seedless, but smaller than the Thompson.

Back in 1872, an Englishman named William Thompson brought to his farm at Yuba City in California's Sacramento Valley a hothouse grape named Lady de Coverly. Some say he had known it in England, but that he brought it from a grapery in Connecticut; others say he found it at Rochester, New York. Who Lady de Coverly was remains a mystery, too. The Yuba City farmer became known as Seedless Thompson, although he fathered seventeen children. When the raisin industry became important around Fresno in the 1890s, vineyardists there began planting Thompson's seedless grape. It became the three-way grape of the valley, salable for fresh use or dried as a raisin, and after Repeal to make neutral-flavored dessert wines and brandy. When the table-wine revolution came in the 1960s, the valley wineries learned that if harvested early the Thompson makes a clean though bland-tasting table wine, called by some cynics "Fresno Chardonnay." It also is useful in making inexpensive champagnes, and because of its neutral flavor has become the vintners' favorite grape to make both brandy and the sweet-flavored and newly popular "pop" or "mod" grape wines.

• 8 •

The other famous mystery grape is Zinfandel, the second most widely planted red variety of California, where it is exceeded in acreage only by Carignane. Except for scattered transplants from California to Oregon and Mexico, Zinfandel is said to be found nowhere else in the world.

Zinfandel is a round, thin-skinned, very sweet and juicy grape, and if eaten fresh in any quantity it has a cathartic effect. Depending on where and how it is grown and vinified, it makes many different wines. In the cool coast counties climates, Regions I to III, it usually makes a fresh, bright-ruby wine with the famous raspberrylike or "bramble" aroma, that is especially delicious when drunk young, like Beaujolais. Grown in Region IV climates, Zinfandel also makes fruity table wines if harvested early, and is useful, blended with other grapes, in making rosés and red ports. In Region V, however, Zinfandel is subject to bunch rot (unless sprayed with the giberellin plant hormone, which makes the berries larger and loosens the bunch), and if harvested late, makes only ordinary port or an alcoholic, flat-tasting table wine. If a well-made coast counties Zinfandel is aged in wood and in bottle for several years, it develops a bouquet as fine as the noble Cabernet. But few vintners age their Zinfandels more than a year or two, because long aging is costly and unprofitable except for Cabernet and Pinot Noir, the prices of which rise steeply as their wines increase in age. Lately some coast counties wineries have also been making delicious Zinfandel rosés, and the David Bruce Winery of Santa Cruz County has produced a Zinfandel Blanc from the colorless juice. I have also tasted recently some 17 percent Zinfandel wines made from late-harvested grapes. The best was a Zinfandel Essence, a very sweet red wine made by the Ridge Winery from Lodi grapes.

Hundreds of articles have been written about the mystery of Zinfandel. Who brought it from Europe, when, from where, and what was its original name? Most wine writers credit "Count" Agoston Haraszthy with introducing the grape to California from his native Hungary between 1851 and 1862. But Zinfandel was never listed among his importations, and no such red grape has been found in Hungary—only a white grape named Zierfahndler or Zierfandel (which are among the many names of Sylvaner). However, a European grape named Zinfandel was grown under glass by William Robert Prince on Long Island, New York, as early as 1830, ten years before Haraszthy emigrated to the United States. Prince wrote in his *Treatise on Grapes*, published in that year, that the Zinfandel came from Hungary. During the 1840s the noted hybridizer, John Fisk Allen, also grew a grape he called "Zinfindal" at Salem, Massachusetts, and his description of it, published in 1848, exactly matches California's adopted foundling, Zinfandel.

Since many of the Vinifera grapes brought to California during the nineteenth century came from eastern nurseries rather than directly from Europe—and it was Robert Prince who first mistakenly called Zinfandel a Hungarian variety—it may well have come from a hothouse in his nursery at Flushing, New York.

If Dr. Austin Goheen, who doesn't claim to be an ampelographer, knows Zinfandel when he sees it on the vine, the mystery of its origin may already have been solved. In the autumn of 1967, Dr. Goheen, the United States Department of Agriculture plant pathologist who originated "mist-propagation," was inspecting the vineyards of southern Italy, studying the damage done by virus diseases. One day, near Taranto in Puglia, he passed rows of vines bearing grapes that looked exactly like Zinfandel. He could not be certain; farmers there called the grapes "Primitivo di Gioia." Back at Davis, Dr. Goheen consulted ampelographies and found another clue—that the Primitivo has also been called "Zingarello." (Cyril Ray, in his *Wines of Italy*, discusses the Primitivo and mentions that its wine can improve with age—a characteristic of California's Zinfandel.)

Dr. Goheen won't say he is positive, but he is willing to bet that when Harold Olmo makes his next trip to Europe and visits the vineyards of Puglia, he will confirm that Goheen has discovered the origin of Zinfandel.

· 9 ·

The many French hybrid wines I have tasted in the eastern, midcontinent, and Canadian wineries have been mostly winy, not grapy, in flavor. Many of the whites and some of the reds could easily be mistaken for fine Vinifera wines. The reds generally tended to be soft and especially pleasant to drink young. Only one red had an outstanding varietal character, easily recognized when tasted "blind." The name of the grape is Baco Noir; the flavor of its wine is more powerful than that of Cabernet Sauvignon.

Great as has been the impact of the French hybrids on the American wine industry outside California, the change these varieties have made in the vineyards and wines of France is far greater. A fact never mentioned in French wine publicity, and therefore not yet realized in the wine trade, is that fully one third of French wine production now comes from the hybrids. Every French vineyard district, including Bordeaux, Burgundy, and Champagne, now grows them extensively, and although the hybrids legally are not permitted to be used in making any of the *appellation contrôlée* wines, many hybrid grapes are specifically recommended by the French Government to be grown for *vins du pays*. (The French, by the way, call them "the American hybrids.")

How and when did this revolutionary change in French viniculture come about? It will be remembered that the phylloxera aphid, accidentally introduced to France on botanical specimens bought from America, spread like a plague and that between 1860 and 1910 it devastated the vineyards of Europe. About 1869, French viticulturists discovered (as was already known in this country) that the tough roots of native American vines are immune to the deadly phylloxera. The French then sent to America for rootstocks and replanted their vineyards with American vines, onto which they grafted their Vinifera. It was thus that American roots saved the vineyards of Europe. But the French winegrowers were not satisfied. They wanted *producteurs directes* (direct producers)—phylloxera-resistant vines that would produce grapes without the painstaking labor and expense of grafting. This started their viticulturists in hybridizing (crossing) the robust American wild varieties with the delicate Vinifera. The first resulting hybrid vines did resist the phylloxera, but the grapes they produced tasted like their wild American parents. Hybridizers in the United States had already made such crosses, with the same disappointing results. The French, however, kept trying, because their motive was more compelling; winegrowing is their nation's chief agricultural industry and supports much of the French population. By 1900 they had succeeded in producing a number of hybrids which made wines resembling Vinifera types. These first nonfoxy hybrids were widely planted in France. But much better hybrids were developed in the few following decades, and still better ones have kept coming from France—and also from grape breeders in the United States and Canada—during the past several years.

The vines Philip Wagner first imported to Baltimore during the 1930s were the early creations of two of the first French hybridizers, Maurice Baco and Albert Seibel. The Baco No. 1 variety was the most successful of the early reds. Most of the French hybrid grapes were named for their originators, such as Georges Couderc, Seibel, Baco, Galibert, Landot, Ravat, Seyve-Villard, and Vidal, and were distinguished by the hybridizers' seedling numbers. Lately, however, those that make the best wines have been given names, which have now begun to appear on varietal labels of the wines. For example, Baco No. 1 became Baco Noir; Seyve-Villard 5276 is now Seyval Blanc, and the black Seibel 10878 became Chelois.*

Bitter controversy surrounds the French hybrids in Europe. Some countries have restricted them or even have prohibited them from being planted, lest they replace the Vinifera varieties that made their wines famous in the past. Germany prohibits them by law; Italy permits some varieties in the cool Alpine foothill regions. Some small plantings made in southern Germany before the restrictions became effective were allowed to remain. In this country, Dr. Konstantin Frank of course has opposed the planting of hybrids, claiming that Vinifera can survive eastern climates as well as the hybrids can. Philip Wagner recommends the hybrids over Vinifera for the East as more likely to produce

---

*Other red-wine hybrids include Bellandais (Seibel 14596), Cascade (S. 13053), Chambourcin (Joannes-Seyve 26205), Chancellor (S. 7053), Colobel (S. 8357), Couderc (Couderc 7120), Florental (Burdin 7705), Landal (Landot 244), Maréchal Foch (Kuhlmann 188-2), Ravat Noir (Ravat 262), and Villard Noir (Seyve-Villard 18315). Among white-wine hybrids with new names are Ambros (Seibel 10713), Aurore or Aurora (S. 5279), Baco Blanc (Baco 22A), Ravat Blanc (Ravat 6), Roucanef (S-V 12309), Verdelet (S. 9110), Vignoles (Ravat 51), and Villard Blanc (S-V 12375).

annual crops. He says the care of Vinifera vines in eastern climates requires a high order of expertise.

• 10 •

The classic Vinifera varieties are known by many different names in viticultural regions around the world. Moreover, like other plants and animals, including people, each Old World variety has changed through the centuries, by cross-breeding and by natural selection to fit particular environments—into different strains or *clones*. The only grapes that have not yet changed and developed clones are the new hybrids, which when planted as cuttings, produce grapes with the same flavors as the original vines.

There are at least 200 clones of Pinot Noir. Consequently, wines made from different Pinot Noir clones, even when grown in the same vineyard, may differ markedly in aroma and taste. There are dozens of strains of Cabernet Sauvignon in California and many more in France. New clones of both old and new varieties are now being developed to make them easier to be picked by the new harvesting machines. (Nurserymen who sell the new heat-treated, virus-free Vinifera vines now call them "superclones.")

Chardonnay is called Weisser Klevner in Germany, Beaunois in the region of Chablis, Auxerrois in the Jura, Pinot Blanc in South America, White Pinot in Australia, and Pinot Chardonnay in the United States. Yet it is not a member of the Pinot family, as are Pinot Noir, Pinot Meunier, and the true Pinot Blanc, another variety that makes fine white burgundies and champagnes.

White Riesling is usually called Johannisberg Riesling because it makes the wines of world-famous Schloss Johannisberg in the Rheingau. It also has many relatives, including such crosses as California's Emerald Riesling and Germany's Müller Thurgau. Most California wines labeled simply as "Riesling" are not made from White Riesling, but from Sylvaner or Franken Riesling, the variety responsible for the Franconian Steinweins. Sylvaner wines are most fragrant and delectable when young, but the best White Rieslings retain their zestful, fruity, tart-sweet character and gain in velvety texture for several years. Grey Riesling, which makes a delicious, mouth-filling young white wine, is not a Riesling, and is called Chauché Gris in France; nor is Missouri Riesling. Multiple names occur among native American grapes, too; the grape called Norton in Virginia is known as Virginia Seedling in Missouri but is called Cynthiana in Arkansas.

Since varietal labeling reached its present height of popularity, vineyardists have discovered that some of the grapes they have been growing for generations are misnamed. Australian wine-growers have recently learned that the grape they have been calling "Riesling" is really the Sémillon of Bordeaux.

The identification of grapes is a science by itself. When varieties closely resemble one another, only an expert can tell them apart. He studies the canes, shoots, leaves, and the sizes and shapes of the clusters, as well as the single berries, which he must select from the center, not the outside of the bunch, or else he may be fooled. Many vineyardists are not certain of which varieties they grow.

Each year from 1949 to 1953, wine juries at the California State Fair awarded the gold medal for Traminer to the Charles Krug Winery of St. Helena, until the vineyard was inspected and it turned out the grapes were not Traminer, but Veltliner, an Austrian variety. In a similar case, the Inglenook Vineyard was winning medals regularly for its Barbera wine until Dr. Albert Winkler studied the vines and identified them as a similar variety called Charbono or Charbonneau. For Inglenook the mistake turned out lucky, for its owners have since enjoyed a monopoly on the hearty red wine labeled Charbono.

Krug meanwhile is back on the market with a wine of the true Gewürztraminer grape. There are several Traminers, but the one called Gewürztraminer has a distinctly "spicy" flavor; Gewürz means "spicy" in German. Incidentally, Gewürztraminer now has a California relative named Flora. UC viticulturist Dr. Harold Olmo developed the Flora by crossing the Gewürz variety with Sémillon. Flora has some Gewürz aroma, yields more tons per acre than its flavorful parent, and shows promise of becoming a popular California "varietal" in years to come.

The viticulturists at Davis say the grape called Petit or Petite Sirah, which makes sturdy young dry red wines (as well as rosés and ports) in California, is probably misnamed. It differs from the Syrah (Sirah or Shiraz) grape of Persia, which contributes a piquant flavor to the best red wines of Tain-l'Hermitage in the Rhone Valley of France, but more closely resembles another Rhone variety the French call Durif.

The red grape called Early Burgundy in California is the variety the French call Portugais Bleu. Folle Blanche, which means "crazy white" and which makes tart wines that somewhat resemble chablis, is called Piquepoul Blanc in France. Dr. Olmo has identified the Bastardo grape of Portugal as the French variety called Trousseau. The red-wine variety named Refosco in Italy and California is also the Mondeuse of France; and so it goes.

A particulary knotty example is the story of the Gamays, the principal grapes of southern Burgundy. There are both red and white Gamays in France, and some red Gamays whose juice is red instead of white. The French call the latter Gamays *teinturiers*, literally "dyers," and use them to darken their burgundies, which often lack color.

The late Paul Masson, on visits to his native France, brought home to his California vineyards many Burgundian grape varieties, including a red grape named Gamay Beaujolais. His successors labeled its rich, flavorful red wine with the name of the grape.

They believed it to be the variety from which the famous red wines of the Beaujolais region south of Mâcon are made, attributing its richer flavor to the differences in climate and soil.

In 1946, when I still was secretary of the Wine Institute, France formally demanded of the United States Government that the Masson Vineyard be stopped from selling its red wine as Gamay Beaujolais, on the ground that only a French wine should be allowed to use the name of Beaujolais. I prepared the reply for our Government, pointing out that the varietal label was true because ampelographies had long recognized Gamay Beaujolais as the name of the grape. The French, on consulting their own ampelographies, were astounded when they found I was right.

Meanwhile, a more productive red grape named Gamay had been planted extensively by California growers, mainly in Napa and Sonoma Counties. Its wine, when young, has a distinct "spicy" flavor quite different from Gamay Beaujolais. The grape became known as "Napa Gamay" and was regarded as an inferior relative of Gamay Beaujolais.

Because Masson's wine brought higher prices than "Napa Gamay," other California vintners obtained cuttings and began planting additional acres of his Gamay Beaujolais. By the mid-1960s, there were almost two dozen California wineries selling their own brands of Gamay Beaujolais wine.

Then Professor Olmo, on one of his periodic trips to Europe, made a startling discovery. Inspecting the vineyards in the French Beaujolais district, Dr. Olmo found that the grape grown there was not the Gamay Beaujolais, but the identical variety the Californians were calling "Napa Gamay." Its common name in France, he learned, is Gamay Noir *à jus blanc*, "black Gamay with white juice." Further research soon convinced Olmo that Gamay Beaujolais is actually one of the hundreds of clones of Pinot Noir.

Dr. Olmo, after announcing his discovery, tried to persuade California vintners to change their Gamay Beaujolais wine labels to "Pinot Noir." Most of them refused, saying that this clone makes wines distinctly different from those of other Pinot Noirs.

Besides, their wines were selling too well as Gamay Beaujolais.

If you find this confusing, you are not alone. Most wine merchants and even most grape growers do not understand it yet. First, remember that Beaujolais is an area in southern Burgundy; it is not a grape. The evidence adds up to this: The "Napa Gamay" is the same grape as the Gamay Noir *à jus blanc*, from which the French make their red Beaujolais wines, and is a completely different grape from Gamay Beaujolais, which is a clone or sub-variety of Pinot Noir.

Now the once-underrated "Napa Gamay," its name corrected to Gamay Noir, is acquiring new admirers because connoisseurs are learning that it is the true grape of Beaujolais. But some vintners are taking advantage of the confusion and are labeling their wines of Gamay Noir (Napa Gamay) as "Gamay Beaujolais," which brings a higher price.

• 11 •

Because the Old World wine grapes have many interchangeable names, vintners naturally choose those which best sell their wines. Before Prohibition, California vineyardists grew a luscious white grape they called "White Zinfandel." After Repeal, when varietal labels were first becoming popular, they learned that one of the names of the grape in France is Pineau Blanc de la Loire, so they began selling its dry wine as "White Pinot." In 1955, the Mondavi brothers of the Charles Krug winery made a semidry version of the wine and introduced it under the grape's other French name, Chenin Blanc. Though their customers couldn't spell or pronounce it, they liked both the name and the wine, which is fresh and delicious when drunk young, like the wines this grape makes in the Vouvray district of the Loire. Other wineries soon emulated Krug, and semidry Chenin Blanc (although some wines under this name are dry) has since become the most plentiful of all California "varietal" white wines. The Christian Brothers make two different wines of the same grape: the younger and sweeter one is called Chenin Blanc, the finer and drier one is their Pineau de la Loire. Krug still sells its dry version as White Pinot.

How much difference a name makes is exemplified by another of the Brothers' wines. For many years, in the vineyard beside their monastery in the hills above Napa, they grew a red grape of uncertain ancestry and sold its tart, chewy wine as Red Pinot. During the 1960s their Red Pinot suddenly began winning medals at the State Fair, whereupon the Brothers remembered that the grape's other name is Pinot Saint-George. They reprinted the label, and their estate-bottled Pinot Saint-George became their most famous red table wine.

Wente Brothers of Livermore during the 1940s sold a dry white wine named for their Ugni Blanc grape, but withdrew it from the market when their customers insisted on calling it "Ugly Blank." The Wentes knew Ugni Blanc is called Trebbiano in Italy, where it is one of the four varieties used to make the classic red chianti. Actually, the grape has a third and more saleable name, St. Emilion, by which it is called in the Cognac region of France. The Bianes, of the Brookside Vineyard at Guasti, later learned this from a knowledgeable nurseryman, and the Bianes are doing a thriving business with their dry white wine called St. Emilion. The Wentes now identify their Ugni Blanc as part of the blend with Chenin Blanc that they call their "Blanc de Blancs."

Sauvignon Blanc, the grape that contributes the spicy taste to fine French sauternes, makes equally spicy white wines in California, but its varietal name on wines has never appealed to very many American buyers. Robert Mondavi remembered that Sauvignon Blanc is also the grape that produces the Loire Valley wine named Pouilly-Fumé, and that its name there is Blanc Fumé.* He conceived of the bright idea of renaming his dry Sauvignon Blanc "Fumé Blanc." His wine became so popular that other wineries began also using the name, with some reversing it to "Blanc Fumé."

• 12 •

Because varietal names project glamour and attract buyers who search for new flavors in wines, some vintners sell "varietals" that don't deserve varietal names. Green Hungarian, for example, is a flavorless grape that is valuable only to make white blending-wines, but its name has an intriguing winy sound. Semidry wines called Green Hungarian, pleasant but with no outstanding flavor, first appeared in 1945 and are now popular throughout the United States. Royalty, Rubired, and Salvador are grapes with red juice, extensively grown in the San Joaquin Valley because they are useful to darken wines that lack color. You can write a letter with their juice in your fountain pen. There now are dry red table wines named Royalty, although that grape has a harsh, unpleasant taste. Palomino, a hardy, tough-skinned grape, is the principal variety grown in the sherry-producing districts of Spain. Its only virtue for making sherry is that its juice rapidly becomes oxidized, a grave fault in making any other type of wine. In California,

*The French say the Sauvignon Blanc grown around Pouilly-sur-Loire has both a smoky and a spicy taste; hence *fumé* (smoked).

Palomino is sometimes miscalled Golden Chasselas, and a few wineries unfortunately use it to make a white table wine under that name. It is not related to the true Chasselas grapes, from which the Germans make their excellent Gutedel and the Swiss make their Fendant.

A century ago, West & Sons of Stockton brought to their El Pinal Vineyard from France a vigorous-growing white grape and named it "West's White Prolific." The late L. K. Marshall of Lodi rediscovered the variety after Repeal and named it Winkler for the famous viticulturist. Dr. Winkler, however, declined the honor and identified the grape as the French Colombard. Because it is prolific, and its high-acid juice is useful in making white wines and champagnes, it has become the principal white-wine variety grown in California, chiefly planted now in Regions IV and V. Although its wine has no varietal personality, a dozen California wineries sell wines labeled French Colombard.

Carignane, the principal red-wine grape grown in California, is not noted for any quality except the vigor and high productivity of the vine. However, when Carignane is grown on coast counties hillsides without irrigation, it sometimes produces an excellent, highly flavorful table wine. On the other hand, the historic Mission grape usually makes poor red table wines, yet is useful in making some good dessert wine types.

• 13 •

"Blanc de Blancs" and "Blanc de Noir" are terms with varietal meanings but which don't name any grapes. "Blanc de Blancs" means "white of whites" and is meant to tell you that champagnes so labeled are *not* made of the principal grape of the French Champagne region—Pinot Noir—but entirely of white grapes, particularly Chardonnay. Most American champagnes are made of white grapes, but were never called "Blanc de Blancs" until Almadén and Schramsberg adopted the term for their special champagnes made mostly of Chardonnay. "Blanc de Blancs" on labels of still white wines, however, merely refers to blends of white grapes and has nothing to do with Chardonnay.

American winemakers used to wonder why the French use Pinot Noir, the black grape with white juice, to make most of their fine champagnes. The answer is in Amerine and Joslyn's 1970 edition of *Table Wines*: "The cool climate [of the French Champagne region]," they say, "necessitates growing the early-ripening Pinot Noir in order to have adequate sugar for a balanced wine." In California climates, white grapes ripen with plenty of sugar every year and black grapes are not needed to make champagne. Nevertheless, two California vintners are now making special premium champagnes containing Pinot Noir. One is Schramsberg's Blanc de Noir, the other is Masson's Blanc de Pinot.

• 14 •

In the eastern and mid-continent states, there are many varietally named table wine types made not of the French hybrids, but of native American grapes. Although the principal variety grown in these states is the Concord, the best "varietal" native wines are Delaware, Catawba, Dutchess, and the Norton or Cynthiana of Virginia and Arkansas. All are less foxy than Concord, and Cynthiana has no foxy flavor at all.

American grapes are tame descendants of the many species of wild grapes that abound in North America. (There are almost no wild grapes south of the Equator.) They are called "slip-skin" grapes because their skins, which are inedible, do not adhere to the pulp. Many of the cultivated varieties are American hybrids, crossed by the early American grape breeders between *Vitis labrusca* and other native species, such as *Vitis riparia*, and Vinifera varieties.

These native "varietal" wines are usually best when consumed young, while their grapy fragrance is at its height. The foxy aroma is said to disappear as the wines age.

Nicholas Longworth, the early Ohio winegrower, always maintained that Catawba improved with age. He had trouble convincing his contemporary, Jean Jacques Dufour, of this. Dufour preferred the Alexander grape, with which he pioneered winegrowing in Indiana. To win his point, Longworth gave Dufour three bottles of Catawba. Dufour drank one after six months, another at the end of a year, and buried the third in his vineyard. In 1827, when Dufour lay on his deathbed, he made a last request to his doctor, that the bottle be dug up and brought to him for a final taste. Dufour was propped up in his bed, the cork was drawn, a glass was held up to the light, and he tasted the wine. "Ah, doctor," he said, "Longworth was right. Catawba improves with age."

Labrusca grapes, such as Concord, are said to be unsuited to the warm climates of California, and California wineries rely on the states of Washington and Oregon to supply them with the Concord juice used in most of their Cold Duck sparkling wines. However, there are some Concord vineyards in the cooler parts of California, and three other Labrusca varieties are now being grown experimentally in the Gallo vineyard at Livingston in Merced County. One is Golden Muscat, the "secret magical

grape" which the Gallos once advertised as the mysterious ingre-
dient in their Eden Roc Champagne. The others are Iona and Ives.

In Chapter 3, you read that the southeastern states have their
own distinctive "varietal" wine called Scuppernong. Scuppernong
and its many relatives of the Muscadine (*Vitis rotundifolia*) family
are the only usable grapes that thrive in the humid lowland areas
of these states. American and Vinifera bunch grapes have often
been planted in Scuppernong country lowlands, but the vines
have always died after producing fruit for a short time. Phylloxera, which does not attack the Muscadines, was long blamed.
During the 1950s, however, plant pathologists discovered that
what killed the northern bunch grapes was not phylloxera, but
the deadly virus called Pierce's disease, which thrives in humid
climates, and to which the Muscadines and other indigenous
grapes of the Southeast are immune.

Scuppernong and other Muscadine vines have been planted
experimentally in the vineyard at UC Davis, and Professor Olmo,
after twenty years of failures, has succeeded in making fertile
crosses of them with several Vinifera grapes, including relatives
of Cabernet, Palomino, and Grenache. Olmo has made wines
from his Muscadine hybrid grapes, and a panel of tasters has
scored them as high as six (good) on a scale of ten. A question
this raises is whether—if Olmo's Scuppernong hybrids, with the
virus- and insect-resistance of their Muscadine parents, were now
to be transplanted from Davis to Scuppernong country and were
to thrive there—they might develop a wine industry based on
bunch grapes in the South.

There was a time, before the Prohibitionists came into control
of agricultural research in this country, when grape breeders in
the southern states thought they could tame their wild Mustang,
Post-Oak, and River-bank grapes and develop winegrowing industries in such states as Texas, Louisiana, Mississippi, Tennessee, Georgia, Alabama, and Florida. The late Thomas Volney
Munson of Denison, Texas, bred a number of promising hybrid
bunch grapes there in the early 1900s, but Munson's object was
chiefly to develop new table grapes, and the results of his experiments are said to have been lost. Independent grape breeders are
again at work in Texas, developing varieties to make wine in
southern climates.

Since 1946, Professor John Mortensen of the University of
Florida experiment station at Leesburg has developed four new
bunch-grape varieties that are resistant to Pierce's disease. Some
of Mortensen's hybrids are already being grown in Florida and
Alabama, both for table use and for wine.

Now that dry influence on the southern agricultural colleges is declining, perhaps horticulturists in these states—who until now have been expressly prohibited from experimenting with grapes for wine—will soon be permitted to engage in this kind of research.

• 15 •

Since wines can be only as fine as the grapes from which they are made, the truly dedicated student of wines must also become a student of grapes.

The only sources of precise data on individual grape varieties are the colorfully illustrated books about vines, called ampelographies. Hundreds of ampelographies have been published in Europe. The greatest is the seven-volume *Traité General de Viticulture* by Professors Pierre Viala and V. Vermorel, the French viticulturists who with some sixty collaborators labored from 1890 to 1910 compiling 24,000 names and synonyms of grapes and gathering paintings of the principal varieties. The first American ampelography to picture grapes in full colors was published by the California Vinicultural Association in 1877, with water-color paintings, made in the vineyards, of ten varieties. In 1908, the Geneva, New York, experiment station published *Grapes of New York*, the monumental work of Professor Ulysses Prentiss Hedrick, in which he described almost 1500 native American grapes.

Dr. Olmo has been compiling a new California ampelography since 1936. After thirty-five years of research, half a lifetime, he published in 1971 his work on a single variety, Chardonnay. It is a four-page folio containing a color photograph of Chardonnay and its foliage, a diagram of its leaf, a history and description of the variety and its many clones and mutations, and a bibliography. Olmo plans to follow with similar folios on forty-nine more varieties, the next ones on Palomino, Pinot Noir, and Cabernet Sauvignon. The Chardonnay folio is priced at five dollars. If the rest sell at the same price, Olmo's complete ampelography of fifty varieties will cost two hundred and fifty dollars, which will make it the most expensive wine book in the world.

But there can never be a complete book of grapes, for there are almost ten thousand different grape varieties from which wines of some sort can be made, including many not yet tried in the United States; and new varieties are continually being created by breeders in France, other European countries, Canada, and the United States.

As still more wines appear on the market named for their grapes, the mystery of wine becomes increasingly fascinating, because we can never know the full story of any grape.

26

Meanings of Some Wine Terms

AMONG the reasons American wines far out-sell imports in this country, apart from their intrinsic value, is that American wine nomenclature is simpler than that of Europe. Old World labels are a maze of unfamiliar European geographic names, of vintage years that mean little to a buyer who hasn't studied a vintage chart, and of mostly unrecognizable names of châteaux, shippers, and importers. American labels, less cluttered with names and dates, are easier to buy.

But American labeling, though simple by comparison, has become increasingly complex in recent years, and some terms have acquired obscure meanings that need explaining.

Why do Finger Lakes District wineries label some of their wines "Finger Lakes," others "New York State," and still others "American"? The same question applies to wineries elsewhere, including California vintners who label some of their wines with such district names as "Napa" and "Sonoma" but call the rest "California." The reason is that as more and more Americans become winewise, the names of viticultural districts that have become known as producing superior wines increase the prices that buyers readily pay for bottles labeled with these names. "Finger Lakes" and "New York State" wines are usually priced higher than New York wines called "American."

The Federal labeling regulation requires that if an appellation of origin is used, 75 percent of the wine in the bottle must be derived from fruit grown in the place stated. If more than 25 percent comes from somewhere else, a broader appellation is used.

European winegrowers have argued for generations over the precise meanings of their famous district names. Disputes over what American district names mean have only begun. Multi-

415

million-dollar decisions on where to plant vineyards and build wineries are already influenced by which geographic appellation can legally appear on the labels of the wines to be produced.

One of the reasons the French hybrid grapes have been so widely planted by the big New York and Ohio wineries is to protect their labels of origin. In order to reduce the strong flavors of their Labrusca wines, they need neutral blending wines, readily available from California. But when their blends contain more than 25 percent of California wine, the labels change to "American." Now, with their locally grown hybrid grapes available to make neutral blending wines, they can use unlimited quantities and keep their local appellations of origin.

The Federal regulation originally required not only that fruit be grown where labels state, but that it be fermented and that the wine be finished there, too. An amendment in 1972 eliminated the requirement that the fermentation take place where the fruit is grown. One reason for the change was that wineries in some lately urbanized California valleys have planted new vineyards elsewhere while the wineries remained where they were. They now can use the appellation of the new vineyard district so long as the fermentation and finishing of the wine take place in the same state. But now, some Napa wineries are seeking a way to prevent wineries elsewhere from using "Napa" on labels of wines they might make from Napa grapes.

California's state regulation is stricter than the Federal in that it requires any wine labeled with a California name to be made 100 percent from California grapes. When some California wineries began bringing grapes and juice from the State of Washington to blend with their own, they changed "California" on some of their labels to "American." There is nothing in the California regulation, however, to prevent coast counties vintners from stretching their locally labeled wines with up to 25 percent of lesser wines from the hot Central Valley.

The United States regulations are much less strict than the *appellation contrôlée* system in France, which has now been copied by Italy. But the American regulations were written to protect the consumer and are strictly enforced. European wine regulations aim primarily to protect the honest grower against competitors. European authorities are also better at writing strict regulations than at enforcing them.

Does "mountain" on a wine label mean that the grapes were mountain-grown? It once did, but it doesn't anymore. In ancient times it was already known that the finest wines are those grown in mountainous regions. Virgil wrote that "Bacchus loves the hillsides." In the

United States, Frank Schoonmaker first used "mountain" in 1939 on labels of two wines from the Paul Masson Mountain Vineyard, when he also used "lake" to designate his "varietal" selections from the Widmer Cellars of New York State. Later, "mountain" having never been defined in terms of how high or steep a vineyard should be, the word began to appear on labels of wines made from grapes grown in any of the hilly California coast counties. Then, through the years, "mountain" gradually became the designation of wines sold by coast counties wineries at much lower prices and of lesser quality than their best.

Are wines whose labels read "Produced and bottled by," preceding the vintner's name, more reliable than others using the words "Made" or "Cellared" or "Perfected" rather than "Produced"? The Federal regulation defines "produced" as meaning that the vintner fermented and finished at least 75 percent of the wine in the bottle. To the buyer, it signifies that the vintner did not just buy the wine or have it made for him by someone else. "Made" once meant that the winery "produced" at least 10 percent of the wine, but this detail has been eroded by time. It now means only that the vintner produces some of his wine and at least blended or changed this particular wine in some way. Some wineries, however, prefer to say "Made" on all their labels, rather than try to keep separate those they actually produce and those they buy or have other wineries make for them. "Produced" formerly meant also that the named vintner actually crushed the grapes, but this provision was eliminated by an amendment to the regulation in 1972. Advanced technology now makes it possible to crush the grapes at the vineyard and deliver the unfermented must in perfect condition to the winery, protected as described on page 274.

What does "Estate Bottled" on wine labels mean? Originally this was the rare designation permitted only for use by the small wine-growing estates. It was equivalent to the French *mise en bouteille au château*, meaning that 100 percent of the grapes were grown in the owner's vineyard and that every drop of the wine was made and bottled in his adjoining cellar. Some wineries still adhere strictly to this meaning and consequently don't have many "Estate Bottled" wines. But recent Federal rulings in individual cases have allowed certain vintners to label whole assortments of wines as "Estate Bottled" when the grapes came from vineyards they do not own, some of them located many miles away from their cellars. The rulings only limit "Estate Bottled" to mean that the vineyards are in the same county as the winery and that the grapes are grown under the winery's control. But neither is *mise en bouteille au château* any longer a complete assurance of genuine château-bottling in France. Trucks with portable bottling equipment now call each year at some small French wineries, making their bulk wines eligible to be labeled as château-bottled.

Why do most American wine labels omit the year of the vintage, which is commonly stated on labels of European wines? Vintage labels on California wines do not serve the purpose for which they are needed on certain European wines, to differentiate the bad-weather years from the good. Vintage labeling on American wines is useful mainly in identifying batches or casks that vary from others in character, and especially in telling you the age of a wine that you lay down for aging in your cellar. Many wineries refuse to use vintage labels because with large reserve stocks, they can blend together wines of different ages, adding the freshness and aroma of the young to the mellowness and bouquet of the old. Such blending also enables them to maintain year-to-year uniformity in the flavor of each type of wine they sell. A further objection to vintage labeling was that the original Federal regulation required 100 percent of the wine in the bottle to be of the year stated. But some wine evaporates while stored in barrels before bottling, and the barrels need to be "topped" (replenished) frequently to keep the wine from being injured by exposure to air. Vintners seldom had enough additional wine of the same age and type with which to do the topping. In 1972, the United States regulation was amended to permit wines to be topped with up to 5 percent of wines of other ages without losing the right to be labeled with the year of vintage. No European government has such a strict regulation. Germany only requires 75 percent of a vintage-labeled wine to be of the year stated.

Why are some champagnes labeled "bulk process," others "fermented in the bottle," and still others "fermented in this bottle"? For two centuries after champagnization was discovered in France, reputedly by the monk Dom Pérignon, all champagnes were given their secondary fermentation in the bottles in which they were sold. In 1907, Eugene Charmat in France developed his method of fermenting them in large tanks, virtually giant bottles, and bottling them under pressure. Because this is a less costly procedure, the Federal regulation requires such wines to be labeled with such words as "bulk process" to show the method used. If the original wines are of identical quality and are given no additional aging, the Charmat process should produce champagne equally good as that fermented in the bottle. However, leading producers who use the bottle-fermentation method also age their best champagnes in the bottles before disgorging (removing the sediment caused by fermentation). Prolonged contact with the sediment gives these champagnes a flavor and bouquet different from those not so aged.

Since the 1950s, many producers of bottle-fermented champagnes have adopted the "transfer method," developed in Germany, of removing the sediment without the laborious process of disgorging each bottle. Instead, the bottles are emptied under pressure, the champagne is filtered to remove the sediment, and then is rebottled. Producers who use the old disgorging process label their champagnes "fermented in *this* bottle" and sometimes add still other terms, such as *méthode champenoise*. In the Champagne district of France, however, only the disgorging process may be used for wines labeled champagne. French wines champagnized by the Charmat process may only be labeled *vin mousseux*, which means "sparkling wine."

What are crackling wines? Until 1972, the Federal regulation defined crackling, *pétillant*, or *frizzante* wines as those made naturally effervescent—but less so than champagne—by a secondary fermentation in the bottle like champagne. An amendment in 1972 permits crackling wines also to be made by the Charmat process, but if so their labels must say "bulk process."

Since many of the new "pop" wines with such names as Spañada and Strawberry Hill are made effervescent by artificial carbonation, why don't their labels say so? "Pop" or "mod" wines first appeared in the United States when the Federal law was amended in 1958 to allow table wines to contain up to half an atmosphere (about 7 pounds of pressure per square inch) of added carbon dioxide without paying the higher Federal tax rate on carbonated wines. These wines may not be labeled or represented as effervescent, because if they were, the higher tax rate would apply. At such low carbonation, they give a slight "pop" when opened, but you seldom see any bubbles; they only cause a prickly sensation on the tongue.

At this writing, a bill is pending in Congress to double the permissible pressure to a whole atmosphere, about 14.7 pounds, compared to almost 90 pounds in some champagnes.

Are there any legal definitions of "dry," "brut," "extra dry," "medium dry," and "sweet"? "Dry," which simply means the opposite of sweet, is the most abused single term in the language of alcoholic beverages. Vintners long ago learned that most American and British buyers prefer wines that are labeled "dry" but that taste at least slightly sweet. Champagnes labeled "brut" are almost dry, but "extra dry" means semisweet, and only "natural" means really dry. There are only two legal regulations of dryness or sweetness in North America. One is the definition of "dry" in

420 THE WINES OF AMERICA

Ontario, Canada. The other is a California regulation that defines the permissible range of sweetness of sherry, dry sherry, sweet or cream sherry, California tokay, and other dessert wine types. Dryness is not a measure of quality, because all wines are sweet until their sugar is fermented to the degree of dryness the vintner desires.

What does "solera" on wine labels mean? Solera is the Spanish name of the fractional-blending system used in the sherry bodegas of Spain. Traditionally, a *solera* consists of tiers of barrels containing sherries of different ages. Wine for sale is taken from the oldest barrel at the bottom, which is left at least half full. The quantity withdrawn is replaced from the next oldest, and so on. New wine goes always into the top tier, thus gradually blending the new with the old. This is why sherries rarely are labeled with the year of vintage. Many American wineries maintain fractional-blending systems for both sherries and ports, equivalent to the Spanish *soleras.*

What do the different bottle shapes and colors used by American wineries mean? Because buyers of European wines are accustomed to finding particular types of wine in the bottles traditionally used in Old World vineyard districts, most American vintners use the same kinds of bottles for their wines of corresponding types. Wines of burgundy types, or made from Burgundian or similar grapes, usually come in the slope-sided green bottles used in Burgundy. The high-shouldered bottle that represents Bordeaux is used for clarets, sauternes, for such Bordeaux "varietals" as Sémillon, Sauvignon Blanc, and Cabernet, and also for Zinfandel, which is considered a claret type in the United States. Rhine types, including Rieslings and Gewürztraminer, come in the tall, slender, so-called "hock bottle," which in Europe is green for rhine wines and brown for moselles. Colored bottles help to protect wines from injury by ultraviolet light, but some vintners, both European and American, use clear glass bottles (called "flint" in the trade) to display the attractive colors of their wines. Many American vintners have given up trying to follow European traditions and have created their own distinctive bottle shapes.

Why is the use of sugar prohibited in making California standard wines while it is permitted within legal limits in other states and in most other countries? The addition of cane or beet sugar to the juice of grapes before fermentation is called chaptalization, named for its originator, Jean Chaptal, the French minister of agriculture in Napoleon's time. It is needed when in cool seasons or districts the grapes lack sufficient natural sugar of their own to produce wine of standard alcoholic content. The use of nongrape sugar is prohibited in producing standard still-wine types in California because there it is almost never needed; grapes ripen every year in the California climates. But sugar may be used in California for sweetening champagnes and flavored wines. Some winemakers say California wines could be improved if the use of sugar were permitted there.

*What do alcoholic content statements mean on wine labels in this country?** Table (light) wines sold in the United States, if labeled with a specific statement of alcoholic content, may vary within a three-degree range. If the label says "alcohol 12% by volume," it means the alcoholic strength is between 10½ and 13½ percent. Appetizer and dessert wines are permitted a two-degree range; a label that reads "18%" means 17 to 19 percent. The strength of the "light" dessert wines sold in Michigan is usually stated as 16 and may be as low as 15, but in that state it does not exceed 16 percent.

Wines up to 14 percent, the maximum reached by normal fermentation, pay a Federal excise tax of 17 cents per gallon. Between 14 and 21 percent, levels usually reached by adding brandy, the Federal tax is 67 cents.

Labels may omit the alcoholic content if they read "table wine" or "light wine," which means they are not over 14 percent.

The original purpose of requiring alcoholic-content statements on labels was to deal with the ancient practice, still common in some countries, of watering the wine before sale. It also serves some other purposes. In Europe, alcoholic strength is regarded as a measure of wine quality. The French legal minimum standard for Beaujolais wine, for example, is 9 percent; if it reaches 10 it becomes Beaujolais *supérieur. Vin ordinaire* in France is sold in three quality grades, 9, 10, and 11 percent; the higher the alcohol, the higher the price. European families value the stronger wines because they can dilute them with water at the table for drinking with meals. For example, the Charles Krug Winery sells a special 14 percent wine named "Fortissimo" under its "CK" brand especially for the Italian trade.

One reason Europeans associate alcohol content with quality is that grapes develop more natural sugar—which ferments to more alcohol—in their years of good weather, the so-called vintage years. By this measure, hot countries should make the best wines, but the opposite is true. Another reason is that in the past, wines

---

*Alcoholic strength of wines is stated as percentage by volume, not by weight as it is for beers, and not as "proof" as it is for distilled spirts. ("Proof" is simply double the percentage of alcohol by volume.)

laid down for long aging were least likely to spoil when their alcohol content was high.

But advanced technology, such as the use of pure yeast cultures, sterile filtration, and aseptic bottling, now make it possible to produce wines that keep sound at much lower alcohol levels than in the past. It is unfortunate that the old association of alcoholic content with quality still prevails among Europeans, because many of the most delicious and most healthful wines are as low as 8, 9, and 10 percent.

The Federal minimum standard permits wines as low as 7 percent, and a bill is pending in Congress that would reduce it to one half of 1 percent. But California still sets a 10 percent minimum for its standard whites and rosés. As mentioned earlier, this does not apply to flavored wines, and some of the new "pop" types are as low as 8 percent.

California for many years required its dessert wines to be at least 19½ percent in order to prevent spoilage when sweet wines, such as ports, were shipped across the country in bulk. Later the California vintners discovered that the 16 percent "light" sherries and ports they were compelled to produce for sale in Michigan did not spoil and that some were more palatable than those they were selling at 20 percent. During the decades when California had ruinous annual surpluses of grapes, the grape growers strongly resisted proposals to lower the California 19½ percent minimum, because the extra brandy required "burned up more grapes." In 1971, when the grape surplus was no longer a threat, California adopted the lower Federal minimums of 17 percent for sherries and 18 percent for other dessert wines.

What do such terms as "Private Stock," "De Luxe," and "Special Selection" on wine labels mean? They usually are an individual vintner's way of distinguishing his higher-priced from his lower-priced wines of the same types. But if a winery sells only one price class of wine, such terms have no meaning.

It is understandable, in our free enterprise system, that every vintner would like to have his winery considered a château and sell his wine at the highest price obtainable. Yet the most important wines that any nation produces are those simply called "red wine," "pink wine," or "white wine," sold young, at low alcoholic content in jugs or returnable bottles, at no higher prices than milk, for consumption with everyday meals.

27

A Brief Chronology of Wine in North America

1524   Cortez, conqueror of Mexico, ordered vineyards planted in the New World with grapes brought from Spain.

c. 1564   French Huguenots in Florida made wine from native Scuppernong grapes.

1595   Philip II, to suppress competition with Spanish wine exports, prohibited further planting of vines in New Spain.

1609–1716   Franciscans brought the Mission (Criolla) grape from Mexico to their missions in New Mexico and made wine for the Mass.

1619–1773   Unsuccessful attempts to grow European grapes by Lord Delaware in Virginia, Lord Baltimore in Maryland, William Penn near Philadelphia, Thomas Jefferson at Monticello, and by others in Alabama, Georgia, Massachusetts, New Hampshire, New York, Rhode Island, South Carolina.

1636   Jesuit missionaries at Québec in Canada made sacramental wine from wild grapes.

1769   Father Junípero Serra founded Mission San Diego, then brought Mission grapes from Baja California. Wine was being grown at most of the 21 Alta California missions by 1824.

c. 1783   The first domesticated native (Labrusca) grape was planted by John Alexander during the American Revolution. The Alexander grape was introduced throughout the East and wine was made from it with varying success.

1801   Jean Jacques Dufour organized the Kentucky Vineyard Society, failed to grow Swiss grapes in Kentucky, then planted the Alexander grape at Vevay, Indiana, and a wine industry prospered there for many years.

1810   Scuppernong wine was being made and sold at many North Carolina farms.

1811   The first commercial vineyard and winery in Canada was established by Johann Schiller at Cooksville, Ontario.

1818   Deacon Elijah Fay cultivated wild grapes at Brocton in the Chautauqua Grape Belt of New York.

1818   At York, Pennsylvania, Thomas Eichelberger began the first commercially successful winegrowing venture in the United States.

1823   Nicholas Longworth planted his first vineyard at Cincinnati, Ohio. In 1842 he made the first American champagne.

1823   Major John Adlum introduced the Catawba grape at Washington, D.C.

1823   The Florissant vineyard was established near St. Louis, Missouri.

1824   The Harmonists established vineyards and wine vaults at Economy on the Ohio River near Pittsburgh, Pennsylvania. Wine was produced in the Pittsburgh area until 1900.

1824   Joseph Chapman founded California's first commercial vineyard at Los Angeles.

1827   Dr. Richard Underhill planted the first large vineyard in the Hudson River Valley; he later established a winery and sold "Croton Point Wines."

1829   Reverend William Bostwick began cultivating grapes at Hammondsport in the Finger Lakes District of New York, but no wine was made there commercially until after 1860.

1833   Jean Louis Vignes imported French vines to California and planted them in his El Aliso Vineyard at Los Angeles.

1840   German immigrants planted vineyards on the Lake Erie Islands and around Sandusky in northern Ohio.

1850–1860   Grape planting boomed in California during and after the Gold Rush.

1854   The Concord grape was introduced by Ephraim Wales Bull of Massachusetts.

c. 1855   The phylloxera vine pest attacked vines in France and during the next half century destroyed most of the vineyards of Europe. Phylloxera was controlled, beginning in 1870, by grafting Vinifera vines to American wild-grape roots.

1856   Kohler & Frohling, the San Francisco vintners, began exporting California wines to England, Germany, Russia, China, and Australia.

1859   Southern Ohio vineyards were attacked by black rot and mildew. Winegrowing then expanded in northern Ohio, Arkansas, the Carolinas, Illinois, Indiana, Missouri, and Tennessee.

1861   Mrs. Abraham Lincoln began serving American wines in the White House.

1861   "Count" Agoston Haraszthy, commissioned to study winegrowing in Europe, sent 100,000 vines of 300 varieties to California.

1862   French viticultural experts, sent to survey American vineyards, reported they found California "capable of entering serious competition with the wines of Europe."

1867   Overplanting of vineyards created a grape surplus in California. Cycles of boom and bust occurred repeatedly in California during the next hundred years.

1869   On completion of the transcontinental railroad, California wines invaded eastern and midwestern markets, competing with Ohio, Missouri, and New York wines.

1870   California became the leading winegrowing state, surpassing Missouri and Ohio.

1870   Drs. Thomas and Charles Welch founded the fresh grape juice industry, introducing "Dr. Welch's Unfermented Wine" at Vineland, New Jersey. The Welch Company moved in 1896 to New York State and later established plants in Pennsylvania, Michigan, Arkansas, and Washington.

1872   William Thompson planted an English hothouse grape on his farm at Yuba City, California, and named it "Thompson's Seedless."

1873   Phylloxera attacked vines at Sonoma. Before it was controlled in about 1900, it destroyed many vineyards in Napa, Santa Clara, and the Sacramento Valley.

1876   American wines won two awards at the Paris Exposition.

1880   The University of California began research and instruction in viticulture and winemaking by order of the state legislature.

1880   Wineries were reported thriving in Alabama, Arkansas, California, Georgia, Illinois, Indiana, Iowa, Kansas, Kentucky, Mississippi, New Jersey, New Mexico, New York, North Carolina, western Oregon, Pennsylvania, Tennessee, southern Utah, and Virginia.

1880   Kansas became the first state to adopt statewide Prohibition. By the First World War, 33 of the 48 states were legally dry.

1887   A California law prohibited the use of sugar in winemaking within the state, but an act of Congress in 1894 allowed its limited use in other states.

1900   American wines won three dozen medals at the Paris Exposition.

1904   The first grapes were planted at Outlook in the Yakima Valley of Washington.

1910   During the Mexican revolution, most of the vineyards of Mexico were abandoned or destroyed. They were revived beginning in the early 1940s.

1916   Eight Canadian provinces adopted Prohibition laws, but Ontario wineries prospered, being permitted to make wine for local sale. Seven of the provinces repealed their Prohibition laws in 1927.

1920   National Prohibition began in the United States. More than 100 wineries continued limited production under government permits, making sacramental, medicinal, and salted cooking wines.

1921–1931   Grape growers prospered by supplying home winemakers and bootleggers during the early Prohibition years, but the grape market crashed in 1925. The Federal Government loaned millions to convert surplus grapes into "Vine-Glo" concentrate for home winemaking, but called a halt when the Drys objected.

c. 1930   The first commercial grape wine in British Columbia was made at Victoria from Okanagan Valley grapes.

1932   Congress legalized 3.2 percent beer and 3.2 percent "McAdoo wine."

1933   National Prohibition ended in the United States, but many states and localities remained legally dry. Oklahoma finally repealed its dry law in 1959, Mississippi in 1966.

1934   Wine consumption in the U.S. was less than 29 million gallons in the first Repeal year.

1934   The Wine Institute was incorporated and California adopted state wine quality standards. Federal wine quality and labeling standards became effective in 1936.

1935   Philip Wagner of Baltimore began importing French hybrid wine grapes, which later spread through the East and Midwest.

1939   Varietally labeled American wines, introduced by Frank Schoonmaker, began their rise to popularity.

1940   Wine consumption in the U.S. reached 86 million gallons, but less than a third was table wine.

1941–1946   War caused a wine shortage. Whiskey distillers bought many wineries, but sold most of them after the war.

1945   The kosher wine type was first advertised to the general public at New York and soon became the best-known North American wine.

1946   The University of California released the first new wine grape varieties bred at Davis—Emerald Riesling and Ruby Cabernet.

1950   "The wine awakening of America" began after the Second World War, and the consumption of table wine began a steady rise.

1950   The American Society of Enologists was organized at Davis.

1950   Research begun after the war produced greater advances in the sciences of viticulture and enology than had been made in the preceding 2000 years.

1951   A Federal move to tax wine on its alcoholic content was defeated, and Congress voted the present tax rates of 17¢ per gallon on table wines, 67¢ on dessert wines.

1956   James Zellerbach brought Burgundian barrels to his hobbyist winery at Sonoma, and California vintners discovered the "complex" bouquet of wines aged in European instead of American oak.

1956   California premium producers began nationwide "blind" tastings to prove their wines equal to Europe's best.

1957   After three centuries of repeated failures to grow Vinifera grapes in the East, the first New York State Johannisberg Riesling and Chardonnay grapes were produced by Dr. Konstantin Frank in the Gold Seal Vineyard at Hammondsport.

1959   Congress authorized wines to contain seven pounds of carbon dioxide pressure without paying an additional Federal tax. Low-alcohol flavored "pop" or "mod" wines became nationally popular a decade later, competing with beer.

1965   Mechanical harvesting machines began picking grapes in New York State, and later in Ohio, Washington, California, and Ontario, Canada.

1968   For the first time since before Prohibition, consumption of table wine exceeded dessert wine in the U.S.

1960–1972   Table-wine consumption more than trebled during these years, causing a nationwide upsurge in winegrowing. Giant corporations in other fields entered the wine industry, buying established vineyards and wineries. Americans drank almost 340 million gallons of wine at the rate of more than 1.5 gallon per capita in 1972, a record likely to double in ten more years.

Acknowledgments and Notes

I N DOING the research for this book I have had generous help from hundreds of individuals and institutions, only a small number of whom are named in the text. In expressing my appreciation, I should make it clear that none of them is responsible for the errors and omissions that are unavoidable when one volume attempts to encompass the whole moot subject of American wines. In particular, because the sections on individual wineries often differ from the romantic versions in their advertising, I should mention that no vintner has read what I have written about him or his vines.

My most valuable single American sources of historical material have been the writings of the great professors of viticulture, George Husmann and Ulysses Prentiss Hedrick; of San Francisco's wine-loving journalist of the 1880s, Frona Eunice Wait Colburn; of Herbert B. Leggett, who in 1941 was the first to attempt a history of the early California wine industry; and of Vincent P. Carosso, who in 1951 published the most complete study of the industry's formative years. Dr. Carosso in turn gives well-deserved credit to the research of Dr. Irving McKee, whom I persuaded in 1943 to undertake his dozen research papers on the histories of California wine counties and their pioneer winegrowers.

Early viticultural and wine journals, such as *The Grape Culturist, Cozzens' Wine Press,* and the *American Wine Press and Mineral Water News,* have provided details of many pioneer winegrowers' histories. For California, I have found the best sources to be the three books privately published since 1954 by Ernest Peninou and Sidney Greenleaf. Ernest Peninou still has an unpublished treasure trove of early California wineries' histories, which he has compiled during three decades of travel and painstaking research at their sites. Some of the key portions of Chapter 12 on California are based on Professor Maynard Amerine's scholarly study, published in 1962, of Professor Eugene Hilgard's life and contributions to California viticulture.

For the many references to "Count" Agoston Haraszthy I have relied mainly on the Haraszthy research project that Paul Fredericksen undertook in the 1940s at the Wine Institute, and on the study in 1969 by Sister Joan Marie Donohoe, chairman of the Department of History at

428

the College of Notre Dame at Belmont, California. Haraszthy's contributions to the development of California viniculture have been exaggerated, but his fabulous adventures could provide rich material for a historical novel.

The tremendous influence of Captain Paul Garrett (1863-1940) on the American wine scene before and following Prohibition became most apparent when my field and library research were virtually complete. After much correspondence with those associated in his many enterprises, I finally obtained from his daughter, Mrs. Emily Barden, the loan of the Captain's own story, dictated on his deathbed, which cleared up remaining questions about his career.

Philip Wagner has been especially helpful in explaining the role of the French hybrids in changing the character of the eastern and midwestern states' wines, and in directing me to many valuable sources of information. Frank Schoonmaker has also been of great help in tracing the development of varietal labeling.

It would have been impossible to cover all of the interesting small vineyards and wineries of the United States without the excellent annual directory of the wine industry published by the industry's trade publication, *Wines & Vines*. Nor can anyone keep up to date on significant developments in the industry without studying every issue of this magazine, which has been published at San Francisco (originally as *The California Grape Grower*) continuously since 1920. Also helpful has been the *California Wineletter*, ably edited by Charles H. Van Kriedt.

For their invaluable help I wish particularly to thank:

The University of California Departments of Viticulture and Enology and Food Science, and especially Drs. Albert J. Winkler, Maynard A. Joslyn, Harold P. Olmo, Maynard A. Amerine, Lloyd Lider, Vernon Singleton, James Cook, Dinsmoor Webb, Mark Kliewer, Professor Harold Berg, and Extension Specialist Amand Kasimatis. Equally generous with assistance have been Dr. Austin C. Goheen, the U. S. Department of Agriculture plant pathologist stationed at UC Davis, and Professor Vincent Petrucci, the head of the viticulture and enology programs at Fresno State University.

The Wine Institute staff, and especially Legal Counsel Jefferson E. Peyser, Roy Camozzi, James Seff, Arthur Silverman, and Henry Gage; the Institute's economic research director, Werner Allmendinger, and his former assistant, Dorothy Huff; Librarians Joan Ingalls and Kay Chadwick; Technical Director Hugh Cook; and my former co-workers, Doris Brown Paulsen, Roy Taylor, wine consultant Louis R. Gomberg, who was the first head of the Institute's research department; the Institute's president, Harry G. Serlis, and the past president, Don W. McColly.

University and government horticulturists, food scientists, and agricultural economists who have supplied much essential data, including Professor Erwin Abmeyer of the Northeast Kansas Experiment Fields, Dr. J. LaMar Anderson of Utah State University, New Jersey Secretary of Agriculture Philip Alampi, William L. Bair of the New York Crop Reporting Service, Dr. H. C. Barrett of the University of Illinois, Drs. J. M. Beattie and Garth Cahoon of Ohio's Agricultural Research and

Development Center at Wooster, Dr. John F. Bowen of British Columbia's Summerland Research Station, Dr. Ralph Crowther and Oliver Bradt of the Ontario Research Station at Vineland; Dr. Robert T. Dunstan of Alachua, Florida; Drs. William B. Nesbitt and Carlos Williams, and Extension Specialist Joe F. Brooks of North Carolina State University; Drs. Walter Clore and Richard Dailey and Professor Vere Brummund of Washington State University; Professor A. E. Cott of Iowa State University; Drs. John Einset, John P. Tompkins, and Nelson Shaulis of Cornell University; Professor R. R. Furgason and Anton S. Horn of the University of Idaho; Drs. H. K. Fleming and Carl W. Haeseler of Pennsylvania State University; Dr. Delbert D. Hemphill of the University of Missouri; Professor Herman Hinrichs of Oklahoma State University; Dr. Byard O. Fry of the Georgia Experiment Station; M. Aubrey Owen of Owen's Vineyard and Nursery at Gay, Georgia; Professor Delbert D. Hemphill of the University of Missouri; Don A. Huber, extension specialist of Utah State University at St. George; Trenholm D. Jordan, extension agent for the Chautauqua-Erie Grape Belt; W. Grant Lee of the Utah Statistical Reporting Service; Dr. N. Horace Loomis of the USDA Horticultural Station at Fresno; Dr. Darrell T. Sullivan and Extension Agents Filiberto L. Marquez and Joseph F. Tondre of New Mexico State University and Dr. Sullivan's predecessor, Horticulturist Arra B. Fite; A. M. McDowell and V. W. Eaton of the Federal-State Market News Service at San Francisco; Drs. Hoya Y. Yang, Ralph Garren, Jr., Professor Porter Lombard, David E. Passon, and Lloyd W. Martin of Oregon State University; Neil W. Miles of the University of Minnesota Agricultural Extension Service; Professor Norman P. Maxwell of Texas A. & M. University; Drs. Loren H. Stover and John A. Mortensen of the University of Florida Grape Investigations Laboratory; Dr. Jesus Moncada of the Centro de Investigaciones at Torreón, Mexico; Dr. George D. Oberle and Charles R. O'Dell of Virginia Polytechnic Institute; Dr. J. P. Overcash of Mississippi State University; Dr. Sigmund Schanderl, formerly in charge of wine research at Michigan State University; Professor Harold J. Sefick of Clemson University; Dr. Sherwood W. Shear of the University of California at Berkeley; Lowell F. True, University of Arizona agricultural agent at Tucson, and the dedicated county farm advisors and agricultural commissioners of California, without whose help the chapters about their districts would be incomplete.

Historians, librarians, and others who performed special research on historical questions include Franklin (Busty) Aulls of Hammondsport, New York; John L. Bree of Modesto, California; Aycock Brown of Manteo, North Carolina; Irvin Brucker of St. Louis, the historian of Missouri wines; Julia L. Crawford of the Philadelphia Library; Elizabeth L. Crocker, historian of Chautauqua County, New York; Christopher B. Devan, director of the New Castle Library at Wilmington, Delaware; Marion Curry Geoble, editor of the Lake County (California) Historical Society Pomo Bulletin; Thomas E. Harman of the Distilled Spirits Institute at Washington, D.C.; Mrs. Renno J. Hawkins, North Carolina Department of Conservation; Mrs. Cornelia K. Lane of Grapevine

Cottage, Concord, Massachusetts; Mrs. Maurine Madinger of Wathena, Kansas; Carl Oehl of Amana, Iowa; Eleanora M. Lynn, head of the Maryland Department of the Enoch Pratt Library, Baltimore; John Matthews, assistant historian of Ulster County, New York; Allan R. Ottley, California Section, California State Library; J. Allen Mays, Taylor Wine Company; Dr. L. Rosser Littleton of Stateville, North Carolina; Research Supervisor Lauritz G. Petersen of the Church of Jesus Christ of the Latter-day Saints; Marie C. Preston, historian of Livingston County, New York; Reverend Arthur D. Spearman, archivist of the University of Santa Clara's Orradre Library; Sam A. Suhler, Local History Librarian of the Fresno County (California) Library; Mrs. C. A. Stoughton of Fredonia, Kansas; Mrs. Helen Schowengerdt of Independence, Missouri; Edwin S. Underhill, III, publisher of the Corning (New York) *Leader*; Wilson B. Tillery of Stevensville, Maryland; Margot Timson of the Boston Library; Roy Wilder, Jr., of the North Carolina Seashore Commission; Rosalie F. Wilson of the Westchester County (New York) Parks Department, and Mrs. Prudence H. Work, editor of the Brocton (New York) *Beacon*.

Additional historical facts of importance were contributed by Allen A. Arthur of Los Angeles, the late Burke H. Critchfield, Andrew G. Frericks, and Louis Stralla of St. Helena; Robert Eaton, Henry Bugatto, and Edmund A. Rossi of San Francisco; Rexford G. Tugwell of Santa Barbara; Peter Valaer of Washington, D.C.; Douglas Moorhead, Sr., of North East, Pennsylvania; Nicholas H. Paul of Widmer's Wine Cellars, Julius H. Fessler of Berkeley, Guy Baldwin of Los Gatos, Evins Naman of Fresno, Wallace H. Pohle of Stockton, and Dick Sherer of Hammondsport, New York.

I am deeply indebted to the following friends who traveled great distances to investigate particular facets of winegrowing for the book: Dr. Paul Scholten, who explored the vineyards of New Mexico; Dr. Thomas N. Poore, who took the trouble to find grapevines in Hawaii, verifying the point that grapes grow in all fifty states; J. Walter Fleming, who found and revisited the old Mormon winery in Utah; Irwin Phillips of San Francisco City College, who continually explores California and Missouri wine districts and reports the changes he finds between my own trips, and Dr. and Mrs. Keith Witte of Monroe, who explored the wineries of Wisconsin in my behalf.

Warm personal thanks are due those who so kindly guided me through their respective winegrowing districts, especially Henry O. Sonneman of Meier's Ohio vineyards and wineries; John K. Couillard, G. W. B. Hostetter, and Philip Torno of the Canadian Wine Institute; Mario Ortiz Rodriguez of Saltillo, Coah., Mexico; Dmitri Tchelistcheff of Ensenada, Baja California; William R. Clayton of the South Carolina Development Board; Grace and Allen Furman of Raleigh, North Carolina; Melvin S. Gordon of Birchrunville, Pennsylvania; Joel Arrington of the North Carolina Travel Division; Walter S. Taylor and Charles Fournier of Hammondsport, New York; Herman J. B. Wiederkehr of Altus, Arkansas, and Frank Koval of the Michigan Wine Institute. I am further indebted to

Marcial Ibarra and Juan Cid y Mulet of the Asociación Nacional de Vitivinicultores of Mexico, who planned my itinerary and the hospitable receptions I was accorded in that country.

Oenothusiasts who supplied invaluable help concerning viticulture and winemaking in their respective localities include Eugene Charles of Seneca, South Carolina; Julien Cornell of Central Valley, New York; Thomas R. Clarke of New Canaan, Connecticut; Bryan H. Doble of Oak Knoll Vineyard, Tryon, North Carolina; Dr. August W. Denninger of Santa Fe, New Mexico; Dr. Arvin T. Henderson of Palo Alto, California; Charles O. Foerster, Jr., of Elsa, Texas; Charles J. Bus of Portage, Michigan; John F. Kistner of Stillwater, Minnesota; Dr. Wilbur P. McDonald of St. Joseph, Missouri; James E. Spooner of Rolla, Missouri; Norman F. Willms of Los Fresnos, Texas; John Wickham of Wickham's Fruit Farm, Cutchogue, Long Island; Dennis T. Willis of Tumcumcari, New Mexico; Dr. Robert Adamson, his wife Dorothy, and Dr. Bernard and his wife Belle Rhodes, whose vineyards are in the Napa Valley; and especially Dr. Ben Fisher of Tonawanda, New York, who for several years has kept me informed of the changing wine scene in upstate New York and in the Ontario wine district of Canada.

Finally, I wish to express thanks to James Field, Gerald Adams, Lee and Jack Pollexfen, and my other wine-knowledgeable friends who have read some of the chapters for clarity and have made many valuable suggestions.

Index

Under the more comprehensive subjects, the page numbers
of the principal references are in *italics*.

A